STEP'97

incorporating CASE'97

STEP
1997

Proceedings

Eighth IEEE International Workshop on Software Technology and Engineering Practice incorporating Computer Aided Software Engineering

July 14-18, 1997 London, UK

Sponsored by

IWCASE-International Workshop on CASE

BT Laboratories, BT plc

IEEE Computer Society-Technical Council on Software Engineering

British Computer Society

IEE

UMIST

Learning Tree International

Edited by

David Budgen, Gene Hoffnagle, Jos Trienekens

IEEE COMPUTER SOCIETY

Los Alamitos, California

Washington • Brussels • Tokyo

IEEE Computer Society Order Number PR07840
ISBN (paper) 0-8186-7840-2
ISBN (microfiche) 0-8186-7842-9
IEEE Order Plan Catalog Number 97TB100145
Library of Congress 97-72008

Additional copies may be ordered from:

IEEE Computer Society
Customer Service Center
10662 Los Vaqueros Circle
P.O. Box 3014
Los Alamitos, CA 90720-1314
Tel: + 1-714-821-8380
Fax: + 1-714-821-4641
E-mail: cs.books@computer.org

IEEE Service Center
445 Hoes Lane
P.O. Box 1331
Piscataway, NJ 08855-1331
Tel: + 1-908-981-1393
Fax: + 1-908-981-9667
mis.custserv@computer.org

IEEE Computer Society
13, Avenue de l'Aquilon
B-1200 Brussels
BELGIUM
Tel: + 32-2-770-2198
Fax: + 32-2-770-8505
euro.ofc@computer.org

IEEE Computer Society
Ooshima Building
2-19-1 Minami-Aoyama
Minato-ku, Tokyo 107
JAPAN
Tel: + 81-3-3408-3118
Fax: + 81-3-3408-3553
tokyo.ofc@computer.org

Editorial production by Deborah Plummer

Cover art production by Joseph Daigle/Studio Productions

Printed in the United States of America by Sony Electronic Publishing Services

IEEE
COMPUTER
SOCIETY

IEEE

Table of Contents

Paper Session P2b: Experiences with OO Development

Paper Session P2c: Project Management Tools

Paper Session P3a: Quality Issues

Paper Session P3b: Experiences with OO Development II

Paper Session P4d: Software Engineering Education

Paper Session P5a: System Development Methods II

Paper Session P5b: Employing COTS Technology

Paper Session P5c: Requirements Specification

Foreword

Welcome to Software Technology and Engineering Practice (STEP'97), the first event to have that name, but the eighth international workshop in the series that includes the International Workshops on Computer-Aided Software Engineering. And welcome to the exciting city of London!

STEP'97 is the premier world event and working meeting for the field of software engineering in practice, drawing together practitioners and researchers concerned with software engineering's role in software and systems development, evolution, and management. The programme of workshops, refereed papers, presentations, and tutorials allows participants to explore and report on the most important and current practical, applied, experimental, and theoretical work that affects software engineering in practice.

The programme will again include the presentation of the Wayne Stevens Lecture on Software Development Methods, sponsored by the IWCASE Board. This year's honoree is Michael Jackson of MAJ Consulting, who will speak on "The Place and Value of Method in Software Development." There will also be two distinguished keynote speakers: Robert Glass of Computing Trends (USA) and Lawrence Regan of Barclays Bank (UK).

A major theme that runs through STEP'97 is creativity and innovation in software development. Increasing demands are and will continue to be placed upon software developers to produce a wide range of software systems and support that provide creative solutions to the needs of industry, commerce, and society.

With many existing approaches to software development failing to meet this demand, there is a need to expand the repertoire of innovative methods, techniques and tools for software production. Balanced against this is the need to perform proper evaluation of new techniques to understand their cost and benefits. STEP'97 seeks to present both the new ideas and a proper evaluation through experience reports. Indeed, the conference programme contains a number of papers reporting on the introduction of software best practice within a variety of organizations. Many of those reports reflect projects funded as part of the European Commission's European Systems and Software Initiative (ESSI) programme.

Software and systems development, evolution, and management are undergoing dramatic change as we approach the 21st century. Economic pressures require systems to be built better, cheaper, and faster. Increased IT awareness and the use of technologies such as object orientation are creating a new generation of system builders who do not necessarily have a traditional software development background. New communication technologies and co-operative working are forcing changes to working practices leading to distributed, 24-hour, and global software development. The result is that the processes, skills and tools that support all aspects of software development will undergo dramatic change during the next few years. STEP'97 prepares participants for that future.

The STEP'97 Programme Committee refereed 107 and selected 47 excellent papers for inclusion in the proceedings and presentations. In the spirit of this series of conferences, those papers serve as launching platforms for the ten workshops created by the Program Committee. The workshops are intended to explore in depth the current and future technologies underlying each subject, expand communication between the development and research communities for each subject, and prepare a summary of the state-of-the-art and the state-of-the-practice for inclusion in a post-conference report. There are also ten tutorials available on a variety of topics of interest to software practitioners.

The final programme of 1997 Software Technology and Engineering Practice is the result of a great deal of effort by many people, world wide. First and foremost, we thank our sponsors. Second, we thank the authors who offered their work for consideration. Third, we are indebted to the members of the Conference Committee for their valuable ideas, generous help, and tireless support throughout the creation of this event. We are, of course, particularly indebted to the members of the Programme Committee, who refereed papers (three or more reviews per paper), came from all over the world to the Programme Committee meeting at UMIST (University of Manchester Institute of Science and Technology) in Manchester, UK, and are serving as session and workshop chairs. And thanks to all the many other volunteers who made STEP'97 possible, and to the staff at the IEEE Computer Society who made these proceedings possible.

Paul Layzell
UMIST
Manchester
UK
General Chair

David Budgen
Keele University
Keele
UK
Program Co-Chair

Gene Hoffnagle
IBM Research
Yorktown Heights
New York, USA
Program Co-Chair

Jos Trienekens
Technical University
Eindhoven
Eindhoven, The Netherlands
Program Co-Chair

Conference Committee

General Chair

Professor Paul Layzell
UMIST
PO Box 88
Manchester M60 1QD
United Kingdom
Voice: +44 161 200 3338
FAX: +44 161 200 3745
Email: P.Layzell@umist.ac.uk

Program Co-Chairs

Professor David Budgen
Keele University
Keele
Staffordshire ST5 5BG
United Kingdom
Voice: +44 1782 583079
FAX: +44 1782 713082
Email: db@cs.keele.ac.uk

Gene Hoffnagle
IBM Corporation 82-205
PO Box 218, Rt.134
Yorktown Heights
NY 10598-0218, USA
Voice: +1 914 945 3831
FAX: +1 914 945 2018
Email: g.hoffnagle@computer.org

Dr Jos Trienekens
Technical University Eindhoven
PO Box 513
MB Eindhoven 5600, Netherlands
Voice: +31 40 472 290
FAX: +31 40 451 275
Email: j.j.m.trienekens@bdk.tue.nl

Tutorial Chair

Kathy Spurr
ADC International
41 Lyndhurst Road
Chichester PO19 2LE
United Kingdom
Voice: +44 1243 775890
FAX: +44 1243 536053
Email: kspurr@adcon.demon.co.uk

Tools Fair and Exhibition Chair

Professor Roger Phillips
Department of Computer Science
University of Hull
Hull HU6 7RX
United Kingdom
Voice: +44 1482 465680
FAX: +44 1482 466666
Email: r.phillips@dcs.hull.ac.uk

Publicity Chair

Alan Brown
Object Technology Branch
Texas Instruments Inc
PO Box 655303, M/S 8373
Dallas, Texas 75265, USA
Voice: +1 214 997 5950
FAX: +1 214 997 5568
Email: awb@csc.ti.com

Local Arrangements Chair

Dr John Jenkins
School of Informatics
City University
Northampton Square
London EC1V 0HB
Voice: +44 171 477 8410
FAX: +44 171 477 8588
Email: j.o.jenkins@city.ac.uk

Publications Chair

Dr Shirley Williams
Department of Computer Science
University of Reading
PO Box 225
Whiteknights
Reading RG6 6AY
United Kingdom
Voice: +44 118 9318613
FAX: +44 118 9751822
Email: shirley.williams@reading.ac.uk

Treasurer

Michael Freeman
UMIST
PO Box 88
Manchester M60 1QD
United Kingdom
Voice: +44 161 200 3304
FAX: +44 161 200 3745
Email: M.J.Freeman@umist.ac.uk

Registration Coordinator

Irene Beech
UMIST
PO Box 88
Manchester M60 1QD
United Kingdom
Voice: +44 161 200 3331
FAX: +44 161 200 3745
Email: I.Beech@umist.ac.uk

Program Committee

IWCASE Officers

IWCASE Executive Board

About IWCASE

Software Technology, CASE, and Engineering Practice

The demand for software to manage information in business, to drive computer-controlled products and manufacturing processes, and to enable advanced scientific exploration is growing faster than our ability to produce it. Simultaneously, there is a growing realization of the vital nature of software in virtually all industry segments. "Mission-critical", a term once reserved for software controlling key military systems, is now widely applied to strategic applications, where a system failure could jeopardize the survival of an entire business, as well as potentially life-threatening commercial applications from automobiles to nuclear reactors and air traffic control systems. Software is not only a larger and more important component of our products and services, it is now a key factor in global competition, and is rapidly becoming a dominant, if largely unnoticed, fact of our daily lives.

How can software development managers and practitioners become more effective? How can they meet the exponentially growing demand? How can they ensure that software is built efficiently and the result is highly reliable? These are questions the emerging discipline of software engineering is trying to answer. Rooted in the "structured methods revolution" of the 1970's, software engineering attempts to go beyond single-domain notations and design strategies, to embrace a comprehensive engineering approach to software development, similar to mechanical, electronic or civil engineering.

In this context, the concept of software technology, the basic elements that make software engineering possible, is gaining wide acceptance. The potential for leveraging the intelligence and creativity of software engineers using the power of computers seems obvious. Yet, advances in Computer-Aided Software Engineering (CASE) have lagged other disciplines -- partly because software developers were too busy automating other industry segments, and partly because the software industry itself grew far more rapidly and with less foundation in formal science than other fields. We also must allow that software, by its very nature, exhibits degrees of freedom not enjoyed by its sister disciplines more securely anchored in the physical world. This freedom, while enabling more abstract and powerful solutions to human problems, creates a daunting challenge to tool builders who would assist software developers in their work. Evidence of this is apparent in the large and growing array of software methods and notations in use, and the highly fragmented character of the software industry itself. As a result, while no one argues about the great potential of CASE methods and tools, the implementation of integrated tool support on an industry-wide basis has proved difficult.

It is now appropriate to talk of a software tools industry of a general kind. Like in the growth of the industrial revolution, attention focused first on the development of particular machines, in our case particular CASE developments, products, and environments. Then, the emphasis broadened to manufacturing itself as machine tools came of age. So it is with CASE moving on to software technology in general for widespread engineering practice.

Industry Forum for Progress and Exchange

There has not been a shortage of effort expended to solve software development problems. Over the last ten years, a CASE industry grew up encompassing hundreds of suppliers from every corner of the globe, then met a gap among expectations, useful and practical achievements, marketing claims, and the realities of technology transfer. Methods have proliferated and research consortiums have added exponentially to the body of knowledge documenting the software problem and potential solutions.

The vast majority of these efforts explore software engineering problems in minute detail, segmenting the problem space and searching for the answer to a single, well-defined question. They foster highly unique perspectives in an effort to create new theories and technology.

Yet, the fragmentation of the software industry, its diversity of constituencies, and its plethora of approaches and perspectives, begs for an integrative force. We need a forum to help researchers, suppliers and users communicate their respective accomplishments and their unmet needs.

It is this need for a "forum of industry participants" that inspired the formation of IWCASE, founded as the International Workshop on CASE Inc., an organization which sponsors workshop events on a regular basis. IWCASE's focus is in bringing together leading-edge users, developers, researchers, consultants and educators for active exchange of ideas and solutions to advance the state-of-the-art and the state-of-the-practice. Historical evolution of the field has led to a broadening of our role to encompass software technology in general. Hence, the new conference name: Software Technology and Engineering Practice (STEP).

As the sponsoring organization, IWCASE is an independent non-profit industry association (U.S. 501(c)(6) tax exempt corporation) with the mission to exchange, synthesize, and disseminate ideas among users, developers, researchers and supporters of software- and systems-engineering technology with the goal of advancing the technology and its effective use. See http://www.iwcase.org/.

CASE workshops, and now the STEP 97 Conference, have been co-sponsored by the IEEE Computer Society's Technical Council on Software Engineering (TCSE) with the cooperation of supporting corporations and universities. See http://www.tcse.org/ and http://computer.org/.

IWCASE also sponsors the annual Stevens Lecture on Software Development Methods (the Stevens Award) to advance the state of software development methods and enhance their continuing evolution.

IWCASE
International Workshop on CASE Inc.
P.O. Box 400
Burlington, MA 01803 USA
iwcase@iwcase.org

Workshop Abstracts

W1a Reverse Engineering and Legacy Systems

Cornelia Boldyreff, University of Durham, UK
Rob Davies, BT Laboratories, UK

Often legacy systems are mission critical to an enterprise, but lack of systemic evolution has resulted in systems which are difficult to change. Reverse engineering offers the possibility of recovering higher level views of the legacy systems and thus establishing the vital system understanding needed to support maintenance. Through application of reverse engineering techniques and tools to legacy systems, it is also possible to recover assets exploitable in evolving the legacy systems.

These recovered assets also can be used as the basis for organizing a component based approach to system development and more generally as a basis for a reuse program underlying future development. Rather than continuing to maintain and evolve existing legacy systems in isolation, through these approaches, it may be possible to identify product lines across a number of legacy systems or elements of those systems leading to a more unified form of support for related legacy systems. This workshop will consider these ideas, as well as pick up on issues raised in the related paper sessions.

W1b Configuration Management

Shirley Williams and Rachel McCrindle,
University of Reading, UK

Software configuration management is now a recognized discipline for controlling the evolution of large software systems and is acknowledged as adding considerable value to the control and visibility of the software development and maintenance processes. This workshop will focus on, but will not be restricted to, two main areas of interest. Firstly it will explore whether current configuration management techniques and practices are adequate for controlling the evolution of today's computer systems such as those of a distributed, embedded or multimedia nature. Secondly, it will consider what features and facilities should be incorporated into future tools and environments for facilitating the configuration management of both legacy and new software systems. Issues will cover both technical and managerial aspect of software configuration management.

W1c Object-Oriented Middleware, Frameworks for Systems Integration

Sri Raghavan, Digital Equipment Corporation, USA
Rudolf K. Keller, University of Montreal, Canada

The objective of this workshop is to share an understanding and synthesize the characteristic strengths and limitations of popular frameworks such as CORBA, Java, ActivceX/DCOM, and WWW for OO system integration efforts; and issues and approaches for successfully practicing OOAD in these contexts. Key challenges in object technology lie in inventing the right set of object abstractions and organizing them so that the objects can interoperate, collaborate, and evolve efficiently. In build-from-scratch projects there is considerable freedom in tackling these challenges. However it is different in systems integration projects which are driven and constrained by the existence of legacy systems and a strong a priori commitment to the use of off-the-shelf components. Since these projects are typically executed in tumultuous organizational context there are significant implications for the practice of OOAD methods.

W2a What Makes for Project Success or Failure?

John Jenkins, City University, UK
Rob Kusters, TUE, Netherlands

Most commentators argue that the reason for IS project failure lies not in Technology but in People. A particular cause being the innate optimism of Systems people which results in the adoption of unachievable targets which are passed off as estimates. This workshop will explore the evidence for this thesis and hopefully identify ways in which the problem can be alleviated. The issue of risk management will be explored.

W2b Net-Centric Computing

Scott Tilley, Software Engineering Institute, USA
Margaret-Anne Storey, University of Victoria, Canada

The explosion of interest in the World Wide Web has given rise to many new developments. One of them is Net-Centric Computing (NCC), the underlying principle of which is a distributed environment where applications and data are downloaded from network servers on an as-needed basis. The adoption of NCC will have significant impact on users, developers, and administrators. Some users may chaff at the limitations of NCC brings with it: the removal of "personal" in PC means users will no longer be able to significantly alter their desktop environment. However, for administrators this means a potential reduction in the cost and complexity of managing a corporate network. For developers, NCC offers an opportunity to greatly increase their customer base: applications written in a NCC-aware programming language, such as Java, means writing code once and having it immediately accessible on multiple platforms. It also means a different development environment, a new deployment model (renting applications versus buying), and new concerns about security. Through focused presentations and open discussion, this workshop will explore NCC and its potential impact on software users, application developers, and system administrators.

W2c Component Based Development

Ben Whittle, British Telecom plc, UK
Andy Ormsby, University of Sussex, UK

Component based development is the latest buzz phrase in the reuse world, but what is a component and how does it differ from the modules and classes that we already deal with everyday? In this workshop we will explore the idea of component based development, what difference will it make in terms of development methods, tools and techniques. We will pick up on themes from previous sessions in STEP'97 (reuse, COTS, OO, legacy systems) as well as bringing in specific ideas related to component technology. The workshop will covers issues such as:

- Is component based development really a paradigm shift?
- How big is a component - and who cares?
- What makes a component any different to a traditional software module?
- Is a component a technical entity or a business entity?
- What is the relationship between COTS and component based development?

W2d Structured Testing

Martin Pol, IP/Software Control Testen, Netherlands
Erik van Veenendaal, KEMA, Netherlands

This workshop will focus on the testing of complete information systems, not just the software, but also the related products and system support features. After a short introduction, the main testing pitfalls will be identified. Next a generic testing approach, applied in over 200 companies of different types will be presented covering the four pillars of structured testing: the testing lifecycle, testing techniques, infrastructure and tools and finally organizational issues. Two case study presentations will show the application of structured testing. Participants will be encouraged to interrupt the presentations and to start discussion which will provide feedback on the earlier collected pitfalls.

W3a Choosing Techniques and Tools for Requirements Specification

Sara Jones, University of Hertfordshire, UK
Mehmet Ozcan, Sheffield Hallam University, UK

The aim of this workshop will be to promote discussion of factors which may significantly influence the choice of methods, tools and notations for requirements specification in a particular project. Discussion will focus on tools and techniques which support the generation of a requirements specification document, but other activities, such as the elicitation and validation of requirements, will also be considered in-so-much-as they affect the choice of tools for specification.

The outcome from this workshop will be the production of an initial categorization of 'project types' and some preliminary notes regarding experiences and lessons learned as to the kinds of methods, tools and techniques which can be, and have been, successfully applied in projects of these types. Where possible, the emphasis will be on real world and industrial projects.

W3b Effectiveness of Software Process Improvement

Erik Rodenbach and Rini van Solingen
Schlumberger Retail Petroleum Systems, Netherlands

In order to manage and improve software development, industry uses many methods and techniques that focus on the development process of software, the so called "Software Process Improvement" (SPI). SPI aims at improving time-to-market, cost and quality of software, in particular by focusing on the process by which it is developed. However, most industrial organizations sell products, not processes. Therefore the effectiveness of process improvements must be visualized in order to decide whether 'changes' are really 'improvements'. This workshop will focus on the effectiveness of software process improvement. Beside a small overview presentation on SPI-methods, some examples from practice will be presented that showed beneficial results of SPI.

W3c Distributed Cooperative Working

Linda Macaulay, UMIST, UK
Pearl Brereton, University of Keele, UK

New opportunities arise from the field of computer supported co-operative working where the merging of computing and telecommunications enables teams to function with individual members residing in different physical locations. The aim of this workshop is to explore the potential of new technologies to support distributed software engineering teams. The workshop will focus on two issues, firstly what technology is available and ready for use today, and secondly whether technology is in itself sufficient for success.

The outcome of the workshop will be the identification of those factors which affect the success of distributed co-operative working for software engineering teams.

Keynote 1

Session P1a

System Architectures

Yasmin: a Component Based Architecture for Software Applications

Luca Deri
IBM Zurich Research Laboratory[1]
University of Berne[2]

Abstract

Object-oriented programming (OOP) has changed significantly the way to produce software applications and allowed many problems that affected traditional programming to be overcome. Unfortunately several object-oriented frameworks misused OOP techniques, failed to address issues such as application extensibility, and have produced monolithic systems hard to manage and tailor.

This paper describes Yasmin, a new object-oriented, component-based architecture for software applications. It allows one to build applications which use system resources efficiently and which can be easily extended and configured in addition to being simple to program and to compose. This is achieved by means of droplets, a new type of software components that can be replaced and modified at runtime and by exploiting novel techniques such as collaboration and delegation.

Keywords: Object-Oriented Programming, Software Components, Application Frameworks.

1. Introduction

The popularity of object-oriented programming (OOP) has increased considerably over the past several years. OOP offers many benefits over traditional programming such as allowing programmers to define objects that can be easily extended and composed in order to build a software application. Although powerful, OOP lacked a standard framework through which software objects created by different vendors can interact with one another. The major result of this trend has been the production of a "sea of objects" that cannot interact across application boundaries in a meaningful way. At the beginning of this decade, the software industry realised that the ability to tie objects together into a closer unit would result in a much more powerful system. For this reason, many frameworks and architectures have been developed to address this problem. Unfortunately applications based on such frameworks often had a monolithic structure mostly because object-oriented techniques such as inheritance have been misused by introducing cross dependencies among classes. The obvious consequence has been that objects were so tightly coupled that even the simplest application had to link the entire system. This has been the reason for the decline or limited diffusion of highly celebrated applications systems [27] [6].

Software components [21] [17] [25] seem to be the answer to all these problems. As its name suggests, component software is based on the notion of a component, which is a reusable piece of software that can be "plugged into" other components from other vendors with relatively little effort. In contrast, traditional applications are monolithic, which means they come pre-packaged with a wide range of features, most of which cannot be removed or replaced with alternatives.

This paper presents Yasmin, a component-based, object-oriented architecture and framework for software applications. Yasmin has been developed with the intent to simplify the implementation of software applications with particular emphasis on distributed networking applications for network management.

Yasmin defines a new style of building applications, based upon established technologies such as OOP [20], software components and novel concepts like cooperation and delegation. This is part of the effort to make computer software easy to use and develop in addition to overcoming typical problems that affect network management applications such as being monolithic and hard to configure and extend. The experience gained by applying Yasmin to selected network management problems allowed us to refine and to transform it into a more general architecture for software applications.

[1] IBM Research Division, Zurich Research Laboratory, Säumerstrasse 4, 8803 Rüschlikon, Switzerland. Email: lde@zurich.ibm.com, WWW: http://www.zurich.ibm.com/~lde/.
[2] Universität Bern, Institut für Informatik und angewandte Mathematik, Software Composition Group, Neubrückstrasse 10, CH-3012 Bern, Switzerland. Email: deri@iam.unibe.ch, WWW: http://iamwww.unibe.ch/~deri/.

0-8186-7840-2/97 $10.00 © 1997 IEEE

2. Yasmin Fundamentals

This section introduces Yasmin: it defines the scope of the architecture, the basic components and how they interact from a high-level perspective.

2.1. Understanding Frameworks

Yasmin is built upon OOP abstractions known as frameworks. A framework is an extensible library of cooperating classes that make up a reusable design solution for a given problem domain. Nevertheless a framework is more than a class hierarchy: a framework is an object-oriented class hierarchy plus a built-in model which defines how the objects derived from the hierarchy interact with one other [18].

When the class hierarchy is constructed prior to running the program, the relations among object classes are static. At runtime, the objects are constructed during program execution, hence the relation is dynamic. The framework defines the architecture itself and provides both dynamic and static parts of the application.

An application framework goes beyond class hierarchies defining a preassembled generic application with a dynamic and static structure that a developer can modify to create a real application. A programmer, instead of writing a main program, instantiates objects that are part of the framework's class hierarchy and provides methods for the framework to call by refining the implementation of some classes. In this way, a developer tailors the generic framework by defining highly specialised classes and methods that are called by the framework itself. Because the developer starts with robust code, the new code is more likely to work reliably, hence reducing the testing and debugging phase.

2.2. Yasmin's Background

The idea to design Yasmin derived from several years of network management application development [7]. Despite the fact that many frameworks and architecture for building software applications are available on the market, most of them are tailored only for GUI development [19] [16] [12]. In the network management world, applications are usually built following the craftsman principle without the adoption of application frameworks. Some companies have developed huge application systems [15] that are composed of several applications and libraries that address every network management need. Although these systems are very powerful and rich in terms of functionality and tools, they do not address problems relating to application development. In fact in order to build network management applications based on those systems, developers need to know in detail many different libraries that have not always been designed to work together and that very seldom are based on OOP concepts. Additionally, due to the interdependencies among those libraries, user applications require the installation of a large subset of the application system in order to run. The natural consequence is that applications are monolithic, difficult to tailor and configure and are system resources-hungry, preventing them from running on hosts of limited power.

Beside this, network management applications quite often have to support different management protocols and object models other than being open to extensions and updates. Since network services should be available most of the time, it is necessary to identify mechanisms which allow to selectively upgrade applications while they remain partially available in order to guarantee a minimal level of service. Additionally, it is necessary to build applications in such a way that it is possible to add new pieces when new hardware devices have to be supported or when users demand new services.

Yasmin attempts to address these issues and to overcome problems that affect conventional network management applications by defining an applications framework characterised by the following properties:

1. light and simple kernel;
2. based upon pluggable software components;
3. built from the ground up on object-oriented technology;
4. founded on cooperation and delegation;
5. extensible, easy to tailor and distribute.

During the design phase, the author has analysed several frameworks and architectures available on the market, in order to verify whether it would have been possible to implement Yasmin using one of them. The result of that survey is that even established standards such as CORBA [26] are not fully suitable for this task in terms of:

- independence of the CORBA implementation being used: there is no CORBA implementation which allows one to write the code once and to deploy it on several platforms ranging from personal computers to powerful Unix workstations;
- interoperability of Yasmin-based applications: CORBA implementations are usually unable to interoperate, although this problem is supposed to be fixed in CORBA V2;
- ease of development: CORBA is rather difficult to use especially in terms of memory management and datatypes generated by the IDL compiler;
- runtime application evolution: it is not simple to develop facilities which allow the behaviour of CORBA objects to be modified at runtime.

The idea behind Yasmin is to build component-based applications that can be composed by the user, who can add or replace components at runtime. By enforcing the component boundaries, Yasmin prevents components from making assumptions on other components, hence reducing component inter-dependencies and making them easy to reuse on different contexts [4]. Additionally, Yasmin loads the components on demand only when they are really needed and unloads them when no longer in use according to the component lifetime defined by its developer. The efficient use of system resources is quite important because it enables complex applications to run on hosts of limited computation power like mobile computers.

An effective way to limit the application size is through cooperation: every component that implements a service of general use makes it available through a well-defined interface. Often, large network management systems need to use a common set of services that sometimes require significant resources. A typical example are encoding/decoding (enc/dec) services needed to transmit information that are often replicated in different applications. As those services are often implemented using shared libraries, there is only one copy of the enc/dec logic in memory. Nevertheless this is not efficient enough because every time the enc/dec service is instantiated in the application, it needs a lot of memory for the allocation of the enc/dec tables. In this case, a single (multithreaded) enc/dec that cooperated with all the local applications would be able to serve all of them without the need to replicate the services and hence require a larger amount of memory.

3. Inside Yasmin

The following picture depicts Yasmin's components.

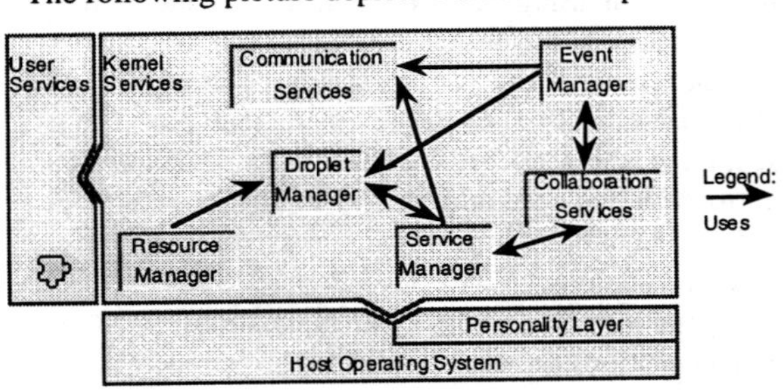

Figure 1. Yasmin's Components

The design goal of Yasmin is to define a style of building applications that make efficient use of system resources whose behaviour can be modified and tailored at runtime.

Yasmin's main characteristic is its simplicity. The kernel is very light and contains only those services that are needed by every Yasmin-based application. Every other service not widely needed is not included in the kernel. This is to prevent adding to the kernel some superfluous logic that takes up memory and disk space. The kernel being rather generic, it is possible to build very different applications that share the same architecture: the applications differ for the number and the nature of their software components[3]. Extensibility and runtime behaviour modification is realised using *droplets* [8], software components implemented using shared libraries having the following specific properties:

- they are not statically linked to the application but loaded at runtime;
- they have the ability to be replaced (i.e. a new version of the droplet can replace a previous one) at runtime while the application is running[4];
- they have a well-defined interface (droplet interface) that makes it possible to communicate with other droplets independently from the type of services provided.

Usually object-oriented frameworks provide a set of object classes that have to be subclassed in order to implement the final application. Yasmin instead uses droplets to implement the application itself. Internally, droplets can be based on different object models and frameworks, and implemented using procedural or object-oriented languages. Basically Yasmin provides the glue between different droplets and makes sure that they can interoperate and cooperate to define the application behaviour. The droplet interface guarantees that droplet internals are not exposed hence that they appear like black boxes which prevents other droplets from using specific droplet characteristics which may change in future releases or which may not be available all the time. Besides this, the droplet interface pushes droplet developers to have a clean design exporting the public services and shielding droplets from using services and resources not available through the interface. Basically developers are free to implement droplets using the tools and technologies that they prefer, leaving to Yasmin the task of ensuring application consistency.

From this perspective Yasmin can be seen as a generic architecture for compound applications because it allows one to build very different applications sharing the very same structure. Nevertheless its lack of specialisation in a specific domain, e.g. GUI, does not allow people to use it as the final solution for all their problems. This is beyond the scope of Yasmin, as its root are in the network management field where there are different standards, object models and APIs that often need to be combined in order to construct the final application [24]. This is Yasmin's problem domain: the integration of many heterogeneous

[3] Despite this characteristic of Yasmin, this does not mean that it is possible to efficiently build every class of applications using a single framework since frameworks are specialized for a narrow range of applications because each model of interaction is domain-specific.

[4] In order to activate a droplet it is necessary to drop it into a certain directory monitored by the running application. Hence the term droplet.

programming models, sometimes deeply different, in a compound object-oriented application. This is achieved through the droplet interface which prevents different application components from influencing each other and hence from creating a monolithic structure. For instance, multiple inheritance, used to combine different classes, creates interdependencies among all such classes with the result that even a minimal application has to include most of the code needed to implement the whole system. Through cooperation, different classes can be associated to perform a certain task without the limitation of creating a monolithic system.

Additionally, by using droplets the system can load on demand the parts it needs and purge them when no longer in use. This mechanism allows Yasmin-based applications to make efficient use of system resources enabling them to run in systems of limited computation power.

Finally the ability to replace droplets at runtime, hence to modify the behaviour of an application while it is running, is quite important on network management. In this field, application lifetime is very long. When an application has to be stopped for maintenance, services that rely on such application become unavailable. This is clearly a major problem when many users rely on those services, like in the case of telephone or network communications. Droplets give the chance to developers to incrementally upgrade their applications without the need to stop them hence to interrupt services that rely on such applications.

3.1. Personality Abstraction Layer

The framework kernel services are designed to run on different operating systems. For this reason it is necessary to abstract the operating system through a thin layer called *personality*. Personalities provide abstractions for low-level services performed by the host operating system. Those services include, but are not limited to:

- threads and semaphores;
- loadable shared libraries with metadata;
- interprocess communication.

If a potential operating system does not support all of these capabilities, it is often possible to run Yasmin too. For instance an application can run in single threaded mode if threads and semaphores are not supported.

The use of personalities allows to keep a single source code tree for different operating systems, whereas the personality contains operating system dependent code. This makes simple to port the framework on different operating systems and to maintain the different versions.

3.2. Droplet Manager

The droplet manager (DM) is responsible for handling droplets. Namely it:

- loads droplets on demand;
- maintains a droplet reference counter that allows droplets to be purged;
- is responsible for detecting new droplet versions or further droplets added at runtime;
- collaborates with the service manager, informing it of newly available services.

A Yasmin-based application stores droplets in a well defined directory (usually named Droplets). The user puts (or drops if drag-and-drop is used) droplets in such directory and is free to replace them during program execution. The DM at start-up time searches for a file named `index` which contains the name of the droplets and the services they implement. If such file is found, the DM verifies that it is newer than all the droplets (this is done by checking the file modification time) to make sure that it is consistent with the current droplet set. If not, or if there is a new droplet, the index file is rebuilt. This operation similar to the registration of the OpenDoc [1] part editors, is done by loading and unloading in sequence each droplet in order to build the list of droplets available and of the services provided by such droplets that are not visible at the file system level because they are usually stored inside the droplet itself[5].

Inside each droplet the droplet lifetime is specified. The lifetime, which ranges from one second to infinity, specifies how long the droplet has to be kept in memory since the last time it was used. This facility is used to avoid keeping droplets in memory that are no longer needed and indicate to the system when it is necessary to purge some resources in case of low memory conditions. If a droplet's lifetime has expired, the DM unloads it and releases all the memory and resources allocated by the droplet by calling the droplet termination function.

The DM is also responsible for detecting new droplets and new versions of them. In this case the `index` file is updated and the service manager (SM, covered in 3.4.), responsible for handling the services, is notified of the new services available and the ones no longer available (this happens when a new version of a certain droplet does not implement all the services implemented by the former version). Besides this, droplet versioning prevents the system from loading and using droplets which have been developed for a different application version which may introduce problems or spurious errors. Similar to the versioning system used by DSOM [11], droplets have a mi-

[5] In some systems such as MacOS™ it is possible to know the set of implemented services by using the resource manager, supposing that for each service there is a code resource that represents it.

nor and a major version number. The major version number specifies what application version can use such droplet version, whereas the minor number it is used to implement the droplet versioning.

It is worth noting that droplets cannot be unloaded when in use, whereas it is possible to have one or more different versions of the same droplet active at the same time. This technique works because the DM is the only entity that maintains direct references (i.e. pointers) to droplets, whereas other entities such as the service manager simply access services through the DM. For this reason, whenever there is a new droplet version, the DM loads it without checking whether someone is still using the old version. In case the old droplet version was no longer in use, then such a version is unloaded and the new version is loaded, otherwise the DM flips the pointer to the droplet. This operation:

- allows the new droplet to be used whenever a new request for such a droplet has to be processed;
- prevents new requests from being processed with the old droplet while the operations in progress (that make use of the old droplet) can continue;
- allows the old droplet to be unloaded whenever all the operations involving the old droplet have been completed.

The DM collaborates with the SM in order to guarantee this behaviour by keeping track of the requests currently in progress for each droplet. A request is considered "in progress" since the time the SM issues a new service request to the DM until the SM notifies the DM that such request has been completed. This mechanism works because services and droplets are accessed only through managers which shield them from the rest of the system.

The access to resources and services exclusively through managers:

- contributes to the global system robustness;
- prevents droplets from being directly dependent on each other, i.e. by means of direct function or method calls;
- allows droplets to be selectively plugged and unplugged at any time because they have no cross dependencies of any type.

3.3. Event Manager

Events are by nature asynchronous and usually indicate that something has occurred. Typical events are mouseUp/mouseDown or network events. Normally, events are processed when they occur and their type is well defined so the program can handle them. In Yasmin, these limitations are relaxed, hence:

- events can specify when they have to be processed;
- droplets can define new event types.

Yasmin represents events as information records containing the type of the event (event type), when it has occurred (event time), and additional information relative to the event itself (event info). Yasmin adds a new field to this record which specifies when the event has to be processed; it may contain an absolute time or a displacement with respect to the time the event occurred. If this field is set, the event is called a *delayed event*. A delayed event is used to implement repetitive tasks and activities that have to be performed at a certain time. Typical examples are chime clock events that have to be executed every hour or system backups that have to be performed every Sunday at 1 am when almost nobody is expected to use the system.

The Event Manager (EM) is responsible for:

- delivering events to the various components;
- handling delayed events;
- allowing different droplets and services to cooperate and interact by means of the events they exchange.

Yasmin defines a set of basic event types and allows droplets to define their own custom event types, specified inside the droplet itself. Hence, whenever a new droplet is loaded/unloaded, the DM notifies the EM about the event types that can be handled. As different droplets can handle the same event type, a string called event destination specified inside the event record is used to identify the type of the received event. Such string can have three values: a droplet name, a star ("*"), or a null value. In the first case the event is delivered to the specified droplet, in the second to all the droplets that handle such an event, in the last to a droplet that handles the event, if any. If an event cannot be handled it is discarded and the memory used by the event is freed.

Yasmin's event flexibility allows communications to be implemented between droplets easily and in a clean way. Delayed events facilitate the implementation of periodical tasks whereas custom events allow different droplets to interoperate in an appropriate way to send a specific event for a certain situation instead of using generic ones that need to be jeopardised in order to express peculiar situations. Additionally, the event destination enables droplets to implement a multi/broadcast facility which is useful when multiple droplets have to be informed of a certain event that is important for all of them (for instance a resourcePurge event which is broadcast by the system in low memory situations).

3.4. Service Manager

The Service Manager (SM) interacts with the DM to handle the services provided by the droplets. When a droplet is loaded, the DM notifies the SM of the services provided by the droplet which are made available to the whole system. When a droplet is unloaded, the DM informs the SM of the services that are no longer available. Services, identified by a unique string, can be of two types: local or remote. A local service can be used only locally whereas a remote service can be used both locally and remotely in an RPC[6]-like way [3] by exploiting the Communication Services (CS, covered in 3.6.). The main difference between local and remote services is that for remote services, the input/output parameters are both strings (hence the service is responsible for marshalling/unmarshalling data) whereas local services can use any type they want. Each service is specified through an entry inside the droplet information record. Such entry contains the name of the service, information about the service and about the input and output parameters specified as strings using the C language convention. Remote services contain "char*" in both input and output parameters whereas local services parameter contain the real type. For instance a local service that takes as input a record containing the name and the age of a person has a service input parameter that looks like "char*, "unsigned short". Service parms are mandatory and are useful for developers whenever they want to access services provided by a droplet written by third parties[7].

When a droplet has to invoke a service request, it cannot call the service directly so the SM does this on its behalf. The droplet provides the service name and the input parameters to the SM, and it gets back from the SM the result of the service invocation or an error if the service cannot be found. This design choice derives once more from the plug 'n play principle which specifies that information access cannot be gained directly (e.g. through a pointer) but has to be mediated by the entity responsible for managing such information.

In Yasmin, service requests must be processed within a limited amount of time in order to leave processing time to other requests. This means that a service request has to terminate and it cannot last for an infinite amount of time (e.g. an endless loop). Services that may need a long amount of time in order to process requests (for instance they may need some resources not yet available) should be divided into subservices that are activated sequentially by means of events. The requirement to complete service requests in a finite amount of time is very important in single-threaded systems, because the whole system is blocked until the service has been completed. In a multi-threaded system, although the system can continue to work, long lasting services occupy resources (for instance threads) hence reduce the global application performance. The SM has no way to guarantee that services do not last for too long since programmers are responsible for this. The only way for SM to prevent application deadlock or wild resource usage, is to run a sort of garbage collector that kills the threads that are apparently in a infinite loop or that are running since too long. Although this solution is not very clean because resources in use by threads may not be freed when the thread is killed, SM has no other choice to guarantee a minimal quality of service and to prevent application deadlock.

3.5. Resource Manager

The Resource Manager (RM) cooperates with other managers to use system resources efficiently. Such resources include but are not limited to memory, communication sockets, and droplets. The RM makes sure that system resources are not wasted and that it is activated periodically like a sort of garbage collector to purge resources no longer needed. The RM:

- informs the DM when droplets have expired their lifetime so they can be unloaded;
- makes sure that threads are used efficiently not starting too many threads, which would decrease the overall application performance;
- is responsible for purging memory and other system resources (including droplets) periodically or when it is required to perform a certain task and the available resources like MacApp does.

Although the RM is a 'hidden' component, it is very important because it allows the system to be run with very limited resources and prevents wasting them. For instance, Liaison, a Yasmin-based network management platform, can perform complex network management tasks using a very low amount of memory because the RM contributes to scale-down network management applications from large hosts to standard machines.

3.6. Collaboration Services

CollaBoration Services (CBS) enable droplets and services to cooperate in order to perform a certain task. CBS, exploiting SM and EM, allow a task to be broken down into many small cooperative subtasks. This solution enhances performance because these subtasks can be performed concurrently. This helps keep the complexity low because each subtask is simpler than the original task. CBS provide facilities for:

- sending requests in multicast/broadcast mode and collecting results;
- synchronising tasks by means of events.

[6] RPC stands for Remote Procedure Call.

[7] In a future version, service parms will be used to do transparent marshaling/unmarshaling, allowing just one type of service accessible both locally and remotely.

It is worth noting that Yasmin implements collaboration not only by means of CBS but also through the SM. In fact droplets collaborate with the rest of the system by providing services that can be of general interest. This avoids services being replicated, which saves development time and keeps the system slim and efficient.

3.7. Communication Services

Communication Services (CS) allow droplets and services to communicate with remote entities (local communications are performed via events). Since Yasmin has been designed with portability in mind, external communications are based on TCP/IP because it is a protocol supported by most platforms especially after the explosion of Internet. In view of the great diffusion of the World-Wide Web, CS includes also support for the HTTP protocol used by the Web to retrieve documents and which is becoming increasingly important even outside this context. Its popularity derives from the fact that it is a simple and efficient protocol which can be used to retrieve information other than to communicate with remote peers possibly located behind firewalls. Developers can exploit CS in order to:

- register/deregister sockets;
- be notified when data is available;
- issue HTTP requests and retrieve results.

CS is also used internally by other architecture components such as the SM which uses it to send transparently remote service requests and to receive responses. In fact an important characteristic of CS is that they allow one to send data in a reliable way and to handle transparently socket and protocol errors, shielding droplets from differences among socket implementations available on various platforms.

4. Yasmin at Work

Yasmin has been designed as an open and general architecture for software applications. Although the base principles of Yasmin have been applied to different fields such as a system for rapid GUI application development and a C++-like interpreter for the manipulation of distributed objects [2], Yasmin has been designed with particular emphasis on distributed networking applications for network management. This section covers the implementation of a Yasmin-based application for multidomain network management and shows how the adoption of Yasmin simplified the design of the application and allowed multiple network management protocols to be supported in a seamless way.

4.1. Liaison: a Yasmin Based software application

Liaison [9] is a proxy application [22] [13] which allows users to manage network resources through the Web using CMIP [5] and SNMP [23], the two dominant protocols for network management. Issues encountered during the design and development of Liaison are mostly related to:

- the great difference between CMIP and SNMP, other than their complexity;
- the need to leave room in order to accommodate future network management protocols/services and to modify the existing ones at runtime;
- the ability to run Liaison on hosts of limited computing power and under different operating systems.

Following Yasmin's principles, Liaison has been divided into two parts: general and protocol-related services. General services constitute the kernel of Liaison and are necessary for an application's execution. They include Yasmin's kernel services and additional ones such as HTTP services that are necessary to allow Web browsers to interact with Liaison, this being the only way for clients to interact with the application.

Protocol-related services, stored inside droplets, implement basic CMIP/SNMP services besides other facilities needed to allow users to manage network resources easily. The great difference between CMIP and SNMP prevented them from having a shared set of services shared by both protocols. Nevertheless the dynamic nature of droplets allowed services to be loaded on demand and to unload them when no longer needed. This has contributed a small application memory footprint and to avoiding the need to mix different protocols, for instance by means of object-oriented techniques such as inheritance. This design solution allowed Liaison's core part to be totally independent from the management protocols and simplified the integration of additional services and protocols that will be implemented using additional droplets.

Yasmin's collaboration services allowed us to reduce the amount of code needed to implement Liaison. Instead of implementing CMIP and SNMP separately, the few services shared by the two protocols have been implemented in a droplet in order to be used by both of them. This allowed us to avoid code duplication and also prevented these services that may not be needed by other protocols from being included statically into Liaison.

Yasmin's event services have been used to handle asynchronous protocol events. Network resources may emit asynchronous notifications when they change state or when a special situation arises. Management applications usually perform some actions prior to receipt of such notifications. Liaison allows droplets to register event handlers that are called when a notification is received. The droplet responsible for receiving notifications posts an event containing the notification itself. Event services then process the event by invoking the corresponding event handlers, if any. This mechanism allows asynchronous events to be handled properly, independently of the type of event and the protocol used to receive it.

The usage of personalities contributed to obtaining a highly portable application with almost no effort. Every platform specific functionality such as thread and shared library management has been encapsulated inside the personality without affecting most of the Liaison's code. This solution allowed Liaison to be ported over different platforms with very little effort.

Liaison has been used to validate Yasmin and to apply the architecture to a real case with strong requirements in terms of resource utilisation and problem complexity. The use of Yasmin has significantly contributed to creating a highly extensible and customisable application, which makes moderate use of system resources and which allows network management resources to be managed easily from the Web.

5. Final Remarks

This paper presented a new object-oriented, component-based architecture for software applications called Yasmin. Its main characteristics are that it is:

- highly portable, configurable and extensible;
- built upon dynamic software components called droplets;
- founded on cooperation and delegation, used to glue components together;
- a slim and efficient kernel which relies on a fast event handler;
- an efficient use of system resources, which enable Yasmin-based applications to run on environments of limited computing power.

Despite Yasmin's native ability to work in a networked environment, this architecture is general enough to be used not only on this applications field. So far it has been successfully applied to break large monolithic applications and to create a new class of web-based applications based on Liaison that integrate heterogeneous network management object models in a single homogeneous application [10]. Finally, the ability to modify and extend its applications at runtime, makes it attractive in dynamic environments where new services and resources need to be supported while the original application must remain active and ready to serve incoming requests.

6. Acknowledgements

The author would like to thank Dr. Wolfgang Kleinöder, Prof. Oscar Nierstrasz and the users and early adopters of Liaison[8] who have greatly contributed with all their comments and suggestions.

References

[1] Apple Computer, *Components Made Easy*, OpenDoc Technical White Paper, March 1995.

[2] B. Ban, *A Generic Management Model for CORBA, CMIP and SNMP*, PhD thesis, University of Zurich, Institut für Informatik, 1997.

[3] A. Birrell and B. Nelson, Implementing Remote Procedure Calls, *ACM Transactions on Computer Systems*, Vol. 2, February 1984.

[4] D. J. Chen and D. T.K. Chen, An Experimental Study of Using Reusable Software Design Frameworks to Achieve Software Reuse, *Journal of Object-Oriented Programming Languages*, May 1994.

[5] International Standards Organization, Information Technology - OSI, *Common Management Information Protocol (CMIP) - Part 1: Specification*, CCITT Recommendation X.711, ISO/IEC 9596-1, 1991.

[6] Cotter and M. Potel, *Inside Taligent Technology*, Addison-Wesley, ISBN 0-201-40970-4, 1995.

[7] L. Deri and E. Mattei, An Object-Oriented Approach to the Implementation of OSI Management, *Computer Networks and ISDN Systems*, Vol. 27, 1995.

[8] L. Deri, *Droplets: Breaking Monolithic Applications Apart*, IBM Research Report RZ 2799, September 1995.

[9] L. Deri, *Network Management for the 90s*, Proceedings of ECOOP '96 Workshop on System and Network Management, Linz, Austria, July 1996.

[10] L. Deri, *Surfin' Network Management Applications Across the Web*, Proceedings of 2nd Int. IEEE Workshop on System and Network Management, Toronto, Canada, June 1996.

[11] IBM Corporation, *DSOM Development Toolkit*, October 1994.

[12] A. Weinand, E. Gamma and R. Marty, *ET++: An object-oriented application framework in C++*, ACM OOPSLA '88 Conference Proceedings, San Diego, CA, September 1988.

[8] A version available for public download can be found at http://misa.zurich.ibm.com/Webbin/.

[13] E. Gamma, R. Helm, R. Johnson and J. Vlissides, *Design Patterns: Elements of Reusable Object-Oriented Software*, Addison-Wesley, 1994.

[14] T. Berners-Lee, R. Fielding and H. Nielsen, *HyperText Transfer Protocol - HTTP/1.0*, Internet Draft, October 1995.

[15] IBM Corporation, *IBM TMN Products for AIX: General Information, Release 2*, GC 31-8016-00, March 1996.

[16] M. Linton and P. Calder, *The design and implementation of Interviews*, Proceeding of USENIX C++ Workshop, Santa Fe, NM, November 1987.

[17] A. Joch, Killer Components, *Byte Magazine*, January 1996.

[18] T. Lewis et al., *Object Oriented Applications Frameworks*, Manning Publications, ISBN 0-13-213984-7, 1995.

[19] Apple Computer Inc., *MacApp 2.0: Programmer's Guide*, 1989.

[20] B. Meyer, *Object Oriented Software Construction*, Prentice Hall, Englewood Cliffs, NY, 1988.

[21] O. Nierstrasz, S. Gibbs and D. Tsichritzis, Component-Oriented Software Development, *Communications of the ACM*, 35(9), September 1992.

[22] M. Shapiro, *Structure and Encapsulation in Distributed Systems: the Proxy Principle*, 6th Int. Conference on Distributed Computing Systems, Boston, Mass., May 1986.

[23] J. Case, M. Fedor, M. Schoffstall and C. Davin, *Simple Network Management Protocol (SNMP)*, RFC 1157, May 1990.

[24] D. Tsichritzis, *Object-Oriented Development for Open Systems*, Proceedings of IFIP '89, North-Holland, San Francisco, August 1989.

[25] J. Udell, ComponentWare, *Byte Magazine*, May 1994.

[26] Object Management Group, *The Common Object Request Broker: Architecture and Specification*, Revision 2.0, July 1995.

[27] Symantec Corporation, *Bedrock Architecture*, 1993.

An Architecture for Designing Internationalized Software

Stavros Kokkotos
National Documentation Centre
National Hellenic Research Foundation
48 Vas. Konstantinou, 11635 Athens, Greece
skokko@iris.ekt.org.gr

Constantine D. Spyropoulos
Institute of Informatics & Telecommunications
National Centre for Scientific Research "Demokritos"
15310 Aghia Paraskevi, Greece
costass@iit.nrcps.ariadne-t.gr

Abstract

This paper presents a modular architecture for designing internationalized software, called ISDA-i. This architecture combines successfully the user requirements for highly personalized applications, with the developer requirements for easily maintained reusable software components, incorporating high localization potential. It enlarges the reusable software libraries and minimizes the size of the program core. All the configurable components of a software application are systematically stored in external configuration and resource files, which a system administrator or end-user may edit in order to modify its appearance and behavior.

1. Introduction

Enterprises as well as individuals all over the world increasingly depend upon computers. Users without prior experience on computers, and in some cases without knowledge of English, are required to efficiently use software applications and understand the conventions, which the developers have embedded in their product. More often than not, these conventions are based on the developer's cultural and linguistic background. Most software developers assume that users of their products have a working knowledge of the English language. This is not always the case, especially in new markets, like Russia and China [8,10,12]. It is necessary, in order to compete in the international market, to adapt software products to the cultural and linguistic background of the users, and not expect the users to adjust to the product. Furthermore, old established markets, like France, impose legal obstacles for software not converted to their language, and large multinational users want their applications adapted to local requirements, while preserving the same look and feel [10,12,17].

Localization is the modification of a software product to meet the requirements of a specific market, or locale. This adaptation does not include only translation of the user interface, and integration of the appropriate keyboard driver and input methods. It must also take care of local conventions, like date, time, currency and number representation formats, collating sequence, perhaps spelling, hyphenation, grammar and syntax rules, ordering, sorting, searching and matching rules, as well as local peculiarities about the use of color, sound and symbols [7,10,12,20]. Internationalization is the development of a software product that is free of linguistic and cultural dependencies and can be easily localized [5,10,12,17]. There exist three methodologies for the internationalization and localization cycle: compilation time, link time and run time localization [8,10,19,20]. The compilation time methodology requires changing the application source code, in order to adapt it to a local market. The link time methodology uses one version of source code, but links different libraries for different locales. The run time methodology uses a single internationalized product, which can use different dynamic libraries, or user-defined local resource files. The most common methodology is the compilation time, with all the disadvantages of having several versions of the same product to support and upgrade. Most efficient and flexible is the run time localization approach.

Many large software companies have realized the advantages of internationalizing their software products [1,2,4,8,9,10,11,14,15,17,18,21]. These companies follow a variety of internationalization and localization strategies: development of internationalized products from scratch, internationalization and localization of existing products, in-house or outsourcing localization, etc. Some of the most well known internationalization methodologies are those followed by Digital, Hewlett-Packard, Microsoft and IBM. On the WWW front some activities exist, which attempt to bring into focus internationalization issues for WWW-enabled applications and URLs [6,16].

In the present paper we propose a modular architecture for developing internationalized software that suits most software types. Each software product needs to integrate only the necessary modules. We call the proposed architecture Internationalized Software Design Architecture (ISDA-i). ISDA-i is based on the run time internationalization methodology. It evolved from the ISDA architecture developed during the GLOSSASOFT[1] project and appeared in a book that describes the GLOSSASOFT results [10]. ISDA-i combines, in a novel way, methodologies currently used by software companies, such as NLS message files and X-Windows resources, with new ideas, such as localized file systems and external configuration of linguistic and cultural methods. ISDA-i is expected to increase the product life cycle and assist the maintenance process by extensive use of reusable modules, as well as to enable the end users to customize and localize the software applications without expert assistance.

In the second section we present the requirements for software internationalization and localization as well as the various software components involved in these processes. In the third section the internationalization approaches of some well-known software companies are briefly described. In the fourth section the ISDA-i architecture is presented. In the fifth section we evaluate and discuss the benefits that result from the use of ISDA-i. The final section of the paper is a general discussion with the resulting concluding remarks.

2. Internationalization/localization requirements and software components

Developing an internationalized software product requires more time and resources than following conventional software development methodologies. Software developers decide in favor or against internationalized products, after examining customer profiles and needs, business prospects as well as any technical restrictions imposed by staff experience and resources [8,9,10,17,18]. Before developing a new product or updating an older version, software companies should thoroughly survey the target markets. The results of the survey, combined with the company's criteria and priorities, will enable the managers to decide upon the internationalization level of the product, as well as upon the localization level for each target market [10].

From the user's point of view a software product should offer full support for the local language and writing script, support for specification of different colors, icons and sounds, easy adaptation to the users needs, as well as self-explained operations.

From the business manager's point of view, internationalization and localization requirements are profits, and legal necessities as well as standing and prestige for the company. A manager should know if the target market needs the localized product, and if the market's size justifies the extra effort. In some cases, a manager will authorize the localization of a product, even if there is not enough profit margin, for prestige or legal reasons. Another important issue for managers is the simultaneous release of a product in as many markets as possible, in order to avoid complaints from local customers and vendors and illegal copies [3].

Technical requirements for internationalization and localization include support for modularized design, sufficient reusability of software components, easy product maintenance and long life cycle. All these requirements ensure that every successive version of the product will be localized using established methodologies and reusable components. Developers consider version control and configuration or localization effort as major problems.

After evaluating these requirements, the managerial staff of a software company must reach a decision [8,10,18]: should the product be internationalized and then localized for every locale, or different source code versions are required? What level should the localization reach in order to satisfy the target market requirements (legal requirements only, level with competition, full localization)? Will the product need to support multiple locales within the same session or as a multi-user product? Will the product interact with networks (LAN, WAN, INTERNET)? Who will do the localization (in-house or outsourcing)?

Generally, the software components that affect localization are categorized as follows [10,13]:

- User Interaction
- Data Encoding
- Software Services
- Networking
- Hardware Devices
- Linguistic Aspects
- Cultural Aspects and Local Practices
- Documentation

User interaction consists of software components that handle user input and screen output, including keyboard drivers, display drivers, application messages, user input processing, window geometry, colors, sounds, icons, symbols, etc. *Data encoding* includes any part of the application that deals with internal representation of data, such as font, character sets, standards, etc. *Software*

[1] GLOSSASOFT was partially supported by the European Community under the contract LRE 61003. Partners were The Open University (GB), NCSR "Demokritos" (GR), Claris (IR), HP Hellas (GR), VTT (FI), Bull (FR).

services include operating system support, inter-process communication, linking and embedding, as well as network communication. *Networking* consists of communication protocols and methodologies that connect heterogeneous computer platforms, often across enormous distances. *Hardware devices* deal with low level support of hardware devices, such as keyboard, display, mouse, pen, CD-ROM, printer, plotter, etc. *Linguistic aspects* include spelling, grammar and syntax checkers, sorting and ordering functions, upper-lower case converters, hyphenation, message generation. *Cultural Aspects* deal with date, time, currency, number representation formats as well as with local practices, methods and formulas, such as revenue and tax computation routines. *Documentation* includes both written manuals and on-line help.

3. Current Internationalization Approaches

In this section we briefly outline the internationalization approaches followed by some of the most well known software companies. Unfortunately, each of the large software companies has developed its own internationalization model, incorporating different architectures. Each of these architectures has advantages and disadvantages. Some offer better message and text localization, while others offer better geometry and color flexibility. Other architectures are suitable for window management systems, while others are better for word processors and spreadsheets.

Digital uses a blend of the link time and run time methodologies [4,10]. All Digital products are highly modularized with the locale-dependent components isolated in different modules. Digital offers two types of products: localizable and multilingual software. Localizable products are created by linking appropriate locale libraries that substitute functions, which are not suitable for the target locale. Multilingual software products use external message and resource files. These files contain language and market specific information, are distributed by Digital separately, and are added to the software at a later time.

Hewlett Packard uses the run time approach [10,11,14]. Its X11-based window manager, VUE, offers the Native Language Support (NLS) system, based upon the X/Open Portability Guide XPG4 [21]. The NLS system uses external files to store resource values and software messages. Applications automatically access the correct message file according to the locale selected by the user. System administrators may add message files for locales not supported by HP. VUE can be localized in-site without re-compilation or re-linking.

Microsoft utilizes a blend of the link and run time approaches with the run time approach more heavily used [10,15]. For window products, DLLs (Dynamic Link Libraries) and resource files are used, in order to enrich the software with locale and language dependent features. The disadvantage of the Microsoft approach is that application messages are included in DLLs, which need compilation after modification. Thus it is difficult for the user to localize a product without expert support.

IBM, in its OS/2 Warp product offers a set of internationalization functions, within an API, which support run-time localization, using locale files and resources [1]. A tool is provided for easy creation of new locales.

Many smaller companies appear to be active in the fields of internationalization and localization, especially regarding character sets (UNICODE), data exchange over INTERNET and cross-platform, cross-culture WWW enabled tools [6,16]. Especially popular today is the idea of internationalized Java applications, which are able to detect the client's locale and adjust the responses of the server to this locale.

4. A New Paradigm Architecture for Internationalized Software

Most of the software components, which we described in the second section of the paper, have to be localized. Approaches for internationalization and localization of these components, followed by software companies, do not really assist the localizer. The various software components are usually spread all over the software and one has to follow a different approach for the localization of different components and different applications. Furthermore, the software architectures, which have been proposed for developing internationalized products [5,19], lack in generality. Most of these architectures are useful for a small set of software types, because they focus on a subset of the software characteristics, like language (software translation) or text direction (for Middle and Far East software). The ISDA-i architecture allows parameterization of all these software components, thus easing their localization. This localization is performed by a centralized utility, which manages all the localizable options of a software application.

The ISDA-i architecture that we propose for developing internationalized software is pictured in Figure 1. An early version of this architecture appeared in [10], together with other results from the GLOSSASOFT project. In the following we briefly outline the proposed architecture.

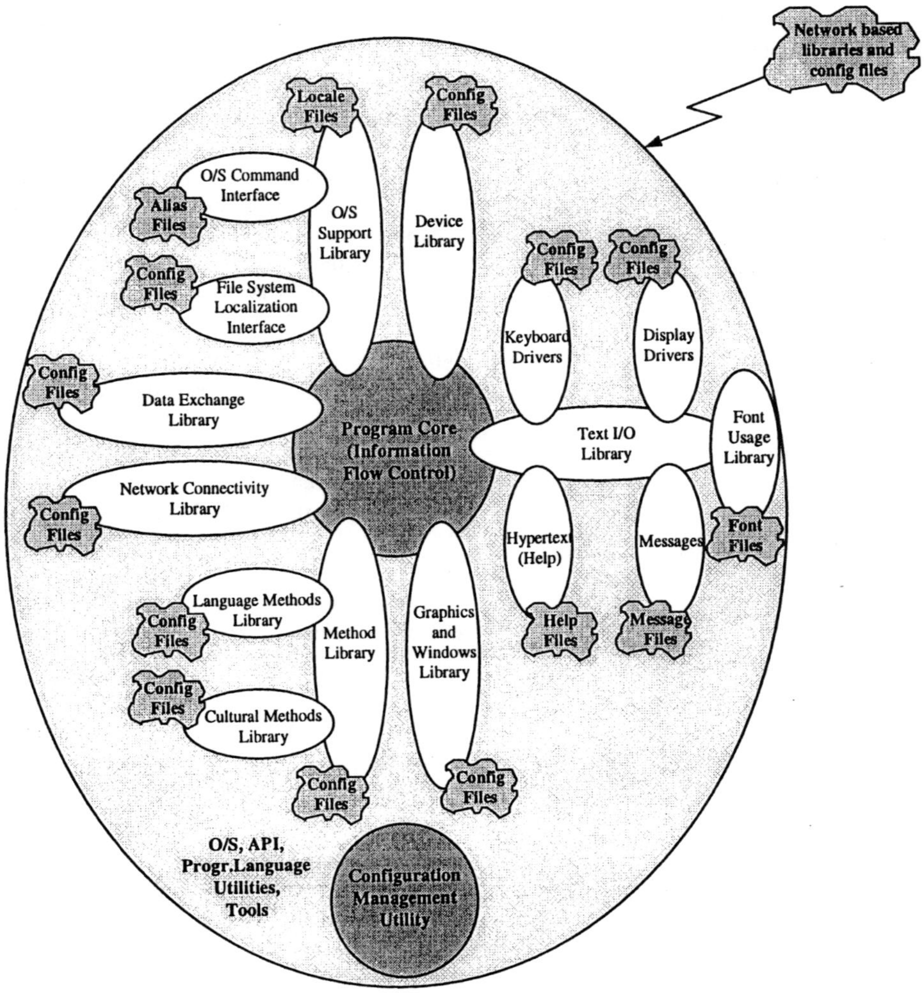

Figure 1. Architecture for internationalized software products.

ISDA-i considers that applications consist of a core, which contains only the basic logic of the software. For example the basic logic of most applications is a repetition the following steps: read a user input (character from the keyboard, mouse movement or click, etc.); react to this input by calling the appropriate functions; update the display; wait for the next input. The core of an application would hard-code these steps, while the implementation of every step should reside partly in the core and partly in external libraries. In Figure 1 the program core is the small circle at the center, labeled "Program Core (Information Flow Control)". The amount of hard coded information is decided by the developer, according to the specific application needs. A general guideline is that maximum localization can be reached using less hard-coding.

The program core, as well as any other software component, is built upon the operating system, using development tools and APIs (Application Programmer Interfaces), which in Figure 1 are represented by the large gray ellipse surrounding the figure. Tools include any utilities offered by the operating system, API tools, programming languages and libraries as well as any application used during the development of the product, or needed at run time.

As we mentioned in the second section of the paper, there exist a variety of components in a software product. These components in ISDA-i have been defined as external libraries. In Figure 1 libraries are represented as white ellipses. The program core calls functions and procedures from these libraries, in order to perform its activities. The libraries in turn perform actions and return the results of the function calls to the program core, or they may call other functions residing in the same or in other libraries. The libraries can be re-configured by altering external resource and configuration files (collectively called configuration files), represented in Figure 1 as clouds over the libraries. According to the capabilities of the operating system the libraries may be DLLs (run-time) or plain libraries (link time).

Most configuration files are text files, editable by the end user using a special utility. This utility, called Configuration Management Utility, is either specific (offered by the application) or generic (offered by the operating system). In Figure 1 it is represented by the circle at the bottom of the figure. There should be some configuration files that contain non-textual data, such as font files or DLLs implementing formulas, rules or methods. By textual data we mean data that the user can read and edit. In most platforms today these data should be written in ASCII, ISO-8859-x or UNICODE formats.

Since most of the functions and resources, contained in the libraries and the configuration files, are universally used, it is permitted for more than one application to use the same libraries and configuration files. As an example the Devices library, which contains the definitions of the hardware or logical device capabilities, and its associated configuration files, could be the same for every application, avoiding redundancy. Furthermore, these libraries and configuration files need not reside on the same computer. If the operating system permits such distribution these libraries and files could be in different computers, communicating over a LAN. A sensible configuration for an enterprise would be to have a pool of libraries in a set of commonly accessible computers, while each user or group of users has its own configuration files. Theoretically, it is absolutely possible for these libraries and configuration files to be obtained even from INTERNET.

We will now describe each of the libraries and configuration files in Figure 1.

The first software component category is user interaction. In ISDA-i, user interaction consists of the Text I/O and the Graphics and Windows Libraries. The first library handles the textual input and output, while the second handles the graphical I/O.

The Graphics and Windows Library contains functions that read the mouse movement and clicks as well as functions that enable the application to draw on the screen. Whenever the program core needs to know the mouse input, open a window or draw in a window, it calls the appropriate library function. This library is connected with a set of configuration files. These files contain directives for the user-mouse interaction, as well as guidelines about the display geometry, such as window, button, label and field sizes, positions, colors, as well as sounds that accompany the user-application interaction. An example of a mouse directive may be "In Window1, Phase A, Selection Of Text: Left-Button-Click", meaning that during the A phase of the application (the program core defines the phases) the user must click the left mouse button in order to mark text in Window1. The interaction descriptions are recognized either by the library functions, if they concern generic descriptions, or by the application for more specialized cases. The user may use the Configuration Management Utility to edit these configuration files, in order to alter the whole application behavior and layout. The application resource files of X11 can be considered as primitive examples of this type of library-configuration file use. In fact these files might be the basis for a Graphics and Windows configuration file standardization. The example in Figure 2 compares the creation of a button using conventional programming practices, and an ISDA-i-based methodology, in a C-like language.

The two approaches in Figure 2 look similar at first glance. All the items of the conventional programming style are present in the ISDA-i approach as well. However, when examined more deeply, the ISDA-i methodology has a major advantage over the conventional: the second "displaybutton" function parameter is not internal hard-coded variable of the program, which has to be recompiled in order to change its appearance and behavior, but it is defined in an external text file, which may be different for every locale. Furthermore in ISDA-i the application passes the minimum set of arguments, and the library function reads the rest from the configuration files. This results to the enlargement of the libraries and the minimization of the application code. Since the libraries are reusable, this enlargement is of small consequence, while the minimization of the application code reduces the cost of consequent application development and improvement. The "displaybutton" function reads the locale from a system variable, opens the appropriate configuration file to read its contents, and then displays the button within the specified base window, using the attributes (size, position, style, color, etc.) defined in the configuration file resources, by calling the low level functions of the Device Library. Then it calls an appropriate text displaying function ("displaytext") to display the text. Thus a differently looking button will be displayed for the "English" and the "Greek" locales. The NLS system from HP (based on the X/Open approach) follows the same methodology, but severely restricted [10,11,14].

The Text I/O Library contains the functions needed for textual input and output. The program core will call these functions whenever it needs to display text or to read something from the keyboard. These functions in turn call other functions in other libraries. Text input functions use the functions of the Keyboard Drivers. These functions control the language, font and writing direction of text input. The associated configuration files contain the control sequences for changing these attributes. The Keyboard Drivers functions handle the keyboard input calling the appropriate functions from the Device Library.

Conventional	Internationalized

#define BUT1WIDTH 30
#define BUT1HEIGHT 12
#define BUT1X 50
#define BUT1Y 80
#define BUT1COLOR BLUE
#define BUT1STYLE SHADOW
#define BUT1LABEL "Cancel"
#define BUT1LABCOLOR RED
#define BUT1LABSIZE 12
#define BUT1LABFONT Roman
. . .
button1=createbutton(basewindow,
    BUT1X, BUT1Y,
    BUT1WIDTH, BUT1HEIGHT,
    BUT1COLOR, BUT1STYLE,
    BUT1LABEL, BUT1LABCOLOR,
    BUT1LABSIZE, BUT1LABFONT);
. . .
/* createbutton is an API function) */
	Configuration file for locale English:
	BUT1*GEOMETRY=30x12+50+80
	BUT1*COLOR=BLUE
	BUT1*STYLE=SHADOW
	BUT1*LABEL="Cancel"
	BUT1*LABEL*COLOR=RED
	BUT1*LABEL*SIZE=12
	BUT1*LABEL*FONT=Roman
	
	Configuration file for locale Greek:
	BUT1*GEOMETRY=50x12+35+80
	BUT1*COLOR=RED
	BUT1*STYLE=RAISED
	BUT1*LABEL="Ακύρωση"
	BUT1*LABEL*COLOR=WHITE
	BUT1*LABEL*SIZE=10
	BUT1*LABEL*FONT=GreekRoman
	
	Program file:
	. . .
	button1=displaybutton(basewindow, BUT1);
	. . .
	/* displaybutton is a library function */

Figure 2. Displaying a button in a conventional and an ISDA-i based approach.

Whenever a message is to be displayed, the Text I/O Library calls the Messages Library. This library connects to the Message files, which contain the application messages, translated into the target locale language. As messages we consider error messages, other messages of the application, as well as button, window, menu and other screen component labels. HP has followed this approach in the VUE System. VUE applications read their messages from external files that can be modified by the system administrator [10,11,14]. Other companies such as Microsoft, Digital, IBM and Apple have followed the same approach in some of their products. The Text I/O Library calls the appropriate functions from the Display Drivers, in order to display messages or other text. This library contains routines that read the writing direction and character set and font from the associated configuration files and display the text using the appropriate method, by calling the appropriate functions in the Graphics and Windows Library and the Devices Library.

In the example of Figure 2 the "displaybutton" function will call the "displaytext" function from the Text I/O Library, in order to display the label of the button. This function identifies the locale, accesses the appropriate configuration file, accesses the Font Usage Library, which returns the specified font, and then displays the appropriate text using the appropriate attributes. Thus the displayed text will be in red and in English for the English locale and white in Greek for the Greek locale. In the same way we could have an unlimited number of other locales, to display differently shaped buttons and texts.

Software developers have used the idea of graphics, windows and text I/O libraries, mainly when developing applications for windowing environments. The new element in ISDA-i is the connection of the libraries with user-defined configuration files, which alter the behavior of the library functions for different applications and different locales.

The second software component category is data encoding. This component consists of the Font Usage Library. This library accepts calls for font retrieval from the other libraries and returns the appropriate font, which it reads from the Font files. This is a standard approach, used in most modern window-based environments. An embellishment of this approach is the substitution of a "similar" font if the requested font does not exist. Something like this has been implemented by Microsoft in its popular MS-Windows environment.

The third and fourth software component categories are software services and networking. Software services consist of the Data Exchange Library and the O/S Support Library with its two associated libraries, the O/S Commands Interface and the File System Localization Interface. Networking consists of the Network

Connectivity Library. The O/S Support Library contains functions that use the Operating System commands, and access the file system. The Locale file contains the basic locale definition (country name, language name, associated fonts, date, time, currency and number format, collating sequence and upper-lower case transformations, names of days, months and numbers, names of the configuration, Message, Help, Font and Alias files as well as any other generic locale information). The locale file is the resource catalog of the application. Each application may contain many locale-specific sets of configuration, Message, Font, Help, Alias and Locale files. In this case the user defines the required locale, the application reads the appropriate Locale file and specifies the other configuration files. Many software developers use locale files, and there already exist standards for their use [10]. However the contents of a locale file depend upon the developer's intentions and the application scope.

The Data Exchange Library contains functions that enable the application to connect to other applications and exchange data between applications and processes. The Network Connectivity Library contains functions that enable data transfer between computers, over LANs, and WANs, including Intranets and the INTERNET. The associated configuration files describe the protocols and standards used for the communications and exchanges. The user or system administrator may tune the performance of the system or alter its behavior, by modifying the underlying configuration files. Microsoft uses a similar approach in MS-Windows by allowing the user to define and configure the network drivers.

The O/S Commands Interface contains functions and aliases that translate the Operating System commands into the locale language. A primitive O/S Commands Interface can be constructed in UNIX using the alias command to define a new name for existing commands. For example the statement "alias delete rm" defines the command "delete" as a synonym for "rm".

The File System Localization Interface uses the associated configuration files as dictionaries that map a locale-specific file name to every system file. Using this library the software may access the files using local names, without altering the actual file names used by the operating system. This mapping is necessary when we have to rename files to a target language that does not use the Roman-English character set (for example Greek, Russian, Hebrew, Arabic, Japanese, etc.). One can view the File System Localization Interface as a set of directory trees, each one a copy of the original directory tree, where the names of files and directories are translated into other locales. When the application needs to display a file name, using the appropriate function calls, it searches for the file in the original directory tree and then finds the file name in the same position into the tree of the current locale. When a user enters a file name, in his locale language, the application finds this file name in the locale directory tree, and then searches for the file in the same position of the original tree. Such sets of directory trees can be constructed in UNIX and MS-Windows using links or shortcuts. However, these trees are not updated automatically.

The fifth software component category is hardware devices. This component consists of the Devices Library, which accepts calls for hardware or virtual device usage directly from other libraries and the program core. It translates the calls to the appropriate low level calls, according to device definition of the associated configuration files. As simple examples of such configuration files we mention the "termcap" and "princap" UNIX files that define, using ASCII characters, the characteristics and capabilities of various terminals and printers. Another example is the driver based, user-configurable hardware device management offered by Microsoft.

The sixth and seventh software component categories are linguistic aspects and cultural aspects and local practices. These components consist of the Method Library. This library accepts calls for linguistic or culture dependent methods from the program core, and passes these calls to the appropriate functions of the Language Methods or the Cultural Methods Libraries.

The Language Methods Library contains linguistic-dependent methods such as spelling, syntax checking, hyphenation, etc. The Cultural Methods library contains culture-dependent methods such as tax computation, salary computation, etc. New linguistic and cultural methods may be added to these libraries by local vendors and developers. A method to facilitate this openness of the libraries is to use different DLLs (Dynamic Link Libraries) for each locale. This is the approach followed by Microsoft in its Office product.

The eighth software component category is documentation. For hard copy documentation (manuals), hard copy translation methods are required. The on-line help facility is served by the functions of the Help Hypertext component of ISDA-i. These functions read the appropriate Help files, based on the selected locale, and pass the text to the Display Drivers for displaying. Furthermore they call the Keyboard Drivers functions and the Graphics and Windows Library functions to interpret and respond to user reactions. Such an approach is followed by the HP VUE system for its on-line help facility.

The Configuration Files Management Utility is either a special utility, part of the software application, or a generic one, offered by the operating system or the window management system. Using this utility the system administrator or the end user may review and modify all the resources and configuration commands, used by the application. For example the user may see every message in a message file, and, if the appropriate permissions are available, modify some messages. A primitive example of a Configuration Management Utility is the Style Manager application, used by the HP VUE System, to alter the windows, display, keyboard, mouse and audio appearance and behavior [11]. Another example is the Control Panel application in the MS-Windows environment. However both these utilities work on the operating system level, while ISDA-i supports the application level.

5. Evaluation of the Proposed Architecture

The proposed ISDA-i architecture is based on a highly modular design. Each system component is clearly separated from other components, resulting in easy maintenance and larger life cycle. Easy maintenance is achieved because only the affected modules must be modified for changes or improvements. Since improvements are so easy the product can be improved repeatedly remaining competitive for a long time.

The cost for developing a software product, by following the ISDA-i architecture, may be higher in the short run, when all the different libraries are developed, but eventually, due to the high reusability degree, product maintenance, as well as new product development, will be lower than average. New software products may use functions from the same reusable libraries. For new products, functions may be added or removed to these libraries to minimize the overall volume.

The Configuration Management Utility centralizes the localization process. Our opinion is that generic applications, like window management systems, or operating systems should offer a generic configuration utility that will be used for their applications, while complex individual applications, such as spreadsheets, word-processors, graphics packages, databases, etc. should also offer tailored configuration tools. Using the Configuration Management Utility the localization of every application aspect is within easy reach and can be done in a very short time. It is easy for a non expert end user to customize or personalize the software, according to specific needs. Customization is defined as the process of adapting a software product to the needs of a small subset of the overall market (like a company), while personalization is the adaptation of an application to the demands of a specific end user. Personalization is usually performed by an experienced user at his/her own risk. The easy localization, customization or personalization, either by the developer/vendor or by a system administrator/end-user, helps lowering the maintenance cost. Using the proposed architecture the localization idea is extended from locales to users. This means that every user can have a different application configuration, layout and messages, according to his personal interests, background and taste. Even a single user can be considered as a different locale. Thus, the localization, customization and personalization of an application are different aspects of the same methodology.

A software product developed following the ISDA-i architecture will possibly require more computing power and resources than a conventionally developed product. However, the rate of improvement of computing power and hard disk access speed is so high that these limitations, which may apply to a small number of applications and platforms today, will be invalid during the immediate future.

Some legal issues will become simpler as well [3]. The adoption of the ISDA-i architecture may solve the legal ownership and copyright issues for localized software versions, since there exist only one master version. This may also help in solving the serious problem of version control. Furthermore, simultaneous release is possible for a large range of markets, adding to the developer's prestige as well reducing the danger of piracy, which is always present in small and badly supported markets [3]. Independent vendors and local developers may offer additional libraries and configuration files, making the product more attractive to the customers.

Parts of ISDA-i are already offered by various software developers as utilities within their operating systems or window-based environments. However none of these utilities supports the full spectrum of the internationalization and localization requirements, as described in the present section. If ISDA-i becomes accepted and supported by the major software developers it will homogenize software development and support across platforms, since applications will follow the same design principles. Before this happens, the international software community has to agree on standards for the locales and the configuration files.

Thus, ISDA-i may also assist the support of multiple platforms. This support can be realized by recompiling the source code of the core program for the target platform, and rewriting some of the libraries to support this platform, while keeping a consistent look and feel of the product. The libraries that most probably may need rewriting for different platforms, are the ones that deal with the hardware and operating system support of the platform, namely the Devices Library, the O/S Support Libraries, the Data Exchange Library and the Font Usage Library.

ISDA-i has been used in a case study for the design of an internationalized word processor [10]. The conclusions of this case study were similar to these expressed by other researchers and developers facing similar problems [8,18]. The initial development, which includes all the different libraries and configuration files, requires more effort, in some cases as high as twice the effort needed to develop the same application conventionally, but subsequent localizations, as well as improvements, modifications and maintenance are much easier. We have not yet implemented an actual application using the ISDA-i approach. We know that the performance of such an application will be worse than the performance of a conventionally developed similar application, in terms of computing power and I/O needed, because of the overhead imposed by the function calls to the external libraries and the use of the configuration files. However, for broad use applications (like most of the PC and workstation applications today) we believe that the difference in performance will be very small, while the advantages we have mentioned will persuade developers for the benefits of our approach.

6. Conclusions

We presented the Internationalized Software Design Architecture, ISDA-i, which is an architecture for developing internationalized software products. Since each large software developer company uses its own architectural model, which often is not general enough to support all the required software application types, we believe that the ISDA-i architecture is a step towards the unification and globalization of software design principles.

ISDA-i enables the users to configure the software products according to their specific needs, altering their behavior and appearance, without need for expert assistance. Software products that adopt the ISDA-i architecture are expected to load different configurations at run-time, depending on the locale. Since there is no limit to the number of locales, and a new locale may be specified based on an old one, it is possible for every user or group of users to be considered as a different locale, enabling the customization and personalization of the software products.

We believe that ISDA-i combines successfully the user requirements for highly personalized applications, with the developer requirements for easily maintained reusable software components, incorporating high localization potential.

References

[1] S. Atkin, K. Borgendale. Developing Applications using Universal Language Support. *Proceedings of the Tenth International UNICODE Conference*, Mainz, Germany, March 1997.

[2] D. R. Carter. *Writing Localizable Software for the Macintosh.* Addison-Wesley, Cambridge, MA, 1992.

[3] J. Daunt. Legal Issues. *Proceedings of the Globalizing Software Product Management Conference*, San Jose, CA, 1994.

[4] Digital Corporation. *Digital Guide to Developing International Software.* Digital Press, Bedford, MA 1991.

[5] M. Farid. Software Engineering Globalization and Localization. *Proceedings of the IEEE International Conference on Systems, Man and Cybernetics*, 491-495, 1990.

[6] A. Freytag. Java Internationalization Architecture. *Proceedings of the Tenth International UNICODE Conference*, Mainz, Germany, March 1997.

[7] N. Gaitanis, S. Kokkotos. Formal Specification of Multilingual Alphanumeric Ordering Systems. *Computer Standards and Interfaces*, 17(5-6):535-552, 1995.

[8] D. Goldstein. Strategies for Globalizing Software. *Proceedings of the Tenth International UNICODE Conference*, Mainz, Germany, March 1997.

[9] D. Greco. Reducing Time to Market and Localization Costs. *Proceedings of the Globalizing Software Product Management Conference*, San Jose, CA, 1994.

[10] P. A. V. Hall, R. Hudson (eds.). *Software Without Frontiers.* John Wiley and Sons, Chichester, UK, 1997.

[11] Hewlett Packard. *How to Develop Internationalized Software.* Hewlett Packard, 1992.

[12] R. Ishida. Internationalization: More than just Character Sets. *Proceedings of the Tenth International UNICODE Conference*, Mainz, Germany, March 1997.

[13] E. Karkaletsis, C. D. Spyropoulos. Internationalization and Localization of Software. *Proceedings of the 4th Greek Computer Society Conference*, Patras, Greece, 629-640, 1993.

[14] T. Madell, C. Parsons, J. Abegg. *Developing and Localizing International Software.* Hewlett Packard Professional Books, Prentice Hall Englewood Cliffs, NJ, 1994.

[15] Microsoft Corporation. *The Windows Interface: International Handbook for Software Design.* Microsoft Press, Redmond, WA, 1992.

[16] G. T. Nicol. Dynaweb: Content Generation Based on Client Preferences. *Proceedings of the Tenth International UNICODE Conference*, Mainz, Germany, March 1997.

[17] M. O'Callahan. Keynote Speech. *Presented at the Globalizing Software Product Management Conference*, San Jose, CA, 1994.

[18] H. H. Preston, U. Flohr. Global from Day One. *Byte*, March 1997:97-104.

[19] D. Taylor. *Global Software: Developing Applications for the International Market.* Springer-Verlag, New York, 1992.

[20] E. Uren, R. Howard, T. Perinotti. *Software Internationalization and Localization, an Introduction.* VNR Computer Library, New York, 1993.

[21] X/Open Company. *Internationalization Guide Version 2.* X/Open Company Ltd., Reading, UK, 1993.

Hypernode Model Support for Software Design Methodology Modelling

Louise Scott

CSIRO - Macquarie University Joint Research Centre for Advanced Systems Engineering,
Macquarie University Sydney, NSW 2109 Australia
E-mail: louise@mpce.mq.edu.au

Abstract

This paper argues that the graph-based hypernode model is a good tool for supporting software design methodology modelling in a software design meta-CASE tool. Unique features of the hypernode model that make it particularly suitable for this task are a nested, graph-based structure, support for meta-data modelling and a high-level, procedural query and update language. These features make it possible for the hypernode model to support the definition of both methodological structures and processes and run-time modification of methodological support in a meta-CASE tool. We demonstrate these features in a prototype meta-CASE tool called CASEMaker.

Keywords: Meta-CASE, software design CASE, methodology modelling, graph-based models

1. Introduction

The large amount of variation in the requirements for software design CASE from companies, projects and individuals coupled with the large amount of resources required to produce such sophisticated software applications drive our interest in meta-CASE tools. There is a need for meta-CASE tools that can be customised and instantiated to meet the requirements of a particular CASE tool, be it to support a new or emerging methodology or to customise an existing methodology to meet specific needs.

Meta-CASE tools need to supply powerful models for design methodologies because software design CASE tools base much of their support for the design process on supporting particular design methodologies. The methodology determines what kind of representation and notation the CASE tool uses, provides rules for checking and analysing the design and dictates the support for the design process embedded in the tool.

This paper shows how the hypernode model provides a uniquely supportive framework for modelling software design methodologies in a meta-CASE environment. The hypernode model addresses aspects of methodology modelling which have not been fully addressed in other meta-CASE tools. In particular, the hypernode model supports the definition and enactment of software design processes, a key aspect of methodology modelling which has been overlooked in many meta-CASE tools. This paper also shows how the hypernode model supports the run-time definition of methodology through support for meta-data modelling.

The related work section introduces methodological models and reviews models used for capturing methodology. From this review emerges a set of key issues to be addressed by a model for capturing design methodology. The hypernode model is then briefly introduced and it is shown how the hypernode model can provide comprehensive support for capturing software design methodology. The paper concludes with a description of a meta-CASE tool that utilises the hypernode model to provide novel features in methodology modelling.

2. Related work

Several meta-CASE tools have been built, some of which are commercially available (e.g. toolbuilder [1], metaEdit [15], and Metaview [17]). Since methodology is central to CASE support for design process, meta-CASE tools rely heavily on the model they use to capture methodology which in turn determines the nature of the functionality they can provide. This section begins by introducing a high level model for software design methodology and then reviews several meta-meta-models used by meta-CASE tools to capture software design methodologies. These models include an entity-

0-8186-7840-2/97 $10.00 © 1997 IEEE

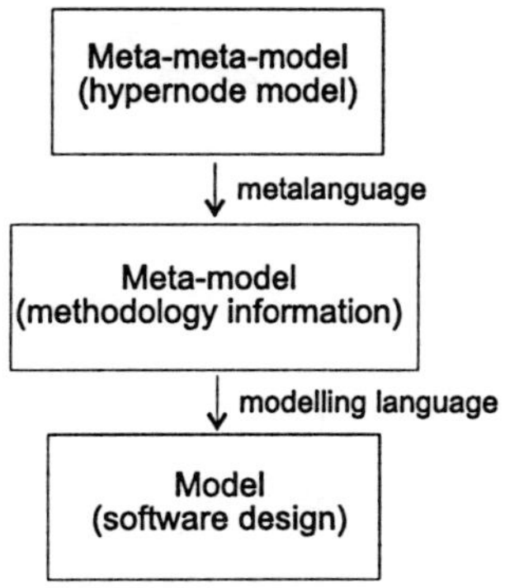

Figure 1. Levels of abstraction in a meta-CASE environment. The meta-meta-model is used to specify the meta-model that captures the methodology which is in turn used to specify the software design (adapted from [9]).

relationship model, an object-oriented model and a graph-based model. This review shows that a meta-model for software design methodology should ideally be able to support:

- definition of both representation *and* process components of methodology,
- capture of complex (nested) objects that are common in software design methodologies,
- definition of rules governing the allowable and "best" structures of artefacts produced using the methodology and,
- preferably allow changes to the methodology to take effect without compilation of models so that fast prototyping of methodology is possible.

The role of models in a meta-CASE environment is shown in Figure 1.

Our model of methodology is based on the one proposed by Reeves, Marashi and Budgen [13] which describes design methodology in terms of *representation*, *process* and *heuristics*. The representation part describes the structure of design artefacts and notations used by the methodology; the process part describes the steps to be followed to develop the design; and the heuristics capture the non-procedural knowledge contained in the methodology such as guidelines gained from experience using the methodology. The authors argue that heuristics can usually be captured as part of the process, making representation and process the most important components of methodology. We therefore concentrate our modelling efforts on capturing methodological representations and processes.

The Reeves, Marashi and Budgen model is compatible with another model for methodology proposed by Welland, Beer and Sommerville [18] who characterise a design methodology as a language with three components - vocabulary, syntax and semantics. The vocabulary describes the set of symbols and notations used to represent the design, the syntax describes the rules governing the organisation and connectivity of symbols on a diagram and the semantics describe rules and guidelines which constrain the design to "good" designs. This model is easily captured by the first by noting that vocabulary and syntax are representation issues and semantics can be expressed as rules on the representation or as processes.

Various meta-meta-models for software designs have been used in meta-CASE tools. A review of three successful models including a graph-based model (GDL) [16] and two entity-relationship-attribute based models (EARA from the MetaView project [5, 17]and GOPHR from the MetaEdit project [11]), shows the following issues to be key issues for methodology models:

- Graph-based models are promising. GDL (Graph Description Language) was created on the realisation that the prominence of graphical representations in software design methodologies makes them particularly suited to capture with a graph-based model. A graph-based model allows a clean and intuitively simple mapping between methodology and model and ensures that structural aspects can be easily captured.
- Nested or complex structures have to be supported. All of the models were at some stage extended to capture nested or complex structures.
- Inheritance among design elements is useful. All of the models have an inheritance construct which allows for generalisation/specialisation of methodological concepts.
- Support for defining rules governing the structure of allowable or "good" diagrams in the methodology is essential.
- Late binding to allow changes to the model to take effect without compilation is desirable. Only GOPHR supports this at present.
- While desirable, none of the models provide intrinsic support for process modelling (although in MetaView and MetaEdit this facility has been

added in tool support on top of the underlying model, the fundamental models do not give any support to this concept).

This paper argues that the hypernode model is a particularly promising model for methodology modelling because it addresses most of the issues identified above. Its nested graph-based structure matches the graph-based structures used in software design methodologies, its hypernode scheme definition framework allows structural constraints on graphs to be defined and enforced and allows meta-data modelling capabilities which means that models do not have to be compiled to take effect. The hypernode model can also utilise the procedural style hypernode query language to specify detailed methodological processes. The only issue supported by the other modelling languages but not supported by the hypernode model is structural inheritance among design elements which, although potentially useful, we have never felt limits the hypernode model's applicability to methodology modelling.

The application of graph-based formalisms in software engineering is not new. The prevalence of graph structures in software design prompted Harel in 1988 to propose *higraphs* as a software modelling tool [7]. Since then, several graph-based meta-models have been proposed, including Progress [4], GOOD [6], Graphlog [3] and PGADT [2]. Many have found application supporting software design CASE tools (e.g. [4, 2]) but none have been specifically applied to meta-CASE or flexible design methodology modelling. The hypernode model also differs significantly from these graph models in that it supports a nested graph structure. This makes it possible for the hypernode model to naturally support the important modelling concepts of encapsulation and hierarchical decomposition, both of which are commonly employed in software design methodologies.

3. The hypernode model

A hypernode is a directed graph comprising nodes and edges, where any node can itself be a hypernode. Thus hypernodes are *nested* graphs. A graphical example is shown in Figure 2. It has been shown that this simple formalism can capture many popular modelling concepts such as object, entity, relationship, attribute, inheritance, records, sets, and many more [10], [14].

An important concept in the hypernode model is that of hypernode schemes. Analogous with graph schemes, hypernode schemes are used to define the allowable structure of other hypernodes. The relationship between a hypernode scheme and its instance is

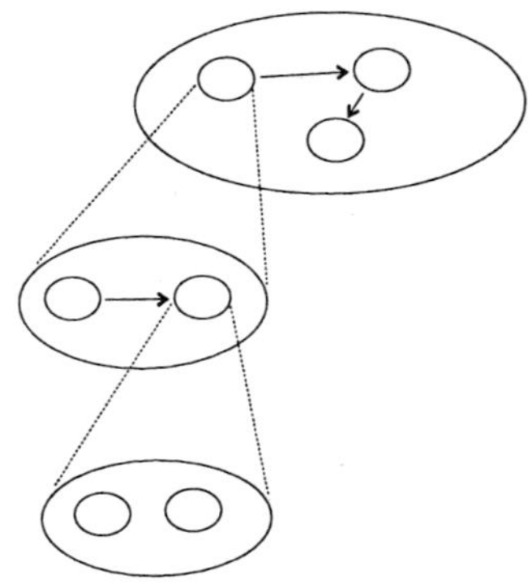

Figure 2. A graphical description of a hypernode. Ellipses are hypernodes, solid lines are hypernode edges and the dotted lines indicate hypernode nesting. A hypernode may contain other hypernodes joined by edges to form a directed graph. Although only three levels are shown here, the nesting of hypernodes can continue infinitely.

that there must be a hypernode morphism which maps the instance onto the scheme. Briefly, this means that there must be a mapping that maps each node in the instance to a node in the scheme and each edge in the instance to an edge in the scheme while preserving the adjacency relationships. A graphical example of a hypernode scheme and instance is shown in Figure 3.

The above definition of hypernode scheme allows a variety of structures to conform to a particular hypernode scheme. In practice it is desirable to allow the mappings to be constrained to only a subset of possible mappings. This increases the expressive power of hypernode schemes, allowing structures to be defined more precisely than is possible with a general hypernode morphism. Such constraints find application in modelling areas such as defining integrity constraints for entity-relationship models.

The hypernode model supports a constraint definition framework which allows users to specify constraints such as how many nodes of a particular type may appear in an instance, how many edges may go from a node of that type to nodes of some other type and whether the appearance of two nodes of different types should be mutually exclusive (for a full explanation of scheme constraints see [14]). Each constraint is given a maximum and minimum value ranging from 0 to "unspecified" (which means there is no value). A textual language for describing scheme constraints has been defined, an example of which appears in Figure 5.

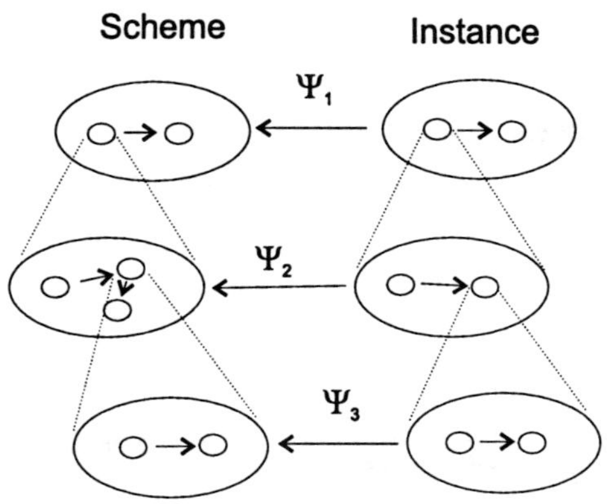

Figure 3. An example hypernode scheme and instance. At each level the hypernode morphism (components of which are denoted by Ψ_i) is equivalent to a graph morphism between the corresponding component graphs.

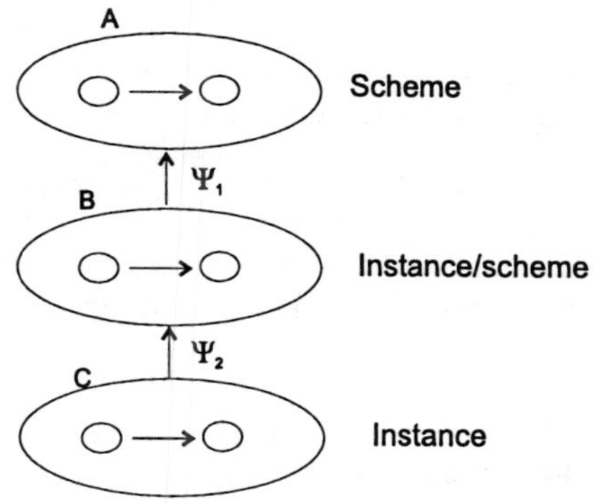

Figure 4. An example of a hypernode scheme hierarchy (hypernode morphisms denoted by Ψ_i) where hypernode B is acting both as an instance of the scheme definition, hypernode A, and as a scheme definition for hypernode C.

Hypernode scheme/instance relationships need not be restricted to two level relationships. There is no reason why a hypernode scheme definition for a particular hypernode cannot itself be an instance of another scheme definition, thus forming a scheme hierarchy as shown in Figure 4.

Hypernode scheme hierarchies make possible the notion of *meta-data modelling* in a hypernode database. Meta-data modelling describes the situation where multiple levels of abstraction can be modelled in a database. One consequence is that the database scheme can be changed by the end user as though it were data in the database (in traditional databases the scheme is fixed at implementation time and only data can be changed by the end user). Meta-data modelling has been found useful in projects such as Conceptbase where it is desirable to combine data from different meta-data models [8], where there is a need to allow data models to evolve over time [8] and where it is necessary to model multiple levels of abstraction in a database [14].

Finally, the *Hypernode Query Language* (HNQL) is a high-level, procedural style query language which provides facilities for the creation and deletion of hypernodes in a hypernode repository, declarative querying of hypernode structures and updating of hypernode structures by inserting and deleting nodes and edges from hypernodes.

4. Methodology modelling with hypernodes

Following the [13] model of methodology as representation and process, we show that the hypernode model can capture many of the concepts required for methodology modelling as identified in Section 2. In keeping with [13] terminology we consider that the design methodology specifies design elements and the relationships between design elements. Instances of design elements are created by the designer and constitute design artefacts. The tool builder (doing the methodology modelling) is distinguished from the tool user, the software designer using the CASE tool built by the tool builder to develop a software design.

4.1. Representation

To model a methodology representation it is necessary to capture the following information,

- the structure of the representation. This includes what elements make up the artefacts produced by the methodology and the rules governing the way these elements are related to each other. This is equivalent to the structural and data modelling viewpoints of [13] and the syntax component of [18]. It also includes some of the semantic rules described in [18] which constrain the designs that can be produced (by constraining the structure of the artefacts).

- the notation. This describes the visual way in which design elements are represented. This is equivalent to the vocabulary component of [18].

The hypernode model provides good support for capturing the structural aspects of representation. While it contains no inherent support for notational aspects it is straightforward to attach symbols to hypernode types in a meta-CASE environment to ensure that the correct notation is supported. We support the view of [16] that it is the underlying information which is the important part of methodology modelling and the graphical representations can be handled separately by the user interface.

To model methodological structures, the abstract structure of design elements is drawn as a hypernode (directed graph) which acts as the scheme for design instances. Elements can be captured as nodes and relationships between them denoted by edges. The hypernode model gives natural support to nested structures, so encapsulated and hierarchical structures can easily be captured. Detailed constraints on the structure of design elements can be specified using the hypernode scheme constraint definition language. In [14] it has been shown that a variety of methodological structures can be captured with the hypernode model including object-oriented, entity-relationship-attribute, state-chart, data-flow and Petri net structures.

A hypernode representation of the abstract structure of a "class" in the object-oriented design methodology is shown in Figure 5. Design elements such as Class, Relationship, attribute name and attribute type are captured as hypernodes. Hypernode nesting has been used to encapsulate the attribute names and attribute types in the class and to allow the recursive reference of the "Class" type. Constraints are added to the scheme definition to more precisely define the allowed structure of the instances. For example, the first constraint shown in Figure 5 specifies that a class must have more than one attribute name. The second constraint specifies that an attribute name must always be connected to either an attribute type or another class. This means that in this methodological description there can be no attribute names defined without assigning them an attribute type.

Once hypernode schemes have been defined in the database, instances of these schemes can be created with no need to compile the scheme definitions. Figure 6 shows an instance of the scheme definition for class. This allows the tool builder to quickly explore the effects of changes to the methodological support in CASE tools. It also means that the tool user (the software designer) can define methodological schemes for design elements if required. This could be used by the

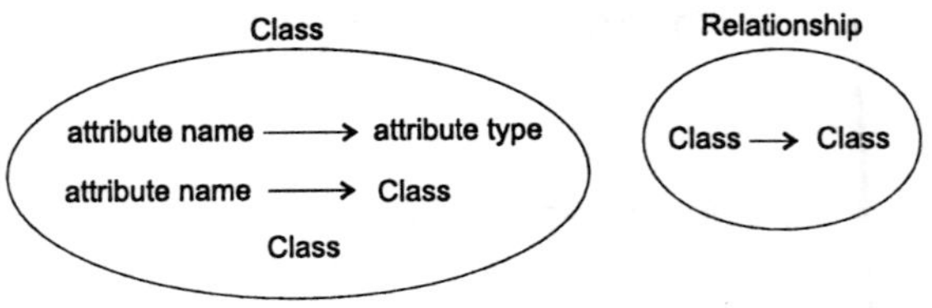

Typechecking Class:
attribute name: (1,unspecified);
attribute type: (0, unspecified), indegree wrt attribute name (1,unspecified);
at least one of outdegree of attribute name wrt attribute type or outdegree of attribute name wrt Class is not zero;
Typechecking Relationship:
Class: (2,many),
at least one of indegree of Class wrt Class or outdegree of Class wrt Class is not zero;

Figure 5. The hypernode scheme definitions for the object-oriented concepts of attribute, class and relationship. Attributes are encapsulated within classes using the hypernode's naturally nested structure. Inheritance is captured by including the superclass object within the subclass, indicating that the subclass contains everything in the superclass as well as extra information of its own. Constraints specify "good" structures, such as an attribute name must be connected to either an attribute type or another class.

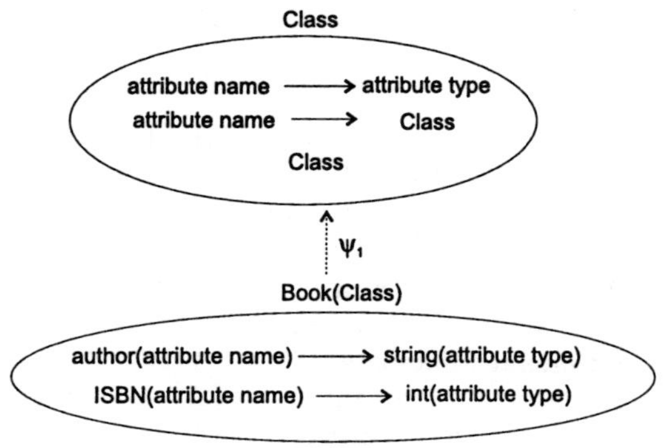

Figure 6. The hypernode scheme definition for "Class" with an instance hypernode representing a "Book" class definition. The relationship between the hypernodes is a hypernode morphism denoted by Ψ_1. Any number of instances of "Class" can be created in the hypernode repository and changes to the structure of the hypernodes "Class" or "Book(Class)" can be made at any time.

software designer to change scheme definitions during a project if the defined methodology was not meeting project requirements (this would have to be allowed by the project management). The meta-data modelling capabilities of hypernodes (where scheme definitions behave as changeable data in the database) provides a lot of flexibility in methodology modelling.

4.2. Process

Many methodologies for modelling the software designing process exist (e.g. Petri nets, state charts, GANTT charts). This section shows how the hypernode model supports the definition of these methodologies and their instantiation as methodological process models. In this way a particular process model for a methodology can be built, either using a common process modelling methodology or one which suits the CASE tool builder, and run to provide CASE support for methodological process. To model methodological process the following concepts must be captured:

- the procedures or steps to be followed to produce design artefacts (in enough detail that the model can be run by the CASE tool to provide support),
- the order of the execution of the steps and any pre- or post- conditions that govern the execution order the steps.

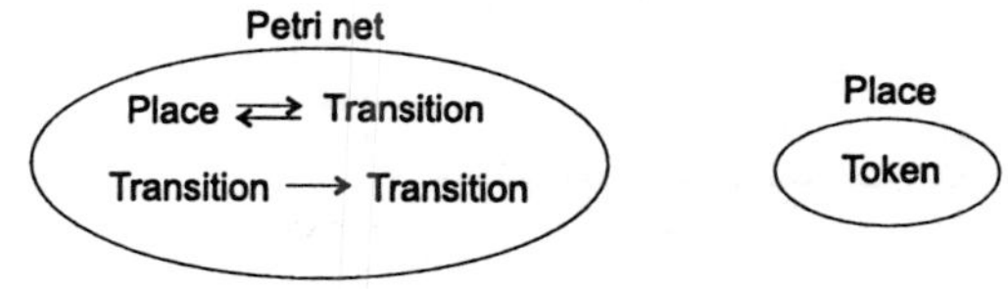

Typechecking Petri net:
Place: (0,unspecified);
Transition: (0,unspecified);

Figure 7. The abstract structure of Petri nets captured using hypernodes.

The hypernode model provides powerful support for methodology modelling through the HNQL. By allowing HNQL scripts to be attached to hypernodes, the overall process structure can be defined as a directed graph, as is common in many process modelling methodologies, and detailed behaviour of processes in these graphs can be defined with HNQL. Process models can be run and HNQL scripts executed to provide CASE tool support for methodological processes.

HNQL scripts can describe a variety of process concepts including preconditions, postconditions and actions. The query facilities of the language support precondition and postcondition definition by specifying that if the repository is not in a certain state then a process can or cannot proceed. Several actions are available, including the facility to call another HNQL script, call another tool, enact the graph within the hypernode, display a hypernode, wait for input from the user and move to (and run) another hypernode (only along an adjacent edge). These instruct the CASE tool as to what support to provide at any methodological process step.

Consider as an example a tool builder who wishes to construct a Petri net based description of the process of a particular methodology. Firstly, he/she defines (or retrieves from the database) abstract structures for the Petri net graphs with constraint definitions, as shown in Figure 7. Notice that these structures do not define standard Petri net structures because a Transition can be joined to a Transition with no Place type between them. This is an example of the hypernode scheme being used to define a modified version of methodological structures.

The abstract structures shown in Figure 7 are now instantiated into a Petri net-based process model for the methodology. The dynamic behaviour of the transitions (i.e. the preconditions, actions and postconditions) are expressed using interpreted HNQL script. Preconditions and postconditions are expressed as

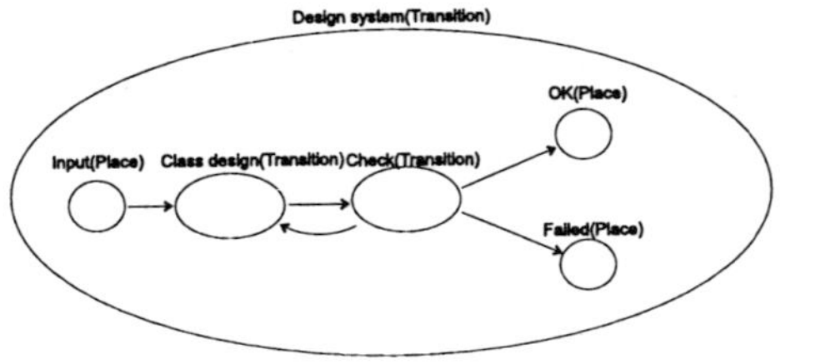

Figure 8. An instance of a (portion of a) design process constructed according to the structural meta-model of Petri net graphs defined in Figure 7.

```
Class design(Transition).hnql
//preconditions
TB
create_node(active);
insert_node "active" into_node "Class design(Transition)";
for_all(v is_adjacent_from(Class design(Transition))
        TB
        if (!v contains_node("token")) then
                remove_node "active" from_node "Class design(Transition)";
        TE
if ("Class_design(Transition) contains_node "active") then
        TB
        // actions
        display_node(Class diagram(Class diagram));
        wait;
        TE
// postconditions
move_to ("Check(Transition)");
TE.
```

Check that the "Place" nodes adjacent from this transition contain "token" nodes

Display the "Class diagram(Class diagram)" node so that the user can work on it.

Move to the next node

Figure 9. The detailed process description of the "Class design(Transition)" hypernode. When the process model is run this script will be run to provide process support in the CASE tool.

graph-based queries on the hypernode repository. For example, the common precondition that each node of type place adjacent from a transition is active before the transition can be fired is checked by querying the database to see if each place adjacent from the transition contains a token type node. This is shown in the first part of the script in Figure 9. Any actions to be taken when the transition fires are now specified. In the example in Figure 9 this involves displaying the class diagram hypernode so that the designer can work on it and then waiting until the designer signals to continue. Postconditions are then evaluated and if these are satisfied the next transition is run.

Once the methodological process model has been specified it can be run to instruct the process support in the CASE tool. This involves navigating the specified directed hypernode graphs and running the associated HNQL scripts.

5. An example hypernode-based meta-CASE tool

The hypernode model is used as the basis for a meta-CASE tool called *CASEMaker*. *CASEMaker* is implemented in Microsoft Visual C++ (4.0) on a Microsoft Windows NT platform and uses a Versant object-oriented database as a repository. The hypernode model is implemented as a set of C++ classes on the object-oriented database. All information for the meta-CASE toolset except the graphical user interface information is stored in hypernode data structures.

The tool builder works in a graphical user interface environment to specify the methodological support for the CASE tool. Firstly, the abstract structures for the design artefacts are specified as hypernodes (directed graphs), or previously defined abstract structures are retrieved from the database. An example of an abstract structure for a data flow diagram is shown Figure 10. Next the tool builder specifies the symbols for specific types in the abstract structure. For example, the tool builder may specify that the hypernode type "data store" has a special symbol in keeping with the data flow modelling methodology. The dialog that supports this symbol specification is shown in Figure 11. Symbols can be attached to the drawing palette to obtain a customised editor for the methodology. Detailed constraints on the structure of data flow diagrams can be specified using the scheme constraint definition framework. It is now possible to draw data flow diagrams which conform to the abstract structure of their schemes and follow the notation specified by the symbol editor.

The tool builder can specify methodological process in a similar fashion. Abstract structures for process models can be drawn or already defined structures can be reused, and structural constraints can be defined. The process model can then be created according to the abstract structures and detailed process behaviour can be coded in HNQL. Once this is done, the process model can be run and the result is a CASE tool with support for both representation and process aspects of methodology.

CASEMaker possesses several novel features due to the use of the hypernode model as its underlying representation for methodology modelling. Some of these are:

- methodological structures (hypernode schemes) and process definitions can be changed at run-time and changes take effect with no need to recompile,
- abstract methodological structures, including process definitions, are data in the database, which

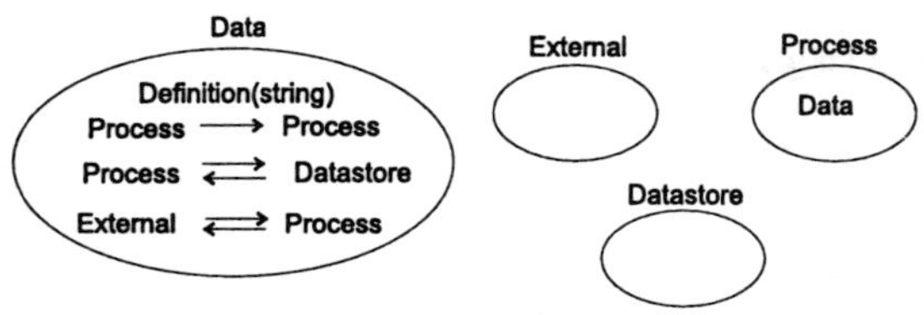

Typechecking Data:
Definition(string): (0,1);
Process: (0,unspecified);
Datastore: (0,unspecified);
External: (0,unspecified);

Figure 10. The hypernode type definitions for capturing data-flow modelling data including the constraint definition for data. Notice how the hierarchical nature of the data-flow diagram has been captured by nesting "Process" within "Process" (via "Data").

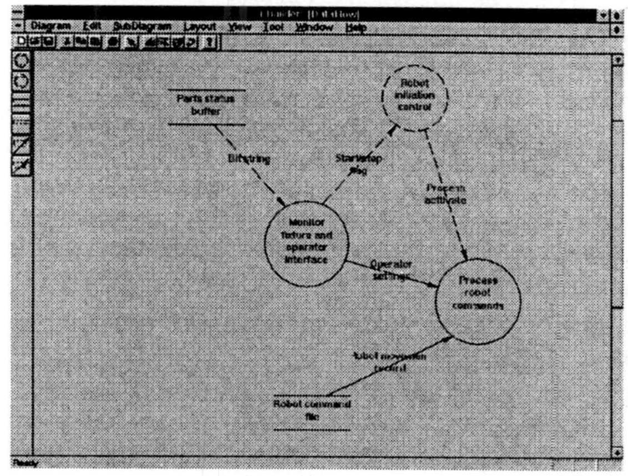

Figure 12. An example of a dataflow diagram drawn using *CASEMaker*. The structure must conform to the abstract scheme shown in Figure 10. The symbols defined for "Datastore" and "Process" have been used to ensure the dataflow diagram displays the correct notation.

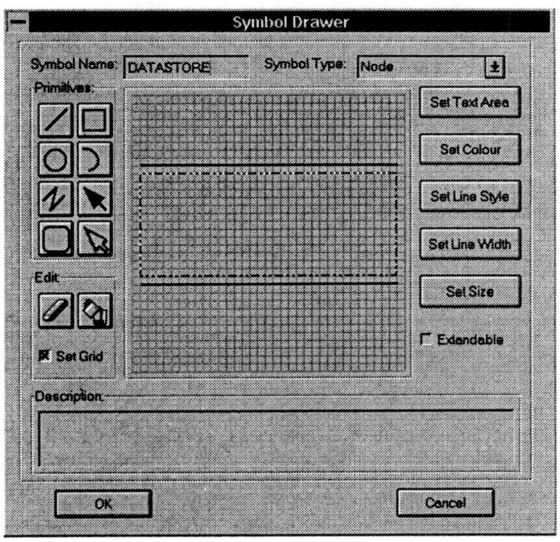

Figure 11. The symbol drawer screen from the *CASEMaker* meta-CASE tool. The "DATASTORE" symbol is linked to the "Datastore" hypernode scheme shown in Figure 10 so that every time this scheme is instantiated this symbol is used.

means the CASE tool user can modify the structures to suit personal tastes or particular project needs during a project. Alternatively, the abstract structures can be locked by the tool builder to prevent user modification of abstract structures depending on company policy,

- type-checking can be active or passive - that is, it can warn immediately a typing (structural) violation occurs or can be user invoked to warn against errors at a time convenient to the user - thus acting as a variable constraint CASE tool,
- abstract hypernode structures can be reused so there is no need to continually define structures for popular methods. Not only can the structures be reused in their entirety, but they can be retrieved and modifications made to suit particular requirements,
- support for methodological process is provided through hypernode graphs and interpreted HNQL scripts.

6. Applications and future work

Immediate work involves continuing the implementation of *CASEMaker* in order to demonstrate the hypernode model's applicability to supporting a meta-

CASE tool. The implementation will allow the application of the hypernode model to methodology modelling to be explored further. For instance, we will be able to explore the expressive power of HNQL as a process modelling language and to evaluate any negative side effects of using meta-data modelling and interpreted support for process enactment, such as performance problems and unforseen loss of functionality due the lack of "hard-coded" methodology modelling constructs. Future work also includes an investigation of hypernode support for modelling other aspects of meta-CASE technology, such as meta-analysis tools (e.g. design measurement tools). Part of this work involves using CASEMaker as a library of C++ classes to form the basis of a tool that supports design process modelling and measurement [12].

7. Conclusions

This paper has argued that the graph-based hypernode meta-data model is a powerful model with which to capture software design methodology. Unique features that make the hypernode model particularly good for this use have been emphasised, in particular the nested graph-based structure, a powerful update and query language and support for meta-data modelling. The nested graph structure of hypernodes matches the nested graph structures used by many design methodologies to describe design artefacts. The query and update language provides powerful support for specification of methodological processes. Finally, support for meta-data modelling means that methodological specifications do not need to be compiled before taking effect.

A meta-CASE tool that uses the hypernode model as the basis for methodology modelling has been described. The tool has several unique features due to the use of the hypernode model including the ability to change methodological specifications at any time with no need for re-compiling the tool, good support for methodological process modelling, a graphical environment for the tool builder that maps easily to the underlying hypernode database structures and a good basis for reuse of methodological specifications. The hypernode model has the ability to support unique functionality in a meta-CASE tool within a simple, graph-based framework and as a result we believe it provides a powerful basis for methodology modelling.

8. Acknowledgments

I would like to thank Gong Maokai for programming and providing the screen dumps from *CASEMaker*. I would also like to thank CSIRO who have partially supported this work through the CSIRO-Macquarie University Joint Research Centre for Advanced Systems Engineering.

References

[1] A. Alderson. Meta-CASE technology. In *Lecture Notes in Computer Science 509, Software Development Environments and CASE Technology*, pages 81–91. Springer, 1991.

[2] R. M. Colomb and A. Eilertsen. Use of a persistent graph abstract data type for representing CASE tool repositories. Technical Report 334, Department of Computer Science, The University of Queensland, 1995.

[3] M. P. Consens and A. O. Mendelzon. GraphLog, a visual formalism for real life recursion. In *Proceedings of the ACM Symposium on Principles of Database Systems*, pages 404–416, 1990.

[4] G. Engels, C. Lewerentz, M. Nagl, W. Schafer, and A. Schurr. Building integrated software development environments Part 1: Tool specification. *ACM Trans. Software Engineering and Methodology*, 1(2):135–167, April 1992.

[5] P. Findeisen. The EARA model for Metaview. A reference. Technical report, Department of Computing Science, University of Alberta, June 1994.

[6] M. Gyssens, J. Paredaens, and D. V. Gucht. A graph-oriented object database model. In *Proceedings of the ACM Symposium on Principles of Database Systems*, pages 417–424, 1990.

[7] D. Harel. On visual formalisms. *Commun. ACM*, 31(5):514–530, May 1988.

[8] M. Jarke, R. Gallerdoerfer, M. Jeusfeld, M. Staudt, and S. Eherer. Conceptbase: a deductive object base for meta data management. *Journal of Intelligent Information Systems: Special Issue on Deductive and Object-Oriented Database Systems*, pages 167–192, 1995.

[9] S. Kelly and K. Smolander. Evolution and issues in metaCASE. *Information and Software Technology*, 38(4):261–266, April 1996.

[10] M. Levene and G. Loizou. A graph based data model and its ramifications. *IEEE Trans. Knowledge and Data Engineering*, 7(5):809–823, Oct. 1995.

[11] K. Lyytinen, P. Kerola, J. Kaipala, S. Kelly, J. Pirhonen, M. Rossi, K. Smolander, V.-P. Tahvanainen, and J.-P. Tolvanen. MetaPHOR: Metamodeling, principles, hypertext, objects and repositories. Technical report, Computer Science and Information Systems Reports Technical Report TR-7, University of Jyvskyl, Finland, 1994.

[12] R. Offen and G. Xia. SQUATter-M conceptual requirements document. Technical Report 96/13, JRCASE,, Macquarie University Sydney, Australia, 1996.

[13] A. Reeves, M. Marashi, and D. Budgen. A software design framework or how to support real designers. *Software Engineering Journal*, 10(4):141–155, July 1995.

[14] L. Scott. Hypernode model support for software design CASE. Technical Report 96/7, JRCASE, Macquarie University Sydney, Australia, 1996.

[15] K. Smolander, P. Marttiin, K. Lyytinen, and V.-P. Tahvanainen. MetaEdit - a flexible graphical environment for methodology modelling. In *Advanced Information Systems Engineering, Proc. Of the 3rd Int. Conf. CAiSE '91*, pages 168 – 193. Springer-Verlag, May 1991.

[16] I. Sommerville, R. Welland, and S. Beer. Describing software design methodologies. *The Computer Journal*, 30(2):128 – 133, 1987.

[17] P. G. Sorenson, J. Tremblay, and A. J. McAllister. The Metaview system for many specification environments. *IEEE Software*, 5(2):30–38, March 1988.

[18] R. Welland, S. Beer, and I. Sommerville. Method rule checking in a generic design editing system. *Software Engineering Journal*, 5(2):105 – 115, March 1990.

Session P1b

Reverse Engineering and Legacy Systems

A System for Generating Reverse Engineering Tools

G. Canfora*, A. De Lucia* and G. A. Di Lucca**
(canfora/delucia/dilucca)@nadis.dis.unina.it

* DIIIE - Dept. of "Ingegneria dell'Informazione ed Ingegneria Elettrica"
University of Salerno, Faculty of Engineering at Benevento
Palazzo Bosco Lucarelli, Piazza Roma, 82100, Benevento, Italy

** DIS - Dept. of "Informatica e Sistemistica"
University of Naples "Federico II"
via Claudio 21, 80125, Naples, Italy

Abstract

Most current reverse engineering techniques start with an analysis of the system's source code to derive structural information, based on compiler technology. As a consequence of the maturity of the field, several formal program models exist that have allowed the automatic generation of language processing front-end. However, the software engineer has to code the data structures that implement the program model and the algorithms that implement the desired analysis. Thus, while the domain of code analysis is well understood, economic convenience leads very often to rigid code analysers that perform a fixed set of analyses and produce standard reports that users can only marginally customise.

We have implemented a system for developing code analysers that uses a unique database to store both a no-loss fine-grained intermediate representation and the analyses' results. The analysers are automatically generated from a very high-level specification of the desired analyses expressed in a domain-oriented language. We use an algebraic representation, called $F(p)$, *as the user-visible intermediate representation. Analysers are specified in a logic-based language, called* $F(p)-\ell$, *which allows the specification of an analysis in the form of a traversal of an algebraic expression, with accesses to, and stores of, the database information the algebraic expression indexes. A foreign language interface allows the analysers to be embedded into C programs to facilitate interoperation with other tools.*

This work is supported by "Progetto Strategico CINI-CNR Informatica nella Pubblica Amministrazione - Sottoprogetto PROGRESS: PROcess-Guided REengineering Support System"

1 Introduction

Previous research has shown that code analysis tools are effective in a number of activities of the software maintenance and evolution process. It has also shown that the construction of a robust code analyser may be costly and error prone if dealt with inadequate technologies and tools.

1.1 The problem

Reverse engineering has been defined as the process of analysing a subject system to identify the system's components and their interrelationships and create representations of the system in another form or at a higher level of abstraction [7]. Although reverse engineering may be performed at any stage of the life cycle and starting from any level of abstraction, most current reverse engineering techniques start with an analysis of the system's source code to derive structural information. To accomplish this, tools apply parsing and control/data flow analysis technologies based on the lexical, syntactic, and semantic rules that determine the correctness of program constructs in a given programming language.

As a consequence of the research conducted in the area of compilers, the domain of code analysis is now well understood and several formal models exist, such as the BNF and the AST, that describe it accurately and exhaustively. These formal models have allowed the implementation of application generators that support the creation of language processing front-end such as the compiler writing facilities Lex and Yacc in the UNIX environment. Nevertheless, the production of robust, fully flagged code analysers remains a very complex task. The manual coding of the parser of a language whose grammar is specified in BNF, while not particularly demanding, is tedious and error prone and can easily run into several thousands lines of code even for relatively simple languages such as C and Pascal. If the parser is constructed automatically from the grammar, like in the case of Yacc, it is still a duty of the designer of a code analyser to select the right data structures to implement the AST (possibly annotated with semantic information such as scope and control flow) and to code operations on them. Finally, he or she has to code the algorithms that implement the desired analysis on the AST and derive the resulting views or reports. Thus, while the domain of code analysis is well understood, economic convenience leads very often to rigid code analysers that perform a fixed set of analyses and produce standard reports that users can only marginally customise.

1.2 Existing solutions and criticisms

Standard forms for intermediate representations have long been claimed as an optimal solution to the problem of writing robust code analysers in a cost effective manner [9]. With a standard intermediate representation, the implementer of any particular analyser is free from the need to deal with the idiosyncrasies of code parsing as any language front-end compliant with the standard adopted may be used. A notable example of intermediate representation is the Descriptive Intermediate Attributed Notation for Ada (DIANA) [11]. DIANA type definitions and associated primitives are given as an Ada package specification which can serve as a complete environment for analyser development once the body is implemented. Unfortunately, commonly accepted standards have not yet emerged and interoperability of both intermediate representations and language front-ends is hard to come by [18].

Proprietary intermediate representations are however largely exploited to implement code analysers. A common approach consists of extracting from code an intermediate representation that is then entered into some form of database. Many systems in this class use relational databases [6, 15] but different forms of databases have also been successfully exploited such as deductive databases [2] and object oriented databases [17]. The analysers are implemented by using the standard query and reporting facilities of the database system. Many systems use the industry standards SQL that is not oriented to the specific domain of code analysis and does not have the power to express transitive closures. The advantage is that SQL may be embedded into a host language to implement complex analyses. Other systems, such as the Software Refinery toolkit [17], offer more powerful languages to implement the analysers. The main drawback is that these systems are usually closed on themselves, i.e. all the components of an analyser (including the language front end and the user interface) have to be realised using the system's facilities. The consequences are a scarce interoperability and the need for the analyser developers to mastering a complete language.

An alternative approach consists of implementing an application generator that can create analysis tools from a high-level specification of the analyses that the tools are intended to perform. A notable example is the GENOA/GENII system [10]. The GENOA sub-system implements a specification language to generate code analysers for a given programming language. The creation of an analyser consists of specifying a traversal of the program syntax tree and the output to be produced during the traversal. The GENII sub-system customises the environment for a particular programming language. One of the main advantages of this approach is the use of an high-level domain-oriented language to define the analyses to be performed. In addition, if the analysers are generated in a largely adopted language, such as C or C++, they are easy to integrate into larger systems. A pitfall is the inability to modify the internal representation and to reuse the results of an analysis for further manipulations within the environment.

1.3 Our approach

We have implemented a system for developing code analysers that combines the winning features of the above approaches while trying to overcome their limitations. The system uses a unique database to store both a no-loss fine-grained intermediate representation and the analyses' results. However, the analysers are not implemented by using the query and reporting facilities of the database system; rather, they are automatically generated from a very high-level specification of the desired analyses expressed in a domain-oriented language.

Figure 1 shows the overall architecture of the system. A front-end compiles the source code into the intermediate representation and loads the database; the application generator receives the specification of an analysis and produces an analyser that implements it on the database. A foreign language interface allows the analysers to be embedded into C programs. This is useful, for example, to implement the user interface of an analyser or to facilitate interoperation of the generated analysers with pre-existing tools.

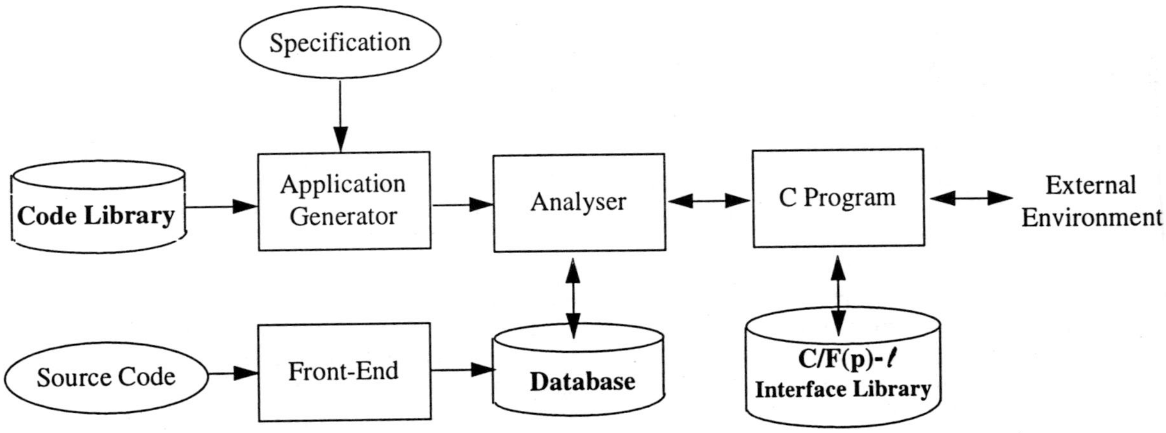

Figure 1: The system architecture.

At the conceptual level, we use an algebraic representation, called $F(p)$, as the user-visible intermediate representation. $F(p)$ models a program in the form of a set of algebraic expressions, one for each program module. Analysers are specified in a logic-based language, called $F(p)-\ell$, which allows the specification of an analysis in the form of a traversal of an algebraic expression, with accesses to, and stores of, the database information the algebraic expression indexes.

The intermediate representation $F(p)$ is discussed in [8], while the analyser specification language $F(p)-\ell$ is presented in [5]; these will be briefly recalled in section 2. This paper concentrates on the foreign language interface that allows the analyser generated from a $F(p)-\ell$ specification to be embedded into a C program. Section 3 illustrates the programming interface as perceived by a C programmer, and section 4 gives a few practical examples of use. Concluding remarks are discussed in section 5.

2 A system for code analyser production

In the current implementation, our system exploits several technologies and languages and runs on most UNIX workstations. We have implemented front-ends for different programming languages, including Pascal and a sub-set of C, using either a conventional programming language or the compiler-writing facilities Lex and Yacc. The use of Prolog and Definite Clause Grammar has also been explored to realise a front-end for PL/1 [4]. The database is realised as a Prolog program dictionary on the top of the SWI-Prolog environment [19] and, accordingly, the analysers are generated in the Prolog language. The application generator also comprises a compiler for $F(p)-\ell$, written using Lex and Yacc.

2.1 The $F(p)$ intermediate representation

$F(p)$ applies to one-in/one-out program modules that have a structured flow of control[1]. Such a program module consists of a set P of test predicates, a set B of blocks of code[2] and a set C of calls to other modules, embedded into a set S of control structures. Calls and blocks are nested into control structures, and these are nested into each other. For each element $x_i \in S \cup B \cup C$, a nesting level $l(x_i)$ is defined which is the number of structures $s_k \in S$ into which x_i is directly or indirectly nested; x_i^j denotes that the element x_i has a nesting level $l(x_i) = j$. For the sake of simplicity, in this paper we will refer to programs structured with respect to the set S = {*sequence, if-then, if-then-else, while-do, repeat-until*}; examples of how $F(p)$ can be used to model other control structures are given in [3].

The flow of control generated by a control structure is a function of the structure itself and the elements it comprises: $s_i^j = s_i^j(x_{i_1}^{j+1}, x_{i_2}^{j+1}, \ldots, x_{i_m}^{j+1})$. Table 1 shows the function corresponding to the control structures considered in this paper; "$\circ$", "/" and "+" denote the

---

[1] We exploit the results of Fenton and Kaposi [FK87] who have shown that every control flow graph is built up from, and can be decomposed into, a family of primes in just one way, i.e. every program is structured with respect to some family of one-in/one-out control structures.

[2] These can be either single statements or maximal sequences of statements where the flow of control is sequential, depending on the level of abstraction desired.

sequence: $seq_i^j = seq_i^j \circ (x_{i_1}^{j+1} / x_{i_2}^{j+1} / \ldots / x_{i_m}^{j+1})$
if-then: $if_i^j = if_i^j \circ (x_{i_1}^{j+1} + \lambda)$
if-then-else: $if_i^j = if_i^j \circ (x_{i_1}^{j+1} + x_{i_2}^{j+1})$
while-do: $w_i^j = w_i^j \circ (x_{i_1}^{j+1} + \lambda)$
repeat-until: $r_i^j = r_i^j \circ (x_{i_1}^{j+1})$

Table 1: Control flow functions.

inclusion, the serialisation and the alternative operators, respectively, and λ is an empty block (i.e. no operation). An algebraic expression $F(p)$ is inductively defined by the two following clauses: (i) every $x \in B \cup C \cup \{\lambda\}$ is an algebraic expression, and; (ii) every *n*-ary function from table 1 applied to *n* algebraic expressions is an algebraic expression itself. Every program module *p* is represented by an algebraic expression $F(p) = s_0^0$; Cimitile and De Carlini [8] prove that a one-to-one correspondence exists between a program module and the relative algebraic expression. Indeed, $F(p)$ uniquely identifies the sets *P*, *B*, *C* and *S*: calls, block and control structures are directly shown as the expression's operands and test predicates are in a one-to-one correspondence with control structures. Because there is no predicate associated with sequences, these are completely described by the serialisation of the relative components: $seq_i^j = seq_i^j \circ (x_{i_1}^{j+1} / \ldots / x_{i_m}^{j+1}) = x_{i_1}^{j+1} / \ldots / x_{i_m}^{j+1}$.
Figure 2 shows a sample C-like program (a) and the relative algebraic expressions (b). For the sake of clarity, we use b_i^j and c_i^j to denote blocks of code and calls, respectively.
Our system uses $F(p)$ as an index to store and retrieve program information; each operand is an access key to relevant pieces of information into the database. Retrieving information from the repository is achieved through a unique function, *get(operand, kind)*, where *kind* identifies the piece of information desired and *operand* is a $F(p)$ operand. Similarly, the procedure *put(operand, kind, info)* inserts a new piece of information into the database (this is attached to *operand*). The identifiers of program items (such as module and variable names) are treated as a special case of operands to access information which is related to the entire item. As an example, a module name can be used to retrieve the module's local variables:

get(module_name, varl_decls)

or the algebraic expression itself:

get(module_name, algebraic_expression).

	`void SAMPLE() {`
b_1^1	`statement;`
r_2^1	`do`
b_3^2	`statement`
	`while (expression);`
b_4^1	`statement;`
if_5^1	`if (expression) {`
b_6^3	`statement;`
w_7^3	`while (expression) {`
if_8^5	`if (expression)`
b_9^6	`statement;`
b_{10}^5	`statement;`
	`}`
	`}`
	`else`
c_{11}^2	`function call;`
	`}`

(a)

$$F(SAMPLE) = b_1^1 / r_2^1 \circ (b_3^2) / b_4^1 / if_5^1 \circ (b_6^3 / w_7^3 \circ (if_8^5 \circ (b_9^6 + \lambda) / b_{10}^5 + \lambda) + c_{11}^2)$$

(b)

Figure 2: A sample C-like program (a) and the relative algebraic expression (b).

2.2 The core $F(p) - \ell$ language

The basic data types available in $F(p) - \ell$ are algebraic expression operands (used to index the database), numbers and strings. During a traversal of an algebraic expression, the function *get_op* allows reference to the operand of the current sub-expression. The language provides users with the constructors for structured data types *tuple*, *set*, and *sequence*. It also furnishes operators to deal with sets (*union*, *intersection*, *difference*, *insert*, and *retract*) and sequences (*head*, *tail*, and *cons*). A special operator *seq_to_set* transforms a sequence into a set.

$F(p) - \ell$ allows the specification of an analysis in the form of a traversal of an algebraic expression, with accesses to, and stores of, the database information the algebraic expression indexes. The result of an analysis on an algebraic expression $s_i^j = s_i^j (x_{i_1}^{j+1}, x_{i_2}^{j+1}, \ldots, x_{i_m}^{j+1})$ is a composition of the results of analyses on the algebraic

```
proc_name: <input_parameters> returns <output_parameters>
on X/Y iff body1 ;
on if ∘ (X + λ) iff body2 ;
on if ∘ (X + Y) iff body3 ;
on w ∘ (X + λ) iff body4 ;
on r ∘ (X) iff body5 ;
on b iff body6 ;
on c iff body7 .
```

(a)

```
proc_name: <input_parameters> returns <output_parameters>
        iff body .
```

(b)

```
module mod_name
uses <list_of_module_names>
public
        procedure_signatures
foreign <list_of_procedure_names>
private
        procedure_signatures
body
        procedures
end
```

(c)

Figure 3: Elements of the $F(p)-\ell$ language.

expressions $x_{i_1}^{j+1}, x_{i_2}^{j+1}, \dots, x_{i_m}^{j+1}$, combined with information associated with the operand s_i^j and retrieved from the database. Figure 3(a) shows the general form of a $F(p)-\ell$ procedure for the traversal of an algebraic expression. $F(p)-\ell$ treats the sequence control structure $seq_i^j = x_{i_1}^{j+1} / x_{i_2}^{j+1} / \dots / x_{i_m}^{j+1}$ as the concatenation of the first element $x_{i_1}^{j+1}$ with the rest of the sequence $seq'^{j}_{i} = x_{i_2}^{j+1} / \dots / x_{i_m}^{j+1}$; the serialisation operator "/" denotes such a concatenation, i.e. $seq_i^j = x_{i_1}^{j+1} / seq'^{j}_{i}$. Whenever seq'^{j}_{i} is the empty sequence, the traversal of seq_i^j reduces to the traversal of $x_{i_1}^{j+1}$. Predicates $body_1$ to $body_7$ define how information has to be recovered from the database and further elaborated (possibly together with the input parameters) to define the result of the analysis. Basic predicates available in the language are relational expressions defined on numeric expressions, *is* and *is not*, to compare two elements of the same type, and *in* and *not in*, to check whether or not an element is a member of a set. The procedure *put* for storing information into the database is treated as a special case of predicate that always succeeds. Finally, simple predicates can be composed through the connectors *and* and *or*. Procedure calls for the traversal of an algebraic (sub-)expression assume the form:

```
proc_name <actual_input_parameters>
        returns <actual_output_parameters> on X
```

where X identifies the algebraic expression to be traversed. In addition to traversal procedures, the language provides also a general purpose procedure as shown in figure 3(b); calling these procedures assumes the form:

```
proc_name <actual_input_parameters>
        returns <actual_output_parameters>
```

```
mc_cabe: <module_name> returns <vg>
        iff ae is get(module_name, "algebraic_expression") and
        compute_mc_cabe <> returns <vg> on ae.

compute_mc_cabe: <> returns <vg>
on X/Y iff compute_mc_cabe <> returns <vg1> on X and
        compute_mc_cabe <> returns <vg2> on Y and
        vg is vg1 plus vg2 minus 1;
on if ∘ (X+λ) iff compute_mc_cabe <> returns <vg1> on X and
        vg is vg1 plus 1;
on if ∘ (X+Y) iff compute_mc_cabe <> returns <vg1> on X and
        compute_mc_cabe <> returns <vg2> on Y and
        vg is vg1 plus vg2;
on w ∘ (X+λ) iff compute_mc_cabe <> returns <vg1> on X and
        vg is vg1 plus 1;
on r ∘ (X) iff compute_mc_cabe <> returns <vg1> on X and
        vg is vg1 plus 1;
on b iff vg is 1;
on c iff vg is 1.
```

Figure 4: An example of $F(p)-\ell$ specification.

As an example, figure 4 shows the $F(p)-\ell$ specification of an analyser that computes the McCabe cyclomatic complexity of a program module [16]. The specification consists of a general purpose procedures, *mc_cabe*, that receives in input the name of a program module and retrieves the related algebraic expression from the database, and a traversal procedure, *compute_mc_cabe*, that actually computes the metric.

3 Integrating $F(p)-\ell$ analyses into a host language

The main focus of $F(p)-\ell$ is on the specification of code analysers in terms of traversals of an algebraic expression. Issues such as operating system and user interfaces are not tackled within the language. On the other hand, these issues would make a domain oriented language more complex than it really needs, and dependent on a particular platform. Rather, it would be desirable a software engineer to be able to write the tools he or she needs using different languages (each of which suitable for a different purpose) and to integrate these tools in a common environment.

Therefore, instead of providing $F(p)-\ell$ with programming facilities for accessing external software and hardware resources, we have built a library to embed $F(p)-\ell$ procedures into a host language, in the current implementation the C language.

3.1 Providing $F(p)-\ell$ with modular programming constructs

$F(p)-\ell$ is a highly modular language: a **module** construct is provided to build analysers in a modular way and to reuse previously built analyses. Moreover, this construct allows tool developers to specify the procedures of a module that can be accessed from the host language. The general form of a $F(p)-\ell$ module is shown in figure 3(c):

- the optional clause **uses** imports the public procedures from the listed modules;
- the signatures of the module's procedures are declared either in the **public** or in the **private** section: public procedures are exported towards other $F(p)-\ell$ modules, while private procedures can only be accessed by other procedures within the module. A module must contain at least a public procedure and may not contain private procedures. The signature of a procedure for the traversal of an algebraic expression has the form:

  traversal proc_name :

  tuple(*type_list*) => **tuple**(*type_list*)

  while the signature of general purpose procedures has the form:

  proc_name : **tuple**(*type_list*) => **tuple**(*type_list*)

```
module mc_cabe_complexity
public
    mc_cabe: tuple(string) => tuple(integer)
foreign <mc_cabe>
private
    traversal compute_mc_cabe:
                              tuple(nil) => tuple(integer)
body
    -- see figure 4.
end
```

Figure 5: An example of $F(p)-\ell$ module.

Each type in *type_list* can be either a simple type, i.e., **integer**, **real**, **string**, and **ae_op** (where **ae_op** is the type of algebraic expression operands), or a structured type, i.e., **tuple**(*type_list*), **set**(*type*), and **sequence**(*type*);

- the clause **foreign** lists the public procedures exported towards the host language. Only general purpose procedures can be exported towards the host language: this decision has been made in order to avoid the host language to directly access and manipulate the intermediate program representation of the analysis tools;
- the **body** part contains the $F(p)-\ell$ procedures as described in section 2.

As an example, figure 5 shows a sample $F(p)-\ell$ module exporting the procedure for the computation of the McCabe cyclomatic complexity.

3.2 Using $F(p)-\ell$ modules into C programs

General purpose $F(p)-\ell$ procedures can be used within C programs, by including the library "fpl" that allows C programs to interface with $F(p)-\ell$ modules. This library is built on the top of the "SWI-Prolog" library which provides facilities for the integration of the languages SWI-Prolog and C. In particular, it allows Prolog types (such as atoms and terms) to be modelled by special C types, Prolog queries to be directly executed within C functions and C functions to be treated as Prolog terms.

The "fpl" library provides special functions to load a $F(p)$ indexed data-base (*uses_db*), to import resources from a $F(p)-\ell$ module (*uses_fpl*), and to call a $F(p)-\ell$ procedure (*call_fpl*). The interface of these functions is shown in figure 6(a). The library also provides a generic type *FPL_ELEMENT* to model $F(p)-\ell$ types. The type of the input and output parameters of the function *call_fpl* (*FPL_ELEMENT_PTR*) is a pointer to elements of type *FPL_ELEMENT*.

Figure 6(b) shows the type declarations used to model $F(p)-\ell$ types. The type *FPL_ELEMENT* is a C *struct* with an enumeration field (*enum fpl_type*), that specifies the particular type of a $F(p)-\ell$ element (string, integer, real, ae_op, tuple, set, sequence), and a union field (*union fpl_union*) that models the different $F(p)-\ell$ types. Structured type values (tuple, set, and sequence) are all modelled as lists by the field *list_val* of type *FPL_LIST_PTR*.

Hidden functions have been implemented to translate (within the function *call_fpl*) elements of type *FPL_ELEMENT_PTR* into elements of the corresponding $F(p)-\ell$ type, and viceversa. Finally, a set of functions is provided to build values of type *FPL_ELEMENT_PTR* (to be passed to the function *call_fpl*) and to visit the *FPL_ELEMENT_PTR* values returned by the function *call_fpl*. For example, the function:

```
FPL_ELEMENT_PTR
make_set_element(FPL_LIST_PTR l)
```

builds a $F(p)-\ell$ set from a lists of elements, while the functions:

```
enum fpl_type
get_type(FPL_ELEMENT_PTR e)
```

and

```
FPL_LIST_PTR
get_list_element(FPL_LIST_PTR e)
```

return the type of a $F(p)-\ell$ element and the list of components of a $F(p)-\ell$ structured element, respectively.

Figure 7 shows a sample C program which uses the $F(p)-\ell$ module for the computation of the McCabe cyclomatic complexity.

4 Examples

In this section we show two examples of analysers that benefit from the integration of $F(p)-\ell$ modules into C. The two examples are a data flow analyser and a tool that derives the control flow graph of a program. In both these examples the foreign language interface has been exploited to improve the presentation of the analyses' results. In the first case this is achieved by producing the results in the HTML format, thus leaving to the user's preferred browser the problem of graphical rendering. In the second case the visualisation of the control flow graph is obtained by realising a bridge towards VCG [14], a tool that displays a graph from a textual specification.

```
void uses_db(char *db);
void uses_fpl(char *fpl_module);
FPL_ELEMENT_PTR call_fpl(char *fpl_fun, FPL_ELEMENT_PTR fpl_input);
```

(a)

```
typedef struct fpl_list    FPL_LIST,     *FPL_LIST_PTR;
typedef struct fpl_struct  FPL_ELEMENT,  *FPL_ELEMENT_PTR;
enum fpl_type {STRING_TYPE, INT_TYPE, REAL_TYPE, AE_TYPE,
               TUPLE_TYPE, SET_TYPE, SEQ_TYPE};

struct ae_elem {
   char *ae_op;
   long nesting_level, id_num; };

union fpl_union {
   char * string_val;
   long int_val;
   double float_val;
   struct ae_elem ae_val;
   FPL_LIST_PTR list_val; };

struct fpl_struct {
   enum fpl_type fpl_element_type;
   union fpl_union fpl_element; };

struct fpl_list {
  FPL_ELEMENT_PTR fpl_elem_ptr;
  FPL_LIST_PTR next; };
```

(b)

Figure 6: Sample functions (a) and type declarations (b) in the library "fpl".

```
#include "fpl.h"

main()
{
  FPL_ELEMENT_PTR e1, e2, e3;
  FPL_LIST_PTR l1, l2;
  char func[10];
  long n;

  uses_db("examp_db");
  uses_fpl("mc_cabe_complexity");
  printf("Function: ");
  scanf("%s", func);
  printf("\n \n");
  l1 = make_elem_list(make_string_elem(func));
  e1 = make_tuple_elem(l1);
  e2 = call_fpl("mc_cabe", e1);
  l2 = get_list_elem(e2);
  e3 = first_elem(l2);
  n = get_integer_elem(e3);
  printf("McCabe complexity of %s: %d \n", func, n);
}
```

Figure 7: A sample C program that uses a $F(p)-\ell$ procedure.

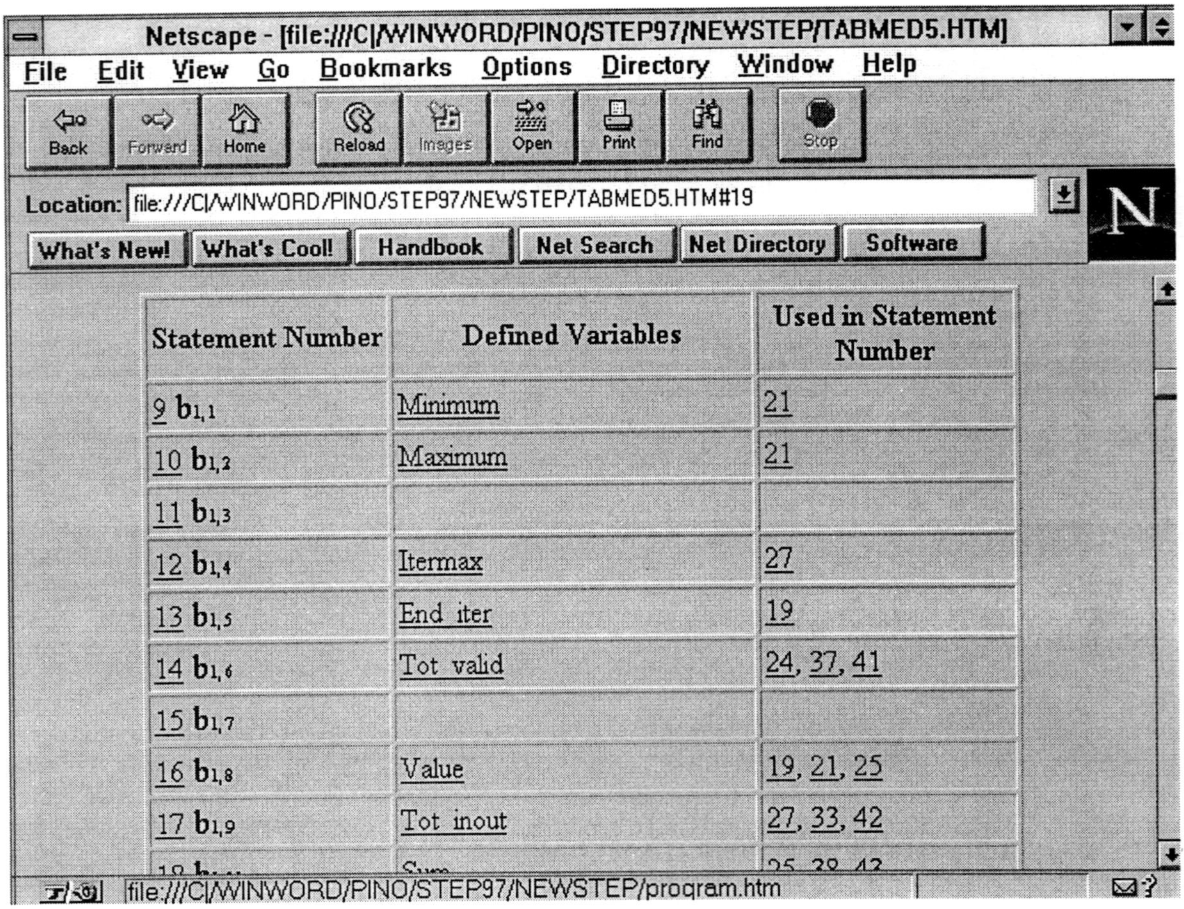

Statement Number	Defined Variables	Used in Statement Number
9 $b_{1,1}$	Minimum	21
10 $b_{1,2}$	Maximum	21
11 $b_{1,3}$		
12 $b_{1,4}$	Itermax	27
13 $b_{1,5}$	End iter	19
14 $b_{1,6}$	Tot valid	24, 37, 41
15 $b_{1,7}$		
16 $b_{1,8}$	Value	19, 21, 25
17 $b_{1,9}$	Tot inout	27, 33, 42

Figure 8: A sample HTML table showing the results of the data flow analyser.

4.1 Computing definition-use relationship

Data flow analysis entails the identification of the definition-use relationships in a program [1]. For statements S_i and S_j, a definition-use relationship exists between S_i and S_j if S_i defines the value of a variable V, S_j uses V, and there is a path from S_i to S_j on which V is not re-defined. A triplet (S_i, S_j, V) which respects these conditions is called a definition-use triplet.

In [5] we have shown the $F(p)-\ell$ specification of an algorithm to compute definition-use triplets. Based on this algorithm, we have realised the intraprocedural data flow analyser described in this section. The algorithm to compute definition-use triplets is used into a C program by calling the foreign $F(p)-\ell$ procedure *data_flow* that takes a module name as its input and returns the set of definition-use triplets of the module. The C program arranges the definition-use triplets into a HTML table consisting of three columns: the identifier of a statement (the source code line in which the statement appears and the relative $F(p)$ operand); a variable defined in the statement, and; the set of the identifiers of the statements that use the value of the variable defined by the statement in the first column. If a statement defines more than a variable, it will appear in the first column of as many rows as the variables it defines. An example of such a table is shown in figure 8. The C program also generates links that ease the investigation of the data flow. Each statement number in the first column points to the relative line in the source code file, while each variable in the second column is a link to the line in the source code file where the variable is declared. Finally, each statement identifier in the third column points to the first table row where it appears in the first column; this allows users to follow arbitrary long chains of definition-use relationships.

4.2 Deriving the control flow graph

A control flow graph is a flow graph in which nodes represent one-in/one-out regions of code and edges depict execution paths among the regions [1, 13].

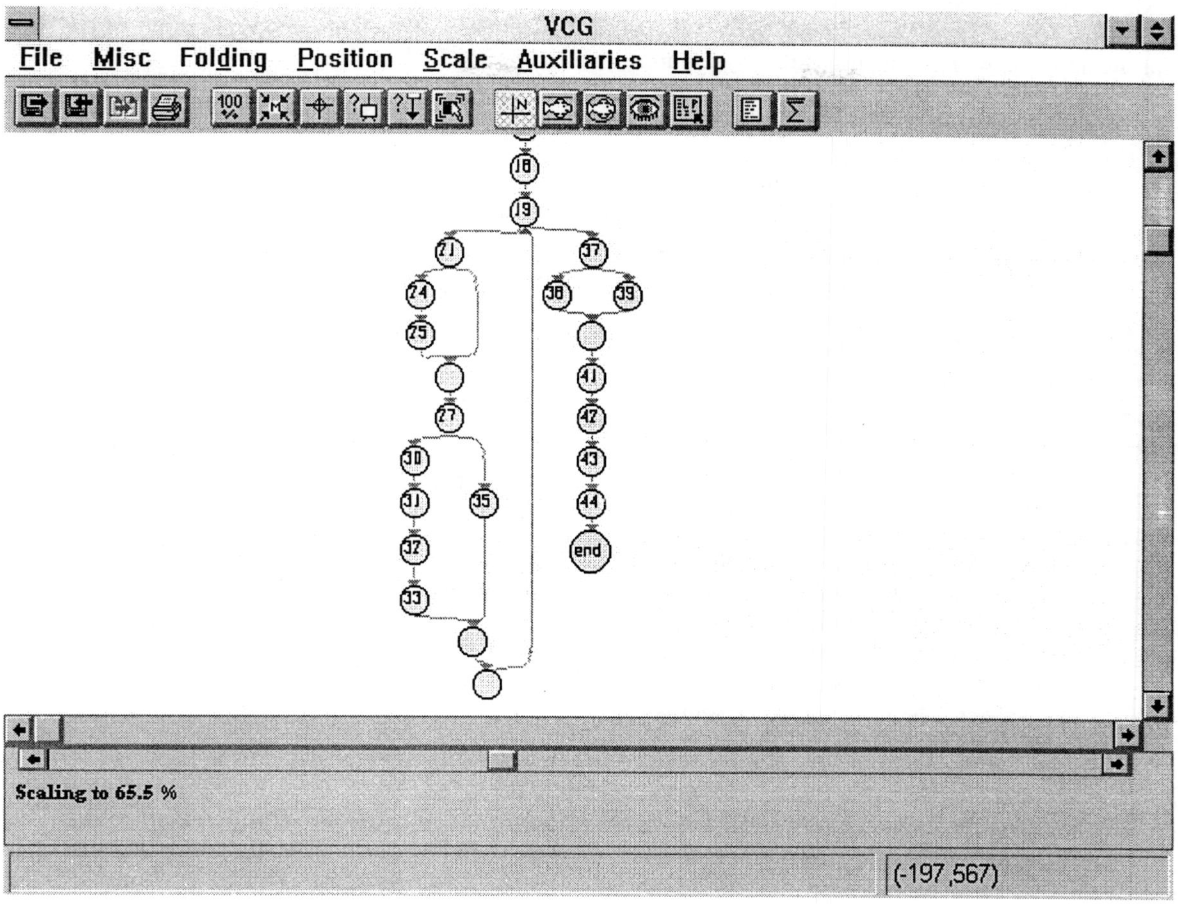

Figure 9: A sample VCG screen that visualises a control flow graph.

Although for compiler optimisation regions are maximal sequences of statements where the flow of control is sequential [1], many code analyses require that each node of a control flow graph correspond to an individual statement.

Based on the algorithm proposed in [8], the derivation of the control flow graph of a program module from its algebraic expression is relatively easy to be specified in $F(p)-\ell$. We have written a $F(p)-\ell$ module that exports the foreign procedure *cfg*; this takes a module name as its input and returns the control flow graph in the form of a set of nodes (each identified by the corresponding source code line) and a set of edges (each consisting of a pair of source code lines). The *cfg* procedure is used into a C program that builds and visualises the control flow graph of a module. The visualisation is achieved through VCG [14], a tool intended to visualise large graphs that are generated by other programs. VCG reads a textual specification of a graph and visualises the graph using several heuristics (as reducing the number of crossing, minimising the size of edges, and centering the nodes) to derive the layout. The C program that calls the foreign $F(p)-\ell$ procedure *cfg* realises the bridging towards the VCG tool; it translates the control flow graph returned by *cfg* into the specification expected by VCG. Figure 9 shows a sample VCG screen that visualises a control flow graph.

5 Concluding remarks

The research described in this paper has addressed the development of code analysis tools that assist designers during the maintenance and evolution of large software systems. We claim that robust analysers may be constructed in a cost effective manner by defining a very high-level language which includes operations, objects and representations characteristic of the particular domain of code analysis. Analysers are then automatically generated from a specification of the analyses they are intended to perform expressed in this domain-oriented language. The generation is performed by an application generator that uses embedded knowledge of the application domain and a library of code templates.

To evaluate this idea, we have implemented a system for the generation of analysis facilities which exploits a high-level specification language, $F(p)-\ell$, based on an intermediate representation of programs called $F(p)$. $F(p)-\ell$ allows the specification of code analysers in terms of traversals of $F(p)$ expressions and does not deal with issues that are not strictly belonging to the domain of code analysis. As an example, issues such as operating system and user interfaces are not tackled within the language. Access to external software and hardware resources is achieved by embedding $F(p)-\ell$ procedures into a host language. We have built a foreign language interface that allows $F(p)-\ell$ procedures to be used by C programs.

Compared to other application generators in the domain of code analysis, such as the GENOA/GENII system [10] our system presents the advantage that analyses are performed on a program model stored in a database. Other systems that use a database to record program information, such as [6, 15], exploit the standard querying and reporting mechanisms of the database to implement code analyses. The main difference with our system is that we exploit a high-level domain-oriented language to define the analyses. In addition, our system integrates the program model and the analyses' results into a unique conceptual model, and this simplifies the reuse of the results of an analysis. Another system that uses a database and a domain-oriented language, both based on an abstract syntax tree, is the Software Refinery toolkit [17]. The main difference with our system is that we do not use an abstract syntax tree. Our specification language is based on a very compact program algebraic representation which furnishes a flexible and powerful indexing mechanism to access the information into the database.

Acknowledgements

We would like to thank A. Cimitile and U. De Carlini for the deep insights our conversations gave to us.

References

[1] A. V. Aho, R. Sethi, and J. D. Ullman, *Compilers, Principles, Techniques, and Tools*, Addison-Wesley, 1986.

[2] F. W. Callis and S. W. Dietrich, "The application of Deductive Databases to Inter-Module Code Analysis", Proc. of *Conference on Software Maintenance*, Sorrento, Italy, IEEE Computer Society Press, 1991, pp. 120-128.

[3] G. Canfora, "Deriving Testability Estimates from Program Algebraic Representations", Unpublished DIIIE Internal Report (available from the author), 1994.

[4] G. Canfora, A. Cimitile and M. Tortorella "Prolog for Software Maintenance", Proc. of *7th International Conference on Software Engineering and Knowledge Engineering*, Rockville, Maryland, 1995, pp. 478-486.

[5] G. Canfora, A. Cimitile and A. De Lucia "Specifying Code Analysis Tools", Proc. of *International Conference on Software Maintenance*, Monterey, California, 1996, IEEE Comp. Soc. Press, pp. 95-103.

[6] Y. F. Chen, M. Nishimoto and C. V. Ramamoorthy, "The C Information Abstractor System", *IEEE Transactions on Software Engineering*, vol. 16, no. 3, 1990, pp. 325-334.

[7] E. J. Chikofsky and J. H. Cross II, "Reverse Engineering and Design Recovery: A Taxonomy", *IEEE Software*, vol. 7, no. 1, 1990, pp. 13-17.

[8] A. Cimitile and U. De Carlini, "Reverse Engineering Algorithms for Program Graph Production", *Software - Practice and Experience*, vol. 21, no. 5, 1991, pp. 519-537.

[9] U. De Carlini, A. De Lucia, G. A. Di Lucca and G. Tortora, "An Integrated and Interactive Reverse Engineering Environment for Existing Software Comprehension", Proc. of *2nd Workshop on Program Comprehension*, Capri, Italy, IEEE Computer Society Press, 1993, pp. 128-137.

[10] P. T. Devanbu, "GENOA - A Customizable, Language- and Front-End independent Code Analyzer", Proc. of *14th International Conference on Software Engineering*, Melbourne, Australia, IEEE Computer Society Press, 1992, pp. 307-319.

[11] A. Evans, K. J. Butler, G. Goos and W. A. Wulf, *DIANA Reference Manual*, Revision 3, Tartan Laboratories Inc., Pitsburgh, PA, 1983.

[12] N. E. Fenton and A. A. Kaposi, "Metrics and Software Structure", *Information and Software Technology*, vol. 29, no. 6, 1987, pp. 301-320.

[13] M. S. Hecht, *Flow Analysis of Computer Programs*, Elsevier North-Holland, 1977.

[14] I. Lemke and G. Sander, *14: A Visualization tool for Compiler Graphs*, The COMPARE consortium, 1993, available from: ftp.es.uni-se.de (134.96.254.254) :/pub/graphics/cdg/

[15] M. Linton, "Implementing Relational Views of Programs", Proc. of *ACM SIGSOFT Simposium on Practical Software Development Environments*, Pittsburg, USA, 1984, pp. 132-140.

[16] T. J. McCabe, "A Complexity Measure", *IEEE Transactions on Software Engineering*, vol. 2, no. 4, 1976, pp. 308-320.

[17] *REFINE User's Guide*, Reasoning Systems, Inc., Palo Alto, CA, 1989.

[18] S. Rugaber and L. Wills, "Creating a Research Infrastructure for Reengineering", Proc. of *4th Working Conference on Reverse Engineering*, Monterey, California, 1996, IEEE Comp. Soc. Press, pp. 98-102.

[19] J. Wielemaker, *SWI-Prolog - Reference Manual*, University of Amsterdam, 1995, available from: http://swi.psy.uva.nl/usr/jan/SWI-Prolog.html

A Practical System of COBOL Program Reuse for Reengineering

Hongji Yang
Computer Science Department
De Montfort University
England

William C. Chu
Department of Information Engineering
Feng Chia University
Taiwan

Yong Sun
Computer Science Department
Queens University of Belfast
Northern Ireland

Abstract

Transformation and reuse techniques have been discussed for many years and it is even more important to apply these techniques in practice. This paper introduces our approach to combining transformation and semantic interface analysis for reuse of COBOL programs. In our approach, COBOL programs are reverse engineered to their designs represented in Entity Relationship (ER) diagrams; both the original code and obtained ER diagrams are used by semantic interface analysis; reusable components are annotated with conditions which are needed for checking suitability and saved in a reuse library for reuse and reengineering.

Our method is demonstrated in detail throughout an example in this paper. Besides being practical, advantages of the approach include that a formal link between the original COBOL program and its design in an ER diagram form is retained, and both the program code and the design can be reused.

1 Introduction

COBOL programs, claimed to constitute almost ten percent of code in the world in terms of program lines, represent a class of programs — in which the complexity is focussed on the design and implementation of data structures rather than the algorithms which are often simple. COBOL language provides complex data structuring mechanisms and high level composite operations to manipulate them. Because of this, COBOL programs are often referred to as *data-intensive programs.*

As one of the oldest serving programming language, COBOL is closely related to the word "evolution", i.e., after having been in service and subject to frequent modification for many years, most of COBOL programs are facing evolution problems, such as reuse and reengineering.

It has been well accepted by the people in software engineering community that one of the important aspects of reengineering is to move COBOL code to its high abstraction level presentation, i.e., to reverse engineering COBOL, because the form at higher abstraction level is easier to be understood.

Reuse of COBOL code in practice needs a careful study. This paper will begin such a study by examining features of COBOL and listing problems specifically associated with COBOL.

Programs written in COBOL have several characteristics, compared with other computation intensive programs, which are important constraints in reverse engineering such programs:

1. Data are represented in records and the operations on records, thus data are therefore heavily record based.
2. Programs are often designed using entity-relationship (ER) diagrams, rather than process based design methods.
3. COBOL allows programmers two different records with different structures to share the same memory location (known as the *aliasing problem*).
4. COBOL programs usually have external calls to the operating systems and database management systems.

0-8186-7840-2/97 $10.00 © 1997 IEEE

5. COBOL programs use many *foreign keys* to represent complex data structures which other languages would use pointers to do.

In order to reuse existing COBOL code through reverse engineering, we need to consider the following essential problems:

a) Are ER diagrams still appropriate for representing a reverse engineered COBOL program at a high abstraction level?

b) Is it feasible to acquire ER models from old, heavily modified source code?

c) What restrictions to the general applicability can be found?

d) How powerful is an approach based on formal transformation technology?

f) What tool support is needed?

g) How scalable is the method?

Solutions to these problems will help us to understand existing COBOL code so as to the code, in particular identifying reusable COBOL code.

2 Related Work and Our Motivation

Relevant work has been done in reverse engineering COBOL, code understanding, semantic interface analysis, etc. and is briefly reviewed in this section.

Sneed's Work and Bachman's Work on COBOL Sneed and Jandrasics use automated tools to support retranslation of software code in COBOL back into an application specification by the process of reverse engineering [14]. Two steps are needed, firstly to recover a program design from source code and secondly to recover a program specification from program design. In the first step, the code of COBOL programs is translated into an intermediate design schema based on a set of normalised relational tables for the modules, data capsules, and interfaces extracted from the source programs. In the second step, the intermediate design representation is retransformed into a specification schema based on the entity/relationship model.

Bachman introduced a CASE tool for reverse engineering COBOL programs [2]. The Reengineering Cycle chart provides an architectural view of this CASE tool, which features both forward and reverse engineering. In particular, reverse engineering begins with the definition of existing applications and raises the applications to successively higher levels of abstraction. At the top level, the design objects created by the reverse engineering steps are enhanced and validated to become the revised design objects used in the forward engineering process. At the lowest level, a new applications system becomes an existing applications system when it goes into production.

Reverse Engineering Using Formal Transformation at Durham The research at Durham (England) carried out under the REFORM project has concentrated on using transformations for reverse engineering, and full details of the theory, methods and tools, and results can be found in [17] [3] [18]. The Maintainer's Assistant (MA) is the name of a system which has been developed in REFORM. Apart from a language dependent front end translator, the Maintainer's Assistant operates totally using a wide spectrum language, WSL. MA would take existing software written in low-level procedural languages, through a process of successive transformation, and turn it into an equivalent high-level abstract specification expressed in terms of a non-procedural abstract specification language (for example, Z). However, software reuse was not yet addressed in REFORM.

Semantic Interface Analysis and Reuse Semantic interface analysis is a formal approach and it has been used in the development of a reuse tool called the Module Integration and Adaptation Tool for Ada Components (MIATAC) where semantic attributes of software components were described by formal notations. Since software reuse includes areas of concern such as representation, retrieval, and adaptation and integration [4], MIATAC attempted to use formal semantic interface predicates in solving these four areas of concerns. In particular, MIATAC focuses on the area of integration and adaptation. In MIATAC, the reusable Ada components are resident in a reuse library and contain formal semantic interface specifications consisting of precondition, postcondition, and obligation predicates represented as specialised Ada comments. An existing reuse library system will provide the initial retrieval mechanism for the selection of candidate reuse components. A candidate reuse component is then inserted into the application system. The application system consists of both newly developed components, and previously adapted reuse components; all of which contain formal semantic predicates. This "syntactically integrated" application system is then transformed by a parser which organises the Ada code and the annotated comments into a Descriptive Intermediate Attributed Notation for Ada (DIANA) Tree intermediate form [8]. The DIANA Tree is then traversed and analysed by predicate logic routines to determine how well the candidate component fits into the application system.

Code Understanding Code understanding is a question that has to be answered when responding to the challenge of software reuse. An obvious reason is that one can not reuse a piece of software before being absolutely sure about the functionality of the software. A basic activity to understand existing code is to gather information. When the documentation of a software system became unreliable, the sole source of information from the software is the code itself. This means that code understanding is typically a code activity. Apart from the information directly from the software, other sources of information can also help with code understanding. These sources are domain knowledge of the application, software development and programming knowledge [15].

Code understanding process is heavily dependent on individuals and their specific cognitive abilities, and on the set of facilities provided by code understanding [16]. This suggests that tools are one crucial factor to help human to understand code.

It is well accepted that code understanding can be enhanced using reverse engineering technologies. Therefore a reverse engineering tool can be seen as a necessary part in a code understanding system. Also, if one can learn more about how programmers understand code successfully, one can build better tools to support the understanding process [13].

Our Motivation The motivation of our work was originated from observing the existing work, in particular those reviewed above:

- COBOL code reuse is of great practical significance.
- MA provided a form foundation to build a program transformation tool for software reuse, and MA has both a firm theoretical foundation and a design which has evolved from case studies, which together provide beneficial results when used with real programs.
- People trying to tackle software evolution challenges use a variety of techniques and representations for understanding programs — most of these representations focus on the control structure of a program such as call graphs, control flow graphs and paths (control-centred code understanding), and data centred code understanding [11] such as data and data relationships.
- There are two basic technical approaches to reuse: parts-based and formal language-based [9]; the parts-based approach assumes a human programmer integrating software parts into an application by hand. In the formal language-based approach, domain knowledge is encoded into either an application generator or a programming language.

Our study on COBOL code reuse focus on the parts-based approach. In parts-based approach, components are required to be found and understood, and then incorporated into the designed system. Reusable parts are identified through reverse engineering via program transformation. Program understanding is done inside the program transformation process. Data structures are the main points to reverse COBOL programs. Based on these observations, we decided that MA can be extended to a new tool for COBOL code reuse.

3 A Method for Reuse in Practice through Program Transformation

A method was proposed in this study to reverse engineer COBOL programs into their reusable forms through program transformation based on a wide spectrum language, RWSL (Reengineering Wide Spectrum Language). A prototype tool, RA (Reengineering Assistant), was built according to this method. RA is influenced by the REFORM project and by the MIATIC project, e.g., RWSL is extended from the WSL in REFORM to include a set of language structs used for Semantic Interface Analysis and Knowledge Elicitation, and RA will not only deal with software maintenance as in MA but also deal with software reuse and reengineering.

3.1 A Method

After carefully studying the existing state of the art in this field, a new method was proposed for RA in identifying reusable components through program understanding. The method consists of following steps:

1. Translating a COBOL program into RWSL.
2. Using initial tidy-up transformations to "clean up" the target program in RWSL in order to reduce the redundant statements introduced during the translation.
3. Looking for functionally self-contained modules. A code module, a function or a procedure in the original software system, are potentially self-contained modules. A reusable component may well be obtained from one of the above modules. A module which is not a function or a procedure may also be transformed into an abstract data type, and hence also a candidate of a reusable component.
4. Taking one module obtained from the above process to work, one at a time. Program transformations are applied to the module to reverse the module into its high-level representation in ER diagrams.
5. The obtained ER diagrams are viewed as reusable components. The ER diagrams, together with the original code, are used by a Semantic Interface Analysis tool to generate semantic predicates and interface predicates for a reusable module in terms of its pre-conditions, post-conditions and obligations. These predicates are used to serve as the rules of describing implicit semantics, characteristics, and interface requirements of each software component explicitly.
6. Storing a reusable module in the Reuse Library, and maintaining a formal link between the reusable module and its high abstraction level representation.

3.2 Prototype of A Transformation and Reuse Tool

The main design philosophy of RA was to build the Browser/Interface component (Figure 1) and use it for integrating other tool components.

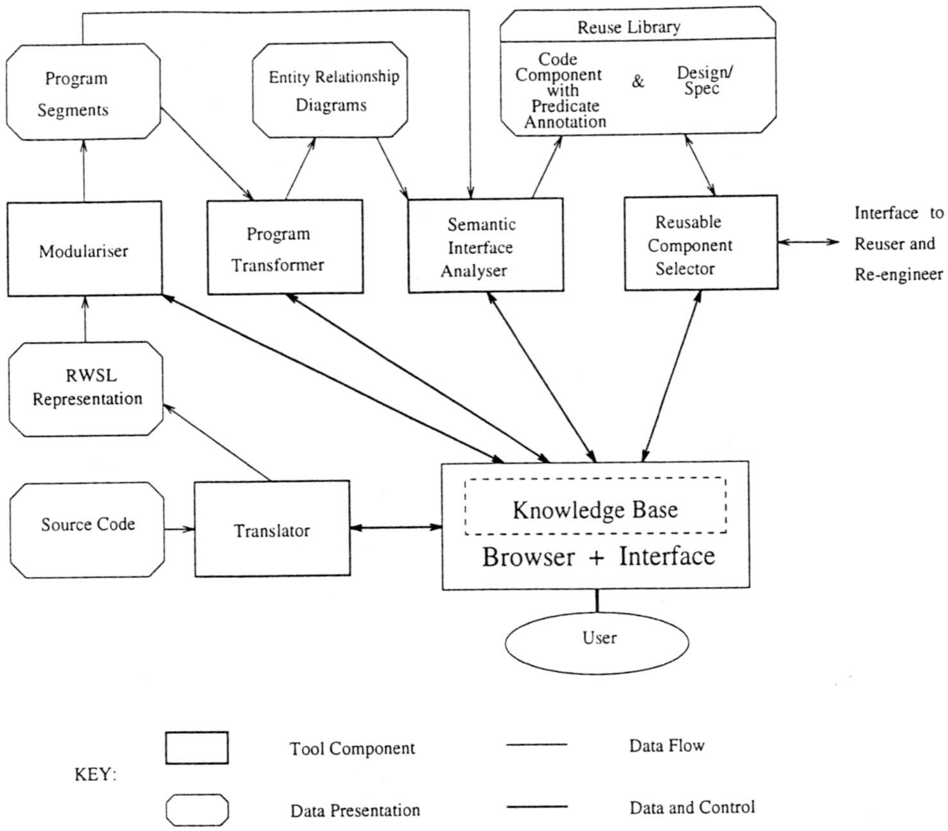

Figure 1: Design of Reengineering Assistant

Use of Entity Relationship Model Entity relationship diagrams are based on *entity models* [5] [12] [7]. ER models provide a system view of the data structures and data relationships within the system. All systems possess an underlying generic entity model which remains fairly static in time. The entity model reflects the logic of the system data, not the physical implementation. ER models provide an excellent graphical representation of the generic data structures and relationships. To reverse engineer code to a high abstraction level representation is to make the original code easier to be understood. Therefore a model at high abstraction level is needed. Because, as discussed earlier, data centred code understanding has many advantages and the ER model has been popularly used for many years, the model is used in RA.

Crossing Levels of Abstraction and Use of Program Transformation Abstraction techniques are heavily used in reverse engineering. In reverse engineering, abstraction is the process of identifying the important qualities or properties of the phenomenon being modelled. They abstract from irrelevant details, describe only those details that are relevant to the problem at hand, e.g., understanding the design.

Usually, program code and its design are not at the same level of abstraction, e.g., the design is more abstract than the code. It is necessary to reduce the amount of complexity that must be considered at any one time, so that certain number of abstraction levels may exist during the specification extraction process. Each "layer" can be considered as a program in a language provided by a virtual computer, implemented by the layer below. In the lowest layer, we have a real machine.

Keeping Formal Links between Reusable Components and Their High-Level Representation The process of transforming a module at the code level to its high abstraction level representation may take a number of steps. The Program Transformer has a built-in facility to keep a full history of the transformation process. The advantage of doing this is that when a route of abstraction fails the Program Transformer can "retreat" to a suitable point and move forward again. At the mean time, this facility maintains a formal link between the original module to every intermediate stage of the transformed module as well as the final version of the module. This provides a facility for reuse of COBOL program designs.

Annotating Predicates for Reusable Components A systematic abstraction for reusable components is based on formal predicates, i.e.:

* annotating a predicate to each component,

* propagating the predicate to a higher level component, and

* recognise the required predicate conditions for abstraction rules (if the predicate conditions hold the abstraction can be achieved).

The idea is to use data semantics and operation semantics in programs to infer a high level abstraction and semantics. An example in this paper (Section 4) is to use semantics of data structure *sequential-file* and a loop of record copy to infer that the module *file-backup*(*File*1, *File*2) has the post-condition, EQU(File1,File2), i.e. we have inferred and abstracted semantics of module *file-backup* from its composed components. However this inference can only be achieved when proper predicates are annotated with software components. Although the annotating process may be an overhead, it usually helps to reveal the embedded semantics, which is needed during the comprehension process. In other words, it should reduce guessing work and clarify the semantics during the process. This approach can be achieved with the help the Knowledge Base in RA.

The Knowledge Base in RA plays a vital role in annotating predicates for the reusable components. Knowledge Base contains two major information: software templates, representing knowledge, including domain independent and specific knowledge of software components in the formal predicate format; abstraction rules, representing conditions for abstraction.

3.3 Acquiring Entity Relationship Models

This section describes in detail the solutions to the problems raised in Section 1, in terms of the source code structures, a summary of the transformations defined, and the ER components that result. Each subsection takes a similar approach: relevant RWSL constructs are introduced briefly; then the transformations that have been designed are described; finally it is shown how they are used to extract a particular component of the ER model.

We have the following observations and approaches for solving the problems concerned.

For the problem of combining both data and code into abstract data types, which has also been studied elsewhere, our own contribution here has focussed on developing a method which is suitable for a transformation approach.

For a class of code constructs where some variable y depends on others x1, x2, ..., i.e. y := f(x1, x2, ..), to view it at a high abstraction level, the crucial information is that the variables are related and the exact nature of the function f is less important.

For the problem of input and output, which is often a substantial part of data intensive programs, we have partially solved this by modelling I/O as operations on high-level data types. The external calls to the underlining operating system and the embedded database can be modelled as external procedure calls and external functions.

For aliasing problem, in which one piece of memory (code) is used at different points in the program for different purposes, writing to the memory may have a side effect. In some languages, the memory may be aliased to variables with different types.

For foreign keys problem, in which a data value in one data structure is used to index another data structure i.e. a[b[i]], the connection between the data structures is only apparent by comprehending the code.

It should be noted that some COBOL constructs are irrelevant for acquiring ER models, and hence are ignored; these include DISPLAY, REMOVE, INITIALIZE, PERFORM, IF, WHEN, UNTIL, GOTO, SEARCH, ACCEPT. Initialising assignment statements are also ignored. In our tool this was done during the translation from COBOL to RWSL.

Transformations developed for extracting ER models in our tool are divided into seven categories and each category will be discussed in each of the following subsections. RWSL is used unless specificly stated.

3.3.1 Basic Data Structures and Entity Relationship Components

Transformations in this category deal with simplifying data objects in basic data types according to the properties of data type.

From record to entity In forward engineering, a "01 level" COBOL record is usually used to implement an entity in an ER model. Therefore, in reverse engineering, a record with just one level of subrecord (syntactically a subrecord in RWSL is still denoted by the keyword <u>**record**</u> for the convenience of defining a sub-sub-record, etc.) can be abstracted to an entity with attributes. For example, a record and an entity abstracted from the record are illustrated below. When the record is transformed into the entity, information such as length and type of each field is thrown away, because the information was not usually in the original data design and was added in by the implementor, e.g:

```
record E1 with
   record A1 [n of char]
   record A2 [n of char]
   record A3 [n of char]
   end;
```

is abstracted to:

```
entity E1 with
   attr A1
   attr A2
   attr A3
   end;
```

Acquiring a relationship from a record with subrecords When a subrecord of a record can be abstracted into an entity and the record can be abstracted into an entity as well, there exists a relationship between the entity derived from the record and the entity derived from the subrecord. For example, in the given record *author*:

```
record author with
    record name [30 of char]
    record address [60 of char]
    record book with
        record title [50 of char]
        record ISBN [20 of char]
    end
end;
```

the subrecord *book* can be abstracted into an entity while the record *author* can be extracted into an entity *author*, according to the knowledge in forward engineering. At the same time, a relationship "write" is abstracted from the logical connection between the record and the subrecord, i.e.:

```
paragraph
entity author with
        attr name
        attr address
  end;
entity book with
        attr title
        attr ISBN
  end;
relationship entity author has one write relation
        with many entity book;
end;
```

Note that information on the implementation details is also thrown away in the process of abstraction.

3.3.2 Transformations for Manipulating Data Items

Transformation in this category deal with manipulating data items for the preparation of applying further transformations, for example, "Swap-With-Next-Record"(when a record is moved to a position closer to another record so permitting them to be joined to form an entity).

3.3.3 Files

File input/output is one of the central problems in COBOL programs. File operations in a programming language usually involve access to external storage. For example, a serial file is a sequence of records, i.e., a record is the unit with which a physical file can be accessed. Though COBOL file operations can be translated into RWSL as external procedures and external functions (i.e., we effectively ignore them, and knowledge of variable usage is lost across calls), more suitable forms of data representations are required to replace these external procedures and functions in order to examine file operations at a high abstraction level. In our tool, a queue data type is proposed to model COBOL sequential files and operations on these files, in order that files (external storage objects) can be transformed into queues (internal mathematical objects). We have not yet addressed random access files, but would model them with arrays.

3.3.4 Aliases

There are two purposes in using aliases. The first purpose is to share storage space and the second purpose is to control storage scope. In languages, which do not have block structure, there is no way to use scope to control storage allocation so the only technique is to use aliasing. The former can usually be determined by the declarations and the latter can be done by defining a function which map from a record to a sequence of bytes (the representation of that record in memory), and from a sequence of bytes to a record. These functions need to know the *structure* of the record in terms of the number of bytes occupied by each component. We first determine which records are aliased and determine a mapping between the aliased records. We then define a function to describe a WRITE to an aliased record as mapping the COBOL data structure to a low level memory model and a function to describe a READ from an aliased record as a mapping in the reverse direction.

For instance, suppose we have a COBOL program as below:

```
01 L                PIC X(6).
01 M REDEFINES L.   PIC X(6).
01 N                PIC X(6).
... ...
MOVE N TO L.
```

It will be translated into RWSL:

```
record l  [6 of char];
record m  [6 of char];
redefine l with m;
record n  [6 of char];
......
l := n;
m := read-rec(m, write-rec(l, n));
```

Here the RWSL struct **redefine** declares that l and m are two aliased records. The function *write-rec* maps a change of l when assigned by n to the low level memory model of l and m; the function *read-rec* describes how the variable m is affected when its aliased record l was written. The second statement in the above program can be simplified by transformations, i.e.:

$m :=$ *read-rec*$(m,$ *write-rec*$(l, n))$;

becomes

$m := n$;

3.3.5 Foreign Keys

A relationship can exist between two entities that both have the same attribute (known as a *foreign key*) and the relationship can be spotted by transformations in the imperative code. This relationship can be abstracted from two entities which have been derived already from source code (e.g. record definitions) and two relations which between two pairs of entity attributes (e.g. assignment statements).

3.3.6 Abstract Data Types

Transformations in this category deal with recognising an abstract data type from constituent data declarations and operations on them.

Transformations for forming abstract data type An abstract data type consists of "objects" and "operations". Objects are usually implemented as variables and operations are implemented as procedures and functions. In reverse engineering, an abstract data type may be formed by looking for a closure of a group of variables and a group of procedures (or functions). No matter whether a closure was originally used for an abstract data type, if an abstract data type is obtained from this closure in the code, it is helpful in viewing the code at a higher abstraction level.

The way of implementing this idea is to provide a structure first in RWSL. Five constructs are defined for the definition of a user-defined data type, user-defined data type procedure call and user-defined data type function call. The key words for these constructs are: **user-adt**, **user-adt-funct**, **user-adt-proc**, **user-adt-funct-call** and **user-adt-proc-call**.

The search for a closure can be started with a procedure definition (or function definition) as well as a variable, and the result is the same, for example:

```
var iset := 0, rest := 0, x := 0, y := 0, m := 0, n := 0,
    int1 := 0, int2 := 0, real1 := 0, real2 := 0 :
    begin
      ......
      iinsert (int1);
      idelete (int2);
      rinsert (real1);
      rdelete (real2);
      ......
    where
      proc iinsert (x) == iset := iset ∨ {x};
      proc idelete (y) == iset − {y};
      proc rinsert (m) == rset := rset ∨ {m};
      proc rdelete (n) == rset − {n}.
```

Here we assume that the variables x and y are not used in (...) parts (this can be easily confirmed by the Program Transformer). If we start with variable x which is used by procedure definition *iinsert*, it is found that variable *iset* is also used by the same procedure definition. There is no other procedure definitions using x, but the procedure definition *idelete* uses variable *iset* and y. Following the same steps, a closure can at last be recognised which contains three variables (x, y , *iset*) and two procedures (*iinsert*, *idelete*). Hence an abstract data type is formed (and named *intset*). The above program can be transformed into the following:

```
var ......
    begin
      ......
      user-adt-proc-call intset.insert (int1);
      user-adt-proc-call intset.idelete (int2);
      ......
    where
      user-adt intset (iset := 0, x := 0, y := 0) (nil)
          user-adt-proc iinsert (x)
              == iset := iset ∨ {x};
          user-adt-proc idelete (y)
              == iset − {y};
      ......
```

From user-defined data types to entity relationship model When a closure is found, a user-defined abstract data type is found. Furthermore, a user-defined abstract data type can be abstracted to an entity while all statements accessing this abstract data type have to be changed accordingly and "ADT->Entity" is such a transformation. By applying this transformation, the above program will be abstracted to

```
paragraph
entity int1
entity int2
entity intset
......
relate int1 to intset;
comment : insert int1 to intset;
relate int2 to intset;
comment : delete int1 from intset;
......
end
```

In this process, the abstract data type *intset* becomes an entity, and so do the two parameters involved. Two procedure call statements become two relations. In order to abstract the program further, useful information is recorded by comment statements.

A **relate** statement has two components of which one is an entity derived from an abstract data type. Then the other component is a variable or a record without any subrecord (these two are equivalent and there are transformations available in the prototype for transforming one into the other), this **relate** statement can be transformed into a relationship. The name of the relationship has to be provided by the user according to the information existing in the code. The program can be transformed into the following RWSL form.

```
paragraph
entity intset;
entity int1
entity int2
......
relationship entity int1
        has one is-member-of relation
                with one entity intset;
relationship entity int2
        has one is-not-member-of relation
                with one entity intset;
......
end
```

```
************************************************************
*                                                          *
*                                                          *
*    THIS PROGRAM SEQUENTIALLY ACCESSES TO TWO SEQUENTIAL  *
*    FILES, ONE IN INPUT MODE AND ONE IN OUTPUT MODE.      *
*                                                          *
************************************************************
 IDENTIFICATION DIVISION.
 PROGRAM-ID. FILE-BACKUP.

 ENVIRONMENT DIVISION.
     INPUT-OUTPUT SECTION.
     FILE-CONTROL.
          SELECT SOURCE-FILE-NAME ASSIGN TO XYZ
              ORGANISATION SEQUENTIAL
              ACCESS MODE IS SEQUENTIAL.
          SELECT TARGET-FILE-NAME ASSIGN TO WXY
              ORGANISATION SEQUENTIAL
              ACCESS MODE IS SEQUENTIAL.

 DATA DIVISION.
     FILE SECTION.
     FD SOURCE-FILE-NAME.
     01 SOURCE-RECORD              PIC X(50).

     FD TARGET-FILE-NAME.
     01 BACKUP-RECORD              PIC X(50).

     WORKING-STORAGE SECTION.
     01 EOF PIC X.

 PROCEDURE DIVISION.
 MAIN.
     OPEN INPUT SOURCE-FILE-NAME
          OUTPUT TARGET-FILE-NAME
     PERFORM, WITH TEST AFTER, UNTIL EOF = "T"
          READ SOURCE-FILE-NAME NEXT;
          AT END
              MOVE "T" TO EOF
          NOT AT END
              MOVE "F" TO EOF
              MOVE SOURCE-RECORD TO TARGET-RECORD
              WRITE TARGET-RECORD;
     END-PERFORM
 * THE STOP RUN STATEMENT CLOSES THE FILES
     STOP RUN.
************************************************************
```

Figure 2: A File-backup Program in COBOL

3.3.7 Functional Relationships

Transformations in this class address how ER models are extracted from code, in particular, from assignment statements, branching structures and loop statements.

An assignment statement is a simple but straightforward measure to implement a relation between two data objects, which, at the data design level, may be two entities. Therefore, an assignment can be usually abstracted to a relation.

A branching statement, such as **if .. then .. else .. fi**, is used as a control structure in implementing programs. But the structure itself did not appear in the original data design and neither did the condition part of the branching structure. These parts will not contribute to the ER diagram and however information appearing in both arms of an **if .. then .. else .. fi** statement may exist in the ER diagram. Therefore, an **if .. then .. else .. fi** statement can be abstracted to a sequence of two groups of statement (each group comes from each arm of the **if ... fi** statement).

Looping statements, such as **while** and **for**, are also used as a control structure in implementing programs but do not appear in the original data design. A looping statement can be treated to enumerate operation on every instance of entities. The condition part of the loop also does not contribute to the ER diagram. So a **while** loop or a **for** loop can be removed just leaving the body of the loop.

```
comment : "program-id:  file-backup";
file source-file-name with
   record source-record with
   end;
end;
file target-file-name with
   record target-record with
   end;
end;
eof := 0;
!p open_file (i var source-file-name);
!p open_file (o var target-file-name);
while (eof ≠ 1) do
      if non_empty? (!f eof? (source-file-name))
        then eof := 1
         else eof := 0;
              !p read_file (source-record var source-file-name);
              target-record := source-record;
              !p write_file (target-record var target-file-name);
      fi;
        od;
```

Figure 3: The File-backup Program in RWSL

4 Experiments

4.1 A Detailed Illustration

The example program used in this illustration was taken from a COBOL text book [10] and its COBOL source code is shown in Figure 2.

This program is translated into its equivalent form in RWSL (Figure 3). The program module was a procedure in the original program and it would be called by a (COBOL) PERFORM statement. This program copies the contents in one file to another file. Figure 3 shows the format of the program when loaded in to the transformation tool of the RA prototype.

The identification division in COBOL is translated into a **comment** statement in RWSL. Information in the environment division will be used when data division and procedure division are translated, i.e., the files in the code are sequential files. In the data division, COBOL records and files are translated into RWSL records and files. COBOL files in this example are sequentially organised and sequentially accessed.

In this program original file operations are translated into RWSL as external procedures (denoted by **!p** which is the RWSL function to call an external procedure for which it is known definitely which variables will be changed) or external functions (denoted by **!f** which the the RWSL function to call a named external function).

The program in Figure 3 is then dealt with by the Program Transformer, which applies transformations to it.

To understand the module, the program transformer first transforms two records in the program into two data entities, i.e., those two records in the module can be viewed as two data entities. The entities keep the same names as the records.

Operations on a sequential file are treated as operations on a "mathematical" queue: to "read" a record being reading a record form a queue, to "write" a record to a file being writing a record to a queue, and to test whether the file operation pointer is pointing to the end of the file being testing whether the pointer is pointing the end of the queue.

When a record is transformed into an entity, any program statement using this record must be changed accordingly. Because transforming a record into an entity is an abstraction, the statement using the obtained entity must be expressed at a higher abstraction level. In this case, the assignment statement in the module should be viewed as those two entities (originally two records) are related or linked.

Other two assignments in the "if" statement, which were used for control purposes, should be viewed as something that would not exist at the high abstraction level and therefore they can be ignored.

The looping statement, **while**, is also used as a control structure in implementing programs but did not appear in the original program design. A looping statement can be treated as enumerating the same operation on every instance of entities. The condition part of the loop also does not contribute to the ER diagram. So a **while** loop was removed just leaving the body of the loop.

entity *source-record* **end**;
entity *backup-record* **end**;
relationship entity *target-record* **has** *one back-up* **relation**
with *one* **entity** *source-record*;

Figure 4: An Entity Relationship Diagram for the File-backup Program in RWSL

The original program is supposed to implement copying all the records from the source file to the target file. At the higher abstraction level, it is to say that there is a "back-up" relationship between the two entities — source-record and target-record. Each record is one instance of an entity. The original program is transformed into (Figure 4):

The final result of the "file-backup" program can be shown by an ER diagram (Figure 5).

When the original program was transformed into an ER diagram, the user can easily decide that the program segment can be a good candidate of a reusable component. Therefore, the component in RWSL (Figure 3 and 4) will also be analysed by the Semantic Interface Analyser (SIA) in order to generate a form annotated with formal pre-conditions, post-conditions and obligations. For details of annotation rules of SIA, please refer to [6].

Based on the predefined software templates for COBOL in the Knowledge Base, predicate analysis and propagation, we can infer that the module *file-backup* contains the predicates as shown in Figure 6.

4.2 Other Case Studies

A number of case studies on COBOL code (including real programs of several thousand lines) were used in experiments. Typically, experimenting with these programs progressed through several stages.

- Some of the "data" statements which are not able to contribute to the eventual ER diagrams are omitted. For example, COBOL statements, such as MOVE 0 TO A-VARIABLE, MOVE SPACES TO A-VARIABLE, MOVE "NOTHING" TO A-VARIABLE, ADD 0 TO A-VARIABLE, SUBTRACT 0 FROM A-VARIABLE, SET A-VARIABLE TO 0, INSPECT statements, COMPUTE statements, etc. were omitted. This represents information not needed in abstraction.

- One line of COBOL code is typically translated into one line of RWSL.

- After the initial tidy-up, the translated COBOL program in RWSL was ready for further transformation. It worth mentioning that information that could be useful in future abstraction was recorded by RWSL **comment** statements.

- Almost all the assignment statements that were originally translated from the MOVE statements in COBOL were abstracted to **relate** statement. So were those assignment statements originally from ADD and SUBTRACT statements. A **comment** statement was usually added along with each abstraction in order to record information which will be used to decided the degree of the relationship between the two entities which would be obtained from the two records linked by the **relate** statement later on.

- The REDEFINES statements in the original COBOL program were translated into **redefine** statements in RWSL. According to observation, all original records to be redefined were of the same data types as that of the redefining records. The conclusion how applying those functions for dealing with aliased records was that aliased records would not affect each other in the abstraction process. Therefore, a record and its redefining record were treated as independent records in this case study.

- Entities were abstracted from records and this is the starting point of moving from the code level to the conceptual level. This was done when restructuring work at the code level had been finished.

- Relationships were mainly derived from the **relate** statements and information recorded by the **comment** statements were used to decide the degrees for the relationships by transformations with a help of human expertise.

- Relationships can also be obtained from other sources. For example, relationships were able to be obtained from the declaration of a record in COBOL. When a subrecord occurs for more than once, the subrecord and the record can both be abstracted to an entity and a relationship between these two entities can also be obtained.

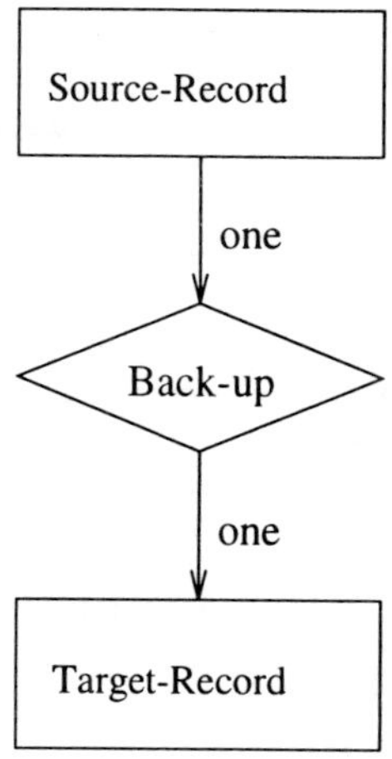

Figure 5: An Entity Relationship Diagram for "File-Backup" Program

- The **comment** statement was translated from the OCCURS construct in the COBOL and was used to decide the degree for the relationship.
- Duplicate entity relationships which might be obtained from different places of the program, and these were checked and removed. All the **comment** statements were removed when the abstraction process was finished.

The method developed in this research can deal with most code in the case studies. In particular, COBOL records and files are able to be represented in RWSL and this is crucial to the implementation of the prototype as well as the successful application of the method. Therefore, it is comparatively easier to extract ER models from a relatively independent (self-contained) segment of COBOL code with record (file) definitions, but it is more difficult for a COBOL segment with many calls to other segments (i.e. with many PERFORM statements) because the structural complexity is increasing. The problem may be helped by building more powerful "restructuring" transformations, which is not a main thrust of the paper.

5 Conclusions

This research described in the paper has focussed on acquiring ER models from data intensive source code to obtain reusable COBOL code components and their designs by combining an analysis of data structures and code. Suitable formal transformations for this purpose have been developed, in particular transformations for dealing with COBOL records and files, aliased records, foreign keys, user-defined abstract data types and functional relationships. These transformations have been used in the case studies. The research brings us valuable detailed understanding in this field and some main problems of acquiring ER models have been solved.

The development of the method and the implementation of the prototype show that this approach has covered a scope from theory to practice for reverse engineering and reuse.

A number of conclusions can be reached:

- The abstracted ER diagrams are able to represent the designs of the original programs and

---

pre-condition
!*Sequential-file*($File1$, *record-type1*)
!*Sequential-file*($File2$, *record-type2*)
!EQU(*record-type1*, *record-type2*)
post-condition
!$EQU(File1, File2)$

file-backup($File1, File2$)

Figure 6: Semantic Interface Predicates Generated

they make original programs much more understandable, which is a great help to identify reusable COBOL components. The correctness of the obtained ER diagrams is at present checked manually based on human knowledge and expertise.

- The method combines analysis of data and code, and therefore it can address two major problems common to data-intensive programs, i.e., aliases and relations (like foreign keys) that affect both data and code.

- The method is sufficiently general to apply to data intensive programs written in other source languages than just COBOL, for example, a program written in the C programming language can be reverse engineered using the approach as long as the C program is translated into RWSL.

- This method only requires source code as its input and it can be applied to heavily modified code typical in systems which have been maintained over many years.

- There are few restrictions on the approach developed in this research. Perhaps the only restriction is that the user needs to supply the source code to be reverse engineered. The approach is, however, fundamentally interactive, and the tool supports the expert maintainer in restructuring code and then extracting designs. It is not automatic. The user-driven mode is common with the approach used in almost all other reverse engineering approaches. The user's role is well taken into consideration when the approach was studied and a user-friendly interface was designed and implemented when the prototype tool was built.

- When the source code scales up, the method developed in the paper would still work well provided program segments in a manageable size could still be found. The scale of the source code would affect the method in a situation where smaller program segments are all not comparatively self-contained, i.e., self-contained segments are already not in a manageable size. One possible solution could be to build an Information Database. When the Program Transformer is working on a program segment which has many calls to other segments, it is the Information Database that collects all the necessary information from the called segments for the Transformer so that the Transformer does not need to load in those segments.

- Semantic Interface Analysis is used and this will give re-users confidence on the reusable components in the Reuse Library.

This research has so far indicated that the approach of program transformation can be practically used in COBOL code reuse, though the real application of this approach will not be seen until an industrial-strength tool has beed built. More research will be conducted to improve the prototype developed in this research into a practical tool.

Example programs used in the experiments were mainly written in COBOL, and they were translated into RWSL. It is expected that more experiments will be carried out on programs written both in COBOL and other languages. Also, in the future work of the research in RA, the results of applying those reusable components identified by the approach described in the paper will give useful feedback on improving the process of identification of reusable components.

References

[1] Arnold R. and Frakes W., "Software Reuse and Reengineering", *Software Reenginnering*, Robert Arnold Edits, IEEE Computer Society Press, Los Alamitos, CA, 1993.

[2] Bachman R., *A CASE for Reverse Engineering* reprinted from DATAMATION, Cahners Publishing Company, July, 1988.

[3] Bennett K., Bull T. and Yang H., "A Transformation System for Maintenance — Turning Theory into Practice", IEEE Conference of Software Maintenance-1992 (CSM '92), Orlando, Florida, November, 1992.

[4] Biggerstaff T. and Ritcher C., "Reusability Framework, Assessments and Direction", IEEE Software, Vol.4, No. 7, pp. 252-257, 1987.

[5] Chen P. P., "The Entity Relationship Model — Toward a Unified View of Data", ACM Transaction on Database Systems, Vol. 7, No. 1, March, 1976.

[6] Chu W. C. and Yang H., "Component Reuse Through Reverse Engineering and Semantic Interface Analysis", IEEE Nineteenth Computer Software and Application Conference (CompSac'95), Dallas, Texas, August, 1995.

[7] Date J., *An Introduction to Database Systems*, Volume I, 4th Edn., Addison-Wesley Publishing Company, Manchester, 1986.

[8] Evans A., Bulter K., Goos G. and Wulf W., *DIANA Reference Manual*, Tartan Laboratories, Inc., Pittsburgh, 3rd Edition, 1983.

[9] Frakes W. B. and Pole T. P., "An Empirical Study of Representation Method for Reusable Software Components", *IEEE Transactions on Software Engineering*, Vol. 20, No. 8, August 1994, pp. 617-630.

[10] Inglis J., *COBOL 85 for Programmers*, John Wiley & Sons, Inc., Chichester, 1989.

[11] Joiner J.K., Tsai W. T., Chen X. P. Subramanian S. and Gandamaneni H., "Data-Centred Program Understanding", IEEE International Conference on Software Maintenance-1994, Victoria, Canada, 1994.

[12] Martin J. and McClure, *Structured Techniques for Computing*, Prentice-Hall International, Inc., Englewood Cliffs, New Jersey, 1985.

[13] von Mayrhauser A. and Vans A. M., "From Code Understanding Needs to Reverse Engineering Tool Capacities", Proceedings of the Sixth International Workshop on Computer-Aided Software Engineering (CASE '93), Singapore, July, 1993.

[14] Sneed H. M. and Jandrasics G., "Inverse Transformation of Software from Code to Specification", IEEE Conference on Software Maintenance-1988, Phoenix, Arizona, 1988.

[15] Soloway E. and Ehrlich K., "Empirical Studies of Programming Knowledge", *IEEE Transaction on Software Engineering*, SE-10, September 1984.

[16] Tilley S. R., Wong K., Storey M. D. and Muller H. A., "Programmable Reverse Engineering", IEEE International Conference on Software Maintenance-1994 (ICSM '94), Victoria, British Columbia, Canada, September, 1994.

[17] Yang H., "The Supporting Environment for A Reverse Engineering System — The Maintainer's Assistant", IEEE Conference on Software Maintenance-1991 (CSM '91), Sorrento, Italy, October, 1991.

[18] Yang H. and Bennett K., "Extension of A Transformation System for Maintenance — Dealing with Data Intensive Programs", IEEE International Conference on Software Maintenance-1994 (ICSM '94), Victoria, Canada, September, 1994.

Support for Modular Parsing in Software Reengineering

Ian Peake, Eric Salzman
Centre for Software Maintenance
School of Information Technology
The University of Queensland 4072
AUSTRALIA
Phone: + 61 7 3365 2097
Fax: + 61 7 3365 1428
{ peaki | eric }@it.uq.edu.au

Abstract

As reengineering increasingly contributes to software engineering, so can software engineering principles contribute to cost-effective reengineering tool development. The cost of modelling languages motivates support for modular parsers which can, like program modules, be assembled cheaply from smaller, tested components. We describe a scheme which achieves this by extending the expressive and flexible combinator parsing scheme using object-oriented constructs (class inheritance and dynamic method dispatch). Related schemes either do not fully support code sharing or sacrifice flexibility. The scheme has been implemented in a prototype reengineering environment and successfully tested on grammars such as Modula-2. Generation time for extensions is linear in the size of the extension. Run time performance is potentially as bad as for general parsing algorithms but can be linear (10 times slower than LALR for Modula-2) after optimization.

1. Introduction

The need to support *modular* language implementations – that is, where components (of a language implementation) can be defined, compiled and tested separately, then integrated – has been widely recognised.

As Koskimies has observed, although modularisation is most commonly seen in a traditional language front end implementation where lexical analyser, parser, linker etc. are separate loosely coupled modules, there is another important form of modularity. This is "...according to the natural units of the language itself," – splitting, e.g., a grammar into logically cohesive units such as "expressions" or "database statements." Because language models are as much "targets" as they are "tools" of software engineering, the benefits of this approach fulfil software engineering objectives. Module size can be more closely managed; modules match natural concepts thus supporting cohesion and coupling; and modules embodying important syntax constructs can be reused in the production of new languages [16].

Increasingly there is a trend toward incorporating principles from programming into language design and implementation [3], including reusability and modularity [15], originally proposed in language extensibility literature [22][25] originating in the sixties and seventies. There are several applications and tools which support various forms of modular language definition [5][7][8][16][26][27].

The need for such support in software reengineering is readily apparent:

- Models for languages such as COBOL are central to translation projects, requiring person months to develop, test or extend, so support for their reuse is highly desirable. However COBOL, like several other mainstream languages, has several independent implementations [23], each with slightly different syntax and semantics, so modifying a copy of an existing grammar might be necessary before it can be used in a new situation.
- The emergence of 4GLs has resulted in hybrid or "embedded" languages, integrating the syntax and semantics of, for example, C and SQL. Defining syntax for such a language necessarily involves new syntax at the connection between two pre-existing syntaxes (i.e.: SQL as C expressions or C expressions within SQL). Implementation would require copying and merging syntax descriptions of SQL and C.

The software engineering problem to be solved is that of the "version fork" resulting from having copied code to create slightly different language models. Later changes to

0-8186-7840-2/97 $10.00 © 1997 IEEE

common behaviour may in general have to be manually propagated to all "derived" grammars, increasing the risk of introducing unnecessary errors.

Ideally language implementers should be able to specify derived language models in terms of a base grammar and a summary of changes. Then, any compiled resources (i.e.: object code) of one language model should be reusable by the compiler when creating resources for derived language models. In other words, object code should behave in ways sympathetic to modular language *specifications* (which emphasise distinctions) rather than language *denotations* which may include large amounts of redundancy.

Figure 1 illustrates the goal by depicting specifications (horizontal lines and arrows), which either fully specify a language (L0) or specify a language relative to another (L1).

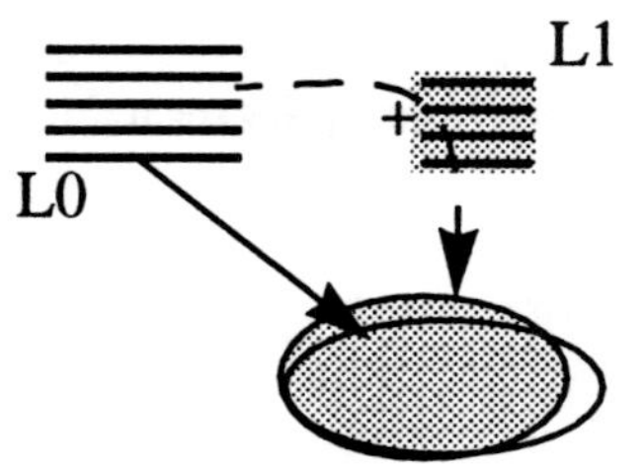

Figure 1. Language specifications vs. language denotations

Ellipses represent derived resources (L0's outlined, L1's shaded). Our goal is to achieve an implementation of L1 which, in terms of the diagram, only creates derived resources not in the intersection of L0 and L1's ellipses.

We use the term *extend* to refer to the way a language model *extension* reuses the specification or implementation of another *base* language model.

The goal does not allow the possibility of a language model specified in terms of more than one other model, but as seen by the examples represents a sufficiently interesting goal which may be useful in achieving more general ones.

We focus on parser specification and reuse, which constitutes a large portion of the language tool implementation effort [4][6]. So the narrowed goal is to create parsers whose code can be reused as though they were modules. Hence we use the terms "grammar" and "language model" as synonyms. For the purposes of this paper we do not consider issues of parse tree construction, so regarding the *behaviour* or *denotation* of some *compiled* grammar as its *recognisor*.

Ideally, any extension to support modularity should be maximally orthogonal to existing parser technology. That is, it should integrate with any existing parsing scheme without compromising any of that scheme's advantages. For reengineering, expressiveness and efficient parser generation are arguably more important than of parse time efficiency.

Expressiveness is important since both the ability to create rapid prototypes and maintainability determine productivity in the reengineering tool building domain rather than parse time efficiency: it is suboptimal to require grammars to be, e.g., LL, LR or unambiguous since this involves more work to transform an otherwise executable language specification into a (perhaps less elegantly expressed) compilable grammar.

Efficient parser generation is important since (i) a grammar will likely be recompiled frequently in a prototyping environment; and, (ii) the cost of recompiling very large grammars (a likely occurrence in industrial scale projects) is nontrivial even when using an established parser generator such as Refine's parser generation system Dialect [20].

Parse time performance is less important since the *primary* concern is the development and maintenance of models for large complex languages. Although software reengineering and related disciplines are often concerned with deployment into large scale applications, overall costs are often dominated by development, maintenance and reuse [2].

Our scheme builds on combinator parsing, which satisfies the criteria above as follows:

- expressiveness: any context free (even ambiguous) grammar is supported (initially with the exception of left recursion but see later);
- flexibility: the basic scheme can be extended e.g. to support semantic actions, increase efficiency or explicitly support expression hierarchies [12] (However we are not necessarily claiming that these facilities are all compatible with this scheme or each other);
- compile time efficiency: creation of top down parsers is typically cheaper than LR style parsers;
- run time efficiency: The apparent equivalence of combinator parsing and chart parsing obtained through optimisations such as memoing [17] suggests polynomial worst case parse time complexity. Nearly linear run time performance is likewise possible through techniques such as the removal of routine ambiguity from "normal" grammars, the use of pragmas [13], and backtracking related optimisations [21].

Parsers for specific grammars are implemented as collections of function definitions. Through the use of a hierarchy of "parseable input streams" (corresponding to a hierarchy of language descriptions) combined with generic functions and methods for nonterminals and productions, parser code (in compiled form) is available to implementation of any derived language model.

Several alternative schemes providing support for modular grammars have been proposed and developed.

Existing schemes either do not retain the flexibility and succinctness of definition of an approach such as combinator parsing or do not fully support object code sharing across multiple language models as required by the examples. We defer detailed comparisons until the section on related work, below.

The technology presented in this paper is being used as part of an extended version of Software Refinery (called the Language eXtension Work Bench – "LXWB" [18]) to implement language tools for, e.g., preprocessors, translators and design recovery tools.

2. Source language

The parsing scheme presented in this paper works for BNF style context free grammars consisting of a set of productions and a set of starting symbols. The scheme is (by design) closely related to Reasoning Systems' Dialect parser generator (see the section on related work below).

Extra clauses are required to identify grammars by (unique) name, and (optionally) specify importation from another grammar by name:

```
grammar Gname1
{extend Gname2}
```

(Braces denote optionality.)

A dependant grammar GY which `extends` a grammar GX implicitly includes all productions in GX, including productions reused by GX from other grammars (that is, transitive extension chains are permitted). The dependant grammar may selectively exclude any nonterminal ("NT") (and its associated productions)

```
excluding NT
```

or any single production by specifying the rule in full:

```
excluding NT -> I1 .. In
```

It is an error for an `excluding` clause to refer to nonexistent nonterminals or productions in the base grammar.

Every grammar must explicitly define its own start symbols.

Grammars containing references to nonterminals which are neither explicitly or implicitly defined (and therefore to nonterminals which have been excluded) are undefined. No grammar may `extend` another grammar in such a way that it transitively depends upon itself.

3. Infrastructure

The scheme is based on combinator parsing and several features found in object oriented and functional (or applicative) languages. We present the scheme using both Refine and Allegro Common LISP, reflecting the fact that our prototype has been built using both. The combinator parsing library is presented in Refine. Parser functions corresponding to user defined nonterminals are expressed in Common LISP.

3.1 Software refinery.

Software Refinery [19] [20] is a reengineering tool development environment built on Allegro Common LISP, which includes the programming language Refine. Lexically, Refine has an Algol-like flavour and is case-insensitive.

Refine functions with signatures of the form

```
function refine-fn (var1: type1, ...) : result-type
  ...
```

are accessible to LISP code as functions of the form

```
(defun refine-fn (var1 var2) ...)
```

and, conversely, LISP functions of the second form are accessible as Refine functions of the first form.

Refine is statically typed and provides some complex types such as `seq` (sequence) and `set`, implemented as LISP lists. The type `tuple` is also implemented as a LISP list. Refine has a class system which does not transparently interact with Common LISP's CLOS (see below). Refine also does not directly support laziness or method overriding, so these features must be accessed via functions implemented in LISP.

3.2 Combinator parsing.

Combinator parsing is an elegant parser implementation scheme which can handle all ambiguous context free grammars not containing left recursion. The scheme involves user defined functions to parse language primitives such as tokens, supported by higher order "glue" functions to combine primitive parsers into more complex parsers.

Our initial implementation of the combinator parser library does not differ substantially from that described by Hutton [Hutton92], although we actually use opaque types instead of the Refine `seq` type for `pstream` and `parser`.

The type of a parser function (expressed in Refine) is:

```
type parser = map (pstream, seq (parse-result))
```

This type describes functions mapping from values of a class `pstream` to a list of objects of class `parse-result`. We assume that `pstream` handles lexical analysis and therefore represents a sequence of tokens (strings).

```
type pstream = seq (string)
```

The definition of the `parse-result` type is

```
type parse-result = tuple (user-object, pstream)
```

that is, two components: a value representing the object successfully parsed (`user-object` denotes the type of all user created objects), and the remaining unconsumed portion of the token stream.

A simple example of a `parser` is a function `p-begin` behaving as follows:

```
p-begin (["begin",..])
  ==>
  [ <"begin", [..]> ]

p-begin (..)
  ==>
  []
```

That is, the function returns a sequence containing a tuple representing the appropriate parse result if its input starts with the "`begin`" token, and the empty sequence otherwise.

"High level" parser *combinators* combine `parsers` to create new `parsers`, achieving the effect of both simple BNF style operators such as e.g. concatenation ("`then`") and alternation ("`orelse`") as well as EBNF operators such as the Kleene star ("`many`").

For example, because in this implementation parsers return lists of possible parses, the alternation combinator is implemented simply as the list concatenation of the application of all parser alternatives to the input stream:

```
function ORELSE (alt1: parser, alt2: parser): parser =
 lambda (s: pstream)
  concat (alt1 (ps), alt2 (ps))
```

3.3 Common LISP.

Although combinator parsers are traditionally defined for functional languages which have lazy evaluation strategies, it is possible to implement the strategy in LISP using demand driven evaluation of function arguments and lexically scoped closures. Demand driven evaluation of a function F's argument A is achieved by wrapping the actual parameter expression as a parameterless first class function. At the first point in the definition of F where A is required, it is passed as an argument to `apply`.

The Common LISP Object System (CLOS) is a library of object oriented programming facilities, including the *generic function* facility. Generics are declared with signatures stipulating the classes of their parameters. Generics may be instantiated with *method* declarations, each of which is a function with a signature specifying the subclasses of the corresponding generic parameter's class for which it applies. For every application of a (unary) generic function to its argument, CLOS determines and applies the *effective method* – the method whose parameter class most closely match the actual parameter's class.

4. Implementation scheme

The translation scheme: (i) is presented as a scheme for implementing BNF style production alternatives as parse combinators (section 4.1); (ii) is extended to handle scenarios where a nonterminal's parse method may include new syntax (section 4.2); and (iii) is further extended to handle scenarios where syntax may be excluded (section 4.3). Finally, the issue of ensuring that names used in parse functions do not collide is addressed in section 4.4.

In what follows we make use of the example grammars in Figure 2. Case is not significant.

```
grammar GA                    grammar GB

 start-symbols Item            extend GA

 item -> item-a                start-symbols item

 item -> item-b                item -> item-c

 item-a -> "A"                 item-c -> "C"

 item-b -> "B1"

 item-b -> "B2"
```

Figure 2. Simple grammars GA and GB

4.1 Basic scheme

For every nonterminal there must be an associated generic function of type `parser`. E.g., for `item-b` in GA above this would be:

```
; parse an item-b from the front of a pstream
(defgeneric p-item-b (pstream))
```

Each of GA's nonterminal generics must be instantiated with methods to call all associated productions. E.g., for `item-b`:

```
; apply the parser for all item-b's productions
; to the pstream s
(defmethod p-item-b (pstream s)
 (funcall (orelse ('p-item-b-ga-1) ('p-item-b-ga-2))
          s))
```

And hence the references to `p-item-b-ga-1` and `p-item-b-ga-2`:

```
(defun p-item-b-ga-1 (pstream s)
 ; consumes a "B1" from the pstream s
 )
```

```
(defun p-item-b-ga-2 (pstream s)
 ; consume a "B2" from the pstream s
 )
```

The names for each production's parse function must be unique within all nonterminals in all grammars, hence the inclusion of "ga" in the names above.

Figure 3 illustrates the use of LISP generics and methods to implement `p-item` according to the scheme so far. In all following diagrams: Ellipses represent generic functions, rectangles represent functions (or methods, with arrows pointing to the instantiated generic) and dashed lines represent calls to functions. Quoted text within rectangular boxes represents a token which would be expected at that point in the input for the recogniser to succeed.

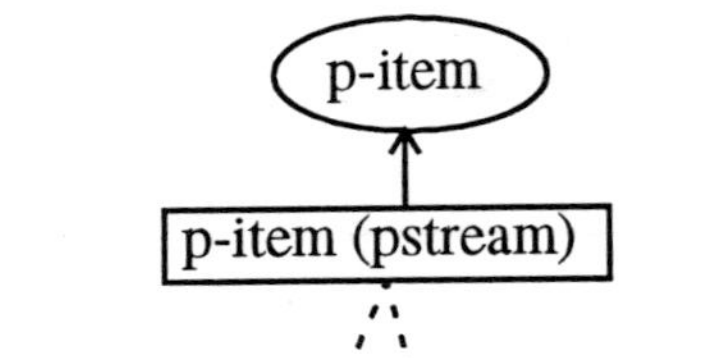

Figure 3. Example of a simple parse-function Implementation

4.2 Using method overriding to allow extension

Consider the grammar GB which `extends` GA. In GB, the syntax definition of `item` is extended to include `item-c`. Thus, "A" is legal in both GA and GB, while "C" is legal only in GB. Below we outline the implementation of parser functions for GB.

Distinguishing Input Streams. First we need to distinguish between "parsing in GA" and "parsing in GB". When any `pstream` is created it must be created as an instance of some subclass of `pstream` uniquely corresponding to its grammar. Classes corresponding to extensions must be subclasses of their bases. So two new subclasses of `pstream` are required:

```
(defclass GA-pstream (pstream))
(defclass GB-pstream (GA-pstream))
```

From now on, methods created specifically for some grammar G must only be applicable to the appropriate `pstream` subclass associated with G. For example, we need to retrospectively specify that methods created for GA have parameters of class `GA-pstream` instead of `pstream`:

```
(defmethod p-item (GA-pstream s) ... )
```

Providing fanout functions to allow reuse of grammar alternatives. To implement GB, two extra productions must be recognised. Consider

```
item -> item-c
```

The method for parsing `item` in GA cannot be changed, or GA will behave differently when "parsing in GA". Instead `p-item` must be re instantiated so as to override the pre-existing `p-item` applicable to `GA-pstreams`.

This requires a further refinement to the scheme: for every NT create a *fanout* function (uniquely named as a function of its NT and grammar). For `item` in GA this is

```
(defun p-item-GA-f (s)
 ; call the generics for p-item-a and p-item-b
 )
```

Ordinarily, the method for a particular NT (e.g., `p-item`) simply calls the fanout function corresponding its NT.

```
(defmethod p-item (GA-pstream s)
 (p-item-GA-f s))
```

When a new method for the same NT is introduced in an extending LM, the new method uses the "`orelse`" combinator to call the fanout for both the base grammar, and a new fanout for the NT in its own grammar. Thus, `p-item` for GB would be implemented as

```
(defmethod p-item (gb-pstream s)
 (funcall (orelse 'p-item-ga-f 'p-item-gb-f) s))
```

where `p-item-gb-f` is an ordinary function implementing the parser which calls the generic for `item-c`.

Implementing

```
item-c -> "C"
```

is itself straightforward since there is no overlap with existing productions in GA.

Figure 4 illustrates the objects created in order to implement GA according to the extended scheme. (In this diagram there are some entities which are functions rather than methods, and hence do not have attached upward solid arrows since they do not instantiate anything.)

Figure 5 illustrates the new objects created to implement GB, and how they link to the existing objects (shaded area).

4.3 Exclusion of syntax in extensions

Let GB be as before, with the additional clause

```
excluding item-b
```

meaning that use of `item-b` is not valid in GB.

The implementation scheme already provides for this possibility: instantiate the `item-b` generic in GB so that

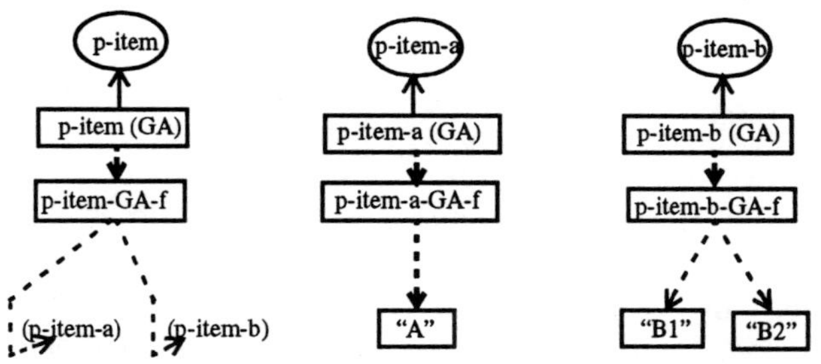

Figure 4: Implementation of grammar GA using fanout functions

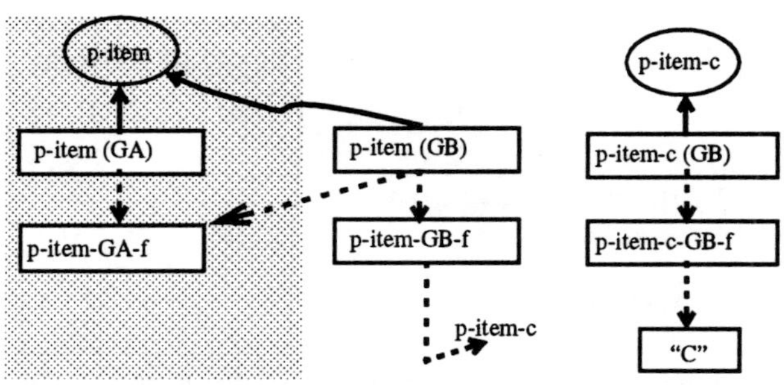

Figure 5. Example of using fanout functions and method overriding to implement production addition

the new method does not call any fanout functions, but rather calls a "null parser" (which always fails by returning an empty set of possible parses.)

GB might alternatively contain the production

```
excluding item-b -> "B2"
```

meaning that the specific production is invalid. This requires that each *production* have its own *production generic*:

```
(defgeneric p-item-b-gb-1 (gb-pstream))
```

(As stated earlier, the name of the generic function must be unique. Ideally the name should correspond uniquely to the production's RHS in order to best satisfy the requirement that a base language model need not be examined by other models.)

The production generic is instantiated by a new method whenever some language model excludes the production. The implementation of the exclusion example above is illustrated in Figure 6.

4.4 Parse function namespace management

Since there are several grammar implementations coexisting within one LISP world, it is important that no unexpected behaviour occur as a result of function name

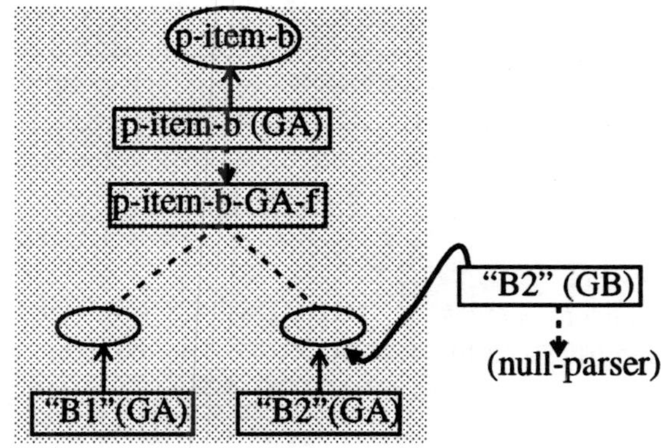

Figure 6. Using production generics and method overriding to exclude productions

collisions arising from coincidental name sharing between language models. But the scheme precludes this possibility: Nonterminal generic function names cannot collide because the inheritance hierarchy partitions the name space correctly: even if two completely unrelated grammars GX and GY define nonterminals with the same name, the two separate instantiations are completely independent by virtue of LISP's method overriding. Fanout functions are again unique by virtue of their naming scheme (note that the naming scheme used here is fallible unless grammar names are restricted from containing hyphens "-"), so there is no danger of name collisions between them.

5. Related work in modular parsing

5.1 Object oriented precedence grammars.

An implementation strategy devised by Bloesch *et al.* [5] based on an object oriented implementation of precedence grammars supports sharing of generated parser code.

The scheme efficiently compiles expression style grammars but requires a worst case $O(n^2)$ transformation to handle empty free, deterministic context free grammars. We believe the need for this transformation makes the scheme unsuitable for preprocessing grammar modules in isolation.

Bloesch described a scheme similar to ours based on recursive descent parsing but the apparent difficulties of using recursive descent led to its rejection.

5.2 Dialect.

Software Refinery includes a language modelling suite called Dialect [20]. In Dialect a grammar may optionally name another grammar as its base. The meaning of the grammar is then determined relative to the base grammar.

Dialect generates parsers for some grammar G by calculating its denoted grammar G' (calculating any changes necessitated if G is an extension), then compiling G' using GNU Bison, an LALR(1) parser generator.

The advantage of using a preprocessor like this is that off-the-shelf parser technology can be reused by augmenting an existing generator with a simple preprocessor.

The major disadvantage is that G will be recompiled in space and time as a function of G', the denoted grammar. Even small changes to a base level language model necessitate regeneration of all dependant language models before their behaviour reflects the changes.

5.3 Lazy incremental generation of parsers.

Heering *et al* [11] propose a tool, IPG, which lazily generates a state table driven (LALR) parser and critique several other possible methods for incremental parser generation. We have not determined whether theirs or any other LALR based strategy can be modified to allow for code sharing.

5.4 Modular recursive descent parsing.

Koskimies [16] developed a parser generation scheme based on specifying modular LL(1) grammars as collections of interdependent Modula-2 modules. Each nonterminal is implemented as a separate function in a recursive descent parser. A "start tree" is constructed lazily at parse time to cache the FIRST and FOLLOW sets required in recursive descent parsing.

Our approach differs from Koskimies in two important respects: first, by making use of combinator parsing, no other special apparatus is required to support top down parsing, and secondly, by making use of dynamic method dispatch, code sharing is more readily achieved.

Koskimies' approach satisfies the first part of the "true sharability" criterion because each syntax component is a separately compilable module and the dependencies between productions are implemented as inter-module dependencies. Consider again our example grammars GA and GB. To implement GA, each NT is declared in its own module, and GA is (presumably) defined as a module which imports the modules for `Item`, `Item-A` and `Item-B`. To implement GB, a (new) module is required for `Item` which must not collide with the previous module for `Item` (how easy this is in Modula-2 obviously depends on the particular compiler in use). GB itself is implemented as a module which imports all GA's modules, substituting the revised version of Item. Thus parser code can be shared, however object code for each module must be copied and re-linked whenever it is used in a new language instance.

5.5 Extended chart parsing.

While enrichments such as memoing and modularisation are being made to top down parsers, there is some justification in asking whether anything new is achieved that has not already been achieved with chart parsers [10]. For example Wegbreit [25] for example showed how dynamically extensible parsing could be implemented using Earley's algorithm [9]. Several authors including Johnson [14] and Norvig [17] have remarked on the correspondence of chart parsing to strategies involving memoing and (simulated) concurrency [24].

We take the position of that given such an equivalence, suitable top down parsers are by no means inferior since they achieve similar results to chart parsers with economy of specification and flexibility.

6. Evaluation / conclusions

6.1 Modularity.

The work presented here satisfies the modularity requirement inasmuch as it supports true sharing of object code. A grammar may `extend` no more than one other grammar, although there is apparently no reason why the scheme could not be extended to allow such (see below).

6.2 Expressiveness / abstractness.

Since the scheme is based on combinator parsing, it admits many enhancements available to that regime. For example, although the scheme presented here does not construct parse trees, combinator parsers readily support the attachment of semantic actions to parser functions.

The elegance with which the existing scheme admits enrichment demonstrates the feasibility not only of building a fully featured implementation for conventional parser specifications, but also extending specification languages to make the modular paradigm for grammar implementation a practical reality.

One drawback of the existing scheme is that grammars containing left recursive definitions are not acceptable, a widely documented deficiency with the combinator parsing scheme as used above – and with most top down parsing schemes [1]. The traditional solution, removing left recursion prior to parser generation is suboptimal, because although left recursion may be removed from each module specification, unexpected left recursion may occur as modules are combined. Alternative combinator parsing schemes based on continuation passing such as that described by Johnson [14] do not suffer from this problem. Initial efforts in merging our scheme with Johnson's have yielded promising results.

Our scheme does not easily admit the use of LR style precedence rules to eliminate routine ambiguity from e.g. expression hierarchies, however there has been some work to create special combinators for expressions which may be applicable [12]. We have not investigated whether these can be admitted into our scheme.

6.3 Compile time and run time performance.

Although still a prototype, the scheme has been used to generate parsers for several grammars, including a pre-existing grammar for Modula-2. Compile time performance of the parser generation has not been isolated from other superstructure in the prototype but is observably faster than Software Refinery's Dialect subsystem when compiling small extensions to large base models. After implementing memoing of fanout functions and lexical analyser calls and removing ambiguity in expressions, run time performance was of the order of 10 times slower than the equivalent Dialect generated LALR parser but arguably acceptable for prototyping purposes.

As with all general parsing strategies, run time performance is compromised both by the possibility of ambiguous grammars (we expect parsers in the worst case to have a run time complexity of $O(n^3)$ in the size of the input) and by the overhead of *allowing* for the possibility of ambiguous grammars even when grammars are not ambiguous; some optimisations to address the latter are possible [21].

6.4 Significance.

As mentioned above in the section on chart parsing, the novelty of this work is twofold: the use of object oriented notation and combinator parser notation to succinctly express powerful, general, composite parsers; and the possibility of capitalising on further developments in combinator parsing which might allow the reuse of efficient (i.e.: linear parse time performance) parsers by "plugging in" extensions without the need for further parser generation or compilation.

The scheme could be therefore be used to support abstract specification and prototyping of truly modular grammars in fields where large scale prototype language models are vital, such as constructing translation tools, CASE tools and even compilers.

Tangentially, the usefulness of object oriented method instantiation for this application could be regarded as a reason for investigating method dispatch implementations.

7. Future work

7.1 Prototyping and validation

The scheme presented here is one of several parser generation schemes integrated into a protype called the Language eXtension Work Bench (LXWB) [18].

As mentioned in the evaluation section above, investigation of combinator parsing schemes for handling routine ambiguity is also needed.

The use of fanout functions is slightly unsatisfactory since base grammars which are also extensions must create fanout functions for whatever NTs they propagate to downstream extensions. A more appropriate technique might be to use the CLOS `call-next-method` facility.

Further work in applying this scheme to new and pre-existing extension hierarchies, is needed to validate the usefulness of the modularity paradigm and the applicability of this scheme in practice.

Further work in integrating alternative combinator parsing strategies with our scheme would both increase the viability of the scheme described here to be used in real language model implementations and demonstrate the flexibility of these schemes.

7.2 Extending concepts of grammar extension and modularity.

Wildman [27] showed the desirability of grammar composition (versus extension); some key composition operations could be implemented elegantly based on the current scheme. For example, the current scheme allows a grammar to use at most one other grammar. Proper support for the second example in the introduction (4GL) requires that multiple grammars be used. Provided existing constraints are satisfied, multiple grammar use could be added by means of CLOS's multiple inheritance scheme. To be consistent with existing semantics, rules must be introduced for resolving name conflicts where the same nonterminal names have different meaning in base models.

Implementing the representative input class for:

```
grammar GZ
extend GX, GY
```

would require the declaration:

```
(defclass GZ-pstream (GX-pstream GY-pstream))
```

GZ would be constructed by implicitly including all of GX's and GY's productions, except where productions were explicitly excluded. Methods instantiated for `gz-pstream` would then override methods instantiated for `gx-pstream` and `gy-pstream`.

Acknowledgements

Ian Peake's contribution to this work was sponsored by an Australian Postgraduate Award and a scholarship from the Australian Defence Science and Technology Organisation.

References

[1] A. Aho, R. Sethi, and J. Ullman. *Compilers: principles, techniques and tools*. Addison-Wesley, Reading, 1986.

[2] P. Bailes, M. Chilvers, and I. Peake. A generic, knowledge-based, re-engineering architecture. In *Proceedings 6th International Workshop on CASE*, pages 190–198, Singapore, 1993. IEEE.

[3] P. Bailes, T. Chorvat, and I. Peake. A formal basis for the perception of programming as a language design activity. In *Proceedings of the 6th International Conference on Computing and Information*, volume 1 of *Journal of Computing and Information*, pages 1279–1294, Trent University, 1994.

[4] A. Berglas and J. Harrison. Evaluation of the ITOC Information System Design Recovery Tool. In *Proceedings of the Workshop on Program Comprehension*, Dearborn, Michigan, USA, 1997. to appear.

[5] A. Bloesch and T. Halpin. An object-oriented approach to extensible parsing. In *16th Australian Computer Science Conference*, volume B, pages 345–351, Feb. 1993.

[6] P. T. Breuer and J. P. Bowen. A PREttier compiler-compiler: generating higher-order parsers in C. *Software - Practice and Experience*, 25(11):1263–1297, Nov. 1995.

[7] L. Cardelli, F. Matthes, and M. Abadi. Extensible syntax with lexical scoping. Research Report 121, Digital Systems Research Centre, Palo Alto, California, Feb. 1994.

[8] J. R. Cordy and C. D. Halpern. TXL: a rapid prototyping system for programming language dialects. In *Proceedings IEEE International Conference on Computer Languages*, Miami, Nov. 1988.

[9] J. Earley. An efficient context-free parsing algorithm. *Communications of the ACM*, 26(1), Jan. 1983.

[10] S. L. Graham, M. A. Harrison, and W. L. Ruzzo. An Improved Context-Free Recognizer. *ACM Trans. Prog. Lang. Syst.*, 2(3):415–462, July 1980.

[11] J. Heering, P. Klint, and J. Rekers. Incremental generation of parsers. *IEEE Transactions on Software Engineering*, 16(12):1344–1351, Dec. 1990.

[12] S. Hill. Combinators for parsing expressions. *Functional Programming*, 6(3):445–463, May 1996.

[13] G. Hutton and E. Meijer. Monadic Parser Combinators. Technical Report NOTTCS-TR-96-4, Department of Computer Science, University of Nottingham, 1996.

[14] M. Johnson. Memoization in Top-Down Parsing. *Computational Linguistics*, 21(3):405–417, 1995. Discussion Paper.

[15] S. Kamin and E. Golin. Report of a workshop on future directions in programming languages and compilers. Technical report, University of Illinois, 1994. NSF CCR-9304990.

[16] K. Koskimies. Lazy recursive-descent parsing for modular language implementation. *Software–Practice and Experience*, 20:749–772, 1990.

[17] P. Norvig. Techniques for automatic memoization with applications to context-free parsing. *Computational Linguistics*, 17(1):91–98, 1991.

[18] I. Peake. User's guide to the language extension work bench version 1. Technical Report 387, School of Information Technology, University of Queensland, 1996.

[19] Reasoning Systems, Palo Alto, California. *Refine user's guide for Refine version 3.0 on Sun computers*, 1990.

[20] Reasoning Systems, Inc., Palo Alto, California. *Dialect user's guide for Dialect version 1.0*, 1990.

[21] N. Rojemo. *Garbage collection and memory efficiency in lazy functional languages*. PhD thesis, Chalmers University of Technology, 1995.

[22] T. Standish. Extensibility in programming language design. In *Proceedings of AFIPS Conference*, pages 287–290, Ahaheim, 1975.

[23] N. Stern and R. A. Stern. *The Wiley COBOL syntax reference guide: with IBM and VAX enhancements*. Wiley, 1994.

[24] D. S. Warren. Memoing for logic programs. *Communications of the ACM*, 35(3):93–111, Mar. 1992.

[25] B. Wegbreit. *Studies in extensible programming languages*. Garland Publishing, London, 1980.

[26] D. Weise and D. Crew. Programmable syntax macros. *SIGPLAN Notices*, 28(6):156–165, 1993. (Proceedings of ACM SIGPLAN '93 Conference on Programming Language Design and Implementation).

[27] L. Wildman and I. Hayes. Composing grammar transformations to construct a specification of a parser. *Australian Computer Science Communications*, 17(1):556–562, 1995.

Session P1c

System Development Methods

Constructing Formal Specifications from Informal Requirements

Robert G. Clark
Department of Computing Science and Mathematics
University of Stirling
Stirling FK9 4LA
Scotland, UK
rgc@cs.stir.ac.uk

Ana M. D. Moreira
Departamento de Informática
Faculdade de Ciências e Tecnologia
Universidade Nova de Lisboa
2825 Monte da Caparica, Portugal
amm@di.fct.unl.pt

Abstract

The Rigorous Object-Oriented Analysis (ROOA) method provides a systematic development process which, starting from a set of informal requirements, produces an executable object-oriented analysis model. The model is expressed in LOTOS and provides a precise and unambiguous formal requirements specification of the static, dynamic and functional aspects of a problem.

There is, however, a wide gap between informal requirements and a formal specification. To help bridge this gap, we propose that a formal and executable model which specifies behaviour in terms of what the environment expects from the system should be constructed initially. This user-centred model will give very early feedback to the requirements capture process and can be used as a step in the construction of the ROOA model. Both models are expressed in the same executable formal language and so they can be composed to verify that the ROOA model is compatible with the user-centred model and the composition executed to validate it with respect to the requirements.

1. Introduction

The Rigorous Object-Oriented Analysis (ROOA) method [8, 9, 10, 11] integrates formal description techniques with standard object-oriented analysis methods such as [3, 7, 12, 14, 15]. Its objective is to provide a systematic development process in which an initial formal requirements specification (the ROOA model) can be created from a set of informal requirements. As requirements are informal, this cannot be a formal process. It is also far from simple as there is a wide gulf between the structure and notation of the specification and of the requirements from which it is to be derived. We have been investigating ways of narrowing this gap.

A formal requirements specification is concerned with modelling an idealised view of the system and its interaction with the environment. It is a system-centred model from which the design and eventual implementation will be developed. However, informal requirements are usually presented in terms of the needs and expectations of the users of a system. A possible addition to the ROOA method is therefore to construct a formal and executable model which specifies the interaction of the environment with the system as seen from the viewpoint of the users.

The construction of this user-centred model has several advantages: it gives very early feedback to the requirements capture process, it provides a stepping stone in the construction of the system-centred ROOA model and it plays an important role in validating the ROOA model. We use the same executable formal language to specify both models. Therefore, we can compose them to verify that they are consistent and execute the composition to validate it with respect to the requirements.

2. Formal models

2.1. The system-centred model

Entities in the real world exist in parallel. As the object-oriented approach supports the direct modelling of real world entities, an object-oriented specification should model requirements as a set of communicating concurrent objects even when the eventual implementation is to be sequential. The formal language used to represent the formal model must support this view. LOTOS is such a language [1].

The ROOA formal specification is expressed in LOTOS and models objects as process instances and message passing by processes synchronizing on an event during which information may be exchanged. The ROOA method builds on the object model produced by an informal OOA method. However, whereas OOA methods such as OMT [14] create

0-8186-7840-2/97 $10.00

three separate models, the ROOA method gives rules for the systematic creation of a single integrated formal object-oriented analysis model whose aim is to give a complete and accurate description of the static, dynamic and functional aspects of a problem. This model is primarily a dynamic model although its structure is directly related to the object model. LOTOS tools enable the model to be analysed for syntactic or static semantic errors and it can form the basis for formal reasoning. As LOTOS is executable, simulation tools can be used in validating the specification with respect to the requirements [4].

2.2. The user-centred model

The user-centred model is a set of *agent views* where each agent view describes, from the viewpoint of an agent, a way in which the system is to be used. The agents are the users of the system, i.e. the environment in which it is to operate, and may be humans, hardware devices or other software systems. An agent view is concerned with the role being played. For example, a person can play different roles and therefore take part in more than one agent view while several different people can play a similar role and therefore take part in different instances of the same agent view. The focus in the user-centred model is on the way agents use the system, not on the system itself.

As the user-centred model is concerned with events, i.e. interactions between the environment and the system, it is best expressed in an executable event-oriented formal language such as LOTOS.

The user-centred model is of value throughout the ROOA method. It helps us to understand and structure the requirements and to construct and then validate the system-centred model. We have previously described how prototyping of the formal ROOA model shows up inconsistencies, contradictions, ambiguities, misunderstandings and omissions in the requirements sufficiently early in the development so that feedback can be given to the requirements capture [8, 10]. The introduction of a formal user-centred model enables such feedback to be given even earlier in the development process.

Hsia *et al.* have shown how a formal user-centred model can be represented using finite state automata [6] while Glinz has shown how it can be represented using Statecharts [5]. However, they do not provide a method for the integration of the user-centred model into the process of developing of a formal system-centred model.

Agent views play a similar role to Jacobson's use cases [7, 13]. However, unlike use cases, agent views only include the interactions between an agent and the system and do not include the consequent internal object interactions. In the early stages of analysis, it is important that we do not get bogged down in detail. This is especially important when an executable formal model is being produced as it necessarily contains more detail than an informal model. That is why we formalise agent views rather than use cases; formalising complete use cases would introduce too much detail and it is only external behaviour that we are concerned with at this stage.

3. The case study

We describe our approach through its application to the following case study.

In a road traffic pricing system, drivers of authorized vehicles can be charged at toll gates without having to stop. Vehicle owners register and then install a device (a gizmo) in their vehicle. The system holds information about authorized vehicles including the owner's personal data and a bank account number from where automatic debits are done monthly.

Each gizmo has an identifier which is read by sensors installed in special lanes at the toll gates. The system stores information so that the specified bank account can be debited. Different types of vehicle pay different rates.

When an authorized vehicle passes through a special lane, it gets a green light and the amount being debited is displayed. If an unauthorized vehicle passes through the lane, it gets a yellow light and a camera photographs its plate number. (Later, the owner will be fined.) There are two kinds of special lane: one where all vehicles of the same type pay the same amount (e.g. at a toll bridge) and one where the amount to be paid depends on the distance travelled (e.g. on a motorway) and the system has to store the entrance and exit point for each vehicle.

In Section 4, we show how we can identify the agents and their views and represent each view as a tree. In Section 5, we describe how both single and multi-agent views can be represented in LOTOS and how the user-centred model can be validated. In Section 6, we show how the user-centred model is used in the construction of the ROOA model and, in Section 7, how it supports the validation of the ROOA model.

4. Describe agent views

4.1. Identify agents, agent views and interface objects

We start by identifying agents. We have, for example, a gizmo installed in a vehicle which has a driver. We regard the composite vehicle-driver-gizmo to be a single agent which we refer to as *vehicle*. Related agents are a vehicle without a gizmo and a vehicle with a broken gizmo. It is likely that we will not be able to distinguish between the behaviour of these two agents. Other agents are the system manager, the bank and owners who have to buy a gizmo and register their vehicle before using the special lanes,

To determine the agent views, we imagine ourselves to be the agent and describe how we use the system. A vehicle agent, for example, uses the system in two different ways: one where it always pays the same amount, the *one-point vehicle view*, and another where the amount paid depends on the distance travelled, the *two-point vehicle view*.

We also identify the interface objects which provide the *external* behaviour of the system and with which the agents interact. This information is used to create an initial object model. Several agent views will often use the services offered by the same object. Creation of the object model helps ensure that different agent views use identical names for objects and services which are essentially the same.

An important interface object is the toll gate. The vehicle agent not only sees a toll gate, it also sees a light component, knows that there is a sensor which identifies its gizmo, that there is a hidden camera and that there may be a display. The vehicle agent also knows that there are different types of toll gate. The resulting object model is shown in Fig. 1. It uses OMT notation [14] and was built using the LOV/OMT Object Editor[1].

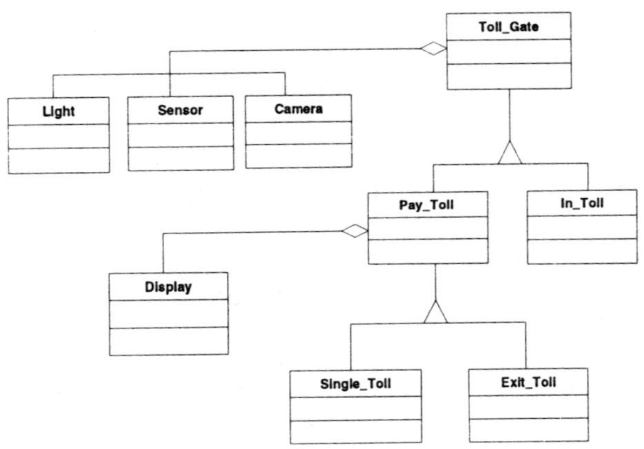

Figure 1. Initial object model

4.2. Represent agent views

Alternative behaviours can occur within each agent view. These possible alternative event sequences are represented graphically in a tree. Each event is represented in the tree as a node with the structure: $\langle interface\ object\rangle.\langle event\rangle$. Each path through the tree represents a sequence of external events and is referred to as an agent scenario.

In the one-point vehicle view, a sensor reads the gizmo identifier and, depending on whether or not it is acceptable, the system either shows a green light and the amount being paid or shows a yellow light and triggers a camera. Another agent view deals with the situation where a vehicle goes through a special lane either without a gizmo or with a broken gizmo which cannot be detected. This shows us that the sensor must take part in two events; it must be able to detect the presence of a vehicle as well as being able to read a gizmo. Initially, we treated the situation where no gizmo was detected as a separate agent view, but then decided that it was really a special case of the normal one-point vehicle view. Identifying agents and agent views is an iterative process and existing views are combined and new views created as we learn more about the requirements.

Focusing in this way on one agent view at a time enables us to determine the different ways in which an agent can interact with the system, and hence the services which the system must offer, without being sidetracked by other issues.

The tree representing the one-point vehicle view is shown in Fig. 2. Trees for other agent views are constructed in

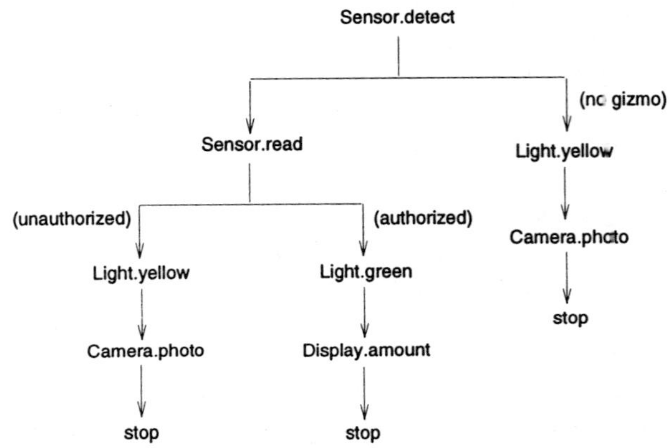

Figure 2. Tree representing the one-point vehicle view

a similar way. As the agent views are developed, new interface objects, together with events which correspond to services offered by interface objects to the environment, are added to the object model.

In general, an agent's interaction with the system involves other agents. One agent may initiate a scenario, e.g. attempt to register a vehicle, but that also involves a second (dependent) agent, namely the bank which checks the owner's account. Initially, we create two *single-agent views*, i.e. one for the vehicle owner and one for the bank. Later, the two single-agent views can be composed to form a *multi-agent view*. The advantage of dealing with single-agent views is their simplicity. They give us a place to start when handling large complex requirements. They provide a separation of concerns; at any one time we focus on a single agent's view of the services the system is to provide. They are therefore

[1] LOV/OMT is a trademark of VERILOG SA

ideal in giving feedback to potential users who can check that their requirements have been interpreted correctly.

5. Formalise agent views

We formalise each agent view as a LOTOS process which requires possible alternative series of services from the system. It is straightforward to construct the outline of a LOTOS process definition from a tree by using the choice operator to offer each branch of the tree as a LOTOS choice expression.

The LOTOS formal model contains more detail than was held in the tree, namely the information that is to be passed between the agent and the system. Adding this extra detail can help clarify the requirements and may involve us returning to the clients to resolve problems. A LOTOS process definition for the one-point vehicle view is given below. It includes a LOTOS gate for communication with each toll gate component. Each event has the structure:

> *<gate> <message name> <object identifier>*
> *<optional parameters>*

Both the toll and gizmo object identifier sorts, `Toll_Id` and `Gizmo_Id`, are specified as ADTs.

```
process One_Point_Vehicle[sen, lgt, dpl, cam] : exit :=
    choice t: Toll_Id []
    sen !detect !t [Is_Single(t)];
    (  sen !read !t ?id_g: Gizmo_Id;
       (  lgt !green !t;
          dpl !amount !t ?am: Cost;
          exit
       []
          lgt !yellow !t;
          cam !photo !t !id_g;
          exit
       )
    []
       lgt !yellow !t;
       cam !photo !t;
       exit
    )
endproc (* One_Point_Vehicle *)
```

The LOTOS SMILE simulator [4] allows the use of uninstantiated variables instead of values. As SMILE is able to determine when a combination of conditions can never be true, a single instantiation of an agent view deals with a set of similar agent instances rather than a particular agent instance. Hence the `Toll` identifier `t` is introduced as a variable in a **choice** expression and is constrained to be a `Single_Toll` identifier by the predicate `Is_Single(t)`. A complete LOTOS user-centred specification for the road pricing system is given in [2].

5.1. Multi-agent views

The interesting case is when a multi-agent view involves the interaction of single-agent views, e.g. a bank only checks an owner's account *after* the owner attempts to register a vehicle and the check determines whether or not the registration is allowed.

LOTOS was designed to be used in the specification of OSI systems. A *service specification* is produced using the *constraint oriented style* where behaviour is expressed as sets of constraints operating at external interfaces. There are *local constraints* which define the order of the services required by a single user and *end-to-end constraints* to enforce the sequencing between users [16].

A similar approach can be used to specify multi-agent views. The owner view `Owner_Agent` and the bank view for account information `Bank_Acc_Agent` can be composed to give a multi-agent view. The LOTOS definitions of the two single-agent views are left unchanged and are composed using the interleaving operator |||. The two processes then synchronise with a new process `Constraint` where we constrain the sequencing of the events.

```
process Owner_Bank_Acc_Agent[rd, bk] : exit :=
    (Owner_Agent[rd] ||| Bank_Acc_Agent[bk])
    ||
    Constraint[rd, bk]
endproc (* Owner_Bank_Acc_Agent *)
```

5.2. Instantiate and verify agent views

The LOTOS process definition of each single-agent view can be instantiated and executed. A simulator such as SMILE creates a tree showing all possible event traces. As this should have the same structure as the original tree representing the agent view, we have a simple check to verify that a view has been correctly specified in LOTOS.

We execute single-agent views independently to demonstrate the possible behaviours that the view expects from the system. When an agent's interaction with the system involves other agents, single-agent views are then composed to form multi-agent views as described in Section 5.1.

Initially, our aim is to understand and to model the given requirements and so it is to be expected that inconsistencies will occur in the behaviour expected by different agent views. When single-agent views are composed, these inconsistencies will be highlighted and it is only at this stage that they need to be resolved. Inconsistencies between agent views will often be caused by inconsistencies, ambiguities or omissions in the original requirements. Their resolution may therefore require us to go back to the users for further or revised information.

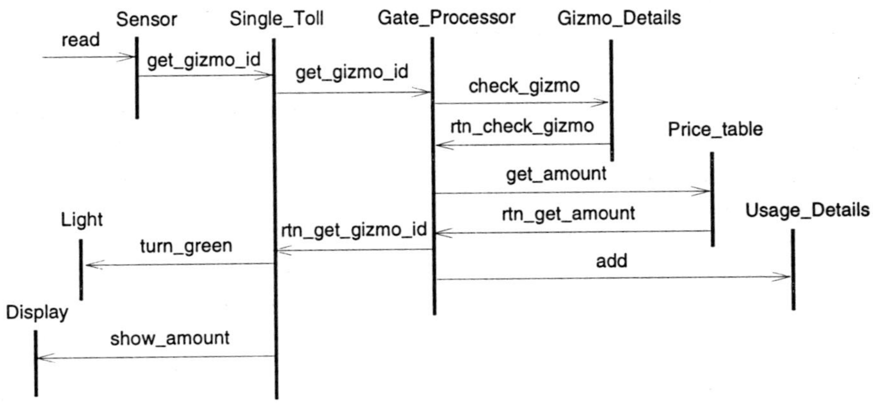

Figure 3. ETD for a vehicle passing a one-point toll gate and getting a green light

We cannot guarantee that all inconsistencies will be detected at this stage. Further inconsistencies may be detected and have to be resolved during the construction of the system-centred model.

6. Create the system-centred model

We do not propose that a complete user-centred model is created before we proceed to the system-centred model. Instead, it is best if an incremental approach is adopted. We are not only constructing formal user-centred and system-centred models, but also prototyping these models both to give feedback to requirements capture and for validation. We therefore have, within the analysis phase, activities which normally take place in later phases. This supports an iterative and incremental approach.

Often, some parts of the requirements will be well understood while others will not. Those parts which are best understood can be modelled first. This subset of the user-centred model can be executed to ensure that it behaves according to the clients' expectations. This gives both analyst and client a better understanding of the system. The corresponding part of the system-centred model can then be created, the models composed and the composition executed. Prototyping of both the user-centred and the composed models gives feedback to the requirements capture process, enabling further agent views to be formulated and existing ones refined.

6.1. Tasks 1 and 2: Build and refine the object model.

The ROOA method involves three main tasks: build an object model; refine the object model; build and validate the LOTOS model. When a problem is primarily data-oriented, an object model can be constructed without paying too much attention to dynamic behaviour. When a problem is process-oriented, as in our example, the dynamic aspects of a problem must also be explored to help identify the static object structure. The user-centred model is of major help in this respect.

Agent views show the interactions between agents and interface objects. The starting event in an agent scenario triggers a series of interactions between objects internal to the system. We describe these interactions by means of event trace diagrams (ETDs). The construction of an ETD may identify new objects and services which are added to the object model. In the one-point vehicle view, the scenario where it gets a green light leads to the ETD shown in Fig. 3. This ETD allowed us to identify new services and the new objects: `Gate_Processor`, `Price_Table` and `Usage_Details`.

We also examine the agent views to identify messages sent to the environment and determine if the relevant interface object must offer a service to some internal object to trigger the external event. For example, in the one-point vehicle view, for `Light` to generate the events `Light.yellow` and `Light.green`, it must offer the services `turn_yellow` and `turn_green`. An object model, including the objects found when considering dynamic behaviour, is shown in Fig. 4. As LOV/OMT has no notation for message connections, we use the relationship notation and name it "calls".

The next step is to collect the information given in the ETDs and build an Object Communication Table (OCT) where we list the class templates, the services offered by each class template and, for each service, the class templates (clients) which require that service and the services that it requires from other class templates.

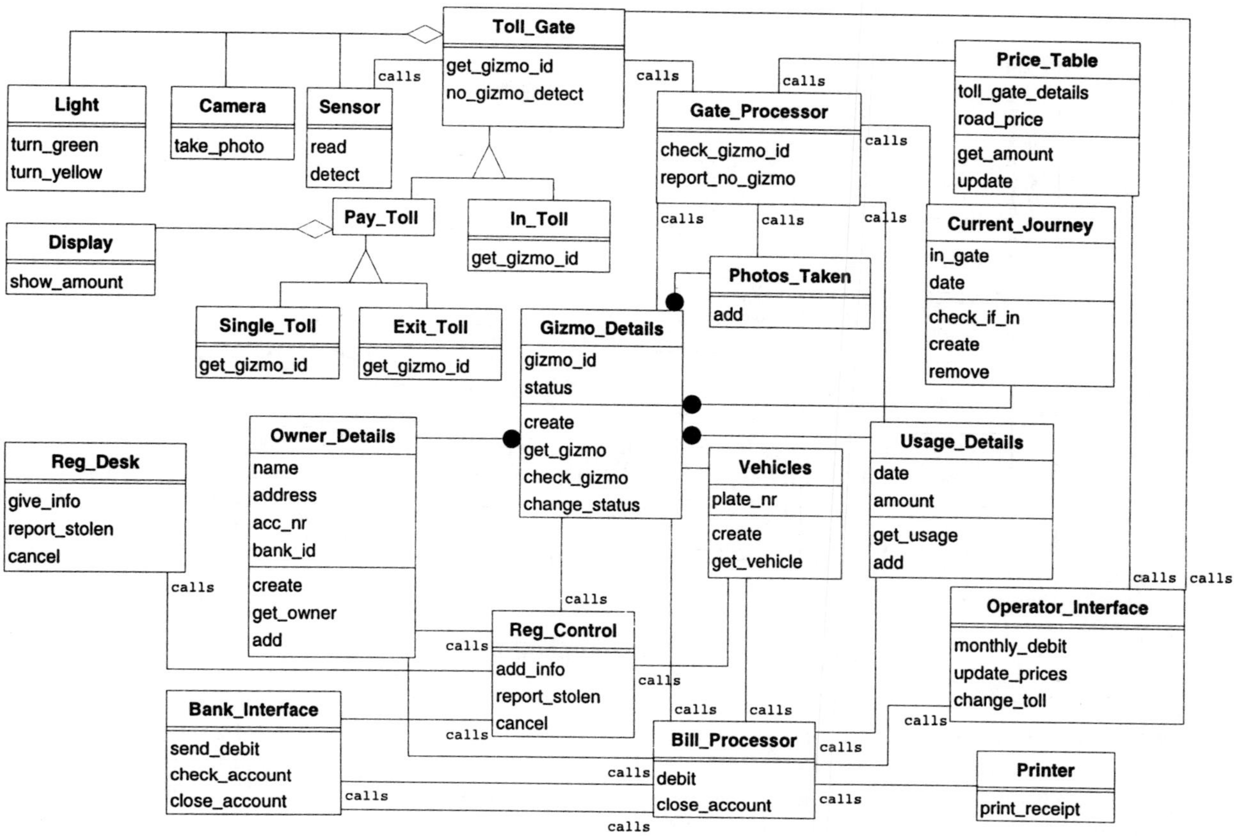

Figure 4. Refined OMT object model

6.2. Task 3: Build the LOTOS formal model.

We extend the OCT to identify the LOTOS gates through which the objects are to communicate and construct an Object Communication Diagram (OCD), i.e. a graphical representation of the ROOA model. It is shown in Fig. 5.

We first specify the interface objects and then proceed to the internal objects. For each event in the LOTOS process definition of an agent view, we create a matching event in the LOTOS process definition of an interface object. The formal user-centred model is therefore used directly in the construction of the LOTOS definition of the interface objects.

The user-centred model shows the information which is to be passed between the environment and the system. The events on which the internal objects synchronise are described in the ETDs, but it is the user-centred model that determines the information which is to be passed during event synchronisation.

Each agent view describes the expected behaviour of the system from the point of view of a particular agent. Some inconsistencies in the requirements are detected when we compose single-agent views. As we are now specifying a system-centred model which has to satisfy all the multi-agent views, this can lead to further inconsistencies being detected in the requirements. Once again we may have to return to the users for clarification. This is a further example of how the development of the user-centred and system-centred models is an iterative process.

All the objects in the system-centred model are specified as LOTOS processes. The processes must then be composed, using the LOTOS parallel operators, into a behaviour expression to specify the overall behaviour of the system-centred ROOA model. To do this, we follow the structure of the OCD shown in Fig. 5. The complete model is given in [2].

7. Validation and verification

The specification of each agent view is composed in turn with the top-level behaviour expression of the system-

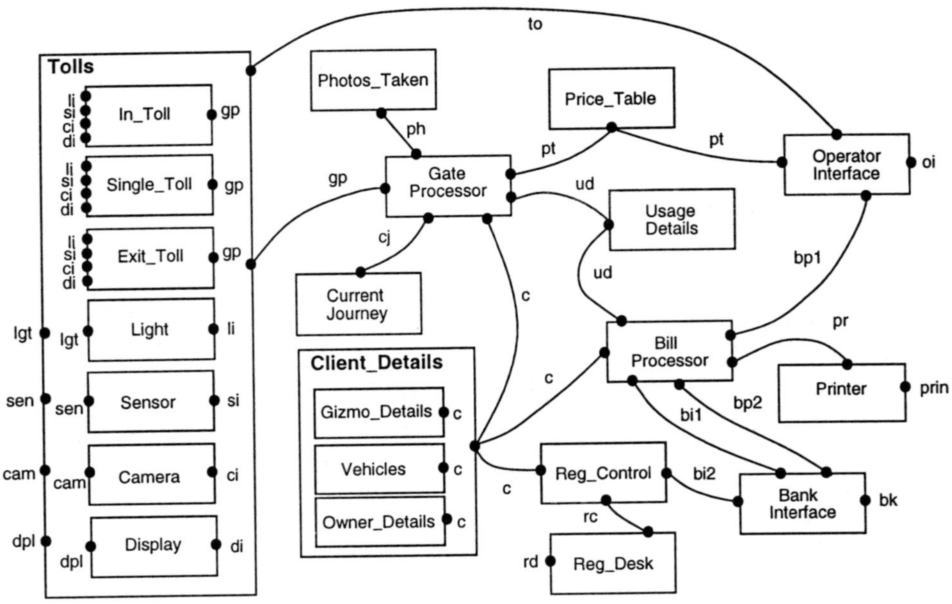

Figure 5. Object Communication Diagram

centred LOTOS specification. We verify that the system-centred model offers all the services required by the user-centred model by checking that each event in the user-centred model has a matching event in the system-centred model. By executing the composed specifications we can validate the system-centred model and ensure that it satisfies each agent view. This is described in [2].

Execution of the SMILE simulator creates an event tree. It may be created either depth or breadth first. The branching is kept within bounds because:

- we simulate with uninstantiated variables rather than with values;
- SMILE does not expand subtrees which it recognises as providing behaviour identical to that already analysed;
- composing the ROOA model with one agent view at a time enables us to focus on a particular feature of the overall behaviour.

Although the ROOA model was developed from the user-centred model it contains extra internal detail and so inconsistencies can be introduced. By composing the two models, and executing their composition, such inconsistencies are identified and so can be resolved.

8. Conclusions

We have shown how the development of a formal user-centred model can be integrated into the ROOA method. The user-centred model consists of a set of validated agent views. Agent views specify the different roles that agents play in the system and enable the description of the behaviour of complex systems to be decomposed into a set of self contained views. Formalising the agent views forces their unambiguous description and identifies areas which are vague or which have not been fully worked out. This enables the analyst to formulate questions to the clients so that these points can be clarified. Therefore, the construction and analysis of the formal user-centred model helps clarify the informal requirements.

We have described how the formal user-centred model can complement the OCD and ETDs in the construction of a formal requirements specification, i.e. the ROOA model. The user-centred and the ROOA models are then composed to verify that the ROOA model is compatible with the user-centred model and the composition executed to validate it against the requirements.

References

[1] T. Bolognesi and E. Brinksma. Introduction to the ISO Specification Language LOTOS. *Computer Networks and ISDN Systems*, 14(1):25–59, 1987.

[2] R. Clark and A. Moreira. Using a formal user-centred model to build a formal system-centred model. Technical Report CSM-140, Department of Computing Science and Mathematics, University of Stirling, Scotland, 1997.

[3] P. Coad and E. Yourdon. *Object Oriented Analysis*. Yourdon Press, Prentice-Hall, Englewood Cliffs, 2nd edition, 1991.

[4] H. Eertink and D. Wolz. Symbolic Execution of LOTOS Specifications. In M. Diaz and R. Groz, editors, *Formal Description Techniques V*, pages 295–310. North-Holland, 1993.

[5] P. Glinz. An Integrated Formal Model of Scenarios Based on Statecharts. In W. Schäfer and P. Botella, editors, *ESEC'95*, LNCS 989, pages 254–271. Springer-Verlag, 1995.

[6] P. Hsia, J. Samuel, J. Gao, D. Kung, Y. Toyoshima, and C. Chen. Formal Approach to Scenario Analysis. *IEEE Software*, 11:33–41, March 1994.

[7] I. Jacobson. *Object-Oriented Software Engineering*. Addison-Wesley, Reading Massachusetts, 1992.

[8] A. Moreira and R. Clark. Combining Object-Oriented Analysis and Formal Description Techniques. In M. Tokoro and R. Pareschi, editors, *8th European Conference on Object-Oriented Programming: ECOOP '94*, LNCS 821, pages 344–364. Springer-Verlag, 1994.

[9] A. Moreira and R. Clark. Rigorous Object-Oriented Analysis. In E. Bertino and S. Urban, editors, *ISOOMS: International Symposium on Object Oriented Methodologies and Systems*, LNCS 858, pages 65–78. Springer-Verlag, 1994.

[10] A. Moreira and R. Clark. Adding Rigour to Object-Oriented Analysis. *Software Engineering Journal*, 11(5):270–280, 1996.

[11] A. Moreira and R. Clark. LOTOS in the Object-Oriented Analysis Process. In S. Goldsack and S. Kent, editors, *Formal Methods in Object Technology*, pages 33–46. Springer-Verlag, 1996.

[12] K. Rubin and A. Goldberg. Object Behaviour Analysis. *Communications of the ACM*, 35(9):48–62, 1992.

[13] J. Rumbaugh. Getting started. Using use cases to capture requirements. *J Object Oriented Programming*, 7(5):8–23, September 1994.

[14] J. Rumbaugh, M. Blaha, W. Premerlani, F. Eddy, and W. Lorensen. *Object-Oriented Modelling and Design*. Prentice-Hall, Englewood Cliffs, 1991.

[15] S. Shlaer and S. Mellor. *Object Lifecycles — Modeling the World in States*. Prentice-Hall, Englewood Cliffs, 1992.

[16] K. Turner and M. van Sinderen. LOTOS Specification Style for OSI. In T. Bolognesi, J. van de Lagemaat and C. Vissers, editors, *LOTOSphere: Software Development with LOTOS*, pages 137–159. Kluwer Academic Publishers, 1995.

Is My Software Process Improvement Suitable for Incremental Deployment?

Lech Krzanik [*#] and Jouni Similä [*#]

[*] CCC Software Professionals Oy
Lentokentäntie 15, FIN-90460 Oulunsalo, Finland. Phone +358 8 5205111. Fax +358 8 5205222

[#] University of Oulu, Department of Information Processing Science
Linnanmaa, FIN-90570 Oulu, Finland. Phone +358 8 5531900. Fax +358 8 5531890
email krzanik@rieska.oulu.fi

Abstract

Incremental delivery policies for software process improvement are anxiously required by the industry. Improvement projects need to show results as early as possible to capture the attention of the organization and to keep things focused on process improvement. Incremental policies are the foundation of building provider-user partnership in software process improvement. Few guidelines, if any, explicitly support such an approach.

In this paper we examine a general approach to incremental software process improvement deployment, and investigate a method for verifying the suitability of conventional models of software process improvement for incremental improvement deployment. We present a framework including the necessary models, an evaluation method and support tools.

Keywords: *Software process improvement. Incremental improvement deployment. Tools for software process improvement.*

1. Introduction

The objective of this paper is to demonstrate a method for evaluating suitability of software process improvement approaches for incremental delivery of improvements. The motivation for such an evaluation is twofold: (1) to be able to select a most useful improvement model, and (2) to make informed decisions about extensions, if any, necessary for the application of an incremental policy. Incremental deployment has two fundamental properties:

• the delivery steps are small, in terms of schedule and budget, and,

• each of the deployment steps delivers perceivable end-user added value.

The incremental approach is a fundamental way to reduce risk on complex projects, also process improvement projects. The extra costs may include more complex management and multiple versions of documentation. Incremental policies are anxiously required by the industry. Software improvement projects need to show results as early as possible to capture the attention of the organization and to keep things focused on process improvement. Incremental policies are the foundation of building provider-user partnership in software process improvement. Few guidelines, if any, explicitly support such an approach.

Section 2 sets the objective of the incremental approach to software process improvement. Section 3 outlines the approach and deliverables. Section 4 considers the motivation and current experience. Subsequent sections introduce and discuss the components of the proposed incremental improvement framework: Section 5 introduces a benchmark incremental deployment model referred to later in the paper. Section 6 discusses matching and verification of improvement models, and presents certain preliminary results of the investigation. Section 7 presents the concept and a prototype of a support tool for improvement model verification (support tool 1). Section 8 introduces the support tool for incremental improvement planning (support tool 2). Section 9 presents case examples. Section 10 summarizes main conclusions.

The authors belong to a development team of the major software process assessment and improvement methodology. The purpose of the work reported here was to investigate approaches to increase effectiveness of software process improvement methods and tools.

The reported work included experience analyses, feasibility studies, prototype tool development, and case studies.

The purpose of this publication is to disseminate information about on-going research and practical experience in order to formulate a broader investigation addressing the issues of incremental improvement of software processes.

2. Objective

The objective of the work reported in this paper has been to:

- shorten the response time of software process improvement projects to about 3-6 months from the current minimum of 12-18 months, under a recognized improvement model based on a capability model such as CMM, SPICE, etc.

Response time is measured by the time from initiating the improvement action and allocating respective resources till perceivable end-user results corresponding to these resources. The improvement project will normally last longer (there will be many improvement cycles), consistently with the current process state and applicable technology transition models. The delay between allocating resources and identifying the corresponding effects should be minimized.

Software process improvement has a profound impact on other technology domains. Effective software process transition has a multiplier effect. The above objective contributes to shortening the time to institutionalized improvements. It also contributes to motivated, informed commitment of key management.

3. Approach and deliverables

Software process improvement must be performed according to an established process *improvement model* (IM). Such a model shall include a process *capability model* (CM) which indicates successive steps in advancing capabilities of software production or maintenance, along with a representation of the relevant technology base. Examples of process capability model are CMM (Paulk et al. 1993), SPICE (SPICE, 1996, Part 2), ISO 9001/9000-3, ISO 12207, etc. Another part of the improvement reference model is a *deployment model* (DM), such as IDEAL (McFeeley, 1996) for CMM, or Part 7 of SPICE (SPICE, 1996). Deployment policies are strongly related to technology adoption models (Rogers, 1995; Fowler and Rifkin, 1990). The type of deployment model of particular interest here is the incremental model, which requires: • small delivery steps, usually of several months, or below 2-5% of total transfer budget and schedule, and • perceivable end-user added value, taking into account both qualities and costs. An example of a model akin to the incremental policy is the Defect Prevention Process (Jones, 1985; Mays et al., 1990). Conventional IM's pay little attention to the incremental characteristics of deliveries though some deployment models claim to support the incremental approach. This paper proposes services suporting verification of such claims. The approach is illustrated in Figure 1.

The approach assumed in this paper introduces a *benchmark incremental deployment model* (BM). BM is used in evaluating IM's for their suitability for incremental software process improvement. We are interested in how much of an incremental policy is already included in a candidate IM. The answer would determine the additional effort necessary to adapt a given

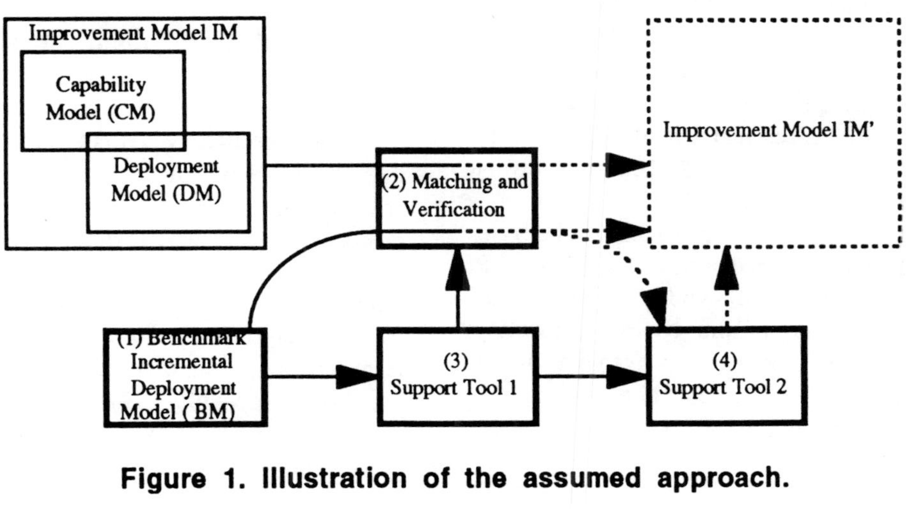

Figure 1. Illustration of the assumed approach.

improvement environment. The proposed method offers more: it provides tools to support the verification (support tool 1) as well as planning the improvement steps (support tool 2). The deliverables include the following components:

(1) the benchmark incremental deployment model (BM)

(2) a matching and verification tool, including rules for creating a derived improvement reference, IM'

(3) tool support for matching and verification

(4) tool support for incremental improvement for a derived IM'.

It is assumed that the initial IM includes one of de-facto standards for CM's. This entails certain assertions about the structure of the models and tools. The matching and verification method is questionnaire-based and can benefit from the specific knowledge of experts taking part in evaluation. The approach is applicable to IM's of various level of generality.

4. Motivation and current experience

Short delivery steps are a remedy for one of most frequent flaws: "All too often, new technologies fail in the marketplace because of flawed assumptions about considerations totally unrelated to technical merit - pricing models, distribution channels, support processes, and, of course, customer needs and perceptions. (...) Initially, some work may be fairly short term in its focus (...) longer term research issues emerge during the initial business entry phase as a first set of products are designed and deployed" (Kuchinsky, 1996). Too big delivery steps are a common deficiency. Bennett (1996) points out that "Researchers tend to have a long-term perspective with a focus on generic values. Developers focus on specific short-term, time-to-market concerns". A specific function of the delivery step may also be suggested: "We should not focus on changing the organizational structure or putting new processes in place. Rather, the best thing we could do was to build bridges to other groups" (Isaacs and Tang, 1996). Pressman (1996) emphasizes that CMM (Paulk et al., 1993) "(...) has been well defined. Unfortunately, it represents a destination, not a road map (...) Create a realistic plan that recognizes that resources will be scarce and some people will be unenthusiasthic about SPI [software process improvement] work". He specifically addresses timely deliveries of the education function: "Continuous software process improvement means continuous education. If you establish a strategy that strives to deliver knowledge in a just-in-time manner, smarter people will result".

Incremental deployment of software projects

In the domain of software engineering, the method of incremental deployment may refer to both software and the software process. One type of the former is known as evolutionary development (Gilb, 1988; May and Zimmer, 1996; Kruchten, 1996). It is a development method and life cycle that replaces traditional development with small, incremental product releases or builds, frequent delivery of the product to users for feedback, and dynamic planning that can be modified in response to this feedback. The method has the following key attributes: multiobjective-driven; early, frequent iteration; complete analysis, design, build, and test in each step; user orientation; systems approach, not merely algorithm orientation; open-ended basic systems architecture; result orientation. When using the method, the product development team divides the project into small increments. Ideally, each increment is less than 5% of the overall effort. The increments are then ordered so that the most useful and easiest features are implemented first and some useful subset of the overall product can be delivered every one to four weeks. Within each cycle, the software is designed, coded, tested, and then delivered to users. The users give feedback on the product and the team may respond by changing the product, plans, or process. These cycles continue until the product is shipped. The method offers opportunities to optimize results by modifying the plan, product, or process at each cycle. Benefits of the method include better matching to customer needs and market requirements, increased productivity and reduced risk, even the risks associated with changing the development process.

Shaw (1996) considered another interesting approach to incremental development of software (rather than process) with special emphasize on the structure of specifications.

Incremental deployment of software process improvement

We are specifically concerned with the application of incremental deployment to software *processes*. The critical success factors of the method are: clear vision, process development planning, quantitative process improvement control. The method requires a new way of thinking about process development. Traditionally, much of an improvement project is spent getting the infrastructure in place before developing any customer-perceivable capability. This is a problem because the method requires earlier development of customer-perceivable functionality to elicit customer response. The existing improvement models are not sufficient for full use of incremental deployment though the method is characterized by relatively wide spectrum of potential users. There are candidate organisations with special types of software processes, products, special cases of small and medium-size enterprises, etc. A family of incremental methods might be needed rather than a single method, allowing for tuning and specialization.

CMM (Paulk et al., 1993) is supported by two potentially (with extensions) incremental approaches: the Defect Prevention Process (Jones, 1985; Mays et al., 1990) embedded in the CMM's level 5, and the IDEAL method (McFeeley, 1996). The CMM demonstrates a dependence of the deployment model on the maturity state of the improved process. The Defect Prevention Process (DPP) is a process to continually improve software development - real-time and integrated in every stage of development. It consists of the following four key elements: causal analysis meetings, action team, stage kickoff meetings, action tracking and data collection. DPP focuses on defect-related actions and process-oriented preventive actions. It provides a systematic, objective mechanism for action implementation. DPP can be applied to any development process as long as the defects are recorded, causal analysis can be performed and preventive actions mapped and implemented. The IDEAL model (IDEAL="Initiating, Diagnosing, Establishing, Acting & Leveraging", for the five phases it describes) is "an organizational improvement model developed by SEI that serves as a roadmap for initiating, planning, and implementing improvement actions. The IDEAL model forms an infrastructure to guide organizations in planning and implementing an effective software process improvement program, and is the founding strategy employed in delivering many SEI services. Organizations that follow the IDEAL approach to SPI can effectively integrate SEI technologies, courses, workshops, and services into a comprehensive method for managing and improving their overall capacity" (McFeeley, 1996).

Of the two, DPP is closer to the incremental policy. The timing of IDEAL is too sparse: during the Diagnosing phase the management steering group must create baselines in order to develop a plan that will achieve the business changes specified in the organization's software process improvement goals. The baselines are intended to be iterative and provide a snapshot of the organization's various capabilities, processes, and measures. Subsequent cycles through the IDEAL model require repeated baselining to show what progress or changes have taken hold in the organization. According to the manual, software maturity baselines should be repeated *every eighteen months to three years.* Metrics baselines should probably be taken *more often, depending on the business cycle* of the organization. If the organization goes through a full cycle only *every two years*, more frequent metrics baselines would probably not be useful. If the organization goes through a product cycle every three months, metrics baselines could be taken *annually*. In the Acting phase, "Pilot projects are used to test out the solutions (...) The solutions will require some tailoring and refinement to fit them into projects across the organization, and the pilots will help determine the tailoring needs and guidelines for the rest of the organization. Several pilots may be run for a solution, and there may be *several iterations* between the solution development and piloting steps to get the solution ready for deployment across the organization".

Other examples include the product-driven improvement approach introduced by the Software Engineering Laboratory (Basili, 1989; McGarry et al., 1994). It is an experience-driven approach. The underlying concept is that any organization must become a "learning organization". However the timing characteristics of the user feedback are far from the incremental delivery method.

Incremental deployment being considered here refers to cases where the deliverables are well determined. More complex cases, beyond the scope of this paper, may include *incremental adaptation* inferring conceptual design structure of legacy systems from existing technology, synthesis of more efficient solutions based on metering of current process' real data, synthesis of new deliverables implied by incremental changes to process' architecture, etc. Current research and development must be improved and matured to provide the necessary technical basis for those activities.

What happens if the delivery step is set too big?

What happens if a delivery step is *too big?* One pattern of behavior might be the following (Baker, 1996): "When an organization sets its rewards on the amount of improvement, then the lower the initial rating, the greater the improvement can be claimed. The improvement is easy, as the organization is already performing at a higher level. Managers are tempted to shade the answers in the initial assessment and play the improvement game. (...) Consultants may not look for signs of deception. With a low rating it is easier to persuade upper management to hire them to improve the software process. Such deception may explain why so

Table 1. Key methods, objects and factors of incremental delivery.

Methods	Objects	Factors
(A0) Setting architecture	Architecture (a0)	Open-endedness Cost of information Evolution Qualitative functions/quantitative attributes decomposition, common for both goals and technology
(A) Setting goals	Goals (a)	Risk, uncertainty, and tolerance intervals included in quantitative specifications User-defined measurements relative to accepted definitions; reference values included; authority specification Measurements defined for both goal setting and technology evaluation Goal qualifiers
(B) Obtaining quantified technology specifications (optional - if specification not provided with problem statement))	Solutions (b)	Risk, uncertainty, tolerance, and performance ranges included in quantitative specifications User-defined measurements relative to accepted definitions with nominal conditions for referenc Reference values included; authority specification Solution applicability qualifiers
(C) Design	Designs (c)	Multiobjective-driven Design patterns Quantitative Risk-conscious Safety coefficients and evaluation protocols Early, frequent iteration Complete analysis, design, build, and test in each step Result orientation; user orientation; perceivable added value Systems approach, not merely algorithm orientation Open-ended architecture
(D) Planning for incremental delivery	Delivery plans (d)	One next delivery step in focus Clear user added value Referring to quantitative, risk-conscious, end-user, safe design Restricted ranges of fundamental resources (schedule, budget, other)
(E) Tracking and controlling the delivery process	Tracks and controls (e)	Sensitive to perceivable added value Immediate user feedback Elements of evolutionary control
(F) Verifying delivery implementation	Delivery proofs (f)	Entry/exit conditions and rules Embedded improvement of the incremental delivery process Extensive use of CASE tools Inspection-based for issues beyond the control of CASE tools

Notes:

(a0) Specification of architecture and certification of exit conditions on architecture.

(a) Specification of goals and certification of exit conditions on the goal setting process.

(b) Specification of solutions (practices with boundary conditions, to achieve certain values of goals) and certification of exit conditions on the solution specification process.

(c) Specification of association of goals and solutions, specification of the verification and /or validation processes for the goals, and certification of exit conditions on the design process.

(d) A staged plan of delivering the goals, specification of the solution delivery processes, and certification of exit conditions on the planning process.

(e) A delivery process event log, specification of controls (solutions), certification of exit conditions on the control process, and certification of exit conditions the event service process.

(f) Certification of exit conditions on delivery verification/ validation processes (eg., an inspection process).

few organizations start with an initial rating above a level 1".

5. The benchmark incremental deployment model

The contents of the benchmark incremental deployment model (Table 1) has a simple structure and focuses on most fundamental issues discussed in previous sections. More detailed discussion is beyound the scope of this paper and is available elsewhere (Krzanik and Similä, 1996). Required model capabilities include: tolerating incompleteness, collecting specifications incrementally, supporting specifications of many properties, propagating new information, invalidating specifications where necessary, search for components that partially match a partial specification, supporting checking specifications and implementations; incremental checking for incremental specifications, supporting flexibility, yielding incremental value for incremental information. The proposed contents consists of required methods (activities), corresponding objects and factors referring to both methods and objects.

The methods correspond to successive stages of the iterative incremental delivery process. All stages, except possibly an optional (B), are necessary for a correct implementation. Because of the inevitable intertwinning of implementation and use of succesive new features in the incremental approach, the states of technology *use* and *efective use*, are not differentiated here, as oposed to many conventional approaches (cf. the study discussed in next paragraph). The information in Table 1 constitutes a first-approximation benchmark model outline. The outline, and specifically the factor information may be further extended and detailed to create more specific representations, following selected architectural principles, eg., object-oriented.

Impact analysis

Significant aspects of the model can be identified with an impact analysis. Such an analysis is necessary in cases of special uses of the method, eg., with regard to selected types of software proces improvement. Such an analysis is demonstrated below. It is focused on introduction and use of CASE tools. The analysis refers to a previous investigation (Iivari, 1996) addressing the factors of CASE tool usage and perceived CASE productivity and quality effects. Now we try to evaluate the impact of an incremental policy on those factors. The results given in Table 2 are qualitative and informal but provide a basis for further investigation. It is expected that most important aspects would have highest impact on significant productivity and quality factors. Often, as in this case, care must be taken because the above study assumes a conventional, non-incremental approach. For instance, *availability of results* is an important determinant of usage and perception of productivity and quality. With regard to timing, often the *reaction time* of technology introduction is a catalyst or a critical variable. As in many analyses of that type, we conclude that stage (A) (Setting Goals) has a profound effect on many factors. More difficult to evaluate is the impact of the stage (F) (Verifying Delivery Implementation). In conventional, non-incremental investigations that stage is often not taken into account.

Selection of the class of improvement models and the respective benchmark model structure

It is important that the architectural style selected for the benchmark model coincides with architectural styles of capability and deployment models of the investigated improvment environment.

Two software process improvement models have been selected for consideration here. They are listed in Table 3. The Capability Maturity Process for Software (CMM) describes the principles and practices underlying software process maturity and is intended to help software organizations to improve the maturity of their software processes in terms of an evolutionary path from ad hoc, chaotic processes to mature, disciplined software processes. Similarly, BPG (Base Practice Guide), a fundamental part of SPICE, defines, at a high level, the goals and fundamental activities that are essential to good software engineering. The BPG describes what activities are required, not how they are to be implemented. In the context of BPG, CMM is an example of a specific BPG for large software-intensive projects and organizations. The models share a similar structure of sets of practices assigned to ordered capability (maturity) levels. The levels determine the recommended order of implementation. Thus the practices are described in terms of their functional asignment to subsequent levels, and also in terms of their non-functional, or capability impact. The structure is also representative for other improvement approaches such as ISO 9001/9000-3, ISO/IEC 12207, etc.

Consistently with these models, we select the structure of a benchmark model. The structure will represent technology practices in two dimensions: a process (functional) dimension and a capability dimension. The latter is quantitative. The process dimension expresses functional constraints on the practices while the capability dimension represents the degree to which goals associated with functions are met. The capability dimension is suitable for expressing quantitative concepts of incremental delivery such as risks.

It should be noted that despite the similarity in structure, the meaning of the dimensions will differ for the two discussed reference models, CMM and SPICE. CMM, for example, represents organisational maturity and is focused on *necessary* practices, while SPICE represents process capability and constitutes a more general framework of practices (Paulk et al., 1994, 1995).

If the improvement model has a variable structure changing with process maturity, then also the selected benchmark model may depend on the current development stage of the improved process.

An important property is the *granularity* of the model, ie., here, the most detailed distinguishable level of the practices. Granularity of the model must be consistent with granularity of the represented concrete practices, and with respective representations on the process and capability dimensions.

Table 2. The impact of incremental delivery on factors of technology usage, productivity and quality.

The first three columns: Class..Variance are extracted from (Iivari, 1996). Columns: (A0)..(F) demonstrate impact of key stages of the incremental policy on the factors. Depending on the extent the impact is marked as 'MAJOR' or 'minor'.

Class of factors	Factors influencing CASE tools usage and perceived effects of productivity and quality	Variance for significant factors in the study (op. cit.)	(A0) Setting architecture	(A) Setting goals	(B) Obtaining quantitative technology characteristics	(C) Design	(D) Planning for *incremental* delivery	(E) Tracking and controlling the delivery process	(F) Verifying delivery implementation
Development process factors. Based on IS implementation research.	Participation (i)			minor		MAJOR	minor		
	Management support (ii)	.21 (1) .27 (2)		MAJOR		MAJOR	MAJOR		
	Training (iii)	.15/- (5) .28/- (6)	minor	minor	minor				MAJOR
	Expectation realism (iv)			MAJOR	MAJOR	minor			
CASE innovation characteristics. Based on innovation diffusion literature.	Perceived complexity (v)	-.30/- (5) -.41/-.32 (6)		MAJOR		minor			MAJOR
	Compatibility (vi) (*)			MAJOR	MAJOR				minor
	Relative advantage (vii)	.27 (2) .44/.31 (3) .52/.26 (4)		MAJOR	MAJOR				MAJOR
Managerial influence	Voluntariness (viii)	-.61 (1) -.69 (2)	MAJOR	MAJOR	MAJOR				minor
CASE usage	1 factor (ix)	.28/.54 (3) .08/.63 (4) .28/.65 (5) .30/.73 (6)							MAJOR
Perceived productivity and quality effects	2 factors (x)			MAJOR					MAJOR

Notes:

(i) Participation of the IS professionals and software professionals in the selection of the case tool and in planning of the organizational implementation (adoption) of the case tool: • number of people participating in the selection of the CASE tool (ie., initiation and adoption, according to Cooper and Zmud, 1990); • number of people participating in planning of implementaion (installation) (ie., adaptation, according to Cooper and Zmud, 1990).

(ii) Controlling the resources needed, identification of behaviours encouraged: • support of top management (selection and implementation, 5 points); • support of IS management (selection and implementation, 5 points).

(iii) Internal (in-house) training, vendor courses, self studies: • adequacy of training; • quality of training.

(iv) Difference of perceived CASE impact *minus* expectations concerning CASE impact. Both measured by (six 5-point items): • impact on the speed of develoment; • functional quality of new applications; • productivity of development; • cost of development; • quality of developed applications; • cost of maintenance.

(v) The degree to which an inovation IS perceived as difficulty to understand and use (perceived "ease of use").

(vi) Consistency with existing values, past experiences, and needs of potential adopters. 5-point scale very_poor...very_good; with factors: • use compatibility; • vendor compatibility; • functional compatibility; • interface compatibility; • project support compatibility; • method compatibility; • hardware compatibility.

(*) Existing standards may be inconsistent with the purpose ot technology transition project. The incremental method provides suitable validation of standards' use.

(vii) The degree to which an innovation is perceived as better than its precursor.

(viii) The degree to which an innovation is perceived as being voluntary, or of free will.

(ix) Extent: • the proportion of projects using CASE; • the proportion of analysts using CASE; • routinization of the CASE use; • the number of phases supported by CASE. Routinization and infusion (5-point scale): • the use of CASE is encouraged as a normal activity; • the use of CASE as a natural activity; • increased organizational effectiveness obtained using the CASE technology; • the use of CASE to its fulllest potential.

(x) As with expectation realism above: • impact on the speed of develoment; • functional quality of new applications; • productivity of development; • cost of development; • quality of developed applications; • cost of maintenance. Additionally: • significantly improved the documentation of software products.

(1) Dependent variable: CASE usage; individual respondents; R^2=.73

(2) Dependent variable: CASE usage; companies; R^2=.84

(3) Hierarchical regression; dependent variable: perceived effects of quality/productivity; individual respondents; R^2=.42/.45

(4) Hierarchical regression; dependent variable: perceived effects of quality/productivity; companies; R^2=.53/.56

(5) Hierarchical regression; dependent variable: perceived effects of quality/productivity; dropped: relative advantage; individual respondents; R^2=.32/.38

(6) Hierarchical regression; dependent variable: perceived effects of quality/productivity; dropped: relative advantage; companies; R^2=.57/.61

Table 3. Software process improvement models and structures considered

Model	Focus	Process dimension	Capability dimension	Other elements of structure (cf. Table 1)
Benchmark model	Generic	• Qualitative functional dimension	• Quantitative attribute dimension	• Methods • Objects • Factors
CMM 1.1 (Paulk et al., 1993)	Organisational maturity	• Level • Key process area • Key practice	• Goal • Common feature • Subfeature	• Practices supporting incremental improvement deployment
SPICE (SPICE, 1996)	Project capability	• Process category • Process • Base practice	• Level • Common feature • Generic practice	• Practices supporting incremental improvement deployment

6. Matching and verification of improvement models

The candidate improvement models are matched against the benchmark model, and evaluated, with the following purpose:

• evaluation of the extent to which a given IM (improvement model) is appropriate for incremental improvement deployment

• deciding upon whether the IM can be used for incremental improvement

• deciding about the changes or extensions, if any, necessary for a given IM.

A central issue here is the matching and verification method and instrument. The result should support the decision whether an IM can be used for incremental improvement, and the obtained adequacy profile should support planning for changes and extensions where necessary.

Matching and verification instrument

We propose a matching and verification instrument which is based on a questionnaire. Evaluations of candidate improvement environments are derived from ratings provided by software process experts. The experts should be qualified assessors, licensed to perform software process assessments and to supervise process improvement projects. Structures listed in Table 3 are evaluated for the items listed in Table 1. We investigate several aspects of matching between the improvement models (IM's) and the benchmark model (BM):

(1) Matching between the structures of capability dimensions of IM and BM.

(2) Matching between the structures of process dimensions of IM and BM.

(3a0)-(3f) How well the practices of IM fit the role of objects of BM (architecture, goals, solutions, designs, delivery plans, tracks and controls, verifications)? BM's factors applied to IM determine suitability of the characteristics.

(4A0)-(4F) How well the practices of IM fit the role of methods of BM (Architecture setting, Goal setting, Obtaining quantified technology specification, Designing, Planning for incremental delivery, Tracking and controlling the delivery process, Verifying delivery implementation)? BM's factors applied to IM determine suitability of the characteristics.

(5) How well the practices of IM fit the roles of incremental solutions under the conditions set by BM? BM's factors applied to IM determine suitability of the characteristics. Note that BM associates solutions with architecture (well-formed), goals (solutions to be matched with goals), designs (matching goals), plans (solution delivery), tracks and controls (solution observability and controllability, controlling solutions), and delivery proofs (solution effectiveness) - all these associations are a source of issues to be asked in the questionnaire.

Major questions are connected with the granularity issue - for example, whether solutions provide a suitable granularity level (practically "small enough" in the sense of critical project resources) and whether they contribute with perceivable added value (practically "valuable enough" in the sense of critical project qualities).

The questions refer to all three: IM structure ((1)-(2)), IM (implemented) policy ((3)-(4)), and the technology to be deployed (5). The answer results from technology evaluation. The evaluation may be difficult if not supported by an appropriate tool (cf. next section).

It should be noted that IM's are often generic and the matching can be determined only after a concrete improvement environment is established. This may restrict applicability of the method at the absence of concrete application environments. A similar argument refers to the improvement lifecycle. Long improvement time scales (several years) make it sensible to consider a given IM only for the current development stage, of a particular software process in question. It is also easier to formulate conclusions about IM's by comparing two or more of them, with a BM derived from the IM's.

Questionnaire

To facilitate the answering process, a questionnaire should include questions related to the individual items (1)-(5) listed above. There should be a distinction between Part 1 including questions corresponding to (1)-(4) and Part 2 dealing with questions (5). Part 1 deals with an IM as a whole, while Part 2 deals with individual practice structures of an IM. First we ask whether an IM provides a suitable process improvement framework. Example questions and answers related to Part 1 are included in Table 4. Part 2 questions are illustrated in Table 5.

Table 4. Samples from Part 1 of IM's evaluation.

Integer scale from 0(none)..5(full corresponding to BM requirements).

Nr	Question	Sample CMM 1.1 rates	Sample SPICE rates	Sample comments
1	Existence of process improvement framework	4	3	
2	Matching of process improvement framework with target process development stage	2	3	Improvement process dependent. Most of CMM's improvement mechanisms reside at upper maturity levels."
3	Efficiency of process improvement framework with target process development stage	2	4	Improvement process dependent. SPICE provides a more flexible structure while CMM tends to stabilize (from L1 to L2) practices to be changed later on."
4	Direct matching between process dimension (IM) and functional dimension (BM)	2	1	
5	Direct matching between capability dimension (IM) and attribute dimension (BM)	3	1	
6	Existence of qualitative functions/quantitative attributes decomposition	2	1	
7	Existence of risk, uncertainty, and tolerance intervals included in quantitative specifications	0	0	The planned new CMM 2 Risk Management KPA will anyway deal with process risks, not the process improvement risks."
8	Reference values enforced	0	0	
9	Existence of user-defined measurements relative to accepted definitions with goal dependency structure.	1	0	
10	Authority specification enforced	0	0	
11	Measurements enforced for both: goal setting and technology evaluation	0	0	

7. Support tool 1

The purpose of the support tool 1 is to provide matching and verification (the instrument), and to standardize and simplify the following:

- comparing the models
- evaluating the models
- derivatinon of an extended-capacity model IM'.

At least these services are needed:

- support for conversion and editing of the structures of the IM's,
- support for evaluation of the structures.

Conversion and editing refer primarily to the following:

Table 5. Samples from Part 2 of IM's evaluation.

Integer scale from 0(none)..5(full corresponding to BM requirements).

Nr	Issue	Rate
101	Function/attribute decomposition	4
102	Risk, uncertainty, tolerance, and performance ranges	0
103	Reference values	2
104	Measurements	3
105	Authority	2
106	Qualifiers	0

• transformation of parts of the process dimension into capability dimension and vv.

• exploding/imploding (decomposition/agreggation, clustering) of practices for the purposes of visualization and planning.

Evaluation refers to:

• performing partial or overall evaluations based on ratings included in the model

• recording, maintenance, and reporting of expert ratings referring to individual structures of the model (eg., practices, capability, etc.)

Conversion and editing are perhaps most difficult. A suitable tool support is unavoidable. Figure 2 shows a screen view from a prototype of such a tool. Functionality of the tool may vary from a simple outliner to an advanced structure editor/evaluating tool. In the prototype it is possible to operate at a wide range of detail level of the model.

Preliminary results of evaluation

A preliminary investigation of the two IM's listed in Table 3 demonstrated that neither satisfsfied more that 40% of requirements for an incremental improvement deployment methodology. CMM 1.1 performed slightly better, a bigger drawback beeing the arbitrary allocation of explicit quantitative process improvement to upper maturity levels. SPICE had an important advantage of more independent, clearly delineated processes. One way to use these de-facto standards with incremental improvement deployment anyway is to define a consistent methodology supplement covering the missing elements.

Inability to define incremental deliveries may be a major problem. Another problem may be the granularity of the models. Although the granularity of both models is similar, the SPICE model can be directly supported by ISO/IEC 12207. That improves granularity of that model. There's no such immediate corresponding references for CMM.

8. Support tool 2

Since the structure of the models used for matching and verification of the software process improvement method is very much determined by the structure of the technology (CMM or BPG in SPICE) - ie., the structure of the deliverables of the improvement project - it is straightforward to apply a similar type of model to support the improvement project itself. In that case however the focus would be on:

• transforming and editing candidate incremental deliverables of the improvement project

• evaluating of the candidate deliverables

• comparing candidate deliverables

• exploding/imploding (decomposition/agreggation, clustering) of practices for the purposes of visualization and delivery planning

• recording, maintenance, and reporting of expert ratings for technology structures (solutions)

• formulation of incremental delivery plans.

In feasibility experiments, a generic version of support tool 1 has been successfully used as support tool 2. Evaluation protocols may be pre-programmed corresponding to criteria and procedures of major process improvement models.

9. Case examples

Apart from the feasibility studies and prototype development described above, an analysis of selected past results has been performed. Two practical cases may be given as examples:

• AH (USA, 1995)

• AB (Europe, 1995).

The improvement deployment at AH had many features of an incremental activity. It was succesful. The model used there was CMM 1.1. On the other hand, application of incremental improvement deployment at AB failed due to lack of almost all critical elements of the incremental methodology. Incremental improvement was forced because of the unusually sharp constraints on schedule (10 months for advancement corresponding to one CMM level difference). The site used a recognized improvement model. Despite difficult schedule constraints there was a favorable distribution of the assessed maturity state and the incremental deployment might actually meet the expectations, or, in the worst case, create a considerable improvement that would satisfy the managers. However, most likely the process group lacked suitable expertise. An important conclusion was that the improvement procedure should have started with an appropriate improvement of the deployment methodology itself - towards using an incremental methodology.

10. Conclusions

Incremental software process improvement deployment provides an important alternative to conventional improvement methodologies and frameworks. Its wider application in practice might contribute to a visible increase in software process

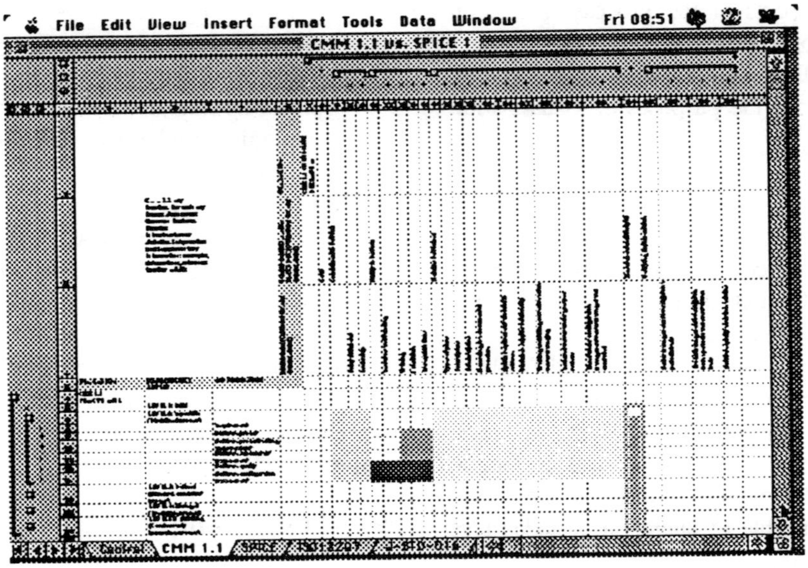

Figure 2. Support tool 1: Practices are configured and evaluated in two dimensions: capability and process. A percentage scale is used for multiobjective metrics (of type "% plan") - useful in manipulations of more complex practice configurations.

improvement success rate. That would follow the advice resulting from studies investigating key factors of software process technology transition.

As results from the introductory investigation reported in this paper, the methodology is consistent with many conventional improvement deployment methods, although mostly not covered by them. For wider application, a new class of specific verification methods and tools is necessary. This report demonstrates a feasible approach to the development and implementation of such tools.

References

Baker, R. Technical opinion. *Comm. ACM 39*, No. 9 (Sept. 1996).

Basili, V. R. Software development: A paradigm for the future. *Proc. COMPSAC'89*, Orlando, FL, Sept. 1989. IEEE, 1989.

Bennett, J.L. Building relationships for technology transfer. *Comm. ACM 39*, No. 9 (Sept. 1996).

Boehm, B. Anchoring the Software Process. *IEEE Software 13*, No. 4 (July 1996).

Cooper, R.B., and Zmud, R.W. Information technology research: A technology diffusion approach. *Manage. Sci. 36*, 2 (1990), 123-139.

Cox, G.M. Implementing the Capability Maturity Model for Software. *Hewlett-Packard Journal 47*, 4 (August 1996), 6-14.

Fowler, P., and Rifkin, S. Software Engineering Process Group guide. *CMU/SEI-90-TR-24*, Sep. 1990.

Gilb, T. *Principles of Software Engineering Management*. Addison-Wesley, Cambridge, 1988.

Iivari, J. Why are CASE tools not used? *Comm. ACM 39*, No. 10 (Oct. 1996), 94-103.

Isaacs, E.A., and Tang, J.C. Technology transfer: So much research, so few good products. *Comm. ACM 39*, No. 9 (Sept. 1996).

Jones, C.L. A process-integrated approach to defect prevention. *IBM Sys. j. 24,* No 2, 1985, 150-167.

Kruchten, P. A Rational development process. *Crosstalk 9*, 8 (July 1996).

Krzanik, L., and Similä, J. Benchmarks for incremental software process improvement. To appear.

Kuchinsky, A. Transfer means more than just technology. *Comm. ACM 39*, No. 9 (Sept. 1996).

Maher, J.H., Jr. Managing technological innovation. In: Przybylinski, S.M., Fowler, P.J., and Maher, J.H., *Software Technology Transition*. Tutorial presented at the 13th Intl. Conf. on Software Engineering, SEI, 1991.

May, E.L., and Zimmer, B.A. The evolutionary development model for software. *Hewlett-Packard Journal 47*, 4 (August 1996), 39-45.

Mays, R.G., Jones, C.L., Holloway, G.L., and Studinski, D.P. Experiences with defect prevention. *IBM Sys. J. 29*, No. 1, 1990, 4-32.

McFeeley, B. IDEAL: A user's guide for software process improvement. *CMU/SEI-96-HB-001*, Feb. 1996.

McGarry, F., et al. An overview of the Software Engineering Laboratory. *Software Engineering Laboratory Series*, SEL-94-005 (Dec. 1994).

Paulk, M.C., et al. Capability Maturity Model for Software. *CMU/SEI-93-TR-24*, Feb. 1993.

Paulk, M.C., et al. Measuring process capability versus organizational process maturity. *Proc. 4th Intl. Conf. on Software Quality*, Wash., DC, 3-5 Oct. 1994.

Paulk, M.C., Konrad, M.D, and Garcia, S.M. CMM versus SPICE architectures. Tech. Council on Software Engineering. IEEE Computer Society, 1995.

Pressman, R., Software process impediment. IEEE Software Vol. 13, No. 5 (Sept. 1996).

Rogers, E.M. *Diffusion of Innovations*, 4th ed. The Free Press, New York, 1995.

Shaw, M. Truth vs. knowledge: The difference between what a component does and what we know it does. *Proc. 8th Intl. Workshop on Software Specification and Design*, March 1996. IEEE, New York, 1996.

SPICE. Software process assessment. Working draft. Limited distribution. ISO/IEC JTC1/SC7 WG10. 26 July 1996.

Thong, J.Y.L., and Yap, C.S., An information technology adoption model for small businesses. K. Kautz and J. Pries-Heje, eds., *Diffusion and Adoption of Information Technology*, Norsk Regnecentral, Oslo, 1995.

Product Development a Chunk At a Time

Kenneth R. Abbott
Rising Tide Software, Inc.
1253 Worcester Rd, Suite 302
Framingham, MA 01701
abbott@acm.org

Abstract

"Chunking" is a product development discipline developed and successfully used at XSoft in the development of InConcert, a software product for workflow management. In chunking, teams of 4-8 developers are assigned to develop a set of related product features in a fixed amount of time, measured in weeks. The team begins with requirements definition and carries development through to unit test. The team can adjust the delivered functionality, but not the schedule. Complex feature-sets are developed in multiple chunks. The benefits of chunking are a high degree of control over cost and schedule, and a high quality product based on developer's understanding of customer requirements. This paper reviews the chunking discipline and explores some pragmatic issues encountered while developing InConcert. The advantages and disadvantages of chunking are recounted from the perspective of various groups involved in product development: Engineering, Marketing, Quality Assurance, and Management.

1. Introduction

"Chunking" is an informal name for a product development discipline developed and successfully used at XSoft in the development of InConcert, a software product for workflow management. Using chunking, we developed multiple releases of InConcert on a tightly constrained schedule and budget.

Chunking is closely related to a technique now commonly referred to as "timeboxing". In timeboxing, a team is given a certain amount of time to develop a result. Whatever the team has produced by the end of the time period is the deliverable; there is no extension. Timeboxing has recently become popular in the context of Business Process Reengineering. It is generally prescribed as a technique for managing early stage prototyping of computer applications to support newly reengineered business processes. Timeboxing is effective in these situations because it limits the amount of resources expended on investigating "the unknown", produces incremental results that can be appreciated by non-technical people, and forces people to be realistic about biting off only what they can chew.

Chunking is timeboxing applied to product development. The benefits of chunking are a high degree of control over cost and schedule, and a high quality product based on developer's understanding of customer requirements.

This paper reviews the chunking discipline and then explores many of the pragmatic issues encountered in actual practice while developing InConcert. The advantages and disadvantages of chunking are recounted from the perspective of various groups involved in product development: Engineering, Marketing, Quality Assurance, and Management.

1.1. What is Chunking?

Chunking decomposes a software product development project into subprojects which can be completed by 4-6 developers in 6-8 weeks. Each subproject addresses a set of closely related, customer-visible features. Within a subproject (chunk), the development team proposes a concept for the work to be performed in the

0-8186-7840-2/97 $10.00

chunk. Upon approval of the concept, the team develops a specification, and then designs, implements, unit tests, and delivers the software to Quality Assurance (QA). Software functions that are too large to develop in a single chunk are developed in multiple chunks. Marketing, QA, and engineering management frequently review progress. Some "unconventional" attributes of chunking are:

- The schedule is fixed, but the functionality to be delivered is not precisely known at the beginning of a chunk.
- There is no written requirements specification at the outset; requirements are developed and communicated orally and implicitly captured in the concept proposal and functional specification.
- Software is developed by teams of 4-6; there are no smaller teams and no larger teams.
- Definition and assignment of work items is done by the development team; involvement of engineering management in day to day scheduling of engineering tasks is an exceptional and anxiety producing event.
- Breakdown of work is based on clustering of user visible features, not software modules. Teams of developers work in all parts of the software affected by the feature; individual developers do not "own" pieces of the system.
- Scheduling of milestones is highly compressed compared to the "conventional model", where longer projects are assigned to smaller groups of people. This correpsonds to a shift in how software developers are perceived: no longer are developers treated as artisans with highly individualized, specialized skills; rather, they are treated as teammembers with general, flexible capabilities.

I refer to chunking as a "product development discipline" rather than a "software development methodology." The reason for this is that chunking is fundamentally a technique for setting the basic parameters of a project (resources, duration, input, output). Within the constraints of these parameters, any conventional software development methodology can be applied. Chunking is equally compatible with a "waterfall" methodology or iterative prototyping.

1.2. When Is Chunking Applicable?

Chunking is not conventional in most respects. It is not uncommon for people newly exposed to the idea to simply deny that it could work, despite the undeniable fact that we actually delivered a working, commercially viable software product using the technique. A common misperception is that chunking is not applicable except in a few specialized cases. Chunking is a general discipline that can be applied in a variety of circumstances. However, it must be applied with intelligence.

Some general guidelines:

- Chunking, as described here, works best with small to medium size projects. Large projects would probably require some form of "hierarchical chunking", which I have not explored.
- Chunking provides the most benefit when requirements are not known in detail. If the requirements are well known, either by precedent (e.g. building another general ledger application) or by abundant specification, chunking is competitive with other approaches.
- Chunking is an excellent choice when budget or schedule is tightly constrained. Chunking is very efficient at keeping budget and schedule constraints visible and actionable to all parties involved.
- Chunking is a good choice when there is a need to release "intermediate" results between scheduled releases. Chunking offers considerable flexibility in structuring releases because each chunk results in working subset of the final release.

A number of comments and reactions to chunking have touched on issues of how to structure work and coordinate multiple people working on the "same thing". Full discussion of these issues is outside the scope of this paper; the point is that chunking is an *approach* to managing and structuring work across multiple teams, and must be *applied* in particular cases.

Some of the specific issues that must be dealt with in applying chunking to a particular case are:

1. How do you develop and maintain a consistent user interface (UI)?

2. How do you develop embedded common software components that are not directly required by end-user features?
3. How do you handle developing multiple feature-sets that all require changes to the same corpus of code?

2. How Chunking Works

2.1. Project and Release Planning

The basic project parameters are: the chunk duration, the number of people assigned to each development team, and the assignment of feature-sets to chunk teams. At XSoft we set the chunk duration at 6 weeks to start with, but increased it to 8 weeks as the product grew. Experience has shown that the most effective team size is 4-6 people. Fewer than 4 people could not achieve the "critical mass" needed for a high performance team; more than 6 people led to communication and coordination problems that wiped out productivity.

Feature-sets are assigned to chunks in the release planning negotiation, where Engineering and Marketing negotiate cost/benefit tradeoffs. The conventional approach to cost estimation requires Engineering to develop detailed requirements for each proposed function, and then derive detailed project plans and costs from them. In chunking cost estimation works differently:

1. Costs are estimated at a gross level, in units of chunks. How many chunks would be required to develop the feature-set?
2. The precision of the estimates is intentionally low. Precise requirements and precise costs will be elaborated later by the development team.
3. Because the requirements and the costs are at the same (low) level of detail, the release planning negotiation can rapidly screen out low-priority or prohibitively expensive feature-sets without wasting time developing unnecessary detailed requirements and costs.

Once the feature-sets are assigned to chunks, engineering management determines the sequencing of the chunks and the team sizes for each of the chunks. This allows some "tuning" of cost estimates: a "big" feature-set might get a 6 person team assigned, while a "small" feature-set might get a 4 person team assigned.

2.2. What Happens In A Chunk

We chose to follow a traditional "waterfall" methodology within a chunk, although other methodologies are possible. We are currently experimenting with combining iterative prototyping with chunking. This is an area for future work. In this section, we describe the "chunk execution process" as we actually used it; however, this is done for clarity in explanation, and is not strictly required by the chunking approach.

In each chunk, there is a sequence of milestones. Each milestone is observed by a formal review (see Table 1).

The development team sequences the work and assigns tasks to individuals. Each team has a team leader, who

Table 1: Milestones Within A Chunk

Milestone Review	Object of Review	When	Who Attends
Concept Proposal Review	Presentation (overhead foils)	+1 wk	Marketing, Engineering, QA, Documentation, Devel Team
Functional Specification Review	Functional Specification (text document, ~7-15 pp)	+2 wk	Marketing, Engineering, QA, Documentation, Devel Team
High Level Design Review	High Level Design (text document, ~15 pp)	+3 wk	Engineering, Devel Team
Design Review	Design Document (pseudocode)	+4.5 wk	Devel Team
Code and Unit Test Review	The Code (C++ source code + headers)	+6 wk	Devel Team
Delivery to QA		+6 wk	

corresponds to a project manager in a conventional environment. The team leader is responsible for facilitating team meetings, for communicating status to and from management, for drawing attention to problem areas, and for maintaining high team awareness of schedule and delivery expectations. As usual in team-oriented approaches, the team leader role emphasizes facilitation, coaching, and communication, and is not an exalted position of authority.

2.3. Rationale

The key reasons for chunking are:

There's never enough time and money to develop the software you'd like. Welcome to reality. An important corollary is: part of software engineering is making tradeoffs to do what you can with the time and money you've got. The chunking discipline provides a framework for efficiently integrating cost/benefit decisions into the software product development cycle.

People work most productively when there is a clear and present deadline. At the beginning of a project, people's awareness of time and deadline is low. This awareness grows as the deadline approaches. Finally, everyone becomes keenly aware of time and people work extra hard to frantically meet commitments right down to the wire. People who have become accustomed to working under frequent deadlines become more efficient at producing results while controlling panic. A key aspect of chunking is to always have a near-term deadline (a review about a week away), a medium-term deadline (end of the chunk, roughly a month away), and a "long"-term deadline (full release, 6-12 months away).

Effective decisions/tradeoffs concerning product content are best made from the perspective of the intended user. The idea behind chunking is to improve the making of cost/benefit decisions by transferring knowledge of "what the customer wants" to the development team. With this understanding, the team is expected to propose a coherent, useful concept that can be implemented by the team in the available time with available resources. This makes it possible for the development team to explore cost/benefit tradeoffs that take into account the user benefits as well as technical costs.

The people best able to tradeoff between the cost to build features and the contents of features are the people doing the building, providing they understand what the features are for. The conventional model for trading off cost and benefit of a product feature is a cumbersome dance between Marketing and Engineering. In theory, there is a back and forth negotiation in which Marketing sets requirements and Engineering proposes and prices solutions, culiminating in a compromise between cost and functionality that is acceptable to both sides. In practice, this process is often confrontational and does not necessarily result in useful compromises. Chunking moderates the formal "back and forth" by chartering the development team (who has the best handle on cost) to develop an acceptable proposal for the delivered feature-set.

2.4. Pros

Productivity. People work effectively because there are visible targets and deadlines.

Quality. Chunking requires team performance and observes the benefits of team oriented work. Frequent reviews and interactions with teammembers bring the strength of many into play.

Project schedules are easier to track and control. Because there are frequent milestones (roughly weekly, in each chunk) and deliveries every 6-8 weeks, schedule problems and slips become visible soon. With chunking, halfway through the development schedule, 50% of the work is 100% done, rather than 100% of the work 50% done.

Tradeoffs are effective and informed. Since the development team is responsible for comprehending and interpreting requirements communicated to them, they are able to make informed decisions about how changes to proposed features will affect customers.

Release planning is simplified. Early planning decisions are made at a coarse level, and are then refined as featuresets are developed.

Release contents are flexible. Since each chunk results in a working, self-consistent feature-set, it is possible to test and generate "intermediate" releases as needed.

2.5. Cons

Unconventional. People are not accustomed to chunking, so even highly experienced product developers and managers need to be sold and educated on "the way to work".

Tradeoffs can lead to less functionality than hoped for. When expectations (or hopes) for results are out of line with the realities of development costs, chunking can appear to shortchange required functionality.

Emphasis on short term deliverables can impair creativity. The compressed schedules characteristic of chunking can lead to a trench mentality, where people fight daily battles but don't raise their heads to see how the war is doing.

Lack of early detailed specifications can lead to misunderstanding about intended deliverables. It's is quite possible to have high level discussions about the intent of a chunk, with representatives from the various groups using the same words to talk about different things.

Requires ongoing buy-in, cooperation, and support of Marketing, Engineering, and QA. The chunking process requires continuous involvement and participation of the various groups.

3. Observations From Experience

The concept of chunking evolved out of experience in working on a variety of software development projects in various business environments. The key observations about software projects were: a) software development works best in teams; b) a small number of motivated, smart developers can outproduce a large number of less capable, less motivated people; c) software under development can expand to consume virtually any schedule and resource level allocated for it.

In looking at the human side of software projects, I believe that software developers want to do the best job possible, and that they are extremely concerned about quality of their output. Despite the software industry's poor record in meeting project commitments, people in the software industry are no more unmanageable or unreliable than people in other industries. However, because software is abstract and intangible, it is especially difficult for people to maintain the connection between user satisfaction (as a measure of quality) and the technical, complex development activities that are required to produce software. As a result, people tend to measure quality based on technical criteria, rather than on less accessible criteria based on user requirements and expectations. This leads to high productivity (as measured by lines of code *written*, not by lines of code *well received by customer*), high technical quality (elegance of code), and low conformance to expectations (about business issues of schedule, cost, and functionality).

The solution to this problem, as embodied in chunking, is to ensure that developers are kept constantly aware of the customer and business ramifications of their actions.

3.1. Case Example

Chunking was used to develop InConcert, workflow management software sold by XSoft, a Division of Xerox. The first application of chunking occurred in the concept stage of InConcert. At this point, 4-5 people were developing the product concept and demonstrating it in a proof-of-concept prototype. The team had approximately 21 weeks to develop the prototype, and elected to split the time into 3 subprojects of 7 weeks duration. For each subproject, the team began by reviewing research literature on the topic, and then proceeded through concept development and prototyping. The team delivered the working prototype on time and received additional funding for the development phase of the project.

Chunking was then refined and used through the commercial development of InConcert, from 1988 to the present. During this time the development group grew from 4 (developers) to a peak of approximately 30 (approximately 20 developers, 4 test/QA, 2 documentation, 4 management), fluctuating around an average of roughly 12 people. Overall, more than 60 labor years of development effort have been expended under the chunking discipline.

3.2. Marketing Perspective

- Marketing does not write a requirements spec and plays an "advise and consent" role in the development process. This role is not conspicuously dominant, but it does communicate the requirements to the intended audience -- Engineering.
- The release definition process is much quicker.
- At the beginning of a chunk, specifications are sketchy. It requires considerable faith and trust on the part of Marketing to defer detailed examination of the proposed functionality until later on.
- Chunking adjusts delivered functionality to meet available time. Thus, tradeoffs always

go in the direction of decreasing functionality. This can lead to the feeling of "being ripped off" by Engineering.

- Chunking provides many opportunities to release partial results before the "big" release date. Every chunk is a potential "interim" release.
- Product planning is always ongoing. Marketing must make decisions about product content and priority throughout the development phase.

3.3. Software Developer's Perspective

- Rather than passively reacting to requirements from Marketing, the development team must absorb, interpret, and understand the requirements. The team must then actively synthesize a technical solution that meets the requirements and can be implemented by the team in the available time.
- Product developers must work in teams. It is not possible to work as a lone individual. Projects are defined, managed, and assigned through the team process.
- Developers contribute through the whole development cycle, from concept through unit test. This requires developers to be flexible about what they do, and to perform a wide variety of necessary tasks.
- There is constant schedule pressure, because there is always a review or delivery of something a week or so away.
- Software integration is a frequent (every 6 weeks) and demanding activity that requires planning, attention, and involvement of the entire development staff.

3.4. Engineering Management Perspective

- In conventional methodologies, engineering spends a lot of time "inventing" detailed requirements in order to derive detailed cost estimates. Chunking encourages a "graduated" approach to estimation, so that early estimates are (fast and) coarse, and become more refined as the requirements become fixed through negotiation.
- Engineering management must make an effort to avoid directing day to day project issues. It must maintain a consistent and inexorable focus on committed dates and deliverables, leaving ownership of the day to day activities to the teams.
- The principal "management" function is the allocation of people to teams. Engineering management must staff the teams correctly, ensure that the number of people on each team reflects the priority and size of the feature-set being developed, and monitor the effectiveness of the teams.
- The amount of time spent in different activities by the chunk teams was quite visible as the teams went through project cycles repeatedly. Our experience was:

  concept formulation and functional specification took approximately 30-40% of the time;

  design took approximately 20-30% of the time;

  implementation took approximately 20% of the time

  unit test, integration, configuration management, and release management assertively demanded a significant portion of time, approximately 20% throughout the chunk.

3.5. QA and Documentation Perspective

- Quality Assurance and Documentation can begin testing and documenting each chunk when delivered. Each chunk produces a set of related features, which works well for developing test plans and producing user documentation.
- Testing and documentation can be performed during the development phase, there is an opportunity to reduce the amount of time spent in QA and writing after the full release to QA.
- Because there are no complete descriptions of overall release contents, both testers and writers must piece together specifications delivered from individual chunks. This requires close involvement with developers.

3.6. Commentary & Observations From Experience

In actual practice, the development teams enthusiastically attempted to address every requirement thrown their way. Development teams consistently and repeatedly overcommitted the amount they could deliver in a chunk. This intensified schedule pressure and caused considerable stress. From a management perspective, the teams did in fact propose the work to be performed, and could have proposed more or less as the team decided. However, developers were quite unwilling to cut quality to meet time constraints, feeling that this was management's job. Unfortunately, when management interceded to reduce stress by cutting back the amount teams proposed, ownership of the schedule fell back in management's lap.

Many developers were uncomfortable with the high level of teamwork and communication required by chunking. Discomfort was particularly strong among programming consultants and contractors. There is a strong cultural history of treating specialist programmers as "lone geniuses", which is at odds with the team-oriented, generalist approach fostered by chunking.

Chunking has a strong effect on the way that marketing interacts with engineering, and how the whole product management function is performed. Conventional product development usually requires one or two blasts of close attention by marketing, followed by periods of intensive (and exclusive) development. Chunking requires continuous marketing review and oversight.

4. Summary And Conclusion

Chunking is a product development discipline developed and used at XSoft in the development of InConcert. InConcert has been well received by customers and industry analysts. It has been chosen by a number of customers following detailed technical evaluations of InConcert vis a vis competitive products. Customers repeatedly cite InConcert's open and configurable architecture and its comprehensive functionality as key differentiators.

Overall, chunking is an excellent development discipline for use when resources are constrained. Chunking is an extremely efficient way to allocate and spend limited resources, and to maximize the return from those resources. The concept of fixing schedule, constraining resources, and then adjusting functionality is unconventional and requires some time to adjust to. Some people do not adjust, and never feel comfortable with the idea that schedule and resource drive everything from concept through delivery.

- Chunking transfers many of the product definition responsibilities from Marketing to the development teams. This improves the accuracy of tradeoffs, but reduces the comfort level of Marketing.
- By running repeatedly through the full development cycle, chunking emphasizes the non-coding aspects of product development, and forces individuals and organizations to become effective at activities such as specification, code integration, and release building.
- Cost/benefit tradeoffs are made by the team actually performing the work. This improves the quality of the tradeoffs, but they are made later in the development phase than people are used to.
- We achieved high productivity and high code quality using chunking, but we also achieved the pressure-cooker schedule and short term orientation characteristic of startups.

There is one pro that should carry considerable weight in the software industry:

> *Using chunking, we delivered a working software product on schedule and within budget. Over a 4.5 year period, which included multiple releases, we met every scheduled external release deadline and stayed on budget.*

5. Acknowledgements

Dennis McCarthy is the other original proponent of chunking. He provided a number of key suggestions, quantified much of the factual background, and helped shape the exposition of the concept for this paper. Sunil Sarin, Diane Smith, and Steve Fox provided valuable suggestions which improved the paper considerably. InConcert was developed at XSoft, a Division of Xerox. InConcert is currently available from InConcert, Inc., 4 Cambridge Center, Cambridge, MA 02142.

Session P2a

Measurement and Metrics

A Process for Asynchronous Software Inspection

Paul Murphy and James Miller

Empirical Foundations of Computer Science Group
Dept of Computer Science
University of Strathclyde, Glasgow G1 1XQ
E-mail: {jpm,james}@cs.strath.ac.uk

Abstract

Although there exists a multitude of different inspection processes, the basic process has remained unchanged since it was first defined by Fagan in 1976. The process has as its central component an inspection meeting which all participants attend. But is this meeting cost effective? Recent work suggests this is not the case.

An inspection model that dispenses totally with the need for the inspectors to be in the same place at the same time is presented. It replaces the meeting with further individual inspections combined with asynchronous communication between inspectors.

A prototype tool has been developed that supports the asynchronous model. In contrast to a previously developed asynchronous inspection tool, it uses electronic mail as the basis for communication and the reasons for this approach are discussed.

The inspection model is evaluated in comparison with the traditional, meeting-oriented approach on a number of criteria. An initial attempt was made to gain quantitive data by carrying out a small-scale experiment, but whilst encouraging results being obtained, the number of subjects was too low for any significant conclusions to be drawn. Larger scale experiments are planned for the future to obtain more data.

Keywords: Software inspection, asynchrony, tool support

1. Introduction

Software inspection has become a widely-used technique [18] since its introduction by Michael Fagan in 1976 [3], and its benefits have been extensively reported in the literature. Some examples of these include: Fagan's own finding that the cost of fixing errors found during inspection is one to two orders of magnitude less than if the errors were not detected until the next phase of development [3, 4]; IBM-Houston's Space Shuttle Onboard Program established that if it cost $1 to fix an error found in inspection, it would cost $13 to fix it after system test and $92 to correct if discovered after delivery [7]; and Gilb and Graham's claim that using inspections can save up to 50% of a project's development time [5]. As a result of such reports, inspection has become one of the few well-known successes of software engineering.

Since its inception, Fagan's technique has been adapted in various ways (see Humphrey [6] for a summary) but still forms the basic process model which the other variants are based upon. To summarise the approach, Fagan divides the process into six phases:

1. Planning. Where rôles are allocated, materials distributed *etc.*
2. Overview. The author briefs the inspection team on the document under inspection.
3. Preparation. Each member of the inspection team goes through the document to locate defects.
4. Inspection. A meeting takes place where the inspection team attempt to find, not correct, defects.
5. Rework. The defects found in the meeting are addressed by the author.
6. Follow-up. The moderator checks that all the defects have been addressed. They then decide whether the document should pass on to the next phase of development or be reinspected.

0-8186-7840-2/97 $10.00

The main focus of inspection is stage 4, the meeting. According to Votta [19], the factor most often quoted when justifying the inspection meeting is **synergy**. To define this term with respect to inspections, Votta states that synergy refers to the belief that the inspection team working in a meeting will do better than any or all of the members working alone. That is, the meeting will find more defects. This is one of Fagan's central beliefs, as he stated [3]:

> ...the number of errors found [by individuals] is not nearly as high as in the inspection operation.

Recently a series of empirical studies [13, 17, 19] have contradicted this, and suggested that holding meetings adds very little to the defect detection process. It is this thread of investigation which is followed up in this paper. The next section discusses the results of these studies, and some of their implications. The paper then continues with descriptions of an inspection model that removes meetings altogether, and a tool that has been developed to support it. We conclude with a short evaluation of the new model contrasted against meeting-based inspection techniques.

2. Related Work

2.1. Votta's inspection study

This paper originates from work done by Votta at AT & T Bell Labs [19], in which he observed a series of inspection meetings involving software professionals working upon industrial projects. From the data gathered, he argues that the reasons for holding meetings are either invalid or capable of being incorporated into a process without meetings. While praising the meeting for providing a set of deadlines, a well-structured process model, and for eliminating 'false positive' defects, his analysis produced results that suggest that the number of defects found in meetings is only 4% greater than the number discovered during individual preparation.

Subsequently he conducted a cost-benefit study that demonstrated that the delay needed for the two-hour inspection meeting to be arranged was not worth such a small increase in defect detection. This lack of effectiveness is put down to the fact that since the inspection meeting is rigidly fixed at two hours (to prevent tiredness), quite often the goal of the inspectors is simply to complete the exercise, not to contribute their skills as individuals. The result is that little synergy actually occurs.

Votta also raises the point that at any meeting, only 2 of the n inspectors can interact at any one time. As a result the meeting becomes a series of sequential conversations, with no opportunity for parallel communication. He also observed that around 30% to 80% of the other n-2 inspectors were actually listening to the current conversation. Clearly, this wastes time and effort for all those concerned.

Votta proposed a range of solutions to these problems: more strictly managed meetings; more focused three-person meetings between reviewer, author, and moderator; or to conduct the inspection meeting through correspondence so that the inspectors never have to meet.

This last suggestion ties in with the work done by McCarthy *et al.* [13], investigating various methods of conducting inspections. They conducted a series of experiments to test two commonly held opinions:

1. Meetings are responsible for the discovery of many faults, and so justify their cost.
2. More faults are found because a meeting is held than would be found otherwise.

They found that the defect detection rate was highly dependent on the personnel who took part. Simply put, the more able the people who participated, the more effective the inspection. They also found that most inspectors approached the process in one of two ways:

- **Preparation - Inspection**. The inspector initially surveys the document in order to become familiar with its content, but not to locate any defects. This is followed by the inspection meeting where defect detection takes place.
- **Detection - Collection**. The inspector goes through the document with the intent of finding as many defects as possible. The subsequent meeting will locate many of the defects already found by the individual inspectors, who are simply reporting their own findings. Note that there is usually a loss of some defects found by the inspectors individually. The effect of this **meeting loss** is considered in the next section.

To test the hypotheses above, they proposed a third method, where no meeting was held. Instead, a second round of individual inspection was substituted in its place, immediately following the first, so that the time that would have been taken up by the meeting is used by the inspectors to continue defect detection individually. This method was called **Detection - Detection**. The results of their experiments showed that Detection - Detection produced the best defect detection rates (46%), followed by Detection - Collection (23%), and finally Preparation - Inspection (19%). McCarthy *et al.* concluded that, on the basis of their study, meetings were not an indispensable part of a successful inspection, but that further study was necessary.

	Porter et al.	Lanubile and Vassagio	Miller et al.
Mean gain	4%	19%	9%
Mean loss	7%	25%	39%

Table 1. The mean meeting gains and losses measured in Porter's experiment and its replications.

2.2. Porter et al. and replications

Porter *et al.* [17] ran a series of experiments in which they investigated which sort of defect detection techniques were most useful in inspections. Following Votta, they also collected data to determine whether or not holding a meeting added anything to the number of defects gathered.

Their work compared meeting gains (defects found for the first time at the meeting) and meeting losses (defects that had been found previously by one of the inspectors that were not subsequently reported at the meeting). They found that there was no significant difference between these two measures. As a result, they concluded that the net gain of holding meetings is approximately zero.

In an attempt to measure the validity of the above results, a series of external replications of Porter's experiments have been carried out. Using a lab kit supplied by the original experimenters, Lanubile and Vissagio [9] in Italy and Miller *et al.* [14] in the UK, have reached a similar conclusion - that inspection meetings produce no net improvement. Their results and those of Porter can be seen in Table 1[1].

The data clearly shows that all three experiments experience a net loss from the meeting exercise. While it should be borne in mind that all of the work listed here has taken place in academic environments with students as subjects, the data that has been produced is broadly in line with Votta's meeting gain data, which was produced from observations of software professionals in real industrial situations.

2.3. Conflicting evidence

A subsequent study of inspection at AT & T by Porter, Siy, Toman and Votta [16], generated data that conflicted with Votta's original paper, and with the work reported above. Over 100 code inspections were studied, and the average meeting gain rate was observed to be 33%, although there was considerable variance in the results. While we will not comment further on this study in this report, it was felt that the existence of contradictory data should be made clear.

[1] Note that the results reported for Lanubile and Vissagio are approximate as the data was reported in a graph, and that all figures quoted in this study ignore one group's data as an extreme outlier.

2.4. Summary

In summary, Votta's industrial study produced data that indicated meetings may not make any significant contribution to the number of defects collected in inspections. Porter's study of defect detecting techniques and the replications of that work has generated support for this theory by finding that meeting losses outweigh meeting gains. In spite of the contradictory evidence outlined above, this forms a body of evidence that suggests that meetings could be removed from the inspection process with no loss of defect finding capability. It was on this basis that an inspection model that dispensed with meetings was developed. This model is described below.

3. Asynchronous Inspection Model

Given the findings described above, it was decided to explore the idea of abandoning the face-to-face meeting altogether and replacing it with another period of individual inspection, combined with asynchronous communication between the members of the inspection team. This was done to combine the most effective defect collection mechanism, detection - detection, with a communication mechanism that eliminates the need for the inspectors to meet. The reasons for this are discussed below.

Initially, the first three stages go ahead as before with the moderator checking that the document meets any entrance criteria, identifying the personnel they wish to take part and inviting them to do so, and selecting any relevant support materials such as checklists.

After they have indicated they are willing to join the inspection, a deadline is set for the inspectors to individually review the document for defects. After this, each inspector circulates a copy of their list of defects to the other inspectors and the moderator for review.

The idea behind review is to allow the inspectors to pick up on any defects they failed to identify. They can then discuss these with the other inspectors using the communication mechanism, which may be e-mail, a bulletin board, or some other medium. The rôle of such tools in supporting the whole inspection process is discussed in the next section.

The asynchronous discussion involved in review mimics a face-to-face meeting, and improves on it in a number of ways:

1. The inspectors can explain themselves in whatever amount of detail they think necessary, and they can include original parts of the document to illustrate what they mean.

2. We no longer have the situation suggested by Votta where members of the inspection team are simply waiting to leave the two-hour meeting and no longer contributing to the process. They can contribute to the discussion at the the time they feel best.

3. An inspector does not have to wait for someone to stop talking, and risk losing their train of thought.

4. Conversations can now proceed in parallel, allowing separate threads of discussion to proceed simultaneously.

After this round of debate, and in possession of the defect lists of the other inspectors, the inspectors go through the product document again. This implements the second round of the detection-detection process. They may generate new defects, reclassify ones they noted before (or delete them as 'false positives'), or include defects from the other inspectors' lists. Each inspector then submits their final defect list before some preset deadline to the moderator.

On receipt of the all the inspectors' defect lists, the moderator compiles a complete defect list to send to the author for rework. The defects that go into this list are selected solely at the discretion of the moderator. This eliminates the inspectors from this phase of the inspection, and hence eliminates the need to gain approval from the group. Thus the need for consensus over defects, one of the main sources of meetings, is removed. This does not mean, however, that the moderator simply ignores the work of the inspectors.

In effect, the model supports **implicit voting**. If an inspector finds a defect during their initial review, or includes one from another inspectors defect list, then the moderator will be able to judge whether or not a majority of the team agree simply by looking at their defect lists.

Finally, the follow-up phase takes place as normal, with the moderator deciding whether or not the document is of sufficient quality to pass on to the next phase of development. If it is, then the inspection is complete, otherwise the document must be resubmitted for a fresh inspection.

3.1. The Inspection Team

Because of the changed nature of the inspection model, some of the tasks that each member of the inspection team has to perform have also changed.

3.1.1 The Moderator

The Moderator is still responsible for planning the inspection process. As usual, this involves selecting the appropriate personnel to take part, choosing and supplying documentation, specifying deadlines, and checking that any specified rework has been correctly carried out *etc*. The additional tasks imposed by the asynchronous model are:

1. Monitoring communication. Since we no longer have a same-time, same-place meeting where the moderator can immediately stop any irrelevant threads of conversation, the moderator must monitor the messages that pass between the inspection team to make sure that they are keeping to the task in hand and not discussing irrelevancies.

2. Compiling the final defect list. The moderator will collate the errors collected into a final defect list that will be passed to the author.

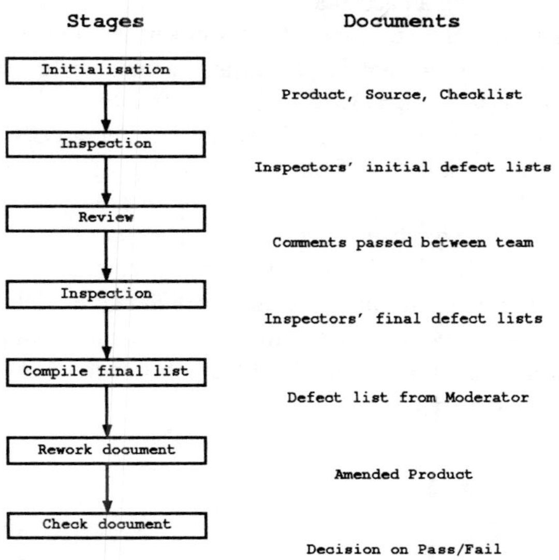

Figure 1. The stages of the asynchronous inspection model and their associated documents.

3.1.2 The Author

Other than being available to answer any questions from the inspectors, it was decided not to give the author any rôle in inspecting the document. This is on the grounds of **cognitive dissonance**. This is the theory, proposed by Weinberg [20], that since most people have the tendency to reject evidence that contradicts their beliefs, programmers are not very good at finding flaws in their own code. As a result of this, asking the author to participate in an exercise designed to find flaws in something they themselves produced seems wasteful as it may lead to too much debate or even friction between the author and the other inspectors.

3.1.3 The Inspectors

The rôle of the inspectors is straightforward - to look for defects. This is an easy requirement to state, but can be hard to fulfill in practice. It implies that the inspectors must be familiar with any notations, domain terminology *etc.* in the document under inspection. If inspectors are not able to understand the conventions used, then they cannot be expected to contribute as fully to the inspection. Having the inspection team consist of such experts is advocated by Parnas and Weiss [15] who argue that inspectors who have the additional task of becoming familiar with a new application area, notation *etc.*, will have to spend considerable amounts of time reaching an acceptable level of fluency. As a result they have less time to inspect the document for defects.

Such a requirement is particularly amenable to asynchronous inspection as such experts are free to conduct inspection in their own time. They are not being called to meetings which detract from their own output. This may be a marked improvement for inspection workers who have their domain expertise called upon frequently. It can also remove the blocking factor that is often encountered when scheduling a synchronous meeting, which can be delayed for a considerable period of time until all the relevant personnel have a mutually suitable block of time to be able to attend the meeting.

4. Tool Support

There are a number of papers describing tool support for the traditional inspection process, of which Macdonald [11] gives an overview, but as meetingless inspection is still very much a research topic, there is very little published information available. However, Mashayekhi *et al.* [12] have identified a number of features that should be supported to support any meetingless inspection process.

Threads of discussion Inspectors must be allowed to discuss defects. In synchronous meetings, this is a serial process with only one discussion proceeding at any one time.

Sharing of Information The documents involved in the inspection process must be accessible to all team members.

Train of thought Those involved must be able to follow a line of argument throughout its lifetime.

Coordination The team must be able to coordinate their activities to ensure that the goals of the inspection are met, and deadlines adhered to.

Mashayekhi *et al.* make use of the WWW to achieve these goals in their AISA tool [12], which has been developed as part of their wider effort to make software engineering activity asynchronous. In contrast, an e-mail based tool, named *InspectA*, has been developed to implement the inspection model discussed in the previous section. Using e-mail still allows all the criteria listed above to be met, as is illustrated below.

Threads of discussion Each inspector can conduct simultaneous discussions with the other inspectors.

Sharing of information Documentation and commentary can be broadcast throughout the group, if that is what is required, or directed to individuals.

Train of thought E-mail allows for replies to be structured in response to messages received, i.e. 're: your earlier message...'. Many e-mail utilities, for example Netscape Mail, automatically format included messages in support of this.

Coordination Deadlines can be issued as part of the structured messages from the moderator, which are sent on initiation of a new inspection.

The reasons for not adopting the WWW approach are that all the defects noted by the inspectors are sent to a single WWW location that is viewable by the whole inspection team, as and when they are produced. This could have the effect of discouraging individual inspectors if they see other team members posting defects on a more frequent basis than themselves. Also, inspectors may be tempted to indulge in premature discussion of the posted defects instead of pursuing their own individual inspections. To overcome this, in *InspectA* defect lists are only circulated when they are all completed.

In *InspectA*, this period of discussion can proceed only after all the inspectors have posted their defect lists. All mail that the inspectors send to each other in the inspection is also copied automatically to the moderator. This fulfills the moderator's obligation to monitor communication, and allows them to intervene when the discussion of a defect is dragging on far too long or is becoming unfocused.

4.1. Using the InspectA tool

InspectA enables the whole inspection process to be automated, from initiation with the moderator selecting and notifying the inspection team, through to follow-up where the moderator checks that all the issues raised during the inspection have been addressed. This section describes how *InspectA* assists the process.

The moderator begins a new inspection by filling in a form that lists the names of the author and the inspectors, and also relevant inspection documentation. Copies of these documents are sent via e-mail to the inspectors, who can then view them and begin to find defects. Defects are entered using a form in the inspection window, which can be seen in Figure 2. The defect's text and a description are included, along with the inspector's estimation of the defect's type and severity.

On completing the initial inspection phase, the tool circulates each inspector's defect list to the other team members. Review and subsequent re-inspection then take place before the team e-mail their final defect lists to the moderator. The moderator then produces a complete defect list which is e-mailed to the author. The final part of the tool supports the follow-up phase and displays this final defect list and the modified product document. The moderator reviews the altered document and then chooses to either allow it to pass or to re-submit it for a new inspection. The first choice generates an e-mail telling all concerned that the inspection has been completed, the second summons the initiation window so that the process can begin again.

The inspection window (Figure 2) was organised in such a way as to allow the document being inspected, its source document, a checklist, and the form for entering defects to be displayed together. This tiled display was chosen because empirical studies have shown that experienced users prefer tiled arrangements, as opposed to overlapping windows [1]. It allows the inspectors to easily cross-reference all the appropriate documentation without having to constantly adjust their display. This approach can also be seen in the review window (Figure 3), where all the inspectors' defect lists are displayed simultaneously.

To help promote the idea of asynchronous working, a notepad facility is available which lets the inspector record comments during their inspection. The notepad is saved automatically when the user closes ends the current session. This aids asynchrony by allowing the inspector to split the inspection up into a series of sessions, instead of having to do the work in a single, possibly tiring, contiguous block.

All e-mails sent between team members are collected and archived. This function allows the messages passed within the team to be analysed post-inspection, which may lead to improvements to the inspection model in the future.

5. Evaluation

In this section we compare the relative merits of asynchronous and synchronous inspections.

Synergy Votta [19] states that synergy makes no or little impact in the synchronous meeting, therefore holding up the inspection process until a meeting can be scheduled wastes time and may delay the development process. In the asynchronous model meetings are removed and the findings of Votta, Porter [17], and McCarthy *et al.* [13] suggest that no loss is incurred in the amount of defects found.

Participation The moderator can very easily see just how much each inspector is contributing in the inspection meeting in both the synchronous and asynchronous models. In the former they can see which inspectors are speaking up regularly and which are not. In the asynchronous model all communications are automatically copied to the moderator, who can build up a database of each inspectors contributions, and so gauge their input over the whole inspection.

Process improvement Following from the above, the keeping of communications passed between inspectors can form a valuable record of inspection experiences, and can be used to improve the process in future. It is hard to imagine such a facility being built into a synchronous meeting, as this would involve recording or transcribing many hours of such inspections.

Peer review In both models the moderator can judge how well an inspector has performed by monitoring their communications, but the database of messages provides evidence for any formal assessment that would otherwise be based solely on opinion.

Conversations Meetings are limited to strictly serial, one-on-one conversations. Asynchronous inspections can

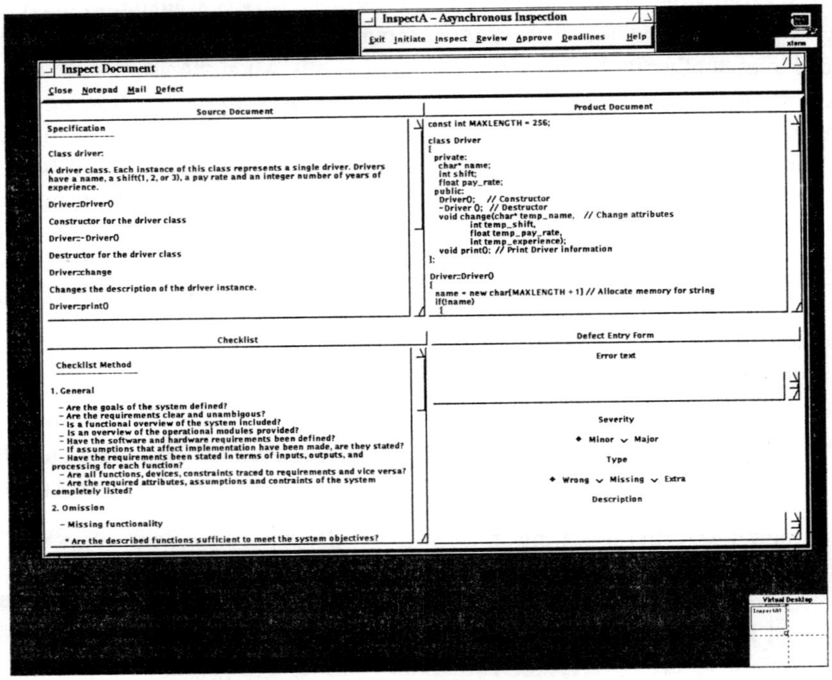

Figure 2. The inspection window in InspectA

have any number of parallel, n-way threads proceeding at any one time.

Automation The traditional meeting can be automated, but usually takes the form of a pen and paper session. The need for a communications mechanism in the asynchronous model may form the basis of tool support for the whole process.

Location The asynchronous inspection can be distributed in space as well as in time. There is no need for the inspectors to be in the same room or the same site. In their paper, Mashayekhi *et al.* describe an inspection team with members in the USA and Japan [12]. In contrast, any tools that have supported the synchronous inspection process have still required the inspection team to be in the same room [10].

Decision Making Deciding whether a proposed defect is to be included or not is usually decided by asking each inspector to vote on the issue. This can cause contention as the inspection team may be evenly divided on the matter, or a minority may refuse to agree with the consensus. The implicit voting associated with asynchronous inspections leaves such decisions to the moderator, who decides whether or not to include a defect on the basis of the inspectors' individual submissions.

An initial attempt was made to gather quantitive data on the performance of both the model and the tool, using students from a practical software engineering class to perform a small inspection. After completing the exercise, the participants completed a questionnaire, with answers on the normal Likert scale.

Due to the small number of participants, detailed analysis is inappropriate, but the responses provided encouragement by their highly positive nature. For example, in response to the question "Overall, what is your impression of the asynchronous inspection model compared to other inspection methods you have used?", all answered four or five, with five being the most positive. Similarly, all liked the support for the model provided by the *InspectA* tool. Larger scale experiments are planned for the future to provide data for more in-depth analysis.

6. Conclusions

A model for conducting inspections has been developed that dispenses with the need for face-to-face, synchronous meetings. These are replaced with two rounds of individual inspection incorporating a review of the other inspectors' defect lists, which potentially increases the amount of time

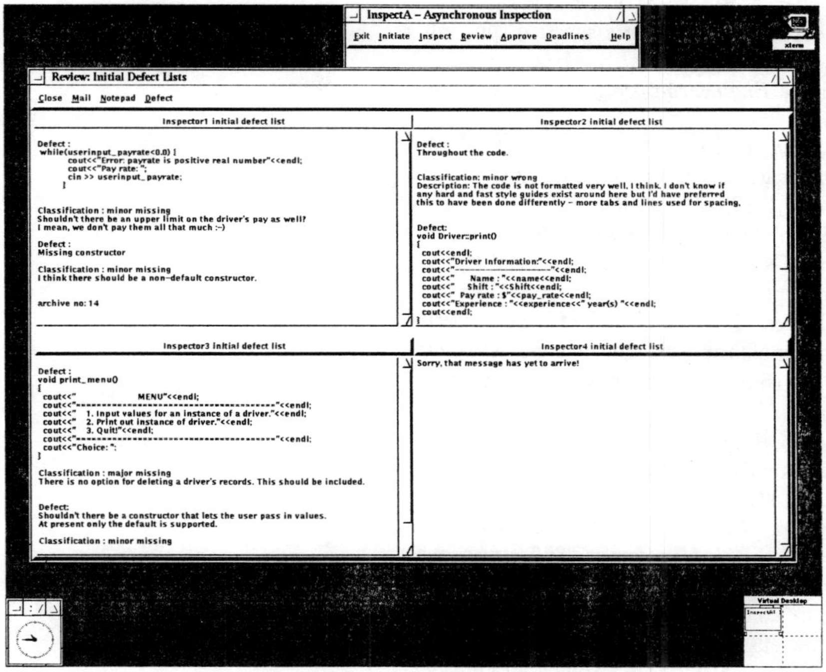

Figure 3. The review window in InspectA

team members can spend looking for defects. This is coupled with an e-mail based asynchronous 'meeting' that satisfies the criteria set by Mashayekhi et al for asynchronous communication [12].

Instead of using explicit voting to clear up areas of contention the moderator gauges the opinion of the inspection team by browsing their individual defect lists, thus removing another reason for holding a meeting.

Possible future directions for this work include incorporating security features such as encryption to allow e-mail to be sent across different sites securely, facilitating greater distribution of inspection teams. Another option would be to allow the asynchronous meeting to function anonymously, i.e. with the inspectors involved unaware of each other's identities. Recent theory suggests that meetings function more effectively when the participants are unaware of each other's identities [2, 8].

Inspection has been demonstrated to be a successful technique for improving software quality. This paper describes an alternative to the traditional inspection mechanism which the authors believe can make the traditional inspection process more efficient by eliminating the need for meetings and the associated delay, increasing the amount of time actually spent looking for defects, and greatly increasing the scope for the discussion of defects between the members of the inspection team. In the near future we hope to be able to present quantitive evidence in defence of these claims.

References

[1] S. Bly and J. Rosenberg. A comparison of tiled and overlapping windows. In *Proc. CHI'86 Conference - Human Factors in Computing Systems*, 1986.

[2] T. Connolly, L. Jessup, and J. Valacich. Effects of anonymity and evaluative tone on idea generation in computer-mediated groups. *Management Science*, 36(6):689–703, 1990.

[3] M. E. Fagan. Design and code inspections to reduce errors in program development. *IBM System Journal*, 15(3):182–211, 1976.

[4] M. E. Fagan. Advances in software inspections. *IEEE Transactions on Software Engineering*, 12(7):744–751, 1986.

[5] T. Gilb and D. Graham. *Software Inspection*. Addison-Wesley, 1993.

[6] W. S. Humphrey. *Managing the Software Process*. Addison-Wesley, 1993.

[7] S. E. Institute. *The Capability Maturity Model*. Addison-Wesley, 1995.

[8] L. Jessup, T. Connolly, and J. Galegher. The effects of anonymity on group process in automated group problem solving. *MIS Quarterly*, 14(3):313–321, 1990.

[9] F. Lanubile and G. Visaggio. Assessing defect detection methods for software requirements inspections through external replication. Technical report, Dept of Informatica,University of Bari, 1996.

[10] F. Macdonald, J. Miller, A. Brooks, M. Roper, and M. Wood. A review of tool support for software inspection. In *Proceedings of the Seventh International Workshop on Computer Aided Software Engineering*, pages 340–349, July 1995.

[11] F. Macdonald, J. Miller, A. Brooks, M. Roper, and M. Wood. Automating the software inspection process. *Automated Software Engineering*, 3:193–218, 1996.

[12] V. Mashayekhi, R. Glamm, and J. Riedl. AISA: Asynchonous inspection of software artefacts. Technical report, Computer Science Dept, University of Minnesota, 1995.

[13] P. McCarthy, A. Porter, H. Siy, and L. Votta. An experiment to assess cost-benefits of inspection meetings and their alternatives. Technical report, Computer Science Dept, University of Maryland, 1995.

[14] J. Miller, M. Wood, M. Roper, and A. Brooks. Further experiences with scenarios and checklists. Technical report, Dept of Computer Science, University of Strathclyde, 1996.

[15] D. L. Parnas and D. M. Weiss. Active design reviews: Principles and practices. *Journal of Systems and Software*, pages 259–265, 1987.

[16] A. Porter, H. Siy, C. Toman, and L. Votta. An experiment to assess the cost-benefits of cose inspections in large scale software development. *ACM SIGSOFT Software Engineering Notes*, 20(10), October 1995.

[17] A. Porter, L. Votta, and V. Basili. Comparing detection methods for software requirements inspections: A replicated experiment. *IEEE Transactions on Software Engineering*, 21(6):563–575, 1995.

[18] C. Ramamoorthy and W.-T. Tsai. Advances in software engineering. *IEEE Computer*, pages 47–58, October 1996.

[19] L. Votta. Does every inspection need a meeting? In *Proc. of ACM SIGSOFT '93 Symp. Foundations of Software Engineering*. ACM, 1993.

[20] G. Weinberg. *The Psychology of Conputer Programming*. Van Nostrand, 1971.

GQM-based Improvement of Embedded, Real-time Software Development Practices

Vassilis Kopanas, Vassilios Sylaidis, Ioannis Nanakis

INTRACOM S.A.
P.O. Box 68, 19002 Peania, Attika, Greece
{vkop, vsyl, inan}@intranet.gr

Abstract

This paper reports on the experiences from an ESSI project, called PITA, carried out at INTRACOM's department developing software for digital telephony applications. PITA introduced the Goal-Question-Metric (GQM) approach via the AMI method and tool, focusing on a typical project as a baseline. Expected benefits from PITA include: reduction of software development cost, shortening of the time-to-market for software products and increased product reliability at customer's site. This paper presents the rationale of the experiment, a brief account of the GQM method and the AMI approach, the objectives and the organisation of the experiment, its relation to other ongoing improvement efforts, the results and conclusions from the experiment, lessons learned and plans for future activities.

1. Introduction

In recent years one can observe a growing interest in the application of measurement techniques in software project management. This trend can be justified as a systematic approach to overcome the effects of software crisis, such as budget and schedule overruns, low quality and reliability and high cost for software quality [1, 2].

According to many studies on the application of metrics and models in industrial environments, measurements should be focused on specific goals, applied to all life-cycle products, processes and resources and should be interpreted based on understanding of the organisational context, environment and business goals. This means that measurements must be defined in a top-down fashion, they must be focused and based on goals and models.

In line with the above trends and studies, and in attempting to alleviate shortcomings of INTRACOM's existing software development metrics framework, the Goal-Question-Metric (GQM) approach was introduced to the company's software development practices through the AMI method. The introduction of GQM was carried out as a Process Improvement Experiment (PIE) named PITA, in the context of the CEC programme ESSI (European Systems and Software Initiative).

This paper aims at presenting the rationale of the experiment (sec. 1, 2), a brief account of the GQM method and the AMI approach (sec. 3), the objectives and the organisation of the experiment (sec. 4), an analysis of experiment activities performed (sec. 5), lessons learned from introducing GQM (sec. 6) and a set of conclusions and plans for further activities (sec.7). Section 8 finally, provides a basic set of references related to software measurements, GQM and AMI.

2. The software development practice

The PITA experiment introduces the GQM method to INTRACOM's software development practices. INTRACOM S.A., the leading Greek telecommunications and electronics firm was founded in 1977. It employs 1500 people (650 are specialised engineers). The company produces a wide range of products (both hardware and software) and turn-key systems covering the needs of modern networks: digital switching and radio links, energy control, telecommunications network management. Other activities include support of installed systems, engineering services, and involvement in several cutting-edge projects in areas such as multimedia systems, image processing and advanced transport telematics applications.

0-8186-7840-2/97 $10.00 © 1997 IEEE

The main area of software development at INTRACOM is the Software Design Centre (SWDC), which mainly designs high quality software products for digital telephony applications. SWDC which hosted the PITA experiment employs 180 highly qualified and specially trained software engineers / designers. Various process improvement activities are pursued at this department within a formal Policy Deployment scheme. Also, software process capability assessment has been effected and upgrade activities have been initiated. Inspections are carried out using a specific process integrated in all stages of the model used for software development. Testing is carried out in specially operated test sites. The utilised software development method is a variation of the classic 'waterfall' paradigm. The software designers attend an initial training course on the development method, tools and the application field.

Prior to the experiment, a basic set of metrics were being used providing a high-level view of the design process and product quality, as well as a basis for bench-marking. However, they did not constitute a set adequately developed and closely linked to actual experiences and problems. Measurements taken within that immature metrics frame had shown some trends but the necessary analysis was insufficient and the results were inconclusive. In addition, the utilised metrics tended to reflect only generic upper management concerns and viewpoints. Thus, metrics usefulness and suitability was often questioned and their acceptance by involved personnel could not be taken for granted, especially when these metrics contradicted everyday experiences. At the same time, there were not adequate measures for monitoring and controlling the progress of improvement actions.

3. Overview of GQM and AMI

Several efforts related to software measurements are reported in the literature [3, 4, 5, 6, 7, 8, 9]. Among them, the **Goal-Question-Metric (GQM)** approach [8, 9] provides a well-defined measurement mechanism. This approach has been developed and proposed for application at software development organisations and is based upon the assumption that for an organisation to measure in a purposeful and efficient way, it must firstly specify the goals for itself and its projects, then it must trace those goals to the data that will define those goals operationally, and finally provide a framework for interpreting the data with respect to the stated goals. GQM was originally defined for evaluating defects for a set of projects in the NASA Goddard Space Flight Centre environment. Since then, the use of GQM has been expanded to a larger context.

The result of the application of GQM is the specification of a measurement system targeting a particular set of issues and a set of rules for the interpretation of the measurement data. The GQM measurement model has three levels:

1. *Conceptual level* (GOAL): A goal is defined for an object (product, process, project or resource), for a variety of reasons, with respect to various models of quality, from various points of view, relative to a particular environment.
2. *Operational level* (QUESTION): A set of questions is used to characterise the way the assessment / achievement of a specific goal will be performed based on some characterising model. Questions try to characterise the object of measurement (product, process, etc.) with respect to a selected quality issue and to determine its quality from a selected viewpoint.
3. *Quantitative level* (METRIC): A set of data is associated with every question in order to answer it in a quantitative way. The data can be objective (e.g. person-hours spent on a task) or subjective (level of user satisfaction).

A GQM model is a hierarchical structure (see Fig. 1) starting with a goal, that specifies purpose of measurement, object to be measured, issue to be measured and viewpoint from which the measure is taken.

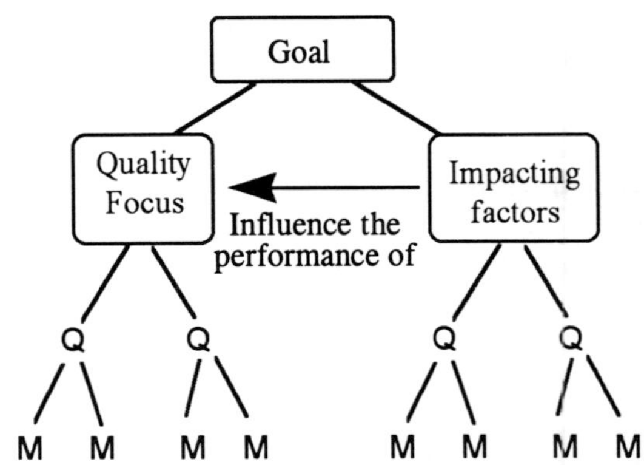

Figure 1. The GQM model.

The goal is refined in several questions, that usually break down the issue into its major components. Each question is then refined into metrics. The same metric can be used in order to answer different questions under the same goal. Several GQM models can also have questions and metrics in common, provided that when the measure is actually collected, the different viewpoints are taken into account correctly (i.e. the metric might have different values if taken from different viewpoints).

GQM provides a method for top-down metric definition and bottom-up interpretation. The GQM approach can be used as stand-alone for defining a measurement program or, better, within the context of a more general approach to software process improvement.

The **AMI method (Application of Metrics in Industry)** [10] is based on the GQM approach and provides a common-sense framework for quantifying software projects. This framework comprises four principal phases:

1. *Assessment* of the organisation's environment to define primary goals for measurement.
2. *Analysis* of the assessment results and primary goals to derive sub-goals and the relevant metrics. The analysis is formalised as a goal tree with a corresponding set of questions to which these metrics are linked.
3. *Metrication* by implementing a measurement plan and then processing the collected primitive data into measurement data.
4. *Improvement* as measurement data are exploited and actions are implemented. Comparison of the measurement data with the goals and questions in the measurement plan provide guidance towards the achievement of the immediate project goals. When measurements show that a goal has been achieved, there is enough improvement attained to reassess the initial primary goals. One improvement cycle in the AMI method is then considered to be complete.

The approach followed by AMI is an adaptation of Deming's widely used Plan-Do-Check-Act cycle for improvement using software measurements. The AMI method is divided in 12 steps with a series of support tools (guidelines, templates and examples), each phase having 3 steps, as shown in Figure 2.

AMI is designed to be flexible enough to employ existing, proven techniques, such as GQM and Software Process Assessment based on SEI's CMM [11]. With the AMI method, the number of metrics that need to be collected is focused on those that correspond to the most important goals. Thus, data collection and analysis costs are limited to the metrics which give the best return. On the other hand, the emphasis on goals and business objectives establishes a clear link to strategic business decisions and helps in the acceptance of measurements by managers, team leaders and engineers.

AMI has a quite flexible structure which allows for it to be easily integrated with other quality and improvement models that may have been already adopted by an organisation prior to AMI. Such is the case, for instance, with CMM which is actually suggested by AMI as the assessment framework to be introduced, if it is not already in use. AMI is designed to support CMM in an effective way by facilitating the implementation of the 'Measurement and Analysis' Common Feature for all Key Process Areas of CMM.

Another such case is ISO 9001 (together with ISO 9000-3 guidelines or even the newer framework provided by ISO 12207 for Software Life Cycle Processes). In this case, AMI provides the necessary foundation for addressing requirements for 'statistical techniques' (ISO 9001), 'measurement' (ISO 9000-3) or 'process improvement data' (ISO 12207). At the same time, during AMI's first step (assessment), besides applying techniques such as CMM assessment, it is recommended to take into account information produced by audits and reviews clearly relating to ISO standards compliance verification.

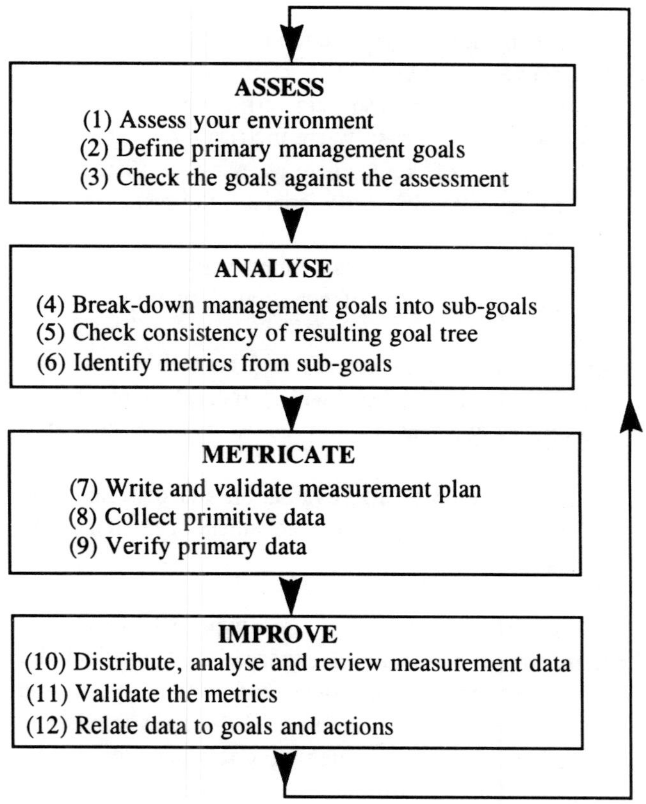

Figure 2. The AMI method.

Based on the experience of AMI users [10], the average cost for the metrication of a project using the AMI approach ranges within 2-5% of the total cost for the software development, decreasing dramatically with the maturing of the metrication process itself (due to reuse of experience). In any case, this cost is much less when compared to the cost of bottom-up metrics approaches, which collect and analyse vast amounts of data.

The AMI method was developed in the context of the AMI project which was funded through the ESPRIT programme to make the technology and techniques of software metrics and measurement available in a simple, straightforward and understandable form that could be easily implemented. The consortium which developed AMI was led by GEC-Marconi and included Alcatel, Bull AG, Objectif Technologie, TECHNOS and South Bank University's Centre for Systems & Software (CSSE).

4. PITA objectives and organisation

The PITA experiment introduces the Goal-Question-Metric approach via the AMI method and tool to INTRACOM's software development practices. The objectives of PITA experiment can be grouped as follows:

- establishment of a systematic GQM-based framework for software metrics
- evaluation of the use and effectiveness of AMI approach to support software metrics
- introduction of a formal assessment (SEI/CMM based) to establish software development process maturity
- identification of process improvement areas and monitoring / support of corresponding improvement actions
- dissemination of experience and know-how on AMI and GQM-metrics, both within INTRACOM and its group, as well as in the Greek and international markets
- continuous monitoring, evaluation and dissemination of results collected from mechanisms established by PITA

A number of benefits are expected from the implementation of the PITA experiment. These include: enabling and focusing improvements, better support and focused follow-up for scheduled CMM assessments and increased capability in achieving goals and controlling processes. Furthermore, it is expected that PITA experiment will result in better software project planning and control, prevention of defects due to requirements and improved product quality. Finally, PITA will contribute to increasing the awareness and motivation of personnel for software process improvement (SPI), as well as, to providing more opportunities for technology transfer and business partnerships.

In the context of the PITA experiment, GQM was integrated as necessary with the selected baseline project. Baseline project selection was based on the availability of new projects, their 'typical' character, and their schedule in relation to the PITA effort. To support the smooth and efficient uptake of AMI method, Objectif Technologie's consulting services were used (training, consulting).

As an **initial step**, setting up of co-ordination and, where required, integration of the experiment with the baseline project was effected. This was done both with the project leader and other key responsible persons, as well as with affected line management and quality engineers. During this step the above personnel was trained in the AMI method. From then on, the basic improvement steps as defined in the AMI method were followed, being implemented at the baseline project. The acquired experience and the confidence built-up for the method allowed similar practices to be gradually taken up in other starting projects as well, even before the experiment was completed.

The four main phases of the PITA experiment, correspond roughly to the 4-step Deming cycle: Plan-Do-Check-Act, supported where possible by the AMI method and tool.

The **first phase** in the PITA experiment, involved the performance of an assessment focused mainly on the baseline project. All relevant information from any preceding projects, any special restrictions, previously available measurements and audit results were taken into account together with the SEI CMM model requirements, ISO 9001 requirements and ISO 9000-3 guidance. The outcome was the definition of primary goals for measurement. In this phase, managers were involved coming both from the baseline project and from other projects as well, representing the viewpoint of the whole software development centre. This activity was co-ordinated by a metrics promoter together with the external AMI consultant.

The **second phase**, concerned the analysis of the primary goals to arrive at sub-goals and relevant metrics. This was formalised as a goals tree with corresponding questions leading to the metrics. This activity was generally carried out by the metrics promoter, the AMI consultant, the project leader, the quality co-ordinator and other experts as necessary.

The **third phase**, concerned the actual metrication, with the introduction of a measurement plan, collection and verification of primitive data which were processed into measurement data. These tasks were initiated and co-ordinated by the metrics promoter with the participation of project personnel.

The **fourth phase** concerned managing the improvement resulting from the implementation of the measurement plan. Goals and questions were used as a guide for the evaluation of measured data and the implementation of corrections or modifications, where necessary. Different sets of data were correlated to validate underlying hypotheses.

In parallel to performing the fourth phase - focused always on the baseline project - the overall evaluation of the degree of success of the experiment took place. All kinds of data stemming from the AMI pilot implementation were utilised for the evaluation. In a follow-up to this phase, data are also becoming gradually available from other AMI implementations in newer projects. As part of the fourth phase, information was disseminated and expertise was transferred to other areas of application, as well as in other departments involved in software development.

The **baseline project** for the PITA experiment was part of a wider project called *FM phase 4.1 Design Project* (FM-p4.1). The purpose of this project was to develop a telecommunications software system for the French market, with a scheduled delivery for June 1997. This system is an improved version of the general part of the operating system for digital telephony exchanges focused on some additional intelligent network functions such as handling of service requests and voice messaging. Additionally, ETSI-ISDN specifications were taken into consideration. This software system will run on Ericsson's AXE-10 digital telephony exchanges.

Baseline project activities were divided among a group of Ericsson subsidiaries and co-operating companies, each undertaking the development of parts of the product's functionality (multi-site development, is a common practice for Ericsson's software development operations).

In the FM-p4.1 project, INTRACOM was responsible for developing a part of the Operation & Maintenance subsystem of the final product. INTRACOM's work focused on Functional Design, Detailed Level Design, Unit Level Test and Function Test phases of the software development process. Function testing was carried out as an autonomous activity. Average resource allocation for the FM-p4.1 at INTRACOM was 10 persons (including a management function) and the budget expressed in development effort was 1,400 person-days.

5. Conducting the experiment

As a first step in the AMI loop, the software process in the software development department was assessed, based on the CMM model. CMM was chosen for the following reasons:

- its recognition as a reference model by many industrial companies and particularly by Ericsson
- the results of a CMM assessment are considered as a credible picture, indicating priorities and general recommendations, as well as being a reusable reference in the future
- CMM is highly compatible both with general INTRACOM's software improvement efforts and the AMI approach

The CMM assessment produced findings that concerned the whole software development organisation. As a reaction, a Software Engineering Process Group (SEPG) was established to address the findings, promote and co-ordinate improvements. The implementation of AMI was since assigned under the overall monitoring authority of this SEPG.

After the CMM assessment, findings were checked with baseline project members and used as a first source of information. Additionally, several other sources of goals were explored, such as Business Goals, project specific priorities, Policy Deployment initiative results, management review findings and audit results (for compliance to ISO 9001 and ISO 9000-3), reports, conclusions and recommendations from previous development projects or past improvement initiatives.

In any case, no attempt was made to systematically cover full CMM compliance with the use of AMI, because of the experimental nature of PITA and for overheads to be minimised. Therefore, only priority issues were covered, based on the judgement of the baseline project team. Still, in the future, AMI could be applied to systematically address full CMM compliance.

In line with the AMI method, a Goal Tree was constructed, aiming at a better development process, but taking also advantage of previous experiments results and integrating different points of view. This tree which is shown below (see Fig. 3), reflects concerns (valid for both the baseline project and the software development department) about simultaneous search of quality and repeatability in planning and reduced time-to-market. As a first attempt, it was deliberately kept simple, while the possibility remains open for other goals to be later included.

The approach taken for implementing AMI was influenced by two different but interrelated factors: the nature of the product from a technical / engineering viewpoint and the business environment together with its priorities.

The software engineering aspect concerns implementation of functionality through software which abides to strict rules, procedures and requirements. Implemented software will have to be integrated within very large systems incorporating critical operations and therefore, demonstrating high level of reliability.

The emphasis is put on early defect detection and prevention, with main focus on implementing systematic and extensive inspections. In this respect, even though there were some goals reflecting CMM Level 2 key process area improvements (e.g. planning and tracking of a project), Peer Reviews from CMM Level 3, which relate closely to technical and product engineering considerations were also addressed as an issue of high priority.

The same argument applies to test efficiency. This is because as long the software design process does not achieve a highly formal and standardised character, there will always be reliance on testing to improve product quality.

Concerning the technology involved in this experiment, even though there exist vast legacy libraries of implemented functions, most of their content is far from a status that could be reused as standard building blocks. Thus modifications required are rather extensive, leading to potentially high defect rates and requiring extra measures for achieving the required quality.

Primary Goal 1. Improve meeting of internal & final delivery date with adherence to process

- **G1.1** Improve preparation and maintenance of the sub-project plan
- **G1.2** Decrease impact of early phases (delays, affected quality) to the later phases
- **G1.3** Improve project monitoring

Primary Goal 2: Improve quality as experienced by the customer

- **G2.1** Improve effectiveness of inspections, reviews
- **G2.2** Improve function test to prevent faults slipping through
- **G2.3** Improve effectiveness of design
- **G2.4** Efficient, adequate technical co-ordination
- **G2.5** Increase competence of people

Figure 3. The PITA experiment Goal Tree.

Improving software quality is thus a key concern of INTRACOM's business as a result of the intensive competition inside the telecommunications domain. Quality is measured based on customer's perception and at regular check-points. At such intermediate points, the measurements / indicators that were introduced reflect several points of view (quality co-ordination, test, design, technical co-ordination). The selected factors should affect positively both the quality directly built into the product (due to design process and personnel competence), as well as the activities that reduce defects (testing, inspection).

Time-to-market is another key element of INTRACOM's competitiveness and is expressed here through delivery dates. This goal has been expressed as improving achievement of delivery dates both internally and externally. Such an objective should be pursued while keeping a coherent and controlled process.

To reach this goal, two major areas of assessment have been addressed simultaneously: planning and tracking. Since achievement of delivery dates is also the result of the whole project life-cycle, the early phases shall be taken into account as real factors, even if in some cases they are not directly controllable. This is, for instance, the case with requirements related to the baseline project which are handled outside INTRACOM. The impact of early phases is therefore taken as a control factor which cannot be directly improved (being out of the scope of the baseline project), but which is measured and monitored. As shown in the assessment report, higher accuracy in estimation and planning lead to increased plan reliability, ability for efficient use of resources and better co-operation.

This work was documented following the general track of AMI, using documentation templates already used internally or recommended by AMI. An example of tabular representation of a particular goal (which is under the primary goal for improving time-to-market) together with its breakdown is given in Figure 4.

Analyse	early phases	*OBJECT*
for the purpose of	decreasing	*PURPOSE*
with respect to	adverse impact	*QUALITY FOCUS*
from the viewpoint of	project team	*VIEWPOINT*
in the environment of	FMp4.1 Project	*ENVIRONMENT*

<table>
<tr><td>Quality Focus
1. Rework effort due to early phase impact</td><td>Factors Impacting on Quality Focus
A. Requirements stability
B. Late events, reviews
C. Open technical issues</td><td>Change/ Control
A. Control
B. Control
C. Control</td></tr>
<tr><td>Baseline/ Current/ Estimated Quality Focus
1. <Current Value of Indicator>
Expected Quality Focus
1. < Indicator Target Value></td><td colspan="2">Factors' Impact on Quality Focus
(Note: +/- means positive/negative trend)
A. The less the requirements change, the less the project is affected (-T)
B. Delaying events can delay decisions and lead to more rework (-T)
C. Open issues can force to rework (-T)</td></tr>
</table>

Figure 4. Goal Breakdown Template.

The next step in refining the GQM plan involved identifying metrics for the quality focuses and impacting factors. As an example, Figure 5 illustrates the case of the goal for improving the effectiveness of inspections and reviews (within the primary goal for improved quality). In this Figure, a combination of focus-impacting factor-question-metrics is presented.

Goal: Improve effectiveness of inspections, reviews

Quality Focus: #3 Relative Effectiveness of Inspection Defect Detection in all life-cycle

Impacting Factor: Inspection preparation

Question: To which degree process and criteria are respected prior to the execution step?

[**Hypothesis**: The document(s) for inspection, according to applied procedure is (are) to be made available to inspectors at least 5 days in advance; if not so, then a postponement is required and the process is still respected according to this factor.]

Metrics:

1. Percentage of documents handed-over at least 5-days before inspection
2. Average actual preparation per inspector
3. Average preparation rate per inspector (inspection object size/effort)
4. Average total preparation per meeting

Figure 5. Metrics identification example

The approach taken in identifying metrics did not involve some advanced process control model but it reflected the actual procedure used and the experiences and maturity of the development team.

This principle was observed throughout the experiment since it is a precondition for ensuring acceptance, participation and commitment of the development team, for which improvement goals and opportunities should derive naturally and in a non-obstructive way.

On the other hand, if one introduces an advanced technique such as Gilb's inspections, as an improvement towards the goal in Figure 5, it will only be natural to use more advanced metrics, based on the mechanics of the new method. This latter approach was outside the scope of the experiment described here, but may be used in the future, AMI inherently having the potential to support such an improvement.

In PITA, the objective was to assess the current process maturity and establish metrics that would entail improvement through better control and exploitation of standard processes or enhanced processes already introduced prior to this experiment.

At the same time, relatively simple metrics were identified and basic statistics and graphs were used as analytical tools, avoiding complex approaches, obscure to the development team who are the main beneficiaries of the introduction of AMI. Thus, quantification did not advance to a level higher than that of existing processes or beyond personnel experiences and maturity.

After the metrics definition step, a measurement plan was set-up including a measurements list (as a table), mechanisms for data collection, roles and responsibilities and a detailed list of possible attributes for measurement description as shown in Figure 6.

Name: (as in a summary and quick reference table)

Goal: reminds goal as a textual information

Collection procedure: how the metric is collected, if more information is required (form and frequencies are defined in the table)

Presentation: the way data are shown, with practical examples

Analysis procedure: how the metric is used, how trends (+/-) are analysed

Responsibilities: for collection, for analysis

Figure 6. Measurement Description Attributes.

Regarding the effort spent for the above tasks, the CMM assessment was performed during one week (excluding the time spent for assessment-related preparation and training). It involved approximately 50 people from all the levels of INTRACOM's software developing organisation and 5 full-time team members. Goal tree derivation and documentation up to the measurement plan preparation involved partially 7 persons, and lasted approximately 4 months. From then on, the project team proceeded with measurement collection, presentation and analysis. The final evaluation, involved a wider improvements addressing team (within the SEPG scope of activities).

A particular aspect of this effort involved establishing an automated on-line environment for data collection, which greatly facilitated the work of the development team and greatly reduced the measurements overhead.

6. Experiences from the experiment

Due to INTRACOM's lengthy software development cycle (18 months till field operation is well under way), data for metrics that have been defined in the baseline project, are still flowing in. The data collection period will be considered finalised towards the end of 1997.

At the same time, other later projects where AMI has been or is being introduced are producing data and thus, a measurement baseline for process capability indicators is gradually being built and allows a realistic and systematic planning and tracking of quantifiable improvement goals. The table in Figure 7, provides an indicative set of metrics results collected from the baseline project.

Goal: Establish behaviour in Inspection / Review Effectiveness (of PITA baseline project)

Metrics Definition - Background	Measured Result
Focus: Relative inspection defect detection effectiveness **G2.1 Metric**: (insp. detected defects)/(total # of defects detected in insp., function +system testing, 6mo. in operation) % Estimated current performance: 68% Target performance: 80% [partial current. - function test defects: 72%]	Partial result available (function test defects) 84% (vs. Current 72%)
A. Impacting factor (question): Inspection planning	
A1. % of inspections on planned date Estimated current performance: 84% Target: 90%	86%
A2. % of inspections with planned composition Estimated current performance: 87% Target: 90%	82%
A3. % of inspections held with experienced moderators Estimated current performance: 95% Target: 100%	98%
A4. % of inspect. held with technical expert Estimated current performance: 90% Target: 100%	96%
B. Impacting factor: Inspection preparation	
B1. % of documents available min. 5 days prior to inspection Estimated current performance: 91% Target: 100%	96%
B2. Total effort / inspection object Estimated current performance: 12.7hrs Target: Not established	14.45hrs
C. Impacting factor: Inspection conduct	
C1. % of inspections lasting within 2±1hr Estimated current performance: 85% Target: 100%	92%
C2. Insp. efficiency: (# Maj. Remarks / Total effort) Estimated current performance: 0.26/hr Target: Not established	0.21/hr

Figure 7. Sample metrics and results from PITA baseline project.

As a comment to the results given in the table above, one can witness an improvement in many indicators, from the ones estimated on partial data available from the past ('current performance'). Indicative 'target' performance is given, (not really an improvement goal yet, as explained below).

It is not possible at this point, to correlate the improvement shown, with AMI application (since this a first application). On the other hand, since this was a pilot application, one should consider the possibility for a Hawthorn effect (enhanced motivation, carefulness which may diminish in future applications).

In any case, the results need several application cycles to become conclusive and stable. In the long run, trends will appear and will be possible to be validated in a positive way, that could be correlated to the result of analysis, feedback, identification of problem areas by development teams, corrective actions etc.

During this exercise and based on experiences and results obtained up to this point, some issues proved to be of particular importance and lessons were learned thereof. A number of important points are summarised below.

AMI method's power has been proven as a means to consolidate various ongoing improvement activities. It is a fact that an organisation like INTRACOM found it necessary or useful in the past to embark on several such initiatives. These were planned and effected in a more or less formal way and conformed to different models and approaches. One problem often experienced with these activities is that they were not consistent with each other. Also for each activity, planning and monitoring were rather inadequate and their overall effectiveness was limited. On the other hand, measurements been collected were not clearly associated to particular objectives or sometimes variations of metrics were used for similar goals, increasing complexity and decreasing comprehension by development teams, eventually having little or no use. The AMI approach provided the unifying structure that was missing for clearly identifying and quantifying goals and for gaining visibility towards their progress.

A particular strength of the AMI approach is the systematic identification of goals based on an assessment of current practices. A suitable form of assessment is the SEI/CMM model (or equivalent). The performance of SEI/CMM assessment at INTRACOM led to a report that presented the findings of weak process areas and included correction / improvement recommendations. Both findings and recommendations in the report were evaluated by INTRACOM management and key personnel, leading to plans for actions to achieve improvements.

This course is co-ordinated and monitored by the SEPG which was instituted as the main improvement body. Implementation of such actions are effected by adopting practices and formalisms being successfully introduced within the PITA baseline project. In this way, process improvements are being significantly facilitated and supported by the application AMI, combined with CMM-based assessments. In addition, other objectives concerned with quality assurance (ISO-9001 based), productivity and lead time reduction are also being integrated in a unified AMI approach to software improvement / metrication.

In cases where there are no extensive and reliable historical data to establish baseline process performance and/or the process is immature and unstable, it was necessary to use essentially *knowledge* instead of *improvement* goals. The focus in this case is on establishing a baseline process performance (to enable better control) instead of attempting big improvements and changes.

Still, the use of even tentative target values for the various measured goals is important to enable indicative analysis of results and validation of the GQM model that was derived. Thus, in all cases during the PITA experiment, target value ranges were defined, either based on historical data when available, or on assumptions and hypotheses that had then to be validated themselves (see example in Figure 7 above).

This is more or less a common occurrence at this stage of maturity in applying AMI. In such cases, more than one cycle of application will be required before the GQM plan and respective performance baseline data stabilise and are validated enough to become reusable in a way that could support planned improvements.

The experience from PITA shows that various goals and measurements may exist before a systematic measurement plan is introduced based on AMI. Thus, as a first step, all such pre-existing goals and measurements should be listed and evaluated. In general, careful and systematic co-ordination of various SPI activities as well as measurements used should be performed to avoid conflicts and duplication.

When analysing results, especially when processes are relatively immature and not effectively controlled, special care should be taken to avoid easily-reached conclusions and judgements. The development team should be involved in such analysis and conclusions should be validated with them, to avoid a risk of reduced buy-in and loss of credibility for the value of the AMI-related SPI activity.

Thus, as explained in the example above (Fig. 7), some favourable changes in the indexes to date, have been analysed but, except for particular instances, no clear conclusions were found whether a positive trend was exhibited.

Still, numerical feedback proved useful in focusing attention on the pertinent issues and especially in these modules where there was significant variation from average. No clear conclusion was drawn even in such cases due to the scarcity of data and to avoid over-reaction to effects that could be attributed to random causes or to the combination of factors (e.g. due to complexity).

Long-term measurements based on late phase results such as testing or field performance, are important in providing the overall picture for both product and process and in validating the derived GQM plan. Such long-term measurements need to be balanced with short-term metrics, based on data and facts becoming available during the progress of the project. These later ones, provide timely feedback to support in-process decision making and enable more effective closed-loop management of project tasks.

Currently, only function test results are collected and give a superficial indication of improvement in some indexes (e.g. effectiveness of inspections) while system test and field use results (defects) are expected later in 1997.

Visibility of GQM results by the development team is very important. Results visibility supports participation and motivation of the development team regarding SPI work. Short-term goals should be set to provide software developers with feedback on SPI results and ensure their involvement and collaboration.

One particular problem in applying the AMI method, especially to long life-cycle projects, is the fact that towards the last phases where system test and operational data are becoming available, most of the project team members have been reassigned to other work (only maintenance/support kernel group is active) to effect meaningful feedback sessions. Still, there has been organisational provision to get as many as possible project members together again to a final evaluation and feedback session.

In the meantime, a permanent organisation being institutionalised under the SEPG and implemented within each application area unit (starting from the one the baseline project belonged), performs ongoing analysis to results collected and provides a continuity in experience, offering input and advice to new projects in order to apply AMI efficiently.

As regards the costs and ROI of the experiment, the general experience of the AMI community is validated by INTRACOM's experience to date, giving roughly a 4-5% overhead to development costs. This overhead concerns initial direct costs to the project, excluding initial training, performance of CMM assessment, institutionalisation of SEPG, establishment of on-line facilities to measurement collection, general evaluation, administrative and dissemination costs required for the experiment. These are costs related to line organisation's support of the experiment and would be amortised over a multitude of projects taking advantage of the experience. If such costs would apply to the baseline project, then the overhead would rise to prohibitive levels (30% or even 40%).

On the other hand, it is expected that in new applications of AMI, the direct overheads will be reduced to around 2% of development effort, leaving room to effect other specific improvements at project level (which AMI will actually facilitate and support).

7. Conclusions and further activities

As the PITA project was progressing, results from the baseline project were validated and analysed. Based on such analysis, specific corrections or further improvements to development processes were proposed (by the development team). Next, an evaluation of the derived GQM plan (model) was effected, in order to validate its correctness and to modify it, if and where necessary.

An overall evaluation of the effectiveness and benefits of the experiment were performed based on latest data. The experience was packaged (in the form of a generic GQM plan and implementation procedure, that can be tailored to the needs of individual projects), so that the approach together with all necessary improvements could be available for reuse within INTRACOM.

Goal tree analysis and metrication based on PITA experience are already being introduced widely (to all new projects) to support specific improvement goals like for instance, improving the effectiveness of software inspections. Enhancing testing effectiveness is another area that is being institutionalised based on PITA experience.

A significant effort is devoted to dissemination activities, both internally to INTRACOM and externally, for interested parties both in the Greek and the European market of software developers.

Internally, PITA was organised and executed in such a way, so as to ensure maximum transferability of acquired experiences. One important provision was the performance of an organisation-wide CMM assessment, setting a context for improvements covering the whole software developing organisation.

The AMI application on the baseline project, was largely based on the outcome of that assessment and the derived GQM plan is expected therefore, to be easily adaptable for other projects.

As a follow-up of the CMM-assessment performed in the context of PITA and in order to improve monitoring of improvements in various key process areas, the 'Light CMM assessment' method was introduced in 1997 based on approach of Daskalantonakis [12].

Particular goals (e.g. inspections related) and measurements from the derived GQM plan could be adopted/standardised across INTRACOM's software developing organisation. This will allow internal bench-marking, in order to identify and promote best practices.

Other goals identified in various SPI activities are also to be analysed and measured with AMI. In particular, the AMI approach will be used to measure the progress and the effectiveness of another CEU-funded ESSI experiment called PIBOP ('Process Improvement through PSP'), introducing Watt Humphrey's Personal Software Process at INTRACOM's software development practices.

Externally, various dissemination activities to present PITA approach and results are scheduled, including participation in conferences, workshops, seminars, publication in magazines, newsletters and the Internet (WEB page that will be kept up to date).

One particular target group involves Ericsson and its subsidiaries, that are seriously engaged in SPI based on CMM. INTRACOM collaborates with those companies, both on software development, and on process improvement.

As a general remark, the approach followed by PITA is quite generic and should be easily replicated or adapted to a wide range of software developing organisations. A particular forum of disseminating PITA experiences, is the AMI User Group, where INTRACOM's experiences and results are compared to similar ones from other organisations having applied AMI.

8. References

[1] B. W. Boehm, "Software Risk management: principles and practices", *IEEE Software*, Jan. 1991, pp. 32-41.

[2] F. P. Brooks, *The Mythical Man-Month*, Addison Wesley, 1995.

[3] *METKIT Software Engineering Measurement Teaching Materials*. Information is available on Web page URL : http://www.sbu.ac.uk/~csse/ metkit.html.

[4] T. Matsubara,"Project Management in Japan", *American Programmer*, June 1991, pp. 41-50.

[5] R. B. Grady, *Practical Software Metrics for Project Management and Process Improvement*, Prentice Hall, 1992, ISBN 0-13-720384 -5.

[6] R.B. Grady, *Software Metrics: Establishing a company-wide program*, Prentice Hall, ISBN 0-13-821844-7, 1987

[7] K. H. Moeuller and D. J. Paulish, *Software Metrics: A Practitioner's Guide to Improved Product Development*, Chapman & Hall, 1992.

[8] V. R. Basili, G. Caldiera, H. D. Rombach, 'The Goal Question Metric Approach', *Encyclopedia of Software Engineering*, volume 1, John Wiley & Sons, 1994, pp. 528-532

[9] C. Gresse, B. Hoisl, J. Wust, *A Process Model for GQM-based Measurement*, Kaiserslautern University (Postfach 3049 D-67653, Kaiserslautern, Germany), STTI Report STTI-95-04-E

[10] K. Pulford, A. Kuntzmann-Combelles, S. Shirlaw, *A quantitative approach to Software Management - The ami Handbook*, Addison-Wesley Publishing Company, ISBN 0-201-87746-5, 1996.

[11] M.C. Paulk, C.V. Weber, B. Curtis, M.B. Chriss, *The Capability Maturity Model: Guidelines for Improving the Software Process*, Addison-Wesley Publishing Company, 1995, ISBN 0-201-54664-7.

[12] M.K. Daskalantonakis, "Achieving Higher SEI Levels", *IEEE Software,* July 1994, pp. 17-24

An Estimated Method for Software Testability Measurement

Jin-Cherng Lin, Szu-Wen Lin & Ian-Ho
Dept. of Computer Science and Engineering
Tatung Institue of Technology
Taipei 10451, Taiwan, R.O.C
jclin@cse.ttit.edu.tw
swlin061@ms3.hinet.net
Tel: (02)592-5252 ext 3295
Fax: (02)592-5252 ext 2288

Abstract

Software testability is becoming an important factor to be considered during software development and assessment, especially for those critical softwares. This paper gives software testability, previously defined by Voas, a new model and measurement which is done before random black-box testing with repect to a particular input distribution. We also compared our measurement results with the one simulated according with Voas's model. It showed that our rough testability estimate provides enough information and will be used as guidelines for software development.

Keywords : software testability, error propagation, data state infection, location execution, domain/range ratio

1. Preliminary

It is believed that software industry is at a risk for a disaster or some kind, a disaster in which the blame will clearly lay to software, and all will be tarred with the brush used on the unlucky developer. Nowadays, many computer systems are used in critical applications such as spacecraft and defense systems. When lives and fortunes depend on software, software quality and its verification demand increased attention. But how can we access the acceptable safety and reliability of such critical software? When can we say that the software is reliable enough; testing can be stopped and the software can be released ?

In the past, much research on software testing has concentrated on methods for selecting effective sets of test data [3], variously based on program specification, on program structure, or on hypotheses about likely faults. Testing tries to reveal software faults by executing the program and comparing the expected output with the one produced so that it can guarantee correctness. Much effort has been put in to answer the question: "what is the probability that the program will fail?" However, software testing can not show the absolute absence of failure unless it is exhaustive [2]. Therefore, if testing is to be effective at all, then non-exhaustive testing must be performed in a manner that offers some degree of confidence that the code is reliable. Here, we ask another question: "what is the probability that the program will fail, if it is faulty?" We present another technique, software testability analysis, that will help developers make the assessment. We focus on some program characteristics that make faults hard to find with random black-box testing.

Assessing a program's testability, T, is a hard task, and much research has explored this problem [14, 6, 4]. However, the analyses of testability in the past were done after testing, especially with random black-box testing. In [13], we got an example of estimating testability for a program finding an integral solution to the quadratic equation $ax^2 + bx + c$ for integral values of a, b, c. The experiment with 121000 input was performed on such a tiny program to get the execution, infection, propagation analysis. We would like to ask, how much test data would be required for a bigger and complicated program? Moreover, how much effort would be made to find the expected results to verify the test data? From this point of view, we suggest another analysis technique to gain the testability of a software by checking the source code instead of testing it. Doing so, it can not only reduce the effort and cost at testing step, but also give a direction for debugging because low testability implies that faults are more easily hidden during testing.

2. Related works

2.1. Fault-failure model

Any assessment of testability must be based on a model of the fault/failure relationship. The following simple model of this relationship has been proposed in [7, 12]:

Each textual location in a program is considered as a possible location of a fault. At a given location, a possible fault could result in a failure if and only if:

1. A fault must be executed.
2. The fault must affect the state of the program in a manner different than what the state of the program would have been had the fault not existed. This is termed as having an infection in the state.
3. The erroneous program state must propagate to an output state.

This model is very simplistic, because it imagines that faults at a single location; however, it can be used to define as practical approximation of testability.

If we confine the possibility of a program's failure to this model, the probability that a fault will turn into a failure will be the product of execution probability, infection probability and propagation probability. Furthermore, a lower bound on testability of a program is obtained as the least product above over all locations in the program.

2.2. PIE

PIE--propagation analysis, infection analysis, execution analysis--is a dynamic technique for statistically estimating the effects that a location of a program has on the program's computational behavior. PIE analysis collects information concerning the semantics of faults. It does not reveal the existence of faults, nor does the technique directly evaluate the ability of inputs to reveal the existence of faults. Instead, it identifies locations in a program where faults, if they do exist, are more likely to remain undetected during testing. The technique is based on fault/failure model and it estimates the probability of the three characteristics of a location:

1. the probability that the location is executed on inputs selected from the assumed input distribution of the software.
2. the probability that if a mutant exists at this location, it will adversely change the data states;
3. the probability that if the data state is adversely changed that that will propagate to the output.

The following is the detailed definition for PIE analysis [14, 11] GLet S denote a specification, P denote an implementation of S, x denote a program input, Δ denote the set of all possible inputs to P, D denote the probability distribution of Δ, l denote a program location in P. Then

$\hat{\varepsilon}_{lPD}$ is the proportion of inputs (selected according to D) that causes location l to be executed.

Let $1 \le y \le z_l$, M_l represents a set of Z_l mutants of location l :$\{m_{l1}, m_{l2}, \ldots m_{lz_l}\}$ (where $1 \le y \le z_l$) [5].

$\hat{\lambda}_{mlylpD}$ of mutant m_{ly} is the probability that the succeeding data state of location l is different than the succeeding data state that mutant m_{ly} creates.

$\hat{\psi}_{alPD}$ for a simulated infection affecting variable a in the data state succeeding location l (where this data state is created by a randomly selected input x according to D) is the probability that P's output differs (from that would normally be produced) after execution is resumed using the simulated infection.

Let θ_l denote the testability of some location l , then

$$\theta_l = \varepsilon_{lPD} * \sigma\left[\left(\min_{m_{ly}}\left(\hat{\lambda}_{m_{ly}lPD}\right), \min_{a}\left(\hat{\psi}_{alPD}\right)\right)\right]$$

where $\sigma(a,b) = \begin{cases} a-(1-b) & \text{if } a-(1-b) > 0 \\ 0 & \text{otherwise} \end{cases}$

2.3. PISCES

PISCES is the commercial software testability tool which is written in C++ and operates on programs written in C. It implements the PIE technique defined in [13, 14]. PISCES produces testability estimates by creating an "instrumented" copy of the program and then compiling and executing the instrumented copy, which is about 10 times as large as the original source code, with inputs that are either supplied in a file or PISCES uses random distributions from which it generates inputs.

If PISCES is performed in its entirety, we will have:

$\hat{\varepsilon}_l$: the estimate of the probability that program location l is executed.

$\left\{\hat{\lambda}_{l,p1}, \hat{\lambda}_{l,p2}, \ldots\right\}$: the estimates of the probabilities, one estimate for each mutant in $\{p_1, p_2, \ldots\}$ at program location l, that given the program is executed, the mutant will adversely affect the program state

$\left\{\hat{\psi}_{l,a1}, \hat{\psi}_{l,a2}, \ldots\right\}$: the estimates of the probabilities, one estimate for each live variable in $\{a_1, a_2, \ldots\}$ at program location l, that given that the live variable in the program state following the program location is perturbed.

Then, a PISCES testability postprocessor inputs all probability estimates and allows the user several choices of how the testability will be displayed: either for a location, a module or for the entire program.

The value of this tool to software quality is two-fold: improved testing, and improved debugging [9].

2.4. DRR

The domain/range ratio (DRR) of a specification denoted by $\alpha : \beta$ [10] is the ratio between the cardinality of the domain to the cardinality of the range. It is one of the important factors in determining whether the software is likely to hide faults. For example, f(x)=2x corresponds to a DRR of $\infty_I : \infty_I$ (the symbol ∞_I denoted the cardinality of integers). The specification f(x) has only one possible input for x for any output f(x). It is a one-to-one function, which implies high testability. The function f(x)=sqr(x), however, mandates a loss of information because both x=5 and x=-5 produce the same internal state after execution f(x). It may be that the negative integer could signal a problem with the software, but f(x) will erase that information in the output. Previous research [8] has also suggested that many-to-one computable function tends to have lower testability since the phenomenon--called internal state collapse--that its internal state is not communicated in its output always occurs. By paying attention to the DRRs, we can potentially give a closer insight for the estimate of testabilities, especially for infection estimate.

3. Software testability analysis

Software testability analysis measures the benefit produced by a software testing scheme to a particular program. There are several ways to define software testability [1]. For instance, it is regarded to as the ease with which some input selection criteria can be satisfied during testing. Thus, a program is said to have "low testability" if it is difficult to find inputs that can satisfy a particular structural coverage criterion (Ex: branch testing) for the given program. Another view of software testability defines it as a prediction of the probability that existing faults will be revealed during testing given an arbitrary input selection criterion C [14]. The former definition focuses on syntactic features, whereas the latter, semantic analysis. In either definition, software testability analysis result is a function of a (*program, input selection criteria*) pair [14]. Therefore, a program may have varying T when presented with varying input selection criteria. Moreover, because T refers to a probability, testability is bounded in a closed interval [0,1].

3.1. Terminology

A ***failure*** is the event where a program's output is not compliment with the specification [1]. Using the definition in [10], a failure occurs because the program enters an erroneous state. Hence, an ***error*** is a part of the state that can lead to a failure. A ***fault*** in a location is the cause of an error. Here, we define a ***location*** as a single instruction--an assignment, input/output statement, a <condition> part of *if* or *while* statement and procedure calls. As for the definition of "***software testability***," we use the one provided in the early 90's Voas [13, 14] : a prediction of the probability of software failure occurring if the software were to contain a fault, given that software execution is with respect to a particular input distribution during random black-box testing. It consists of three estimates, similar to PIE [15] at each location:

Execution estimate: The likelihood that the location is executed on inputs selected from the assumed input distribution of the software.

Infection estimate: The likelihood that if a mutant exits at certain location, it will change the data state.

Propagation estimate: The likelihood that if the data state has been changed, the change will propagate to the output.

For any test case to reveal a fault at a specified location, execution, infection, propagation must occur; without these three events occurring, the execution will not result in failure. Thus for a specific fault, the product of the estimates of these three events occurring yields an estimate of the probability of failure that would occur when this location contains a fault. This is the testability of that location. We then take the location with the lowest non-zero testability to be the testability overall program.

3.2. The model of testability measurement

We determine testability by the code's structure and semantics, and by an assumed input distribution. Thus two programs with the same function may have different testabilities. Since a fault can lie anywhere in a program, we should take all places in the source code into consideration when estimating testability.

In the paper, we consider that the fault might exist at any location in the program. We have purposely limited the faults to single faults to avoid the explosion that occurs in the number of combinatorial changes that could be made at each location. Furthermore, the faults considered in our research are limited to faults of arithmetic expressions and predicates. For arithmetic expressions, the faults considered are limited to single changes to a location--this is similar to the mutations used in mutation testing [5]. For assignment predicates, the faults include: (1) A wrong variable/constant substitution, (2) a variable substituted for a constant, (3) a constant substituted for a variable, (4) a wrong operator. For boolean predicates, the faults considered included: (1) wrong variable/constant substitution, (2) a wrong equality/inequality operator substitution, (3) exchanging *and* and *or*.

Estimate for "E"

Case 1: For any sequential statement, E =1.

Case 2: For any *if* or *while* statement, E is still 1.

Case 3: For the statement in execution body of *if* or *while*,

if there is some clear domain/range ratio for the <control> part of *if* or *while*, we can estimate the execution rate as domain/range ratio or (1-domain/range ratio), depending on whether location l is in *yes* or *no* execution body of if or while.

if there isn't, then we give a weight of certain branch according to the graphic theorem: the number of branches on data flow diagram at location l

Since there might be a lot of paths from the program beginning to a specified location, and the program structure might be complicated--there might be nested branches, we conclude that the estimate for "E" as follows:

For any location l, there are n paths from the program beginning to l --with k branches on every path, the execution estimate of l would be the summation of execution rate along i-th path. Thus,

$E = \sum_{i=1}^{n} E_{p_i}$ where E_{p_i} is the execution rate of a specified location on the i-th path

$E_{p_i} = \prod_{j=0}^{k} e_j$ where e_0=1

e_j is the domain/range ratio, (1-domain/range) ratio, or branch weight at the j-th branch on i-th path before l

See appendix for detailed calculation.

Estimate for "I"

The estimate for "I" is much related with the number of tokens--operands and operators--in a location. If location l is an assignment, we only consider the right-side of the assignment because any incorrect variable substation on the left-side is hard to predict and control. Furthermore, we treat the constants as variables and their I_{l_opd}=1. The following is the calculation of I for location l :

- If location l is an input/output statement, we give every input/output variable a unique infection estimate. For example: if the location is a statement like "read(a,b,c)", then it will have three infection estimates: $I_a = I_b = I_c = 1$
- Others:

$$I_l = \frac{1}{n} \left(\sum_{i=1}^{op} I_{l\_opr_i} + \sum_{j=1}^{od} I_{l\_opd_j} \right)$$

op: the number of the operators or built-in functions on the right -side of the assignment, boolean predicate, or in the <condition> part of *if* or *while* statements.

od: the number of the operands on the right-side of the assignment, boolean predicate, or in the <condition> part of *if* or *while* statements.

n: the number of tokens; op+od=n.

$I_{l\_opr_i}$: the infection weight, I_w, of the i-th operator or built-in function See Table 1 for I_w of some operators and built-in functions.

operator, built-in function	I_w
+, −, ×, /	1
>, <, =, ≦, ≠, ≧	DRR or 1
a mod b (b is a constant)	(b-1)/b
a div b (b is a constant)	([a/b]-1) / [a/b]
others (ex. Trunc, round, div, mod, even,...)	1/2

Table 1. I_w for some operators and built-in functions

$$I_{l\_opd_j} : \begin{cases} \text{variable} & I_{l'} \\ \text{constant} & 1 \end{cases}$$

$I_{l'}$: the infection estimate at some location l', where the j-th operand is lastly defined.

Also see appendix for detailed calculation

Estimate for "P"

The estimate for P here is much different from the one defined by Voas. Voas considered all of the input variables and the variables which were assigned during the program. They were all treated as perturbed variables. According to the definition provided in [14], the propagation probability for location l is the minimum value among the probabilities got by perturbing all the perturbed variables. In our research, however, we only considered the variable *used* in the <condition> part of *if* or *while* statement or the definition of variable v at location l as the perturbed variable. We think that it will have much affect on the propagation analysis at location l.

Here we would like to define ***use*** or ***definition*** of variable v first :

A *use* of variable v is an instruction X in which this variable is referenced. A use can be in a test instruction (the <condition> part of *if* or *while* statement), on the right-side of an assignment instruction or an output instruction.

A *definition* of variable v is an instruction X which assigns a value to that variable. A definition can be an assignment instruction or input instruction.

Now the algorithm for estimating P is as follows :

1. For a specified location l, find the variable v, which is defined.
2. From location l', find location l', where v is used after it is executed at location l. And l', is the new specified location.
3. Get $I_{l'}$ of location

Repeat step 1, 2, 3 until we reach the output statement.

If we can't reach the output statement, then $I_{l'}$=0

else $P_l = \prod I_{l'}$

See appendix for detailed calculation

Loop, while Repeat

We treat the whole loop as a single statement. We give the whole loop a testability score which is the smallest testability score among the ones for every statement in the body of the loop.

If the loop is finite, no matter how many times the loop will iterate, the testability score of the loop is estimated by running the loop body once because we can extend the loop like a series of sequential statements.

4. Performance discussion

We have implemented our new model of measurement to a simple program. The following is the source code of the simple program, and Table 2 is our measurement for the program's testability compared with those based on Voas's model. Every location has two results. The first row of the result is gained by simulating Voas's algorithm, whereas the second row is our measurement based on our model.

```
Location No.
 1       read(a,b,c);
 4       if a <>0 then begin
 5          d:=b*b-4*a*c;
 6          if d<0 then
 7             x:=0
            else
 8             x:=(-b+trunc(sqrt(d))) div (2*a)
         end
         else
 9       x:=-c div b;
 10      writeln(x);
```

No.	Fault	E	I	P	T
5	b*b-5*a*c	0.9090	0.8264	0.9009	0.6767
		0.9090	0.9090	0.7664	0.6333
5	b*b-4*c*c	0.9090	0.7438	0.9009	0.6091
		0.9090	0.9173	0.7665	0.6391
5	c*c-4*a*c	0.9090	0.9083	0.9009	0.7438
		0.9090	0.9000	0.7847	0.6420
5	b*b+4*a*c	0.9090	0.8264	0.9009	0.6768
		0.9090	0.9090	0.7664	0.6333
8	x:=-a+trunc(sqrt(d)) div (2*a)	0.9014	0.9082	0.8186	0.6701
		0.9996	0.8106	0.8106	0.6558

Table 2 Testability Estimates

From Table 2, we can find that the testability derived from our model is almost close to the one got by simulating Vaos's PIE model. Since a program's testability is depend on its input data distribution, our results are still accurate when comparing with the results gained by exhaustively testing based on Voas's model.

Please note that it doesn't make sense to say which model is neither only according to the higher testability it gets because a program testability is related with its input data distribution and neither Voas' model nor our model proposed is exhaustive testing in Table 2.

As for the application of testability, other papers showed that testability can help us make decisions about debug testing [13] and make predictions about reliability [9]. Furthermore, the measures of testability which is proposed in this paper can be used to draw inferences on program correctness because a program has passed a certain number of tests without failing--with a high value of testability and implies a high probability that the program is correct.

5. Concluding remarks

Software testability is becoming an important factor to consider during the software development and assessment. We contend that the preliminary results of our software testability analysis are sufficient to motivate additional research into quantify software testability analysis. Not only do we think that this technique may help assess critical systems but it is also acknowledged as a technique that should be further explored for its enormous impact on assessing ultra-reliable software.

Though our testability analysis is somewhat time-consuming, we have felt that our new model of measurement is worth to make a prediction for software testability without any testing. Obviously, our research does have great contribution on software testability measurement since a tiny program proposed in [13] would need more than 100000 input data, it is without mentioning that any program with more functions and complicated structures would extremely take lots of time. Our future research will focus on empirically exploring different strategies. We expect that the model of measurement will be implemented as a tool for further testability predictions.

Appendix

We work through the program of finding the integral solutions of a quadratic function.

Location No. e_j

```
1        read(a,b,c);
4  e1    if a<>0 then begin
5          d:=b*b-4*a*c;
6  e2        if d<0 then
7              x:=0
           else
8              x:=(-b+trunc(sqrt(d)))div 2*a)
         end
         else
9          x:=-c div b;
10         written(x);
```

Here is the execution (E), infection (I), and propagation (P) estimates with different mutants.

Example 1:

l_5: $d = b*b - 5*a*c$

Execution estimate(E)：

$E = E_{p_1} = e_1 = {}^{10}\!/_{11}$ the range of a is [0,10]

∴the execution rate of "a<>0" is ${}^{10}\!/_{11}$

Infection estimate(I)：

For "b*b-5*a*c" op=5, od=4

$$I_{l5} = {}^{1}\!/_{9}\left[\sum_{i=1}^{op} I_{l\_opr_i} + \sum_{j=1}^{od} I_{l\_opdr_j}\right] - \text{information loss}$$

$=1/9[(1+1+1+1+1)+(1+1+1+1)]-1/11=10/11$

information loss :

For "d=b*b-5*a*c", information loss will occur when either a or c is 0. Since location 5 is in the right execution body of the branch, that means a<>0, the probability that information loss will occur would be 1/11 (when c=0).

Propagation estimate(P)：

$P_5 = I_{l_6} \times I_{l_8}$ Because d is defined at l_5 and used at l_6 and l_8, get I_{l_6};x is defined at l_8 and used at l_{10}, get I_{l_8}

where $I_{l_6} = 1/3[10/11+1+1] = 32/33$

I_{l_8} : The infection estimate for location 8 is done by eliminating the parentheses step by step. For example :

I(sqrt(d))＝10/11 ∵d is defined at location 3 with infection estimate 10/11

I(trunc(sqrt(d))＝1/2×10/11＝5/11 ∵I_w of the built-in function "trunc" is 1/2

I(-b＋trunc(sqrt(d))) ＝1/4[1+1+1+5/11]＝19/22

I(2*a)＝1/3[1+1+1]＝1

I(-b＋trunc(sqrt(d))div(2*a))＝1/3[19/22+1/2+1]＝26/33＝I_{l_8}

$P_5 = I_{l_6} \times I_{l_8} = 32/33 \times 26/33 \fallingdotseq 0.764$

Example 2

l_5: $d = b*b - 4*c*c$

Execution estimate(E):

$E = E_{p_1} = e1 = {}^{10}\!/_{11}$

the range of a is [0,10]

$\therefore$ the execution rate of "a<>0" is ${}^{10}\!/_{11}$

Infection estimate(I):

For "b*b-4*c*c" op=5, od=4

$$I_{l5} = \frac{1}{9}\left[\sum_{i=1}^{op} I_{l\_opr_i} + \sum_{j=1}^{od} I_{l\_opdr_j}\right] - \text{information loss}$$

$=1/9[(1+1+1+1+1)+(1+1+1+1)]-(1\times10\times1000)/(11\times1000\times11)$

$=111/121$

information loss :

For "d=b*b-4*c*c", information loss will occur when either a or c is 0. Since location 5 is in the right execution body of the branch, that means a<>0, the probability that information loss will occur would be 10/121 (when c=0,a==1~10, b=1~1000).

Propagation estimate(P):

$P_5 = I_{l_6} \times I_{l_8}$ Because d is defined at l_5 and used in l_6 and l_8, get I_{l_6}; x is defined at l_8 and used at l_{10}, get I_{l_8}

where $I_{l_6} = 1/3[111/121+1+1] = 353/363$

I_{l_8} : The infection estimate for location 8 is done by eliminating the parentheses step by step. For example:

I(sqrt(d))=111/121 $\because$ d is defined at location 3 with infection estimate 111/121

I(trunc(sqrt(d))=1/2×111/121=111/242

$\because$ I_w of the built-in function "trunc" is 1/2

I(- b ± trunc(sqrt(d)))=1/4[1+1+1+111/242]=837/968

I(2*a)=1/3[1+1+1]=1

I(-b+trunc(sqrt(d)) div (2*a))=1/3[837/968+1/2+1]=2289/2904= I_{l_8}

$P_5 = I_{l_6} \times I_{l_8} = 353/363 \times 2289/2904 \fallingdotseq 0.7665$

Reference

[1] Antonia Bertolino, Lorenzo Strigini, "Using Testability Measures for Dependability Assessment," IEEE 17TH International Conference on Software Engineering, 1995.

[2] O. J. Dahl, E. W. Dijsktra, and C. A. R. Hoare, "Structured Programming," Academic Press, 1972.

[3] R.A. Demillo, et al., Software Testing and Evaluation, The Benjamin/Cummings Publishing Company Inc., Menlo Park, California, 1987

[4] Richard G. Hamilet, "Probable Correctness Theory," Information Processing Letters, pp. 17-25, April 1987

[5] William E. Howden, "Weak Mutation Testing and Completeness of Test Sets," IEEE Trans. On Software Engineering, SE-8(4):371-379, July 1982.

[6] K. Miller, L. Morell, R. Noonan, S. Park, D. Nicol, B. Murrill, &J. Voas, "Estimating the Probability of Failure when Testing Reveals No Failures," IEEE Trans. on Softw. Eng., 18(1): pp. 33--44, Jan. 1992

[7] Larry Joe Morell, "A Theory of Error-based Testing," Technical report TR-1395, University of Maryland, Department of Computer Science, April 1984.

[8] J. Voas and K. Miller, "Improving Software Reliability by Estimating the Fault Hiding Ability of A Program Before It Is Written," In Proceedings of the 9th Software Reliability Symposium, Denver Section of the IEEE Reliability Society, Colorado, 1991

[9] J. Voas & K. Miller, "Improving the Software Development Process Using Testability Research," In Proc. of the 3rd Int'l. Symp. on Softw. Reliability Engineering, pp. 114--121, October, 1992, RTP, NC, Publisher: IEEE Computer Society.

[10] J. Voas & K. Miller, "Semantic Metrics for Software Testability", The J. of Systems and Softw., Elsevier Science Publishers Ltd. 20: 207-216, March 1993

[11] J. Voas & K. Miller, "Software Testability: The New Verification," IEEE Software Appeared May 1995

[12] J. Voas & K. Miller, "Substituting Voas's Testability Measure for Musa's Fault Exposure Ratio," Proc. of the Int'l. Communication Conference, June 1996, Dallas, TX.

[13] J. Voas, L. Morell, & K. Miller, "Predicting Where Faults Can Hide From Testing," IEEE Software, 8(2):41--47, March 1991.

[14] J. Voas, "PIE: A Dynamic Failure-Based Technique," IEEE Trans. on Software Engineer, 18(8): p.717--p.727, August 1992.

[15] J. Voas, "Formal Testability Analysis," In the Encyclopedia of Softw. Engineering, John Wiley & Sons, pp. 517--518, 1994

Bibliography

[1] Bogdan Korel, "PELAS--Program Error-Locating Assistant System," IEEE Trans. on Software Engineer, VOL. 14. NO. 9. Sept. 1988

[2] T. M. Khoshgoftaar, R. M. Szabo, & J. M. Voas, "Detecting Program Modules with Low Testability," In Proc. of ICSM'95, Nice, France Oct. 1995

[3] L. Morell & J. Voas, "A Framework for Defining Semantic Metrics," The J. of Systems and Softw., Elsevier Science Publishers Ltd. 20: 245- 251, March 1993

[4] J. Voas, K. Miller, & R. Noonan, "Designing Programs that do not Hide Data State Errors During Random Black-Box Testing," In Proc. of the 5th Int'l. Conf. on Putting Into Practice Methods and Tolls for Information System Design, September 1992, Nantes, France.

[5] J. Voas & K. Miller, "Dynamic Testability Analysis for Assessing Fault Tolerance," High Integrity Systems Journal. 1(2): pp. 171-178, 1994, Oxford University Press.

[6] J. Voas & K. Miller, "Putting Assertions in Their Place," In Proc. of the Int'l. Symposium on Software Reliability Engineering, November pp. 6-9, 1994, Monterey, CA.

[7] J. Voas, K. Miller, & J. Payne, "Designing Programs That are Less Likely to Hide Faults," J. of Systems and Softw., Elsevier Science Publishers Ltd. 20: 93-100, January 1993

[8] J. Voas, K. Miller, & J. Payne, "Dynamic Testability Analysis for Software Safety," Proc. of the 2nd IASTED Int'l. Conf. on Reliability, Quality Control and Risk Assessment, October 1993, Cambridge, MA, Publisher: IASTED-ACTA Press, ISBN: 0-88986-181-1.

[9] J. Voas, K. Miller, & J. Payne, "Software Testability and It's Application to Avionic Software," In Proc. of Computers in Aerospace 9, October 1993, San Diego, CA. Publisher: AIAA.

[10] J. Voas, K. Miller, & J. Payne, "A Comparison of a Dynamic Software Testability Metric to Static Cyclomatic Complexity," Proc. of 2nd Int'l. Conf. on Software Quality Management, July 1994, Edinburgh, Scotland, Publisher: Computational Mechanics Publications.

[11] J. Voas, "A dynamic Failure Model for Predicting the Impact that a Program Location has on the Program," Lecture Notes in Computer Science Series, Vol. 550: Proc. of the 3rd European Softw. Eng. Conf., pp. 308--331, October 1991, Italy, Publisher: Springer-Verlag, A. Van Lamsweerde & A. Fugetta (Eds.).

[12] J. Voas, "Dynamic Testing Complexity Metric," Softw. Quality J., 1(2):101--114, Chapman & Jall, June, 1992.

[13] J. Voas, J. Payne, R. Mills, J. McManus, "Software Testability: An Experiment in Measuring Simulation Reusability," In Proc. of ACM Sigsoft. SSR'95, Seattle, April, 29-30.

Session P2b

Experiences with OO Development

An Object-Oriented Framework for Transaction Capture Using Co-operating Business Rule Components

John Rivett-Carnac
Ainsworth & Associates (Consulting) Limited,
3 Onega Gate, London SE16 1PR
Email: JohnRivett-Carnac@msn.com

Abstract

In a dealing-room system at a London bank, the transaction capture programs had been built using a GUI-based prototyping approach. This had led to programs with superficial similarity but inconsistency of internal structure which made maintenance difficult. To re-engineer the programs a control framework was devised separating the GUI interface (presentation layer), business rules and persistent storage. The framework allows business rules to be developed as independent, co-operating components. This makes it easier to develop and add new function or re-use previously-developed function. Business rule components are developed and tested separately, then used as building blocks for development of more complex components. They are re-usable because the same business constraints and calculations apply to many different transaction types.

1. Context and issues

In relatively large-scale commercial systems development projects (exceeding 10 man-years of effort) the use of rapid application development (RAD) and prototyping have not lived up to the promise which appeared possible from the success of smaller-scale use of these techniques. In a recent project at a London bank RAD techniques were used to develop a suite of transaction capture applications for a dealing room system. Although the user interface of the various transaction types appeared to behave in a reasonably consistent way and class libraries of business objects were used to provide business processing, the GUI-oriented development approach for transaction capture had led to poorly-structured, inconsistent and unnecessarily complex programs.

The poor structure and complexity of the programs could probably have been avoided by more careful definition and enforcement of program design and coding standards, but this would have increased the timescale for delivery in what was intended as a rapid delivery project. Further, the pressures on developers in a strongly commercial business environment to show results quickly tended to emphasise pragmatic short-term gain over longer-term thinking. This 'pragmatic' approach meant that maintenance of the existing implemented function was becoming increasingly difficult. Development of new function on top of that already in place compounded the problems further.

It was clear that the situation could not be allowed to continue so a new program structure was sought as a template to re-engineer the existing applications and form a sound basis for extension of the system. A particularly important objective was to achieve re-use of function so as to reduce development and maintenance costs.

A framework for transaction capture programs was devised, which defines a set of classes, available as components in for the developer, to implement a transaction capture process. Programmers use the framework components as the basis for developing further re-usable components implementing business-related function.

Insights were gained into the way in which co-operating components could be built, and the best way of presenting components to developers to maximise re-use.

2. The transaction capture process

2.1 Overview

Transaction capture is the process by which details of

0-8186-7840-2/97 $10.00 © 1997 IEEE

a change occurring outside the bounds of a system, are captured, validated and applied to the system.

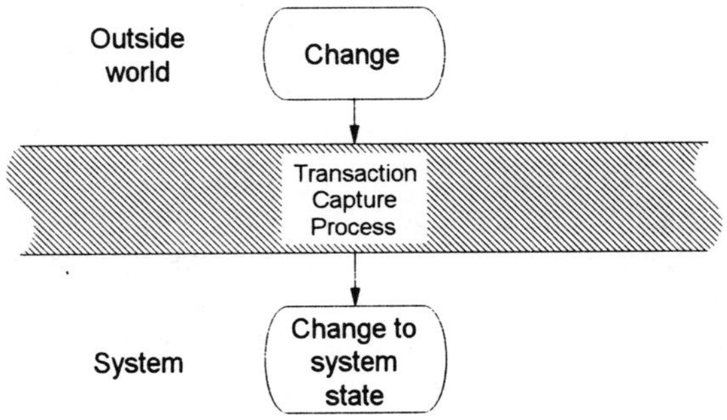

A change in the outside world leads to a change in the state of the system through the transaction capture process

The transaction capture process is divided into three main parts:

Capture of the transaction data
Validation of the transaction by rules
Committing the transaction to storage

These three parts must co-operate to achieve the successful capture of a transaction. In an on-line system the input and validation parts are tightly coupled so that the user can be informed immediately of any errors in the input data. The user of the transaction capture process can change any of the input data at any time. The transaction needs to be revalidated as soon as a change

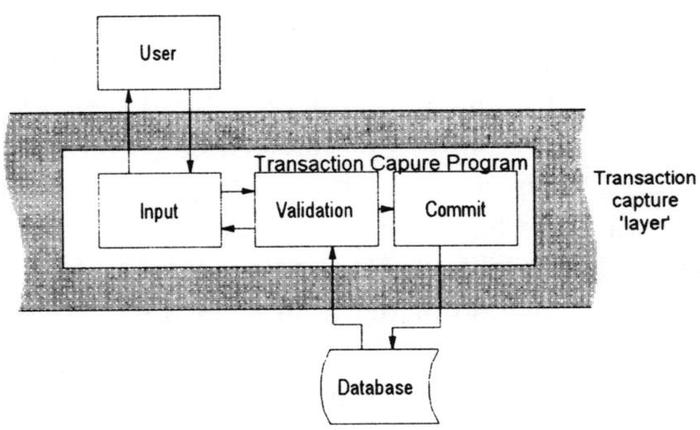

The main parts of a transaction capture program

occurs so that the user can see the effect of the change on the status of the transaction. Commit of the transaction to the system files is done once the transaction is valid and the user confirms it.

The functions of each of the three parts of transaction capture are described in more detail below. The following chapter describes how the Transaction Framework implements this structure and incorporates business function though the use of separately-developed components.

2.2 Capture of the transaction data

This part forms the interface with the outside world. In screen-based transaction capture programs this is the GUI interface to the user and the logic controlling its behaviour.

The responsibilities of the input part are:

- to collect data representing the transaction to be applied
- to pass the data on to the Validation part for checking
- to communicate the results of validation back to the user
- to initiate commit of the transaction when the user confirms it

When an input field is changed, basic validation of that field and the transaction as a whole in the light of the amended field is carried out immediately to detect errors, and any errors or warnings are indicated to the user for correction.

2.3 Validation of the transaction

Validation ensures that a transaction being committed to the database is correct. This is the most complex part of the transaction capture process, requiring understanding of the business domain and involving cross-validation between different data items of the transaction and checking of data on the database. The validation part incorporates business knowledge, so it is principally involved with the aspects of the system specific to the application domain.

We define three types of validation function: *format validation*, *list validation* and *business rules*.

Format validation. Format validation determines whether a single piece of information has a valid layout or structure for the field concerned - for example, that a customer number is numeric, or that a date has a correct layout. There is no dependence on the context, so the same format validation can be applied to all fields of the same type. The code for performing format validation is re-usable in most transaction capture programs.

List validation. List validation checks that the information entered in a single field is (or is not) a member of a given list - for example, that the customer number does indeed correspond to a customer record in a customer table, or that a payment code is one of a defined set of codes. The list of currently valid values can be displayed to the user to make a choice.

List validation usually involves reference to other data in the transaction and access to the database to construct the valid list. For example, the currency list for a transaction may be limited to those currencies for which a) the appropriate agreements with the proposed counterparty are in force and b) the indicated instrument is available.

Business rules. Business rules validation is the core of the transaction capture function. In this part the relationships of different fields of the proposed transaction with each other and with data on the database are checked to ensure that the overall transaction is indeed valid and can be applied to the data base. Derived data required to complete the transaction may be calculated or obtained from the data base.

The business analysts working on the functional requirements of the application can identify business rules. Generally they can be simply stated. For example:

Settlement date must be a working day
A settlement date for an amount in any currency must be a working day in that currency, unless the dealer specifically overrides the check.
Start/Maturity date rule
The start date must be earlier than the maturity date.

These are statements representing business rules. The first one relates three fields involved in a transaction - a date, a currency and an override - and identifies that reference must be made to the calendar for the currency to provide the validation. The rule is applicable to any settlement date in any transaction, because the rule is a general statement of a common piece of business logic.

The second rule defines a relationship between two dates, the start and maturity dates of a loan or deposit transaction.

Each rule is a separately-defined, independently-applied piece of business logic which can be considered in isolation. Many rules may apply to one field of a transaction. All the rules must be checked to ensure full validation of the field. In the example rules above, the Start Date and Maturity Date to which the first rule is applied are settlement dates, so each one would have the Settlement Date rule applied too.

2.4 Committing the transaction to storage

This stage of the processing applies a valid transaction to the system database, usually when the user confirms that the transaction should be applied, for example by pressing the 'OK' button.

In a system based on a relational database, the commit part interfaces to the database server through SQL calls, stored procedures or other intermediate functions. In a system with an underlying object model, this part would apply changes to persistent objects and/or construct new objects.

This part of a transaction capture program is primarily concerned with the design of the persistent data model, and ensuring the integrity and recoverability of the system. In considering the approach to integrity the designer of the commit part must consider which resource locking strategy to use - depending on the type of transaction and the type of business being undertaken, it may be appropriate either to reserve resources as soon as they are referred to, or to take an 'optimistic' strategy and leave resources unlocked until the user indicates that the transaction should be committed.

3. The Transaction Capture Framework

3.1 Overview

The Transaction Framework implements the model for transaction capture programs described in the preceding sections. The framework implements objects such as Transaction fields, Format checkers, List checkers and Business rules, which have complex but well-defined interactions of a generic nature.

The Transaction Framework provides the connections and standardises interactions between these objects so that business function can be contained in software components which 'plug together'. Developers manipulate these components in the development environment. They can wrap simple components together to build other components with richer function. Finally, a "Transaction" Component is constructed which incorporates many other lower-level components. The Transaction component has no presentation behaviour. The value and status of each field of the transaction can be manipulated only by connecting to it another framework component, the Input Connector. The Input Connector publishes methods and events for connection to generally-available display components to provide the visual representation of the transaction in a transaction capture program.

To illustrate of the way in which business rule components are connected, we shall consider the examples of business rules described in the previous section. The Settlement Date and Start/Maturity Date rules are both separately defined pieces of business logic. In well-designed transaction capture systems, these might be implemented as library functions. However, in most systems developed using rapid development techniques, the 'rules' are probably not separately identified and are likely to have been recoded for each field that requires validation. Even the better approaches, such as using library functions are prone to inconsistency and programming error and are expensive to test and maintain.

In contrast, the Transaction Framework requires rules to be developed as 'components' - objects which provide individual pieces of validation function available to the developer.

A business rule is developed as a component with connectors to the fields to which it relates - but the connections are left open. The Settlement Date rule described above has connections to three fields, as shown in the diagram.

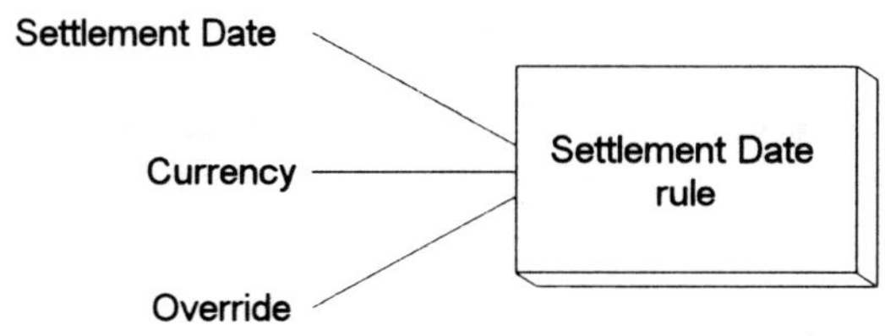

Settlement Date rule connects to three fields

Similarly, the Start/Maturity date rule, which checks that the Start date is earlier than the Maturity date, is developed as a component with two open connections.

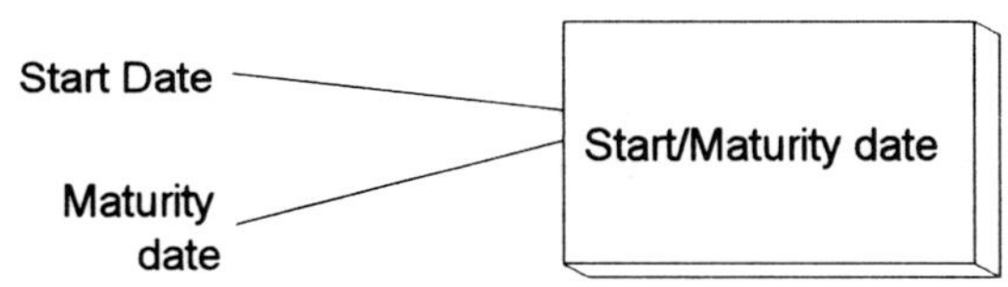

Start/Maturity date rule connects to two fields

The developer uses these rules as components which connect to fields of the transaction, as illustrated in the diagram below, showing four fields connected to three rule instances.

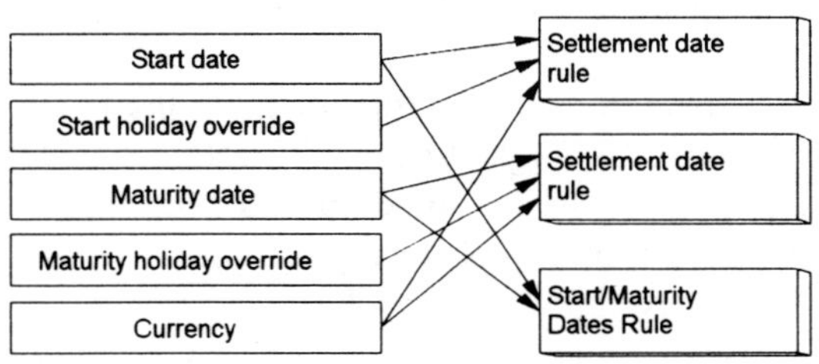

The developer connects the rules to fields of the transaction. This example shows the use of the same rule twice, and fields being connected to two different rules.

When the program is being run, if the user changes the currency then both instances of the Settlement Date rule will be triggered to re-check the dates. Similarly, the start and maturity dates are subject to validation by both the Settlement Date and the Start/Maturity date rules. The Transaction Framework automatically informs the rules of any changes of value in any of their connected fields so that the rules can do the appropriate validation or re-calculation. Rules are not aware of the existence of other rules and operate quite independently of each other.

Rules can also change the value of a field of the transaction, so that a change which the user makes will be reflected in other fields. For example, interest calculation is often done as part of a loan or deposit deal capture, so a rule may be defined which takes the start date, maturity date, principal amount, interest rate and interest basis, and calculates the amount of interest. Any change made to any of the other fields will cause the

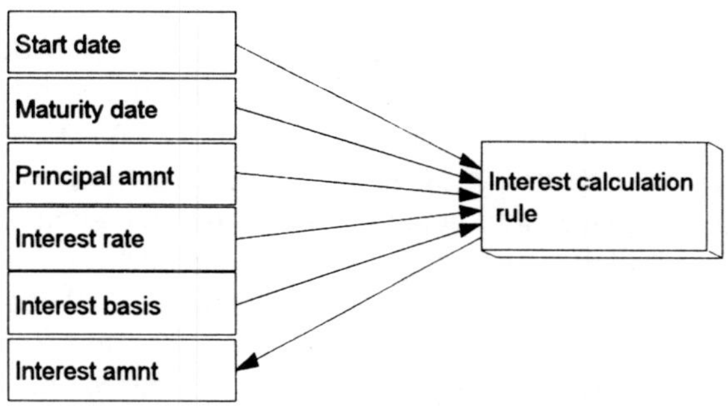

Changes to the value of a connected field can cause a rule to change the value of another field

interest calculation rule to be triggered, and the new interest amount will be calculated.

One field may be connected to many different rules. If one of the rules changes the value of the field, then the other rules are informed so that they can carry out consequent processing. For example, if the currency is changed then the interest basis may change. The Interest Calculation rule must recalculate the interest amount. The programmer does not have to worry about ensuring this happens, as it is part of the in-built behaviour of the Framework.

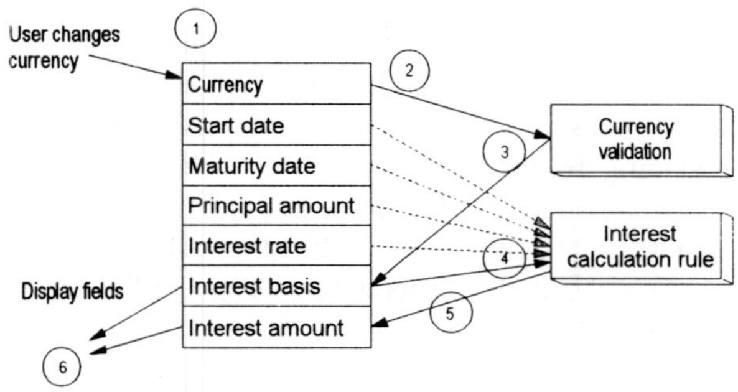

1 User changes currency
2 Framework informs currency validation rule of change to Currency
3Currency validation rule changes Interest Basis
4 Framework informs Interest Calculation rule of change to Interest Basis
5 Interest Calculation rule changes Interest Amount
6 Framework informs GUI to change display of interest basis and interest amount.

Simplified sequence of activity

3.2 The Transaction Framework classes

The initial work on specifying and developing the transaction framework concentrated on the interactions between the classes in the run-time environment. This requires framework mechanisms for notification of changes to fields entered by the user, triggering of rule processing to validate the entry and recalculate dependent data, updating the GUI display and informing the user of any warnings or errors which may arise. This initial implementation of the framework required the programmer to write code to connect rules explicitly with their corresponding fields. As work progressed, it became clear that to improve productivity there had to be better mechanisms by which the GUI, transaction fields, rules and other components achieve connections. As a first step the services offered by the framework were improved so that the connections could be made without coding, by setting properties on components manipulated in the development environment. Then more 'intelligent' connection services were added to the framework components. When a business rule is introduced into a transaction the framework examines the open connections on the rule and the available transaction fields to find good candidates for connection based on 'business types' and 'roles'. So, provided that standard types/roles are defined and their use enforced, most connections between components can be resolved without programmer intervention.

It is not possible to go into detail on all the interactions between the component classes within the scope of this paper, so the descriptions given in the sections below cover the principal attributes and behaviour of each of the Framework classes, to give an overall understanding of the way in which the framework operates.

Transaction Attribute. This class is used by the developer of a Transaction Component to hold the value of an attribute of a transaction. It provides the central connection point between the GUI (i.e. the user) on one hand and all the checkers, rules and committers inside the Transaction Component on the other. The value of a Transaction Attribute is expressed as a string for display to and setting by the user.

A Transaction Attribute has a name, string representations of its value in two forms ('as entered' and 'normalised'), a 'business type' and a transaction role. It also has properties indicating current applicability to the transaction (not applicable, optional, mandatory), format validity, list validity, and business rule validity (valid, warning(s), error(s)).

When instantiated, a Transaction Attribute automatically registers itself with the Transaction Control object, which keeps a list of all the connected Transaction Attributes.

The Transaction Attribute itself maintains a list of connected Rule Attributes. The Rule Attributes give access to the methods for informing Business Rules of changes to the value and/or status of the Transaction Attribute. In the running program a business rule indicates the validity and applicability of its attributes - as determined by that rule alone - by setting the corresponding attributes of its own Rule Attributes. Each related Transaction Attribute determines its own applicability and validity by examining the corresponding status reported by its connected Rule Attributes. For example, if any one (or more) connected Rule Attributes indicates an error, then the Transaction Attribute will report an error status via its Input Connector back to the GUI, and hence to the user.

When the value of the Transaction Attribute is changed (either by the GUI layer or by a Business Rule) the framework does the following:

- Raises the DoFormatCheck event on the connected Format Check Connector (if any). The assigned event handler can set the ValueNormalised string of the Transaction Attribute.
- If the format check is successful, raises the DoListCheck event on the connected List Check Connector (if any).
- Raises the OnChangeWarning events of all the connected Rule Attributes. This gives each rule a chance to decide whether or not it should be checked, and if so to queue itself to be checked.
- If any Business Rules have queued themselves for checking and rule checking is not already in progress, the Transaction Control object will start firing the queued rules in turn.

Input Connector. This component is used by the developer of the GUI layer to gain access to the value of a Transaction Attribute and to be informed through events when its value or other state changes.

The GUI developer has available:

- Properties to access the ValueAsEntered and ValueAsNormalised properties of the underlying Transaction Attribute.
- Read-only properties indicating the validity, applicability and amendability of the Transaction Attribute
- Events which are raised whenever the value or other property of the connected Transaction Attribute changes. The GUI developer can attach event handlers to modify the GUI display as

appropriate when the value or state changes. For example, the background colour of an edit box may change if the applicability changes from 'optional' to 'mandatory'.

Transaction Control. This component is automatically instantiated by other framework components to provide the linkage between the Transaction Attributes, the Business rules and the Committer object which make up the complete validation and commit parts of the transaction capture program.

The Transaction Control object publishes only its name and a few control properties to the developer, but performs some essential work in co-ordinating the connections and operation of the transaction framework components:

- It holds a list of all Transaction Attributes, which is maintained through registration and de-registration calls from the Transaction Attributes themselves. This list is used when a new business rule registers itself to attempt an automatic match between the Transaction Attributes and the Rule Attributes.
- It holds a list of all connected Business Rules which is maintained through registration and de-

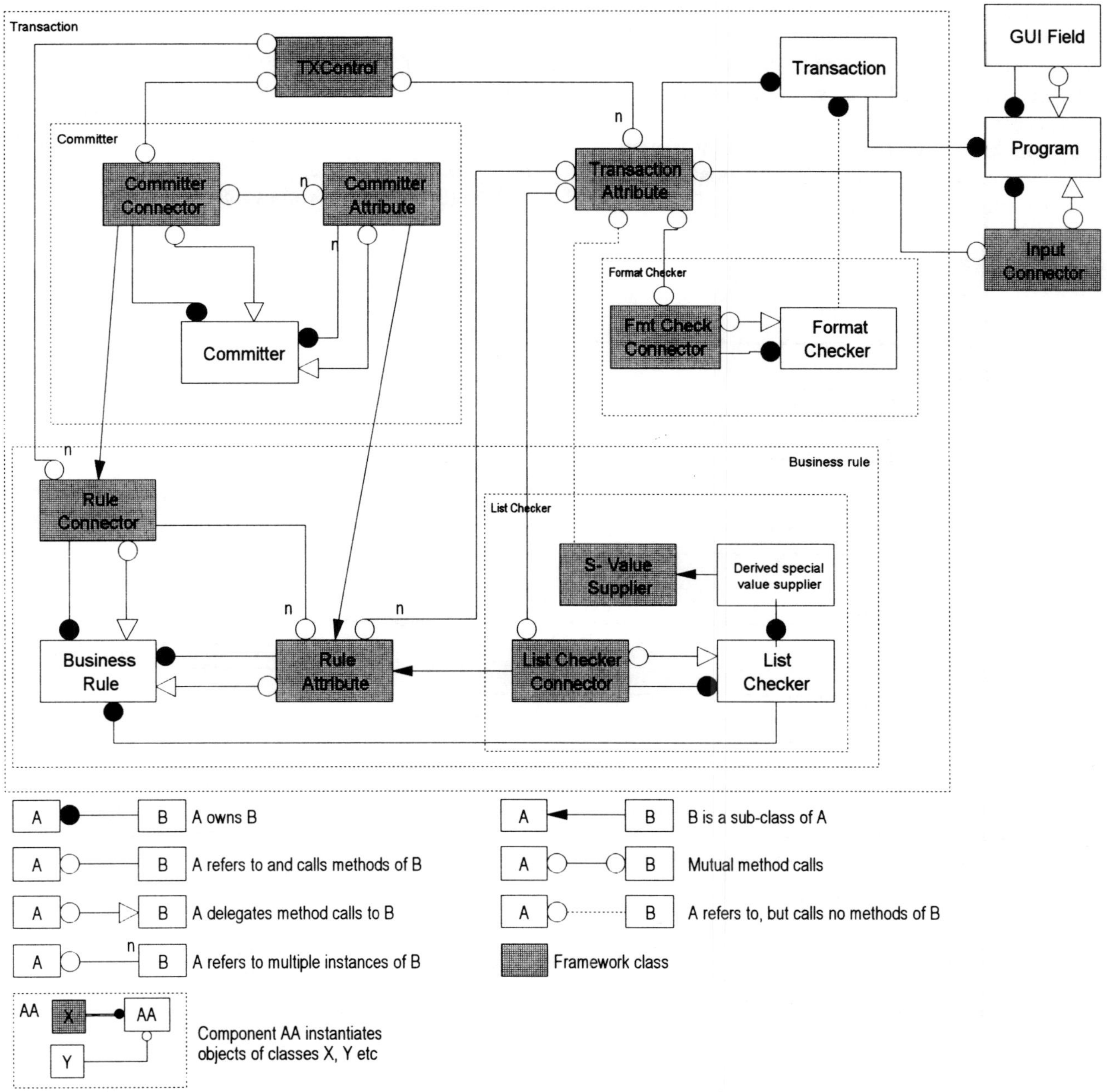

registration calls from the Business Rule Connectors. This list is referred to when a new Transaction Attribute registers itself: open (unconnected) Rule Attribute connections may be matched to the new Transaction Attribute.

- It holds a queue of Business Rules waiting to be checked, and triggers rule checking by calling the (delegated) DoCheckRule event of the Rule Connector component for each rule in turn. A Business Rule puts itself in this queue if it determines that it needs to be checked as a result of a change to one of its connected attributes.
- It keeps track of change sequence numbers so that it is possible to tell the sequence in which changes to the values of Transaction Attributes are made. This is required in some forms of validation and calculation, in which the sequence of changes is significant.

Format Checker Connector. This component is used to provide format checking on a Transaction Attribute. Format checking depends only on the type of field, and is generally independent of the context in which a field appears. For example, a format checker might be applied to a customer number to determine that the entered number conformed to the rules for forming good customer numbers.

The Format Checker Connector publishes an event (DoFormatCheck), ValueAsSet (read-only) and ValueAsNormalised (read-write) string fields, and a method to indicate if a format error is detected. If a format error is reported, most Business Rules attached to the attribute will not elect to queue themselves for checking. There is little point in attempting to validate against a field which is, by definition, incorrect whatever the transaction context.

List Checker Connector. This component is used to provide list content checking for a Transaction Attribute. The connector publishes the DoListCheck event and a set of list supply and navigation events for which the developer can provide event handlers.

The list of possible valid values for an attribute can be

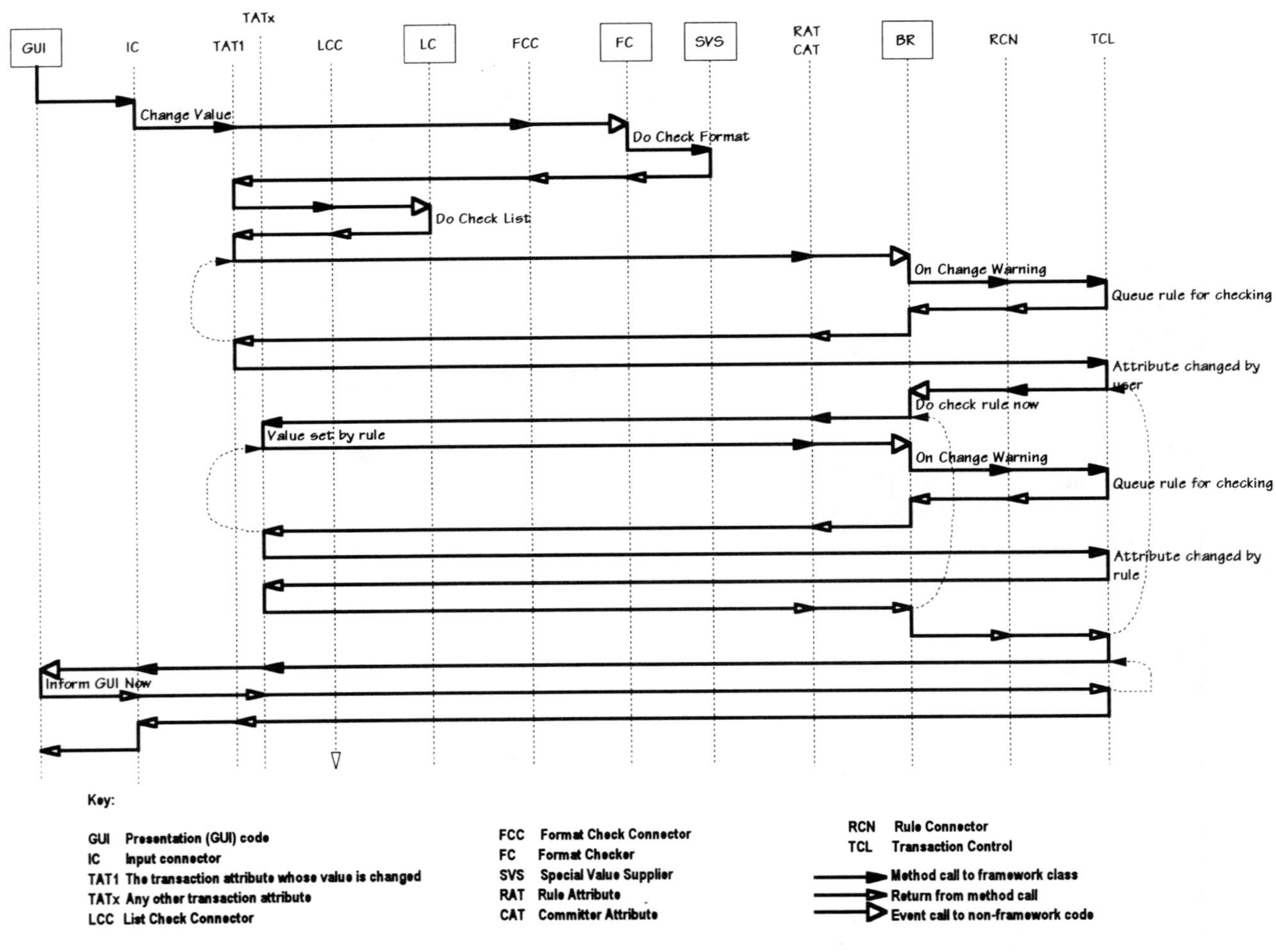

Diagram of method calling sequence arising from an initial change to a Transaction Attribute by the user

affected by other attributes of the transaction. Therefore, the List Checker Connector is included in a Business Rule which may have other Rule Attributes to connect to other fields of the transaction - for example, the list of currencies available may depend on the Counterparty. If the Counterparty changes, this may cause a list error to be raised against an already-entered currency.

Special Value Supplier. This is a base class used for defining classes which contain data related to the current value of an attribute. It may contain alternative internal representations of the string value of the Transaction Attribute, and/or references to other objects. It can be attached to a Transaction Attribute so that it is accessible to other parts of the transaction capture program. The Special Value Supplier is attached to the Transaction Attribute by either the Format Checker or the List Checker.

Rule Attribute. This component is used by the developer of a business rule component to provide the connection between a business rule and a Transaction Attribute. The Rule Attribute publishes:

- Events to report changes of value and state of the connected Transaction Attribute.
- ValueAsNormalised and ValueAsSet properties to allow the rule to read and change the value of the Transaction Attribute.
- RuleApplicability and RuleValidity properties to allow the rule to indicate the status of the attribute as determined by application of the rule.
- A message attribute which may be set by the rule if reporting a warning or an error. The messages applying to an attribute are accessible through the Input Connector, so can be displayed to the user by the GUI layer in whatever way is appropriate.

All the Rule Attributes in a rule are connected to the Rule Connector for the rule. This connection is made by setting the RuleConnector property of the Rule Attribute, which then registers itself with the Rule Connector. The Rule Connector maintains a list of the rule attributes.

Each Rule Attribute is also connected to one Transaction Attribute. This is done either explicitly by the Transaction Component developer, by setting the TransactionAttribute property of the Rule Attribute, or automatically by the Rule Connector, which attempts to match the Rule Attributes with the Transaction Attributes registered with the Transaction Control object.

When a Transaction Attribute's value is changed by the User or a Business Rule, it informs all its connected Rule Attributes. The Rule Attribute publishes a 'change warning' event to which the developer of the rule may attach an event handler to determine whether or not the rule checking should be invoked and, if so, to place the rule in the queue of rules waiting to be checked.

Rule Connector. This component is used by the developer of a Business Rule to provide connection between a business rule and the Transaction Control object. It publishes a method which is used by the rule to put itself into the queue of rules to be checked. It also publishes an event, DoCheckRuleNow, which is raised by the Transaction Control Object when the rule reaches the head of the queue. The developer of a business rule attaches the event handler, which carries out the business logic represented by the rule, to this event property.

The rule connector establishes a two-way connection with the Transaction Control object, and also triggers the attempt to match the Transaction Attributes with the Rule Attributes when the rule is first instantiated.

Committer Attribute. This component is an extension of the Rule Attribute, which has the additional capability to set the amendability state of a Transaction Attribute. This makes it possible for the commiter component to control which of the Transaction Attributes can be changed by the user or another business rule depending on the state of the transaction.

Committer Connector. This component, which is derived from the Rule Connector class, is used by the developer of a Committer component to connect the committer to the Transaction Control object. It publishes additional events and methods for co-ordinating commits of transactions to the database.

4. Outcomes, insights and lessons

Overview. The exercise of re-engineering the existing transaction capture programs provided the opportunity to establish a more formal structure for such programs, in particular to analyse the existing capture function in order to identify and separately define the GUI, business function, persistent storage and control elements. Two things were unexpected. Firstly, the extent and complexity of the control part (which became the Transaction Framework classes) were significantly greater than expected. Secondly, the way in which the classes could establish inter-connections without developer intervention to increase productivity significantly only became clear as the work progressed.

There were also interesting insights into the best way of presenting components and their attributes for the use of developers. We moved away from using inheritance with overridden/virtual methods, and towards event handlers for events published by 'connectors', as this technique seems to be a more productive model in the development environment being used. Development of components which are aggregations of other components is an effective way of managing complexity: groups of simple business rules can be bundled up into components with more complex function and wider interfaces - more Rule Attributes.

New areas for investigation are the potential for distributing business function and for dynamically connecting business rules. New business rules would be instantiated as applets downloaded from a remote server and the connections to the Transaction Control objects and transaction attributes would be established dynamically.

Standardisation of program structure. The standardisation of structure means that developers can quickly understand the function of a transaction capture program, although previously unfamiliar with it. Developers are more quickly productive and can work on different areas of the system at shorter notice.

Also, as each component used to build a program is essentially free-standing and covers a well defined subset of the function of the transaction, it is easier to pinpoint problems and apply fixes.

Sequence of development. Each of the parts of a transaction capture program are considered separately, operating through defined interfaces to the other parts. Each part can be separately developed and tested. The framework helps to break down the development process into clearly identified and manageable units.

Flexibility of GUI design. The GUI part relies on an underlying Transaction Component which does not contain any assumptions about the way in which the GUI interaction with the user will be implemented. This allows flexibility of GUI design and also makes it easy to have multiple versions of transaction capture programs targeted at different end-users and different delivery platforms. Although the GUI design may differ, all have the same underlying transaction component.

Business rules promote re-use. The business rule components have a direct correspondence with business function. The rules are known to and understood by business analysts. The business-level awareness of rules, their separate development and testing, and the ease of 'plugging' rules into a transaction make them highly re-usable.

Prototyping. The transaction framework emphasises the distinction between presentation and function. The GUI part and the business part each have their own development and test cycles, following parallel but distinct prototyping paths. As issues are identified and resolved, each part can adapt appropriately. The framework ensures that the changes are made to the right parts of the program and that the business and GUI issues do not become intertwined.

Distribution of function. The Business Rule components are available in the development environment, but hide their implementation details. Within its implementation, a business rule can use an interface to a server process running on another machine to provide remote function. There is great potential for generalising the techniques for distribution using ORB technology.

Planning and development management. The business components are developed and tested separately, so the work can be allocated to more developers working independently, and there is much more flexibility in the way in which the development work can be reallocated if part of the development takes longer than planned. Progress in the development is more easily verified and tracked, as each component is limited in scope and can be developed and tested separately.

An Experience in Deploying Object-Orientation for Business Applications

Ramkumar Ramaswamy
Education and Research Department, Infosys Technologies Limited
3rd Cross, Electronics City, Bangalore 561229 India
Ramkumarr@inf.com

Abstract

Object-orientation is emerging as a development methodology that promises highly modular software that is easily maintainable and reusable. Object-oriented (OO) methods have been deployed in a variety of fields ranging from OLTP business systems to real-time and embedded software. Interestingly, current OO literature makes barely a passing reference to some of the most outstanding ideas of Structured Analysis that, in fact, continue to be indispensable in the OO context. Also, there are relatively few reports of real-life experiences in deploying the complete OO lifecycle from requirements specification through coding and testing for business systems, which can serve as a starting point for practical guidance on configuring and managing an OO project. This paper presents the experiences of one company in deploying a combination of Structured Analysis and OO design for the development of a set of client/server business applications for a large public utility firm in the US.

1. Introduction

The last few years have seen an explosive increase in the popularity of object-orientation (OO) as a methodology for systems development. OO promises software systems with a considerably higher degree of modularity, with consequent benefits by way of maintainability and reusability. With its emphasis on data abstraction and encapsulation, OO is a particularly natural choice for designing and architecting Client/Server applications, where multiple layers of software are required to work together at different layers of abstraction.

A considerable amount of literature exists today that addresses a vast spectrum of issues in OO development. As concerns analysis and design methodology, those of Rumbaugh [11], Jacobson [9] and Booch [2] have been particularly prominent, and a unification of these is currently under way [3]. It is interesting (and, according to us, unfortunate) that OO literature makes barely a passing reference to some of the outstanding ideas of Structured Analysis that, in fact, continue to play a key role in the OO context. On the contrary, an impression is conveyed that adopting OO requires abandoning traditional methods altogether, an impression that often causes valuable techniques and lessons learned in the context of Structured Analysis to be ignored or forgotten even if they are relevant in the OO context. The notion of "system essence" in distinguishing logical from physical requirements, and the technique of event partitioning are cases in point [10]. OO literature also has relatively few reports of real-life experiences in deploying the complete OO lifecycle from requirements specification through coding and testing, for business applications, which provide practical guidance on configuring and managing an OO project.

In this paper we describe our experiences with deploying Structured techniques for the analysis and OO techniques for the design and development of a set of client/server business applications for a large public utility firm in the US (referred to henceforth as "the client organization" or simply "the client"). Our choice of this "mixed-mode" engineering approach is motivated not only by the desire to build on the lessons of Structured Analysis, but also by the dearth of precise, shop-usable guidelines for analysis in OO literature. In fact, there is scope for considerable saving on the OO learning curve because of the use of familiar, proven traditional techniques where applicable. We discuss this in detail in section 2.

The organization of the remainder of the paper is as follows. In section 2 we elaborate on the issues we faced in requirements specification, with specific reference to

0-8186-7840-2/97 $10.00 © 1997 IEEE

the nature and role of process models and object models. In section 3 we describe the salient features of the application design and architecture. In section 4 we describe the key features of our development strategy. The final section presents our observations and conclusions.

2. Requirements specification

2.1 The setting

A common scenario that exists today is that of the conversion of a legacy system to a client/server setup. Typically, this involves repositioning the corporate mainframe as a centralized database server, while end-users' terminals are replaced gradually by client workstations with attractive graphical user interfaces (GUIs). In many of these situations, the client typically begins with the capability of handling mainly presentation logic, while the bulk of the business and data management logic resides on the server. In due course, some business logic is expected to trickle up to the client. In the present context the backdrop was a 25 year old legacy Customer Data System[1] (CDS) running on an IBM mainframe with VSAM data. Much of the functionality of CDS, essentially a billing system, was being ported to a new Customer Assistance System (CAS). CAS would run on the same machine and access a DB2 database. It would in addition support new functionality and would have to be flexible enough to adapt to the changing business needs of the client organization.

2.2 The nature of requirements

The actual customer for Infosys was the IT wing—the Automated Systems Division (ASD)—of the client organization. ASD had a dedicated team of business analysts for providing business inputs to our team. These business analysts were primarily IT people. The work at hand was to be done in two phases. The first phase involved server-end work. The design of the centralized DB2 database was more or less already in place, and our task in this phase was to write a suite of data-access services that would be used by client applications. This service-based architecture was intended to encapsulate the database structure from all client applications. In the second phase, our task was to write client applications for three end-user groups, comprising over 500 users in all, that would use these data access services on the host. It is worth mentioning that there was considerable difference of opinion about whether this sequencing of phases was right or wrong, particularly since the server-side team's experience in designing client/server applications was limited. Some end-user groups also felt that we would not get a true picture of the business processes involved and the specific needs of end-users unless some analysts spoke to the end-users directly. In fact, the head of one user group even went so far as to assert that initially we would do well to physically stay away from the building that housed ASD!

We thus realized that though a considerable amount of work had already gone into the server-side (mostly in the design of the database and some into the design of services), it would be inappropriate to have the design of the client GUI applications driven entirely by the server-side design. The client-side design would have to be driven, at least in part, by requirements stated by end-users, with consequent rework on the server side design where necessary. To the extent that interaction with end-users was required to understand their business process and system requirements it would be necessary to create analysis models. We now describe the nature and role played by the two key analysis models, namely process models and object models.

2.3 The nature and role of process models

It has been remarked (see e.g. [5]) that OO analysis is only superficially different from traditional Structured Analysis. While this fact is recognized in the literature to the extent that object models are often treated as extensions of data models, it is not immediately apparent that traditional process models have a legitimate place in the object-oriented project. We elaborate on this aspect in the following subsection, in which we describe our experiences with process modeling for a key end-user group, the Exception Billing Center (EBC). EBC personnel, called book keepers, are responsible for manual intervention when CDS signals that it is unable to compute a bill. In such a circumstance, CDS reports an "exception" which is queued for action by a book keeper. A book keeper's sole responsibility is to respond to and act on these exceptions. This activity is called exception billing, so that the process under study was the "exception billing process."

The use of event partitioning. The concept of use cases is by now common to most OO Analysis methodologies. A use case is defined as "a sequence of related transactions performed in a dialogue" [9]. This definition is, however, not precise enough to be shop-usable. As Larry Constantine points out in the preface to [9], use case analysis is kin to the idea of event partitioning introduced in the seminal work of [10]. In

[1] For reasons of confidentiality, all references to systems, departments and individuals at the client organization have been disguised.

event partitioning, the process under study is seen as responding to events that occur *outside* the process boundary. (To avoid confusion with the many other interpretations of the term "event," we use the term *external business event* (EBE) to refer to such events.) Once an EBE is processed, the system comes to rest and *remains at rest* until another EBE activates it. The key step in event partitioning is to identify the EBEs of interest. The response of the process to each EBE is then modeled as an independent chunk. The net result is a highly modular and maintainable process model. In our experience, the emphasis on EBEs injects a considerable degree of objectivity into a traditionally subjective modeling activity. We thus found it useful to think of a use case as *the sequence of activities that takes place as a result of the occurrence of a EBE, before the process can again come to rest.* Given the nature of exception billing, the choice of event partitioning was natural.

We found a fair abundance of information on exception billing. Some of this came from the book keepers' reference manuals, and some of it came from flowcharts diagrammed by business analysts at the EBC (not to be confused with those at ASD). This led us to decide that our use case descriptions would not be completely detailed, but would instead contain suitable pointers to existing documentation. What was the value that our use cases added? The flowcharts produced by the EBC business analysts were not drawn using any process modeling methodology. As such, they were fairly unstructured and tended to lack consistency in the level of detail. In addition, they tended to be monolithic rather than modular, causing tremendous difficulties in understanding, maintaining and extending them. For instance, one flowchart attempted to describe all the possible outcomes of the exception "Idle usage" (which indicated that electricity was being consumed at an apartment thought to be vacant). This flowchart attempted to show, in one breath, the activities involved in notifying a Field Services Representative (FSR), getting a meter inspected and replaced, advising the occupant to apply for service, and setting up a customer account! In contrast, the event partitioned model for the exception "Idle usage" had distinct EBEs such as "Idle usage is reported," "Meter is tested" and "Occupant is found at premises." Each of these EBEs had its own, self-contained flowchart. The flowchart for the EBE "Idle usage reported" terminated with the book keeper sending a notification to the FSR; that for "Meter is tested" terminated with the test result and the new meter information (if the meter had been found defective and replaced) being recorded in the database, and the flowchart for "Occupant is found at site" terminated with a notice to apply for service being sent to the occupant. Each of the above flowcharts had clearly defined boundaries, and contained but a handful of actions and decisions. Clearly, our contribution was to structure existing information in a modular form that would be understandable, maintainable and extensible.

Focus on the essential process. The book keepers at the EBC had to resort to "transaction-level" thinking to be able to use CDS. Given an exception, they had to know which transaction codes to fire to be able to resolve it. (These transaction codes were cryptic 4-letter codes such as BHSI, HIST, and GPRC). A senior supervisor in the EBC made it clear to us that his primary motivation in considering a GUI application was to move the book keepers away from this "transaction world view" and help them think "closer to the business" as it were. In this respect, the flowcharts diagrammed by business analysts at the EBC had a serious flaw: they had explicit embedded references to the low-level transactions being invoked by book keepers to perform exception handling *in CDS*. We perceived a requirement here to concentrate on modeling the *essence* of the process. To recall the definition of essence from [10], "...the essential activities are all those tasks that the system would have to do even if you could implement it using perfect technology." The concept of essence is valuable because it considerably sharpens the boundary between logical and physical requirements. (Unfortunately, as we have noted, this concept is practically ignored in OO literature.) As the authors point out, the assumption of perfect technology does not extend to the world outside the process boundary. In our model, the essential activities included those tasks which were being done by the book keepers, so that the assumption of perfect technology, while it did not extend beyond the boundary of the process under study, did extend beyond the boundary of automation provided by CDS and that to be provided by CAS. The purpose of this was to identify opportunities for further automation.

2.4 The nature and role of object models

In Structured methodologies, there is a clear cut distinction between analysis models and design models. In the OO context, many authors (e.g. [4]) advocate obliterating the distinction between the two. However, we believe that there continues to be a need to distinguish between the complexities of modeling user requirements and those of designing a set of objects to meet those requirements, and thus chose to closely follow Jacobson's approach [9] by having distinct models for analysis and design. Unlike traditional data models which drive database design, object models in OO have a dual purpose in that they also drive the program (class) design. The role of the object models in our context was not to influence the database design (which was very nearly complete), but to focus on documenting our understanding of the business entities and their relationships, and to drive program design. Our analysis model, called an essential object model (EOM), was driven by the concept of system essence and was practically identical to a traditional logical data model, except for the use of inheritance notation for the explicit depiction of is-a relationships, and the use of aggregation notation to explicitly depict consists-of relationships. The design model, called the Physical Object Model (POM), was arrived at by drawing event traces for each use case, using the EOM as a starting point. The role that the POM played for program design was analogous to that which is played by the physical data model in database design (see e.g., [8]). That is, classes and relationships in the POM represented the structure of classes and their relationships in the actual client program. An interesting fallout of this is that the scope of these two models was somewhat different. The EOM, consisting of about 15 classes, turned out to be (not surprisingly) a subset of the EOM that might have been drawn for the entire billing process. The POM on the other hand had objects that were specific to the application that we had conceptualized for exception billing. These were chiefly objects to provide functions such as controlling screen-level navigation, utilities for estimating a bill or prorating a meter reading, and utilities for generating statistics on exception frequency and handling. We provide more details on the application architecture in section 3.

While drawing the EOM, we found significant ambiguity in the definitions of certain key entities which had been used for the server-side design. There were 5 key entities called "the big 5," of which one, called `installed service`, had at least three different definitions in as many documents: one called it "a measurement device," another said "it deals with money," and a third simply said "it stores customer-related information" (when there was clearly a big 5 `customer` entity to do the job!). We discovered that an instance of `installed service` typically represented the set of sources of measurements required for computing a monthly bill. (For example, the installed service for a grocery store consisted of the set of installed meters, along with the number of lamp posts of each type in the store's parking lot.) Similar problems arose with another big 5 entity called `site`, which was defined simply as "any point on earth which is of interest to the company." We discovered that instances of `site` were typically used to record the precise location of a meter, and were typically of the form "the front gate of house #432, Elm St." We thus found the act of drawing the EOM to be particularly useful in pinpointing sources of ambiguity in the business definition, even though the purpose of the EOM was limited to driving the design of the POM and not the design of the database.

3. Application design and architecture

Object Oriented Design (OOD) is significantly different from Structured Design. OOD is class-centered, and, being driven by the classes identified in the problem domain (i.e., in the EOM), lends itself to greater traceability. In addition, the packaging together of data and function makes an OO design highly modular and cohesive. In this section we point out the most interesting aspects of our design. We first describe the use of *control objects* to encapsulate navigation logic specific to an application. We next describe the use of an *interface object* called `Host` to encapsulate the mechanism of host data access, and the use of *transaction objects* to encapsulate data requirements for a transaction. We conclude this section by describing the hierarchical organization of object libraries according to levels of potential reuse.

3.1 Control objects

The key activity in OO design is to decompose functionality into methods and attempt to assign each method to a class to which it most naturally belongs. Most functionality gets assigned to *entity* objects, which are typically objects in the POM that correspond to entities identified in the EOM (see [9]). Functionality that does not belong naturally to any entity object or window is usually assigned to a separate control object. Control objects can in turn be categorized into two types depending on their level of reusability. A control object that applies a complex formula to calculate a surcharge to be paid by a customer is generic enough to find use in multiple applications for the same organization without significant modification. On the other hand, a control object that controls the sequence of screen invocations for a particular use case is so specific to the application for which it was originally designed that it is best to keep its scope limited to that application. We refer to the second category of control objects as application controllers, or just *controllers*. Each major use case had an explicit controller associated with it. Each window also performed the role of a "localized controller" for certain types of interactions. For example, the `customer_selection` window had a `new` button (to allow the creation and subsequent selection of a new customer if the desired one did not exist), so that invocation of a `new_customer` window from the `customer_selection` window was left to the customer window to control; control would then return to the use case controller only after the original customer window was closed.

The use of control objects enabled a clean separation of application-specific logic from organization-wide business rules, and made it easy to pinpoint bugs and localize the effects of changes to the designs in response to requests from end users.

3.2 Transaction objects and the Host interface

The client/server architecture used for the project was based on the Net Gateway product from Sybase. This Gateway product is an OpenServer application (see, e.g., [1]) that performs two functions. First, it allows TCP/IP clients to interface with an SNA host. Second, it makes the host mainframe look like a Sybase System 10 server, i.e., it allows client applications to access mainframe data in exactly the same way as they would access a Sybase System 10 server. Each CICS transaction on the mainframe is made to look like a stored procedure (SP) to the client application, and access is done using the RPC call mechanism used for SPs. Since this client/server architecture was under review and was likely to change as the number of users grew, it was decided to have a class called Host that would encapsulate the specifics of talking to the host mainframe. There was one method on Host for each Gateway "SP", and this method was responsible for translating its input arguments to format suitable for invoking the "SP". The advantage of such a design is clear: if an alternate access mechanism to the mainframe needs to be tried; all it requires is a new Host class to be plugged in, without the need to change the code of any client classes. A beneficial side-effect was that of effectively simplifying the RPCs: while each RPC required parameters such as terminal_id (which we refer to as "technology parameters"), Host methods had only "business parameters" such as customer_no. For the most part, arguments to methods on Host were *not* object-valued, in order that each argument list faithfully mirror the arguments to the corresponding RPCs.

Translation of the attribute-level view to the object-level view was done by a layer of ***transaction objects***. Each transaction object's responsibility was to maintain associations with all objects about which information was required to fire the transaction. For example, a "Turn On" (which set up service for a new customer at a specified address) for a customer required information about, amongst other things, the customer and the metering equipment at the service site. For this we had a turnOn object that had pointers to the corresponding classes called Customer and InstalledService. The transaction would be fired by invoking a method called submit() on turnOn, whereupon the relevant Host method(s) would be called. An added benefit of having the transaction object layer was that more complex transactions could be built out of simpler ones. For example, there were three RPCs to perform a search of customer addresses, depending on what search criteria were specified: one RPC took a partial name, another took a partial meter number, and a third took a partial address. For this we created a transaction object called searchCustAddress which had as attributes the union of the search criteria of all three RPCs. When submit() was invoked, this object would examine the values of the search criteria and call the appropriate RPC (well-defined priority rules were used in case multiple criteria were specified).

The use of transaction objects also helped us resolve a problem of insufficient cohesion in many of the existing RPCs. Consider for example, a RPC named cssut_p_ts1x that we encountered. If supplied the flag REQUESTCODE = 'M' and CUSTNAME = 'Jo', this RPC would retrieve partial details for all customers whose name started with 'Jo.' However, with REQUESTCODE = 'I', and CUSTNUM = '126', it would retrieve all the details of the (single) customer whose id equaled 126. Finally, with REQUESTCODE = 'X', and CUSTNUM = '126,' the RPC would lock the corresponding (single) customer record for updation. For this example we chose to have transaction objects called getCustListByName, getCustForId, and lockCustById, each of which invoked cssut_p_ts1x. The use of transaction objects thus lent considerable conceptual clarity to the design process.

3.3 Organization of object libraries

There is potential for considerable reuse when a suite of applications is to be developed for a single organization. We defined three sets of object libraries according to their projected reusability. At the lowest level in the architectural ladder were foundation class libraries; these included "data structure objects" such as collections and hash tables, as well as hierarchies of UI widgets such as command buttons and list boxes (development was on PowerBuilder). Foundation classes were intended to be usable across all PowerBuilder applications in our company. The next level consisted of a group of "Generic" libraries. This consisted of objects that would be usable across all applications for the client organization. Generic classes were typically entity objects such as the "Big 5" alluded to earlier. It may be argued that windows such as a maintenance window would be equally generic. However, we decided against including any windows in the generic library so as to allow complete freedom for different user groups to exercise their individual preferences for the user interface. At the top of the architectural ladder were application-specific libraries, containing a mix of controllers and windows for each application.

4. Development strategy

We have described the methodology we followed in requirements analysis, and the salient features of our application design and architecture. In this section we focus on the key aspects of our macro development strategy, namely, the use of the offshore development model, the technique for configuration management, and, finally, our strategy for incremental integration.

4.1 Work breakdown structure

The development model used for the project was the *offshore development model* [7]. In this model, development work is done predominantly at offshore development centers, with a small team being stationed at the customer's site. From the software vendor's point of view, the onsite team has the advantage of being in close contact with the customer, while the offshore team has the advantage of being in close proximity to sources of knowledge and information on technical issues. As such, the onsite team, in addition to performing the necessary process modeling and essential object modeling, took responsibility of conceptualizing the user interface of the applications to be built. The offshore team, on the other hand, "encapsulated" the responsibility for the application design and architecture.

Testing a client application offshore can be troublesome because of the response time of the data link to the onsite machines. To ameliorate this problem, we had a second implementation of `Host` which had the same method interface but accessed instead a Sybase database offshore. One developer "specialized" in the implementation and testing of the class `Host;` his responsibility was to periodically test the real `Host` class with the onsite data link and keep the dummy `Host` in sync with the real one.

4.2 Incremental design and integration

Jacobson et al. [9] recommend an incremental integration strategy, in which functionality is incrementally added onto whatever has already been built and tested. A use case usually forms the convenient unit for an incremental addition of functionality. However, even a single use case can be too large a dose for a team that has never been exposed to OO before, and is internalizing much of the paradigm during the course of the project. To allow for sufficient opportunity to learn by doing without unduly setting the project off course, we decided to split the first use case into three "subsets," and employ a subset-driven design and implementation route rather than a strictly use-case driven route. Each subset built on the previous one by adding a piece of well-defined and reasonably self-contained functionality. Correspondingly, there were three stages of testing for the first use case: each stage was to test, in a system test environment, all the functionality built up to that point. There was no separate unit testing. This approach did away with the risks of one-time "big-bang" integration. More importantly, it allowed us to learn from our design decisions and design patterns from a previous subset and refine these in building the next subset. It must be mentioned that the temptation to verify program correctness caused the subsets to be tested in a somewhat less-than-system test environment! This caused time-consuming changes to the program at the actual system test phase.

4.3 Design to code effort ratio

One of the key issues facing a development team is the question of the "ideal" ratio of design to coding effort. With a GUI builder like PowerBuilder that comes with its own integrated debugging environment, it is tempting to try a quick-and-dirty proof-of-concept approach in which design and code are developed up to the point where an initial run can be made; reliance on the debugger then takes over as a means of unearthing bugs and verifying program correctness. While this approach is tempting, it is hardly recommended for systems of nontrivial size. We decided to invest extra effort in design and design reviews. The "default" design to code effort ratio was decided to be unity, and would be revised depending on our experience. The emphasis on investment in design led to significant payoffs; in one case, 8 hours of effort were expended in the detailed design and review of a particularly complex dialogue, following which a developer with just a year's experience in programming took barely over two hours to provide the complete compiled code for testing! (We estimated that had we cut down on the time for design to a third, it would have taken at least 3 more days for the dialogue to have been coded and made available for testing due to design shortcomings surfacing during coding.)

4.4 Configuration management and version control

The conventional notion of unit testing is inapplicable in the OO context. To perform a unit test, the developer must typically write stubs that return dummy data. In traditional development, the size of such stubs is invariably much smaller than the size of the function being stubbed. In a typical OO design however, most methods are but a few lines long, so that it does not make sense to write stubs in the conventional sense. The convenient unit of OO development is a class, whereas the convenient unit of test is usually a group of related classes. This must be taken care of in devising a suitable configuration management plan. The method adopted by us is illustrated here by a simple but representative example.

Consider a scenario involving 2 developers Jack and Jill, and the classes `Customer` and `Host`. Suppose Jack is to work on class `Host`, and Jill is to work on class `Customer`. Each developer has his/her respective class checked out from the shared development directory on the LAN, into a [PowerBuilder] library in his/her personal directory. Suppose now that the method `getCustForId` is to be implemented on class `Host`, and this method is to be called by the method `load()` on class `Customer`. To allow Jill (coding `Customer`) to use the definition of `getCustForId`, the method signature is also defined on the copy of `Host` in the shared development area on the LAN. This allows Jill to compile her code for `Customer`, but not run it till class `Host` is made available by Jack. When both Jack and Jill finish with their coding and error-free compilation, `Customer` and `Host` are both moved to a common test area, and tested together as a unit. Following successful testing, the classes are baselined. For this approach to work well, it is desirable that the quantum of work assigned to each developer is approximately the same, so that they finish with their coding just in time for the test.

Version control was done at the class level, using LBMS' Object Manager. A new version was created, after each cycle of testing, for all those classes that had undergone modification since the previous testing cycle. As our testing cycles were initially driven by subsets of use cases rather than the use cases themselves, not all the versions that were produced were directly of relevance to the client. Nevertheless, we expect each testing cycle to ultimately coincide with an incremental release once the team is sufficiently at home with the new techniques (at the time of writing this has not yet happened).

5. Summary and conclusion

This paper described the experiences of one company, Infosys Technologies, in deploying Structured techniques for the analysis and OO for the design and development of a set of business applications for a large public utility firm in the US. We described the nature of requirements specification and the role of process and object models in a scenario where a server-side design was already largely in place. We described our experiences in using the concepts of event partitioning and system essence for analysis modeling, initially proposed in the context of Structured Analysis. We then presented the salient features of the application design and architecture. We described briefly the roles played by the onsite and offshore teams. Finally, we described the key elements of our development strategy, including our approach to configuration management and incremental integration and testing.

The first client application to be built using the approach described consisted of about 60 PowerBuilder objects of which the key classes constituted about a dozen and visual objects about 20. This application, which formed the basis of most of our observations in this paper, took up about 20 person-months of effort. Work on CAS client applications has since consumed about 100 person-months of effort, and is still in progress.

In our experience, traditional event partitioning and entity-relationship diagramming was of considerable use in clarifying and documenting our understanding of the business processes as seen by the end-user. The use of traditional techniques had the added benefit that the on-site team had little difficulty in relating to the analysis models used. The clean separation of analysis and design models facilitated a clear breakdown of tasks between the offshore and onsite teams, while retaining the seamlessness of the analysis-design transition that characterizes the OO approach. The most palpable benefit of the OO design has been the ability to pinpoint and localize the effect of changes to requirements or design, and to pinpoint bugs.

While the on-site team did not have much difficulty in relating to the essential object model or to the use cases, the offshore team experienced a significant learning curve with the new OO design techniques; it took about two months before there was a certain sense of comfort with the new design paradigms. We find that there is a tendency to underestimate the learning curve for OO design by a large margin, a tendency which arises usually because the developers are already comfortable with the OO programming language *per se*.

Significant benefits from reuse at the code level have not been felt as yet, primarily because the bulk of the applications are still being conceptualized. It is worth pointing out that while there is a conscious attempt to reuse design ideas, we have avoided pinning our expectations of OO on code-level reuse.

In conclusion, we point out that our overall approach as described in this paper is applicable to the development of business applications in general, and is not limited to client/server development or to situations requiring the migration of legacy systems. The process of migration to OO is not easy particularly due to the paradigm shift in OO design; however, this process can be eased considerably by the judicious use of proven, shop-usable traditional techniques for analysis, as we have demonstrated.

We have, in this paper, said nothing about effort or size estimation. This continues to be a weak area particularly in a context where server-side design is more or less a given and OO is limited to client-side development, as is typically the case with legacy systems.

Acknowledgments

The author thanks Pankaj Jalote and S. Yegneshwar for their comments and suggestions.

References

[1] Berson A. and Anderson G. *SYBASE Client/Server Architecture*, McGraw-Hill, NJ, 1995.

[2] Booch G. *Object-Oriented Analysis and Design with applications* (2e), Benjamin/Cummings, CA, 1994.

[3] Booch G. and Rumbaugh J. *The Unified Modeling Language for Object-Oriented Development Version 1.0.*, Rational Software Corporation, 1997.

[4] Coad P., North D. and Mayfield M. *Object Models: Strategies, Patterns, Applications*, Prentice-Hall, NJ, 1995.

[5] Fichman R. G. and Kemerer C. F. "Object-oriented and conventional analysis and design methodologies: comparison and critique," *IEEE Computer*, October 1992.

[6] Gamma E., Helm R., Johnson R. and Vlissides J. *Design Patterns: Elements of Reusable Object-Oriented Software*, Addison-Wesley, 1995.

[7] Gopalakrishnan S., Kochikar V. P. and Yegneshwar S. "The offshore model for software development: the Infosys experience," *Proc. ACM SIGCPR Conference on The Virtual Workplace*, Denver, Colorado, April 11-13, 1996.

[8] Howe D. R. *Data Analysis for Database Design*, Edward Arnold, London, 1989.

[9] Jacobson I., Christerson M., Jonsson P., Overgaard G. *Object-Oriented Software Engineering*, Addison-Wesley, 1992.

[10] McMenamin S. J. and Palmer J. F. *Essential Systems Analysis*, Prentice-Hall, NJ, 1984.

[11] Rumbaugh J., Blaha M., Premerlani W., Eddy F. and Lorensen W. *Object Oriented Modeling and Design*, Prentice-Hall, NJ, 1991.

Experiences with Object Oriented Model-Driven Development

Monique SNOECK
Guido DEDENE

Katholieke Universiteit Leuven
Faculty of Economics and Applied Economics
The Leuven Institute for Research on Information Systems
Naamsestraat 69
B-3000 Leuven, Belgium
telephone: + 32 16 32 67 12, Fax: + 32 16 32 67 32
email: {Guido.Dedene, Monique.Snoeck}@econ.kuleuven.ac.be

Abstract

Model-driven development finds its origin in a reframed version of Zachman's Information Systems Architecture. This framework recognises levels of abstraction, which is not the same as levels of detail, in the systems development process. If the model-driven approach is applied in addition to object oriented analysis concepts, significant benefits are to be expected on the side of maintenance cost. Indeed, one of the main benefits of the model-driven development process is the perfect modular structure of the developed systems. This facilitates maintenance dramatically. However, in order to prove such a statement it is necessary to wait until sufficient experience is gained in the maintenance of systems developed according to this approach. M.E.R.O.DE. is an object oriented development based on two principles: model-driven development and specification by contract. The method was developed around 1988 and has been used by customers since 1991. This paper presents the result of a small scale and informal inquiry amongst the M.E.R.O.DE. users. As many systems they developed have been subject of maintenance, their experiences should allow us to asses or reject the hypothesis that model-driven development facilitates maintenance dramatically. Although the results presented here pertain to one particular method, the model-driven approach can be adopted by users of ***any*** *object oriented analysis method.*

Keywords: Software Engineering - Model-driven development - Object Oriented Analysis - Maintenance

Improving the maintainability of object oriented systems

The object model developed in the analysis phase defines a set of object classes, their features, methods and interactions. In general, object oriented analysis methods do not partition this set of classes in different categories. As a result, the analysis models of large software development projects are complex networks of communicating objects. Some methods provide techniques such as the definition of subject areas to handle this complexity. However, a more systematic partitioning of analysis objects is necessary to keep specifications (and implementation) surveyable and maintainable. When such partitioning techniques are absent, the danger truly exists that object oriented analysis will -to a certain level- suffer from the same flaws as functional decomposition: the starting points are still the user requirements, only now these are expressed in terms of objects rather than in terms of functions. This shift from functions to objects is not a sufficient solution to maintainability problems in information systems development. The shift to the object oriented paradigm certainly offers some benefits, but there is still room for significant improvement.

In order to achieve a better maintainability, one should take account for the fact that specifications are not all alike. There are different types of specifications that each have their own nature and change rate. For example, the change rate of user interface requirements is much higher

0-8186-7840-2/97 $10.00

	strategy *why*	analysis *what*	design *how*	people *who*	timing *when*	locali-sation *where*	measu-rement *how much*	quality *how good*
SCOPE								
BUSINESS								
FUNCTIO-NALITY								
TECHNO-LOGY								

Fig. 1 The reframed Zachman framework for Information Systems Architecture

than that of domain knowledge [1]. Each specification unit will give rise to a number of object type definitions. These object types will have the same change rate as the specifications they originated from.

Rather than having one single set of object definitions in the analysis model, object classes should be grouped into layers according to their change rate. The inner layer must contain the most stable object types. Subsequent layers contain object types with increasing change rate. Classes are allowed to use the services of classes in the same or more inner layers, but not the services of objects in outer layers. This ensures that modifications on objects in an outer layer have no effect on objects that are in an inner layer. By putting stable object classes in the inner layer, they can remain unchanged when classes in outer layers are modified.

In order to obtain such a layered set of objects, specifications should be layered as well. How this can be done, is described in the next paragraph. The second paragraph exemplifies the presented concepts by developing specifications for a small example according to the model-driven approach. The fourth paragraph then presents the results of the inquiry among M.E.R.O.DE. users and finally, the last paragraph draws some conclusions and presents possibilities for further research

Model-driven development: What is it ?

The model driven approach is based on the reframed framework for information systems architecture of Zachman (see Fig. 1) [5, 9]. This framework allows to view information system development in a wide context, possibly with multiple systems and where a wide range of aspects (one per column) and several levels of abstraction (one per row) are considered. The columns and rows in the framework have no order. Note that levels of abstraction are not the same as levels of details. In fact, each level of abstraction can at its turn be described at several levels of details. In this paper we are mainly concerned with the enterprise or business model and the functionality model.

The concept of model-drive development have been integrated in the object oriented analysis method M.E.R.O.DE., developed at the Department of Applied Economic Sciences of the K.U.Leuven. M.E.R.O.DE. stands for **M**odel-driven **E**ntity-**R**elationship **O**bject oriented **De**velopment. The different rows in the reframed Zachman framework define the set of models in the M.E.R.O.DE. system development process (Fig. 2) .

SCOPE MODEL	Model of strategy and goals of the development project
BUSINESS MODEL	Model of domain knowledge; Enterprise Model
FUNCTIONALITY MODEL	Model of the required Functionality
TECHNOLOGY MODEL	Technical design and implementation

Fig. 2 Layers in the M.E.R.O.DE. modelling process

The main characteristic of model-driven development is that it separates domain knowledge specifications from functionality specifications. When users describe systems, they usually tend to mix both types of requirements. Fig. 3 shows a subset of specifications that can be classified in different cells of the Zachman framework. It is clear that only statements 2 and 4 are defining the domain, while statements 3, 5, 6 and 7 are a description of the required functionality. Finally statement 1 should be classified in the technology modelling row of the framework.

Objects that exist in the problem domain are, generally speaking, quite stable and change very little. On the other hand, the change rate of functionality requirements is much higher. Design for maintenance should take account for this different probability for change. In order to manage all possible change in a controlled way, objects should be grouped by their level of stability. This can be achieved by separating objects of the problem domain from objects that embody functionality. The result is an analysis model that consists of two submodels: an enterprise model (or "domain model" or "real world model" or "business model") and a functionality model.

1. The pharmacy system must run on a network.
2. Restricted products should only be delivered upon medical prescription.
3. Doctors connected to the pharmacy by means of a network, must be able to send prescriptions to the pharmacy electronically.
4. The system must be able to handle several types of medicines and products for general sale.
5. It must be possible to request an overview on screen of all data related to a patient by means of maximum three keystrokes and print this overview on paper.
6. The system must keep a history of medicines delivered to patients and check new deliveries for incompatibilities with currently taken medicine.
7. It is possible to have an surveyable list of selected products on screen and to print this list on paper.

Fig. 3 Example of User Requirements

As pioneered by the J.S.D.-methodology, modelling the real world or 'domain' allows to construct a solid nucleus for a software system [4]. The complexity of most systems is driven by the complexity of the reality that it has to deal with. In addition, statements about the required functionality always have some underlying assumptions about the real world which should be made explicit. On the other hand, there is no sense in building a real world model without some functionality in mind. Hence, both models are an integral part of an analysis model with equal importance.

It is important not to confuse the separation between analysis and design with enterprise and functionality modelling. From Fig. 1 we can see that analysis and design match the second and third *columns* while enterprise and functionality modelling match the second and third *abstraction layers*.

The enterprise modelling step results in the definition of domain object classes and business events. The domain object classes form a stable kernel on top of which functionality is modelled as a set of independent functions. Each function results in the definition one function object class and a set of user interface object classes and control object classes (that determine the flow of control in an application). Functions never communicate with each other directly. Output functions extract information from the domain object classes and present it to the user on paper or on screen. Input functions collect data from the user and pass it to the domain object classes by triggering business events. On top of this functionality layer, a user interface layer provides user with facilities to trigger, interrupt and resume the execution of functions. The result is a very flexible application architecture

The main advantage of this architecture is a major productivity gain during maintenance. Because functions are independent modules, they can easily be plugged in and out and domain object classes can be added to the enterprise model without ripple effect on existing functions. In addition, the set functions that is affected by the modification of domain object classes is easy to determine. This allows to better estimate the cost of modifying the enterprise model. It would probably be clarifying to look at a concrete example to better understand how the model-driven approach results in a flexible and maintainable architecture.

Model-driven development: An example

The development of an information system with M.E.R.O.DE. will be illustrated by means of a small library example:

In the Small Library members can borrow books, possibly several at a time. The privileges of a member determine the allowed duration of a loan. If a member has a book that is more than week overdue, the library system automatically generates a letter to this member to remind him/her to return the book. If after that the book still is not returned, the book is registered as lost and possibly the member is withdrawn some privileges. The library provides its members with an online catalogue with search facilities of all available books.

For each development project two models must be developed: an enterprise model and a functionality model. The following sections will briefly outline each of these models for the given case. For a more extensive explanation and for the exact syntax and semantics of the techniques used in M.E.R.O.DE., the reader is referred to [2, 3, 5]

Enterprise Model

In the scope model it has been defined that the library wants an information system for the administration of members, loans, books and reminding letters. The bookkeeping and ordering administration will be done manually.

First of all, we have to search for object types that occur within this scope and are relevant for the system to be constructed. In this case, we retain three object types: MEMBER, LOAN and BOOK.

The static or structural aspects of object types are modelled by means of an object relationship diagram, represented in Fig. 4. In this diagram, the relationship type LOAN between MEMBER and BOOK specifies that a book can be borrowed by at most one member at any one time and that a member can possibly borrow many books at any one time.

Fig. 4. Object Relationship model for the library

The dynamic aspects of object types are described by means of two types of diagrams: JSD-diagrams (equivalent to finite state machines [2]) and an object event table. The latter type of diagram results from the special view that M.E.R.O.DE. takes to object interaction.

An analysis model is supposed to specify *what* the information system should do while the design model specifies *how* things should be done. When interaction between objects is modelled, message passing is much closer to the *how* than to the *what*. For this reason, in the M.E.R.O.DE. enterprise model objects do not communicate with each other by means of message passing. The formalism of synchronous participation to events is used instead. For example, in the library environment, the fact that books can be borrowed, gives rise to the definition of an event type *borrow*. The fact that a member and a book are involved in this event type van be expressed by specifying a message that is sent from BOOK to MEMBER on occurrence of a *borrow* event. Or it might seem more natural to have MEMBER send a message to BOOK. Rather than debating on the direction of the message, it is much more essential to model the essence of this type of communication. In **reality**, none of the objects is sending a message to the other. What really happens is that when a *borrow* event occurs, two objects are involved in this event: one member and one book. For this reason, in M.E.R.O.DE., objects do not communicate by means of message passing but they communicate by jointly participating in events. For the library example this means that both the MEMBER and BOOK object types are provided with a method called 'borrow' and it is agreed that object types have to synchronise on common events. Of course, at design time this synchronous participation to events will be transformed to message passing, provided an object oriented technology is used for implementation. The concept of communication by means of joint participation to business events gives rise to a new enterprise modelling technique. In general OOA methods provide in an Object Relationship diagramming technique, Finite state machines or Harel Statecharts for modelling the dynamic aspects and an interaction diagramming technique [8]. In M.E.R.O.DE. we also have the Object Relationship diagram and Finite State Machines (expressed as JSD-diagrams), but the interaction diagram is replaced by the Object Event Table. This table provides a list of all relevant event types and indicates which object types are involved in these events together with the type of involvement (create, modify or delete). The OET for the library is depicted in **Fig. 5**. Relevant event types for this administration are:

enter =	a person becomes a new member.
leave =	a person ceases to be a member.
borrow =	a book is borrowed.
renew =	a loan is renewed.
return =	a book is returned to the library.
lose =	a book is registered as lost.
acquire =	a new book is acquired.
catalogue =	an newly acquired book is catalogued.
dispose =	an old book is disposed of.

	BOOK	LOAN	MEMBER
Borrow	M	C	M
return	M	D	M
renew	M	M	M
lose	D	D	M
enter			C
leave			D
acquire	C		
dispose	D		
catalogue	M		

Fig. 5. Object-Event Table for the library

Secondly, per object type a structure diagram is drawn according to Jackson's principles of System Development [4]. This structure diagram describes the sequence restrictions each object type imposes on its event types. In this kind of diagrams a '*' indicates the iteration of a structure and a 'o' indicates an alternative in a selection structure. The event types in the structure diagrams of

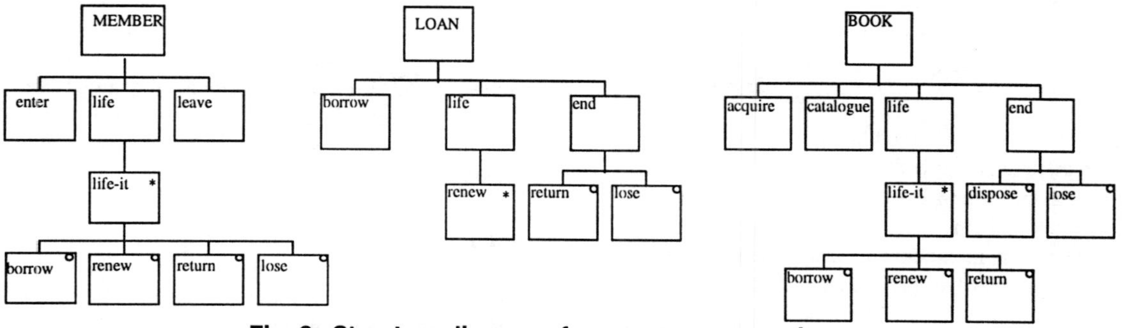

Fig. 6. Structure diagrams for MEMBER, LOAN and BOOK

MEMBER, BOOK and LOAN (Fig. 6) are exactly those event types for which a 'c', 'm' or 'd' is drawn in the OET.

Once the static and dynamic aspects of object types are defined, the business model is further refined by defining attributes for object types and specifying what happens to an object type when a particular event type occurs. This results in the definition of one abstract data type per object type which contains the state vector for that object type and one method per event type in which this object participates. We exemplify this by defining the state vector for MEMBER and the event-method for *enter* in Fig. 7.

The enterprise model can also be refined with additional business rules. This type of rules emerges when other attributes than the "state" form pre-conditions for other event types. This type of rule is expressed by means of the indication of the event type within the object class and the conditions that contain object class attributes which constrain the event type. An example could be a rule that limits the number of books in loan to 10:

borrow: member.number_in_loan < 10

These conditions may involve event attributes as well as object attributes of all the object classes involved in the event type.

MEMBER
state vector: code : unique identification of person; name : name of this person; address : address of this person; zip : postal-code of the city; category : depending on the category, persons have different privileges; number_lost : counts the number of books this person has lost; number_in_loan : counts the number of books this person has in loan.

event-methods:
...
MEMBER.enter (input-code; input-name; input-address; input-zip; input-category)
code := input-code;
name := input-name;
address := input-address;
zip := input-zip;
category := input-category;
...

Fig. 7 Abstract Data Type for MEMBER

Functionality model

The functionality model defines how information functions provide the end-users of the information system with input and output facilities. The functions are designed as a layer on top of the enterprise model. Three types of functions can be identified:

Output functions provide the user with output facilities in the form of predefined screens or printed reports.
Input functions provide input facilities to end-user and generate events that are transmitted to the enterprise model.

Both types of functions can be on-line as well as batch and they are initiated by some external agent (typically the user interface). Input functions will often be of an interactive type: in order to increase the user-friendliness of the interface, facilities can be provided that allow user to search for existing objects. For example, a pick-list allows users to search for a customer whose address is to be modified. Strictly speaking, interactive functions are a combination of output and input functions. The third type of function is the *control* function.

Control functions differ from input functions in that they are initiated by the enterprise model. Initiation of a control function depends on the internal state of the objects of the enterprise model. When triggered, control functions generate events that are transmitted to the enterprise model.

Examples of functions for the library are

F1 = register a new member

F2 = catalogue a new book

F3 = register a loan

F4 = For each member who has a loan that is more than a week overdue, print a letter to remind him/her to return the book.

F5 = print a list of all books that should have been returned yesterday.

F6 = Withdraw privileges of a member when this member has a book that is more than two months overdue.

Functions are allowed to inspect the state vector of objects in order to retrieve information. This is depicted by means of a diamond connected to the function and to the object type. A double bar across the connection between diamond and object type indicates that the function inspects the state vector of more than one object type occurrence. Events are depicted as circles. The functionality model with the six functions defined earlier is shown in Fig. 8. This figure also demonstrates that functions are modular components independent of each other, that can easily be plugged in and out the enterprise model.

Functions never introduce essential changes to the enterprise model. A final element in the functionality model is the definition of transaction objects. Events are atomic units of action which do not always keep the database in a consistent state (e.g. the deletion of a member while there are still loans registered for that member). Therefore transactions are defined. Basically, transactions produce streams of correct event messages that leave the database in a consistent state.

Implementation

While usually it is assumed that an object oriented implementation environment is to be used, the concept of communication by joint participation to events makes it is perfectly possible to implement object oriented specifications in a classical environment. Both for implementation in *classical* environments and in object oriented technology, the object event table is taken as starting point. If horizontal cuts are taken in the object event table, we obtain one procedure per event that can be implemented in classical technology, whereby the object state vectors are stored in a database that will be accessed by these event procedures. The transformation to *object oriented* technology is achieved by taking vertical cuts in the object event table: each column defines the abstract data type of an enterprise object. Events are also giving rise to the definition of an object class responsible for broadcasting the event occurrence to all participating objects. Around this kernel, functions are implemented as independent clusters of control object classes. The final layer consists of a set of interface objects that allow to trigger functions. In this way, a layered set of objects is obtained as shown

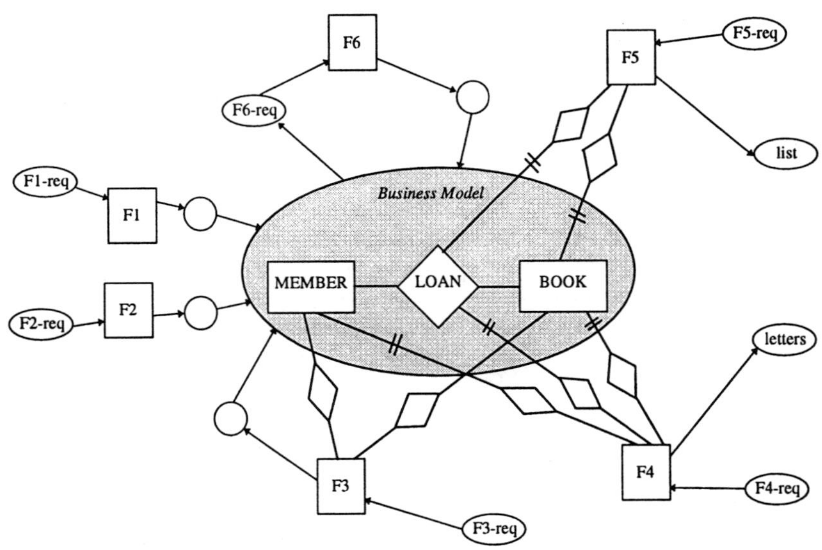

Fig. 8. Functionality model for the library

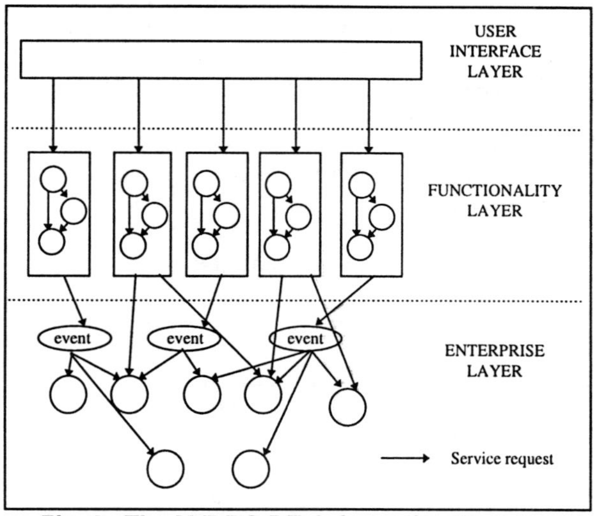

Fig. 9. The M.E.RO.DE. Information Systems Architecture

in Fig. 9.

Model-driven development: Experiences

When the M.E.R.O.DE. method was developed, it was expected that the model-driven approach would result in significant benefits during maintenance. As functions are independent components, they are easy to plug in and out when functionality requirements change. The model-driven approach is also based on the idea that changes to the functionality model will occur more often than changes to the enterprise model. In order to be able to assert these assumptions, it was necessary to wait until the first projects developed with M.E.R.O.DE. were subject to maintenance. Informal contacts with users confirmed that today it should possible to evaluate the approach.

By the end of September 1996, a questionnaire (see Appendix) was sent to 23 companies we believed are users of M.E.R.O.DE.. Only 12 companies returned the questionnaire. We assume that companies that did not return the questionnaire are not using the method. The main purpose of the questionnaire is to identify the users and to have an idea of the extent to which M.E.R.O.DE. has been used so far. Out of the 12 respondents, 2 are not using the method, 1 company is interested in the method, three are testing it and six have definitively chosen for M.E.R.O.DE..

The questionnaire contains 14 general questions and one sheet that must be filled in per project. A total of 27 projects have been/are being developed with the method, but only for 19 projects a documentation sheet was received. The size of the projects in terms of number of business object types, business event types, attribute types and number of functions is given in Fig. 10.

Most of the projects have been implemented using relational databases (Oracle, DB2 and ADABAS) for storage of persistent objects and third or fourth generation languages (COBOL, PL1, Natural) for coding. One company is using Informix and Smalltalk for implementation purposes.

Unfortunately none of the companies could provide us with a project size estimation in terms of function points. As a result, the effect of model-driven development on the development cost of information systems can not be quantified and we have to rely upon the subjective perception of the individual respondent. If function point

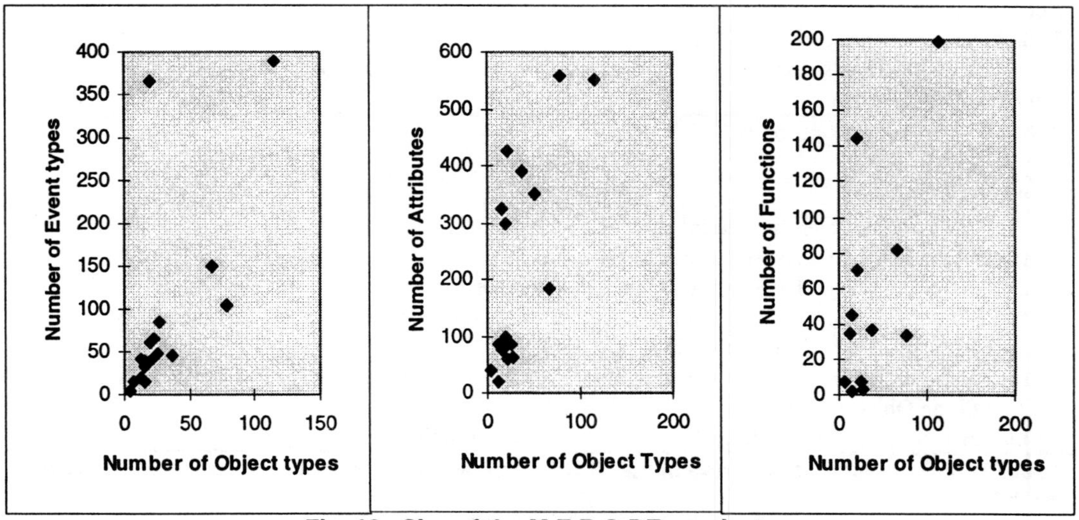

Fig. 10. Size of the M.E.R.O.DE. projects

measurements had been available, it would have been possible to compare the development effort with the development effort of classical projects with a similar size.

Out of the 14 general questions, three were meant to discover the perceived advantages of the model-driven approach. Main advantages in order of number of citations and average score are listed in Table 1. Main disadvantages in order of number of citations and average score are shown in Table 2. A score of 1 indicates the most important (dis)advantage and a score of 5 the least important. The main reason why M.E.R.O.DE. was chosen in stead of other methods are listed in Table 3.

The last three general questions were trying to establish the perceived change rate of the business model and the functionality model. Due to the lack of registration systems, users were mostly enable to answer this questions. But those who answered were unanimous: the change rate of functions is higher than that of the business model.

Conclusion and Lessons Learned

These results confirm that the model-driven approach

Advantage	number of citations	average score
Good modular structure of developed system	9	1,66
Maintenance is faster	8	2,25
Analysis phase is shorter	6	3
Implementation must not necessarily be done in OO technology	6	3,4
Better documentation of the project	6	3,5
Object oriented analysis method	5	3,6
Implementation phase is shorter	2	4
Method is effective help for specification	1	4
Separation of enterprise model and functionality model	1	2
Results are transparent for developers	1	5

Table 1. Advantages of M.E.R.O.DE.

Disadvantage	number of citations	average score
No case-tool available	7	1,4
Method is insufficiently documented	4	2,75
Analysis phase is longer	3	2
Inadequate documentation of project	2	2,5
Method unknown to many developers	2	2,5
Not enough opportunities for education	2	2,5
Techniques are too abstract for end-users	2	3,5
Connection with organisational aspects is missing	1	1
method still incomplete	1	2

Table 2. Disadvantages of M.E.R.O.DE.

- the strict separation of business and functionality requirements (3 users).
- the clear and transparent structuring of developed systems (2 users).
- the fact that the method is well-structured (2 users)
- that the object relation model allows to model the business in a formal way.
- that the methods supports the natural way of thinking and reveals errors in the thinking process.
- the transactional aspect of the method.
- the precise definition of the development process (what, how, documentation) based on scientific research.
- that it is an Object Oriented method.
- that analysis according to M.E.R.O.DE. results in better insight in business processes.

Table 3. Main reasons to choose M.E.R.O.DE. in stead of an other object oriented analysis method

in combination with object oriented analysis is experienced to have a positive impact on the modularity of the developed system and hence on the maintenance cost. As nearly all users are implementing their systems with classical technology, the benefits can not be the consequence of the use of object oriented implementation technology.

From the reasons why M.E.R.O.DE. was chosen above other methods (Table 3) it appears that the separation of business knowledge from functionality requirements also has other advantages: it allows for a better understanding of the rules that govern the functioning of the business, it results in transparent systems and the modelling techniques have the ability of revealing errors in the thinking process. Although the model-driven approach is typical for M.E.R.O.DE., nothing should prevent users of other object oriented analysis methods to apply this approach on top of their favourite method.

To further validate the intuitive perception of our respondents, a measurement system must be set up that measures the development effort spend to maintenance. Although function points are originally intended for the estimation of new development projects, the technique can be adapted to measure the size of maintenance projects [7]. By comparing the efforts spent on maintenance projects for systems developed according to the model-driven approach with efforts spent on maintenance of systems developed in a classical way, the benefit of model-driven development would become quantifiable. We are aware of the fact that this small scale research can only be a first step in the assessment of the hypothesis that benefits on the side of maintenance cost are (only) due to the model-driven approach (and not to the use of object oriented analysis for example).

The impact of the model-driven development process on the initial development cost is not clear: 4 users think the analysis phase is shorter, while two users think this phase is longer compared to classical development methods. It is to be expected that the initial development cycle will not be significantly shorter. Indeed, business modelling is often the starting point for rethinking and reengineering the business processes.

None of the disadvantages relate to the model-driven concept nor to any principle underlying M.E.R.O.DE.. However, it is clear that CASE-tool support is seen as a crucial element in using a method, just as the availability of the proper method documentation. Both points were also mentioned by several users as priority for the further development of this method. The latter problem can be resolved quite easily, but the development of a CASE-tool is not an easy task. One of the future research in the M.E.R.O.DE. project is to investigate to what extent current CASE-tools of third parties can satisfy the needs of M.E.R.O.DE. users.

Finally, a point that clearly appears from the inquiry results is that users are eager to use the object oriented paradigm for analysis, but that they are rather reluctant to use an object oriented implementation technology. The concept of communication by common events (at the business modelling level) and the object event table are techniques that enable the implementation of an object oriented analysis in classical environments. We believe that in this way, the users can gain experience with object orientation without too much a risk of failure, because implementation can be done in a technology well known by the development staff. On the longer term, experiences with object oriented analysis will ease the way for the introduction of object oriented implementation technology.

References

1. Coad, P., Yourdon, E., Object-Oriented analysis, Prentice Hall, Englewood Cliffs, New Jersey, 1991
2. Dedene Guido, Snoeck Monique, Formal deadlock elimination in an object oriented conceptual schema, *Data and Knowledge Engineering*, Vol. 15, pp. 1-30, 1995
3. Dedene Guido, Snoeck Monique, M.E.R.O.DE.: A Model-driven Entity-Relationship Object-oriented DEvelopment method, ACM SIGSOFT Software Engineering Notes, Vol. 13, No. 3 (1994) 51-61.
4. Jackson, M. A., System Development, Prentice Hall Englewood Cliffs (N.J.), 1983, 418 pp.
5. R. Maes, G. Dedene, Reframing the Zachman Information System Architecture Framework, Tinbergen Institute, discussion paper TI 96-32/2, 1996, 20 pp.
6. Snoeck M., Dedene G., *Existence Dependency: Conceptual Modelling by Contract*, Working Paper, Katholieke Universiteit Leuven, Dept. of Applied Economic Sciences; Submitted for Publication to IEEE TSE.
7. Snoeck Monique, Productivity Measurements in Maintenance, *Proceedings of the 31st G.U.I.D.E. Spring Conference*, May 29 - June 1, 1990
8. Snoeck Monique, Wijsen Jozef, Dedene Guido, Formal Specifications in Object Oriented Analysis: A comparative View, Proceedings of the Workshop on Evaluation of Modelling Methods in Systems Analysis and Design, CAiSE*96 conference, Crete (Greece), May 20-21, 1996
9. J.A. Zachman, A framework for information systems architecture, *IBM Systems Journal*, 26(3), 1987, 276-292.

Appendix: Questionnaire

GENERAL QUESTIONS

Question 1: Name of the company:

Question 2: Size of the company:
Total number of employees :
Total number of employees in EDP :
Total number of employees in systems development:

Question 3: Which of the following statements most accurately describes the use of M.E.R.O.DE. in your company ?

❍ We are interested in M.E.R.O.DE. as possible development method

❍ We use M.E.R.O.DE. on trial

❍ We choose M.E.R.O.DE. as development method

❍ We don't use M.E.R.O.DE.

Question 4: Has your company already used M.E.R.O.DE. for the development of information systems ?

❍ Yes ❍No

Question 5: What are according to you the most important <u>advantages</u> of M.E.R.O.DE. compared to other development methods (traditional as well as object oriented). Rank from 1 tot 5, 1 indicating the most important and 5 the least important.

.... Analysis phase is shorter
.... Implementation phase is shorter
.... Better documentation
.... Better insight in business
.... Good modular structure
.... Maintenance is faster
.... Object Oriented Analysis
.... Implementation must not necessarily be done with OO-technology
....
....

Question 6: What are according to you the most important <u>disadvantages</u> of M.E.R.O.DE. compared to other development methods (traditional as well as object oriented)? Rank from 1 tot 5, 1 indicating the most important and 5 the least important.

.... Analysis phase is longer
.... Implementation phase is longer
.... Bad project documentation
.... Bad modular structure
.... Maintenance is slower
.... No case-tool available
.... Method is insufficiently documented
.... Not enough opportunities for education
....
....

Question 7: What are topics that should be given priority in the further development of M.E.R.O.DE. ?

QUESTIONS FOR USERS ONLY

Question 8: What is the most important reason your company has chosen M.E.R.O.DE. as development method ?

Question 9: Since when are you using M.E.R.O.DE. ?
....

Question 10: How many projects were development using M.E.R.O.DE. ? ....
We would like collect a few data on these projects. You can provide us with these data by filling the separate sheet enclosed with this questionnaire. Please return one sheet per project.

Question 11: Were the systems developed with M.E.R.O.DE. already subject to maintenance ?
❍ Yes ❍No

Question 12: Was this maintenance easier and faster or more difficult and slower than usual ? To which amount ?

Question 13: Is maintenance of functions more frequently required than maintenance of the business model or is it the other way round ?

Question 14: Can you provide us with an estimation of the frequency of business model maintenance and functionality model maintenance ?

Question 15: What tools are used for producing project documentation ?

❍ Case-tool. Which one ?

❍ Word processor

❍ Drawing tool

❍ Others:

QUESTIONNAIRE PER M.E.R.O.DE. PROJECT

General

In which phase of the development process is the project:

- ❍ business modelling
- ❍ functionality modelling
- ❍ implementation
- ❍ maintenance

In case there was an estimation of project size by means of Function Point Analysis, what is the number of Function Points for this project ?
Raw Function Points: ....   Netto/Weighted Function Points: ....

The complexity of the project mainly resides in

- ❍ the business model
- ❍ the functionality model
- ❍ both models
- ❍ implementation

Business model (including later additions):

Number of object types :
Number of event types:
Number of levels in the existence dependency graph:
Total number of attributes:
Total number of business rules (only of business rules were documented separately):
Number of object types with life cycle more complex that the default life cycle (create.(modify)*.delete):

Functionality model

Number of functions in the functionality model (including added functions):

number of	input functions	output functions	interactive functions
Batch:			
On-line:			

Implementation

Implementation environment:
hardware:
operating software:
database software:
programming language:
TP-system:
additional tools such as 4GL-environment, report/screen-generator, CASE-tool:

Maintenance

How often was the business model modified (not extended)?

How many functions were modified as result of bugs or changes in required functionality ?

Session P2c

Project Management Tools

Project Performance Indicator Workbench (PPIW)

A.T.M. Aerts J. Blijenberg F.J. Heemstra R.J. Kusters L.J. Somers
Eindhoven University of Technology
P.O. Box 513, 5600 MB Eindhoven, the Netherlands
wsinlou@win.tue.nl

Abstract

A prototype has been developed of a generic tool set and accompanying methods that enable a customizable approach towards project tracking and benchmarking. The underlying data model describes a generic project life cycle. The prototype has been applied to an iterative development life cycle in a number of field tests.

Keywords. Multi-project management, Process assessment and improvement, Software process metrics, Software process modeling, Software quality.

1. Introduction

Control of projects in the IT-world is mainly based on knowledge and experience. Intuition, and political and social skills play an important part in successful project execution. However, more and more customers refuse to accept vague promises and arrangements. More often hard demands are formulated that are aimed at preventing budget and lead-time overruns and insufficient product quality. Customers demand insight in the expected and agreed project performance at the start of the project, during project execution and at its end. Most of the time project management cannot give this insight. This statement holds for the (operational) project management responsible for the execution of IT-projects and for the multi-project management responsible for initiating, planning, assessing and evaluating projects.

Project managers in most software development organizations use various methods, tools, and procedures. Examples are Function Point Analysis [2], Project Management Workbench [1] and Work Breakdown Structures [7]. Despite all these existing tools and aids, project assessment in the end relies mainly on experience from the past of the people involved. This is a highly subjective ground on which to base decisions. This subjectivity hinders the free exchange of experiences, it seriously hampers the collection of meaningful project data, and it trivializes the discussions needed to reach a further understanding of the development process. Furthermore it is difficult to convince someone (management, customers, ..) on the basis of these subjective arguments. Finally, in practice these assessments have proven to have limitations, as can be illustrated by the many software development project failures that have been widely reported.

If we look at the current state of affairs with this in mind, we notice that the IT-industry recently has invested much effort in process improvement. There is an increased interest in ISO certification (ISO 9000-3) [16]. The main focus in ISO is structuring and formalizing the business processes by means of the development of manuals, guidelines and procedures. Also, the IT-world pays much attention to 'process-assessments' [17], that is to the determination of the maturity level of an IT-development process. The Capability Maturity Model [10] is the best known example in this area. Depending on the maturity level specific actions have to be carried out in the field of project control and/or information system development.

ISO- and CMM-activities try to give customers insight into the performance level of the development organization. However, they do not provide a guide for identifying the data that need to be gathered in order to support assessment, evaluation, and benchmarking of projects.

Apart from ISO and CMM, AMI (Application of Metric in Industry) is a successful approach to assess projects on a quantified basis [3]. One of the basic AMI assumptions is that measuring increases management insight in results and problems and employee's insight in business goals. AMI claims advantages like: improved methods for project planning and project management, improved tuning of the software development process and business goals, improved cost control, and improved communication during project execution. The AMI approach leads to a goal-driven approach of which attribute to measure. This goal-driven approach is based on the Goal-Question-Metric approach [4], which in turn has much in common with Deming's quality improvement cycle [8]. However, AMI does not provide the support needed to identify and gather relevant project data either. In particular, AMI is aimed at running projects in detail. The problems described above are focused at a higher level of abstraction.

The conclusion can be postulated that literature and IS development practice provide a number of successful approaches for the solution of the problem stated above. However, none of the solutions are immediately applicable to the identified problem area because they are primarily focused on supporting project management and not on supporting multi-project management, sales management and customers. The existing methods moreover fail to indicate which data have to be collected and stored and have to be transformed into control information.

2. Objectives

The Project Performance Indicator Workbench (PPIW) discussed in this paper has been developed for the purpose of supporting multi-project managers, project managers, sales managers, and customers.

They are involved in actions related to (planned) execution of projects such as submitting tenders, tracking and/or intervening in a project in progress, and accepting or rejecting a tender. These actions are based on their assessment of the status of the current project and the previous record of the organization in handling projects. The PPIW is to support this assessment:

- Assessment for the multi-project manager means answering questions such as: how is the project doing; should I, as multi-project manager, do something?
- For the project manager assessment means answering questions such as: how is the project doing related to other similar projects; how is the project doing related to the original expectations/estimates/planning?
- The sales managers is interested in answers on questions like: what can I promise to the customer; how do I convince the customer?
- The customer finally wants an answer on questions like: how good is this project team; what can I expect from this organization?

Starting point of the PPIW project is, that it is both useful and possible to support the assessment processes discussed above by collecting project-related data and by comparing these with historical data. Project-related data are in themselves a useful commodity. By offering a fixed set of data a 'language' emerges which enables a more effective and efficient communication process with regard to the projects. If in addition to this an explicit link can be made with past projects, which have been registered in a similar way, the project can be discussed in the light of what was and what was not possible in the past. In this way the PPIW gives a contribution toward making projects more visible.

3. Development

The first step in realising the PPIW objectives is the development of a so-called conceptual framework [9]. This framework shows - on a high level of abstraction - what assessment and control of an information system development project means for the target group. It concerns topics like: what does a sales manager control and why, what are the criteria for a successful assessment or control, and which data are worth transforming to control information. Based on the framework methods, techniques, tools, and procedures can be developed.

The framework assumes that software is developed following a structured approach or life cycle (e.g. linear development; iterative development). Within each type of life cycle a number of objects can be distinguished that are relevant for control purposes. These controlled objects will include items such as the project itself, subprojects, and project phases. Using a critical success factor approach [13] and taking into account relevant cost drivers [6] for each of these controlled objects, one is able to identify a number of performance indicators. These indicators provide sufficient information to serve as a basis for tracking and benchmarking purposes.

Based on the framework methods, techniques, tools and procedures can be developed. A major part of the PPIW project is the development of a tool set. In its final form this tool set will support the structured development of a coherent set of performance indicators for a specific life cycle that is in use within a software development organization. Additional tools that use these indicators will be provided to track and benchmark development efforts.

The development of the PPIW tool set went through several stages. First, some experiments have been done using a paper version of the various forms needed to collect the project information. The advantage of using paper forms is that they are easy to construct and in that way are suitable for early prototyping.

Based on the experience gained from this paper version a prototype electronic version has been constructed. The user interface of this version closely followed the layout of the paper forms, but it was refined to make the life of the project manager, who has to enter the data, as easy as possible by using the facilities offered by modern programming environments, such as sliders and pop-up windows. Some sample input screens are shown in figure 1.

The advantage of the electronic version over the paper one is that, once the necessary infrastructure is in place,

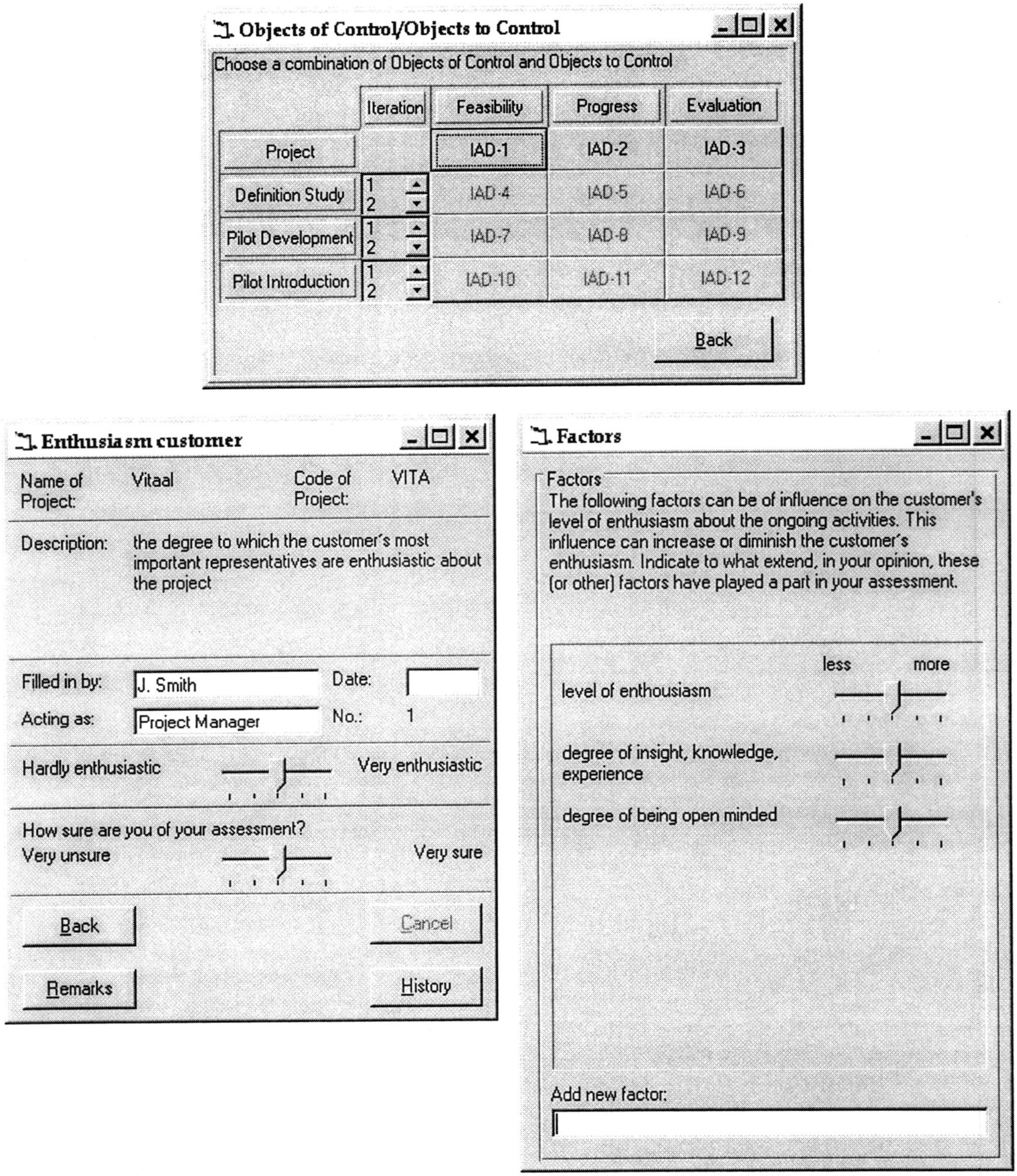

Figure 1. Examples of various input screens of the prototype. In total, the prototype offers over 60 different input screens.

electronic data can be communicated more easily in a form that is directly fit for use by other tools, for instance for the purpose of analysis. The disadvantage is that the tools are harder to construct.

The electronic version was designed to handle information from projects with possibly different life cycle models and development strategies. The underlying data model had to be sufficiently general in order to be able to accommodate this variety. Another requirement was that the tool should be able to access also data from a number of tools for collecting other kinds of project data, such as ESTEEM (the commercial successor of the MERMAID estimation tool set [11]), PMW [1] and SQUID [14]. The PPIW data model therefore should contain as a specialization the relevant parts of the data models of these tools. This led to the data model displayed in figure 2.

General data model: generic part. The left hand side of figure 2 represents the generic description of life cycles and their composition. Life Cycle defines a number of Controlled Objects. An example of a Life Cycle is IAD [15, 18], which defines the Controlled Objects (phases) 'Definition Study', 'Pilot Development', and 'Pilot Introduction'.

A Controlled Object may contain a number of Measurements. Objects defined by Measurement could be the moments of measurement that are defined by the measurement framework. An example of such an object is the moment of measurement with respect to the feasibility of the Pilot Development phase.

A Performance Indicator is used to define the measurement of a property for a particular Measurement, for example 'risk' or 'planning'. This definition can be given by means of separate Aspects and Submetrics.

Since Aspect can only measure one-dimensional values, the measurement property has to be split up into one-dimensional parts. To be able to define clusters of related Aspects, the additional entity type Submetric has been introduced. For example, the Performance Indicator for the measurement property 'risk' contains a risk Top 10. Since this does not yield a one-dimensional value, it has to be divided into 10 separate parts. In order to make it possible to retrieve the relation between these parts, a Submetric is used which defines the various values that have to be measured for one risk. The Submetric has a relation with Aspect for all of these values.

A Submetric can again contain new Submetrics. For example, the Submetric for risk contains a Submetric to define that for each risk a group of measures can be determined. This last Submetric then has relations too with Aspect to determine the values that have to be collected for a measure. This clustering is the only function that Submetric has.

An Aspect may be given an arbitrary value or a value from a predefined list. The entity type Ord/nom Value models the fact that such predefined lists of items are available, so that an item can be chosen to assign it to an Aspect. For example, this could be a list of possible risks or project characteristics.

General data model: specific part. The right hand side of figure 2 shows the specific data about an existing project and the entities that are created for it. Every entity type at the right hand side of the figure represents the fact that actual values are assigned to the attributes that are defined by the entity types at the left hand side of the figure for (parts of) a specific Project.

At the right hand side of figure 2, some additional constraints hold. For a particular Project, there can be more than one Project Phase for each Controlled Object that is defined for the Life Cycle according to which the Project is carried out, if the phase can be gone through iteratively. The same holds for the relations between Project Phase and Project Measurement, and between Project and Project Measurement, but here it depends on the iterative character of Project Measurement. For example, the measurement with respect to 'progress' (and an IAD phase) can be repeated a number of times, whereas the measurement with respect to 'feasibility' (and the same phase) can be done only once.

In the case of the relation between Project Performance Indicator and Project Submetric, the maximum number of Project Submetrics that can be related to Project Performance Indicator are given by an attribute of Submetric. For example, the Submetric of the Performance Indicator for the risk Top 10 defines the aspects that have to be measured for one risk. Furthermore, it determines the maximum number of risks that can be clustered. This number in its turn determines the maximum number of Project Submetrics that can be related to the Project Performance Indicator.

For the various relations between Project Measurement, Project Performance Indicator, Project Submetric and Project Aspect there can be as many relations as defined by the corresponding relations at the left hand side of the model. For example, the Project Measurement with respect to the 'evaluation' of the Pilot Introduction phase can have relations with three Project Performance Indicators, namely 'Enthusiasm customer', 'Involvement customer', and 'Lead-time'.

All entities that are created for entity types at the right hand side of the figure have to be related to an existing entity that is higher in the hierarchy defined by the model. Filling in data for a Project Performance Indicator does not make sense if there is no Project Measurement to relate it to. For Project Measurement and Project Aspect the same holds, with the difference that these entities can be re-

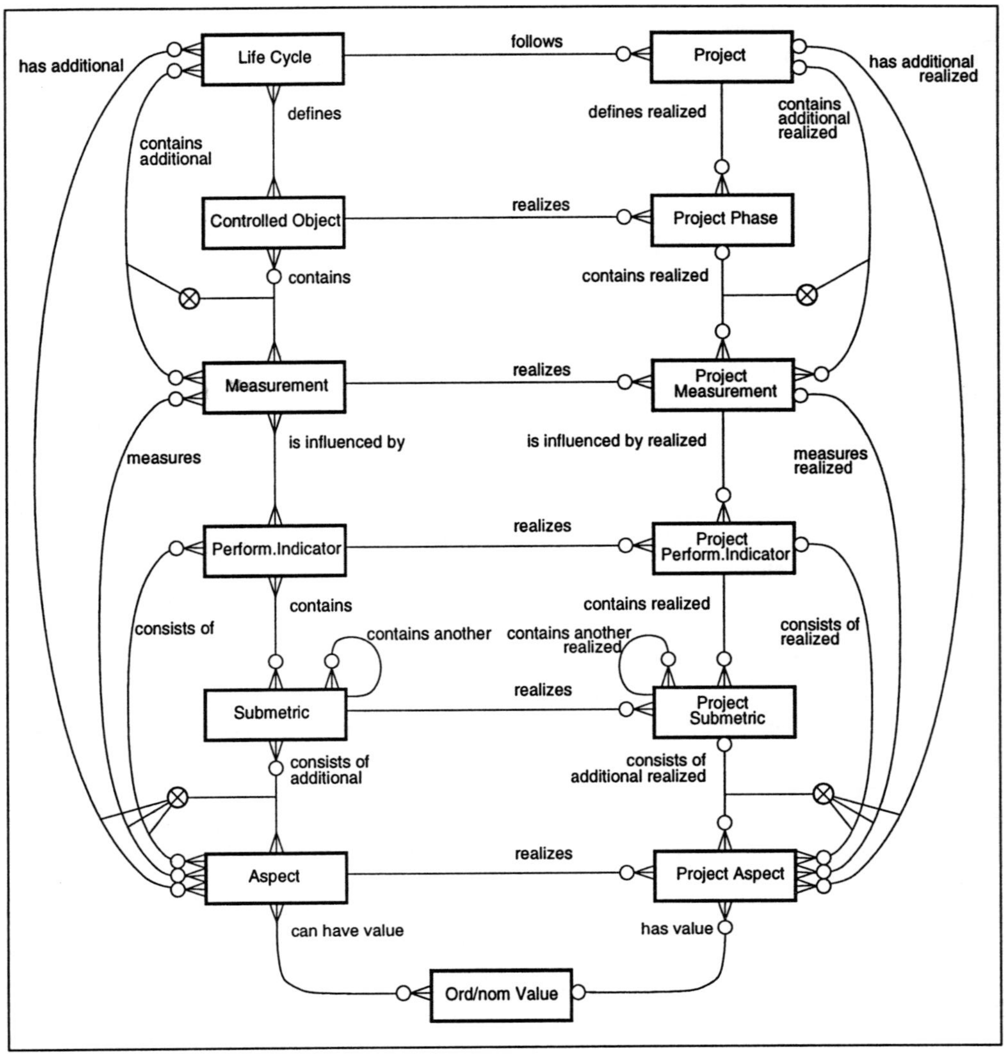

Figure 2. The ER-diagram [12] of the general data model.

lated to more than one higher entity. Because of the exclusion on these relations, they can only be related to exactly one of the other entities.

Prototype data model. The data model of the prototype (called Collest [5]) used in the pilots was a specialization of the general model, suited for IAD-projects. It is the data model in figure 3. Collest stands for collection of data for ESTEEM, referring to the fact that this tool is intended for collecting data in a form that can be analyzed by the ESTEEM-tool.

We see that in this data model the following things have changed. Since this model is specific to IAD, the generic component of the former model has been dropped, and only the right hand side of figure 2 has been kept. Also Project Submetric has been remodeled to a choice of the three simple metrics that a Project Performance Indicator in this case may consist of: Risk Metric, Standard Metric, and Planning Metric.

The Project Aspect of figure 2 we find back in a number of places, where they have been made explicit. Aspects of the Risk Metric are Risk and Risk Measure with their respective value sets Risk Category and Measure. Aspects of the Planning Metric are the Planned and Realized entities representing the planned and realized amounts of work. Aspects relating to the Project as a whole are called Factor and Project Factor, representing predefined factors and user defined, project specific ones respectively. This distinction leaves room for the customization of the factors that influence a project. New developments may give rise to new influences on a project. Another type of aspect, which is not associated with Measurement but represents information about a Project as a whole, are its Characteristics.

From the comparison between figures 2 and 3 we see that the former is a quite general one with a very open structure.

Reporting facilities. The prototype not only offers numerous input facilities, but is also able to generate various reports. For example, after selection of a Controlled Object, a spider graph can be generated for each Measurement that contains all Performance Indicators. For each Performance Indicator a bar graph can be generated showing the values of estimations and their confidence level. Some sample report screens are shown in figure 4.

4. Experiences

The tool set has been tested, first on paper, and later by means of a prototype in two different environments. One test took place in a large Dutch software house. The other took place in the EDP-department of the Dutch Central Statistics Agency. In each setting a number of IAD-project teams participated and used the measurement system. On the basis of the data gathered and a series of interviews the measurement system was adapted. The main result of the field tests was, apart from a number of practical suggestions, that participants indicated that the measurement system tallied with their present working methods. They stated that they already performed similar activities, but not in such a structured way. In other words: they are able and willing to use it. The interest of all the parties involved was raised. They all agreed to participate in a follow-up experiment.

The first prototype was developed specifically for a single project approach (IAD) within a single environment (the software house). The tool was used in another setting (the government agency) and was used successfully there, but a number of adaptations to local circumstances were needed. The requested adaptations mainly referred to the layout of the input screens and the possibilities to generate reports.

Work is in progress to expand the tool. As was discussed above, the aim of the project is a generic tool that can easily be adapted to different project approaches and to different environments. The main functionality of the generic tool would be:

- The possibility to design a specific set of definitions for a specific project approach within a specific organization.
- Maintenance of a locally defined set of definitions.
- The use of this set of definitions to:
  - estimate new projects: the tool offers possibilities to look for comparable, but completed projects (comparable with respect to selected features), so information for planning and estimating a new project can be provided.
  - For a project in execution, the tool has a possibility to look for relevant data of comparable, but completed projects (comparable with respect to selected features), so information to control this project can be provided.
  - Analyzing finished projects.

The finished tool set will provide the generic PPIW this project was aimed at: a generic tool set and accompanying methods that enable a local for local approach towards project tracking and benchmarking.

From the experience gained in this project we conclude that the framework proposed in [9] provides the right information for controlling projects. Note that the kind of metrics needed at the multi-project level is rather different from the more quantitative metrics used to measure daily progress in a project. Further research is needed to find out whether (part of) the information gathered by the tool set can be made more quantitative.

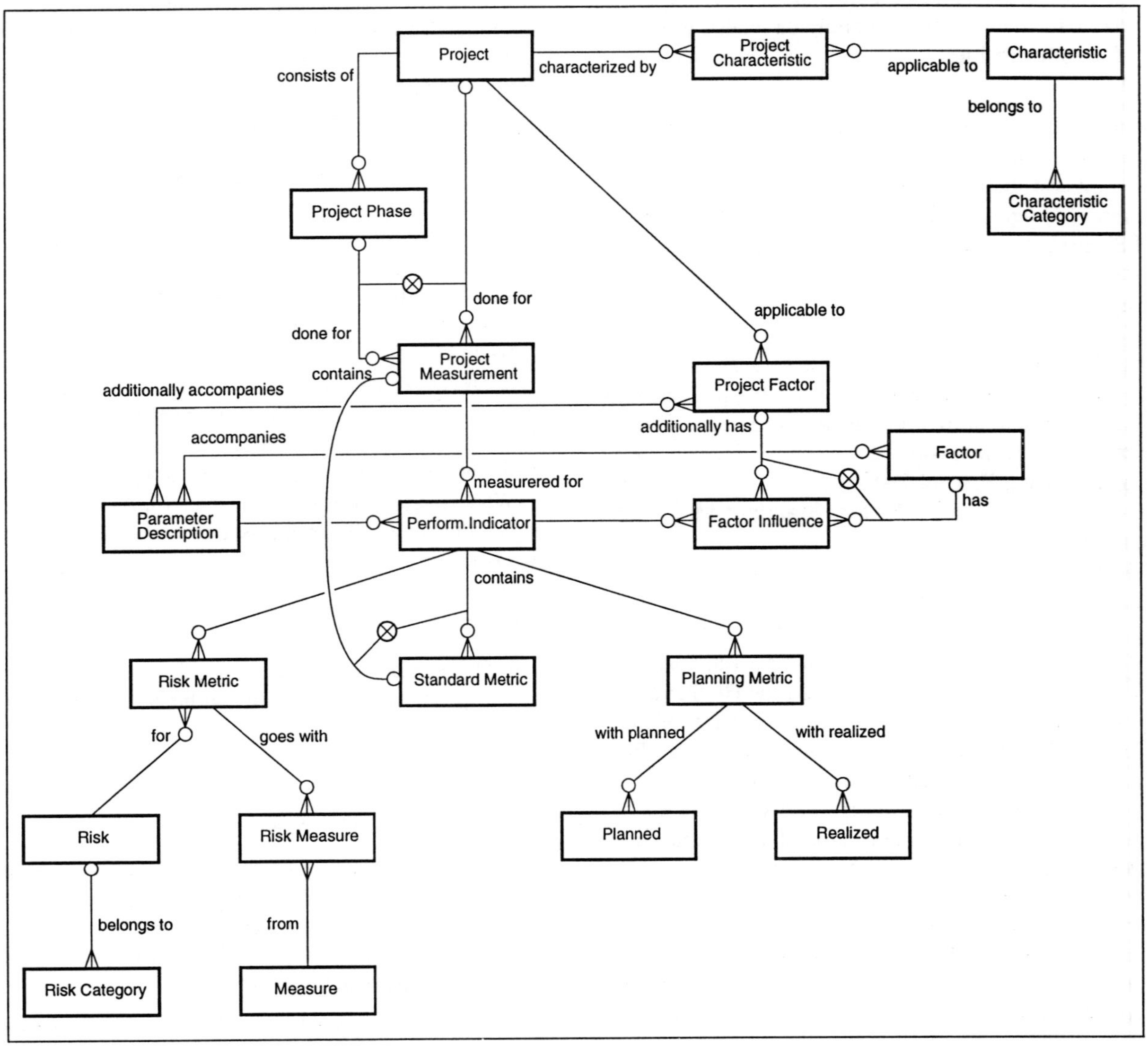

Figure 3. The prototype data model.

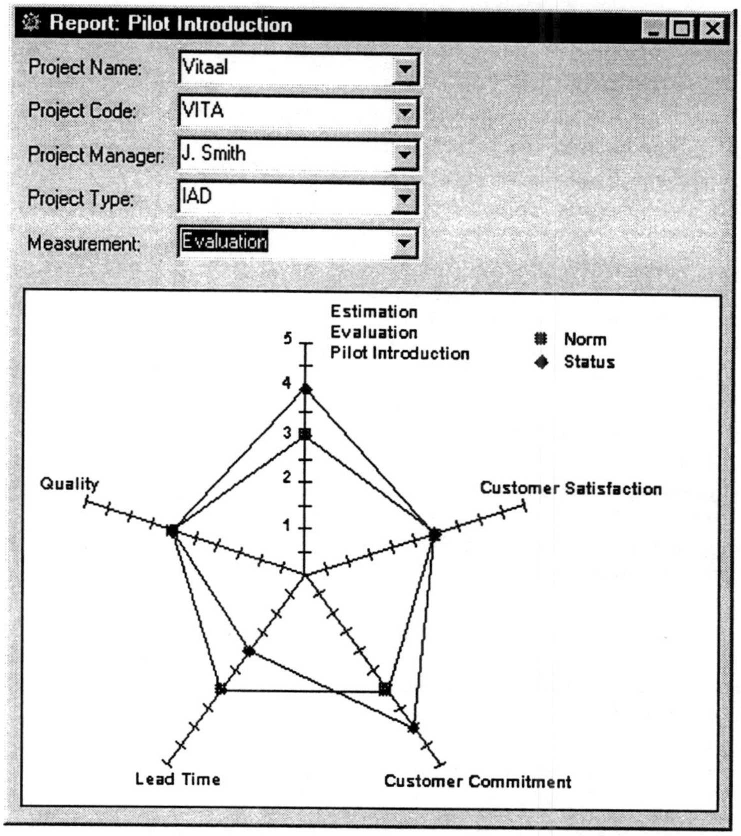

Figure 4. Some reports of the prototype.

References

[1] ABT Corporation, http://www.abtcorp.com/pmw.html, New York. *Project Workbench PMW.*

[2] A. Albrecht and J. Gaffney. Software function, source lines of code, and development effort prediction: a software science validation. *IEEE Transactions on Software Engineering*, 9(6):639–647, 1983.

[3] AMI Consortium c/o The AMI User Group. *AMI Application of Metric in Industry, Metric Users' Handbook.* ISBN 0 9522262 0 0.

[4] V. Basili and H. Rombach. The tame project: Towards improvement oriented software environments. *IEEE Transactions on Software Engineering*, 14(6):758–773, 1988.

[5] J. Blijenberg. Developing a project performance indicator workbench. Technical report, Stan Ackermans Instituut, 1996. ISBN 90-5282-671-4.

[6] B. Boehm. *Software engineering economics.* Prentice-Hall, Englewood Clifs NJ, 1981.

[7] A. Case. *Information systems development: principles of computer aided software engineering.* Prentice-Hall, Englewood Clifs NJ, 1986.

[8] W. Deming. *Out of Crisis.* MIT Center for Advanced Engineering Study, 1986.

[9] F. Heemstra, R. Kusters, H. Ruys, O. Salomons, and W. Aendenroomer. Vitaal: a framework for designing metrics. In A. Cowderoy, editor, *Proceedings of the 7th European Software Control and Metrics Conference*, pages 39–64, London, 1996. CSR.

[10] W. Humphrey. *Managing the Software Process.* Addison Wesley, Reading MA, 1989.

[11] P. Kok, B. Kitchenham, and J. Kirakowski. The mermaid approach to software cost estimation, esprit project 2046. In *ESPRIT'90*, pages 296–314. Kluwer Academic Press, 1990.

[12] R. Rock-Evans. *Analysis within the systems development life-cycle.* Pergamon Infotech, Maidenhead, 1987.

[13] J. Rockard. Critical success factors. *Harvard Business Review*, pages 81–91, March-April 1979.

[14] Squid, esprit project 8436.

[15] R. Tolido. *IAD.* Academic Service, 1995.

[16] J. Trienekens. *Time for Quality.* PhD thesis, Eindhoven University of Technology, Eindhoven, the Netherlands, 1994. (In Dutch).

[17] M. Van Genuchten and F. Heemstra. Surviving is not a must. *De Automatiseringsgids*, November 1993. (In Dutch).

[18] E. Yourdon. *The decline and fall of the American programmer.* Prentice-Hall, 1993.

A Methodical Approach to Establishing a Process Management Infrastructure in an Organization

Vivek Nanda Sylvain Lemire

Ericsson Research Canada
8400 Decarie Boulevard,
Montréal (Québec)
Canada H4P 2N2
E-mails: Vivek.Nanda@ericsson.com & lmcsyll@lmc.ericsson.se
Phone: (514) 345-7900 Ext:5288 Fax: (514) 345-7982

Abstract

This paper describes a practical, methodical and substantiative approach to setting up the essentials of a process management infrastructure in an organization. The paper discusses the key elements of a process management infrastructure, as being implemented in an ongoing process improvement program at Ericsson. The catalysts for this improvement effort were: management need, customer demand, process capability assessments and competitive pressure.

Keywords

Process management; process management infrastructure; process improvement; process baselining; process metrics; process analysis

1. Introduction

Ericsson is an international leader in telecommunications. It is recognized for its advanced systems and products for wired and mobile telecommunications in public and private networks. Ericsson's 90,000 employees are active in more than 130 countries. Ericsson invests heavily in research and development, maintaining some 40 research centres in 22 countries.

'Cellular Systems - American Standards' is a major business unit of Ericsson's 'Radio Communications' business area. It includes companies in Sweden, Canada and USA. This paper describes the process management efforts initiated in Cellular Systems - American Standards and its sub-contracting suppliers (also Ericsson companies) in Mexico and Ireland.

This paper primarily focuses on the *path* identified and adopted for implementing a basic Process Management Infrastructure[1] (PMI) within a main process area of Cellular Systems - American Standards: the Product Development Flow (PDF) process. PDF details the processes to be followed in the development of Ericsson's radio communications products. Note that, this process management effort is focused on the operative[2] (technical) processes within PDF and, for now, management and support processes are not included in this improvement effort. However, since operative, management and support processes are closely entwined together [1, 2], the significance of the managerial and support processes in impacting the overall process efficiency cannot be overlooked. Institutionalizing process management and continuous process improvement within PDF's operative processes is regarded as a *starting point* for the long term process improvements envisioned within Ericsson, and these also envisage process management of management and support processes in the near future.

The primary contribution of this paper is that it describes a practical, methodical and substantiative approach to setting up the essentials of a PMI in an organization.The

1. the underlying framework which includes organizational structures, policies, standards, training, facilities, and tools that support process management [5].
2. include both software and hardware development processes with almost equal content.

0-8186-7840-2/97 $10.00 © 1997 IEEE

paper is organized as follows: in Section 2, we present some pertinent background material. Section 3 describes the establishment of the PDF process management project and the key activities to be performed in order to establish a PMI in an organization and, finally, Section 4 concludes the paper.

2. Background

In the context of improving organizational maturity, 'process management' is simply defined as: establishing a process infrastructure to uniformly support and guide a project's work [3]. 'Process improvement', on the other hand, specifically refers to improvements in process capability and performance. A process management system facilitates process improvements by providing process metrics (and empirical data) to assess process capability and performance.There is an enormous body of literature that explores the reasons for the growing interest in companies in managing and improving their processes [4, 5, 6] and the positive impact on the businesses of organizations which have successfully implemented process management and improvement [7, 8, 9, 11]. Though the intent of process improvement, v.i.z., improving product quality, increasing productivity and decreasing the cycle time for product development is enticing for the corporate management, there are other equally compelling reasons which motivate companies to implement process management: *customer demand* and *competitive pressure* [10]. The above motivators for implementing process management are true for Ericsson as well. Eventhough Ericsson enjoys more world market share in cellular systems than that of its next two competitors combined, we realized that in order to make this situation a competitive asset, we needed to reinforce and coordinate the process improvement work on an international basis.

With the above stated purpose as the precursor, the PDF Process Management project was established in Sept. 1996. The goal was to *establish a PMI which is capable of improving the capability of the internationally distributed Cellular Systems - American Standards's PDF in terms of: lead-times, productivity and quality by march 1997.* Also, as cogent evidence of the success of the process management system, the senior management wanted a concrete proof in the form of a process certification by an independent assessment. The certifying body was chosen to be the British Standards institution (BSi), for its international reputation and familiarity with Ericsson's business processes.

2.1. Process Management Status before the Project

Although, prior to the start of the project, some initiatives for process management already existed in Cellular Systems - American Standards, there was no true framework to handle internationally distributed process management. Most of the process management was "championed" by certain individuals (with few significant results) and although process teams[1] had been established, their efforts were uncoordinated and there was a lack of a common objective to bind them together into a cohesive unit.

Previously, Capability Maturity Model (CMM) [4] assessments (both internal and external) of PDF processes had concluded that Cellular Systems - American Standards was still at the Initial Level (Level 1 of CMM) and although some practices from level 2 and 3 of CMM were in place, they were not effective. These assessments had recommended that Cellular Systems - American Standards focus on implementing a comprehensive process management infrastructure to act as a platform to base all process management and improvement activities upon.

2.2. Implementation Strategy and Expectations from the Project

The key elements of the implementation strategy were: Firstly, The project was to achieve its objectives by taking advantage of existing process assets. As previously stated, initial attempts at establishing process management had met with limited success and everyone agreed that old assets could be reused, as appropriate, in the new project. Secondly, all PDF processes were to focus on a common set of minimum rules. Thirdly, wherever applicable, Ericsson's corporate quality standards were to be used. For instance, the Ericsson Quality Institute, had spent considerable resources on detailing a methodology for process identification, process definition, process analysis, continuous improvement, process redesign and process reengineering. This methodology, outlined in the Ericsson Business Process Management (EBPM) guidebook, was recommended to be used. Fourthly, to overcome the obstacle of geographical scattering of the project teams, Ericsson's 'intranet' was to be used as a

1. the process teams were comprised of highly competent individuals. As members of these teams, there were both experienced process engineers and senior practitioners of the company (with a good insight into the development processes).

communication media and, finally, whenever possible, tools were to be used to simplify process management tasks.

Prior to the commencement of the project, it was also clarified that this project was *not* to be regarded as an "all encompassing solution", but, as the first step in an evolutionary process. It was to serve as an essential initial part of the long term goal of climbing higher maturity levels of the CMM.

Thus, the PDF process management project was set up with the challenging task of rectifying the present situation of process management by enabling the consistent definition and establishment of PDF processes so as to usher Cellular Systems - American Standards into a continuous process improvement phase.

3. Project Establishment

The PDF process management project was established with the following 7 objectives to be met upon completion:

- All PDF processes/subprocesses defined
- All PDF process/subprocess interfaces handshaked
- Process metrics defined and target[1] value set for all applicable processes
- Process analysis started for applicable processes
- Resources in place and appropriate employees trained for their respective responsibilities regarding process work
- Education on PDF operative processes and process management completed (first round)
- Other PMI components in place (v.i.z., improvement tracking and reporting, process configuration management, process documentation guidelines and a preliminary process assets library)

The senior management "buy-in" and total commitment were repeatedly stressed and demonstrated by the provision of adequate resources. In all, 17 process teams (with an average size of 7 members) were allocated for the project. It was estimated that the work of approx. 2000 employees was to be directly impacted by this improvement initiative. A substantial budget was allocated for the entire project; the project was to be completed by early March 1997 and, upon completion, the ownership of the PMI was to be transferred to organization X (to be determined) by early May 1997. Organization X was then to take charge of the PMI and perform routine maintenance and improvement tasks.

In the following sub-sections (3.1 to 3.6), we describe the approach that was to be adopted for achieving the objectives of the project: The effort was to commence with a preparatory process seminar, followed by: process baselining; an internal audit; definition of process metrics; process analysis; formal phase completion; and finally, process management education. At the time of writing this paper, process baselining was nearing completion, the internal audit was being planned and the individual process teams were initiating work on defining process metrics for their processes.

3.1. Preparatory Seminar

The PDF process management project started off with a two day process seminar (more like a huge "kick-off" meeting!) with managers, process owners[2], process team members and senior practitioners from all the participating Cellular Systems - American Standards companies. The process seminar was conducted as a series of informal meetings and information sessions interspersed with four workshops, each with a unique purpose: first, all the people working in the same process were grouped, to produce a preliminary process map; second, people working in two different horizontal processes (producer and consumer processes in different time frames) were grouped, to discuss the process interface objects; third, producer and consumer processes in the same time frames (concurrent processes) were grouped, to discuss process interface objects and critical interdependencies; and, finally, an orderly distribution of some people to their neighbouring processes was done, in order to provide them with an insight into how their producers/consumer processes work.

The purposes served by the seminar were manifold: it helped chalk out an action plan on how the project was to be executed; it helped determine control mechanisms to be built into the project for efficient execution; it helped define the organizational structure to be adopted for the project execution; PDF processes were discussed and mapped; major PDF process interface objects were discussed; process related concerns were addressed; and, perhaps, most importantly, it provided an opportunity to everyone to understand the involvement of different people in the various processes and establish the "right"

1. the 'goal' to be achieved for a metric in the next year, for instance, if the present planning precision was 70%, then the "target" value could be fixed at, say, 80%.

2. heads a process team and is responsible for the definition, consistency, deployment, measurement, analysis and improvement of his/her process.

contacts for coordination purposes and status reporting.

The action plan produced at the end of the process seminar called for: an initial process definition, process mapping and process interface handshaking exercise; an internal audit to ascertain if the fundamental process definition had been done correctly so as not to jeopardise the project later; deployment of process metrics to measure process performance; initiation of process analysis activities; establishment of the PMI components (as mentioned in the project objectives); and, finally, education of the practitioners and process owners on their processes and basic process management concepts. This action plan was tied to a stringent time schedule containing 11 'milestones' defined at appropriate intervals to track project progress and associated with clearly defined passage criteria. In addition, weekly progress reporting was to be honoured by all teams. The 'project coordinator' was to work with a high-level core team responsible for designing the PMI and all the process teams were to report to and get guidelines from the PMI core team. Inputs from individual process teams were also to be solicited by the PMI core team on the various PMI elements and the finally synthesized guidelines were to be communicated to all the process teams.

The process seminar, in fact, was as much an exercise to determine the path to follow in project execution, as an exercise to weed out any possible impediments that might have hampered progress [13].

3.2. Process Baselining

A 'process baseline' is the formally reviewed and agreed upon process specification, that thereafter serves as the basis for further development, and that can be changed only through formal change control procedures [4]. An initial process baseline: helps forge a common understanding of how tasks are performed (or are supposed to be performed!); enables comparisons with actual project execution; provides a basis for analysing and improving processes; and, helps managers plan for specific development projects [14, 15].

As part of the PDF project, process baselining was carried out by: 'process definition'[1] and 'process mapping'. For the purpose of process definition, to ensure uniformity and an agreement on formalism, a common process description template was to be followed by all process teams. The template contained pertinent information of the process like: purpose, description, scope/limitations, competency requirements, owner, version, inputs and input producers, outputs and output consumers, entry/exit criteria and references to process templates and instructions. The information recorded in the process description templates was to be entered in the corporate Process Documentation Tool (PDT), which was to automatically generate process maps and with the help of SOPRAN, a process management software, hypertext links to all associated process documentation were to be generated. The PDT entries were to be accessible via Ericsson's intranet. The construction of process "wall-charts" (which were found to be more beneficial!), though not mandatory, was also encouraged.

The process maps were largely descriptive functional process models [15, 17, 18] with a minor prescriptive [19] content. This was because, though the stress was on ensuring *process fidelity* [16], some improvements had been proposed by the senior practitioners, who were of the view that these could be easily introduced. Moreover, it was argued, having these minor improvements already documented, would help in introducing minor changes to the work procedures.

The process maps developed were generic (applicable across different projects) and were of a fairly high 'granularity' [1]. Process tailoring guidelines for individual projects were to be developed by the PMI core team. All process baselining was prepared by the individual process teams, in close association with the practitioners and upon completion, all the process owners had to handshake their mutual interfaces. Also, by the end of this phase, the PMI core team was to propose: a preliminary mechanism for tracking the disposition of process improvement suggestions; a preliminary mechanism for tracking the progress of process teams and for follow-up actions arising from process management activities; a preliminary mechanism for the storage and access of information (process maps, process descriptions, work instructions, process templates and other relevant reference material) from the 'process asset library' (PAL); a preliminary mechanism to enforce the integrity of the process assets stored in the PAL, i.e., a mechanism for 'process configuration management'; and, preliminary process owner and process team guidelines (roles, responsibilities and training) for all future work.

3.3. Internal Audit

The internal audit of the PMI established so far was to be performed by Ericsson's quality auditors (not directly involved with the project) and the objective of internal audit was to be to primarily ascertain: "Have we made a

1. an implementation of a process design in the form of a partially ordered set of process steps that is enactable [16].

sound start to base all future work upon?". The prime importance of establishing a good process baseline cannot be overstressed, more so when many of the process teams were geographically dispersed. The process auditors were to ensure that all the process teams had correctly, consistently, and completely defined their operative processes. They were also to check for the validity of the mechanisms developed by the PMI core team for process improvement tracking, PAL, process configuration management and guidelines for process owners and process teams.

The auditors during the course of their review, were to issue corrective action requests for those PMI elements, which, in their opinion, were weak or incorrect or ineffective. The effected process teams, then, were to satisfy all the recommendations in the corrective action requests and gain final approval from the auditors before commencing work on the next phase.

3.4. Process Metrics Definition and Process Analysis

Measurements are a key concept of process management. They play a crucial part in planning and controlling software projects, as well as improving software processes, products and projects over time by providing empirical data about current performance and trends [20]. For the purpose of measuring process performance and process capability, 'process metrics' are used.

Since the quality of a product depends on the quality of the process that produces it, the overall performance of a process can be regarded as the combined performance of productivity (P), product quality (Q) and delivery performance (T). A well defined PQT approach to measuring product quality is already in place in Ericsson. Some of the PQT measurements in use are 'planning precision' (Planned lead time/Actual lead time), 'mean fault density' (No. of defects per thousand lines of non-commented source code) and productivity (Thousand lines of non-commented source code/ Man-hours). However, since the existing metrics were primarily 'product metrics', the PDF project participants were of the view that there was a need for defining process metrics. The process metrics, along with target values, were to be derived from business objectives, following the G/Q/M approach [21] and there were to be procedures defined for data collection and storage, data presentation and guidelines for data interpretation. It was decided that, initially, the process metrics were to be a small, yet consistent set, throughout all the process teams. These process metrics were to be based primarily on the 'time' spent in each process and calculations thereof, for instance, effort estimation (Planned effort to be spent in a process/Actual effort spent), cost performance index (Planned cost of process execution/Actual cost of process execution), defect detection precision (No. of errors detected before product release/Total number of product defects 'before and after' release) and the like. Such measures, in conjunction with product metrics, were to yield vital information regarding the distribution and utilization of resources in the various processes (human resources and money), quality of process outputs, accuracy of defect detection procedures and other potential benefits. Once this preliminary set of core metrics were defined, they were to be extended (beyond the scope of the current PDF project) to make the set more comprehensive.

Process analysis was to be performed to give the process owners and process teams an idea of the current performance and capability of the processes, and the underlying causes. In addition, the analysis was to give a view of what apparent possibilities existed for improving the processes. The process analysis was to be primarily 'informal deductive' or 'retrospective', similar to that described by Wolf et al. in [22]. The retrospective process analysis was to be based on the analysis of empirical data gathered from several enactments of the process with the help of previously defined process metrics. The 'informal deductive' analysis was to be performed by all the practitioners and process team members as an "every-day" job and the improvements suggestions were then to be handled by the mechanism proposed for that purpose by the PMI core team (see Section 3.2). Again, it was recognized that the process improvement challenge was going to be: separating the performance information that is an artifact of a particular project's circumstances, from the performance information that could be related to the generic process model [1].

3.5. Phase Completion

The phase completion was envisioned as another crucial milestone, which primarily was to ensure that the preliminary mechanisms demonstrated (for the internal audit) for process improvement tracking, PAL and process configuration management were finally established and *deployed*[1]. Notice that, the stress now was

1. we make a subtle difference between establishment and deployment of the infrastructure: establishment concerns the "construction of the infrastructure" while deployment concerns the "actual use" of the infrastructure built.

on the deployment of the PMI established and this was the last major milestone to identify any major flaws in the PMI establishment or deployment before the end of the project.

3.6. Process Management Education

Towards the end of the PDF project, two types of comprehensive training were planned for the process owners, process team members and practitioners. Firstly, training on the operative processes that had been documented. As part of this training, education was to be imparted on: what were the operative processes; people working in the operative processes; how they were documented; where all pertinent information related to the processes was stored; how the processes were to be measured and analysed; how the improvement suggestions were to be handled; procedures to follow to create new or update existing processes; competency requirements for processes and other pertinent information. Secondly, training was to be imparted on general process management such as CMM, EBPM and other process improvement methods. This training was to be both in-house and outsourced. There was unanimity that general process management would make everyone more "process focused" and provide them with essential competencies to implement the more stringent demands of level 2 and 3 KPAs of CMM in the near future.

4. Conclusion

While the PDF project is part of the many improvement initiatives[1] launched by Ericsson and it is still in the execution phase, some ambitious improvement initiatives in other (or related) domains have already been identified. One of these initiatives relates to P-CMM of the Software Engineering Institute [4], a conceptual model based on the state-of-the-art workforce practices to help companies characterize and improve the maturity of their workforce.

Other projects in the pipeline and being attached prime importance by the management are: CMM Level 3 certification for the PDF operative processes and further advancements; PMI for PDF management and support processes; an integrated and comprehensive software, product and process measurement program by capitalizing on the existing measurements infrastructure; a Team Assignment and Support Process (TAPS) to help transform Cellular Systems - American Standards into a team based organization by standardising, supporting and aligning the teams to assist in the realization of Cellular Systems - American Standards's business goals; and, piloting of 'User-Centred Design' concepts in product development to focus on product users, while also maintaining a focus on the product customers. Perhaps, the PDF project could be best described as a "first iteration" of the traditional quality-improvement program as described by Deming [12].

1. perhaps the most important initiative is the Total Business Improvement (TBI) program, an umbrella project for executing improvements in the time-to-market, product quality, process maturity and employee satisfaction.

References

[1] M. Dawson, "Software Process Themes and Issues", IEEE Transactions on Software engineering, 1993

[2] N. Madhavji, "The Process Cycle", Software Engineering Journal, Sept. 1991

[3] W. Humphrey, "Managing the Software Process", Addison Wesley Inc., 1989

[4] M. Paulk, C. Weber, B. Curtis amd M. Chrissis, "The Capability Maturity Model: Guidelines for Improving the Software Process", Addison Wesley, 1995

[5] W. Humphrey, D. Kitson and T. Kasse, "The State of Software Engineering Practice: A Preliminary Report", In Proceedings of the 11th International Conference on Software Engineering (Pittsburgh, PA.), IEEE Computer Society, 1989

[6] D. Kitson and S. Masters, "An Analysis of Software Process Assessment Results: 1987-1991", IEEE Transactions on Software Engineering, May 1993

[7] W. Humphrey, T. Snyder and R Willis, "Software Process Improvement at Hughes Aircraft", IEEE Software, July 1991

[8] H. Wohlwend and S. Rosenbaum, "Schlumberger's Software Improvement Program", IEEE Transactions on Software Engineering, Nov. 1994

[9] Raymond Dion, "Process Improvement and the Corporate Balance Sheet", IEEE Software, July 1993

[10] D. Stelzer, W. Mellis and G. Herzwurm, "Software Process Improvement via ISO 9000? Results of two surveys among European software houses", In Proc. of the Twenty-Ninth Annual Hawaii International Conference on System Sciences, Wailea, Hawaii, USA, Jan. 1996

[11] F. Zocholl, A. Völker amd M. Gonauser, "Why Maturity Matters", In Proc. of Vision'96: Process Improvement Symposium: Towards an International Vision, Montréal, Canada, Oct. 1996

[12] W. Deming, "Out of the Crisis", MIT Center Advanced Eng. Study, Cambridge, Mass., USA, 1982

[13] R. Pressman, "Software Process Impediment", IEEE Software, Sept. 1996

[14] H. Krasner, J. Terrel, A. Linehan, P. Arnold and W. Ett, "Lessons Learned from a Software Process Modeling System", Communications of the ACM, Sept. 1992

[15] B. Curtis, M. Kellner and J. Over, "Process Modeling", Communications of the ACM, Sept. 1992

[16] P. Feiler and W. Humphrey, "Software Process Development and Enactment: Concepts and Definitions", Technical

Report, CMU/SEI-92-TR-04, SEI, Carnegie Mellon Univ., USA, Sept. 1992
[17] M. Dowson, "The structure of the software process", ACM SIGSOFT Software Engineering Notes, 11, (4), 1986
[18] J. Wileden andM. Dowson, "The software process and software environments", Proceedings of Int'l Workshop, Coto de Caza, Trabuco Canyon, California, Aug. 1986
[19] P. Zave, "Let's put more emphasis on prescriptive methods", Proceedings of Int'l Workshop, Trabuco Canyon, California, Aug. 1986
[20] M. Daskalantonakis, "A practical view of software measurement and implementation experiences within Motorola", IEEE Transactions on Software Engineering, Nov. 1992
[21] V. R. Basili and D. M. Weiss, "A methodology for collecting valid software engineering data", IEEE Transactions on Software Engineering, Nov. 1984
[22] A. Wolf and D. Rosenblum, "A study in software process data capture and analysis", IEEE Transactions on Software Engineering, Feb. 1993

Supporting Impact Analysis and Change Propagation in Software Engineering Environments

Jun Han
Peninsula School of Computing and Information Technology
Monash University, McMahons Road, Frankston, Vic 3199, Australia
phone: +61 3 99044604, fax: +61 3 99044124, e-mail: jhan@monash.edu.au

Abstract

Impact analysis and change propagation are among the major issues of software change management. In this paper, we introduce an approach to providing impact analysis and change propagation support as an integral part of software engineering environments, so that they can be applied during both software development and maintenance. In this approach, the activities are carried out on the original representation of software artifacts in the environment, rather than on a separate system model extracted. This very fact enables automated direct support for the process of actually carrying out and propagating the changes. Dependences and properties of software artifacts are used for impact analysis to achieve increased flexibility and expressiveness. Both impact analysis and change propagation are a combination of guided user intervention and automatic processing based on codified change patterns and propagation rules.

1. Introduction

The development and maintenance of a software system involves a large number of software artifacts, capturing the system's requirements, designs, implementations, testing suites, maintenance records, and so on. Traditionally changes to a software system are referred to those related to software maintenance. During the initial development of the system, however, there are also on-going requirements for change due to changed requirements, error correction and development improvement. Therefore, the requirement for change is an inherent characteristic of the software development and maintenance process. In any case, the required changes are eventually reflected in changes to the software artifacts involved. Since the software artifacts are logically related to each other, an initially proposed change may involve a large number of modifications to various artifacts. As such, the process of software changes needs to be managed and, if possible, assisted by automated tools.

The issues of software change management range from identifying the need for change, assessing the impact of a proposed change in the entire system, carrying out the initial and consequent modifications, managing the versions of the changed artifacts, to collecting change-related data [15]. Over the years, we have seen efforts addressing these issues. They include process models for change management such as Prism [15], frameworks for comparing impact analysis methods such as [2], specific techniques for change impact analysis and change propagation such as program slicing [18, 12] and program dependence graphs [16, 14, 1], and approaches to tool support for change management [13, 4, 7, 5].

In this paper, we address the tool support issues for software change management, in particular for *impact analysis* and *change propagation*, in the context of a (generic) software engineering environment [19, 8, 9]. In our approach, the kernel of the software engineering environment, augmented with specific features for change management, can be seen as a generic tool for change management. The policies, models and methods for change management in a particular application context (e.g., a specific software development and maintenance project) can be codified to specialise the environment kernel, so that the resulting environment provides the specific change management support (as well as other support) as required by the application context. As such, this approach recognises the varied needs of different application contexts, which may be due to the nature of the particular system to be developed, the different development methods and languages to be used, and so on. In particular, our approach has the following characteristics:

1. The original representation of the software system (artifacts and dependences) as developed and maintained in the environment is directly used for change management support, so that there is no information extraction or re-formulation required.

2. In addition to artifact representations and dependences, artifact properties and change patterns are also used for change impact analysis, which has greatly increased the flexibility and expressiveness of the approach.

3. The use of the original system representation allows automated direct assistance to change propagation (i.e., actually carrying out the modifications) based on the impact analysis results and additional change propagation rules.

4. Both change impact analysis and change propagation are a combination of automatic processing (based on change patterns or propagation rules) and guided user intervention.

These are in clear contrast to most existing approaches, where the impact analysis activities are usually performed based on an *extracted* system representation involving only artifact structures and dependences (without their contents), and as such the *actual* change propagation process is not *directly* supported.

In general, our approach provides support for system representation, impact analysis, and change propagation. They are discussed in sections 2, 3 and 4 respectively. In section 5, we present an example to demonstrate the use of our approach. After discussing related work in section 6, we conclude in section 7.

2. System representation

Fundamental to any software change management system is the representation of software artifacts and their dependences. In the context of a proposed change, the software artifacts are objects of modification, and their dependences are among the means to realise the impact and propagation of modifications. We also use the consistency properties of software artifacts and dependences for change management. While not usually addressed in the literature as such, the use of consistency properties provides additional flexibility and expressiveness in specifying and managing change activities (see below).

In our approach, the change management activities are performed on the actual software artifacts and their dependences developed and maintained in the software engineering environment. The requirements for system representation are largely met by the general representation facilities of the environment. Here we only give a brief overview of these facilities, and further details can be found in [8, 11, 9]. Examples can be found in section 5.

Artifact representation. Artifact representation in our environment has the following characteristics which are particularly relevant to change management:

1. The representation is based on syntax trees and uses an augmented EBNF notation for specification [8]. Therefore, it is fine-grained, and facilitates flexible references to various levels of artifact components. If desired, component types at intermediate levels can be identified as atomic for change management purpose. As such, it satisfies the flexibility requirements when referring to artifact components during change management [2].

2. The artifacts and their components are typed in the representation. As such, it will better support the change management capabilities [5].

Dependence definition. Dependences related to change management can be captured using the relationship definition mechanism provided by the environment kernel, where a relationship connects one artifact (component) to another artifact (component) and possibly with its own content and attributes [8]. In fact, the dependences should be among the relationships that are required, introduced and maintained during artifact construction and manipulation. As such, there is no separate dependence representation required for change management. On the other hand, we may exclude certain relationships from consideration with respect to change management.

As in the case of artifact representation, this representation of dependences has the following major characteristics relevant to change management:

1. The dependences can be defined accurately, due to the fine-grained artifact representation. This will enable us to more precisely locate dependence-based consequent modifications.

2. The dependences are typed, which provides the necessary expressiveness required by impact analysis and change propagation.

Consistency properties. Most of the literature on software change management addresses change impact analysis and propagation in terms of dependences, in view of modifying an *existing* set of software artifacts.

This is not surprising as change management is primarily about changing existing software artifacts. In order to implement the changes, however, it is often necessary to introduce new artifacts such as a new module, or remove existing artifacts which are no longer required. In general, the consequences of introducing or removing an artifact or dependence should also be taken into account during impact analysis and propagation. Dependences alone do not *adequately* facilitate identification of the impact related to the introduction and removal of artifacts and dependences. Consistency properties provide an additional mechanism to deal with the issue.

As an example, consider the following property of a given development methodology:

> *"a design module in a design document must be related to one or more implementation modules in the corresponding implementation document."*

Accordingly, the introduction of a design module into the design document may possibly imply the introduction of one or more new implementation modules and associated dependences between the implementation modules and the design module.

In general, properties related to change management can be stated using the environment kernel's property specification mechanism [8, 11]. Again, properties that are not relevant to change management can be excluded from consideration.

3. Impact analysis

An essential part of software change management is to predict the system-wide impact of a change request before actually carrying out *modifications* to the system – *impact analysis*, so that appropriate decisions related to the change request can be made, such as planning, scheduling and resourcing. Impact analysis starts with a set of *initial modifications* to some software artifacts and possibly their dependences, directly reflecting the change request. For a given type of modification, potential *consequent modifications* can be identified along relevant dependences and according to relevant consistency properties. Whether a potential modification is a *required* modification can be decided by the system (based on a codified change pattern) or by the user (interactively). Then the required consequent modification is regarded as a new *initiating* modification to identify further consequent modifications. This process continues until no further consequent modifications can be identified. In this section, we discuss in detail the relevant issues.

Objects and types of modification. The object of a modification is a software artifact, an artifact component, or a dependence. The types of possible modifications for an object are *update, introduction* and *deletion*. While introduction and deletion are self-explanatory, update is applied to an existing object and does not change its type. In general, therefore, a modification is characterised by a pair, (obj, m_type), where obj is the object of modification and m_type is the type of modification. Sometimes, we also write this characterisation as $(obj : obj\_type, m\_type)$ or (obj_type, m_type) to emphasise the object type.

Consequent modifications. For an initiating modification (obj_I, m_type_I), the potential objects of immediate impact are the objects that are involved with obj_I in dependences, properties, derived dependences, or derived properties. The cases based on derived dependences or properties capture the situations where a potential consequent impact can not be directly captured by a defined dependence or property. In general, these situations can be captured by *a change pattern* (see below for detailed definition).

As mentioned above, the determination of a potential consequent modification can be carried out through an interactive process between the user and the system. That is, the system prompts the user, and the user decides (1) whether or not the potential modification is a required modification, and (2) if so, the type of the modification. When a potential modification is identified as a required modification, it is linked to the initiating modification for traceability purpose. For certain cases, however, this process can be automated by codifying change patterns into the support environment.

Automatic impact analysis. A change pattern takes the following format:

$$\{mod_{I1}, mod_{I2}, ...\} \rightarrow \{mod_{C1}, mod_{C2}, ...\} : exp_B;$$

where

1. $mod_{Ij} (j = 1, 2, ...)$ describes a pattern of initiating modifications, and takes the form of $(obj_{Ij} : obj\_type_{Ij}, mod\_type_{Ij})$ with obj_{Ij} being an object variable, obj_type_{Ij} an object type (i.e., an artifact (component) type or dependence type) and $mode\_type_{Ij}$ a modification type;

2. $mod_{Cj} (j = 1, 2, ...)$ describes a pattern of consequent modifications, and takes the form of $(obj_{Cj} : obj\_type_{Cj}, mod\_type_{Cj})$ with obj_{Cj} being an object variable, obj_type_{Cj} an object type and $mode\_type_{Cj}$ a modification type;

3. exp_B is a Boolean expression about the object variables concerned: $exp_B(obj_{I1}, obj_{I2}, ..., obj_{C1}, obj_{C2}, ...)$.

The pattern states that modifications of type $mod\_type_{Ij}(j = 1, 2, ...)$ on object $obj_{Ij}(j = 1, 2, ...)$ of type $obj\_type_{Ij}(j = 1, 2, ...)$ will result in modifications of type $mod\_type_{Cj}(j = 1, 2, ...)$ on $obj_{Cj}(j = 1, 2, ...)$ of type $obj\_type_{Cj}(j = 1, 2, ...)$ if and only if the Boolean expression exp_B holds. The Boolean expression usually states the relationship of the objects involved. During impact analysis, a potential modification will be resolved automatically when it matches a change pattern.

A *potential* change pattern for impact analysis based on derived dependences and properties is described in the following form:

$$\{mod_{I1}, mod_{I2}, ...\} \rightsquigarrow \{mode_{C1}, mod_{C2}, ...\} : exp_B;$$

Note that normal change patterns resolve potential consequent modifications *automatically* while potential change patterns only identify potential consequent modifications to be resolved by the user.

Summary. For a potential consequent modification (identified based on either dependences, properties, or derived dependences and properties), in general, the environment will first try to find a matching change pattern. If found, the pattern is applied and the potential consequent modification is resolved. Otherwise, the scenario is presented to the user for resolution.

Upon completion of impact analysis, we are left with a set of required modifications together with the *impact relationships* between them. In fact, they form a directed acyclic graph (DAG) structure with the nodes denoting the modifications and the edges denoting the impact relationships, which we call the *impact graph.*

4. Change propagation

The next step following impact analysis is to actually carry out the identified modifications – *change propagation.* Ideally, the modifications should be made in an order dictated by the impact relationships. On the other hand, it is also possible to carry out the modifications independently and even concurrently without following the impact relationships, as long as the requirements for the modifications concerned are clear. The consistency among the software artifacts can be re-established after the modifications. In the following discussion, we concentrate on a process of change propagation according to the impact relationships.

Interactive change propagation. At a given time, in general, the modifications concerned can be divided into four categories:

$$(past, current, next, future)$$

where the *past* modifications are the ones that have been completed, the *current* modifications are those that are being carried out, the *next* modifications are the ones that can be selected next according to the impact relationships, and the *future* modifications are the rest. At the beginning, the sets of *past* and *current* modifications are empty, the set of *next* modifications contains the initial modifications, and the set of *future* modifications contains all the identified consequent modifications. At a given time, the set of *next* modifications may contain more than one modification, and therefore more than one modification can be selected as *current* modifications if so desired.

The change propagation process is as follows:

1. Upon on selection by the user, an identified modification from the set *next* will become a *current* modification. The sets *current*, *next* and *future* are adjusted accordingly.

2. The user will then carry out the selected modification as required.

3. When a *current* modification is completed, it will be moved to the set *past*.

4. The selection-modification-completion cycle continues until all the identified modifications are completed (i.e., all in the set *past*).

After a modification being moved into the set *past*, the user may later want to make further updates to the object concerned, and the modification sets should be adjusted accordingly.

In general the environment will maintain the impact graph and the related categories (sets) of modifications. It is also responsible for realising the adjustments to these categories as the change propagation process progresses. On the other hand, the user is responsible for making the actual changes. As such, the above change propagation process is an interactive process.

Automatic change propagation. For well-defined cases, the impact of certain modifications can be propagated automatically according to codified *propagation rules.* In general, there are two kinds of change propagation rules. The first case is that certain modifications are fully realised automatically as the consequence of other modifications. This type of rules take the following form:

$$\{mod_{I1}, mod_{I2}, ...\} \rightarrow \{mod_{C1}, mod_{C2}, ...\} : exp_B \textbf{ by } action;$$

which means that the consequent modifications $mod_{Cj}(j = 1, 2, ...)$ are realised by the *action* as the consequence of completing all initiating modifications $mod_{Ij}(j = 1, 2, ...)$. The *action* is a code segment or function call that can access the objects involved. The firing of this rule is subject to the satisfaction of the Boolean expression exp_B.

Note that the above propagation rule is similar to a change pattern, except that it has an additional action. In general, if the scenario captured by a propagation rule is the same as that captured by a change pattern, the *action* can be specified together with the change pattern.

The second type of propagation rules are to deal with cases where only part of the consequent modifications can be done automatically due to the effect of some initiating modifications. This type of rules are particularly useful when the granularity of impact analysis is relatively coarse (but change propagation can be carried out at a lower granularity). The propagation rules of this type take the following form:

$$(obj_{I1} : obj\_type_{I1}, ...) \rightarrow (obj_{C1} : obj\_type_{C1}, ...) : exp_B \textbf{ by } action;$$

where $obj_{Ij}(j = 1, ...)$ are objects involved in the initiating modifications, $obj_{Cj}(j = 1, ...)$ are objects involved in the consequent modifications, and exp_B is the condition to be evaluated before activating the *action* to realise the partial effects of the consequent modifications. The triggering of such propagation rules will not cause any category change for consequent modifications, because not all impact effects are realised. For reference purpose, however, the consequent modifications are annotated with the rules to indicate the partial realisation of the impact.

Summary. In general, all the relevant propagation rules are fired (if possible) whenever a modification completes (no matter that it is due to the interactive or automatic process) and the rules match. As such, automatic and interactive change propagation works in an interwoven fashion.

5. An example

In this section, we present an example to demonstrate how our software change management approach can be applied. For simplicity, we consider a partial software development methodology that involves a design document developed in the Booch method [6] and its corresponding implementation document in C++, with certain customisation to ascertain a clear development process. Furthermore, we will show only the relevant formalisation of the methodology in a particular application context, i.e., a simplified version of the weather monitoring system presented in [6].

The weather monitoring system is to provide automatic monitoring of various weather conditions, and in particular measuring wind speed and direction, temperature, barometric pressure and humidity (further details can be found in [6]). As Booch suggested, after the system has been developed there may be a change requirement to measure rainfall as well, which we use as the change request in this case study.

5.1. System representation

A design document developed in the Booch methodology may contain class diagrams, state transition diagrams, and a number of other types of diagrams. Here, we only consider a class diagram capturing the architecture of the software system, and state transition diagrams capturing the dynamic behavior of individual classes of the class diagram. Figure 1 shows a partial design of the weather monitoring system, containing the class diagram and an illustrative state transition diagram [6]. The class diagram involves ten ordinary classes and three abstract classes, with "association", "has" and "inheritance" relationships between them (please ignore the class `RainfallSensor` for the moment). The state transition diagram `IMstd` details the class `InputManager`'s state changes upon pressing different types of user input keys (not shown). The relationship between `InputManager` and `IMstd` is captured by a `hasSTD` relation. Some high-level type rules (in an EBNF form) for the representation of this design are

```
DesignDoc = ClassDiagSpec { STD };
ClassDiagSpec = { Class } { AbsClass };
```

The relevant relations/dependences can be defined as

```
association =
    <Class | AbsClass, Class | AbsClass>;
has = <Class | AbsClass, Class>;
inheritance =
    <Class | AbsClass, Class | AbsClass>;
hasSTD = <Class, STD>;
```

Note that a relation type rule defines a relation type (on the right hand side of `=`) using types of the document components to be connected (in arrow brackets

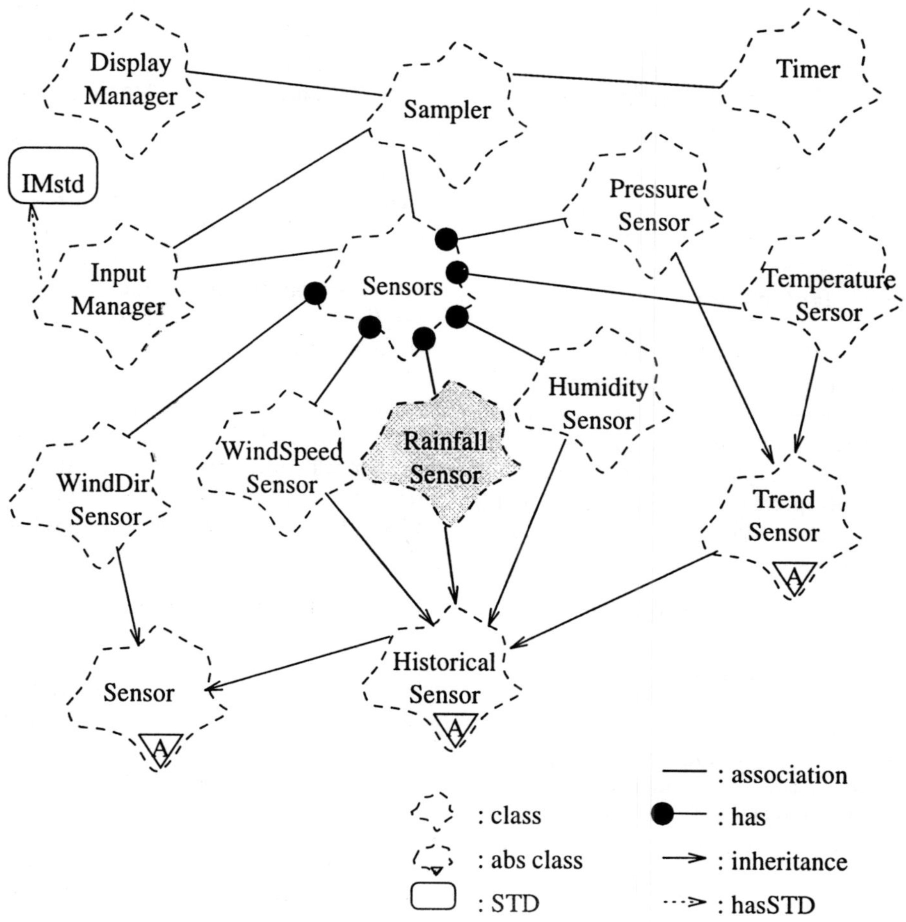

Figure 1. A partial design of a weather monitoring system.

on the right hand side). For example, a `hasSTD` relation connects a `Class` to an `STD`.

The implementation document is a C++ program, in which there is a C++ class for each design class. Among these C++ classes, there are relationships/dependences mirroring the association, has and inheritance relationships between their corresponding design classes. In addition, other components may present, containing entities such as the `main` function and simple type declarations. A particular type declaration is the one enumerating the different types of sensors [6]:

```
//Enumeration of sensor names
enum SensorName {Direction, Speed,
        Temperature, Humidity, Pressure};
```

which can be used by various implementation classes. In particular, `ImpDisplayManager` (i.e., the implementation class corresponding to `DisplayManager`) uses it to discriminate the display functionality according to the sensor type of the data to be processed. So there is a `typeToUse` dependence between the above type declaration and the implementation class `ImpDisplayManager`. Besides, we may introduce a relationship of type `enumToImpClassH` between the above enumerated type declaration and the root of the inheritance hierarchy in the implementation document (i.e. `ImpSensor`) to indicate that the values in the enumerated type declaration reflect the concrete classes on the inheritance hierarchy.

Some type rules for the implementation document are

```
ImpDoc = CppProgram;
CppProgram = { ImpClass } { ImpAbsClass }
    MainFunc { TypeDec } ...
TypeDec = EnumDec | ...
```

There are also the following types of

relations/dependences:

```
impAssociation =
    <ImpClass | ImpAbsClass | MainFunc,
    ImpClass | ImpAbsClass>;
impInheritance = ...
impHas = ...
enumToImpClassH =
    <EnumDec, ImpClass | ImpAbsClass>;
typeToUse = <TypeDec,
    ImpClass | ImpAbsClass | ...>;
```

Between the entities of the design document and the entities of the implementation document, there exist different types of relationships. In particular, there is a **designToImp** relationship between the entire design document and the entire implementation document, and a **hasImp** relationship between a design class and its corresponding implementation class. The relevant relation type rules are

```
designToImp = <DesignDoc, ImpDoc>;
hasImp = <Class, ImpClass> |
    <AbsClass, ImpAbsClass>;
```

As an example consistency property, consider the requirement that there must be an implementation class for each design class in the development. This implies that a mathematical relation formed from all the `hasImp` relationships is total relative to the set of all design classes:

$$\mathbf{propHasImp} = \mathbf{total}(\mathtt{hasImp}, \mathtt{Class});$$

where **total** is a primitive predicate.

5.2. Impact analysis

To work out the impact of the suggested change request about the weather monitoring system, we first need to identify the initial modifications required:

1. **introRS**: A new design class `RainfallSensor` needs to be introduced (see Figure 1). This modification is characterised by or has the type of, (`Class`, *introduction*).

2. **introRSInh**: The new design class inherits from the abstract class `HistoricalSensor`. This modification has the type of (`inheritance`, *introduction*).

3. **introRSHas**: The design class `Sensors` will have instances of the new design class. This modification has the type of (`has`, *introduction*).

4. **changeIMstd**: Since there is a new key in the user interface for `Rainfall`, the state transition diagram `IMstd` will need to be changed. This modification has the type of (`STD`, *update*).

Note that the modifications are provided with a name for reference convenience.

The initial modifications are all relevant to the design document. As the first step, let us examine if there are any consequent impacts in the design document. First of all, the introduction of the new design class (i.e. **introRS**) does not have direct impact in the design document. Since the new class is not directly connected to any artifact component, there is no change pattern required to indicate the above effect.

Next, the introduction of the inheritance relation (i.e. **introRSInh**) does not have direct impact on the parent class in the design document. To identify this null-effect automatically, we have the following change pattern:

$$\{(i : \mathtt{inheritance}, \textit{introduction})\} \rightarrow \{(b, \_)\} :< *, i, b >;$$

where "_" indicates that no modification is required, and $< *, i, b >$ indicates that the relationship i relates an artifact component to b.

As to the introduction of the has relation (i.e. **introRSHas**), a potentially impacted object in the design document is the `Sensors` class. When the case is presented to the user, the user decides there is no change required, i.e., an interactive impact analysis step.

As to the update to **IMstd** (i.e. **changeIMstd**), the candidate object for potential direct impact is the `hasSTD` relationship. In fact, no modification is required for `hasSTD`, as captured by

$$\{(a : \mathtt{STD}, \textit{update})\} \rightarrow \{(r : \mathtt{hasSTD}, \_)\} :< *, r, a >;$$

In general, therefore, there is no consequent modifications in the design document. However, there are consequent modifications in the implementation document following the relevant dependences and properties. First of all, the introduction of the new design class `RainfallSensor` will cause the introduction of a corresponding implementation class `ImpRainfallSensor` and the introduction of a **hasImp** relationship between the two classes. This impact can be captured by the following change pattern:

$$\{(a : \mathtt{Class}, \textit{introduction})\} \rightarrow \{(b : \mathtt{ImpClass}, \textit{introduction}), (r : \mathtt{hasImp}, \textit{introduction})\} : < a, r, b >;$$

This change pattern allows the support environment to carry out the above impact analysis automatically. We give the two consequent modifications the following names respectively: `introImpRS` and `introRSHasImp`.

Instead of the above change pattern, we may rely on the consistency property `propHasImp` to analyse the impact. The introduction of the design class affects this property, and consequently the system will present to the user all the possibly affected objects according to the property, i.e., a new implementation class and a new `hasImp` relationship between the classes. The user then confirms the need for their introduction.

The introduction of the inheritance and has relationships in the design implies the introduction of the corresponding relationships in the implementation. This impact analysis can be done by the system according to the following change patterns:

$$\{(r_1 : \texttt{inheritance}, \textit{introduction})\} \rightarrow \{(r_2 : \texttt{impInheritance}, \textit{introduction})\} : < a_1, r_1, b_1 > \wedge (a_1, a_2) \in \texttt{hasImp} \wedge (b_1, b_2) \in \texttt{hasImp} \wedge < a_2, r_2, b_2 >;$$

$$\{(r_1 : \texttt{has}, \textit{introduction})\} \rightarrow \{(r_2 : \texttt{impHas}, \textit{introduction})\} : < a_1, r_1, b_1 > \wedge (a_1, a_2) \in \texttt{hasImp} \wedge (b_1, b_2) \in \texttt{hasImp} \wedge < a_2, r_2, b_2 >;$$

We name these two consequent modifications as `introImpRSInh` and `introImpRSHas` respectively.

The addition of the new implementation class to the inheritance hierarchy causes change to the enumerated type `SensorName`. To identify this impact, we provide the following potential change pattern:

$$\{(a : \texttt{ImpClass}, \textit{introduction})\} \leadsto \{(b : \texttt{EnumDec}, \textit{update})\} : (b, c) \in \texttt{enumToImpClassH} \wedge ((a = c) \vee (a, c) \in \texttt{impInheritance}^+);$$

As such, the introduction of the new implementation class `ImpRainfallSensor` will lead to the identification of the `SensorName` declaration as a potential candidate for update. When presented to the user, this impact is confirmed. We name this modification `changeEnum`. Note that we formulate the above change pattern as potential ($\leadsto$) – that is, there is no automatic resolution – because not every introduction of an implementation class will lead to the update of an enumerated type declaration.

The consequence of `changeEnum` would be the impact on places using `SensorName`. Following the `typeToUse` dependences, the implementation class `ImpDisplayManager` is confirmed by the user as an actual impact point for update to reflect the specific display requirement of `ImpRainfallSensor`. We call this modification `changeImpDM`.

According to our development methodology, adding a has relationship to a design class will lead to changes to the corresponding implementation class. This can be captured by the following change pattern:

$$\{(h : \texttt{has}, \textit{introduction})\} \rightarrow \{(c : \texttt{ImpClass} \cup \texttt{ImpAbsClass}, \textit{update})\} : (a, c) \in \texttt{hasImp} \wedge < a, h, * >;$$

As such, the introduction of the `has` relationship between `Sensors` and `RainfallSensor` will identify `ImpSensors` as an object for update. We name this modification as `changeImpSensors`.

Similarly, the change to a design class' state transition diagram will affect its corresponding implementation class. This can be captured by the the following change pattern:

$$\{(a : \texttt{STD}, \textit{update})\} \rightarrow \{(b : \texttt{ImpClass} \cup \texttt{ImpAbsClass}, \textit{update})\} : (c, b) \in \texttt{hasImp} \wedge (c, a) \in \texttt{hasSTD};$$

According to this pattern, `ImpInputManager` is automatically identified as requiring update due to the change to `IMstd`. We name this new modification as `changeImpIM`.

In summary, we have four initial and eight consequent modifications. Together with their impact relationships, they form a DAG structure (see Figure 2).

5.3. Change propagation

When actually carrying out the above changes, the support system will provide assistance to the user as to what the next logical modifications are and the major reasons for a modification (as indicated by the impact relationships). In addition, we may introduce an automatic propagation rule to let the system automatically introduce a class skeleton for `ImpRainfallSensor` and the relevant `hasImp` relationship, and add to the set of modifications a new *update* modification on `ImpRainfallSensor` for filling in its details. This can be achieved by adding an action to a relevant change pattern defined earlier:

$$\{(a : \texttt{Class}, \textit{introduction})\} \rightarrow \{\textit{mod} : (b : \texttt{ImpClass}, \textit{introduction}), (r : \texttt{hasImp}, \textit{introduction})\} :< a, r, b > \textbf{ by}$$

$$\textbf{begin } b = \textit{introImpClass}(); \; \textit{introRel}(a, b, \texttt{hasImp}); \; \textit{introMod}(b, \texttt{"update"}, \textit{mod}); \; \textbf{end};$$

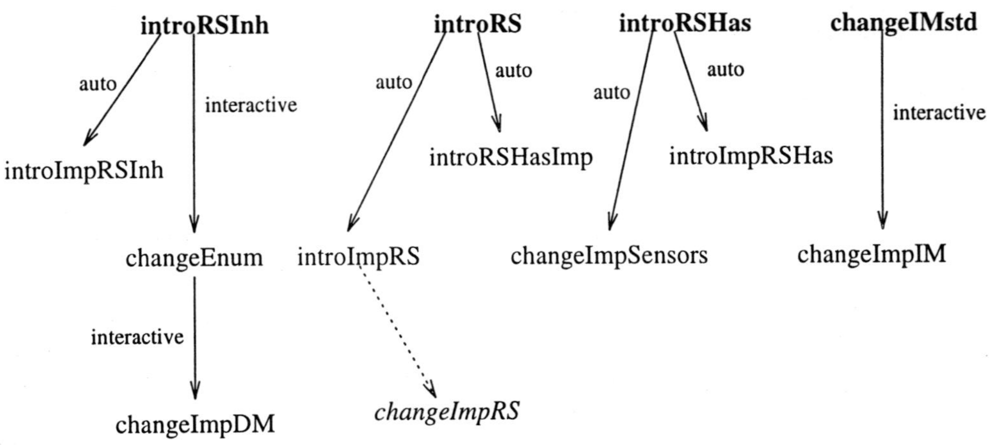

Figure 2. An impact graph of a weather monitoring system.

where *introImpClass* is a function for introducing a skeleton implementation class, *introRel* is a primitive function for introducing a relationship, and *introMod* is a function for introducing a new modification, $(b, update)$, which is related to the initiating modification mod. We name the new modification `changeImpRS` (see Figure 2).

Another example would be a propagation rule for automatically introducing the inheritance relationship in the implementation document following the introduction of the inheritance relationship in the design document and the introduction of the implementation class `ImpRainfallSensor`:

$$\begin{aligned}&\{(r_1 : \texttt{inheritance}, \mathit{introduction}),\\&\quad (a : \texttt{ImpClass}, \mathit{introduction})\} \rightarrow\\&\quad \{(r_2 : \texttt{impInheritance}, \mathit{introduction})\} :\\&\quad < a_1, r_1, b_1 > \wedge\, (a_1, a) \in \texttt{hasImp} \wedge\\&\quad (b_1, b_2) \in \texttt{hasImp} \wedge < a, r_2, b_2 >\\&\quad \textbf{by } \mathit{introRel}(a, b_2, \texttt{"impInheritance"});\end{aligned}$$

Note that this propagation rule is similar to an earlier change pattern, but they are different. In particular, there is an additional precondition for the rule to be fired, i.e., the completion of an additional initiating modification regarding the introduction of the implementation class. This indicates that a propagation rule may contain more initiating modifications than its corresponding change pattern. Also note that this rule is not a change pattern and is not used in impact analysis. Similarly we can define a propagation rule to introduce the has relationship in the implementation document automatically.

6. Related work

Traditional impact analysis approaches based on program slicing (e.g., [18, 12]) and program dependence graphs (e.g., [16, 14]) concentrate on impact analysis of program code. They mostly exploit the data dependence and control dependence as implied in the language definitions [3]. As such, other dependences such as the one between the enumerated type declaration and the concrete classes on the sensor inheritance hierarchy in the given example can not be captured. Besides, most of these approaches perform impact analysis on an extracted system representation, and therefore usually do not provide *direct* support for the change propagation process.

The approaches suggested in [1, 7] concentrate on assistance to change propagation, instead of impact analysis. They achieve this through the use of consistency rules. In [1], the violation of a consistency rule by a modification to the program is reported to the user, and the user is supposed to take action. In [7], message passing is used to propagate changes in order to enforce consistency rules, and to report consistency violations. In [4], an approach based on expert systems is proposed. Software dependences in terms of change are codified as rules in the expert system for impact analysis. Rules are also used to provide advice for change propagation. However, it is not clear how the system would directly support the actual change propagation process.

In [5], an impact analysis tool is reported. It is based on an extracted dependence graph model of system representation, where the nodes and edges are typed and are used to model artifacts and their dependences. It supports the specification of actual and potential impact analysis rules in terms of the system representation. Impact analysis according to the rules is an automatic process with potential impacts marked through a "weight" system. The potential impacts are then interactively validated by the user. The effectiveness of the automatic impact analysis solely based on codified rules in this approach is unclear. This is in clear contrast to our approach, where the dependences, properties and change patterns are all used for impact analysis to give a broader coverage and on the other hand the change patterns are also used to reduce the number of potential impacts for user validation.

7. Conclusions

In this paper, we have presented an approach to software change impact analysis and propagation in the context of a software engineering environment. In clear contrast to existing approaches, our approach uses the environment representation of software artifacts and their dependences. As such, there is no extracted, separate system representation required. Impact analysis and change propagation are performed directly on the actual (typed and fine-grained) software artifacts and dependences, and can be used during both software maintenance and initial system development. Besides, other environment facilities are also available for use during impact analysis and change propagation, including those for defining high-level operations and presentation views [19, 9].

In addition to dependences, we have used properties about software artifacts and dependences for impact analysis. This has greatly increased the flexibility and expressiveness of the approach, and made it possible to provide the capabilities of both traceability and dependence analysis based approaches [3]. Consequently, our approach is able to handle both source code and other types of software artifacts. In particular, our approach is able to identify impacts concerning the introduction and deletion of software artifacts and dependences, which is not usually addressed by existing approaches. The impact analysis process in our approach is a combination of automatic application of codified change patterns and interactive confirmation of potential impacts.

The use of the system representation in the environment has enabled automated direct assistance to change propagation. This is in contrast to most existing approaches, where impact analysis is performed on an extracted system model and no direct propagation support is provided. Again, the change propagation process is a combination of automatic propagation based on codified rules and interactive user guidance based on the impact analysis results.

A prototype experiment of the proposed approach is currently being undertaken in a C++ programming environment developed using the Synthesizer Generator [17]. Its full-scale implementation in our software engineering environment is to follow. Some of the issues for further investigation include incorporation of change rationales, integration with configuration and version management capabilities [10], and management of changes to artifact properties, change patterns and propagation rules.

Acknowledgment. The author would like to thank Hardeep Singh and the anonymous reviewers for their valuable comments on earlier drafts of this paper. The work reported here was partially funded by the Australian Research Council.

References

[1] R. Al-Zoubi and A. Prakash. Program view generation and change analysis using attributed dependence graphs. *Software Maintenance: Research and Practice*, 7:239–261, 1995.

[2] R. Arnald and S. Bohner. Impact analysis – towards a framework for comparison. In *Proceedings of 1993 International Conference on Software Maintenance*, pages 292–301, Montreal, Canada, September 1993.

[3] R. Arnold and S. Bohner, editors. *Software Change Impact Analysis*. IEEE Computer Society Press, 1996.

[4] G. Avellis. CASE support for software evolution: A dependency approach to control the change process. In *Proceedings of Fifth International Workshop on Computer-Aided Software Engineering*, pages 62–73, Montreal, Canada, July 1992.

[5] S. Barros, T. Bodhuin, et al. Supporting impact analysis: A semi-automated technique and associated tool. In *Proceedings of 1995 International Conference on Software Maintenance*, pages 42–51, Nice, France, October 1995.

[6] G. Booch. *Object-Oriented Analysis and Design with Applications*. Benjamin/Cummings, second edition, 1994.

[7] K. Gondow, T. Imaizumi, Y. Shinoda, and T. Katayama. Change management and consistency maintenance in software development environments using object oriented attribute grammars. In *Proceedings of First JSSST International Symposium on Object Technologies for Advanced Software*, pages 75–94, Kanazawa, Japan, November 1993.

[8] J. Han. Software documents, their relationships and properties. In *Proceedings of 1st Asia-Pacific Software Engineering Conference (APSEC'94)*, pages 102–111, Tokyo, Japan, December 1994. IEEE Computer Society Press.

[9] J. Han. A document-based approach to software engineering environments. In *Proceedings of 5th International CASE Symposium*, pages 128–133, Changsha, China, October-November 1995.

[10] J. Han. Providing configuration management support in software engineering environments. In *Proceedings of 2nd Asia-Pacific Software Engineering Conference (APSEC '95)*, pages 282–291, Brisbane, Australia, December 1995. IEEE Computer Society Press.

[11] J. Han. Specifying the structural properties of software documents. *Journal of Computing and Information*, pages 1333–1351, 1995.

[12] S. Horwitz, T. Reps, and D. Binkley. Interprocedual slicing using dependence graphs. *ACM Transactions on Programming Languages and Systems*, 12(1):26–60, January 1990.

[13] G. Kaiser, P. Feiler, and S. Popovic. Intelligent assistance for software development and maintenance. *IEEE Software*, 5(3):40–49, May 1988.

[14] J. Loyall and S. Mathisen. Using dependence analysis to support the software maintenance process. In *Proceedings of 1993 International Conference on Software Maintenance*, pages 282–291, Montreal, Canada, September 1993.

[15] N. Madhavji. Environment evolution: The Prism model of changes. *IEEE Transactions on Software Engineering*, 18(5):380–392, May 1992.

[16] A. Podgurski and L. Clarke. A formal model of program dependences and its implication for software testing, debugging, and maintenance. *IEEE Transactions on Software Engineering*, SE-16(9):965–979, September 1990.

[17] T. Reps and T. Teitelbaum. *The Synthesizer Generator: A System for Constructing Language-Based Editors*. Springer-Verlag, New York, 1989.

[18] M. Weiser. Program slicing. *IEEE Transactions on Software Engineering*, SE-10(4):352–357, 1984.

[19] J. Welsh and J. Han. Software documents: Concepts and tools. *Software — Concepts and Tools*, 15(1):12–25, 1994.

Session P3a

Quality Issues

User-perceptions Of Embedded Software Quality

R.J. Kusters (rku@tm.tue.nl), R. van Solingen (rso@tm.tue.nl), J.J.M. Trienekens (jtr@tm.tue.nl), Eindhoven University of Technology, Department of Technology Management, P.O. Box 513, 5600 MB Eindhoven, The Netherlands

Abstract

Many researchers and practitioners have recognised that the perception of 'quality' is largely influenced by personal view and application context. Depending on personal goals, interests and background, the interpretation of the quality concept is different per individual. In this paper, an approach is suggested by which the different user perceptions on quality are modelled, and can be addressed. This Multi-party Chain model supports the explanation of the various views on product quality of all users. Discussion among the parties involved is therefore enabled. Based on consensus the appropriate measures can be selected. The model should operationalise the basic relation between process and product, it enables the definition of metrics to evaluate process improvements, and links engineering activities to user requirements. The usefulness of the model is validated in a case-study.

1. Introduction

An information system, especially a complex embedded system, does not end up being 'high quality' just by accident. Often much effort and resources are spend to achieve quality. The developers, often of several disciplines, each contribute in the development of a high quality product. In their design and implementation, quality is a self-evident ambition which forms the basis of good engineering practices. As such, quality can be seen as the result of a large number of explicit and implicit control activities, and measures, often deeply implanted in the professional engineering knowledge and actions of the experts involved.

In practice however, quality is not always easy to achieve. Two common problems will be mentioned. Firstly, building functionality within plan and budget is often given higher priority than achieving quality attributes such as for instance quality. Secondly, quality of the complex systems of today must be achieved by combining the experience and knowledge of the disciplines involved. Combining disciplines means co-operation of experts from different fields, probably causing communication difficulties. Human failures become more likely and can easily lead to lower quality (e.g. less reliable or even unsafe systems).

In this paper we present an approach which puts user expectations on product quality as being the ultimate requirement to be fulfilled. An information system should either fulfil all requirements as desired by all parties involved or it should be made clear that some of these desires cannot be fulfilled within the existing constraints. This statement entails at least two types of problem:

1. Requirements are not always made explicit by the people involved, but they do expect the system to adhere to them none the less.
2. We are most of the time dealing with many different involved parties. Differences between users occur related to for example a persons job, responsibility or role and their specific use of the system. Even people that will not "use" software like the manager of the users or the person who is responsible for buying the software are involved. Also individual preferences exist based on intellectual skills, background or interests. The result of these differences is that 'quality' is being defined differently among the different users.

As a result we have to recognise that quality is a *multi-dimensional* concept, that it means many things for many people. This concept is explored further in this paper.

First we will take a look at the existing definitions of quality. In section 3 we will develop the multi-dimensional concept of quality. Based on this, in section 4 a control model for defining and implementing quality is presented. This model is developed further in section 5 where the multi-party chain approach is presented. This approach supports tackling the problem of identifying and controlling product quality. It is based on modelling the organisational chain for a product life-cycle and relating the different parties, roles and requirements to explicit actions to be taken during development. Our approach explicitly defines quality requirements for all users, and facilitates communication of those quality requirements among all parties involved. Therefore it seems highly applicable for application in multi-disciplinary development teams.

A data model to support this model is also presented in section 5. A number of ways to use the model is described in section 6. In section 7, by means of a case study, the validity and the usefulness of the approach is illustrated. The paper ends with some conclusions.

2. Present approaches and problems.

The distinction between functional and quality (or non-functional) requirements is a common one in the IS-field (see e.g. Boehm et.al. 1978 [2]; Cavano and McCall 1978 [3]; Deutsch and Willis 1978 [5], Bemelmans 1991 [1]; Delen and Rijsenbrij 1992 [4]). Examples of these quality requirements are quality, user friendliness, maintainability and portability of an information system (Boehm et al, 1978 [2]). Most of the literature in this area is based on the work of Boehm et. al. (1978) [2] and of Cavano and McCall (1978) [3]. In their view quality is expressed in a number of *quality attributes* of a software product. These attributes can be derived from a set of aggregated *quality factors*. The next step is to define metrics which can be used to test if the final product adheres to these attributes. Over the years this approach has been further refined by several authors (Willmer 1985 [12]; Deutsch and Willis 1987 [5]; Keller, Kahn and Panara 1990 [10]), and in particular the relation between the attributes have been described in a more realistic manner.

The current state of the art can be found in two standards: ISO 9126 (ISO, 1991 [8]) and the IEEE software engineering standards collection (IEEE, 1994 [7]). Both definitions are made for engineers by engineers and provide specifications in engineering terms that can be used as part of a design contract. In doing so, they both provide a vital service. Developing information systems, especially complex embedded systems, will usually take place on the basis of a set of well worked out requirements.

However, the very nature of these solid technical definitions also provided a problem. The greatest objection to this type of definition is that principals and potential users are not supported in the formulation of their quality requirements (see e.g. (Kaposi and Kitchenham, 1987 [9]). It is not clear how an organisation can determine the level and type of quality required that is relevant in its specific situation and in which language this can be formulated (Trienekens, 1992 [11]). This implies the need for a wider look at quality than is provided by either ISO or IEEE.

3. Quality: a wider outlook

Different parties have different ways of looking at a product from the point of view of quality. It might theoretically be feasible to translate all these different 'visions on quality' into one common definition which can then be used to communicate between all those parties involved. This seems the objective of the above discussed standards. In practice however, we deem this to be not feasible. Even if this common terminology could be developed, it is unlikely that it would provide a sufficient basis for discussion with *all* the parties involved. For one it is unlikely that all parties involved will be willing to adopt this technical 'engineering' language. We will therefore take an approach in which explicit account is being taken of locally defined assessments of quality.

In this paper we assume that product quality is related to its *use*. This brings us to the conclusion that to create a reliable product one must first define the function it is intended for, and collect all local definitions of its required quality level. This required quality level can now be derived from the characteristics of the situation within which the system has to function (Heemstra et.al., 1995 [6]). Another approach is to assume that product use is related to the responsibility of the users involved. Different parties, i.e. stake-holders such as buyers, users, project principals, developers etc., have different requirements regarding product quality. Quality appears to be a multidimensional concept, both in theory and in practice. As a consequence different concepts are used to express quality, different measures are carried out to determine and/or to establish quality, and different standards are used to validate and to evaluate the level of quality of a product.

This multi-dimensional concept of quality, as described above, is not intended to displace the more traditional quality concepts of ISO and IEEE. These will still be needed to provide accurate specifications for development engineers and will form the basis of any discussion on product quality. However we do claim that a wider look at quality is needed, if one wants to be able to define the type and level of quality required in such a way that users both understand and agree to what is being proposed. We will take this premise as a starting point when designing a control model for implementing quality.

4. A control model for implementing quality

For product development various activities are needed. A typical breakdown of activities for the development of embedded software systems is:

- initiation
- specification
- design
- implementation

The development activities produce the system and thereby will determine the system characteristics, including its quality. Further phases in the life cycle, such as operation, maintenance and disposal will also change the system quality in time. For simplicity, we will not discuss this and focus on the development phase of the life cycle, since those phases are assumed to have a higher impact.

Within the development process, several activities can be noted that specifically contribute to the quality of the system. If we make this activities explicit they can be seen as control measures on all activities within the development process. We can depict this in a control model (figure 1).

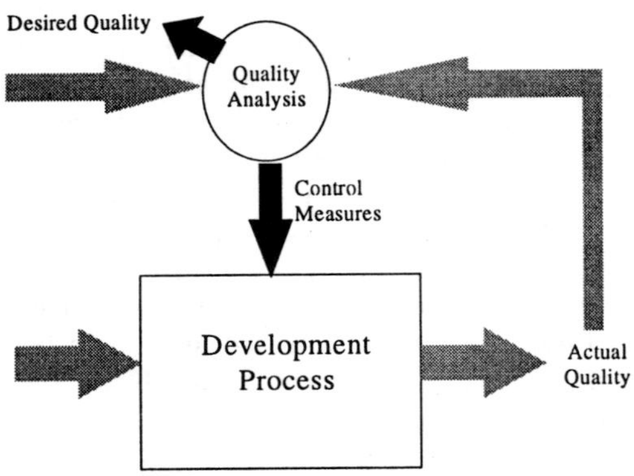

Figure 1: quality control model

In this model the flows of information and corresponding processes are:

- *desired quality* is the quality as stated or intended by the different users, the law or by ethics. It might also be influenced by taking into account results from a *quality analysis*.
- *control measures* are all required activities that should take place in the development process in order that the actual quality will equal the desired quality. These control measures are selected on the basis of *a quality analysis*.
- *actual quality* is the quality of the end product or the intermediate results of the development process, as perceived by the actual user of that product.

The goal of any development project is to create a system that conforms to a pre-specified level of quality. Depending on both the type of quality required as well as the level required a certain amount of measures are selected to result in the required product quality. In order to select the right mix of measures from the numerous possible options, and to achieve a closed control loop we need to be able to assess the result obtained (actual quality) to be able to determine if the proper mix of measures was selected in order to satisfy the required quality, which has to be stated explicitly. More in detail:

1. Assessment of *actual quality*. Product use is the ultimate quality check, but during development specific data collection appears to be applicable to give a representation of product quality. Keeping in mind that control measures will be taken, it seems logical to include data collection activities to track whether those measures give their intended effect.
2. Selection of *control measures* during the development processes. To select the appropriate measures to fulfil quality requirements, a supporting method is required.
3. Make the *desired quality* explicit while taking into account the multi-dimensional nature of the concept of quality as was discussed in the previous section.

The one thing to be kept in mind is that whenever a product must be reliable, measures are required to result in the required level of quality. Selection of measures is a difficult topic, and is done in practice mostly implicit and/or based on experience. What is required in both practice and science is a technique to describe the user-perceived quality requirements for their specific context of use. Whenever this description is available measures can be selected with a clear goal, and evaluation (read: measurement) can be implemented. Such a methodology is not found in literature or practice, but will be described in the next chapter: the Multi-Party Chain model.

5. Multi-party chain model

Measures are considered to be activities/actions that aim to increase the quality of an embedded software product. Both measures as well as the effect they will have will tend to be expressed in an engineers' language. Given this, communication between stakeholders is essential in order to achieve mutual understanding and consensus between the different parties involved which has to lead ultimately to agreed upon operational measures and metrics to realise and quantify the quality of products.

To enable this communication the different interpretations of quality have to be understood. Given a specific product, if it is known which party specified a specific requirement for this product and especially for which reason, then a basis for discussion has been created. If this specification is available it becomes possible to translate different interpretations and it becomes possible to negotiate and discuss those specified requirements. In the end, this enables us to link specific measures (in engineering terminology) to requirements of the different parties involved as expressed in their local terminology.

In this chapter we will present a model to facilitate the identification of all parties involved and of their concerns with quality. This model, the 'multi-party chain' model (MPC), can be used in a specific situation to identify concerns and to facilitate communication among the parties involved.

In a data model of this multi-party chain (MPC) the main entity types and their interrelations are represented. The data model supports the identification of the different parties involved, their interrelations, their roles, their requirements etc. The focus of the data model is on the determination, the realisation and the evaluation of quality in embedded software products by taking the right measures. By taking a specific measure, one aims at increasing one (or more) aspect of quality. The key question is therefor which set of measures suit best to the set of requirements for a specific product.

The data model that represents this approach will be shown in Figure 5. We will not impose this model upon the reader directly, but we will transfer the control model of the previous section stepwise according to the points 1-3, into the MPC-model.

5.1. Assess the actual quality of the output from the development process

The first step to take is to evaluate (e.g. by means of the ISO standard (external) metrics (ISO, 1991) [8]) the actual quality of the product. Therefor we need to perform data collection on that product. Theory on software metrics has learned that metrics on the total development process are required in order to gain insight into actual quality of a product. Figure 2 shows the data model of the development process. For simplicity we have defined that a development consists of a unique set of actions taken in a specific order. Those actions (measures) are taken on the product, the process, the resources and on the project management. Evaluating the actual quality of a product will consist of data collection on all of those entities.

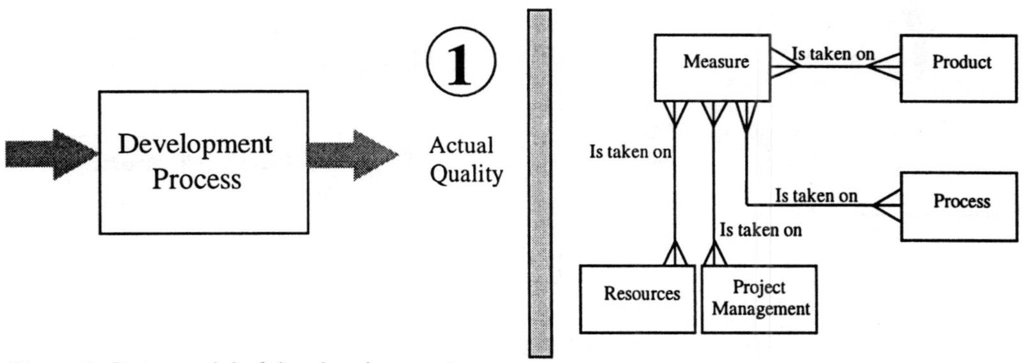

Figure 2: Data model of the development process.

The main entity types in the Figure 2 data-model and their definitions are:

- *Measure*: Activity that influences the type and/or degree of quality that is attained in a given product
- *Project management*: Those activities that guide the execution of the project
- *Resources*: Those resources that are used during project development and use

- *Product*: An imbedded software product seen as part of a larger system
- *Process*: The process of developing, maintaining and managing the product

5.2 Select control measures to fulfil quality requirements

The second step to take is the definition of control measures that aim at fulfilling specific quality requirements. Those requirements can be very diverse like: all software faults in the user-interface have been removed, or the most critical part of the system is fault tolerant. A certain quality analysis has to be executed on which measures can be selected. Figure 3 shows the data model in which control measures to fulfil quality requirements are opposed upon the development process. Note that the data-model of Figure 2 is included in this figure. The new entity type in this data-model and its definition is:

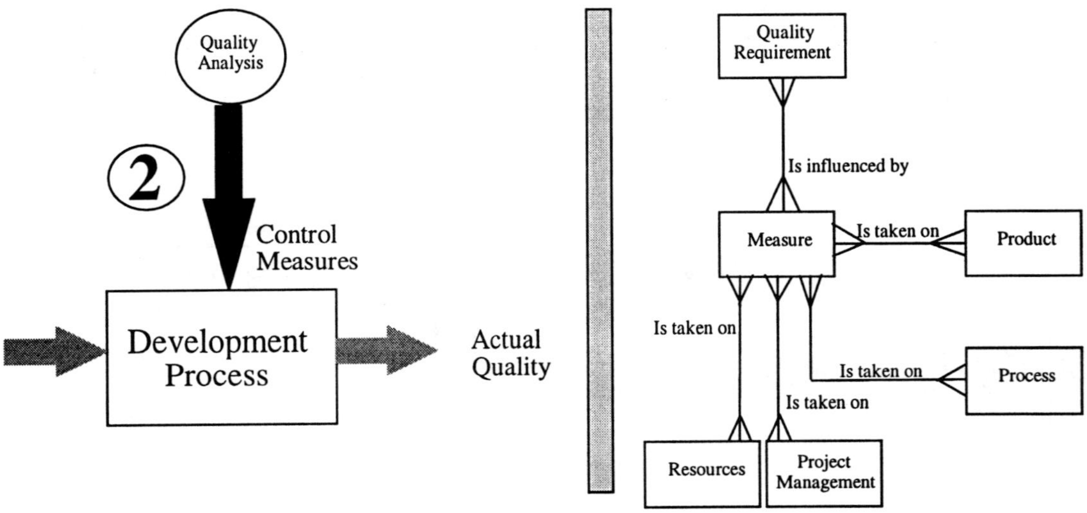

Figure 3: Data model of selection mechanism to fulfil quality requirements.

- *Requirement*: A statement regarding the type and degree of quality that is required from the product as seen from the point of view of a party in a given role

Requirements have to be expressed in terms of a specification. Examples of quality requirements of users: 'the system may not fail (go down) more than two times a month', 'when the system fails (goes down) an engineer must be able to fix it within one hour', or 'I will not have my customers annoyed by this system'. The first requirement can be expressed (in 'engineering language') into the quality aspect "availability". The second requirement can be expressed into the quality aspect "recoverability". The last requirement will need further discussion and clarification in order to find out what is really required, so that this requirement can be translated into requirements in the 'engineering language'. Consequently, measures and metrics (pertaining to project management, process, resource, and/or product) will have to be determined.

5.3. Make the desired quality explicit

The final step to take is to make the desired quality of the system explicit. As described before we will apply an approach in which all local definitions of all users are captured. Therefore a modelling technique is required which models all users and their view on quality. As described before we focus on parties, underlying roles and related quality requirements. Figure 4 shows the data-model by which we describe the chain of parties involved. In this way it becomes possible to make quality requirements explicit and it is possible to trace where they are originating from, based on roles and parties.

This is a 'chain' model, because we assume that a number of customer-supplier relationships exist between the different parties. An important relationship is the 'representation' relationship. Take for instance a system for controlling a fuel pump. Some relevant parties are customers, fuel station managers, oil company managers, oil company purchasing officials, and vendor representatives. We see here a chain of representation. The fuel station manager represents the interests of the customer. The oil company represents the interests of both the customer and the fuel station manager. The oil company purchasing official represents al of those. Also, The oil company purchasing official influences (and is influenced in his turn by) the vendor representative. To chart this area a 'chain' approach is taken.

The main new entity types in this part of the MPC data-model and their definitions are:

- *Party*: An identifiable person, group of persons of organisation who has a legitimate interest in the degree of quality of the product
- *Role*: An area of responsibility of the party determining a view on the type and degree of quality required

A *'party'* was previously defined as an identifiable person, group of persons of an organisation who have a legitimate interest in the degree of quality of the product. This 'legitimate interest' may come to light in one or more phases of the product life cycle. Examples of parties are: principals, customers and users (of different types, e.g. employees from marketing, purchasing, production etc.), project managers, engineers, maintenance people. Parties can also be stake-holders that are not directly involved in one or more specific phase of the life cycle, for instance governmental parties that develop and control policies, rules and constraints for quality of branch organisations that set their specific requirements.

A *'role'* was defined as an area of responsibility of a party that determines which view exists on the type and degree of quality required. A party can have more than one role. Example from Schlumberger, a producer of petrol dispensing machinery: The Schlumberger OPCO (the national sales and service organisation) has the responsibility to represent Schlumberger towards customers and vice versa (customers towards Schlumberger), but also to represent the national government of the country it is servicing and their policies towards Schlumberger. So the OPCO has several roles to play in communication on quality.

Relationship types relevant to the chain approach are:

- Parties may have different responsibilities. This is represented by the different 'roles' that a party may assume. This relationship type allows an inventory of quality requirements which are relevant to this party through the intermediate entity type 'role'.
- Parties can represent, both officially and unofficially, other parties.
- Finally parties may control and/or influence other parties. The last two relationship types allow us to build the multi-party chain by identifying the links between the different parties.
- Roles may be linked to several parties which in that case would be expected to have identical quality requirements.
- A role may be concerned about one or more quality requirements.
- A quality requirement can be linked to several roles. In that case these roles, from a different motivating background, are expected to agree as to the required degree/type of quality.
- Some quality requirements can be 'translated' into another definition of quality. This enables communication and agreement between different parties.
- Requirements can be influenced by measures/actions.

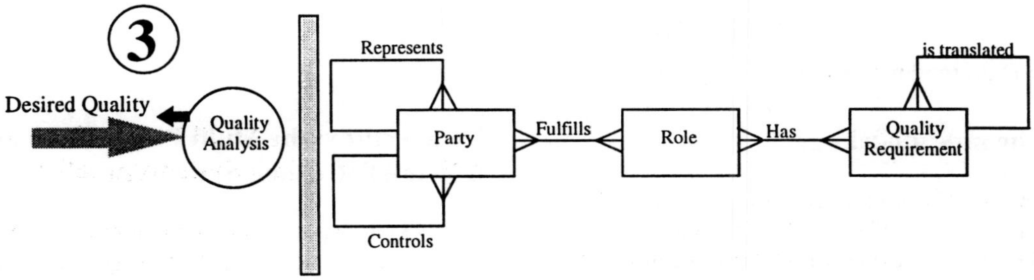

Figure 4: Data model to make quality requirements explicit from the context of use.

5.4. The Multi-Party Chain Data Model

If we combine the steps taken before into the overall Multi-Party Chain model we get the data model as represented in figure 5.

- how to identify and express generic descriptions of quality measures and specific descriptions of measures and how to make distinctions
- how to make distinctions between 'internal' parties (e.g. developers) and 'external' parties (e.g. customers).

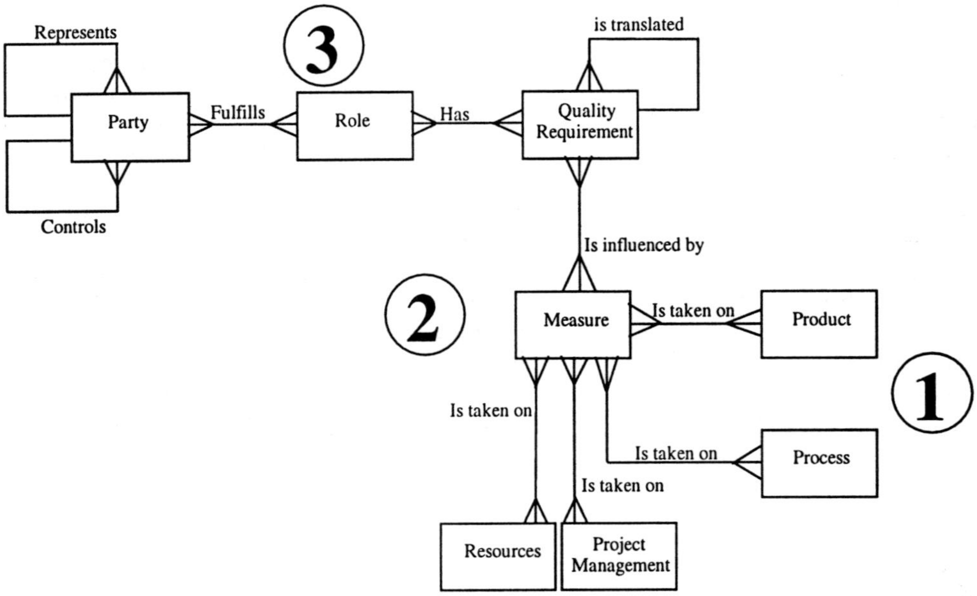

Figure 5: Data model of the Multi-Party Chain.

6. Using the mpc model

The MPC model can serve different objectives. The model can be used initially to fill in the entities and attributes for a specific embedded software product in a specific organisation, i.e. for positioning the different parties and the different types of requirements that can be distinguished. But it can also be applied for identifying the different types of measures that are executed, for investigating differences in opinions etc.

Based on such a 'case-study' the MPC data model can be used for answering questions such as:

- how to identify gaps between quality interpretation, and how to bridge them (e.g. between 'fitness for use' interpretations and 'conformance to spec' interpretations; this to enable communication in the area of quality
- how to distinguish measures, metrics, standards (e.g. ISO9001, usage of test scripts, the gathering of measurement data, informal reviews of developers), and how to store and supply this information in a user-friendly way

7. Case study: the Multi Party Chain applied at Retail Petroleum Systems practice

The Multi Party Chain approach has been applied to make a model of the Schlumberger RPS situation regarding the way that different specialists deal with different interpretations of software quality. First some information is given about the Schlumberger RPS organisation and its products. Subsequently, selected results from interviews with different types parties within Schlumberger are presented to support the basic ideas behind the mpc-model. The second part of the case study shows how it is possible to use the mpc-model in analysing user quality requirements. The case study ends with a number of comments.

7.1. The organisation and its environment

Schlumberger is a world-wide leading supplier of services and technology to the international petroleum industry. Schlumberger concentrates its expertise in three groups: Oil field services (exploitation and production services for the petroleum industry), Measurement & Systems (technologies for optimising the distribution of gas, water and electricity), and Omnes (communication and information technology solutions). The interviews have been carried out at Retail Petroleum Systems (RPS) which is a part of the Measurement and Systems group. RPS serves the major service station networks and offers the oil companies and independent retailers, products for dispensing fuel and transferring funds. The customers of Schlumberger RPS include most of the large oil companies.

The software products of Schlumberger RPS are typically real-time embedded systems. RPS develops and manufactures systems for self-service fuel stations. Examples of these products are fuel dispensers, forecourt control systems, point of sales, and credit card systems, training and maintenance programs and 24-hour customer service.

RPS is divided in six departments, Quality & Marketing, Research & Development, Sales & Service, Manufacturing, Finance and Personnel. Manufacturing is carried out in three factories, of which Schlumberger RPS Bladel The Netherlands is one. Schlumberger RPS is represented in a large number of countries by so-called OPCO's (OPerational COmpanies) which serve national markets in terms of product sales, installation, training, and service.

To better understand the meaning and the importance of software quality in Schlumberger RPS products, hereafter some relevant information about the products, the customers and the organisational policy is given.

The Products

All products of Schlumberger RPS contain software. The software is often incorporated in the hardware (in EPROM chips) or is implemented on a hard disk. Products can be divided in three categories:

- Dispensing systems (Fuel-dispensers)
- Payment Terminals (mostly for out-door purposes)
- Cash register devices (for in-door purposes)

All systems consist of both hardware and software. Some of these products are called "complete" products because the OPCO's do not (have to) carry out customisation activities on the software in these systems. For Point of Sales terminals the core software is released separately, and customised by engineers at the OPCO to meet specific market and user requirements, e.g. regarding customer names, logo, currencies, etc. For these particular systems the difference between software and hardware is very relevant. The product consists of a core system, to which additional functionality such as card applications, back-office applications, supply management, can be attached. Some of these systems have sophisticated man-machine interfaces, for example the Point of Sales terminals, but currently also the payment terminals are increasingly provided with such interfaces.

The Clients

A distinction can be made between two types of clients:

- users who really work with a system (e.g. a manager or operator (e.g. cashier) at a fuel-station).
- customers who decide to buy a system, e.g. a representative of an oil company.

A *user* does not distinguish between hardware and software. Whenever the product does not fulfil its promised function or does not have the quality that has been promised , it is not relevant for a user to know whether it is hardware or software that causes the problem.

Some *customers* do distinguish between hardware or software regarding a product. The number of customers who prescribe acceptance criteria and required test approaches is likely to expand. OPCO's are increasingly specifying those criteria explicitly for the development department.

Mostly products are sold to the major oil companies. A percentage of the customers are independent customers which own and exploit a fuel station. The major oil companies are important customers for which the first releases of a product is intensively supported.

The Policy

Sales at Schlumberger RPS is targeted on high quality products. The importance of software for the fuel station systems has increased during the last years. For example customers ask more and more for systems that operate in local- and wide area networks. Risks of software, and fuel station systems in general, are in particular economic risks. Risks are that transactions are lost, or non-operation of a system causes the station not to sell petrol. Schlumberger RPS invests large efforts in reducing those risks to an absolute minimum.

7.2. Interpretations of quality

A first objective of the case-study was to determine the way that practitioners in Schlumberger RPS deal with the determination and implementation of the quality of software in their products. The concept of quality has been approached from a user or customer perspective. Interviews with different types of practitioners have been carried out to test the assumption that the different involved parties have different roles and tasks (to meet customer requirements), approach quality in different ways, and consequently carry out different activities to strive at an optimal level of quality.

The different parties, their roles and their particular ways of dealing with (quality) requirements have been identified. Also the interrelations between these parties, in terms of co-operation and translating system and quality requirements from one party to another, are investigated. Consequently a description of the Schlumberger environment is developed that consists of parties and their interrelations. The parties in the Schlumberger RPS cyclic chain are respectively: Client, User, Fuel-station, Oil-company, OPCO, Production, Development, Marketing (Figure 6).

In the model both the flow of the demands and the flow of the delivery of the products are visualised. Each step can be considered as a consumer/producer relation. For example an OPCO is often both consumer of products from Development and Production, and producer of customer-specific products for fuel-stations.

In Schlumberger RPS interviews were performed to discuss the interrelations between the different parties and their roles in the chain model, in particular the ways that each party dealt with software quality. The interviews have been carried out in respectively the departments Marketing, Research & Development in The Netherlands and in two OPCO's in Turnhout Belgium and Ridderkerk The Netherlands.

- In the central Development department a project manager has been interviewed who is a technical co-ordinator for the release of a fore-court control and cash register product. His job contains of training, demo's and presentations, evaluating requirements, and co-ordinating test phases. He has relevant experience in software development.

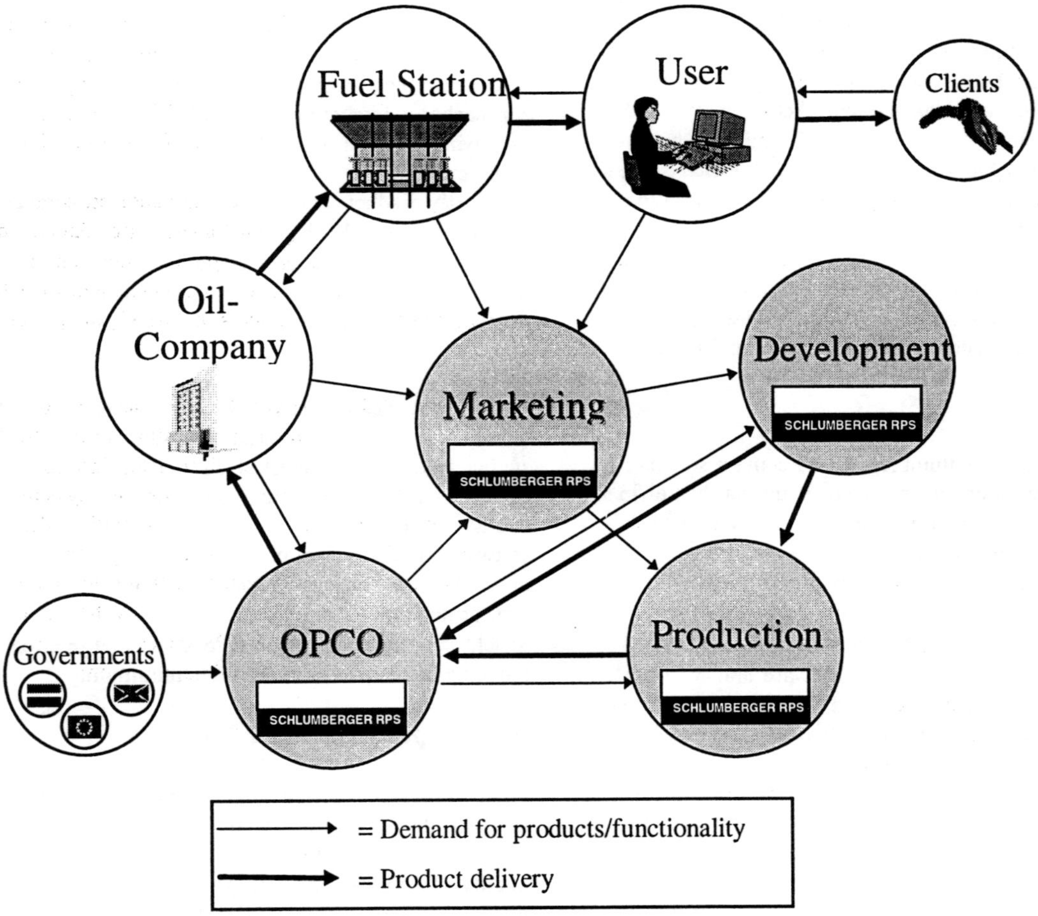

Figure 6: the Schlumberger RPS environment

- In the Marketing department the interview was carried out with a marketing manager who is responsible for the release of a fore-court control and cash register product to a large oil company.

At OPCO two interviews were carried out.

- One interview with an OPCO manager and an operator trainer who has relevant experience in how people use the products. This interview focused on embedded software products such as Point of Sales terminals, since this is the software that is customised by OPCO departments.
- In a second OPCO interview a Sales manager and a support engineer were interviewed. The Sales manager has sound experience, and frequent contacts with Schlumberger RPS' *customers*. The Training and Support engineer has frequent contacts with *end-users*. The fore-court and cash control systems played a central role in each of the interviews.

In the following the main interview results are presented in three system development stages that were identified as most important, respectively:

- requirements elicitation (c.q. identification and definition),
- establishing system/software requirements and
- software testing.

The quality chain model is used to position the Schlumberger practitioners and their particular opinions and activities in a coherent framework. As such the differences of their view points on quality could be presented, discussed and clarified.

Requirements elicitation

Marketing is the central entity in the multi party quality chain model (see Figure 6). Marketing supports the process of specifying the system requirements of the "consumers". In the requirements identification and definition processes Marketing considers 'all' requirements from 'all' consumers. All users, operators, clients, customers, OPCO's and developers are being considered as consumers. As a consequence Marketing has to deal with a large variety of different (quality) requirements. Also the complexity of these requirements continuous to grow.

Marketing considers its role as a highly interactive iterative and concurrent process of:

- investigating new product opportunities and (im)possibilities of developers and producers;
- identifying the implicit and explicit customer (e.g. oil-companies) requirements and wishes;
- identifying the implicit and explicit user requirements and wishes;
- taking decisions about a product's functionality and quality, how to present a product to the customers and when to the market, and how to describe product requirements for the developers.

Marketing specialists are confronted with more and an increasing complexity of the requirements of consumers. Two trends were identified:

- customers, in particular the large oil companies, start prescribing acceptance criteria and required test approaches. This trend is likely to expand. Although formal international standards for development processes are applied, such as ISO9000, product quality standards such as ISO9126 are not applied.
- Customers, require more and more information from the fuel-station. This trend demands for systems that operate in large networks, and that provide information to manage several fuel-stations centrally. The role and the position of the fuel station manager is therefore changing.

Establishing system/software requirements

This section is in particular based on selected results from the interviews of respectively the project manager from the central Development department and the OPCO employees (see Figure 6).

Often, the wishes and needs of the customers and users do not reflect a distinction between hardware and software. Customers want to specify a system and to buy a system (functionality) for a certain price. The translation from system requirements to hardware and software is then made by the developers. One of the main issues that has been addressed was the translation of quality requirements into measurable quality characteristics of a product. Although requirements for quality of systems are not explicitly specified, quality characteristics (e.g. for the Quality of a system), including metrics, are becoming important and are specified. Examples of metrics are "Mean Time Between Failure" (MTBF) or "Mean Time To Repair" (MTTR). The quality characteristics have to be checked by an OPCO, during in-house testing. Sometimes a quality characteristic such as Quality can also be covered by an agreement between developers and customers about the application of specific test sets and test criteria.

It is difficult to develop systems for all European countries that meet all requirements. The reason is that each country has different demands and government regulations. Therefore Schlumberger RPS develops so-called core-systems that have a specific set of basic functionalities. OPCO's customise these systems in accordance with the particular wishes and requirements of a specific country (or customer). On the one hand, this creates time saving, because the core-system is developed only once. On the other hand, the time-to-market is lengthened, because products have to be customised, which takes extra time and effort.

Software Testing

This section addresses the experiences of Schlumberger professionals with testing. Testing is considered as an important area in that quality has to be evaluated and consolidated. The selected interview results that will be presented hereafter have been gained from interviews with the project manager from the central Development department and the OPCO employees (see Figure 6).

The risks of developing systems with more functionality creates higher risks. As stated before, risks of fuel station systems are economic risks. Developers strive at decreasing the risks involved in using software in the systems by using extended testing and debug facilities, 4th generation languages, libraries of software components. Software development itself is getting more mature also because of the use of quality control systems. Risk reduction has an important place in such a quality system. Risk reduction at Schlumberger RPS is mainly based on thoroughly testing of the software-intensive systems and on intensive co-operation with customers during development and testing.

It is recognised that testing should be based on a well-defined test strategy and plan. Based on that the targets for testing can be set and the time and effort planning for the testing can be carried out. Systems should be tested very intensively. For adequate testing it is important to know which the most critical components are of a specific system and what the failures are that have occurred with similar systems before. Only then testing will improve the quality of a product. In the interviews two main issues of software quality have been identified:

- failures and causes of failures
- testing from a customer perspective

To be able to carry out testing in an adequate way, i.e. increasing the quality of the system, practitioners should know about possible *failures* that (can) occur as well as their causes.

There is currently no real consensus among the practitioners about the most important causes of system failures. This underlines the assumption that individual viewpoints influence the perception of product quality. One interviewed person told that most failures are caused by hardware defects. Another one told that most failures of the system are caused by software faults. In his opinion it could be expected that after some time when the stability of the software has increased most defects will be caused by the hardware.

If possible, *customers* should be involved in the testing activities. Actually, they have to be convinced about the quality of a product. At Schlumberger RPS customers respond to the increase of the importance of software in products. Sometimes also a customer is asked by Schlumberger specialists to approve temporary deliverables, and they are kept informed on current status and progress.

To reduce the number of fatal faults in the system before it is released to a large number of fuel stations, it is normal to keep field-tests. Field-tests are trial installations of a system in practice, but in a very small number (1 or 2). During such a first field-test, a developer (engineer) will stay at the fuel-station. There will also be 24 hours support for that station, during the first week of operation.

In this way faults in the system, that were not found during test, are detected before the system is installed at a large number of stations.

7.3. Using the MPC model

In the second part of this case study we will demonstrate how the MPC-model can be applied. For the sake of clarity we will confine the further discussion to a single aspect of quality, namely reliability. Also, again for the sake of clarity and brevity, we will only look at external (from the point of view of Schlumberger) parties. We continue the case within the following setting:

A specific customer of Schlumberger is demanding that each new product is first installed in a pilot installation where it has to be operational for a period of time before the final role-out can proceed. Those pilot installations are called: "Field-tests", and the question is why this customer is demanding those tests, and whether an alternative solution can be offered that fulfils the same underlying requirements.

A first step in using the model is by identifying all relevant parties (see Figure 6), their roles and the reliability requirements that may be derived from these roles. This was done by means of a series of interviews within the Schlumberger organisation. Interviews were conducted with:

- an *operator trainer* for RPS products, with relevant experience in how people use RPS products,
- an *OPCO manager*, who is responsible for all activities performed in a national representative company,
- a *marketing manager* who is responsible for the release of a product to a large customer.
- a *technical co-ordinator* involved in the release of the same product,

- an experienced *sales manager* who has frequent contacts with Schlumberger RPS customers,
- a *customisation engineer* who has frequent contacts with end-users.

The results, an operational version of the MPC-model, are presented in tables 1 and 2.

Table 1: Overview of external parties and roles

Party	Roles
Government	1. Protect the environment
	2. Guarantee safety
	3. Collect taxes
	4. Translating the law into certification procedures
	5. Certifying
Oil-company	6. Buying systems that fulfil the oil-company requirements, customer requirements, and fuel-station requirements
	7. Deliver (fuel) products to fuel-stations in time
Fuel-station	8. Responsible for revenue of a fuel-station
	9. Responsible for fast payment by customer
Customer	10. Responsible that exact amount of fuel is delivered
	11. Paying

Using these tables we will now analyse the customers' demand for a field test. The first step to be taken is to identify the roles that originate to the demand for a field-test. Result: The MPC-model shows that a representative of an oil company has two roles:

- Buying systems that fulfil the oil-company requirements, customer requirements, and fuel-station requirements
- Deliver (fuel) products to fuel-stations in time

It is clear that the request for a field-test mainly addresses the first role of the representative of an oil-company. The difficulty for that specific role is that it has the responsibility to address requirements of many other parties, therefor this person will demand a test (validation of requirements) that is able to check all of the implicit and explicit requirements: practice. This shows the reason behind the demand for a field-test.

Based on this conclusion it is possible to offer the person with that specific role an alternative solution which fulfils his needs. For example showing that person the same product already operational for some years on an other fuel-station. Note: In real-life this request came for a product that was in it's first release to the market, so no operational systems were available, which explains the emphasis of that role for a field-test.

Table 2: Overview of (external) roles and related reliability requirements

Role	Reliability Requirements
1	Safety of environment
	Environment is not at risk, according to the law
2	Safety of people
	People are not at danger, according to the law
3	Security of payment transactions
	Payment transactions are secure, according to the law
4	Operational inspections that show no unreliability
	Operational inspections that show reliability
5	Conform certification procedures
6	Availability
	Maturity
	No (known) failures
	Recoverability
	Support in case of failure
	All implicit reliability requirements are addressed
7	Availability
8	Availability
	Performance
	Support in case of failure
	Accuracy
9	Usability
	Sufficient feedback
	Performance
	Availability
10	Usability
	Accuracy
	Performance
11	Security
	Performance
	Accuracy

But before drawing premature conclusions, it is better to focus on the underlying reliability requirements of the representative of an oil-company. In this example this means focusing on the first role. The underlying reliability requirements according to the MPC-model are [8]:

- Availability
- Maturity
- No (known) failures

- Support in case of failure
- Recoverability
- All implicit reliability requirements are addressed

Again, it is shown that very diverse reliability requirements are included in this role, which declares why this person will ask for a field-test, since it seems difficult to address those different requirements together in one measure. The overall requirement of a product seems to be that it is continuously operational, which is being addressed by four of the above reliability requirements: availability, maturity, no failures, and recoverability. For a representative of an oil-company: it just has to work. It has to be 'good'. One can think of an alternative measures to address these issues, like lab-tests, formal proof, measurement results, or proven operation on a fuel-station in practice.

Two other requirements are still left: support in case of failure, and fulfilling implicit requirements. From the role of the representative the support issue is clear: a fuel-station must be available, so whenever it fails fast support must be guaranteed. One can think of contracts that guarantee support with penalties when those are not kept, but testing this kind of support in field-test is not suitable, because support is mostly important in situations where there is no special attention for a fuel-station, and during a field-test there is special attention because it is a test-case. So it can be concluded that a field-test is not addressing this requirement.

The second requirement left, is about implicit requirements which really show the need for testing in the field, in order to verify those implicit requirements. But, it does not imply that the product needs to be tested at a station of the customer. Involvement of end-users during design, or the intensive enhancement of the user-interface in an external usability-lab may be a sufficient measure to address this reliability requirement of the oil-company representative.

An alternative solution to field-testing might therefor be showing that the product is already operating in practice with success. This can be implemented by showing the successful operation of the system at the station of competitors of that oil-company. But the most likely alternative for a field-test is: testing a product on a fuel-station of Schlumberger. Customer specific enhancements of a product are then not validated, but in that case a lab-test of the additional functions may be sufficient to convince the representative that his responsibilities are being addressed.

One remark that must be added, is that the requirements above may not always be totally stated by the oil-company representative himself. It is very likely that the demand for a field-test is done by someone else in the company who is translating those requirements. Examples are the marketing manager of an OPCO, who needs to prove that the requirements of an oil-company are met, or the manager of a fuel-station who does not want to take any risk. Anyway it is possible to show the reasons behind a measure (expected effects). Look for example at the roles and reliability requirements of a station-manager, or OPCO-marketing. One will see that the demands for a field-test originate mainly from validating all possible requirements on a fuel-station.

7.4. Case comments

Quality is not a concept that can be dealt with by one particular person, or for that one specific specialist should take all the responsibility. The interviews made clear that there are important differences between the viewpoints on quality of different parties, i.e. types of practitioners, and their roles. From the Marketing point of view quality has to be determined starting from the large variety of different customers' wishes and needs and their increasing complexity. Central Development and the OPCO's have to translate these wishes and needs into (measurable) quality characteristics of a product. From the developers' point of view, both in the central Development department and in the OPCO's, actions have to be carried out to evaluate and to verify (i.e. to test) the quality of a product. Preferably, these activities should be a joint effort of Schlumberger specialists and customers. The interview results in the first part of the case show that the different points of view on quality of different parties can be visualised and clarified by means of a cyclic multi party quality chain model.

This example presented in the second part of the case illustrated how the MPC-model can be used to analyse user requirements. As such it can provide important input into the negotiation process will result into 'hard' engineering requirements.

8 Conclusions

It appears that a general definition of quality to which all people: developers, users, managers, etc., agree is not available. It has been concluded that the interpretation and view on quality is influenced by the responsibility, or role of a person. Those different views of quality rightfully exist and cannot and should not be ignored. In this paper a multi-party chain model was presented. It can be used to chart the various views on product quality in such a way that discussion among the various parties involved is enabled. A number of different scenario's for dealing with quality can be distinguished by using the model. Also, the definition of quality issues for different roles can be supported. This will enable the definition of metrics for quality issues and eventually the formation of a link between engineering actions and customers requirements.

Further research within the context of the Spirits project (see appendix) will be aimed at populating the data model with more case material, at further empirical research into the uses of the model, and at developing a series of connected tools that support this approach.

References

1. Bemelmans T.M.A., Bestuurlijke Informatiesystemen en Automatisering (Management Information Systems and Automation), Stenfert Kroese, The Netherlands, 1991.
2. Boehm B.W. c.s, Characteristics of Software Quality, New York, 1978.
3. Cavano J.P., J.A. McCall, A framework for the measurement of software quality. In: Proceedings of the software quality and assurance workshop, 1978.
4. Delen G.P.A.J., D.B.B. Rijsenbrij. The Specification, Engineering and Measurement of Information Systems Quality. Journal of Systems Software, 1992.
5. Deutsch M.S., R.R. Willis, Software Quality Engineering, Prentice Hall, 1987
6. Heemstra, F.J., Kusters, R.J. en Trienekens, J.J.M., From Quality Requirement Factor to Quality Factor: an end-user based method, *Proceedings of the 6th European Software Cost Modelling Meeting*, Kerkrade, May 1995, pp. 18.1 - 18.19.
7. *IEEE Standards Collection*: Software Engineering, Institute of Electrical and Electronic Engineers, 1994.
8. ISO/IES 9126, *Information Technology - Software Product Evaluation - Quality Characteristics and guidelines for their use,* International Organisation of Standardisation, 1991.
9. Kaposi A. and Kitchenham B., The architecture of system quality, *Software Engineering Journal*, 1987.
10. Keller S.E., L.G. Kahn, R.B. Panara. Specifying Quality Software Requirements with Metrics. In: R.H. Thayer and M. Dorfman (eds.), Tutorial: Systems and Software Requirements Engineering. IEEE Computer Society Press, 1990.
11. Trienekens J.J.M. Quality Management in Software Production, A Customer Oriented Approach. In: *Proceedings of the IFIP 5.7 Working Conference on Integration in Production Management* (ed. J.C. Wortmann ed.), North-Holland, Elsevier Amsterdam, The Netherlands, 1992.
12. Willmer H., Systematische Software Qualitätssicherung anhand von Qualitäts- und Produktmodellen, Springer-Verlag, Informatikfachberichte, 1985.

Appendix: about the Spirits project

'SPIRITS' is an acronym which stands for Software Process Improvement in embedded IT environments. SPIRITS is a research project of Schlumberger Retail Petroleum Systems (RPS) which is executed in co-operation with two research institutes in the Netherlands. SPIRITS will develop concepts and methods for process improvement to accomplish high and quantifiable reliability of embedded products. The main objectives are the design of:

- methods for process improvement in embedded systems development;
- methods for measurement and evaluation of the effectiveness of process improvement activities on the reliability of embedded products.

The practical application of the concepts and methods is validated in several case studies within Schlumberger RPS. The set of instruments will be based on practical experiences and will be scientifically founded and validated in a number of pilot projects.

Extending the ami approach to encompass the Foundation activity

John Gorbutt
UK Division
GPT Limited
New Century Park
PO Box 53
Coventry CV3 1HJ
United Kingdom

Email:
john.gorbutt@cab.png.cv.gpt.co.uk

Paul Layzell
Software Management Group
UMIST
PO Box 88
Manchester M60 1QD
United Kingdom

Email: p.layzell@umist.ac.uk

Abstract

The ami approach is a common sense framework for applying metrics to software development projects. This paper proposes an extension to the ami approach, based on industrial experience within a large Telecommunications supplier, which encompasses the very early stages of a measurement programme.

Formalising the initial stages of a measurement programme helps reduce the risk of missing fundamental issues that affect the overall programme, and reduces the likelihood of project failure. Formalisation is achieved through completing the three distinct steps of the Foundation activity; Construct Programme Terms Of Reference, Produce Project Plan, and Conduct Project Launch. To aid in completing these three steps a Foundation Checklist was developed, based on Pulford's five pre-requisites [1] and the work conducted within Telecommunications supplier.

1.0 Introduction

In today's challenging telecommunications market, competitive advantage is gained through understanding and achieving excellence in those processes considered critical to the company's success. To achieve excellence in any field one must continually strive to successfully use and apply the most appropriate methods and techniques available.

The *ami* (Application of Metrics in Industry) approach [7] has been successfully used in a number of industrial projects. The *ami* approach, which was a created through a collaborative ESPRIT project, is a common sense framework for quantifying software projects. It consists of four distinct activities, *Assess*, *Analyse*, *Metricate* and *Improve*. These four activities each consist of three steps that if systematically followed help the introduction of goal oriented measurement into a software development environment.

For a number of years GPT, which is the UK's leading supplier of communications solutions, has been involved in the field of software measurement. The largest group within GPT is the Public Networks Group who design, develop and manufacture public network switches, services and platforms, access and transport equipment and network management products. Significant investment is put into in the continual enhancement and development of new features for a large software legacy systems. Due to GPT's extensive commitment to quality, various process improvement programmes are championed throughout the organisation. This paper is based on one programme, to introduce goal oriented measurement into a specific part of the organisation using a form of the *ami* approach.

This paper concentrates on the initial stages of the *ami* approach. This includes the fundamental activities that should be undertaken before the *Assessment* activity of the should take place and which are necessary

0-8186-7840-2/97 $10.00

for an effective implementation of the *ami* approach.

Section 2 provides an overview of the previous measurement activities conducted within GPT. Specific focus is given to the problems associated with the original measurement programme. Section 3 then discusses the re-launch of the measurement programme.

Section 4 discusses the five pre-requisites that Pulford [1] identifies as important in implementing the *ami* approach. These pre-requisites are expanded upon, by providing five more important questions that must be asked before *Assessment* should take place. These constitute what is called the *Foundation activity*.

Section 5 concludes with the identification of a *Foundation Checklist* that can be used as the basis for completing the three distinct steps of the Foundation activity, namely *Construct Programme Terms Of Reference*, *Produce Project Plan*, and *Conduct Project Launch*. It is these steps which the programme described in this paper believes are fundamental to the successful implementation of a measurement programme.

2.0 The Original Measurement Programme

In 1993 a Metrics Working Party (MWP) was formed at GPT. The major objective of the MWP was to introduce metrics into the software development part of the business. At its peak, the MWP consisted of approximately twelve members, whose positions ranged from software engineer to development head. The MWP met on a bi-monthly or quarterly basis to discuss specific issues to do with metrics definition, collection, automated collection and analysis tools, progress, and problems encountered.

The major aspect of their work concentrated on developing a *metrics template* for the Development Teams within the business. Developed by influential members of the MWP over a number of months, the *template* focused on product and process measures and consisted of:

i. a list of metrics that each team was required to collect.
ii. a brief description of the required metrics.
iii. how the metric should be calculated.
iv. how the metric should be reported.
v. where the metric data could be collected from.

Each of the twelve Development Teams were required to collect metrics throughout the development phase of the project and provide a completed metrics report at the end of the development phase. It was then the responsibility of the MWP to collect, collate and analyse these Development Team metrics reports and produce a collated report which gave an overall picture of the software development phase. Actions were then raised on each Development Team to improve specific aspects of their process.

There were a number of problems associated with the original measurement programme.

2.1 There was a lack of senior management commitment

It is recognised that many measurement programmes fail due to the lack of senior management commitment [1, 8]. Improvement cannot be brought in as if it were a software tool. Management must take the lead in initiating measurement, defining goals and asking for feedback information.

Grady [2] states that the people who you recruit to implement your objectives send a signal to the rest of the organisation that indicates the importance of the programme. Although the measurement programme had a Development Head as the Chairman of the MWP, Director level commitment was also required to bring additional credibility and visibility.

2.2 The internal and external customers of the measurement programme were not precisely defined

Originally, metrics were being collected by the Development Teams and supplied to the MWP. Over time, further metrics "customers", both internal and external to the company, were identified, each requiring metrics for different reasons. Development Teams who supplied the information required metrics for local analysis and process improvement; the MWP required information to provide a collated view of the whole development phase, enabling them to suggest organisational process improvements; the internal company quality function also required information to provide and improve standards; whilst external customers required information to provide them with confidence in the product supplied to them.

2.3 Imprecise objectives with no clear strategy

From the outset of the measurement programme the overall objectives were not formally documented or declared. In addition, there was no Terms Of Reference for the MWP, or high level schedule. This resulted in members of the MWP not fully understanding the direction in which the MWP was heading or when it should get there.

Imprecise objectives also resulted in many of the metrics seemingly being collected for no apparent reason other than "What data can we collect ? Then lets collect it !", rather than deriving the metrics from the goals of the business.

In addition, there was no formal project plan or defined schedule. All process improvement initiatives should be managed like software development projects. They should have an overall project plan identifying key activities, when they should be done, and who should perform them.

2.4 Conflicting commitment requirements on the members of the MWP

All of the representatives on the MWP had a dedicated role outside of the field of measurement. Often, due to the normal everyday workload, many of the measurement related activities were "put on a back burner", to be done when the individual had some "spare time". Many of the MWP representatives did not have any "spare time" and therefore activities relating to the measurement programme were either rushed or not done.

2.5 Naivity lead to being over ambitious

In hindsight it was felt that much of what was being asked of the Development Teams was too ambitious based on the limited training, resources and tools available to them. It was relatively easy to define a seemingly useful metric that could be collected by all Teams. The reality being that hundreds of metrics can be collected but they must be used to achieve a specific goal.

In addition, as Pulford [1] points out, not matching the measures to the capability of the software development process is a recipe for disaster.

Many of these problems were thought to be fundamental issues that future measurement programmes should learn from.

3.0 The Re-launched Measurement Programme

After a period of stagnation (mainly due to the lack of success of the original measurement programme) the MWP was re-launched in late 1995. The re-launch was mainly due to the beginning of a cultural change, with the realisation that metrics and process improvement were vital ingredients in providing quality software solutions to quality, time and cost.

The beginning of this cultural change can be traced back to the appointment of a *Process Improvement Manager* whose role was to facilitate and manage various process improvement related activities within the business. This same Process Improvement Manager was also appointed as the new chairman, or *Metrics Initiator* of the MWP.

Pulford [1] states the *Metrics Initiator* is likely to be a senior manager with sufficient financial responsibility to allocate a budget for use on the measurement programme. Pulford goes on to state that the *Metrics Initiator* typically has several projects under his control and will be responsible for the organisation of the measurement programme although not necessarily the person who does most of the actual work. In addition, the *Metrics Initiator* is the person who justifies the programme in business terms.

At the same time, resource for giving the re-launched measurement programme some impetus was made available through the UK government's *Teaching Company Scheme* involving co-operation with a UK University in experienced graduates who are specifically employed to provide assistance in the adoption of new technologies.

It was decided that the *ami* approach would be used as a framework for identifying, defining and applying the goal oriented metrics. To co-ordinate a successful process improvement project it was essential that a firm foundation was established, from which the remaining programme could progress. An extension to the *ami* approach was therefore identified that catered for many of the "soft issues" associated with starting up a major improvement initiative. This was called the *Foundation activity*.

4.0 The Foundation Activity

The standard *ami* approach states you must firstly *assess* you project environment to define primary goals for measurement. The next activity is to *analyse* the primary goals to derive sub-goals and the relevant metrics. The third activity is to *metricate* by implementing a measurement plan and then process the collected primitive data into measurement data. The fourth and final activity is to *improve* by using the measurement data to implement actions.

After some consideration, it was felt that there was an additional activity that precedes the Assessment activity. This *Foundation activity* provides the firm basis from which measurement programmes can progress (Figure 1).

Pulford [1] in his description of *ami* states that before starting the Assessment, there are a number of important pre-requisites that must be addressed. These pre-requisites can be highlighted by the following five questions:

i. *Do you have managers' involvement ?*
ii. *Is there a budget ?*
iii. *Do you have someone who can be the metrics champion ?*
iv. *Is there sufficient consensus on the strategy that it will remain unchanged for long enough ?*
v. *Is there commitment to training ?*

These questions attempt to address the fundamental "soft issues" associated with starting up a major improvement initiative. The importance of answering these questions before commencing the *Assessment* activity can not be stressed enough. It was therefore decided to incorporate Pulford's pre-requisites, plus number of equally important questions into the *Foundation activity*. Pulford's pre-requisites will now be explained further.

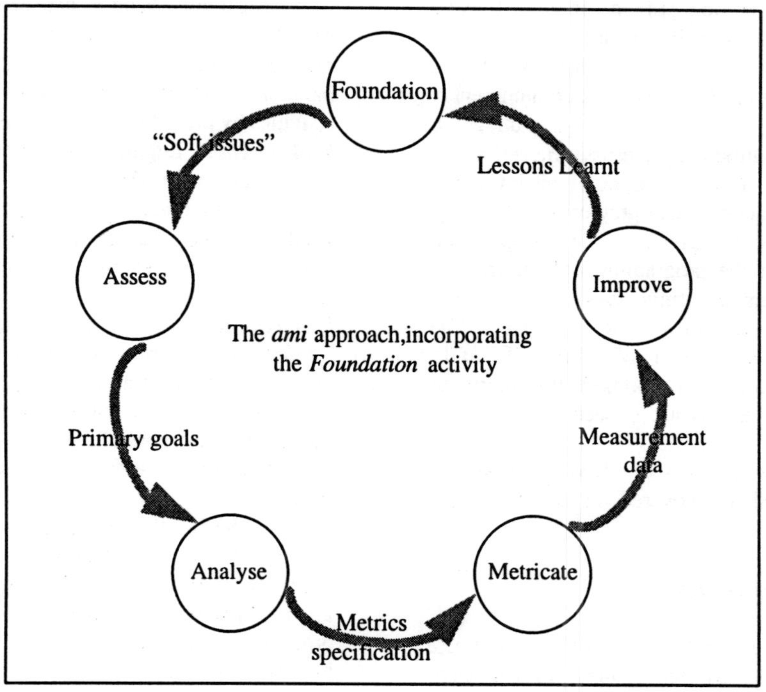

Figure 1: The ami approach, incorporating the Foundation activity

4.1 Management involvement

Both Pulford [1] and Grady [2] agree that it is of up most importance that managers are involved in any measurement programme, and that management must take the lead in initiating measurement, defining goals and asking for feedback results. Therefore, the question that should really be asked is "do you have managers' involvement *and commitment* ?".

Often, in addition to being the key customers of the measurement programme, management are the main suppliers of funding. Therefore, to obtain long term commitment to the programme it is necessary to demonstrate the benefits of measurement. Management needs to be convinced that measurement will improve their business. Ashley [3] suggests managers want answers to the two fundamental questions of "what are the benefits ?" and "how much will it cost ?".

The specific benefits of implementing a measurement programme would depend on the overall goals of the customers, but high level benefits can be identified as:

i. The generation of quantifiable information to help decision making
ii. An ability to determine the impact of changes
iii. An ability to help identify where changes are needed, and
iv. The generation of a more effective development environment

It must be noted that as part of ensuring continual management commitment it is important to be realistic in promoting the benefits of introducing metrics. Managing the expectations of the customer is an important part of any measurement programme. Formally declaring and agreeing the scope and objectives of the programme will ensure that the customers are fully aware of what the programme is meant to achieve. The programme will be declared a failure if you do not deliver what you promised. It is therefore important to be realistic in declaring what you can achieve.

The question of "how much will it cost ?" will be covered in the following section.

4.2 Defined Budget

Like all successful software development projects any measurement programme must have clearly allocated resource and have a budget so that all those concerned will be able to put in the required effort.

Pulford [1] suggests to enable costs to be estimated it is important to look at the various measurement tasks and resources involved. It is therefore important to construct a high level plan and schedule, which identifies the various key tasks and resources required. Pulford goes on to highlight six factors which cause variations in the costs of a measurement programme:

i. The level of data collection already present

Before introducing a measurement programme it is worth looking at existing data collection costs, as most organisations collect some data, such as effort spent on developing specific software modules, or correcting errors.

Pulford does not explain the difficulties associated with collecting data collection costs. Often the activity of looking at data collection costs is difficult because the information required to analyse the true costs of data collection does not exist. If the cost data does exist, it is often inaccurate or incomplete and therefore does not give a accurate representation of the true costs that go into collecting the data.

Timesheets were being used within the organisation to monitor project related costs, such as how much effort was being spent developing specific software modules, fixing software errors, etc. This was done by assigning unique project booking codes to a specific activity. Using a *time sheet* engineers would then record how much effort they exerted on each activity. It was decided to monitor the effort exerted on metrics related activities by providing engineers with a *metrics booking code*. Engineers would then use this *code* every time they exerted effort on a metrics related activity. The data collected would then be used to monitor how much effort was being exerted on metrics related activities.

ii. Organisations with visible and controlled development processes have reduced costs

Pulford states that organisations which are certified to ISO9001 or have a well defined process normally have procedures in place that can be used in measurement data analysis.

Within the organisation the overall development process had been defined and ISO9001 accreditation had been given. As previously stated *time sheets* were used by the organisation to monitor effort exerted on specific activities.

iii. The more metrics for which data is collected, the greater the cost

The more metrics which are used, the more issues are covered, with a corresponding increase in implementation and analysis costs. Pulford suggests that it is possible to build up over time a useful set of metrics without excessively increasing costs. This is achieved by automating key data collection and analysis activities.

Due to a number of problems associated with the previous measurement programme is was decided to re-look at the overall programme using the *ami* approach, identifying metrics that would be of more use. Automating data collection and analysis would then help to reduce costs of the overall programme.

iv. There is a "trial and error" learning curve to introducing a measurement strategy into the development process

Pulford states that as the *ami* approach is a structured method for introducing metrics, errors that may have been introduced by not using a structured method will minimised. This point is true, a structured method provides a sequence of necessary activities, that if followed help produce the desired outcome. Although, there is still the learning curve of understanding the *ami* method itself.

Also the "trial and error" costs were reduced by learning from the mistakes of the previous measurement programme.

v. Monitoring the programme itself helps control the costs associated with it and leads to it becoming more cost effective

Pulford suggests that the *ami* approach has to prove its effectiveness throughout the measurement programme. He suggests that this can be done through assessing the satisfaction of the parties involved in the programme.

This was thought to be slightly academic and not really measuring the cost of the measurement programme, just the subjective views of the individuals involved. It was thought that as regular MWP meetings would be taking place any concerns individuals had could be aired and addressed at these meetings. A separate activity of assessing the satisfaction of the parties involved was therefore not required.

Effort exerted on the measurement programme would be monitored by the MWP on a regular basis. This would then be related to the overall project plan to determine how well the project was progressing.

vi. The suitability of the goals and metrics

Selecting over ambitious goals and metrics, not suited to the needs of the organisation, increases metrication costs. Pulford states that "using *ami* helps you find appropriate goals". This is incorrect, as the *ami* approach only provides a structured method for introducing metrics, "finding the appropriate goals" is really down to understanding of your own processes.

Process modelling was used as technique for defining the overall process. The models that were developed provided the basis for identifying the metrics that were required to satisfy the business goals. It was deemed that starting with a small number of goals which lead to a small number of metrics would be the appropriate path to follow. These goals could then be increased as and when it was deemed necessary.

Pulford states that the average cost for the metrication of a project using the *ami* approach was found to be 2-5% of the total cost for the software development. This was the initial cost for the first iteration of using *ami*. He goes onto state that many of the benefits cannot be measured in terms of cost, and some benefits are indirect such as greater customer satisfaction from improved product quality.

It was known that financial benefits were often difficult to identify, especially in a dynamic organisation where there are often multiple process improvement activities running concurrently. It was therefore decided that there would not be a pre-defined budget, but a project plan that would be monitored on a regular basis by the MWP. Effort exerted on metrics related activities would also be monitored by the data collected from *time sheets*.

As there was no pre-defined budget it was therefore important to ensure continual management commitment. This would then ensure sufficient resource was made available to he measurement programme. Managing the expectations of managers was catered for by regular feedback sessions by members of the MWP. Often these feedback sessions were informal conversations on how the project was going, although there were mechanisms for providing more formal feedback sessions if required.

4.3 Identification of a Metrics Facilitator

Pulford [3] suggests that there must be a *Metrics Facilitator* appointed to the measurement programme. The *Metrics Facilitator* is responsible for the co-ordination and organisation of the measurement programme on a day-to-day basis, responsible for co-ordinating execution of the steps, writing the measurement plan, implementing and supervising data collection, and writing the analysis reports. The role of *Metrics Facilitator* was filled by a person who was dedicated full time to process improvement activities.

4.4 Consensus on strategic direction

There must be an environment in which goal oriented measurement is feasible. Pulford suggests that the essential criterion is not project size or maturity level but continuity of management strategy. There is little point in investing in an improvement programme if there is no element of continuity between projects.

Whereas the previous incarnation of the MWP only concentrated on the Software Development discipline the new strategy was to focus effort on System Design, Software Development, and System Proving disciplines. The strategy involved using the *ami* approach to define a set of goal oriented measures for the Software Development discipline, as this was deemed to be the most mature in the field of metrics. Effort would then be exerted on defining goal oriented metrics for the System Design and System Proving disciplines at a laterdate

The strategy for the introduction of goal oriented metrics into the Software Development discipline was defined in the project Terms Of Reference. It must be noted that no strategy should be set in stone. If during the running of the project it was decided that the strategy chosen was incorrect or should be modified then the you must do so. There is little point in attempting to follow a strategy that is clearly incorrect does not satisfy your goals.

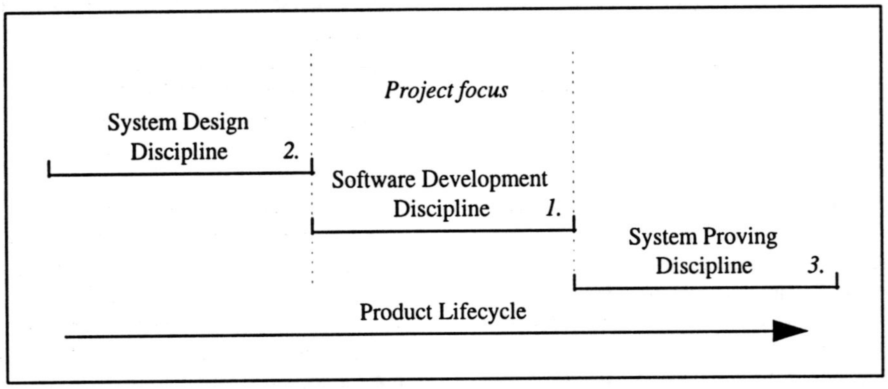

Figure 2: The Metrics Strategy.

4.5 Commitment to training

Finally, Pulford stresses the importance of training, and that measurement in the workplace is an emotive issue for all members of staff. Typically the initial reaction is "You cannot measure software production". Another common reaction is fear of having your customary working practices subjected to scrutiny and laid bare to criticism.

To address this it was decided that the MWP would address training in two ways, via *selling* and *training*. *Selling* involves exchanging products of services for money. The MWP was not concerned in selling for money, but selling to receive commitment to the measurement programme. This commitment comes from various classes of customer, such as senior management, project management and engineers. As Grady [2] states, the key to any successful sales campaign is to know the customer well. One of the first activities of the MWP was therefore to identify the different customers. The selling of the measurement programme was then tailored according to the needs of that customer. For example, senior management were more concerned about the overall costs of the programme and the long term benefits of introducing metrics. Whereas engineers were more concerned about how metrics could improve their day to day software development activities.

Throughout the programme there were various training sessions. Initially the MWP had to be trained on how to use the *ami* approach, the GQM technique and process modelling. These training sessions usually consisted of half day workshops on how to use the technique.

The various *customers* of the metrics programme were also given different types of training. The first session consisted of a short (approximately two hours) *selling* presentation. This presentation was conducted by the Director of the business, the *Metrics Initiator* and various members of the MWP. The purpose was to sell what metrics were, how they were derived, the advantages of introducing metrics and what it meant to the business and the individuals involved.

The next stage was a series of half day workshops which described the metrics that each Development Team were required to collect. This presentation was attended by representatives form each development team including the Team Leaders, and allowed for more in depth question and answer sessions. The final of training involved series of half day hands-on *MetricsWizard* workshops. *MetricsWizard* was the automated data collection and analysis tool that was developed.

Addressing these five issues ide ntified by Pulford were key to the success of the measurement programme. In addition, it was thought that there were a number of fundamental questions that still required action. These questions are:

vi. *Have all the "key players" been identified ?*

vii. *Has a formal plan been drawn up and milestones agreed ?*

viii. *Has the programme team been identified ?*

ix. *Has the overall intent of the measurement programme been communicated to all those affected ?*

x. *Has the Terms of Reference for the programme been drawn up ?*

The rationale behind these questions will now be discussed.

4.6 Identification of key players

It is of up most importance to identify the "key players" at the very beginning of the programme. In discussing client centred consulting Cockman *et al* [5] highlights the usefulness of identifying "Who knows ? Who cares ? Who can ?". If we apply these three questions to the measurement programme, we can ensure that we involve the correct people at the beginning.

- *Who knows* - about the area under investigation or has most of the information that we need to be able to understand and put metrics in place is often the person doing the job. These are the people who take an active part in the every day running of the process.
- *Who cares* - that the measurement programme is put in place might well be the manager who has identified an inadequacy within the process, and believes it could be rectified with the introduction of metrics. However, there may be other people who care about the problem who also have to be considered as part of the programme.
- *Who can* - do something about the programme ? If those involved in the measurement programme have to ask for authority or approval to implement part of it, if more resources in terms of money, time or people are required, then it is important to identify these people at the beginning.

One of the first activities that was performed as part of the *Foundation activity* was to identify those individuals who know, care and could do something about the metrics programme. Often this list is not static and changes as a better understanding of the process is gained.

4.7 Defining a project plan

A good plan should describe, in as much detail as possible, everything that needs to be done as part of the measurement programme. Milestones need to be identified and agreed by all parties to ensure that the overall programme runs as effectively as possible. It is important to note that the plans continually change due to unforeseen circumstances. One must also note that it is likely that many of the low level activities may not be identified until the programme is well underway.

To aid in developing a project plan *ami* identifies seven key activities:

i. Assessment of the project environment
ii. Definition of primary goals
iii. Derivation of subgoals and metrics
iv. Writing the measurement plan and designing collection forms
v. Data collection
vi. Data analysis
vii. Goals and assessment review

Including "producing the foundation", these eight activities were then used as headings on the project plan. Where possible each heading was then decomposed into individual activities. The rationale behind the decomposition of headings into individual activities was based on previous experience. As no member of the MWP had gone through the *ami* approach before, an estimate was made of the activities which made up each heading, and the effort required to complete that activity. The milestones that were identified and agreed mainly coincided with the completion of major activities, such as completion of the Terms Of Reference, Writing the Measurement Plan, Issuing The Metrics Analysis/Collection Tool, etc. After the initial project plan was drawn up it was reviewed by members of the MWP. The regular MWP meetings were then used as the forum for reviewing and amending the plan.

Pulford seems reluctant to provide much information on the planning stages of the *ami* approach. Other than indicating the major steps which comprise the *ami* approach, there is no indication of the amount of effort required to complete each stage. This information would have provided useful input into the early planning stages as well as project budgeting.

4.8 Identification of programme team

DeMarco [6] argues for a completely independent team responsible for collecting and analysing data on the grounds that:

- development staff are more likely to trust an independent group and so give them accurate data;
- an independent team will provide objective analysis and will not be tempted to present "political" interpretations of the data.

It was impractical to have a totally independent team due to the limited resources available. It was also thought that having a team with an in-depth understanding of the problem domain would provide additional benefits when attempting to define metrics. Whereas the previous incarnation of the MWP only concentrated on the Software Development discipline, membership of the re-launched MWP came from the System Design, Software Development and Software Proving disciplines.

Grady [2] states that the people who you recruit to implement your objectives send a signal to the rest of the organisation that indicates the importance of the programme. It was therefore vital that the members of the re-launched MWP were fully committed to the programme, had an interest in metrics and process improvement, had some previous experience and were capable of implementing any necessary changes.

4.9 Communication of overall intent of the measurement programme

Once the "key players" and the team had been identified it was important to communicate the overall intent of the programme. To ensure buy in from those affected by the programme it was decided to conduct an official project launch presentation.

The first activity was to ensure the MWP were aware of the overall project and its activities. This is discussed in section 4.5. The next stage was to educate senior management. As Kitchenham [4] explains often measurement programmes fail without the whole hearted support of senior management. Getting support from senior management ensures support from their subordinates; if your manager requires you to report in quantitative terms, you become far more motivated to support a measurement programme. Senior management was presented with the fundamental objectives of the project, highlighting the overall project plan, and perceived costs and benefits. This was sufficient to enable them to get a basic understanding of the overall programme.

The final stage was to conduct the official project launch. This involved presenting the overall objectives of the measurement programme to the software engineers and team leaders that it affected. This presentation was conducted by two members of the MWP, and the *Metrics Initiator*. In addition, the Director of the Network Switching Business attended the presentation and pledged his support and commitment. This provided much needed credibility, in light of the problems with the previous metrics activities. The agenda for the project launch presentation was as follows:

i. Introduction and history
ii. Why we are here
iii. High level objectives of the measurement programme
iv. High level description of the *ami* approach and the GQM technique
v. What was required of attendees of the presentation
vi. The benefits the attendees will receive from the programme
vii. The next stage
viii. Questions and answers

It is important to manage the expectations of all those involved in the programme. Expectations can be managed by continual feedback of information. It must be noted that different "customers" require different information. Therefore it is important to selectively filter information depending on the audience.

4.10 Defining the Terms Of Reference

The Terms Of Reference should draw together many of the points discussed above. The first task of the new MWP was to draw up a Terms Of Reference. The purpose of this document was to formally define the role of the MWP and its members. This document therefore contained information on the MWP Mission Statement, the scope of the MWP, the high level goals, membership, the responsibilities of the members, the reporting structure and the overall schedule.

It was thought that a Mission statement would provide direction to the MWP. It was vital that the Mission Statement was visionary as it was likely to persist for a significant period of time. This is important as detailed objectives and strategies can be developed, delivered and changed over time, relative to the Mission Statement. In addition, the Mission Statement clarified the main purpose of the organisation, and the reasons why it exists.

The Mission Statement that was drawn up was as follows:

"The purpose of the MWP is to identify both product and process metrics, based on specified business objectives. These metrics will provide the foundation for process improvement and project tracking. In addition the MWP will promote metrics use by example and training."

It was felt that a set of high level goals should be drawn up, based around the Mission Statement. These were defined as:

i. The continual development and refinement of goal oriented metrics. This also includes responsibility for software metric standards, and the change and approval of these standards.
ii. The communication of easily understandable information. This includes research into state of the art metrics literature, and the internal publication of information and results.
iii. The promotion of metrics through selling and training.
iv. Liaising with the rest of the organisation to ensure consistency of ideas and principles.
v. The investigation and promotion tools for automatic data collection and analysis.

It was felt that the combination of t he Mission Statement and the high level goals would provide an initial foundation from which to base many of the measurement programme activities.

Additionally, it was felt that it was important to define the major responsibilities of the members of the MWP. These responsibilities were to:

- Attend the MWP meetings or nominate a replacement in their absence.
- Champion metrics in the area of the business they represent.
- Help to identify and implement metrics best practice within the organisation.
- Liaise with other parts of the organisation to ensure consistency of ideas and principles.
- Help communicate easily understandable metrics information.
- Continually keep abreast of new and emerging literature and technologies.

As mentioned in the previous section many of the members of the original MWP had conflicting commitment requirements due to their everyday workload. In an attempt to address this it was decided that each member must be able to spend at least half a man day per week on activities relating to the measurement programme.

5.0 Conclusions

Pulford [3] states that the application of goal-oriented measurement in an organisation requires a structured method. Without a method, it is not possible to build a coherent framework and the result does not reflect real needs. The organisation wastes a lot of time discovering and trying out more or less successful methods, resulting in measurement often being abandoned before a method is allowed to take root.

Based on the experiences within GPT it was felt that more often than not people would dive straight into identifying metrics without giving enough thought to the initial stages. Many of the problems associated with the previous metrics programme were due to inadequacies in addressing the underlying principles. To avoid these problems re-occurring it was decided that the *Foundation activity* would encompass the pre-requisite questions defined by Pulford and the additional questions identified through previous experience.

The first step of the *Foundation Activity* is the completion of the *Foundation Checklist*. This checklist consists of ten questions based on Pulford's five pre-requisite questions and five questions developed from the work within GPT (Figure 3).

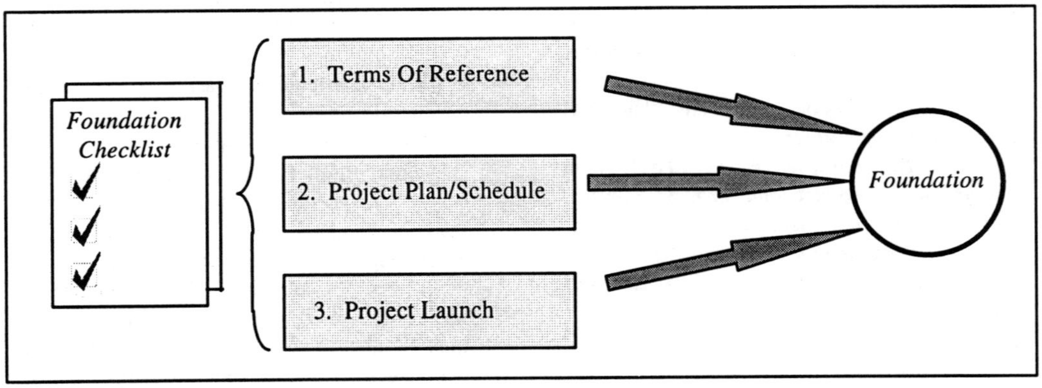

Figure 3: Foundation steps 1 - 3.

This *Foundation Checklist* constitutes three key steps that need to be performed before attempting the *Assessment activity*. These three steps are:

i. Define Terms Of Reference
ii. Define Project Plan
iii. Conduct Project Launch

The first stage is to define t he Terms Of Reference. The purpose of this document is to formally define the Mission Statement, the scope of the Metrics Party, the high level goals, the party membership, the responsibilities of the members and the overall scope of the metrics programme.

The second stage is to draw up the Project Plan. This should encompass the key activities and milestones, identify an estimate of the amount of effort required for each task and identify the resource that will conduct that activity.

The third and final stage of the Foundation activity is the formal project launch. This brings together the Terms Of Reference, the Project Plan and the team to highlight the importance of the overall programme and their role in ensuring the programme is successfully completed.

Finally, the beginning of any project is often turbulent. Formalising the early stages of this measurement programme into the *Foundation activity* helped GPT control and manage many of the "soft issues" associated with starting up a major programme. The actual *Foundation activity* only took approximately 5% of the total effort of the overall measurement programme.

Acknowledgements

The ideas presented in this document have been influenced by various people, who I have had the pleasure of meeting and working with over the last few years. I would especially like to thank Paul Layzell of UMIST, and my work colleagues Kieran Doyle, Jeremy Grammer, Derek Peddie, Mike Stephens, Rob Touch and Kay Winterburn.

Finally, I would like to thank both Martin Shepperd and Steve Webster, of Bournemouth University, who many years ago gave me such an interest in the ever expanding field of software development, process improvement and software metrics.

References

[1] Pulford, K., Kuntzmann-Combelles, A. and Shirlaw, S. (1996). *A Quantitative Approach to Software Management: The ami handbook*. Wokingham, England. Addison-Wesley Publishing Company.

[2] Grady, R.B. and Caswell, D.L. (1987). *Software Metrics: Establishing A Company Wide Program*. Englewood Cliffs, NJ. Prentice-Hall International.

[3] Ashley, N. (1994). *Blueprint For Setting Up A Measurement Programme*. Starter Kit/BMP/Issue 4.

[4] Kitchenham, B.A. (1995). *Measurement for Software Process Improvement (Issue 1 Draft B)*. Manchester, England. National Computing Centre.

[5] Cockman, P., Evans, B. and Reynolds, P. (1992). *Client-Centred Consulting: A PracticalGuide for Internal Advisors and Trainers*. McGraw-Hill Training Company.

[6] DeMarco, T (1982). Controlling Software Project. Management, Measurement and Estimation. Englewood Cliffs, NJ. Yourdon Press.

[7] Ami User Group. Ami Metric Users' Handbook. South Bank University, London.

[8] Moller, K. H. Paulish, D. J. (1993). Sofware Metrics. Chapman Hall.

Promoting the Software Design for Testability Towards a Partial Test Oracle

Jin-Cherng Lin, Pu-lin Yeh, and Shou-Chia Yang
Dept. of Computer Science and Engineering
Tatung Institute of Technology
Taipei 10451, Taiwan, R.O.C
Email: jclin@cse.ttit.edu.tw
FAX: 886-2-5925252ext2288

Abstract

Software testing is one of the most powerful methods to improve the software quality directly. Usually, testing costs on the large scales of 50% during software system development phase. How to reduce the testing cost thus becomes an important issue. The software design for testability maybe a new direction to solve this problem. Using the strategy of software design for testability, we develop a technique called "test condition oracle" to check the program's correctness. The performance evaluation shows that this technique is an effective method for promoting software testability.

Keywords: Software Test, Test Oracles, Software Testability, Software Design for Testability, Test Condition.

1. INTRODUCTION

Software reliability becomes significant while software are applied to more critical applications. High reliability software means that the software works properly and meets the user's requirements. How to promote the reliability of software is one of the most noticeable things for the software system developers. Software testing is one of the most powerful methods to check whether the software errors occur. It improves the software reliability directly.

Software testing has been proved to be an important and valuable activity for determining whether a software system has faults. The purpose of testing is to evaluate if a software system meets its specification and to evaluate the correctness, reliability, and failure rate of the software. General testing methods range from functional (or "black box") methods to structural (or "white box") methods [1]. Since there is no perfect software in realistic applications, the selected testing method is expected to help software developers to detect faults easily. Furthermore, testing costs on the large scales of 50% during software system development phase [2][3]. How to reduce the testing cost thus becomes an important issue in the software engineering strategies.

Testing task is usually not emphasized by software system designers traditionally. The designers consider that the work is belonged to the testers. Therefore, how to persuade the designers to embed testing mechanism early at design phase to reduce the testing cost is a new alternative in software testing strategy. And this new direction seems significant and valuable. The designers should consider how to make the software more easily to be tested (i.e., promote the software testability) during designing it and thus cut the testing cost down in the testing step. That is, we hope the designers to consider software testability early in the design phase. Designers/programmers should apply some kind of techniques to assisting testers to reveal the software errors while they develop the software. Software testability ought to be considered and emphasized during designing. Software design for testability must get its proper attention in order to reduce testing cost and promote software reliability. (Software testability means that a piece of software has some properties, characteristics, or features that will facilitate the testing process. Software design for testability is the process of applying techniques and methods during the design phase in order to reduce the effort and cost in testing its implementation [4].)

Testability is an ability to reveal software error while testing the software in various testing phases. To make a software system "testable" means the software system can be easily revealed errors and can be checked

0-8186-7840-2/97 $10.00

easily and precisely against specifications. The testability of a software also depends on various testing strategies. For example, a program may be with high testability for data flow oriented testing strategies but has a low testability for branch testing strategy. It is very important and valuable to develop better design for testability techniques to promote the software quality and reduce the testing cost.

Furthermore, the tester usually requires large number of test data in testing process to satisfy selected testing strategy. It always spends a lot of time to manually prepare the test data and verify the test results. Software design for testability, which embeds test oracle into the program, is an effective method to solve this problem. The test oracle is evaluated for each test execution to determine if the program behavior is acceptable.

Some test conditions about software design for testability are proposed in this article to verify the correctness of program behavior. These conditions can be integrated to be a test oracle that is used to verify the program in testing step.

2. RELATED WORKS

2.1 Assertion

Assertions are used to check and maintain programs. The primary goal in writing assertions is to specify what a system is supposed to do rather than how it is to do [5]. When assertion tests failed, the program is aborted. The advantage of adding assertions is that we can make an automatic checking while developing the software system.

But there still have a lot of problems for assertions: (1) Previous assertion processing did not integrate easily with existing programming environments. (2) It is not well understood what kinds of assertions are most effective at detecting software faults [5]. (3) The assertion techniques are little widespread use in practice. (4) Existing assertions processing system is not easy-to-use.

2.2 Annotation Pre-Processor for C

Annotation preprocessor (APP) for C [5] uses assertion technique to check the consistency of software system. It expands the C extended comment to check the run time consistency. It also provides some classification to prompt the user how and when to add the checking. But that the user have to learn new syntax make its application limited.

2.3 Robust C

Robust C [6] uses assertions to restrict and check the C programs semantics. In other words, Robust C enhance some insufficiency of C compiler such as out of rang checking for arrays. This kind of enhanced C compilers have been developed by various version of C or C++ languages. Such language can only solve limited error that is because of C compiler's insufficiency.

For a lot of structure errors or errors about the specification of system output, Robust C can not check out them. At the same time, its preprocessor does not add checking at proper place in software. These are the disadvantages of Robust C.

2.4 Specification Based Test Oracle

Specification based test oracle [7] is designed from system specifications. It checks the outputs by corresponding test data. The checking is said failed when the output does not match with the oracles. This kind of outputs checking, usually uses some particular specification languages, determines whether the system is correct or not. This method has to redesign different test oracle rules against different applications and thus can not reuse the test oracles.

2.5 Automated Test Oracles

Automated test oracles [8] are used to check the outputs if the system is correct or not. When a large number of inputs are executed, automated test oracle can help the user to check the outputs. It will take a few time for user to learn specification languages since such kind of methods usually base on specification languages.

3. TEST CONDITION ORACLE

3.1 Test Conditions

Basic data structure, graphic structure, and set theory are three fundamental ingredients in software. Most softwares use them to operate objects. If we could maintain the consistency and integrity of these ingredients, we have solved lots of existing error-prones in software. Some generally test conditions about data structure, graphic theory, and set theory are thus developed in this article. The software developers can use these conditions to construct a test oracle to verify their softwares. For using these test conditions, users need not to learn any new language or syntax. They are constructed by some simple and basic mathematical relations and logic symbols. They are user friendly and easy to use.

3.2 Test Conditions about the Size in a Data Structure

Some test conditions are shown in Table 1, where S and T are two data structures, |S| represents the cardinality of S, and n is an integer. The symbols are the same as those in set theory. For example, user can combine these test conditions to check the consistency and integrity between the relations of domain size and range size. Other examples are given as the followings:

$\|S\| > \|T\|$	$\|S\| <= \|T\|$
$\|S\| < \|T\|$	$\|S\| = 0$
$\|S\| = \|T\|$	$\|S\| <> 0$
$\|S\| = \|T\| + n$	$\|S\| = n$
$\|S\| = \|T\| - n$	$\|S\| <> n$
$\|S\| = \|T\| * n$	$\|S\| = \|T\|^n$
$\|S\| = \|T\| / n$	$\|S\| = (\|T\|)^{1/n}$
$\|S\| >= \|T\|$	$\|S\| = a^{\|T\|}$
T := S (Save S to be T)	

Table 1. Test conditions about the size in a data structure.

(1) $|S| <> 0$; $|S|=0$. The pre-condition or post-condition of many operations need to make sure that the number of element in a data structure is (or is not) empty. Any operations in systems such as popping, deleting, removing, sorting, initialization, and database querying from a set of structure can use these checking conditions. These operations are widely used in stack, queue, or database operations for subroutine calls, recursive procedure operations, tree traversals, general graph traversals, forest traversals, sort algorithms, job scheduling in operation systems, priority queues, disk input/output scheduling, spooling, stack languages such as post-script, stack computers such as HP3000, assembler system operations, macro expander system operations, compiler system operations, ...etc.

(2) T := S (Save S to be T); $|T| = |S| + n$; $|T| = |S| - n$. We observed that after some operations the number of elements contained in a data structure may increase or decrease. All we have to do is to verify this post-condition -- save S to be T and then, after some operations in which S is modified, check if $|T| = |S| + n$ or $|T| = |S| - n$. (See detailed examples in section 4.2.)

These are very useful test conditions. There are many applications which can be checked by these conditions. Take instances, pushing/popping operations in stack, inserting/deleting operations in queue, and adding, removing, querying operations, ...etc. These operations are widely used in many software systems.

Note that the new concept proposed here differs from traditional testing strategies. Our method allows users to dynamically verify any segment in a program between the start point that we save its status and the ending point that we intend to verify it. It is more flexible than traditional testing strategies, in which only the output result on the exit point of a program can be checked.

(3) $|T| = |S|$; $|T| < |S|$; $|T| > |S|$. There are many applications which can be tested by these conditions. We observed that after some operations the number of elements in a data structure may be equal, less than, or greater than that in the original one. The most trivial examples for $|T|=|S|$ are sorting algorithms.

3.3 Test Conditions about Elements in a Data Structure

Some test conditions are shown in Table 2, where S and T are two data structures, and x is an element. These operations are widely used in many real software described in section 3.2.1. For instance, we can check the post-condition to make sure that the items which we pushed have been in the stack or to make sure that the items which we popped have not been in the stack.

For example, consider $x \in S$ and $x \notin S$. In some cases we have to make sure that some elements x's must be (or must not be) in a data structures S. These checking conditions can be applied to many applications, such as push/pop operations in stack, insert/delete operations in queue, add, remove, query operations, tree insertion/deletion ...etc.

$x \in S$	$x \notin S$
$x \in (S \cap T)$	$x \notin (S \cap T)$
$x \in (S \cup T)$	$x \notin (S \cup T)$
$x \in (S \Delta T)$	$x \notin (S \Delta T)$
$x \in (S - T)$	$x \notin (S - T)$

Table 2. Test conditions about elements in a data structure

3.4 Test Conditions about Set Relations

Some test conditions are shown in Table 3. The most popular examples are sorting programs. When any kind of sorting programs being executed, the relation between input set S and output set T must satisfy both $T \subset S$ and $T \supset S$. This results from that we do not want the contents and the number of elements to be changed after sorting.

$S \subset T$	$S \supset T$
$S \subseteq T$	$S \supseteq T$
$S \,!\!\subset T$	$S = T$
$S \subset (T \cap W)$	$S \subset (T \cup W)$
$S \subset (T \Delta W)$	$S \subset (T - W)$

Table 3. Test conditions about set relation.

3.5 Test Conditions about Order Relations

In some situations, we want the elements in a data structure to be ordered. This characteristics should also be checked. The test conditions about order relations are listed in Table 4. The most widely used applications for this kind of conditions are database system operations and various sorting/searching programs.

ORDER(S, $\geq$)	ORDER(S, $\leq$)
ORDER(S,>)	ORDER(S,<)

Table 4. Test conditions about order relations.

3.6 Other Test Conditions

Graph theory is often used in computer programs. There are many basic and widely used structures in the graph theory. The characteristics of these structures can be used in verifying if the programs work properly.

Assume G(V,E) is a graph, V and E are the vertex and edge set of G, respectively, $v \in V$ and $e \in E$.

(1) check_cycle(G)

Check if these exists at least one cycle in G.

(2) check_noncycle(G)

Check if G is without cycle.

(3) check_cycle(G,v)

Check there is a cycle in G passing through v.

(4) check_tree(G)

Check if G is a tree structure.

(5) check_tree(G,v)

Check if G is a tree structure with root v.

(6) check_connected(G)

Check if all vertexs in G are connected.

3.7 Low Level Test Conditions

(1) t: = s; u $\neq$ v; u = v; u > v; u < v

s,u,v are simple variables in a program. The t:=s saves s's value into a temporal variable t. The others check the relations between the values of two variables.

(2) a <= x <= b. We can use this condition to make sure a variable x in a specific range. It is usually used in verifying the value of a variable in a reasonable range, or the subscript of an array not out of its bounds.

(3) x = c; x $\neq$ c; x < c; x > c. x is a simple variable in a program, and c is a constant.

(4) p $\neq$ NULL; p = NULL

(5) $\forall$ x/y, y $\neq$ 0

(6) $(\mathit{Pattern}) \in S$

(Pattern) means a data pattern, while S represents a data structure. An evident example is to check if '\0' exists in a string to verify it a legal string.

4. THE EXPERIMENTAL EVALUATION

4.1 Program Examples

The test conditions described in this article are used in the programs to improve the software testability. The test conditions are written in the comment field and enclosed by "/*@...@*/". Two examples are shown here to illustrate the usage.

The first example is about stack operations, which is shown in Figure 1. The user writes "T := S " and "| S | = | T | + 2" test conditions to check if the number of elements in the array increment by two after the push operations being executed.

Another example of bubble sort is shown in Figure 2. The precondition is to make sure the array not empty. The post-conditions make sure the values in array X are in non-strictly increasing order and the number of elements in the array is the same as that before sorting. In addition, the user also verify if the content of each element is unchanged.

```
int S[8], top;
void push (char int)
{ S[top++] = char;
}

void main()
{      .
        .
   push(14);
   push(39);
        .
}
```

Figure 1(a). Original Program Segment in First Example.

```
#include <oracles.h>
int S[8], top;
void push (char int)
{ S[top++] = char;
}
void main()
{       .
        .
   /*@ T := S @*/
   push(14);
   push(39);
   /*@ | S | = | T | + 2 @*/
   /*@ 14∈S @*/
   /*@ 39∈S @*/
        .
        .
}
```

Figure 1(b). Program Segment with Test Conditions

```
#define Max 15
int X[Max], *p;
void Bubble_Sort (void)
{
   int i, j, OK=1;
   for ( i=1; i<Max; OK=1,i++ )
   {
      for ( j=0; j<Max-1; j++ )
      {   if ( X[j] > X[j+1] )
          {
             Exchange (X[j],X[j+1]);
             OK = 0;
          };
      }
      if ( OK )
         break;
   }
}
```

Figure 2(a). Original Program Segment in Bubble Sort Function

```
#include <oracles.h>
#define Max 15
int X[Max], *p;
void Bubble_Sort (void)
{
   int i, j, OK=1;
   /*@|X|>0@*/
   /*@T := X@*/
   for ( i=1; i<Max; OK=1,i++ )
   {
      for ( j=0; j<Max-1; j++ )
      if ( X[j] > X[j+1] )
      {
         Exchange (X[j],X[j+1]);
         OK = 0;
      };
   }
   if ( OK )
      break;
 }

/*@ ORDER(X,≤)@*/
/*@ |X|=|T| @*/
/*@ X= T   @*/
}
```

Figure 2(b). Bubble Sort Function with Test Conditions

4.2 An Experimental System and Performance Data

An experimental preprocessor system was developed to support the strategy and technique of software design for testability proposed in this article. The preprocessor translates these kinds of simple and high level conditions, which are enclosed by "/*@...@*/" in comment fields, into executable functions, those were developed and included in "oracles.h". While the program is tested, the test conditions in the program are verified. The system will print message if any test condition violated.

The experimental system shows some advantages in software testing practice. The system checks the test conditions automatically. This checking is done automatically instead of manual inspection, which usually causes mistakes especially in inspecting large number of test results. Besides, the test conditions are written according to the program specification and/or system requirements. Therefore we can test the program according to the specification and thus overcome some disadvantages of white-box testing and black-box testing, while in white-box testing the program is tested only based on existing codes; in black-box testing a large number of test data are needed.

Fifteen programs are tested to evaluate the effectiveness of proposed technique. A fault is seeded to each program. Two kinds of test strategies, conventional assertion technique and test condition oracle proposed in this article, are applied to these programs respectively. Test data are randomly generated and executed to evaluate the effectiveness of test strategies. The experimental results are shown in Table 5. The data in the table show that the proposed test strategy is feasible and effective. It also shows that the new test strategy is more precise and more effective than conventional assertion technique.

The Property of Software	Line of Code	Number of Seeded Fault	Number of Assertion	Fault Detection	Number of Oracle Rules	Fault Detection
Bubble Sort	251	1	7	yes	2	yes
Selection Sort	272	1	8	yes	2	yes
Insertion Sort	281	1	10	yes	2	yes
Stack Operation_1	101	1	4	no	2	yes
Stack Operation_2	104	1	5	no	2	yes
Queue Operation_1	118	1	5	no	2	yes
Queue Operation_2	122	1	5	no	2	yes
Binary Tree Creation	119	1	6	yes	2	yes
Tree In-Order Traversal	109	1	7	yes	2	yes
Tree Pre-Order Traversal	109	1	7	yes	2	yes
Tree Post-Order Traversal	108	1	7	yes	2	yes
Linear Search	101	1	4	no	2	yes
Fast Search	104	1	4	no	2	yes
Binary Search	96	1	4	no	2	yes
Inter-polation Search	119	1	5	no	2	yes

Table 5 The experimental results for assertion technique and test condition oracle

5. CONCLUDING REMARKS

5.1 Some Coding Guidelines

It is important how to embed effective test conditions into a program. There are two aspects in the practice of applying this technique into real cases. (1) How to select "effective" test conditions. (2) Where to put them in a program. The first problem is concerned in case by case analysis. On the other hand, embedding the test conditions into a program should not affect the program's behavior, should avoid to regard them as a part of the program and should avoid to embed them without significance. Usually, these test conditions are put on the entry point and/or exit point of blocks, structures, modules, or functions of a program. In fact, they can be put in any place of a program to verify any kind of data relations such as data consistency, data range, and function characteristics. The details of these problems are under studying and to be the future works of this research.

5.2 Conclusion

This article proposes a technique of software design for testability in order to reduce the testing effort and improve the software quality. The technique involves the testing characteristics of data and functions of the program into the source code to guard against the program faults. It promotes the software testability in programming step.

The proposed test conditions can be applied to most programs of any kind of application. Users can easily find the suitable and useful conditions to his/her programs.

The future works include (1) Expending the test conditions to be more complete. (2) Use the strategy of software design for testability to guide how to choose suitable test cases in test step. (3) Use the strategy and technique of software design for testability proposed in this article to develop a software tool to help the software design/test engineers in practical cases.

REFERENCES

[1] R. S. Freedman, "Testability of Software Components", IEEE Transactions on Software Engineering, June, 1991, pp.553-564.

[2] D.J. Mosley, "The Handbook of MIS Application Software Testing", Yourdon Press Computing Series, Englewood Cliffs, N.J., 1993.

[3] B.W. Boehm, The High Cost of Software, in Practical Stratages for Developing Large Software System, Edited by E. Horowitz, Reading, MA: Addison-Wesley, 1975.

[4] S. T. Chanson and A. F. Loureiro and S. T Vuong, "On the Design for Testability of Communication Software", Proceeding of IEEE International Test Conference, 1993, pp.190-199.

[5] D.S. Rosenblum, "A Practical Approach to Programming With Assertions", IEEE Trans. on Software Eng.,January 1995, pp.19-31

[6] D. W. Flater and Y. Yesha and E. K. Park, "Extensions to the C Programming Language for Enhanced Fault Detection", Software-Practice, June, 1993, pp.617-628.

[7] D.J. Richardson, "Specification-based Test Oracles for Reactive Systems", ACM, 1992, pp.105-118.

[8] J.M. Bieman and H. Yin, "Designing for Software Testability Using Automated Oracles", IEEE International Test Conference, 1992, pp.900-907.

Session P3b

Experiences with OO Development II

An Object Oriented Petri Net Language for Embedded System Design

Robert Esser
Computer Engineering and Networks Laboratory
Swiss Federal Institute of Technology (ETH)
CH-8092 Zurich, Switzerland
esser@tik.ee.ethz.ch

Abstract

In this paper a modelling language is described for the automated design of embedded systems. Constraints such as price, performance etc. often imply that embedded systems are implemented as communicating heterogeneous components. Today these components can no longer be classed as software or hardware but as more or less programmable with specialised languages being used to define their functionality and structure. The proposed modelling language consists of a class of high level time Petri nets, augmented with object-oriented mechanisms. It is formal, ensuring unambiguous specification, supports a high level of analysis and is general enough to support other more specialised formalisms. This language constitutes a major part of the CodeSign design methodology [8] developed at the ETH for embedded system design.

Keywords: embedded systems, Petri nets, multiple formalisms, object technology

1. Introduction

Recent gains achieved in efficiency and the mastering of complexity during the design of embedded systems have been due to the introduction of languages and methodologies that add additional levels of abstraction. These enable designers to view the ever increasing system complexity at appropriate levels of detail. However introducing further levels of abstraction results in an increasing gap between system models and their implementation. Embedded systems often have complex behaviour that may not be able to be completely or easily described in a single formalism, so it is desirable to support a number of formalisms that are well suited to modelling particular parts of an embedded system. The modelling language presented in this paper supports the use of multiple formalisms, representing different models of computation within a single system model. This not only allows parts of a system to be modelled naturally but is used to bridge the gap between high abstraction and implementation by providing efficient code generation and system analysis.

Using an object oriented Petri net based kernel language, it is shown how other, more application specific formalisms, can be defined in terms of the kernel language. The advantage of this approach is that the interaction semantics between formalisms are given by the underlying formal kernel language which results in a well defined formal system model. Furthermore embedded systems are often implemented on heterogeneous components, for example general purpose microcontrollers, application specific hardware or specialised programmable hardware (digital signal processors etc.) Cost effectiveness requires that an implementation architecture be chosen that meets a particular set of functional and non functional constraints. The language described here offers mechanisms for design exploration based on flexible system configuration functions and version management.

2. Modelling Language

The modelling language is a combination of object oriented concepts and Petri nets. The Petri net class used is a composition of high level Petri nets [10], [13], [18] and *time* Petri nets [16], [17]. It defines the minimum set of expressiveness needed to describe the functional and behavioural aspects of the target systems. Time plays an important role in all embedded real time systems and any language that purports to model such systems in any level of detail must include a concept of time. Time models for Petri nets and their analysis are described in [3] and [23]. Two basic Petri net models for handling time have been proposed - *time* Petri nets [16], [17] and *timed* Petri nets [22]. *Timed* Petri nets associate a finite firing duration with each transition of a net. The firing rule of these Petri nets is modified to include the time it takes to fire a transition under the assumption that a transition occurs as soon as it is enabled. These Petri nets and the subsequently developed *stochastic* Petri nets [1] have been mainly used for performance evaluation.

0-8186-7840-2/97 $10.00

Time Petri nets associate a finite enabling duration with each transition in a net. For a transition to occur it must have been continuously enabled for at least the minimum duration and for not more than the maximum duration. Time Petri nets are more general than timed Petri nets, i.e. a timed Petri net can be modelled with a time Petri net, but the converse is not true. Time Petri nets are adequate for expressing temporal constraints. Analysis techniques for formal verification of time dependent behaviour in time Petri nets are described in [3]. More interesting is the technique described in [5] where a compositional approach to the analysis of time Petri nets components is proposed.

Figure 1 shows an example of high level time Petri nets. This class of Petri nets is an extension of standard place-transition Petri nets where tokens carry data and transitions have associated functions and time constraints. Figure 1 shows a model of a system containing four transitions (squares) representing a process fork, concurrency and synchronisation. The transitions are inscribed with tuples (α, β) representing time constraints, guard functions $g_x(in)$ that define additional enabling conditions and functions $f_x(in_1, in_2)$ to determine the type and values of tokens produced as a result of a transition occurrence.

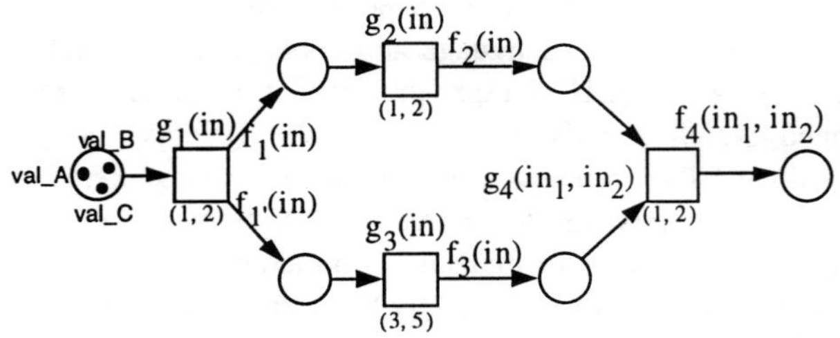

Figure 1. A high level time Petri net where tokens represent data and transitions contain time intervals and functions.

The use of high level time Petri nets as a kernel language has several advantages:

- intuitive graphical representation;
- simple formal definition, reducing the possibility of ambiguous interpretation of system models;
- operational semantics that support simulation and execution;
- analysis techniques that prove a number of interesting structural properties;
- ability to be analysed for temporal properties;
- successful use in many different application areas.

2.1. Combining Object Oriented Concepts and Petri Nets

The absence of both powerful structuring primitives and composition mechanisms in Petri nets is still a major weakness [12]. Various forms of graphical folding mechanisms [7], [20] have been proposed but only aid in information hiding and not in the composition of nets. Modularisation, including composition, proposals include those described in [2], [9] (which also presents module refinement techniques) and Hierarchical Coloured Petri Nets [13].

Recently there have been attempts to combine the structuring techniques of object oriented programming with Petri nets [6], [14], [24]. Allowing behaviour to be described with a Petri net enables complex concurrent behaviour to be modelled together with the data that it manipulates. In high level Petri nets data is modelled as tokens residing on places. Thus classes can define functions, executed within transitions, and a Petri net where (token) data and behaviour are encapsulated. However as discussed above this is not enough, as it is also necessary to support code (net) reuse and sharing. This, in an object oriented context, implies some form of inheritance and polymorphism.

Most existing object oriented Petri net approaches only consider token data to be object oriented. The approach chosen in this paper is similar to that taken in LOOPN++ [14] where not only the token data is object oriented but also the Petri net itself. Conceptually every element is an object and can be used in every context. Hence token data are objects that may also contain a Petri net, enabling multi level systems to be modelled e.g. an operating system controlling a number of processes. Two major differences to LOOPN++ are the addition of a concept of time and the concept of system instantiation, where a system is instantiated to represent a particular configuration in a step preceding the start of execution.

In the object oriented approach taken, every object is an instance of a particular class. An extension to the high level time Petri nets defined above is the addition of a type system, i.e. the values of tokens on places are constrained to be of a particular type. In this approach a type is synonymous with a class hierarchy, therefore class refinement also implies type refinement. This is an important mechanism in refining a model so that it can ultimately be efficiently implemented on a heterogeneous target architecture. For example, a filter can be described as a data flow graph transforming numerical data. The performance requirements may require that the filter be implemented on a DSP. As many DSPs only efficiently handle numbers of fixed bit length a further refinement could involve defining the number of bits used to represent this data and how an overflow is handled (truncation, rounding or exception).

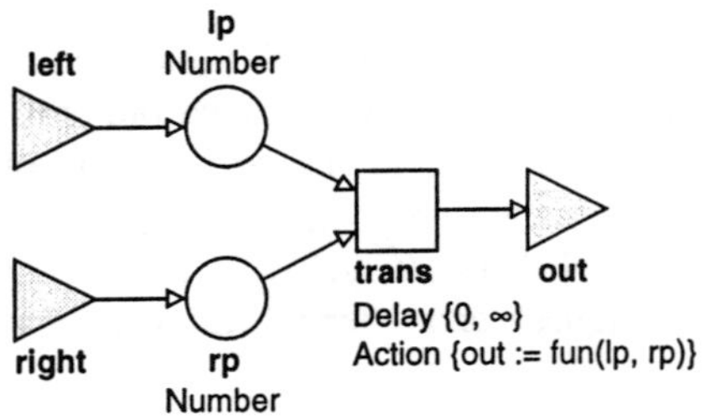


```
FUNCTION fun (a,b:Number):Number
"a function template"
{<ABSTRACT>
   RESULT := 0
}
```

Figure 2. Showing the abstract superclass of classes *Adder* and *Multiplier.* It defines the behaviour and state with the above Petri net and also an abstract function *fun*. Interfaces are represented as triangular shaped elements.

2.2. Components

In the object oriented approach systems are modelled as communicating components or objects. Components have behaviour which is modelled with the kernel language or another formalism described with the kernel language. Components communicate by sending and receiving objects to and from one another. Components are hierarchically structured, i.e. contain other components, which leaves scope during the instantiation process to decide which particular component will be inserted. This mechanism allows design exploration and configuration to be supported in a convenient way. Unlike other approaches where only special communication objects may be sent, communicating standard objects allows for introduced interfaces to wrap protocols around objects if necessary.

Figure 3 shows a component that implements the function $f(a, b) = res = 2a + b^2$ and contains three embedded components using the object oriented high level time Petri net kernel language. Components have defined interfaces over which objects are communicated. Here it is possible to imagine a partitioning that places the three embedded components on different implementation target devices and different configurations with implementation specific components that represent this partitioning. The model of $f(a, b)$ does not assume sequential semantics, as depending on how the system is partitioned, a schedule is determined that ensures that it is functionally correct and also meets its performance constraints, for example it can be seen that a schedule that allows pipelining could be used.

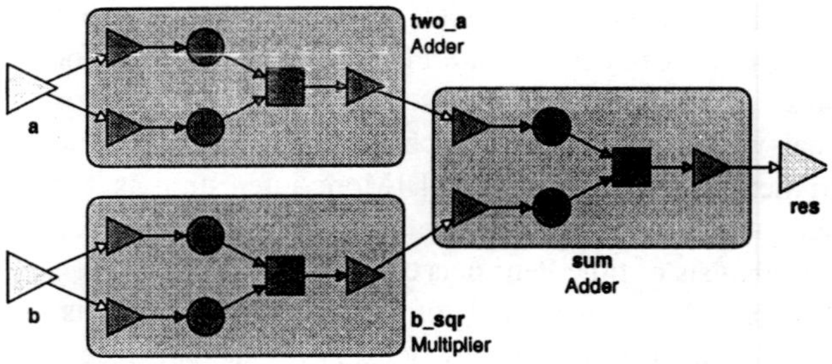

Figure 3. Graphical representation of a component containing embedded components.

3. Support for Other Formalisms

An embedded system design methodology should allow designers the flexibility of choosing the most appropriate set of formalisms for the particular system to be modelled. The approach proposed in this paper is based on a formal object oriented kernel language and concepts from graph grammars [19], [21]. Graph grammar productions are defined which specify the editing rules (syntax) of a formalism. The semantics are modelled using kernel language components to represent the elements of a formalism. Multiple formalisms communicate with one another with semantics defined by the kernel language. An advantage of this approach is that tools need only consider the kernel language rather than each formalism individually, therefore only one simulator, code generator and refinement mechanism etc. is needed. It is however still possible to capitalise on formalism specific tools and methods, for example, for efficient code generation.

As all components are instances of a class it follows that any formalism assembled from components is also fully object oriented. Thus all the benefits of code reuse, abstraction and refinement provided by the object oriented kernel language are also applicable to all derivative formalisms. Figure 4 shows the model architecture used to implement the ideas presented in this paper.

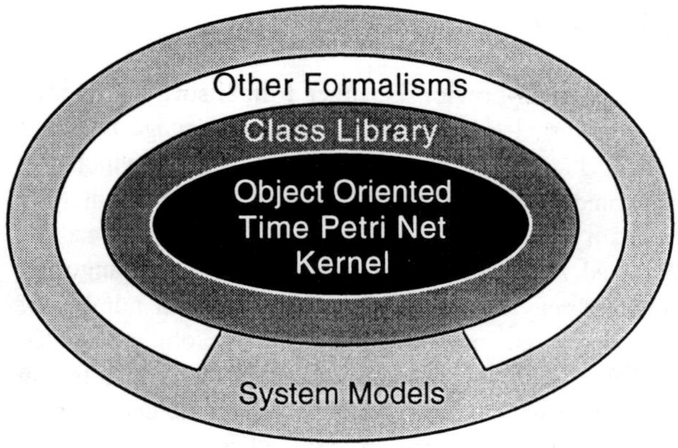

Figure 4. The model architecture.

4. Describing a Formalism

The following steps illustrate how a new formalism is supported. These steps use the expressiveness of the kernel language in which elements of a formalism and editing rules are described:

1. The syntax rules of a new formalism are represented as graph grammar productions. Productions define how elements of a formalism are edited to create models, e.g. the insertion of an element or the connection of two elements. These productions are called Syntax Graph Grammar (SynGG) productions [21] and are described completely in terms of the new formalism;
2. An object oriented time Petri net component class is associated with every element in a formalism. These component classes may be already existing classes where an element of a formalism is directly represented by a kernel language component or they may be new classes representing other behaviour. The resulting class hierarchy represents the elements of a formalism and should reflect that elements may have similar behaviour, which can be inherited. Care must also be taken in how communication between the proposed formalism and its environment is defined - often a class will represent a part of a model described wholly by a single formalism and in which only classes representing the elements of a formalism may be instantiated. These classes can be defined abstractly and, through subclassing, have the ability to be refined and reused. Thus all formalisms are object oriented and models may use the refinement techniques afforded by the object oriented approach;
3. Complementing every SynGG is a Semantic Graph Grammar (SemGG) production which describes the semantics of the syntax defined by the SynGG. These semantics are defined in terms of the kernel language (i.e. object oriented time Petri nets) and involve the component classes defined to represent the formalism's elements.

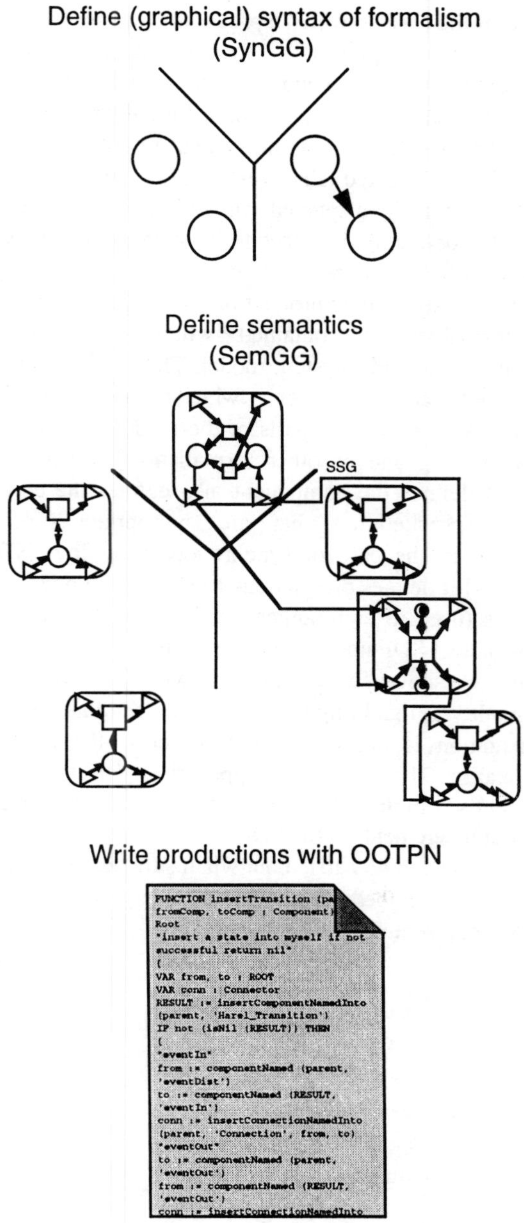

Figure 5. Syntax, Semantic and implementation Graph Grammar productions describing the addition of a state-transition in a simple Finite State Machine formalism.

4. The productions defined by the SemGG are more complex than those represented by the SynGG as they describe how kernel components are composed to represent the semantics of a formalism including the syntax (editing rules) represented by the SynGG.
5. Functions are then written representing the productions defined by the SemGG and are associated with a particular class in the object oriented environment, i.e. they are

defined for the class in which a production can be executed. These functions represent the conditional arcs and the actual subgraph selection and replacement mechanisms;

6. To complete the description of a formalism, functions are created that define how an element of a formalism is graphically represented (shape, weight etc.) including how its current state is displayed. In addition functions are created that define the interface to the editor. This allows a formalism specific editor to be generated in which actions cause previously defined productions to be executed.

A formalism is contained within a component representing the (sub) system model. This component has kernel interfaces through which the formalism communicates with other parts of the model described by the kernel language or other formalisms. Therefore the class that defines the component also defines the editing facilities (productions) that are appropriate for the formalism. In the case of synchronous data flow (SDF) graphs [15] it defines productions to insert SDF nodes and interfaces (used to communicate with other components) and to connect SDF nodes with one another.

Figure 6 shows a component with an equivalent functionality as that in figure 3. It can be seen that the SDF representation is better suited to describe the required functionality. The use of an appropriate formalism can significantly simplify the representation of a component. The round elements are SDF nodes representing an operation that can be carried out when sufficient input data is present. An embedded component in figure 3 shows a Petri net representation of a SDF node.

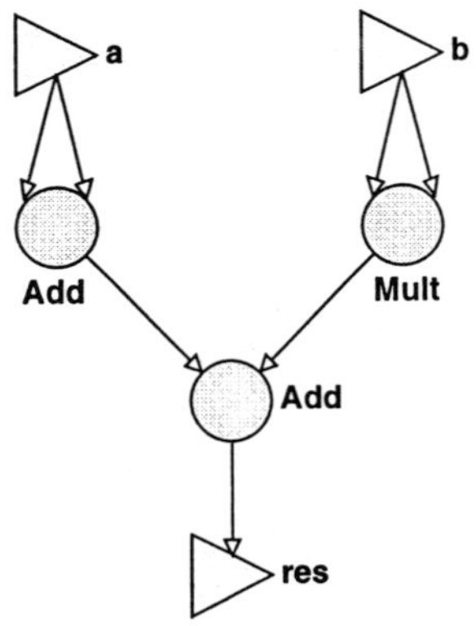

Figure 6. Synchronous data flow (SDF) representation of a component containing embedded components with an equivalent functionality as that in figure 3.

7. Other Formalisms in an Object Oriented Environment

As described previously, other formalisms are defined using the kernel language. This kernel language is object oriented, facilitating the creation of classes which are instantiated in a number of contexts. Any element of a formalism described as a component of a class can be subclassed. As with the components of the kernel language, a subclass may be extended and refined in a number of ways. This is an important feature of the object oriented approach and when applied correctly results in considerable gains in productivity [4]. In object oriented systems results are reused by either subclassing or embedding.

The subclassing of elements of a formalism allows a refined element to be used in place of the standard one. Kernel language inheritance rules ensure that the refined element will always be able to be used correctly. Subclassing may be prevented by defining a class to be monomorphic. This ensures that only suitable classes are able to be refined. Assuming that the functions representing SemGG productions allow a choice of component classes to be instantiated, subclassing is available to all formalisms. This enables abstraction and refinement to be used.

Embedding is a formalism specific feature and usually represents hierarchical structuring. Formalisms that do not support hierarchy, such as SDF, cannot make use of embedding at the formalism level. In contrast StateCharts [11] does support hierarchy and can benefit from the advantages of code sharing.

The following figures show an example of subclassing and reuse using the StateCharts formalism and implemented using the object oriented time Petri nets kernel language. Three classes are used to build a state machine able to count to 4 and 8. Figure 7 shows a subclass of *Abstract_Sequential*. This class implements a simple two bit counter. It does not define a state-transition from state *b1* and state *b0* as this would prevent any subclass from implementing a larger counter.

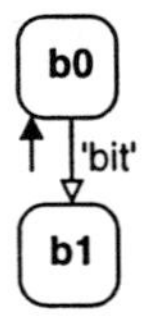

Figure 7. The class *Bit_2* implementing a 2 bit counter.

Figure 8 extends the 2 bit counter to 4 bits. It is a *subclass* of *Bit_2* and has been enhanced with the addition of two states (*b2*, *b3*) and 3 state-transitions. The states and transitions inherited from the class *Bit_2* are shown as being shaded. The state-transition from state *b3* to state *b0* produces an event named *'nibble'*. This event is broadcast throughout the state machine and, in addition, is made available through the external event interface from where it can be used by other parts of a model, possibly modelled with different formalisms. Class *Bit_4* reuses the states and state-transitions defined in class *Bit_2*.

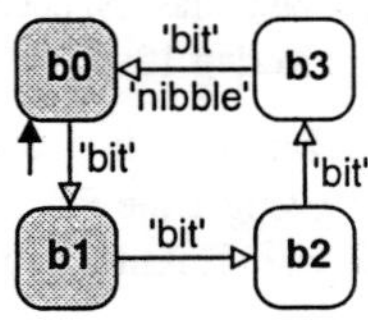

Figure 8. The class *Bit_4* implementing a 4 bit counter.

Finally in figure 9 the class *Bit_8* is shown to consist of two *embedded* components of class *Bit_4*, one of which is marked as the initial state. As the two component hierarchical states are instances of the same class they only differ in their dynamic state information. Ignoring the internal states of both components of class *Bit_4* the system can be regarded as only having 2 states (*b_0_3*, *b_4_7*) and 2 state-transitions that occur when event *'nibble'* is present. The state-transition from state *b_4_7* to state *b_0_3* produces the event *'byte'* to indicate that 8 bits have been counted.

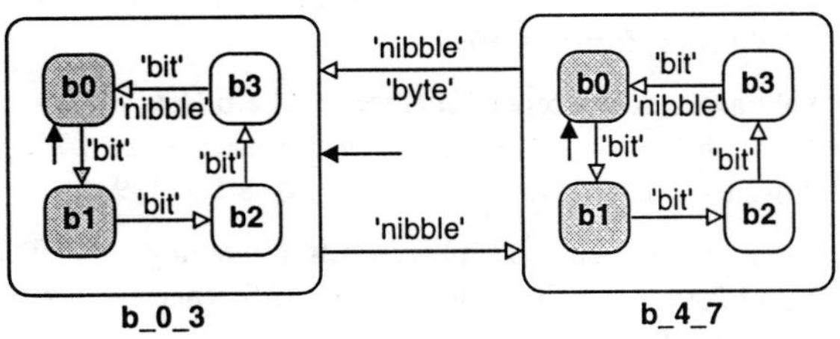

Figure 9. The class *Bit_8* implementing a 8 bit counter.

Figure 10 shows part of the class hierarchy used to implement the 3 classes above.

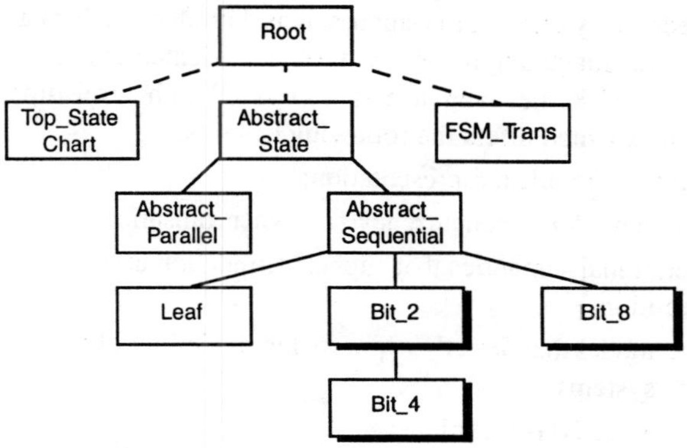

Figure 10. Class hierarchy tree for StateCharts classes implementing an 8 bit counter.

Figure 11 shows part of the instantiation tree for a component of the class Bit_8. This component can be embedded within another class or used directly within a subclass of *Top_StateChart* where a production will connect the event mechanism to the component. This figure does not show the kernel components used to implement the elements of the StateCharts formalism. The components marked *inherited* are defined in the parent class of the defining class.

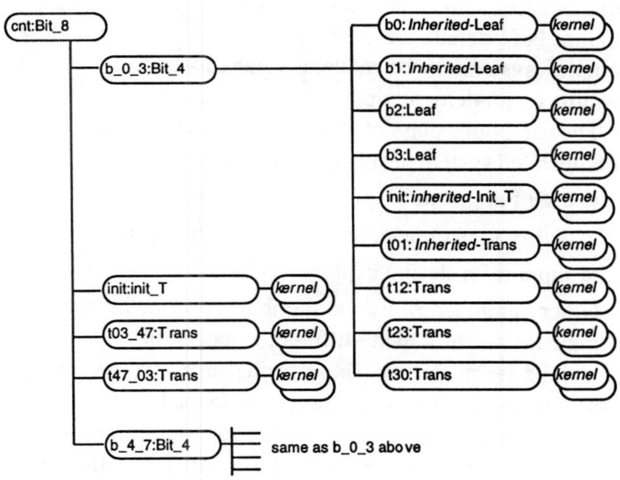

Figure 11. Instantiation tree of the class *Bit_8* (figure 9).

8. Conclusions

This paper presents a new approach to the design of embedded systems. This approach is based on a formal kernel language augmented with object oriented concepts. The formal kernel language is a class of high level time Petri nets which offers the following benefits:

- intuitive graphical representation;
- simple model of concurrency and synchronisation;
- operational semantics that support simulation and execution;
- time model that directly supports the modelling of real time systems;
- proven analysis techniques.

The inclusion of object oriented concepts provides facilities for creating components that encapsulate behaviour and state, and thereby supports:

- abstraction;
- refinement;
- encapsulation;
- reuse and sharing.

Components are described with classes that define how inheritance properties are propagated and provide mechanisms for configuration, reuse and sharing. A system is a composition of communicating components at every level of abstraction. During the design of an embedded system classes are defined, refined, reused and configured. Refinement is supported by substituting less refined components with components containing an increased amount of detail. Abstraction and refinement allow complex systems to be modelled and successively refined towards an implementation.

The use of this class of Petri nets allows relevant aspects of embedded system design to be addressed. These include:

- the use of application specific formalisms;
- the ability to parameterise or configure models;
- the support for design exploration.

Other approaches use a number of domain specific formalisms with which different aspects of a systems behaviour are modelled. These formalisms may be wholly formal methods or a combination of formal methods and informal ones. They often neglect the question of the semantics of the combination of formalisms within one specification.

The proposed approach uses only a single object oriented time Petri net kernel language for modelling both systems and formalisms. In addition the semantics of combining multiple formalisms are completely given by this underlying kernel language. The flexibility supported by the formal language is available to all other kernel based formalisms as they are also object oriented and can be refined and reused in the same manner as the kernel language.

9. References

[1] Ajmone Marsen M., Balbo G., Conte G., Donatelli S., Franceschinis G., Modelling with Generalized Stochastic Petri Nets, Wiley Series in Parallel Computing, 1995

[2] Bernardinello L., De Cindio F., A Survey of Basic Net Models and Modular Net Classes, Lecture Notes in Computer Science 609, Springer Verlag 1992

[3] Berthomieu B., Diaz M., Modeling and Verification of Time Dependent Systems Using Time Petri Nets, IEEE Transactions on Software Engineering Volume 17 Number 3, 1991

[4] Booch G., Object Oriented Analysis and Design With Applications, The Benjamin/Cummings Publishing Company Inc. Redwood City, Calif. 1994

[5] Bucci G., Vicario E., Compositional Validation of Time-Critical Systems Using Communicating Time Petri Nets, IEEE Transactions on Software Engineering Vol. 21, No. 12, 1995

[6] Christensen S., Toksvig J., DesignBeta V2.0.1 BETA Code-Segments in CP-nets, University of Aarhus, Internal report, 1993

[7] Dähler J., Ein Werkzeug für den Entwurf verteilter Systeme auf der Basis erweiterter Petri-Netze, DISS. ETH Nr. 8770. PhD Thesis Swiss Federal Institute of Technology, 1989

[8] Esser R., An Object Oriented Petri Net Approach to Embedded System Design. PhD Thesis ETH Zurich 1996, VDF Verlag Zurich, 1997.

[9] Fehling R., A Concept of Hierarchical Petri Nets with Building Blocks, In Lecture Notes in Computer Science 674, Advances in Petri Nets 1993, Springer-Verlag, 1993

[10] Genrich H.J., Lautenbach K., System Modelling with High-Level Petri Nets, Theoretical Computer Science 13, North Holland, 1981

[11] Harel D., StateCharts: A Visual Formalism for Complex Systems, Science of Computer Programming 8 (1987) 231-274 North Holland, 1987

[12] Jensen K., Coloured Petri Nets: A High Level Language for System Design and Analysis, Advances in Petri Nets 1990, G. Rozenberg (ed), LNCS 483, Springer-Verlag, 1990

[13] Jensen K., Coloured Petri Nets: Basic Concepts, Analysis Methods and Practical Use - Volume 1: Basic Concepts, EATCS Monographs in Computer Science, Vol. 26, Springer-Verlag, 1990

[14] Lakos C.A., Keen C.D., LOOPN++: A New Language for Object-Oriented Petri Nets, Department of Computer Science, University of Tasmania, 1994

[15] Lee E.A., Messerschmitt D.G., Synchronous Data Flow, Proceedings of the IEEE, Vol 75 No. 9, September 1987

[16] Merlin P., A Study of the Recoverability of Computer Systems, Thesis, Department of Computer Science, University of California, Irvine, 1974

[17] Merlin P., Faber D.J., Recoverability of Communication Protocols, IEEE Transactions on Communications, Vol. Com-24, No. 9, September 1976

[18] Murata T., Petri Nets: Properties, Analysis and Applications, Proceedings of the IEEE, Vol 77, No. 4, 1989

[19] Nagl M., A Tutorial and Bibliographical Survey on Graph Grammars, Bericht Nr. 69/78 Abteilung Informatik, Universität Dortmund, 1978

[20] Oswald H., Esser R., Mattmann R., An Environment for Specifying and Executing Hierarchical Petri Nets, 12th International Conference on Software Engineering, Nice, France, 1990

[21] Pezzé M., Cabernet: A Customizable Environment for the Specification and Analysis of Real-Time Systems, Dipartimento di Elettronica e Informazione, Politecnico di Milano, 1994

[22] Ramchandani C., Analysis of Asynchronous Concurrent Systems by Timed Petri Nets, Massachusetts Institute of Technology, Project MAC, Technical report 120, February 1974

[23] Starke P. H, Analyse von Petri-Netz-Modellen, B.G. Teubner Stuttgart, 1990

[24] Verkoulen P.A.C., Integrated Information Systems Design: An Approach Based on Object Oriented Concepts and Petri Nets, University of Technology: Eindhoven PhD Thesis, 1993

Object-Oriented Requirements Analysis for Air Traffic Control Systems

Jan Wortmann
Technische Universität Berlin
Sekr. E-N 7, Einsteinufer 17,D-10587 Berlin, Germany
email: jwortman@cs.tu-berlin.de

Ingo Claßen
Fraunhofer ISST
Kurstr. 33, D-10117 Berlin, Germany
email: Ingo.Classen@isst.fhg.de

Gerd Klawitter
Centre Expérimental Eurocontrol
B.P. 15, F-91222 Brétigny-sur-Orge, France
email: Gerd.Klawitter@eurocontrol.fr

Abstract

This experience report documents the results of the project "Data Modelling for Advanced Flight Data Management" of the research group "Computergestützte Informationssysteme" at Technische Universität Berlin and the Eurocontrol Experimental Centre (EEC) Brétigny-sur-Orge France. A combination of classic object-oriented approaches, such as OMT, the Booch method and Jacobson's use case driven approach have been combined for the creation of an analysis model, describing sector handover procedures in the context of Air Traffic Control (ATC). Due to the complex dynamic properties of ATC systems, Message Sequence Charts (MSC) and statecharts, have been used within this project for requirements analysis, although they are usually considered as design related.

1 Introduction

In the context of EUROCONTROL' s [1] European Air Traffic Control Harmonization & Integration Program (EATCHIP) extensive requirements analysis are on their way for the design of new Air Traffic Control (ATC) systems for the year 2010 and beyond. The complexity of the problem domain requires extensive efforts for the clarification of the initial problem statement. Moreover, due to the extremely long lifespan of ATC systems, stable and robust analysis models enabling the integration of new operational scenarios in the future are crucial for this kind of large-scale software systems. This paper documents the experience of the project "Data Modelling for Advanced Flight Data Management" of the research group "Computergestützte Informationssysteme" at Technische Universität Berlin and the EUROCONTROL Experimental Centre (EEC) Brétigny-sur-Orge France [6].

It describes our approach of using object-oriented techniques for requirements analysis in the ATC domain with special attention on understandable, unambiguous and extensible requirements models. Our working environment in the project was characterized by little experience of using object-oriented techniques on a large-scale with special emphasis on requirements analysis. Furthermore ATC is traditionally related to functional decomposition techniques and ADA83 as programming language.

In section 2 the application domain Air Traffic Control (ATC) as central part of the overall context Air Traffic Management (ATM) is described. Section 3 introduces our requirements analysis approach and in section 4 we draw some conclusions of our work and indicate topics for future research.

2 The Application Domain Air Traffic Control

Similar to computer science, Air Traffic Control (ATC) is a comparatively young discipline. Driven by the rapidly growing amounts of traffic and the progress in aircraft and radar technology ATC, is one of the most innovative and demanding clients of information technology. Reliability, availability and safety

[1] EUROCONTROL - The European Ogranisation for the Safety of Air Navigation

0-8186-7840-2/97 $10.00 © 1997 IEEE

are prominent examples for the special requirements within this application domain. The general objectives of Air Traffic Control can be characterized as follows:

- guarantee safe separation between aircraft in the air;
- assist in preventing collisions between aircraft and between aircraft and obstructions;
- expedite and maintain an orderly flow of air traffic;
- provide information useful for the safe and efficient conduct of flights;
- notify appropriate organizations regarding aircraft in need of search and rescue aid, and assist such organizations as required [4].

In order to meet these objectives, air traffic control service is provided and takes the form of:

- Flight Information Service (FIS)
- Aerodrome Control, controlling aircraft taking off and landing on a given aerodrome or moving on the manoeuvring area, which is usually organized by the tower;
- Approach Control, controlling arriving and departing traffic within the terminal manoeuvring area, located either at an aerodrome or an Area Control Centre (ACC);
- Area Control, controlling the en-route traffic, which is organized by an ACC.

Operational ATC comprises all phases of a given flight from take-off to the arrival at the airport of destination. Along the route the aircraft crosses a series of sectors, each controlled by at least one radar controller, located at one of the mentioned ATC service providers. Radar data and Flight PLans (FPL) are the central information sources for controllers. Radar systems determine the aircraft's current position and altitude (flight level), while flight plans state the pilots intentions, i.e. the pilot's preferred route towards the destination airport. Today, flight plans can be correlated to aircraft equipped with transponders (Mode C) via a four digit octal code, the so called SSR code. At the end of the 1960s computer technology was introduced for the storage and correlation of radar echoes and digital flight plans, in order to improve the controller's information sources. Modern area control centres, like the Maastricht UAC, are supplied with modern digital controller working positions, supplying controllers with the set of information as in Fig. 1.

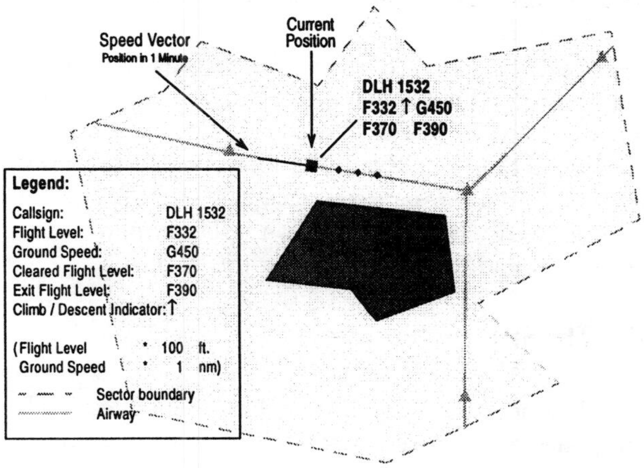

Figure 1. Screen Layout for Modern Digital Controller Working Positions

Analysing sector-hand over procedures was the goal of the project "Data Modelling for Advanced Flight Data Management", carried out at the EUROCONTROL Experimental Centre (EEC). When an aircraft leaves a sector it has to be handed-over to the controller in the next sector, in order to establish clear responsibilities for controllers and pilots. Modelling the business process including behavioural and static aspects has been the central objective of this project. This approach was used for the evaluation of EUROCONTROL' s On-line Data Interchange (OLDI) protocol, designed for the automation of sector-handover procedures. Necessary data structures (classes/objects) combined with all relevant services have been modelled within this project, in order to evaluate the OLDI proposal, which will become an international standard in the next years.

3 Object-Oriented Requirements Analysis

As Davis points out, the central idea of problem analysis is the clarification of the initial problem statement and creating a stable model, which can be used for the design of the system later-on [3]. Due to the complexity of the application domain it soon became obvious that a distinct requirements analysis phase independent of any design considerations is necessary to clarify and finally understand the problem. Additionally it became clear, that different formalisms, namely class diagrams, message sequence charts and statecharts had to be used in the requirements analysis phase to satisfy different needs, such as understandability versus unambiguity. Usually these two aspects are in conflict.

Section 3.1 describes what formalisms have been used to solve this conflict. To enhance understandability our extensions of Jacobson's use case model is given in Section 3.2. Examples for extended use cases and the derived message sequence charts are presented in section 3.3. Finally Section 4 will summarize the experience made in the modelling process.

3.1 The Strategy/Process

To balance the requirements between understandability and preciseness a combination of use case models and message sequence charts has been employed. The initial problem statements was described as a set of use cases according to Jacobson and combined with a domain object model as a rough structural outline of the problem domain ATC [5]. Afterwards the use cases have been used for the refinement of the domain object model. Structural aspects within the use cases lead to new classes. Letters of agreement describe for example transfer conditions between adjacent centres and therefore had to be part of the static structure, the class diagram.

Behavioural aspects within individual use cases have been modelled using message sequence charts (MSC) and statecharts. Interaction between different objects, the inter-object behaviour, has been modelled using message sequence charts, while internal state changes of given objects, the intra-object behaviour, have been modelled using statecharts. Fig. 2 demonstrates this strategy.

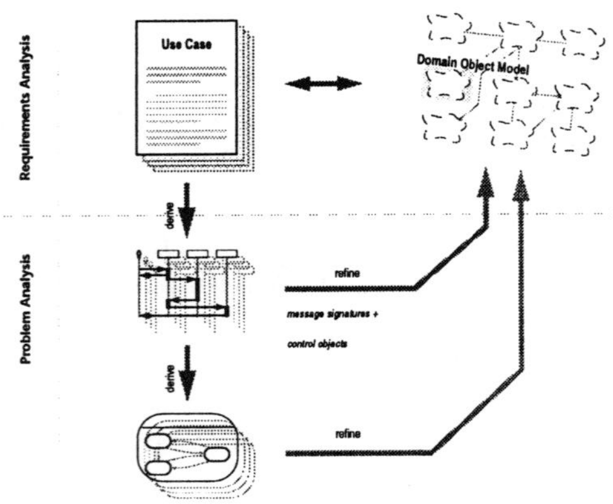

Figure 2. Phases and Modelling Techniques for Object-Oriented Requirements Analysis

Behavioural system properties have been modelled on a per use case basis, i.e. the analysis of each use case led to a set of refinements in the domain object. After the evaluation of 17 different use cases and iterations of the domain object model, the first version of an analysis model has been published.

Note that MSC are usually used for the design of systems. In our approach they have been used to model and clarify behavioural requirements within the analysis phase[2]. This kind of design must not be confused with the actual design of the system with respect to implementation.

3.2 An Extended Use Case Model

During the creation of the requirements model it turned out, that complex business processes, such as "Standard Transfer of Control" could be composed from a set of atomic use cases. Unlike other approaches, where the internal structure of use cases has been formalized, e.g. through the introduction of episodes [1], our approach favoured a sound composition and decomposition mechanism. Path expressions according to Campell and Habermas, seemed to be a suitable solution for this objective [2]. So we did not structure the use case' s internal course of events (sequence of steps and tasks), but we decomposed use cases into atomic units, without alternate courses or iterations. In order to introduce additional clarity for the invocation of atomic use cases through path expressions, we defined pre-, post-, and error conditions, which resulted in the following structure:

```
Use Case <No>: <Name>  - A sequential number and a
                         unique name for use cases
 Assembly:             - Referenced atomic use cases
 Actors:               - Involved Actors
 Precondition:         - Conditions for the invocation of
                         this use case
 Description:          - The plain text description of the
                         business process
 Error Conditions:     - Potential Error conditions
 Postcondition:        - Constraints to be met at the end of
                         a use case
 Author:               - For traceability reasons
 References:           - Traceability of information sources,
                         referenced models & documents
 Questions:            - Identifying vagueness, ambiguity,
                         omissions in the description
```

A primitive form of requirements traceability has been introduced through the notation of the author and used textual references, like company rules, interviews or other referenced data models. Uncertainties in the textual description, ambiguities in the problem statement can be addressed in the question section, which

[2]During the writing of this paper we recognized that a similar approach has been proposed by Edward Yourdon et al. for the development of business applications at Software AG [7]

proved to be very helpful for the resolution of misunderstandings or organisational problems within individual business processes. All these items have been used to add structure, enable modularity and introduce traceability to use cases and have been expressed through textual descriptions of business processes. The resulting use cases were compact and did not contain any redundancy.

3.3 Example for extended use cases and the resulting message sequence chart

The following use case and the derived message sequence chart (see Fig. 3) are intended to give an impression of the results of the project. This example describes the notification of a controller in the next sector. The controller, currently responsible for a given flight, notifies his colleague in the next sector that the given flight will arrive in a predefined amount of time. Notification therefore ensures, that flight plan data can be forwarded to the next sector, in order to synchronize the available information for the two controllers. The business process has been modelled using an atomic use case, while Fig. 3 presents the same business process in a more detailed and technical manner.

Use Case 1: Notify Receiving Controller

Assembly: -

Summary:
Notification of the adjacent sector using the "ABI" message.

Actors:
Transferring Controller (TRACO), Receiving Controller (RECO)

Preconditions:
1. Aircraft under control of the transferring controller (TRACO)

Description:
The TRACO first checks the aircraft's route, as stated in the FPL, in order to identify the next relevant sector. Depending on the current ground speed of the aircraft the TRACO calculates a point where an "ABI" message has to be sent. This point, here referred to as "ABI Point", advises that the aircraft will arrive in a mutually agreed amount of time at the coordination point (COP). The coordination point itself is a mutually agreed point close to the sector boundary, where the RECO will assume control of the given flight. When the "ABI Point" is reached an "ABI" message is sent to the receiving controller in the adjacent sector. The "Advance Boundary Information" contains the following information:

- Message type;
- Message number;
- Aircraft identification;
- ...

The reception of an "ABI" message will be stated automatically with a Logical Acknowledgment Message ("LAM"). The FDPS now checks the availability of a corresponding FPL. If no corresponding FPL is available a new instance of the class "System FPL" will be created. If a corresponding instance is available, the values of its attributes will be compared with the values within the "ABI" message. In case of discrepancies the instance of class "System FPL" and the "ABI" message will be "referred to an appropriate position for resolution" [OLDI sec.6.2.3.2.3, p.22].

Exceptions:
If the "LAM" message does not arrive within a mutually agreed time restart this use case (Use Case 1).

Postconditions: "LAM" message received

Authors: Jan Wortmann

References: OLDI Standard [OLDI95]

Questions:

- Is there an override protection for instances of the class "System FPL", i.e. new estimates may destroy data chosen by the planning controller.
- Who is responsible for the resolution? Should be either the executive or the planning controller on the receiving side.
- Procedures for sector reentry

3.4 Experience

Generally spoken, our experience with object-orientation techniques for the requirements analysis Process was very positive. It proved its applicability especially as a basis of discussions with the domain experts. Nevertheless decisions between different modelling options became difficult. Common heuristics for the definition of classes and operations, described by prominent OO authors, proved not to be sufficient. Flight plans, for example, are the central entities of interest within ATC. As an international standard, flights plans are paper forms, which consist of 19 fields, defining the route and flight level for an aircraft from departure to destination. So it seems quite obvious to create a corresponding domain object named "FPL". While having a closer look, the complex character of this real-world entity becomes obvious: flight plans change their character over time. During the boarding procedure at the passenger gate the only information available for ATC concerning a planned flight is the flight plan itself. Right after the take off of an aircraft new information becomes available, the radar track.

In a first approach a class named "Flight" was introduced, comprising the component classes "FPL" and "Radar Track". This structure seemed to provide an adequate model of the real world entity, without hard-coding temporal aspects in the static, i.e. data part of the model. Both components class "FPL" and class "Radar Track" can be instantiated individually, while the aggregate class "Flight" provides a common interface for other client classes.

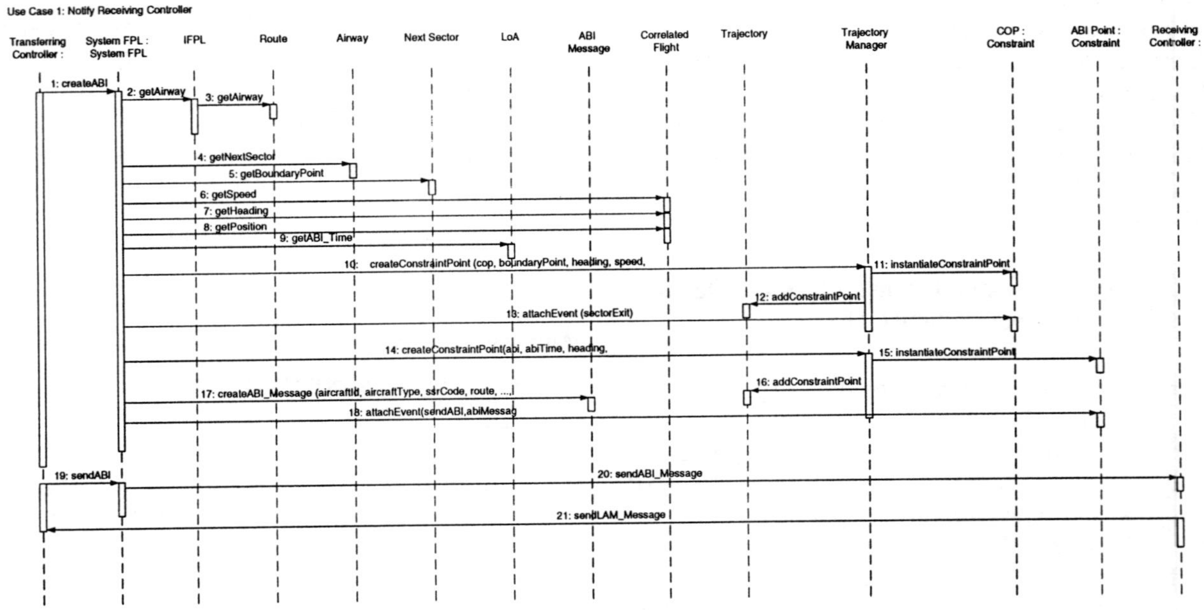

Figure 3. Modelled Inter-Object Behaviour for Use Case 1

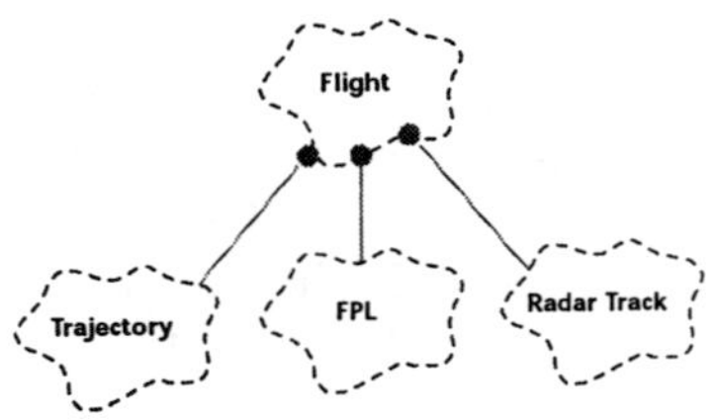

Figure 4. First Model of the Domain Class "System Flight Plan"

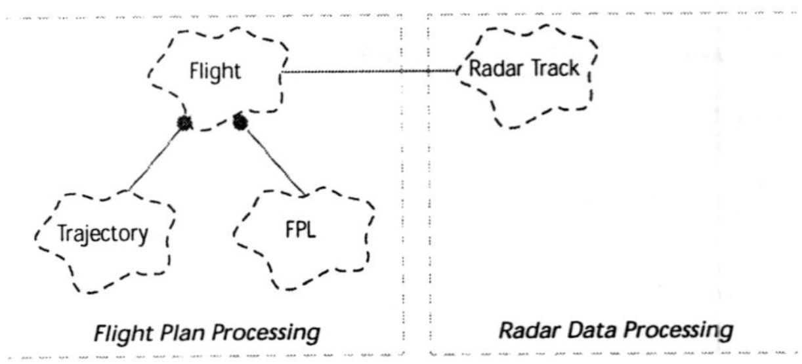

Figure 5. Final Model of the Domain Class "System Flight Plan"

Other ATC experts stressed the importance of an individual existence of the class "Radar Track". This approach implies a greater amount of system security, because two individual representations of the same real-world entity can be regarded as a primitive form of fault-tolerance. Although the experts favoured the approach in Fig. 5, no alternative seemed to be able to express all static aspects of this rather complex real-world entity.

For the analysis of behavioural aspects of the ATC problem domain, classic formalisms, such as message sequence charts and statecharts, have been used. Central objective for this project was a clarification of both behavioural and static problem properties. ATC systems cover all three characterizations of external software behaviour proposed by Davis, namely data, control and algorithm [3]. Towards the end of the project it became evident, that different class categories of the analysis model could be related to one of these aspects. The class category "Flight Data Processing" could be characterised through its algorithmic and control complexity, while the class category "Airspace Environment" can be considered data intensive. Data intensive parts, such as "Airspace Environment" can be characterized through so called get and set operations. Compared to the services in areas with algorithmic complexity, like "Flight Plan Processing", this kind of inter-object behaviour seems less important for the understanding of behavioural system properties. To shift the client's/analyst's attention towards control or algorithmic inter-object behaviour new abstraction mechanisms for inter-object behaviour would be very helpful for the analysis of large-scale systems.

4 Conclusion

Object-oriented requirements analysis using modular and decomposable use cases proved to be a very powerful method for the analysis of large-scale ATC systems. All modelling primitives can be used for a robust and minimal model of the application domain covering static and behavioural system properties. Partitions, abstractions and viewpoints can be used for the investigation of large-scale complex application domains. Especially the introduced modularity for decomposable use cases adds a complete set of new features for requirements analysis, such as traceability and simulation of business processes. Through the creation of object models, i.e. modelling static and behavioural aspects of the system at hand, a stable and robust problem description can be created. This process also facilitates the participation of staff members / users, who are not directly skilled for object-modelling.

Although Edward Yourdan's book "Mainstream Objects", which appeared more or less at the same time, addresses the development of business applications, we feel very confident, that this approach is equally suitable for the air traffic management domain [7]. But compared to business applications behavioural properties of ATC systems are far more important. Tajectory prediction for example includes complex point-mass models for the simulation of aircraft behaviour. Meteorological conditions, such as head winds, provide an additional set of variables for prediction of trajectories.

Further research activities are planned for the traceability of requirements on a broad scale. In this context the consistency and clarity between the different modelling techniques used within this context is very important. For the simulation of use case sequences, composed by path expressions, an automatic and animated simulation tool seems to be very helpful. The design of such kind of system is determined by a deeper understanding of the relationships and perspectives of the used modelling techniques use cases, class diagrams, message sequence charts and statecharts. Especially the pragmatics for the relationships and dependencies between the used modelling techniques within this approach have to be clarified. Another aspect directly determined by requirements traceability is the question off- tool support. What kinds of the best off-the-shelf tools can be combined in an environment to support requirements traceability.

While this project has been entirely dedicated to analysis, the question of object-oriented design and its implication has to be analysed. Object-oriented requirements analysis provides an ideal and stable model of the application domain. But in the design phase a set of new implications induced by operating systems, programming languages, database systems and middleware platforms have to be reflected in the object models. These technologies, so called target platforms, lead to a new set of refinements/iterations of the analysis models. A clear separation of domain specific and target platform related requirements seems to be a first step on the way towards a smooth evolution of large-scale ATM systems.

Another important question is the impact of new user requirements on operational system. Unlike the comparatively stable evolution of analysis models, new user requirements may impact different distinctive levels. New classes and services, as a result of new operational scenarios, may also imply changes in the target platform. This class of changes might imply a reorganization of the complete class/object structure. Such category of changes only seems to be manageable through a detailed understanding of requirements and trace tools, that are able to relate all kinds of textual requirements to parts of the system.

References

[1] J. B. B. Regnell, M. Andersson. A hierachical use case model with graphical representation. In *Proc. of IEEE International Syposium on Engineering of Computer-Based Systems*, 1996.

[2] R. H. Campbell and A. N. Habermann. *The Specification of Process Synchronization by Path Expressions*, volume 16 of *Lecture Notes in Computer Science*. Springer, 1974.

[3] A. M. Davis. *Software Requirements - Objects, Functions and States.* Prentice Hall, 1993.

[4] A. Field. *International Air Traffic Control 2nd ed.* Pergamon Press, 1985.

[5] I. Jacobson, M. Christerson, P. Jonsson, and G. Övergaard. *Object-Oriented Software Engineering — A Use Case Driven Approach.* Addison–Wesley, 1993. Revised Fourth Printing.

[6] J. Wortmann. Object-oriented analysis for advanced flight data management. Technical Report EEC Report No. 306/FDM/1996, Centre Expérimental EUROCONTROL, 1996.

[7] E. Yourdan, K. Whitehead, J. Thomann, K. Oppel, and P. Nevermann. *Mainstream Objects—An Analysis and Design Approach for Business.* Prentice Hall, 1995.

An Overview of Object-Oriented Design Metrics

R. Harrison, S. Counsell, R. Nithi
Department of Electronics and Computer Science,
University of Southampton, Southampton, SO17 1BJ, U.K.
email: rh@ecs.soton.ac.uk

Abstract

In this paper, we examine the current state in the field of object-oriented design metrics. We describe three sets of currently available metrics suites, namely, those of Chidamber and Kemerer, Lorenz and Kidd and Abreu. We consider the important features of each set, and assess the appropriateness and usefulness of each in evaluating the design of object-oriented systems. As a result, we identify problems common to all three sets of metrics, allowing us to suggest possible improvements in this area.

1. Introduction

Various sets of object-oriented metrics have been proposed as a means of assessing whether systems under investigation exhibit characteristics of quality software [6, 7, 14, 5, 15]. In this paper, three sets of such metrics are considered. The first set were proposed by Chidamber and Kemerer [7], the second by Lorenz and Kidd [15], and lastly, those proposed by Abreu [5]. All three sets attempt to capture the key elements of object-oriented software: *encapsulation* (information hiding), *abstraction* and *inheritance*.

In Sections 2, 3 and 4 respectively, each of these sets of metrics is analysed, and the important features of each highlighted. The intentions of the designers of the metrics, in terms of what the metrics were intended to measure, are also discussed. Various problems with the three sets considered are highlighted as a result, and these are then discussed (Section 5); possible future directions are then considered, taking account of these shortcomings (Section 6).

2. Description of Chidamber and Kemerer Metrics

In keeping with the key elements of object-oriented software, the set of six metrics developed by Chidamber and Kemerer (C&K) [7] attempt to identify certain design traits in object-oriented software, for example, inheritance, coupling and cohesion etc. The six metrics can be summarised as:

1. Weighted Methods per Class (WMC). This metric counts the number of methods in a class. WMC was designed to measure the complexity of a class. However, since C&K offer no definition of complexity, it is considered to be unity. WMC is therefore a measure of size, and equivalent to the number of methods in the class.

2. Depth of Inheritance Tree (DIT). This metric measures the maximum level of the inheritance hierarchy of a class; the root of the inheritance tree inherits from no class and is at level zero of the inheritance tree. DIT was intended to indicate the potential for reuse, and to indicate the complexity of the design.

3. Number of Children (NOC). This metric counts the number of subclasses belonging to a class. C&K suggest that the NOC can be used to indicate the level of reuse in a system, and hence be used as a possible indicator of the level of testing required.

4. Lack of Cohesion in Methods (LCOM). This metric purports to measure the lack of cohesion in the methods of a class. It is based on the principle that a variable occurring in many methods of a class causes that class to be less cohesive than one where the same variable is used in few methods of the class. As one would expect, C&K view a lack of cohesion as undesirable.

5. Coupling Between Objects (CBO). This metric measures the level of coupling between classes. Coupling between two classes is said to occur when one class uses functions or variables of another class. C&K suggest CBO as an indication of the effort needed for maintenance and testing. A high CBO is considered undesirable.

0-8186-7840-2/97 $10.00 © 1997 IEEE

6. Response For a Class (RFC). This metric counts the occurrences of calls to other classes from a particular class. In other words, the set of all methods which can be invoked in response to a message to an object of the class. C&K view RFC as an indication of class complexity (and hence a reflection of the testing effort required).

3. Description of Lorenz and Kidd Metrics

We now describe ten metrics proposed by Lorenz and Kidd (L&K). We note that many other metrics were suggested by L&K in [15]. However, the ten metrics described give a fair cross-section of the broad areas covered. Unlike the C&K metrics, most of the L&K metrics are direct metrics, and include more directly countable measures, e.g., the Number of Methods (NM) metric, and the Number of Variables (NV) metric. Although relatively simple to collect, doubt can be cast on the usefulness of such metrics because they give only a limited insight into the architecture of the system under investigation. For each of the metrics considered, L&K offered some justification for the existence of that metric and we include that justification in the following analysis. The ten metrics can be summarised as:

1. Number of Public Methods (PM). This simply counts the number of public methods in a class. According to L&K, this metric is useful as an aid to estimating the amount of work to develop a class or subsystem.

2. Number of Methods (NM). The total number of methods in a class counts all public, private and protected methods defined. L&K suggest this metric as a useful indication of the classes which may be trying to do too much work themselves; i.e., they provide too much functionality.

3. Number of Public Variables per class (NPV). This metric counts the number of public variables in a class. L&K consider the number of variables in a class to be one measure of its size. The fact that one class has more public variables than another might imply that the class has more relationships with other objects and, as such, is more likely to be a *key class*, i.e., a central point of co-ordination of objects within the system.

4. Number of Variables per class (NV). This metric counts the total number of variables in a class. The total number of variables metric includes public, private and protected variables. According to L&K, the ratio of private and protected variables to total number of variables indicates the effort required by that class in providing information to other classes. Private and protected variables are therefore viewed merely as data to service the methods in the class.

5. Number of Methods Inherited by a subclass (NMI). This metric measures the number of methods inherited by a subclass. No mention is made as to whether that inheritance is public or private. In a language such as C++, we have to consider the possibility that the inheritance may be private, Then, any classes using methods from a subclass would not necessarily have access to all of the inherited methods.

6. Number of Methods Overridden by a subclass (NMO). A subclass is allowed to re-define or override a method in its superclass(es) with the same name as a method in one of its superclasses. According to L&K, a large number of overridden methods indicates a design problem, indicating that those methods were overridden as a design afterthought. They suggest that a subclass should really be a specialisation of its superclasses, resulting in new unique names for methods.

7. Number of Methods Added by a subclass (NMA). According to L&K, the normal expectation for a subclass is that it will further specialise (or add) methods to the superclass object. A method is defined as an added method in a subclass if there is no method of the same name in any of its superclasses.

8. Average Method Size (AMS). The average method size is calculated as the number of non-comment, non-blank source lines (NCSL) in the class, divided by the number of its methods. AMS is clearly a size metric, and would be useful for spotting outliers, i.e., abnormally large methods.

9. Number of times a Class is Reused (NCR). The definition of NCR given by L&K is somewhat ambiguous. We assume the metric is intended to count the number of times a class is referenced (i.e., reused) by other classes. In this sense, we could view reuse in a similar way to coupling. We could then consider NCR as a measure of the extent of inter-class communication, and in this respect, a high value for NCR as undesirable.

10. Number of Friends of a class (NF). This metric measures, for each class, the number of friends of that class. Friends allow encapsulation to be violated, and as such should be used with care. A high number of friends within a class could indicate a potential design flaw, an oversight in design, which has filtered through to the coding stage; we note in passing that friends are a concept specific to the C++ language. NF is a measure of class coupling, since friends may rely on a particular class (or classes) to operate properly.

4. Description of Abreu Metrics

The set of six metrics developed by Abreu [5] were intended to be *design* metrics. The emphasis behind the development of the metrics is on the features of inheritance, encapsulation and coupling. The six metrics can be summarised as:

1. Polymorphism Factor (PF). This metric is based on the number of overriding methods in a class as a ratio of the total possible number of overridden methods. Polymorphism arises from inheritance, and Abreu claims that in some cases, overriding methods reduce complexity, so increasing understandability and maintainability.

2. Coupling Factor (CF). This metric counts the number of inter-class communications. There is a similarity here with the NCR metric of L&K. Abreu views coupling as increasing complexity, reducing both encapsulation and potential reuse and limiting understandability and maintainability.

3. Method Hiding Factor (MHF). This metric is the ratio of hidden (private or protected) methods to total methods. As such, MHF is proposed as a measure of encapsulation.

4. Attribute Hiding Factor (AHF). This metric is the ratio of hidden (private or protected) attributes to total attributes. AHF is also proposed as a measure of encapsulation.

5. Method Inheritance Factor (MIF). This metric is a count of the number of inherited methods as a ratio of total methods. There is a similarity here with the NCR metric of L&K. Abreu proposes MIF as a measure of inheritance, and consequently as a means of expressing the level of reuse in a system. It could also claim to be an aid to assessment of testing needed.

6. Attribute Inheritance Factor (AIF). This metric counts the number of inherited attributes as a ratio of total attributes. Just as for the MIF, Abreu proposes AIF as a means of expressing the level of reuse in a system. It is claimed, however, that too much reuse causes a deterioration in understandability and testability.

5. Analysis of the three metric suites

Each of the individual metrics in the three metric suites just described purport to measure some attribute(s) of an object-oriented system. Various shortcomings emerge when we begin to consider criteria important in designing, using and interpreting object-oriented metrics for real systems. The first consideration concerns that of *validity*.

5.1. Validity of Metrics

The theoretical approach to the validation of metrics requires us to clarify what attributes of software we are measuring, and how we go about measuring those attributes [12, 4, 1, 8]. A metric must measure what it purports to measure.

Fenton [9] describes the *representation condition*, satisfaction of which is the pre-requisite for any metric to be viewed as valid. The representation condition states that any measurement mapping must map entities into numbers, and empirical relations into numerical relations, such that those relations are preserved. In other words, our observations in the real world must be reflected in the numerical values we obtain from the mathematical world.

Kitchenham et al. describe a list of features of metrics which must hold for that metric to be valid [12]. A direct metric must not exhibit any unexpected discontinuities, should use the appropriate measurement scale, should be dimensionally consistent and be based on an explicitly defined model of the relationship between attributes.

5.2. Example 1

Consider the Weighted Methods Per Class metric (WMC) of C&K. It was intended to be a measure of complexity, but, in the absence of any definition of complexity, is a measure of class size. We can not view WMC as an indicator of the effort to develop a class, since a class containing a single large method may take as long to develop as a class containing a large number of small methods. The same can be said of the L&K Public Methods (PM) metric.

5.3. Example 2

Consider the Depth of Inheritance Tree metric (DIT) of C&K. It was intended to be an indication of the potential for reuse, but is actually a direct count of the levels in an inheritance hierarchy. It is easy to envisage an inheritance hierarchy which was very deep and yet reused the same number of methods as a shallow, wide hierarchy; using the DIT metric in this case would, however, give very different answers for the two systems.

5.4. Example 3

Consider three metrics: the Response for a Class (RFC) metric of C&K, the Number of Methods Inherited by a subclass (NMI) metric and the Number of times a Class is Reused (NCR) metric, the latter two both of L&K. In each, there is some ambiguity in exactly what the respective designers meant the metric to measure. This forces the user to guess what they think the metric was intended to measure.

Clearly, there is a need for a formal definition of each metric so that there is no ambiguity in its interpretation. It is difficult to validate a metric if its definition is ambiguous.

5.5. Example 4

Consider the Number of Variables per class (NV) metric of L&K. It is claimed that the ratio of private and protected variables to total number of variables is an indication of the effort required by that class to provide information to other classes. However, some would claim that all variables should be be hidden, so maximising encapsulation.

5.6. Example 5

Consider the Polymorphism Factor (PF) metric of Abreu. It is defined as the ratio of overridden methods to total possible overridden methods. Hence, if there is no inheritance in the system under consideration, then the denominator of the metric calculation is zero (giving an infinite value for the metric itself). This would seem to contradict a feature stated by Kitchenham et al [12], i.e., that a metric should not have any unexpected discontinuities.

5.7. The need for empirical evaluation

Numerous authors have suggested that theoretical validation of any set of metrics should not be the only support for a proposed set of metrics. It should be accompanied by empirical evaluation, using proven statistical and experimental techniques; in this way, the practical applicability of any new metrics in the field can be assessed [4, 1, 2, 17]. For example, in [4], Briand et al. describe metrics for cohesion and coupling, showing how an in-depth empirical evaluation demonstrated and supported the usefulness and significance of the set of metrics they proposed. Again, we give a number of examples to illustrate the ideas.

5.8. Example 1

Consider the Number of Friends (NF) metric of L&K which suggests that too many friends indicates a design flaw, and is indicative of oversights in design. This thesis could be supported by perhaps trying to identify a relationship between NF and the number of modification requests (MR's). A high number of MR's indicates a poor design and so the existence of a relationship between the two would add weight to this claim.

5.9. Example 2

Consider the Coupling Factor (CF) metric of Abreu. Coupling is viewed as undesirable, and is claimed to increase complexity and reduce both encapsulation and potential reuse. The thesis regarding increased complexity would be supported more strongly if an empirical evaluation were performed to identify any correlation between CF and, perhaps, a subjective measure of the complexity of each class (provided by the system designer). The thesis regarding encapsulation would be supported by identifying a relationship between CF and private/protected methods of a class; the reuse thesis would be supported by identifying a relationship between CF and a measure of reuse, such as the number of methods reused.

5.10. Example 3

Consider the Number of Children (NOC) metric of C&K. It is claimed to give an indication of the level of testing required. One way to support this thesis might be to investigate the relationship between NOC values and the testing times for each class. Such times can be easily and accurately collected during testing.

5.11. Data Collection

One of the main problems with the three sets of metrics proposed is the difficulty in collecting raw data from the code in order to calculate the metric values. For large systems, collection of the more involved metrics becomes prohibitively time-consuming. For example, calculation of the Lack of Cohesion in Methods (LCOM) metric (C&K), requires careful consideration of the use of variables in a class, and so is only practical for systems with a small number of classes; similarly for the Coupling Between Objects (CBO) metric (C&K). We also note that, in systems with no inheritance, the collection of metrics such as C&K's, L&K's and Abreu's becomes relatively trivial. Although this makes the metrics collection easier, our understanding of the system being analysed is then limited by a large number of metrics with values of zero.

5.12. Tool Support

There is very little tool support for metrics collection. The tool used to produce some of the values in [10], and which collects Abreu's set of metrics, tends to consume a lot of machine resources, and it is not entirely clear how the results obtained have been calculated. Performing a manual collection (where possible) from the code to validate the results is a painstaking, yet necessary task.

5.13. The over-emphasis on code metrics

Many of the metrics outlined are simply **code** metrics in the sense that they are measures of the code's characteristics. The WMC and LCOM metrics of C&K are two prime examples of this. Yet, the three set of metrics studied claim to be high-level design metrics, and to indicate features of object-oriented systems design. It would be more useful to have metrics which measured the quality of the design at a much higher level of abstraction. Flaws in the design could then be identified before they filtered through to the code. This might just possibly alleviate the maintenance and testing problems with which all systems seem to suffer. The many object-oriented design and modelling techniques currently available could be used as a basis for these high-level metrics [16, 3, 19, 18].

5.14. Quality models

The metrics described give suggestions as to what aspects of quality object-oriented software they would be useful for measuring. Quality factors such as reusability, maintainability and testability are frequently quoted.

However, no concrete notion of what constitutes quality is provided by the designers of the metrics studied. Since quality for the systems developer is perceived differently to quality for the manager or end user, a set of metrics must make clear what it is they are trying to measure and who they are directed at. Metrics based on a properly defined quality model, incorporating ideas from many of the current standard quality models [11, 13] would clarify what quality aspects were being considered, and why they were being considered.

6. Future Directions

From our analysis of the three metric suites considered, a number of problems have been shown to exist with currently available metrics:

1. many of the metrics are suspect in terms of their validity, and often do not measure the attributes of software they purport to measure.
2. there is ambiguity in some of the definitions.
3. very little empirical evaluation exists to support the claims made of the individual metrics.
4. in the absence of tool support, manual collection of metrics can be cumbersome and time-consuming.
5. there is currently an over-emphasis on code metrics.
6. a proper definition of quality, based on rigorously defined quality models has been largely ignored.

Future directions in this field are clearly for metrics which are valid (and unambiguous), are aimed at a higher level of abstraction (the design stage of development), are based on a rigorous model of what constitutes software quality and, finally, are supported by appropriate tools and proper empirical evaluation.

7. Conclusion

In this paper, we have described three sets of object-oriented metrics, the problems associated with those metrics, and suggestions for future directions in this field. The main point to note is that, just as our use and understanding of object-oriented systems is still in its formative stages, so the same is true in the field of object-oriented metrics. As a way forward, we should therefore seek to learn as much as possible from the problems we are currently encountering in this area, and adopt solutions to overcome these problems.

8. Acknowledgements

This work is supported by UK EPSRC project GR/K83021.

References

[1] V. R. Basili, L. Briand, and W. Melo. A validation of OO design metrics as quality indicators. *Technical Report CS-TR-3443*, 1995.

[2] V. R. Basili and H. D. Rombach. The TAME project: Towards improvement-oriented software environments. *IEEE Transactions on Software Engineering*, 14(6):758–773, 1988.

[3] G. Booch. *Object-oriented design with applications.* Benjamin-Cummings, 1991.

[4] L. Briand, S. Morasca, and V. R. Basili. Defining and validating high-level design metrics. *Technical Report CS-TR-3301*, 1994.

[5] F. Brito e Abreu, M. Goulao, and R. Esteves. Toward the design quality evaluation of OO software systems. In *5th Int Conf on Software Quality*, 1995.

[6] S. R. Chidamber and C. F. Kemerer. Moose: Metrics for object oriented software engineering. In *Workshop on Processes and Metrics for Object Oriented Software Development, OOPSLA '93, Washington*, 1993.

[7] S. R. Chidamber and C. F. Kemerer. A metric suite for object oriented design. *IEEE Transactions on Software Engineering*, pages 467–493, 1994.

[8] N. E. Fenton. Software measurement: a necessary scientific basis. *IEEE Transactions on Software Engineering*, 20(3):199–206, 1994.

[9] N. E. Fenton and P. S. L. *Software Metrics, A Rigorous and Practical Approach.* International Thomson Computer Press, 1996.

[10] R. Harrison, S. Counsell, and R. Nithi. Empirical assessment of object-oriented design metrics. In *Proceedings of Empirical Assessment in Software Engineering (EASE) '97, Keele, UK*, 1997.

[11] ISO/IEC. Joint technical committee: Information technology - software product evaluation - quality characteristics and guidelines for their use. International standard, ISO/IEC, 1991.

[12] B. A. Kitchenham, S. L. Pfleeger, and N. Fenton. Towards a framework for software measurement validation. *IEEE Transactions on Software Engineering*, 21(12):929–944, 1995.

[13] B. A. Kitchenham, J. D. Walker, and I. Domville. Test specification and quality management - design of a qms subsystemfor quality requiremnets specification. Project Deliverable A27, Alvey Project SE/031, Nov 1986.

[14] W. Li and S. Henry. Maintenance metrics for the object-oriented paradigm. In *Proceedings of the First International Software Metrics Symposium, Baltimore Maryland*, pages 52–60, May 1993.

[15] M. Lorenz and J. Kidd. *Object-oriented Software Metrics*. Prentice Hall Object-Oriented Series, 1994.

[16] J. Rumbaugh, M. Blaha, W. Premerlani, F. Eddy, and W. Lorenson. *Object-oriented modelling and design*. PHI, 1991.

[17] N. F. Schneidewind. Methodology for validating software metrics. *IEEE Transactions on Software Engineering*, 18(5):410–422, 1992.

[18] S. Shlaer and S. Mellor. *Object-Oriented Systems Analysis: Modelling the World in Data*. Prentice Hall, 1988.

[19] R. Wirfs-Brock, B. Wilkerson, and L. Wiener. *Designing Object-Oriented Software*. Prentice Hall, 1990.

Session P3c

Configuration Management and System Interconnection Tools

Software Configuration Management Tools

Angus K.F. Chan
City University of Hong Kong
Department of Computer Science
83 Tat Chee Avenue, Kowloon, Hong Kong
kfchan@cs.cityu.edu.hk

Sheung-lun Hung
City University of Hong Kong
Department of Computer Science
83 Tat Chee Avenue, Kowloon, Hong Kong
cshung@cityu.edu.hk

Abstract

Software Configuration management is concerned with the identification, organizing, and controlling the configuration of and changes to a system under parallel development environment. It should encompass all system components. However, most existing software configuration management tools have emphasized too much on version control of source files and have neglected some of the other vital functionality. In this paper, recommendations are made to the desirable features that should be incorporated in future tools to make them truly effective in the software development process.

1. Introduction

Software Configuration Management (SCM) is concerned with the identification, organization and control of the software components known as configurable items in a software system under a parallel development environment. The configurable items should include all system components such as source codes, documents, test plans etc. The goal of SCM is to maximize software productivity and improve quality by minimizing mistakes [1]. Software quality is ensured through managing changes that occur during the software development process. IEEE provides definitions for SCM activities known as Configuration Identification, Configuration Control, Status Accounting, Audits and Reviews [2]. As a result of the lack of general framework to guide software engineers in their implementation of tools to support the defined SCM activities, there exists a great deal of confusion in the interpretation of the terminology and functions. The problem is further complicated by most of the tool designers whose concern is with larger scale software development. It is the belief of the authors that SCM has an important role to play for small and medium size projects and the definitions of the SCM activities should be modified and be extended to provide more concrete but at the same time more flexible guides to all SCM tool designers. This paper aims to review some of the important SCM activities and discuss the relevant implementation issues. In the following, the authors attempt to identify some of the problem areas associated with standard SCM activities.

1.1. Identification

One of the basic requirements of SCM tools [3] is to provide information on all software configurable items. The information includes description of each configurable item, linkages and interdependencies with other items. Identifying the correct item is important for many reasons. For example, if the wrong version of a software item is being used, bug fixes in a program can quite easily resurfaced when the older version of the item is inadvertently used with other modules. Items interdependence are especially important during system build where the software items are combined and compiled into derived objects. The interdependency information can be used as blueprints for the construction of derived objects, e.g. the description may be the version number and the options of the components to be used in the particular system build. In the case of a distributed system build, the problem is complicated by the need to combine objects which may reside into different physical systems into an executable object. Identification has been implemented in a number of SCM tools but their effectiveness have rarely been evaluated. Some of the observed problem areas with these tools include:

0-8186-7840-2/97 $10.00 © 1997 IEEE

1. Most of the current tools focus on identifying the correct version of source and object files. However, few facilitate the identification of documents such as specification and test plans.

2. It is important to understand the structures of software objects. If a constituent item of a software object is changed, all affected items should be changed. A kind of bill of material is required to facilitate developers' awareness of the inter-dependencies between the configurable items. Graphical support to display the structural dependencies should be most valuable but is currently unavailable in the market.

1.2. Configuration Control

No system developments are immune to changes. Changes to software configurable items should be properly controlled and monitored. Changes can occur not only to the source and executable files, but to other configurable items such as documents. Change requests from members of the development team should be vetted by a change control board (CCB) which either approves or disapproves the changes. Current SCM tools have very rigid approval procedures and change control board composition. An area for improvement should be to allow flexibility in the composition of the CCB and the procedures to reflect the size and scope of the software project. For medium to small projects, the substantial delays and overheads incurred are normally unacceptable. To further expedite the change request process, an efficient means of communication is required. CCB and development team members may reside at geographically dispersed areas and a good email service is required in support of the change request process.

Another essential element of configuration control is the check-in/out facility. The check-in/out facility controls the manner configurable items are being modified. Software development normally involved a team working concurrently. Without proper management and control of these concurrent activities, to maintain the software system's integrity [4] is a difficult if not impossible task. An Example of the problem associated with parallel software development is in the modification of a source program by several programmers with one programmer accidentally destroying the work of another programmer. Parallel software development can involve a development team spatially dispersed over a wide area but sharing same source files and derived objects residing in computers with different hardware and software configurations. SCM tools should provide remote access over heterogeneous computer networks [5] and to provide distributed transaction management for the shared software objects [6]. Logical changes to programs such as bug fixes or enhancements are usually complex and slow, traditional transaction management models are probably too costly and some new forms of conflict management are required. An example is the more elaborate transaction model. Up to date, there is no commercial implementation of well designed distributed transaction models in SCM tools.

Many authors [7], [8], [9] has made many discussion on version and revision control as it is the heart of configuration control. Unfortunately, there is still a great deal of confusion on the usage of the terms revision control and version control in most commercial tools. Revision should refer to the sequential evolution of a module. For example, when a module is edited, the result is known as a revision of that module. On the other hand, a version represents a variant of a given module for another application. A release occurs only whenever a version of the module is ready for sale as a product or has become official. Of the many features in configuration control, traditional SCM tools have focused mainly on revision, version and release control but isolated from other aspects of software development [10]. One of the major weaknesses of all existing tool is the integration of version and release management with the development tools and environment. A seamless integration can streamline the development process and improve productivity as developers are not forced to waste time on the SCM tool.

1.3. Status Accounting

SCM tools should keep a continuous record of all changes and problems to insure against disasters as well as to ensure the quality of the software development process. However, there is confusion as to the type of information to be recorded in such a process. Most traditional SCM tools which claim to have implemented the function offer nothing more than simple information such as the release, level, date and time of creation, etc. In the authors' view, they are inadequate and is of little use in the quality assurance process. Few SCM tools actually keep track of changes to configurable items in terms of defects and enhancements for productivity and project progress assessment. The process of logging and displaying the relevant information should be highly efficient so as not to create overheads on the development process.

1.4. Configuration Audit

Proper authorization procedures should be in place to ensure the accuracy of the product. Configuration audit helps to ensure the software product is as specified by the system requirement. The software development process should be verified, validated through formal reviews and inspections performed on all source files and documents. Mechanisms to automate or semi-automate the review and inspection process should be an interesting research area which are not currently supported in most commercial tools.

1.5. Vendor Control

Subcontracting, outsourcing, the use of shareware and reusable components are fast becoming the a major part rather than a trend for the software industry. Few SCM tools have built in facility to control the usage of third party software. Vendor Control refers to the monitoring and control of all third party software and extends to all relevant documents, plans, tools and tests etc. There is currently few guidelines or discussions in the literature on how this should be carried out. With their ever growing importance, there is great urgency in formulating some formal methodologies in the area.

Of the above mentioned SCM activities, all earlier SCM tools tend to emphasize on version/release (or revision) control of source files. Well known examples are MAKE (A Program for Maintaining Computer Programs) [11] and SCCS (The Source Code Control System) [12]. To a certain extent, they have also control over some of the documents, but they do not possess full documentation control functions. The identification function in these tools concern primarily with identifying the revision numbers of the source files. As a rule, the identification of the inter-relationships between software configurable items (including library functions) is non existing in any of the tools. The Revision Control System RCS [13] differs from others in its change control feature in the form of check-in/out facility. RCS also distinguishes itself in its ability to freeze a revision for baselining [14]. Current SCM tools have increasingly focused on the importance of distributed software developments across homogeneous as well as heterogeneous computer networks [15]. However, distributed transaction management other than simple locking is absent from nearly all commercial implementations. Although a number of tools have facilities for status accounting, they are rarely comprehensive enough to offer much help in improving the quality of software products. With few exceptions, most SCM tools offer no support in the areas of configuration audit and vendor control.

In section 2 of this paper, a survey is presented of some of the popular SCM tools and their main design features. Direct comparison between SCM tools is difficult as each tool tends to focus on SCM activities and adopting different terminology. In section 3, a functional evaluation based on a measure of the expectation from the users' viewpoint is presented with recommendations on some new design features. In section 4, the conclusion is drawn with suggestions on future work.

2. Survey on Current SCM tools

Since the establishment of Software Configuration Management as a discipline of Software Engineering, many SCM tools are available commercially. However, the majority have over emphasized on version and release control of source files but have neglected other equally important requirements of SCM. An example is configuration audit which has received little attention to-date. In this section, the authors present a brief introduction to some of the more popular SCM tools currently available in the market. The SCM tools can be broadly classified into first and second generation tools. The first generation tools focus mainly on version and release control whereas the second generation tools pay much more attention to network support for parallel software development.

2.1. First Generation SCM tools

Of the many first generation SCM tools, three tools namely SCCS, MAKE and RCS stand out as the most important. Other than simple version/release controls, they all have unique features which cannot be found in similar tools of the same generation.

2.1.1. The Source Code Control System (SCCS) [12] : SCCS is a UNIX based source code revision control system. It can store multiple revisions of source files in the form of an ancestral tree structure. It is one of the early systems which incorporated change control and status accounting features.

Its Change Control Mechanism controls changes to source files through a couple of security features. The SCCS's protection facilities control what modules a programmer can add to, and in which software release. SCCS keeps a list of releases that should be *locked* for each module. Consequently, programmers cannot add to the locked releases. Some implementation may in addition keeps a *name access list* for each module or maintains *release passwords* to control the addition to a password protected release. SCCS requires an administrator's password in order to perform administrator functions such as setting locks and passwords, changing the *name access list*, creating or deleting modules etc. SCCS treats each software module as a set of related sequences of source code, each member represents one version of the module. Versions are consecutively added into the set as each time the original module was changed (the term versions should be treated as revisions). AS all versions of a module are stored together in the same file, storage space requirement is extremely high. In order to save storage, source codes common to more than one version is not duplicated. SCCS makes use of the concept of *delta* storage [16] to achieve this end.

In order to determine the correct version of the source code, SCCS places identification information as a set pre-defined *identification keywords* within the source code provides. Each keyword represents one piece of information, e.g. R stands for the release, L stands for the level, D stands for the date, etc.

Status Accounting is another distinct feature of SCCS is documentation generation. It automatically records the time when the programmer adds a new delta, the places of source lines change. However, the reason for the delta change must be provided the programmer manually. SCCS makes use of this documentation to provide several reports, e.g. whenever a module is accessed, SCCS display a chart that shows the release, level, date and time of creation, who added it, why added etc. This information is useful when something goes wrong with a program. Status accounting is achieved through logging this information for each revision.

SCCS is often combined with the SCM tool known as MAKE to expand its functionality.

2.1.2 MAKE [11]:

MAKE allows the programmer to maintain, update, and regenerate groups of computer programs. It is a simple tool by itself and are normally used with other SCM tools. It's adaptability explains why it has been widely used by UNIX programmers since 1975. One of its most distinct features is the provision of software structure identification (information on the inter-dependence between software items) in support of its version control mechanism. A software system is normally composed of a group of dependent computer programs, e.g. program file B may depend on file A. If a change occurs in B, A may be required to be updated. MAKE maintains the dependencies through a file called *makefie*. It contains a description of the dependencies in form of a dependency line between a target and a source. Each dependency line is followed by one or more commands. Whenever a source is newer than its corresponding target, MAKE executes commands in the makefile to update the target. By keeping track of the status of the components in the system, it ensures the final system is built from the correct component pieces. The makefiles can also act as the configuration specifications by providing information such as how and what compilers should be used to compile a particular source file. It can synchronize the source with its object with auto-compilation.

It supports an auto-checkout (a very simple form of change request control). It is often called a front-end tool because of its common usage with other SCM tools.

2.1.3. Revision Control System (RCS) [13]

RCS is UNIX based SCM tool that provides revision/version control. Revisions are organized into an ancestral tree that permits easy management. One of the powerful features of RCS is that it provides several methodologies in its implementation of delta storage. One of its distinct features is Check-in/out control and baselining.

It supports check-in/out function**...xx** but not really suitable for a multiple developers environment as lock overriding (breaking) is permitted. Simple security control is implemented through access lists. Revisions can be frozen for baselining..**xx**.

Logging is supported in support of simple status accounting. RCS can be combined with MAKE to handle configuration processing.

The following is a list of a few SCM tools which are little more than simple revision control systems:

2.1.4. CLEAR/CASTER [17]

It is one of the earliest of the SCM tools. It provides simple revision control on the source files together with documentation and messages. This tool provides control over the whole developmental process.

2.1.5. Software Development Control System [18]

It is a very simple revision control system with no more than 2 revisions at a time. A complete log of the old revisions are kept as a form of status accounting. It is sometimes used with MAKE.

2.1.6. DEC Code Management System (CMS) [19]

A very simple revision control system for DEC computers. It manages tree-structured revisions in groups. It is often used with MAKE.

2.1.7. Others

ENDEVOR/MVS works in the MVS/TSO environment with text-mode interface only. It main distinctive features are change request processing, configuration control board (CCB) and very good security control. auto-compilation (synchronization of source and object) is another important feature but it suffers from the lack of user-friendly GUIs. *Lifespan* supports packaging implying that related components can be automatically packed into a package. *Change and Configuration Control/Development and Maintenance CCC/DM* is a tool which supports four configurations: development, test, approved and production. It does not allow modification of any previous released items. Another important feature is the support for emergency changes.

2.2. SECOND GENERATION SCM TOOLS

2.2.1. Aollo's DSEE [20]

Domain Software Engineering Environment (DSEE) is designed to manage large-scale development where data are normally spread among many locations. To support this distributed network computing environment, it provides configuration management (system building) and history management (source code control) to satisfy the need of programming-in-the-large under the parallel environment. It aims to fully utilize the computing resources distributed over a wide area network. DSEE provides very efficient support for parallel software development in a network environment.

<u>System Builder</u>

System building can be performed in parallel. In DSEE, system building is based on three principal concepts:

A *system model* that describes the components of a system and their dependency relationship. It also provides sufficient information to decide which components can be built in parallel.

A *configuration thread* that describes the version of each components to be used for a particular system build and specifies the options to be used during translation of each component. A configuration thread tells us which revision one is working on in a particular revision group (e.g. A may be working on revision 1.1. and B on revision 1.2 of the same revision group).

A *derived object pool* that contains a collection of arbitrary versions of binary files and other objects produced by translators during system building.

When you want to build all or part of a system, an appropriate system model and configuration thread are selected. The configuration manager combine the system model and configuration thread to produce a desired version description. This description is used to search the derived-object pool. If a component is found, its associated derived objects are reused; otherwise, an appropriate translator is invoked to rebuild the component in accordance with the desired version description.

<u>Building Arbitrary Configurations in Parallel</u>

The source code control system (DSEE history manager) is closely integrated with the system builder to support rebuilding a component according to a specific version description. It uses delta system to save storage space for source element. It enables transparent access to any version of a source element by using a per-process version map, which allows simultaneous building of different system versions from same set source elements. This ability is essential for building arbitrary configurations in parallel.

<u>Parallel System Build</u>

DSEE includes a parallel builder which support concurrently building several components by using the available network computing resources. When the configuration needs to build several components, it starts a parallel building process. The scheduler continues to submit builds in accordance with the partial ordering of the system model as long as there are buildable components and available build servers. The builders on remote computers automatically read source codes from various file servers and write the results to file servers that contain the derived object pools. Overall status and progress of the building process can be seen from a continuously updated graphics display.

Other than the parallel build features, DSEE is very similar to SCCS in functionality. It also provides a mechanism to alert maintainers about the need for system rebuild after a change.

2.2.2. Micro-focus & Intersolv PVCS Option [21]

PVCS is a well-known tool for software configuration management with the LAN environment. It consists of a family of tools that gives you capabilities for version management, reporting, problem and change request tracking, configuration building , promotion and transfer to production. The family consists of Version Manager, Configuration Builder, Reporter and Production Gateway.

Version Manager

The Version Manager has a good document handler that supports revision management, version management and promotion management, access control (security), item locking to permit parallel development, very comprehensive status accounting facilities and delta storage between revisions. An additional feature is its ability to allow developers to add services (user configurable). For revision management, it helps manage the revisions of any program source, executable, graphic or text or binary file. Any change to the system is automatically organized and recorded. For version management, , it clearly defines and manages versions of program builds. For promotion management, it provides the ability to define your project in a promotion model. Consequently, programmers can know the status of their code in the development, and manager can control the movement from one step to the next and to ensure that fixes are tested and included in the production system. The version manager also provides support for code sharing across all development platforms, and locks across the network are possible to prevent unnecessary overwrites.

Configurable Builder

The Configuration Builder is a system constructor that automates the process of reliably reconstructing a software system It eliminates build errors by using a built script that enable repeatable, automated builds of your software development projects. One of the most important feature of the configuration builder is 'footprinting'. It is something like putting remarks in source programming. It is automatically added to source codes. The problem of tracking is made easier by providing this historical data.

Production Gateway

Production gateway permits multi-platform operation. It can be used with IBM's Software Configuration & Library Manager (SCLM) and other IBM products.

2.2.3. Parallel Software Development (CVSII) [33]

Besides revision/release control, UNIX based CVSII distinguished itself for its multiple developers support. It allows concurrent access with build-in conflict resolution. It has Check-in/out facility but no user request control. It cannot remember 'who' has checked out a copy of the source. It is one of the few systems that provide subcontractor (third party vendor source) tracking. User configurability is another one of its important feature. One of the major weaknesses of CVS II is the lack of security on the source repository and baselining and is often used together with RCS.

2.2.4. Network Software Environment (NSE) [22]

Multiple developers can transparently access the same configuration and to work in their private workplace (child environment). These private workplaces are isolated from each other but their relationships are maintained through NSE. It offers good team work support since each developer can work in its workplace but NSE can still coordinate and synchronize the change in the workplaces to the parent environment.

2.2.5. Parallel Configuration Management System (PCMS) [23]

PCMS works under UNIX, Ultrix and VMS environments. Besides providing revision/release control and tracking (status accounting), PCMS was designed for heterogeneous distributed networks (LAN) environment with client server support with ORACLE as the relational database management system. Other than parallel development support, it offers additional features such as:

- Documentation change control.
- Security and integrity are enforced.
- Change requests control in place through emails for feedbacks and event processing.
- Status accounting is provided with fault reporting facility.
- Check-in/out facility for all modified items.

PCMS has many nice features but the lack of WAN support is one of its major weaknesses.

Most of the first generation SCM tools focus mainly on version/revision control whereas the second generation tools distinguish themselves from the first generation SCM tools in the parallel development support.

3. SCM Tools Evaluation

3.1. Identification

One purpose of identification is to provide the ability to recognize, maintain and access the correct version of source and object codes. Most tools that provide this function are very similar in nature. The source and object code are normally stamped with predefined identification strings and keywords that contain the essential information of the configuration items. One typical string may contain the revision number, date, time and author. An example is RCS which identifies items through a stamping string containing the revision number, date, time and author. In some cases, the information can actually be customized to the user environment [13]. SCCS identifies the correct version of source code item by placing the identification information within the source code itself which will appear when the module is loaded at runtime. SCCS has a set of predefined keywords for pieces of information such as release, date etc.

In the identification of the correct version of source items and the dependency between them (e.g. RCS), there are no shortage of SCM tools. **However, there is a general lack of tools to link the source items to non-source items such as design documents, test cases and test data. This capability is vital to the developer for ensuring making the relevant changes to the documentation whenever there is a change to the source item. In addition, it is also important when an item is tested, the system should allow team members to identify the correct test plan and test cases.**

3.2 Configuration Control

3.2.1. Version Management

a) Versioning

The term versioning actually implies parallel develpment support whereby the system is evolved into variants to fulfill user requirements as a result of different operating environments. To support this mode of development, the SCM tool should provide branching capability to facilitate with ease in the creation of variants from the main development line (the trunk). If necessary, the variants should be allowed to merge back to the trunk. SCCS, RCS, PVCS and DSEE all have simple commands for branching the individual items from the trunk and merge back to the trunk. They also provide commands to compare and print the differences between versions of the same configurable item. NSE views branching in a much more general context by treating it as a function that applies to different versions of the system. In making a branch to a particular version of the item, changes including those of other versions are reconciled and merged back to the original environment [24]. The advantage of such an arrangement is that with other child environment, the change can be made immediately available to others after mergiing. This achieves effective synchronization and sharing of the changes.

b) CM Model

There are currently four different kinds of version management adopted by SCM tools. They are commonly known as Configuration Management (CM) models. Detailed discussions on these models can be found in Feiler [25]. They are:

- Check-in/Check-out Model
- Composition Model
- Transaction Model
- Change Set Model

Of the four models, only the first three models are implemented in commercial systems. Check-in/Check-out model provide independent versioning of the individual configuration item in the system. Concurrent modification of configuration items are facilitated through the use of locking, branching and merging. This model is the most widely adopted in the earlier commercial systems. The composition model improves on the check-in/check-out model by adopting a two steps approach. In the first step, a system model is built to provide information on the composition and structure of the system. Version selection rules are then applied to the system model to choose the required version of the system. Transaction model manages system evolution as a whole. The result is a series of atomic changes for each version of the system configurations (transaction model needs further elaboration). Transaction model provides better support for concurrent modification in a team environment.

UNIX based tools such as SCCS, RCS and PVCS adopt the check-in/check-out model, DSEE is a typical example of the composition model and the transaction model is best represented by NSE. Check-in/check-out tools provide good version management for individual configuration items. It concentrates on the management of the repository but fails to provide support for coordinating the users' workspace. This places severe limitation for team development.

C) Storage

A common problem associated with version control is the requirements to store all versions of each configurable item. In order to save space, the technique known as delta storage is employed to better utilize storage. SCCS and RCS create delta based on longest common sub-string proposed by [16]. However, this method cannot produce minimal delta because it does not cater for crossing block move. DSEE uses algorithm proposed by [26] to detect crossing block move and hence produce a better delta. A faster algorithm was proposed by Tichy [27] to produce a more minimal delta.

There are two techniques adopted for delta storage: the forward delta and the backward delta. In forward delta, system stores the complete first version but only the differences between successive versions. In backward delta, system stores the complete latest version but the differences of all previous versions. Backward delta saves time for accessing new versions whereas forward delta requires less space when there are many lines in a delta tree. SCSS stores items in forward delta, whereas RCS, PVCS, DSEE and NSE all use backward delta. As access time rather than space is of more concern to most tool designers, it is obvious that backward delta is the preferred choice for the more recent tools.

D) Project Structure

Hierarchy of directories are very useful means of managing project files. Large projects are normally composed of many sub-projects and it is important that developers can concentrate on their sub-project but can at the same access system codes of other sub-projects for system builds and integration testing purposes. However, it is interesting to find that few SCM tools support such project structures, e.g. SCCS, RCS and DSEE all do not support hierarchical project directories. Others such as PVCS, which appear to support hierarchical directories are in reality flat directories systems. Versioning should be performed on all items of a sub-directory as a composite.

3.2.2. Change Management

It is of vital importance that any change to the repository should be tightly controlled. Change request should be subject to authorization to determine either to approve or reject the change. Change request control can also provide good source of information for tracking changes. SCCS, RCS, DSEE and NSE all do not provide change request mechanism. PVCS is one of the few tools which provide comprehensive change request control. It also provide requesters update information on the status of his/her request.

Change request besides providing the means of submitting, controlling, evaluating and tracking of changes, should have the capability of modifying multiple source, header, program documentation and test data together. In other words, the SCM tool should allow the change requester to group related items to be modified as a single logical unit.

3.2.3. Access Control/Promotion Level Control

a) Access Control

All changes to the repository of a software system should be guarded against unauthorized or accidental access. Users and groups of users should be assigned with specific privileges and restrictions at both project and individual item level. Access rights should include read, modify, add and delete. SCCS, RCS, DSEE, NSE have additional security features on top of what is provided by UNIX, e.g. RCS has its own access control list for individual item and only users on the list can perform update operation on the item. PVCS is a tool with all its own sophisticated security features. It provides a set of predefined base privileges and restrictions. For groups with similar privileges and restrictions, one can predefine composite privileges and restrictions in an effort to simplify the procedure for defining access rights. One of the major security fault of PVCS is that file archives can be accessed directly outside PVCS.

Security control is in general weak for PC and UNIX based SCM tools. For projects with geographically dispersed team members, better security is required.

b) Promotion Level

Software development goes through well defined phases known as the life cycle. Promotion level defines the progression from one phase to the next phase. It is important that control should be applied to items at each level, e.g. only software testers can access test level items. SCCS, RCS, DSEE and NSE all do not provide mechanism for defining promotion levels and PVCS is the only one that supports such a function. The concept of promotion level works well at the project level but is impractical when the items are shared between several projects. A confusing situation will occur when the same item is being used by different projects at different promotion levels.

Promotion level control for shared projects has yet to be implemented in commercial tools.

3.2.4. Release Management

Release specify the collection of specific revisions of configurable items which construct a particular software system to be distributed to users of the system. There are two aspects of release management to be considered;

namely Release Production Control and System Delivery. Release production control refers to the identification of all configurable items for a particular release and the tracking of all releases. It should ensure that all items of a release has the full approval by an authorized body such as the configuration control board (CCB). In addition, records should be provided of the inter-dependence among different software systems' releases. System delivery on the other hand is concern with the distribution of the right releases to the target users. It must ensure that all items in the configuration list are properly packaged in the software release. None of the tools to-date pay much attention to release management. A primitive form of release control is provided by PVCS in the form of version label to identify software releases.

In general, there is weakness in software release delivery. Most of the delivery system to-date is manual in nature. An ideal scenario should allow developers to semi-automate the process of packaging the correct versions of items for a specific release. The items should include not only the software items but all the relevant documentations. The software release should be distributed directly and electronically through Internet. The system should support transparent browsing and retrieval by users irrespective of their physical locations. SCM tools should preferably have remote installation capability to allow the automated installation of new releases on sites of the customers.

3.2.5. Automatic System Build

System building refers to the process of collecting the correct source items and transforming them into the required system. The process should preferably be made automatic to minimize or even eliminate human errors. System builds in most of the tools involve the use of build scripts which define system architecture and the inter-dependencies among the items. Earlier tools such as SCCS and RCS all lack system build capabilities. They are often used with MAKE to support system build. PVCS's configuration builder is similar to MAKE which makes use of build scripts for automatic system construction. The dependency scanning feature of PVCS allows the computation of item dependencies which can be used to update the build script for system construction later. DSEE went a step further by combining its system build model with the configuration thread to obtain the Desired Version Description for the release. The description is used to search the derived object pool for the desired object items. If the item is found, it is reused whereas the item will be retrieved from the repository. DSEE also provides the outstanding parallel system build feature for concurrent system builds.

Configurable items are normally distributed across a network, but with the exception of DSEE, few tools provide the support needed for distributed system builds.

3.3. Development Environment

3.3.1. Project Management

Software development is always a team effort and requires a great deal of coordination . Although tools such as PVCS do provide project team management in the form of controlling access to project files and the way different team members can modify different parts of the same project, there is no build in coordination and management of the project team.

Enhancements should be made in the area of control access and project coordination in the context of parallel development.

3.3.2. Communication Support

The distributed nature of the software projects requires efficient and powerful communication support. SCM tools should provide efficient communication channels among project team member as well as other related project team members. Related personnel should be informed of changes to configuration items. The underlying communication architecture should provide the necessary mechanism in support of software activities such as software integration testing.

Though quite a few second generation SCM tools provide simple communication support, few of them available commercially can meet all the requirements.

3.3.3. Integration with Development Environment

All SCM tools should seamlessly integrate with the development environments in support of software activities such as design, coding and testing. The integration should provide users with the transparency that eliminates the need for detailed knowledge of the SCM tool [28]. None of the tools available commercially can provide such kind of integration, e.g. the command co in RCS for checking out files should preferably be replaced by the command ci to assimilate the UNIX environment. The closest to providing this kind of integration is PVCS which has an Application Programming Interface (API) to enable developers to build interfaces which integrate PVCS services with the user application.

Little consideration has been paid to the manner SCM tools should be integrated with the development environment and tools.

3.4 Status Accounting

Status accounting is absent in many of the SCM tools. Good status accounting should track all activities on configuration items. It should inform users of the what, who and why on the item. It should provide flexible but informative reports for management reviews and development reviews. Tools such as SCCS offers simple status accounting information such as the release level, date and time of creation etc.

3.5 Configuration Audit

This is an area rarely implemented in any of the commercially available SCM tools. As most software projects involve end-user departments as well as developers who may be dispersed geographically, the authorization procedures can be extremely troublesome. **Some form of workflow system should be in place to ensure proper procedures are followed.**

3.6 Vendor Control

CVSII is one of the few systems that provide <u>subcontractor</u> (third party vendor source) tracking. The extensive usage of shareware in many software implementation projects has increased the importance of such control mechanism.

3.7 Visual Support

Visual search capability should be provided to pan and zoom across the project hierarchical structure. Users should be able to start from the top level with a more abstract view of the system. They can then navigate down to the subsystem level to retrieve the desired item. Wein [29] has discussed the perceptual issues relating to the benefits of visual support for version management.

Visual supports are general provided but with very limiting function.

3.8 Flexible Project Structuring

Configuration items for a software project normally come under the categories corresponding to different stages of the development life cycle:

1.Requirement and Design Specifications (documents)
2.Product
3.Plans
4.Tools & Libraries
5.Test & records

Category 1should include all user workflow as well. The term product should include both source and object programs for the project (preferably with program logic). Category 3 includes plans such as the test plan, the installation plan, the implementation plan and quality plan. Tools are the tools used in the project. Libraries are the library functions included in the object programs. Test should include all the test cases and test sets used. Results of the tests should be properly recorded. All project structures should be designed in a flexible way to allow users to choose different combinations, e.g. for a programmer, the project structure should only contain 1,2, 3 and 4.

System configuration should include all constituent items of the system. SCM tools should identify the correct version of items to be used as well as identifying the content (constituents) and the dependent relationships among each items. Another important function of identification is to identify the overall structure of the software system. This is important on three counts:

1. User can gain a better understanding of the system and the inter-dependency to facilitate development and maintenance,
2. The build process will run without error.
3. whenever an item is changed, only those affected components need to be changed.

Both SCCS and RCS fail to provide management of the configuration as they solely rely on MAKE to compose the configuration. MAKE maintains dependency information of items in makefile. One of the disadvantages of MAKE is that if the operating environment does not record adequate timing information on items, MAKE cannot determine which file is out of date. In MAKE, the system is broken down into subsystems which stores in sub-directory under the system directory. On system construction, an activation file which stores all revisions is executed to retrieve items for composition.

Domain Software Engineering Environment (DSEE) [20] provides configuration management for system building. It includes a system model that describes the constituent items and their dependencies. It also defines a configuration thread that defined the version required for each item. By combining the configuration thread with the system model, one can identified the desired system configuration. PVCS on the other hand supports a feature called footprinting. It is in a way like a bill of materials that stores a list of items for the whole system. It has a dependency scanning feature that provides an accurate representation among items. With NSE, the system structure is maintained by objects (mostly files) which contain attributes and link type to describe relationship among items [30]. Makefile information is used to track the dependencies between source and derived objects. In addition, NSE supports the logical system structure regardless of the physical location of items through the component concept [24].

4. Conclusion

Most of the existing SCM tools have been designed with mainframes or mid-range development environments and their most of their interfaces are operated in command text mode rather than user-friendly GUI mode. More recent developments such as Intersolv's PVCS have improved user interfaces but are limited to PC and UNIX platforms only. Too much emphasis has been placed on source code and, the problems of identification and documentation control are rarely addressed. An area of confusion is in the usage of the terminology revision, version and release. Very few tools have actually implemented release control. Although some form of status accounting has been implemented in most of the tools, very little emphasis has been placed on problem tracking in relation to project quality and progress assessment. Distributed processing support has so far concentrated to LAN environments and should be extended to multi-platform WAN environments. Almost as a rule, configuration audit is not implemented in these tools. There is also a general lack of vendor control. In order to make SCM tools more effective, the authors proposed the following features should be incorporated:

1. As a norm, source code control is the main thrust of current tools, identification and documentation control should be implemented to improve the effectiveness of these tools.
2. SCM tools should preferably be run on PC platforms with remote access to different hosts (multiple-platforms). User-friendly GUIs are readily supported in Window environment. Security features should also implemented to protect files downloaded form the hosts.
3. Tools must have the ability to support parallel development in a WAN environment TCP/IP should be used to allow developers to perform parallel software development on Internet.
4. Efficient email or communication support should be a standard feature in the implementation of user change request control.
5. Status accounting should include problem tracking and progress review reporting.
6. For the longer term, configuration audit should also be incorporated to enhance the functionality of these tools.

Although Research on software configuration management is maturing, the authors suggest that future research work can focus on the following area to lead to a new generation of SCM tools.

First, can a standardized and unique CM model be evolved instead of continuously proposing different model such as composition and transaction model? The standardized model should combine the merits offered by each CM models. It is a major challenge to SCM tool design. However, the first step for next generation SCM tool should incorporate multiple CM model together in harmony and try to establish a framework that offer the core concept and functionality for the new tool.

Second, should the new SCM tools have a more detailed representation of software architecture? Today's SCM tools only focus on the configuration items for building compiled and executable objects. For example, the system model and configuration thread in DSEE just concentrates on building the executables. In fact, a good SCM tool should represent all configuration items such as include sources and objects, documentation, test data and libraries that all are related to a software product architecture. For example a set of test data are used by a particular source program for unit testing. The relationship among different type of configuration items should be represented. Besides, a good SCM tool should also represent other important architectural information, such as data or control flow connections among the modules[31]. These information facilitate parallel development since a software system can easier to divide into several distinct sub-systems based on the inter-connection information of modules.

Third, should SCM be integrated with CASE tools so as to provide a unique user interface, maximize data sharing and hence minimize redundant data, and allow effective control and coordination on individuals? Obviously, it is a good news on the users' point of view. However, CASE/CM integration face many technical problems. For example, different SCM tools use different

CM models and different CASE tools use different methodologies. Is it necessary to make fundamental change to the implementation of CASE and CM tools that obviously is not welcome by most vendors? Wallnau try to address key issues of integration of CASE and CM from a third-party integrator's perspective in [32].

Finally, with the rapid development of world-wide inter-networking, there is a trend that team development will be distributed. Team members will be physically located in different sites. Future SCM tools should focus on the support of a distributed and parallel development that are suitable for Internet and Wide Area Network (WAN). The SCM should have a good communication support and ensure synchronization of activities on different sites.

References

[1] Babich W., "Software Configuration Management". Prentice Hall, Englewood Cliffs, N.J. 1980.

[2] "IEEE Guide to Software Configuration Management", ANSI/IEEE std 1042-1987, The Institute of Electrical and Electronics Engineers, Inc, September 1987

[3] James A. Mcdonough, "A Structured Menu of Software Configuration Management", IEEE, 1993

[4] Bersoff V. & Henderson S., "Software Configuration Management-An investment in Product Integrity", Prentice Hall Inc., Englewood Cliffs, N.J., 1982.

[5] Leblang D. & Chase R., "Computer-Aided Software Engineering in a Distributed Workstation Environment", SIGPLAN Notices, Vol. 19, No. 5, pp. 104-112, May 1984.

[6] Peter Feiler, Grace Downey, "Transaction-Oriented Configuration Management: A Case Study", Technical Report CMU/SEI-90-TR23, Software Engineering Institute, November 1990.

[7] Bernhard Westfechtel, "Revision Control in an integrated Software Development Environment", Proceeding of the Second International Workshop on Software Version and Configuration Control, ACM, 1989, pp. 96-105

[8] Ian Thomas, "Version and Configuration Management on a Software Engineering Database", Proceeding of the Second International Workshop on Software Version and Configuration Control, ACM, 1989, pp. 23-25

[9] David B. Leblang, "The Challenge : Configuration Management that Works", Configuration Management (Edited by Tichy), Wiley, 1994, pp. 1-37.

[10] Susan A. Dart, "The Past, Present and Future of Configuration Management", Technical Report CMU/SEI-92-TR-8, Software Engineering Institute, July 1992.

[11] Feldman & Stuart, "Make-A Program for Maintaining Computer Programs", Software practice and Experience, Vol. 9, No. 3, pp. 255-256, March 1979.

[12] Rochkind M., "The Source Code Control System", IEEE transactions on Software Engineering, Vol. SE-1, No. 4, pp. 364-370, Dec. 1975.

[13] Tichy W., "RCS-A System for Version Control", Software-Practice and Experience", Vol. 15(7), pp. 637-654, July 1985.

[14] Tichy W. , "Design, Implementation, and Evaluation of a Revision Control System", Proceedings of the 6th International Conference on Software Engineering, pp. 48-67, ACM, IEEE, IPS, NBS, September 1982.

[15] Arthur Lampert, Shaye Koenig, "Configuration Management in a Heterogenous Target Environment", Proceedings of Third Israel Conference on Computer Systems and Software Engineering, IEEE, 1988, pp. 148-158.

[16] James W. Hunt and M.D. McIlory, "An Algorithm for differential file comparison", 41, Computing Science Technical Report, Bell Laboratories, June 1976.

[17] Brown H., "The Clear/Caster System", Nato Conference on Software Engineering, Rome, 1970.

[18] Habermann M., "A Software Development Control System", Technical Report, Department of Computer Science, Carnegie-Mellon University, Jan. 1979.

[19] Digital Equipment Corporation, "Code Management System", Document No. EA-23125-82, 1982.

[20] Leblang D. & Chase R., "Parallel Software Configuration Management in a Network Environment", IEEE Software, Nov. 1987.

[21] Micro Focus, "Micro Focus PVCS Option u5.1", Micro Focus Product Announcement, 1980.

[22] Courington, William, "The Network Software Environment", Technical Report, Sun Microsystems, Inc., 1989

[23] PCMS Overview. SQL software Ltd 1991,1992.

[24] Peter H. Feiler, "Transaction-Oriented Configuration Management: A Case Study", Technical Report CMU/SEI-90-tr-23, Software Engineering Institute, November 1990.

[25] Peter H. Feiler, "Configuration Management Models in Commercial Environments", Technical Report CMU/SEI-91-TR-7, Software Engineering Institute, March 1991.

[26] Heckel P., "A Technique for Isolating Differences Between Files", Communications of the ACM, Vol. 21, No. 4, pp. 264-268, April 1978

[27] Tichy W., "The String-to-String Correction Problem with block moves", ACM Transaction on Computer Systems,2,(4), pp. 309-321, 1984

[28] David Whitgift, "Methods and Tools for Software Configuration Management", John Wiley & Sons Ltd.,pp.35,185, 1991.

[29] Wein, Wm Cowan and W.M. Gentleman, "Visual Support for Version Management", Proceedings of the 1992 ACM/SIGAPP Symposium on Applied Computing (SAC), pp. 1217-1233, March 1992.

[30] Terrence C. Miller, "A Schema for Configuration Management", Proceeding of the Second International Workshop on Software Version and Configuration Control, ACM, 1989, pp. 26-29.

[31] Andre van der Hoek, Dennis Heimbigner, and Alexander L. Wolf, "Does Configuration Mangement Research Have a Future?", In Proceedings of the 5th International Software Configuration Management Workshop, Seattle, USA, April 1995.

[32] Wallnau K., "Issues and Techniques of CASE Integration with Configuration", ", Technical Report CMU/SEI-92-tr-5, Software Engineering Institute, 1992.

[33] Berliner B., "CVSII: Parallelizing Software Development", Prisma Inc., 1985.

An Experience in Setting-Up a Configuration Management Environment[1]

Gianpaolo Cugola[‡], Luigi Lavazza[†‡], Valeria Nart[†], Serena Manca[§], Maria Rosaria Pagone[§]

† CEFRIEL - via Emanueli, 15 20126 MILANO (Italy)
‡ Politecnico di Milano - Dipartimento di Elettronica e Informazione
p.zza Leonardo Da Vinci, 32 20133 MILANO (Italy)
§ SIA - v.le Certosa, 218 20156 MILANO (Italy)

Abstract

Configuration management (CM) is widely recognized as one of the most important practices that have to be established for developing software in an ordered and controlled way. Despite this, the process of setting-up CM has obtained till now very little attention.

This paper reports the lessons learned in establishing CM at SIA (Società Interbancaria per l'Automazione), the organization in charge of running, developing, and maintaining the National Inter-bank Network of Italy.

1. Introduction

Configuration management is widely recognized as one of the most important practices that have to be established for developing software in an ordered and controlled way. For instance, the Capability Maturity Model [1] defined by the Software Engineering Institute of the Carnegie-Mellon University lists CM as one of the key practices that an organization has to own to go beyond the chaotic level of development.

However, the importance of CM had been recognized even earlier [2,3,4,5], and several tools have been developed in order to support the activities concerning CM [6,7,8]

Researchers have also addressed the problem of modeling the items and relationships participating in configurations.

However, the process of setting-up CM has obtained till now very little attention. As a consequence, when a software process owner decides to establish CM procedures, she/he has to perform several activities and to take several decisions with practically no guidance from the literature.

This paper aims at describing the activities that were performed to establish CM in SIA (Società Interbancaria per l'Automazione), the organization in charge of running, developing, and maintaining the National Inter-bank Network of Italy. In fact, in establishing CM in SIA the authors experienced that lack of a path to CM, and had to devise a sequence of steps to reach the goal. These steps were:

1. To make a model of the process and product. The model of the product was clearly necessary to understand the nature of the items that should be put under control of CM. The model of the process was also needed, because the CM process had to be integrated as seamlessly as possible with the rest of the process (including technical and managerial activities).
2. Implementing the CM procedures. This implied to choose a CM tool and to customize it according to the models developed during the preceding step.
3. Deploying the CM procedures. This implied (besides the rather trivial installation of the tool) to transfer the software artifacts into the tool repository and to provide training and support for the users, i.e., for the developers.
4. Monitoring and optimizations. The management of SIA wanted the prove that the established CM procedures actually provide the benefits that had been anticipated, and they wanted to control whether the procedures were correctly applied and suitably modified where needed.

Although the work was carried out in a specific development environment, it is possible to highlight a set of lessons learned that can be of interest to any organization that have to start the set-up of CM procedures.

[1]This work was partly supported by ESSI Project n. 21244 MIDAS (Measurable Improvement of Development, deployment and operation of interbank Automation Software).

0-8186-7840-2/97 $10.00 © 1997 IEEE

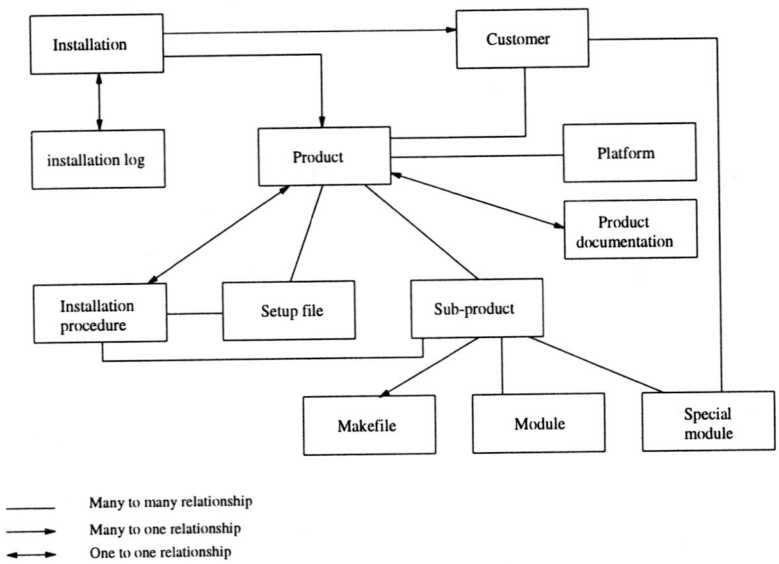

Figure 1: The software product diagram

Section 2 describes SIA's environment, the process evaluation that preceded the establishment of CM, and the kind of effectiveness evaluation that was required by the management. Section 3 describes the process of establishing CM, articulated in the aforementioned phases. Section 4 illustrates the lessons learned, while the last part of the paper draws some conclusions and illustrates future work.

2. Software development in SIA

SIA is a small-to-medium enterprise whose mission is to provide interbank services to all Italian banks and financial institutions. SIA's products and services include network services, banking services, and financial markets operations. To produce the software needed to operate these services, SIA has adopted a mixed approach based both on internal development and on subcontracts to independent software houses and IT technology providers.

In recent years, SIA experienced a variety of problems:

- The management of subcontractors was becoming more and more difficult as the dimension and criticality of the applications increased.
- It was becoming more and more difficult to estimate costs, to track projects and to have full control of the source code, especially of the code developed by subcontractors.
- The interaction with customers was made difficult by the variety of different responsibilities and interaction points for the same customer.
- The banking and financial markets were demanding for higher quality systems, especially as far as availability and reliability of the services are concerned.

To address the above issues, SIA started in 1994 a process improvement program. The first result was an assessment of the SIA software process, that has been carried out according to the Capability Maturity Model Ver. 1.1 of the Software Engineering Institute [1]. The assessment terminated in November 1994 and indicated a list of improvement actions, the top priorities being:

- improvement of configuration management policies and tools;
- introduction of requirement engineering processes.

In addition, the assessment reinforced the idea – already conceived by the management– of reorganizing the company by horizontal (product and customer oriented) processes, replacing the existing vertical, functional structure, recognized as a possible source of delays in the reaction to users requests.

The above plan has now been partly implemented. The company has been reorganized in three departments, each of them taking care of one of the three classes of services (and customers) mentioned above: banking applications, financial markets, and network infrastructure.

CM before and during the assessment was carried out manually, with the only support of RCS [8] under UNIX and of similar tools in other environments. As a consequence of the assessment, a well-studied configuration management process, supported by powerful tools, have been established for one of the most important SIA products (called NRO), dealing with the development of the new generation of SIA's networking software, that has to be completed and deployed in a number of subsequent releases.

SIA's management required that the usage of CM in

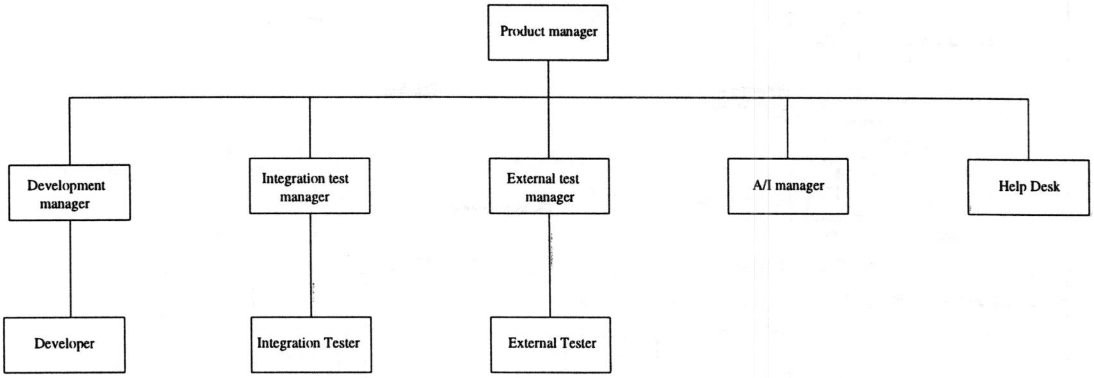

Figure 2: CM roles[2]

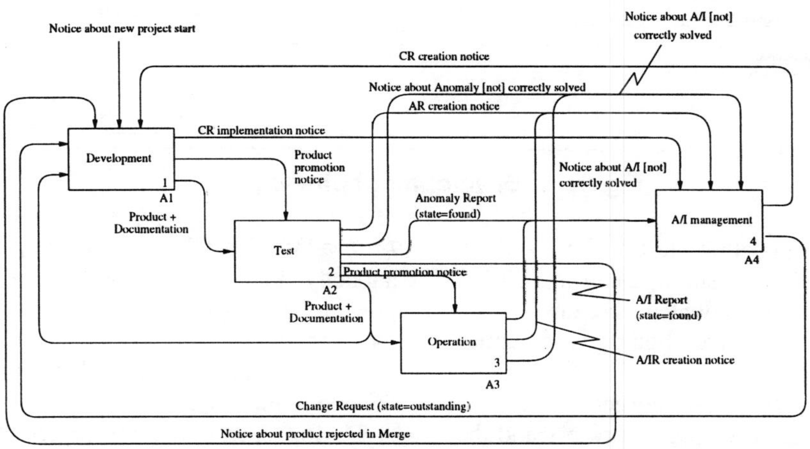

Figure 3: Product life cycle (A0)

the NRO process would be quantitatively evaluated. In particular it was required that the effectiveness of the development process was assessed before and after the introduction of CM, in order to allow a comparison. This request translated into the need to instrument the CM process with measurement capabilities. In this paper we do not report the results of the measurement program, while indications are provided on how measures have been obtained.

3. The process of establishing Configuration Management

3.1 CM process modeling

Modeling the software process is the first step that has to be performed in order to implement an effective CM process, i.e., a CM process that seamlessly integrates with existing development process. This section describes the software process adopted by SIA, focusing on the anomaly management activity only, for the sake of brevity. The other activities are described at an higher level of abstraction[3]. Anomaly management has been chosen because it is usually a complex and critical activity.

The software product and the CM roles. Before modeling the activities which compose the software process, a description of the typical software product developed by SIA was derived. Figure 1 (a simplified version of the E/R diagrams produced) sketches the relationships between products, components and SIA customers.

The roles involved in the CM activities, where also identified, and represented in a hierarchy (see Figure 2).

A detailed description of the roles is omitted, since the hierarchy is derived in quite straightforward way from the product life-cycle (which is a variant of the classical water-fall life-cycle) by establishing a responsibility for each phase or group of phases.

The SIA CM process. After modeling products and

[2] A/I stands for anomaly correction or feature addition (i.e., improvement).

[3] The detailed description of the process is available in the deliverables of the MIDAS project [9,10].

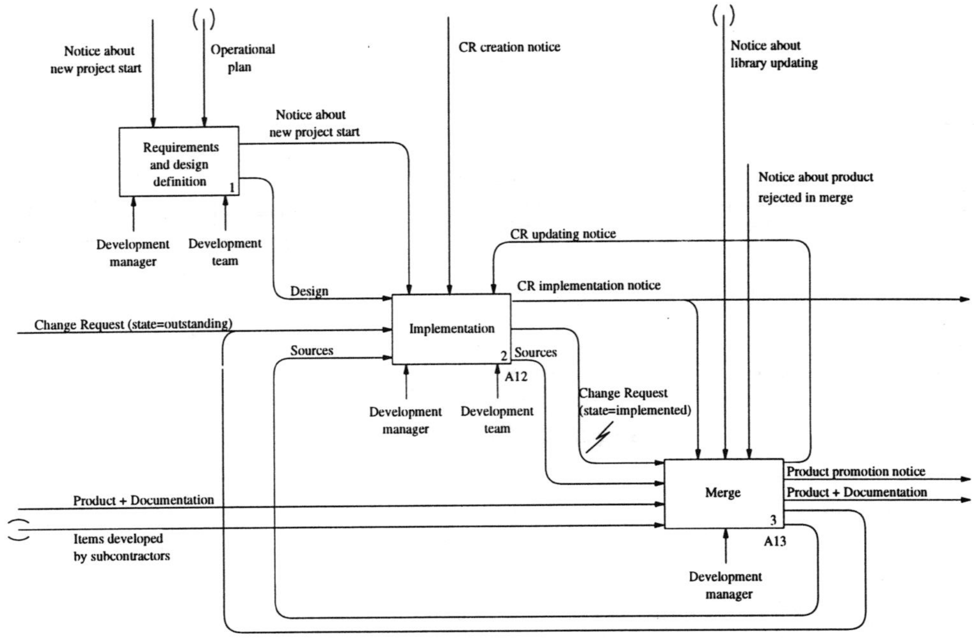

Figure 4: Development phase (A1)

roles, the actual process modeling started. This activity was carried out in a top-down fashion, using the IDEF0 notation [11]. IDEF0 was adopted because it is sufficiently intuitive and expressive, though its semantics is not formally defined.

The model derived is a trade-off between the faithful representation of the actual development process and the definition of an "ideal" process, equipped with CM. The resulting model is similar to the current practice (therefore it does not require a big effort to be adopted), while implementing the most important features of the ideal process, especially as far as CM is concerned.

Figure 3 sketches the top level description of the SIA software.

Software development begins when a new project starts or when some module has to be modified in order to accomplish a request for change (CR). When the development phase ends the product goes to the testing phase and a notice about this transition (the `product promotion notice`) is sent to the people that are in charge of performing tests. Moreover, if the development activity was started to accomplish a request for change, a notice about change request implementation is sent to the anomaly/improvement manager.

Testing starts when the person responsible for this activity receives the notice about the promotion of the product to the test phase. If some tester finds a new anomaly during the test activity, she/he creates an `anomaly report` (AR), whose state is set to `found` and sends a notice regarding this creation to the anomaly manager.

The test activity produces also a `Notice about Anomaly [not] correctly solved` for each anomaly that should have been solved during the previous development activity. These notices are sent to the anomaly/improvement manager.

When the test activity ends the product is promoted to the operation phase.

During operation users report to the Help Desk the anomalies detected during the product usage. As a consequence, the Help Desk creates new anomaly reports describing these anomalies. The same happens if users ask for improvements to the product functionality (in this case the Help Desk creates an improvement report for each improvement requested). Anomaly and improvement reports contain similar information and are managed through the same set of operations.

During the anomaly/improvement management activity, anomaly and improvement reports are carefully analyzed and, possibly, change requests to solve them are issued to the development team.

Figure 4 describes the development activity in detail.

The development phase is executed to develop new products or to modify existing ones. When a new product or a new major version of an existing product has to be developed, the development team first defines requirements and design for the new product or version. At the end of the design activity, the development team starts the product implementation activity. This activity produces a first version of the source code of the product.

At present the process of modifying the requirements specification and the design in order to fulfill a request for change is not modeled. In other words, we suppose that change requests do not involve requirements or

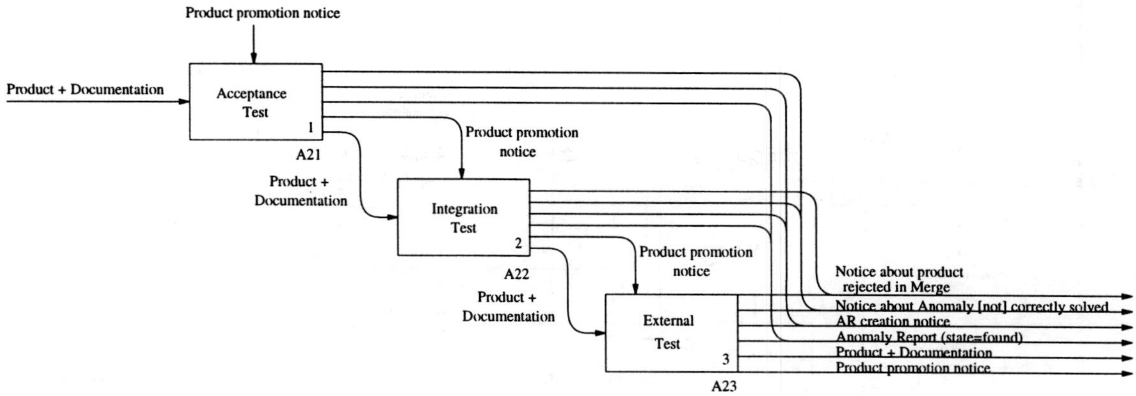

Figure 5: Test phase (A2)

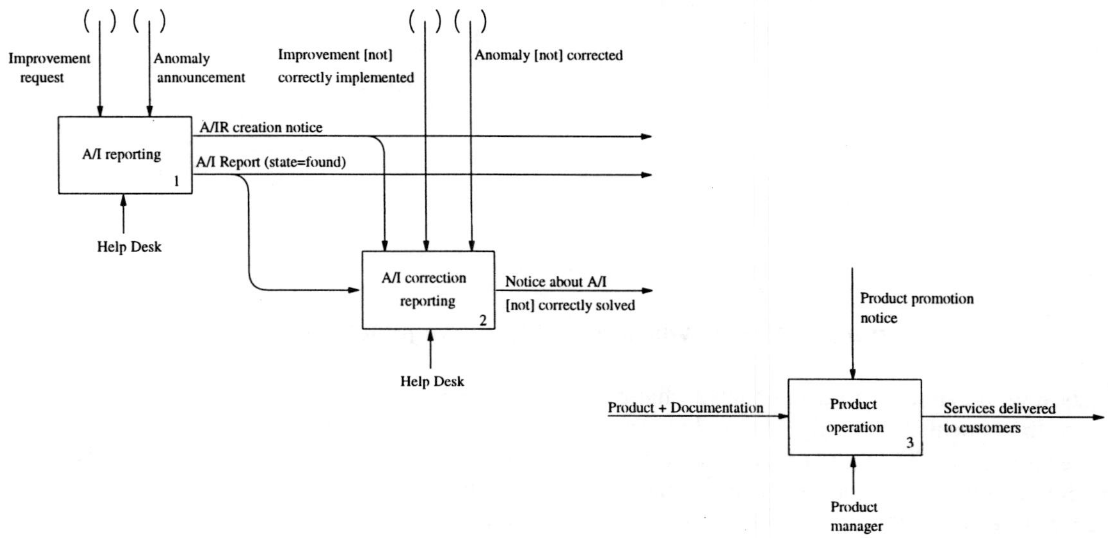

Figure 6: Operation phase (A3)

design modifications. This assumption simplifies the CM process that do not have to deal with artifacts other than the source files that compose the product. Future work will relax this assumption, and both requirements specification and design documentation will be put under configuration control too.

Given the previous simplification, a request for change immediately triggers the implementation activity. Using change request information, the development team performs the required modifications and produces new versions of the product source code.

When the implementation activity ends, merge activity is executed: the different changes made to the same source file during concurrent developments are merged, inconsistencies, if any, are solved, the modules developed by subcontractors are integrated into the product, and, finally, a new release of the product is built. Moreover, using the information about the change requests that were eventually solved, a new version of the documentation that contains the software release notes is produced. At the end of the merge phase, the product is promoted to the test phase.

`sources`, `product` and `documentation` are all collections of versioned artifacts.

Figure 5 describes the test phase.

If an anomaly is detected during one of the testing phases an anomaly report is created and a notice of this creation is sent to the anomaly/improvement manager. The anomaly report contains information like the name of the tester that found the anomaly, the date of detection, the modules affected, the anomaly severity (blocking, high, medium, and low), the date of solution and a description of the anomaly.

The test team also checks that previously found anomalies have been correctly solved and that previously defined improvements have been correctly implemented. Finally, the test team produce `notices about A/I [not] correctly solved` to inform the anomaly/improvement manager of the results of these checks.

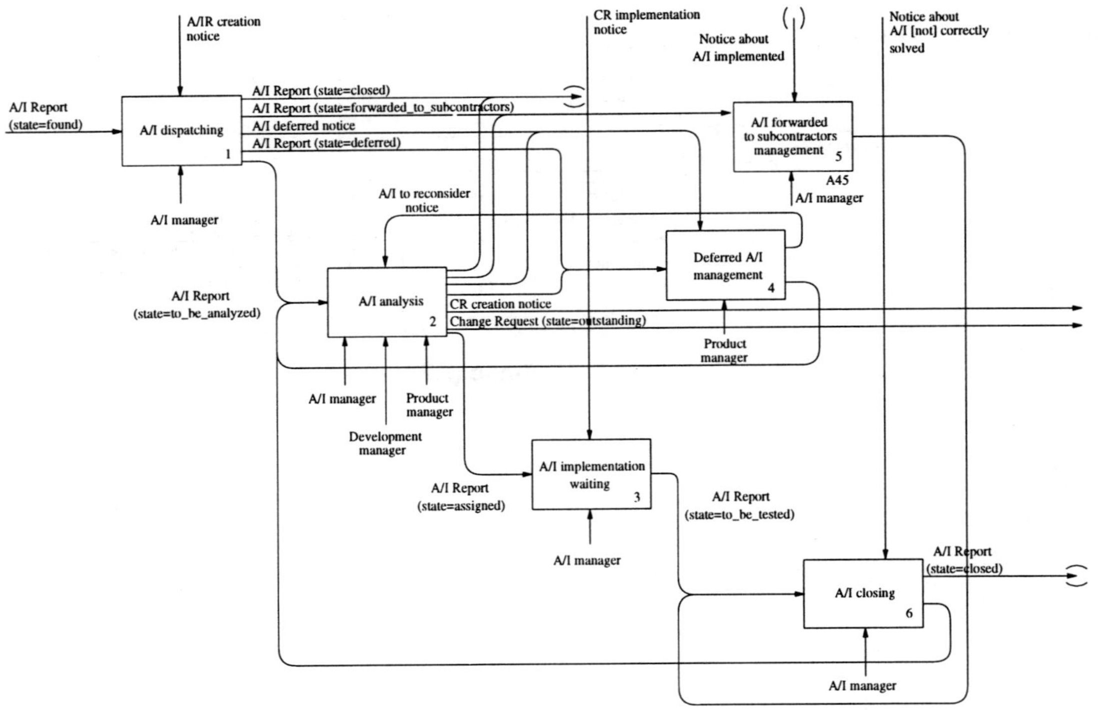

Figure 7: Anomaly/improvement management phase

During tests it is possible to find out that a change request was not implemented correctly. If this happens, the product is sent back to the merge phase and a notice of this transition is sent to the development manager. When the development manager receives this notice, she/he changes the state of the change request that was not correctly implemented from `implemented` to `outstanding` and sends a notice about this updating to the development team. As a consequence of receiving this notice, the development team starts a new implementation activity in order to find the correct solution for the change request under examination. At the end of the implementation phase (i.e. during the merge phase), the new version of the sources are merged with the old ones, the new version of the executables that were modified are built and they replace the old ones that were sent back in merge to produce the new version of the whole product.

Figure 6 describes the operation phase in detail. The Help Desk collects anomalies announcements and improvements requests from the users and produces an anomaly/improvement report (similar to the anomaly report) for each anomaly announced and for each improvement requested.

Figure 7 details the A/I management phase.

The A/I manager is notified of the creation of an A/I report. She/he analyzes the A/I and modifies the state of the report to reflect his/her decision about the A/I. In particular:

1. If the anomaly report does not describe an actual anomaly of the product i.e., it describes a normal execution that was erroneously reported as anomalous, its state is set to `closed` and it is archived.
2. If the A/I report describes an A/I that affects only modules developed externally, its state is set to `forwarded_to_subcontractors` and it is sent to the `A/I forwarded to subcontractors management` activity.
3. If the A/I report describes an A/I that does not demand for an immediate solution, its state is set to `deferred` and it is sent to the `deferred anomaly/improvement management` activity.
4. If none of the previous conditions holds, the state of the A/I report is set to `to_be_analyzed` and it is sent to the `A/I analysis` activity.

Even during `A/I analysis` it is possible to discover that cases 1, 2 or 3 hold. In such cases, the anomaly report is managed as described in the corresponding point. Otherwise, the A/I report is carefully analysed and a request for change report to solve the anomaly and to implement the improvement is created. Next, the A/I report state is set to `assigned` and it is sent to the activity `A/I implementation waiting`.

During the A/I implementation waiting, the A/I manager waits for the notices about the implementation of the different requests for change delivered. When the A/I manager is notified about the implementation of a change request, she/he sets the state of the related A/I

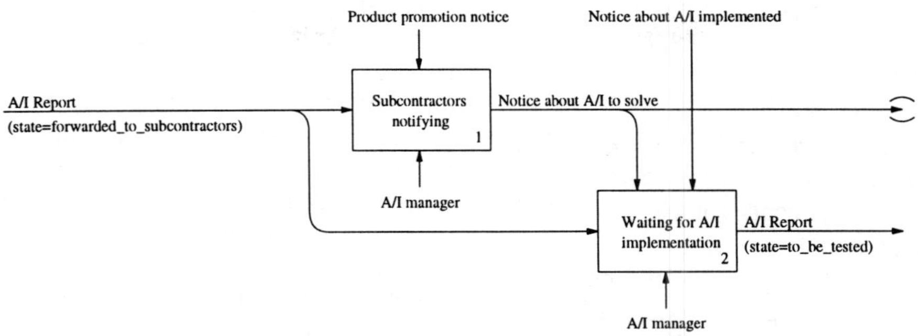

Figure 8: A/I forwarded to subcontractors management activity (A45)

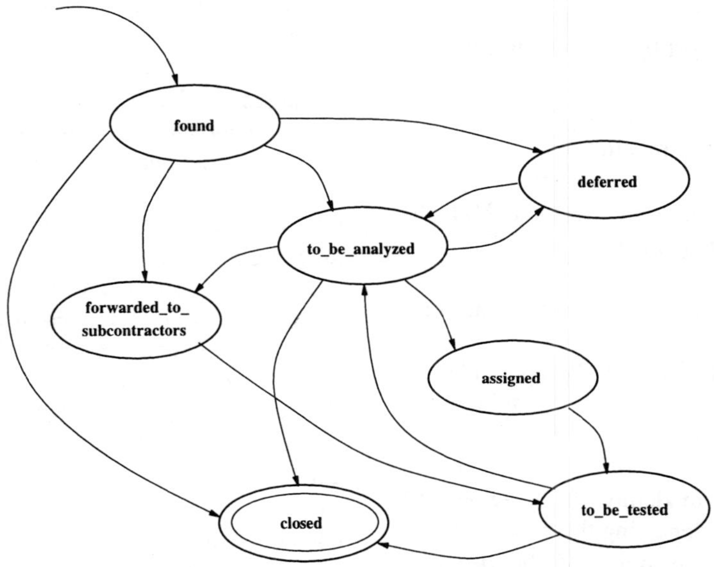

Figure 9: Anomaly-improvement report state diagram

report to `to_be_tested` and sends it to the A/I closing activity.

The `A/I forwarded to subcontractors` activity is detailed in Figure 8.

To better explain the activities performed during the anomaly/improvement management phase, Figure 9 describes the state diagram of the anomaly/improvement report.

3.2 Implementing CM procedures

CM tools evaluation. CM is often based on a set of repetitive activities and procedures whose description can be coded in some formal language. CM tools can be used to automate these activities providing support to the people involved in the development process.

In the last years a great number of commercial system have become available to support CM procedures. One of the preliminary task that were accomplished to introduce CM practices in SIA was to find the most suitable CM tool to support the CM procedures defined in Section 3.1. To achieve this goal, different tools for supporting CM procedures have been compared. The tools evaluated were: CCC, Continuus, ClearCase, Endevor, PCMS and PVCS. They were chosen looking at the OVUM report [12] that describes and compares the most popular CM tools.

The following list describes the requirements that a tool for supporting CM has to fulfill in order to be suitable for supporting the NRO product development.

1. Platform supported:
   - UNIX on hp9000 and IBM RS6000
   - [not mandatory] MVS
2. Version control:
   - Ability of supporting different versions of the same product
   - Support for concurrent development, variant releases and parallel releases
   - Support for external development of software components, i.e. some components of the NRO product are developed by external software

companies and the chosen tool has to assist such kind of practice

3. Configuration control:
   - Definition of configurations
   - Ability of managing configurations composed of different kinds of artifacts like source code, various kinds of documents (in particular MS Word for Mac), etc.
   - [not mandatory] Ability of defining and maintaining relationships among different artifacts. For example, it must be possible to define a relation between the document that describes a software component and the set of files that implements that component
   - [not mandatory] Support for impact analysis
4. Change Control:
   - Support for change management
   - Support for problem tracking (reporting and metrics)
   - [not mandatory] Integration with QuickMail[4] to support problem management
5. Build and release support:
   - Support for automating the process of building releases
   - [not mandatory] It should be possible to customize the releasing process to follow the procedures adopted by SIA
6. Process management:
   - Ability of formally modeling the development process and ability of enacting this model
   - Ability of relating the states of the different artifacts with roles and actions
7. Customizability:
   - [not mandatory] It should be possible to define objects, roles, states, state transitions and access rights
8. Usability:
   - It must be possible to gradually introduce the usage of the tool in an existing project reducing the impact of this introduction on the ongoing activities
   - [not mandatory] Ability to easily integrate the CM tool with other developments tools adopted by SIA

After a comparison of the six tools mentioned, CCC was chosen. It was the only one completely satisfying the requirements listed above.

Appendix A reports a brief description of CCC, focusing on the features that were used to implement the CM process described in Section 3.1.

CM procedures implementation in CCC. As a first step, a different user group was defined in CCC for each role defined in the software development process model. Access permission were also defined to enable the different users to accomplish only the activities they were expected to carry out, thus limiting the chances to perform unexpected actions. The access permissions reflect the responsibilities and the access rights of each user. As an example, only users that belong to the `development_team` user group are allowed to check out the sources that have to be modified during the implementation activity and only the users that belongs to the `development_manager` user group are allowed to start the merge activity.

As described in Section 3.1, the NRO product is composed of a set of sub-products. It was decided to define two CCC environments for each sub-product that composes the NRO product. They are the *Development* environment and the *AIManagement* environment.

The development environment is used to support development, test and production phases of the software life cycle, while the AIManagement environment is used to manage the anomalies and improvement reports, i.e., it is used to support the phase of anomaly and improvement management as it is defined in Section 3.1.

A different state was defined in CCC for each activity of the software development process model. The development environment contains the states `implementation`, `merge`, `acceptance test`, `integration test`, `external test` and `operation`; while the AIManagement environment contains the states `found`, `forwarded to subcontractors`, `deferred`, `to be analyzed`, `assigned`, `to be tested` and `closed`. Packages containing source modules, executables and documentation or packages representing anomalies or improvement reports flow through these states during software development.

Different views of the repository containing the sources, executables and documentation of the product under development are defined for the development environment. They are used to separate the files visible in the different states of the environment. For example, the `MTP_product` environment defines three views. One is used for the phases of development and testing (i.e., it is associated to the `development`, `acceptance test`, `integration test` and `external test` states of the development environment) one for the merge phase and the last one for the operation phase.

On the other hand, the AIManagement environment does not have any view of the repository. It simply manages the packages containing anomalies or improvement reports. These packages carry the information related to the anomalies found or to the improvements proposed in a CCC form linked to the

[4] A mail client for Macintosh computers.

corresponding packages. Working in the AIManagement environment the A/I manager may create the packages that describe the anomaly and improvement reports and the corresponding change requests, she/he may link the change request packages to the sources that have to be modified in order to implement the requested change, and finally she/he may move these packages to the development environment were the requested changes are implemented.

CCC processes were used to automate the different activities involved in the software process. A CCC process has been defined in the development and AIManagement environments for each activity defined in the software development process model.

Electronic mails were used to exchange notices among people participating in the development process. The feature provided by CCC to automatically send e-mails when packages move from a state to another has been used to automate the notification process.

Finally, the tool to support the merging of different versions of the same artifact, provided with CCC, has been profitably used to support the development manager during the merge activity.

3.3 Deploying CM procedures

The deployment of the CM procedures involved two main activities:

- the creation of a real working environment using the customized CCC;
- training and support of the developers.

The former activity was carried out by exploiting the features of CCC which allows the existence of different environments. Once the working environment was set up, the upload of code into the system could start. This was done incrementally, i.e., transferring into the system the code of one component of NRO at a time. This gradual introduction of the CM implied two relevant benefits: only few people at a time had to be supported in their first approach to the CM system, and the CM system itself could be gradually adapted to the users needs according to the feedback provided by the early users.

The training of the users was carried out exploiting several means: written documentation, seminars, and an on-line hypertextual guide. A hot line support was also established, and extensively used.

Thanks to the smooth introduction of CM, both the written and on-line documentation could be gradually enriched with a "frequently asked questions" section, which proved very useful to provide solutions to common problems.

3.4 Process Optimization

During the first months of use of the new CM procedures and tools, a lot of feedback were generated by the NRO developers. Analyzing this feedback, it was possible to optimize the CM procedures to better reflect and support the SIA's development practices.

The most relevant result was the understanding that the software development and maintenance process modeled in Section 3.1 and used as a basis to implement the CM process did not correctly describe the actual SIA's software process. In fact, the patching activity performed by the SIA's developers to eliminate bugs whose solution can not be delayed to the next release of the product was omitted. The reason of the exclusion was that the NRO product was not yet released and thus there was not any need to patch it when the process had been modeled.

Other minor changes were also made to increase the overall quality of the CM process:

- the testers or users that discovered an anomaly are notified when it is closed;
- development manager is notified whenever the product is promoted to the following phase;
- the amount of information automatically inserted into the release notes was increased to include the complete list of the files that compose a release, the compatibility list, and the modification history.
- It was decided to store the executable files in the file-system instead of storing them in the CCC repository, thus reducing the size of the CCC repository and increasing performance.
- A number of reporting procedures were implemented to help the department heads in evaluating both the product and the process quality.
- Finally, it was formalized and standardized the procedure that the anomaly manager has to follow in order to refuse an anomaly that was erroneously reported as caused by the sub-product she/he is responsible for.

Another problem that was taken into consideration is that deviations of the actual process from the modeled one are possible [13], because of errors, which were classified in two categories:

- Incorrect use of the tool. Belong to this category the errors made using the CCC forms to store the information about the anomalies found or the improvement requested.
- Use of the CM procedures not consistent with the CM model. Belong to this category the errors in management of duplicated anomalies, the errors resulting in incorrect state transition of packages, and the wrong associations between an anomaly report and

the related change request.

To detect these deviations, a number of report procedures were implemented and the information obtained was used to modify the CM procedures to better support the user needs and to reduce the occurrences and consequences of deviations. In practice the process was enhanced with:

- procedures that prevent deviations, e.g., by guiding or constraining the user in some operations;
- procedures that detect real or "suspected" inconsistencies and notify them to the correct role.

Finally, the CM tool was provided with procedures to extract data that were required by the measurement program. Several measures are extracted automatically whenever given actions are performed (e.g., the promotion of a package to the next state). Other measures are collected upon request from the CM system administrator.

4. Lessons learned

The CM process has to be built around the existing software development process. This allows a smooth transition to the new way of working.

The availability of a process model driven the customization of the commercial CM tool adopted to support the process and to automate trivial activities.

The selection of the tool was not easy because of the rich variety of tools on the market, and had to be carried out according to precise criteria.

The human factor was –as usual– extremely important. A good deal of effort was spent in training and in customizing the tool to adapt it to the user requirements. Another important activity was to convince the users to adopt CM, overcoming the natural resistance to the introduction of new procedures, which are initially perceived as obstacles.

The feedback from the users was absolutely essential in adapting the CM procedures and tool to the actual needs of the developers. In particular we were able to design tool enhancements that allowed to cope with a more realistic and effective development process, to improve the CM system performances, to control deviations from the official process, to produce reports for the management concerning product quality.

5. Conclusions

The reported experience shows that a sound configuration management process can be established following the sequence of steps described above:

- process modeling, incorporating the current practice and the desired CM procedures;
- tool selection;
- tool customization to fit in the defined process;
- deployment, including user training and support.
- adaptation, according to the users' comments.

The work reported was meant to define and deploy an effective CM process for the NRO project. Although the measurement program has not yet been completed, it is already clear that the new CM process has made software development at SIA more effective.

Future work. It is SIA's intention to provide every project with a sound CM process. Nevertheless, every project has a unique development process: therefore it is in principle necessary to adapt the pilot project's CM process to the various situations. This is especially true considering that SIA is organized in four production units, each developing specific kinds of software, with different tools, HW/SW platforms and with people having different skills.

In order to provide a basis for the establishment of CM practices and tools in other projects and departments of SIA, the following actions have been planned:

- Characterization: other SIA processes are being studied, in order to understand their specific features, and differences with respect to the NRO project.
- Recommendations for transition: the recommendations for the establishment of CM practices and tools in other departments of SIA will be formulated, reporting all the relevant information concerning the different processes.

References

[1] Software Engineering Institute, *The Capability Maturity Model: guidelines for improving the software process*: Addison-Wesley, 1995.

[2] W. A. Babich. *Software Configuration Management*. Addison-Wesley, Reading, Massachussets, 1986.

[3] Fletcher J. Buckley. *Implementing Configuration Management: Hardware, Software, and Firmware*. IEEE Press, Los Alamitos, CA, 1992.

[4] S. A. Dart. Concepts in Configuration Management Systems. In Peter H. Feiler, editor, *Proceedings of the 3rd International Workshop on Software Configuration Management*, pages 1-18, Trondheim, Norway, June 1991.

[5] S. A. Dart. The Past, Present and Future of Configuration Management. Technical Report CMU/SEI-92-TR-8, Software Engineering Institute, 1992.

[6] S. A. Dart. Spectrum of Functionality in Configuration Management Systems. Technical Report CMU/SEI-90-TR-11, Software Engineering Institute, December 1990.

[7] P. H. Feiler. Configuration Management Models in Commercial Environments. . Technical Report CMU/SEI-91-TR-7, Software Engineering Institute, March 1991

[8] W. F. Tichy. RCS - A System for Version Control. *Software Practice and Experience*, 15(7):637-654, July 1985.
[9] G. Cugola and L. Lavazza. Definition of the Configuration Management Process for the MIDAS Pilot Project. CEFRIEL, April 1996. Document code: CMPDD2.1/GNR/0101T/MIDAS
[10] G. Cugola and L. Lavazza. CM Optimized Process Definition. CEFRIEL, December 1996. Document code: CMOPD2.1/GNR/010A/MIDAS
[11] Integration Definition for Function Modeling, *IDEF0.* Federal Information Processing Standards Publications, December 1993.
[12] P. Ingram, C. Burrows, and I. Wesley. Configuration Management Tools: a Detailed Evaluation. Technical Report, Ovum, 1993.
[13] G. Cugola, E. Di Nitto, A. Fuggetta, C. Ghezzi, A Framework for Formalizing Inconsistencies and Deviations in Human-Centered Systems, *ACM Transactions on Software Engineering and Methodology,* July 1996.
[14] Softool Corporation. *CCC User's Guide*, August 1995.

Appendix A. An overview of CCC

CCC Architecture

Developed by PLATINUM technology inc., (formerly SOFTOOL Corp.) CCC [14] is a client/server application built to support distributed development environments and to take advantage of the strengths of various platforms. It uses a three-tier client/server architecture that allows users on a variety of client platforms to communicate with the server across a TCP/IP network, among departments.

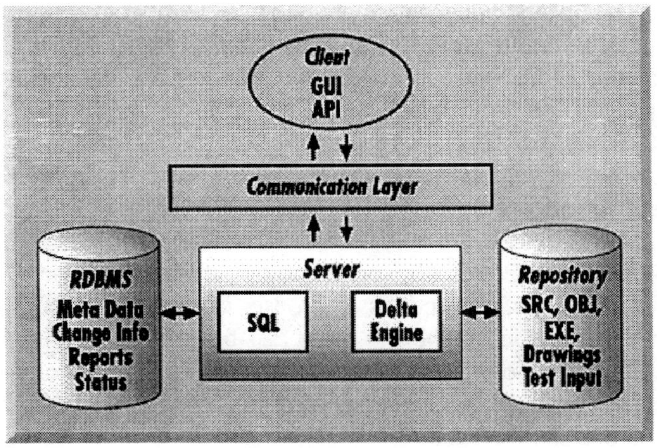

CCC architecture

The CCC client consists of the graphical user interface (GUI), command line interface, and application programming interface (API). CCC clients are available in UNIX, Windows, and MVS.

The following figures show the CCC administrator and user interface. Both use a GUI interface and represent the client side of CCC.

The server contains the majority of the CCC logic. It includes two major pieces: the delta engine and the SQL layer.

- The delta engine communicates with the CCC repository. The CCC repository is a set of operating system directories used to maintain delta files. The delta files contain the changed lines to items under CCC's control.
- The SQL layer communicates with a relational database (RDBMS) such as Oracle, Informix and Sybase. The relational database is used to store detailed information about items under CCC's control. CCC uses the RDBMS to maintain information about logical structures like packages and package groups. In addition, the RDBMS maintains control data describing the physical versions, including the version ID, user, date/time, remarks, and package information.

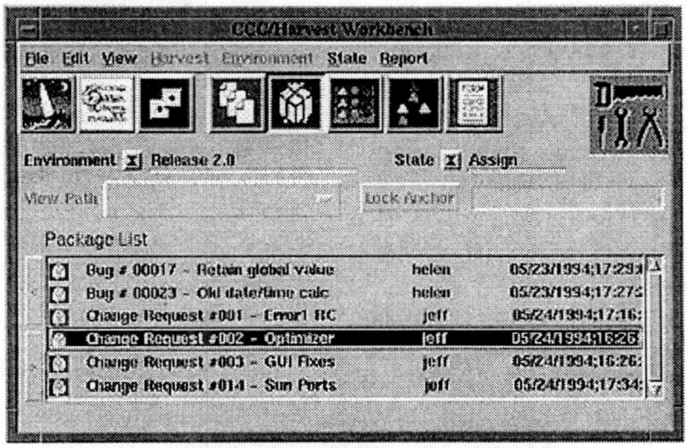

The CCC user interface

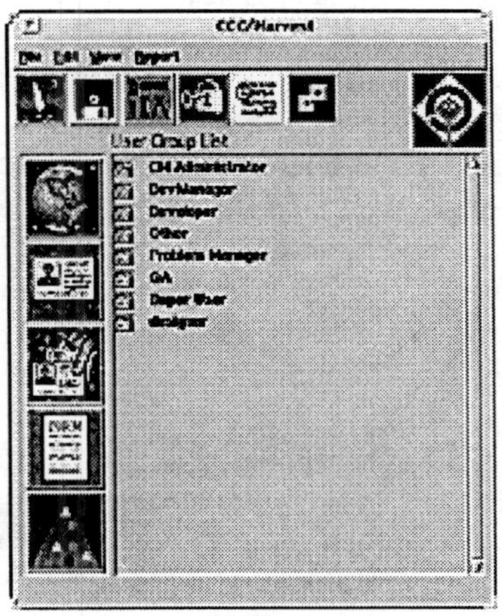

The CCC administrator interface

A communication layer provides the connection between the CCC clients and the server. The clients, server, repository, and relational database may each reside on different heterogeneous platforms.

CCC main features

Traditional CM tools have often viewed CM as an isolated, technical function that can be performed off to the side of the main flow of development activities. On the other hand, the basic purpose of CCC is to provide a unified framework supporting all the core functions in the software development and maintenance process.

To obtain this result, CCC provides a small number of basic objects. Using these objects, it is possible to build any kind of software development and maintenance model. These building blocks include environments, life cycles, states, transitions, processes, views, packages, package groups, and forms.

An *environment* is the control framework supporting a particular development and maintenance process. It includes a *life cycle*, made up of *states* and *processes*. An environment specifies how data is accessed, the processes allowed to execute, how different artefacts move through the development cycle, and user responsibilities. Most CCC functions are only available when an environment has been selected. A site may have a number of different environments, depending on the number of applications being controlled and the kind of development activity undertaken. For example, there may be one environment for maintaining an already released version of an application, another for developing the next release, and a third for maintaining code shared among various applications.

The *life cycle* is the part of the environment that defines a model for a particular development and maintenance process. This model is defined in terms of a set of states and the valid transitions between these states. A life cycle can include many or few states, depending on each site's individual requirements. A common development scenario might include states for assigning change requests, making changes, testing changes, integrating changes, and releasing a completed product.

States represent stages in a life-cycle. After defining a set of states, a life cycle can also define the *transitions* or pathways for work to flow from one state to the next.

Processes are the actions that can be performed at each state along the life cycle. These processes appear to users who are working in that state. Each state can have its own unique list of available processes which can be dynamically updated even while the life-cycle is in use. CCC comes with a number of different process types that can be configured by an administrator. Examples of process types supplied with CCC are: check in, check out, notify and merge. In addition, processes can be defined that invoke other user-supplied programs. This feature allows the administrator to integrate the use of existing development tools into the CCC life cycle.

Views define the kind of data that can be accessed from within an environment. Each environment has one master view, which defines the items to be operated on. The items themselves are maintained in a physical repository, which can be shared by more than one environment. Additional views can be created based on the master view. Within a life cycle, each state may have a particular view associated with it. The view determines which item versions are accessible to users in that view.

A *package* is the basic unit of work that moves through the life cycle. The package is the user's link to the actual data accessed during the change process. Each package must be within a particular state of the life cycle. Associated with a state is a view. The view defines the data and its versions accessed by a package in that state. All packages in the same state share the same view. For example, consider a set of packages that share a Development view of an application. Changes made for each package sharing the view are immediately visible to the others sharing the same view. However, these same changes are not visible from the Test view until the changes are promoted to Test.

A *package group* provides a higher logical level for operating on related packages. A particular package may belong to one group or several, or it may not belong to any. Any operation that can be performed on a package can be performed on all packages in a package group. For example, a user can promote all packages in a group from one state to the next.

Forms represent a way of maintaining and organising information within CCC. Forms can be used in much the same way that paper forms are used. For example, they can be used to track issues and problems or as a structured method of communication. Forms attain their greatest usefulness through association with packages. This association provides the link between the problem tracking and change tracking functions in CCC. Forms can also be associated with other forms, allowing information to be cross referenced. All the information gathered through a form is also directly accessible from the associated package.

CCC provides also access control facilities. The access control is based on the combination of users or user groups, objects, and actions. Each user can belong to any number of groups. The life cycle can be defined so that certain users or user groups must give their approval before a package can move forward through the life cycle from one state to another.

CCC supports concurrent development through a tool that make it easy to merge two parallel releases of the same artefact. Moreover, it uses a modified version of the GNUmake application to define relationships between different artefacts and to automate the building process. Finally, files produced using RCS or SCCS can be automatically converted into the format used by CCC.

Stevens Award

Stevens Lecture on Software Development Methods

Keynote 2

Session P4a

CASE

CASE in the 21st Century: Challenges Facing Existing CASE Vendors

Alan W. Brown

Texas Instruments Software
6620 Chase Oaks Blvd., M/S 8515
Plano, TX 75023, USA.

a-w-brown@ti.com

Abstract

Established CASE vendors face a number of major challenges in upgrading their product lines to support the development and maintenance of large-scale distributed, web-based applications. This paper describes the characteristics of future applications, examines the challenges they pose to established CASE vendors, and suggests activities within the software research community that can help to address these challenges. As a result, the main contributions of the paper include a vision of how CASE products will evolve as we enter the 21st Century, and an analysis of the problems that will need to be overcome by established CASE vendors to realize that vision.

1. Introduction

Technology advances lead us to conclude that future applications in almost all domains will be distributed across many sites, access data from multiple sources, and have web-based interfaces [1, 11]. Developing and maintaining these applications involves a wide range of skills in distributed systems, databases, and web technology. This is in addition to the software engineering skills required by any application developer of large-scale software-intensive systems.

As a result, automated tools for building such applications are essential, and are becoming commercially available. We can identify three major sources of those tools:

- A plethora of small start-up companies have sprung up, producing a wide variety of tools that aid application developers in many aspects of web-based software development. However, these tools tend to suffer from typical first-generation software problems: instability, poor support, and concentration on single-user, small application development.
- The vendors of infrastructure technology (databases, messaging systems, browsers) have produced their own tools that help developers to apply their products. The main limitation of these tools is that they tend to be very closely tied to a particular infrastructure product, and may not allow use of a competitor's product, or a combination of products.
- The established CASE vendors are evolving their existing product bases to address the problems of falling sales in their established markets, and to embrace the opportunities opened up by the new distributed, web-based applications market. The problem with these tools is that they are so slow to reach the market place. The CASE vendors are performing an interesting balancing act between on the one hand evolving their products sufficiently quickly to address the market needs, while on the other maintaining their existing product base and customers.

While a detailed analysis of each of these three tool-producing communities would be valuable, in this paper we concentrate on the third category above, and consider the challenges facing the established CASE vendors as they attempt to address the distributed, web-based applications market. At first sight this community is perhaps in the best starting position of the three categories of tool producers, with an established customer base and marketing channels, experience in tool development, and a large body of development, maintenance, and research staff. However, on closer analysis the challenges to this community are particularly severe. Established CASE vendors must not only completely revolutionize their tools to support the creation and maintenance of distributed, web-based applications, they must also reengineer their own toolsets to be similarly architected. They must achieve this with an existing code base of many millions of lines of code, running on a variety of platforms that range from MVS to many flavors of Unix, and with an established methods

0-8186-7840-2/97 $10.00 © 1997 IEEE

and consultancy business based on 1980's-style structured methods producing traditional mainframe and client-server applications.

The remainder of this paper is organized as follows. Section 2 discusses the principle drivers for change and provides motivation for the key issues to be addressed by the established CASE vendors. Section 3 considers the past, present, and future evolution of CASE by describing the kinds of applications being developed and the CASE tool support available. Section 4 discusses 4 key areas that must be addressed in future CASE tools: creating and managing large-scale distributed systems architectures, component-based development, developing new methods and methodologies, and pragmatic issues for established CASE vendors. Section 5 contains a short summary of the paper.

2. Change Drivers

It is difficult not to be overwhelmed by the speed at which new technologies are being announced - hardware price/performance ratio is increasing fast, web-based technologies are appearing at an astounding rate, and various distributed infrastructure standards and technologies for connecting independently-developed applications are now sufficiently mature that they are being used in large-scale mission-critical applications.

Fuelled by these technology advances, it is useful to consider the two critical change drivers for future applications, as these technologies are the basis for many of the new requirements being placed on future CASE tools.

2.1 World Wide Web

The popularity of the world wide web has revolutionized computing. While there are many aspects to the impact the web is having in society as a whole, in terms of the requirements on application development and CASE tools it is useful to focus on four main areas.

First, the metaphor of "surfing the web" has become universally accepted as the way in which a user searches for relevant information, displays that information within a web browser, and interacts with applications though web-based forms. In a few short years it seems that web browsers are the de facto standard for user interface look and feel.

Second, the location of information and the underlying infrastructure that delivers the information to a user is becoming less visible, and consequently less important to the user. In most cases, the user can be unaware of whether the information is stored on a machine in the next office or on another continent (ignoring network latency of course!). In fact, users now accept that information will be distributed across many machines at many locations, but expect that such distribution does not change the nature of their task.

Third, it is no longer acceptable that information content consist solely of text and tables of numbers. Users expect rich multi-media display of information involving graphics, sound, video, animation, and so on. Web browsers handle many formats of data automatically, and know automatically how to compress and decompress such information for efficient transmission across a network.

Fourth, as the technology of the web is becoming more deeply understood by a wider constituency, a commodity market has developed in all kinds of tools and components for creating and manipulating web content. Users expect to be able to obtain a wide variety of resources for free or at very low cost, and to be able to combine those resources effectively to create sophisticated data content, or data manipulation applications.

As a result, these four areas have had a significant impact on the attitudes and expectations of users developing and using applications in terms of how they view information, where that information resides, the format of that information, and what it is expected to cost to build and evolve applications using that information.

2.2 Distributed Computing

Enterprise-level application development in the late 1980's was characterized by a move away from monolithic, single-machine applications toward client-server computing. In most cases this meant using the graphical capabilities of a users' desktop personal computer (PC) to provide remote access to an application across a local area network. Typically, the desktop client programs provided local display processing and command interpretation, while the central server program performed the compute-intensive activities, maintained shared databases, and so on. This has sometimes been called the "thin client, fat server" model of computing [13].

However, over a short period of time the rapid improvement in performance and reduced cost of PCs began to change the kinds of processing that was performed on the client versus the server. The client PCs could now be used for operations such as query optimization, and could be customized to perform user-specific data visualization and analysis. This migration of functionality from server to client, together with increasingly more reliable, high bandwidth networks, led to software architectures that provided a great deal of flexibility over what functionality was performed on which machine.

The result of this evolution is a change in the way such applications are perceived, designed, implemented, and updated. An application is now considered to be an interacting set of services in which each service is as self-contained as possible, accessed through a well-defined interface. Such a modular approach has many advantages, but relies on a number of elements to be in place:

- design approaches, methods, and tools that support service-based software architectures;
- a shared infrastructure that facilitates specification of service interfaces, allows potential service providers to be identified, and brokers interconnections among service providers;
- a marketplace of services from third party suppliers in the form of components that can readily be connected through the shared infrastructure.

The key to these elements is a set of common agreements concerning service interface specifications, and the availability of a range of products that support service interconnection using those interfaces. Two dominant approaches to providing this have arisen.

The first approach is to make the infrastructure a specific product or platform. This is seen in the Microsoft products. Over the past few years a wide range of encapsulated executables have been made available in the form of Visual Basic Controls (VBXs) and ActiveX Controls (renamed from what was previously called Object Linking and Embedding (OLE) Custom Controls (OCXs)). A large market place has been created for VBXs and ActiveX Controls, with over a thousand VBXs available that sell for anywhere from $25 to $3000. Essentially, a VBX is a packaged set of functions that can be used as an add-on to Visual Basic. These functions can be as simple as visual buttons, or as sophisticated as a database front-end and report generator. Many leading tools can import VBXs into their pallets and use them to construct visual forms and client front-ends [13].

The second approach is to create an industry-consortium which defines public standards and encourages vendors to create products that conform to those standards. This has been provided by the Interface Definition Language (IDL) and the Common Object Request Broker Architecture (CORBA) developed by the Object Management Group (OMG). This large consortium of companies has cooperated to define CORBA and IDL, and at least 5 CORBA implementations are now commercially available. With the availability of these CORBA implementations, a range of services common to many applications are being provided, design methods for developing CORBA-based applications are becoming available, and large-scale applications beginning to appear [14].

3. CASE Evolution

Given the changing technological infrastructure available to software developers, it is not surprising that application development support has been required to evolve substantially to generate applications that are able to take advantage of these changes. Here, we illustrate the evolution of CASE tools as they try to keep up-to-date with application developers' needs. We do this by contrasting CASE tool support of the past (in the late 1980s) with current CASE tool support (mid 1990s), and speculating on the support that will be needed in the future (by the year 2000).

3.1 Past

Application development in the 1980s was characterized by a move from mainframe-based to client/server applications. While this move has been implemented in many ways, the approach is characterized by data-intensive applications which were re-engineered by separating remote database services from local desktop display functions. The functions that manipulated the data were initially executed on the server, but migrated to the desktop as the performance of desktop machines improved. This architecture is illustrated in Figure 1.

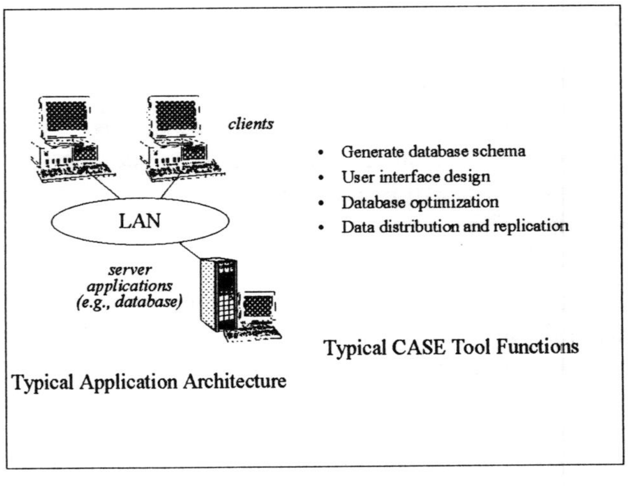

Figure 1. Past Application Architectures and CASE Tool Functions

CASE tool support for client/server architectures typically revolved around the generation and maintenance of the database on the server side, and a series of user interfaces to access and update that database on the client side. Some CASE tools also provided support for database optimizations, inter-operation between databases from different vendors, and synchronization of replicated data sources.

3.2 Present

With the advent of the internet and the world-wide web, application developers are demanding 2 major changes in the way in which current applications are developed:

- Web browser interfaces to data retrieval and update. As a consequence of the popularity of the web, browser interfaces are now a familiar and comfortable metaphor for accessing all types of data. This provides a common look and feel for all applications.
- Commonality of interface across heterogeneous client platforms. Today it is common in any organization to have a large investment in a variety of desktop machines running different operating systems and support software. Applications should be able to execute on any of these without requiring custom changes for each desktop configuration.

To achieve this, CASE tool vendors are extending their products to combine the enterprise-level services of client/server architectures, with the platform independence and commonality of interface provided by a web server. An example of such an approach, adapted from [15], is illustrated in Figure 2.

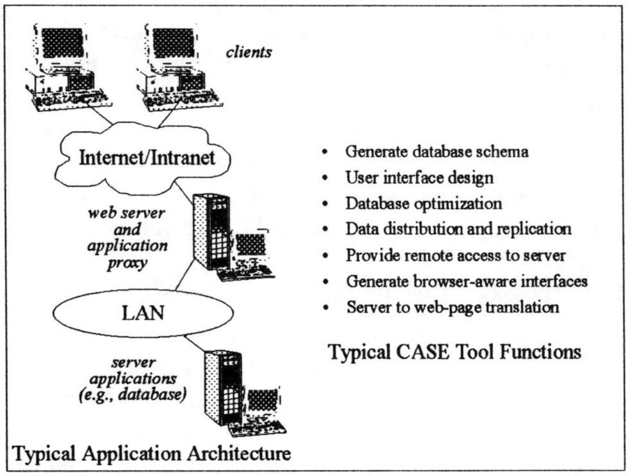

Figure 2. Current Application Architectures and CASE Tool Functions

In the example illustrated in Figure 2, an application end user views an application as a series of interconnected web pages from a browser on any machine connected to the internet/intranet. The user interacts with the web browser by selecting links or by entering information into fields on a web-based form. This information is transmitted across the internet to the web server which recognizes requests for external data and passes the request to an application proxy on the web server who's task is to map data requests to application queries on the server. The application server services the request, and the proxy converts the returned information into a web page which it passes to the web server for display to the end user.

In this example, the CASE tool in now responsible for providing the proxy application server that maps between web-based requests and application services, and vice-versa. Typically, the CASE tool provides a set of templates for this which the application developer can use to create user dialog screens in HyperText Markup Language (HTML) or Java.

The result of this approach is not only an application which can be accessed from a browser anywhere on the internet (security restrictions permitting). Additionally, high-performance local clients can still be developed using the client/server approach illustrated in Figure 1.

3.3 Future

In the future, organizations would like to move toward greater reuse of the results of previous development efforts, leading to application development primarily through component-based assembly. To achieve this requires a number of changes both in the way applications are developed, and in the resultant architecture of developed applications.

Applications must be developed as independent sets of interacting components, offering well-defined interfaces to potential users of the services provided by the components. Similarly, supporting technology must be available to allow application developers to browse collections of components, select those of interest, and assemble those components to create the desired functionality. Such an approach is illustrated in Figure 3.

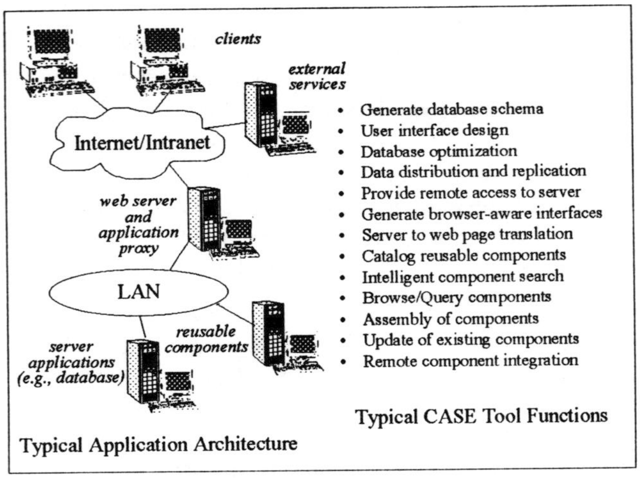

Figure 3. Future Application Architectures and CASE Tool Functions

The illustration in Figure 3 shows a supply of reusable components available to the application developer. These may be drawn from local sources such as previous development projects, or may be acquired externally by browsing the internet, or purchased from a third-party supplier. In any case, having gathered the components a CASE tool must provide support for browsing, querying, and assembling the components within the context of the current application.

Note that the architecture of the applications may be significantly more complex that the simple client/server model of computing typical of the late 1980s. In particular, shown in Figure 3 is an example in which a service provider is accessible somewhere across the internet. In this example the application makes use of external components from that service provider on a fee-for-service basis. Such approaches to distributed systems may become common as a component-based development marketplace is established.

4. Key Issues for the Future of CASE

In summary, we see that application developers for any large-scale system know that their applications must be distributed over many sites, access commercial database management systems (both relational and object-oriented), interact with legacy applications and data, and be web-enabled to allow a browser interface for display and query on heterogeneous machines across the internet. This seems to be true whatever the application domain, whether the system is a real-time command and control system, an enterprise management system, or a materiel tracking system.

Given these characteristics, the developer is faced with a bewildering set of choices. The questions to be addressed include:

- What architectural possibilities exist for a distributed system, and what are their advantages and disadvantages?
- What should the architecture of my solution look like, given the specific requirements of my domain?
- What is a good method of designing my system? Should I use an OO analysis method? A structured method? Do these work for developing web-based applications?
- How can I make use of the existing data and applications I have around? Can I reuse them? How do I wrap them?
- I've heard that all the functionality I need is available either somewhere on the net, or as commercial packages. How do I find them, evaluate them, integrate them, and test them to build my system?
- What support tools and technologies are around to help me? Are there good toolkits? Good libraries of design templates? Useful examples?

Developers of CASE tools and technologies must provide solutions which directly address these questions. These solutions must be well-crafted, and provide a reasonable return on investment for a software purchasing community that is increasingly becoming used to buying and installing low-cost shrink-wrapped software from their local computer superstore.

In this section we analyze three key aspects of future software applications which we believe CASE tools must directly support to be successful: the architecture of large-scale distributed systems, the move toward component-based software development, and the changing requirements for appropriate methods and methodologies. To conclude the section we discuss some of the pragmatic issues which are often the cause of considerable concern for established CASE vendors.

4.1 Large-Scale Distributed Software Architecture

As a consequence of recent advances in network technology, future applications will more frequently be constructed from collections of discrete functionality distributed across a range of machines. For application developers this can bring a number of new problems to the fore. In particular, designing, implementing, and managing large-scale distributed applications is a complex, error-prone task. CASE tools supporting future application development must address the challenge of simplifying the task of creating appropriate architectures for large-scale distributed systems.

Making things more concrete, for a large-scale distributed system an application developer typically has to make decisions at three levels of abstraction [16]:

- At the most abstract level, which we call the architecture level, the developer must decide on the basic "shape" of the solution. That is, the "architectural style" of a solution which determines the primary characteristics of the application's non-functional properties [2]. While Garlan and Shaw analyze these styles based on their inherent qualities, pragmatic factors seem to play a preeminent role in a developer choosing from among them. Typically, the fact that the developer has previously built a similar system dictates that the new system will have a similar style, or will differ in response to that experience. The resulting architecture must be examined with respect to the required functional (i.e., what the system must do), and non-functional (e.g., fault-tolerance, usability, portability, performance) attributes, as dictated by the specific application domain, the users' needs, and what the users are willing to pay to get them.
- At a services level the developer has to consider the interfaces among the major architectural pieces and how they will interact. This level of thinking must consider the operations, their signatures, and their abstract behavior. However, this level must also be concerned with the coordination, or structure, of the way in which they communicate. For example, it may be determined that two components of the architecture (regardless of their function) must synchronize in a particular way, communicate results via certain channels, or allow access to intermediate results through a shared persistent data area (i.e., blackboard). Also dealt with at this level are issues such as replication of service, tolerance to certain faults, unavailability of data, and so on.
- At a mechanism level the developer really does have to choose specific products, languages, platforms, etc. and make the system work. Even here the choices are numerous. For example, having chosen, say, to use Orbix, Oracle, Netscape, Java, etc. the simple question of "where do I start?" is far from straightforward. Each of these products claims some sort of integration with some subset of the others. Yet each does so on its own terms - "I integrate with ABC as long as I am in charge, you don't use features XYZ, and you compile in exactly this order!".

One of the most intriguing and challenging problems is that the designer of a large-scale distributed system must think at these three levels *at the same time*. Each level directly influences and shapes the others. For example, choosing to use an infrastructure product such as a particular CORBA implementation has a significant impact the services you design and how they interact. While software is sufficiently malleable that you can do almost anything with any product, the products make some things so difficult that the system you have designed is just too brittle, too hard to build, or too complex to maintain.

Currently the topic of software architectures is a major research area, with many technologies being developed including architectural description languages (ADLs), collections of specific styles and their inherent properties, and analysis techniques for determining appropriate architectures given a set of specific domain needs [12]. Much of this work is still in the research and prototyping stage. However, there is the promise that these ideas will be supportable by CASE tools in the very near future [4].

4.2 Component-Based Development (CBD)

For more than a decade the dream of software engineering managers has been to have "software factories" where standard components are selected from a catalog, assembled with some value-added local pieces or castigations, and sold on to a willing public. In the 1980s this vision was pursued by considering relatively broad application domains, gathering components (or more generally "assets"), and waiting for the flood of customers to make use of them [4, 5]. It didn't work. The majority of "reuse initiatives" did not succeed, and in hindsight it is for all of the obvious reasons: cataloging was hard, the assets were diverse and of varying quality, the interfaces and behavior of assets was poorly defined, and the culture of reuse undervalued and insufficiently rewarded by organizations.

The mid-1990s has seen a massive revival of reuse initiatives under the banner of "component-based development" [10]. There appear to be two separate stimuli to this. First, the economic push of moving toward greater use of commercial off-the-shelf (COTS) products. Particularly in government the use of COTS is seen as a way to reduce costs, speed up technology refreshment, and improve interoperability [6]. Second, the popularity of the world wide web and easy-to-use browsers lead to the belief that "if you want it, it will be somewhere on the net!". Indeed it is true that you can find a great deal of free software in many languages, in every application domain.

Of course, both of these stimuli are fundamentally flawed. Composing a system from COTS applications often requires a great deal of specialized integration code, and in many examples has led to systems that are brittle, impossible to upgrade, and hence very expensive. Similarly, obtaining software from the net is very much a hit-and-miss affair. There is some very good software, but after a lot of effort to find, download, and evaluate, most of it is found to be useless.

But all is not lost. There are some reasons why CBD may be more effective in the mid 1990s than it was in the 1980s. These reasons include:

- Object-oriented languages have a better structure for facilitating CBD than traditional 3GLs. C++ and Ada95 are in the best position to have an impact. As these OO languages gain a foothold in the mainstream software development community the libraries of classes available will increase.
- Into this we must also factor in Java. It's OO structure makes it ideal for creating Java component libraries, and building Java applets and applications from them. It has the added advantage that Java byte code is portable, and contains sufficient information that interface and inheritance details can be determined from a Java component even when you don't have the component's source. Standards concerning the structure of Java applets such as JavaBeans further increases the ease with which Java components can be interchanged and assembled.
- Domain-specific libraries and frameworks are starting to appear. Concentrating on domain-specific component libraries means that a number of assumptions can be made about the likely architectures of applications in the domain, and the ways in which components usually interact. This will make the cataloguing and composition of components much easier to manage. It may also mean that the integration code can be pre-defined to some extent to include some intelligence about its tasks.
- The current CBD initiatives are being vendor-led and supported. Inevitably this means some of what is produced is hype and market positioning. However, it also means that robust technology support, an established market and distribution channels, and near-term orientation will provide usable tools in a reasonable timeframe. These will underwhelm the research community, but are likely to provide some measure of simple, effective tools and techniques for developers writing applications. CBD strategies and tools have already been announced by companies such as TI, PowerSoft, Centura, and NeuronData.
- The web infrastructure is maturing. While there is a great deal of chaos and competing technology, there is also some basic shape to the infrastructure that allows collections of independently-developed software applications to be searched, remotely invoked, communicate, and share data. There is at least a hope that the technologies will converge, or at least interoperate sufficiently well that selecting among them will be based on price and performance rather than which integration strategy you want to be tied to.
- There finally appears to be some real interest and research from the academic community that is leading toward a deeper understanding of component interfaces, component integration, and the ways to detect, avoid, and repair mismatches among components. Papers by Garlan [2], Wallnau et al [8], and Kaiser [9] are good examples.

For established CASE vendors, the move to CBD will be an evolution from their current strategy and tool base. This is far from straight forward, and will probably proceed in iterative fashion. For example, a first step may consist of simply trying to "componentize" existing applications generated using the CASE tool by reengineering them to conform to a set of "component integration guidelines". This may simply be a set of naming conventions, specific required annotations on design elements, and so on. However, this will be sufficient to allow user of the CASE tool to share and exchange application designs. Additionally, this will allow users to develop new discrete pieces of applications that can be catalogued and reused (although purely within the context of that specific CASE tool).

The second step may be to take one of the major competitor's applications and allow them to be imported into that CASE tool by automatically converting them to conform to the integration guidelines. Then add another competitor's applications, and try to make the guidelines and the solution more general. The result of this evolution will be a set of translation filters for the component integration guidelines that have been shown to work with a reasonable set of applications, and experience with the processes that are carried out when developers follow a component assembly approach involving a "select and integrate" rather than "design and build" philosophy.

4.3 Methods and Methodologies

It is an unfortunate fact that structured methods as defined today are rarely used in any consistent, concerted way by the majority of software developers. Studies have found that such methods use abstractions which don't relate to the designers' perceptions of the system, are too inflexible with respect to changing the design, require too much effort to maintain once coding begins (so aren't), and do not tell maintainers of the system what they need to know to evolve the applications.

These problems are likely to become more acute with the changes in technology, and the need to develop large-scale distributed systems with significant use of CBD. The challenge for method definers is to more closely couple the methods to a development approach that:

- encourages and supports CBD as the primary approach to building an application. Hence it is the component interfaces, interactions, and dependencies that are the focus for the method.

- is more closely aligned to what designers really do when they design: a continuous cycle of "conjecture, explore, evaluate" based on experiential knowledge of what has worked before. (This cycle concludes when the money runs out, the deadline is reached, or the requirements are sufficiently scaled-back to claim you are done -- which ever comes first!).

- documents what maintainers really need to know; design rational and decision points rather than graphical representations of call graphs and inheritance trees (which can more accurately be generated from the code).

It is encouraging to see some recent technology advances which are directly addressing each of these challenges.

Addressing the first challenge, the Unified Modeling Language (UML) is proving to be an interesting focus for creating a notation which can accommodate the modeling of components and interfaces as first class objects [17]. As the UML develops, it is likely that there will be even greater pressure for it to become the standard for component modeling, responding to the influential voices of contributors to UML such as Texas Instruments and ICON Computing.

Addressing the second challenge, a new wave of development methods is being defined centered upon the notions of CBD, modeling component interconnextions, and reusing patterns of component collaboration. Methods such as Catalysis [18] and Synopsis [19] exemplify these new approaches.

Addressing the third challenge, has been a long line of work which can now take advantage of the many developments in multimedia to produce tools which weave documentation, code, audio, and video artifacts to create a complete picture of a product's design and manufacture. Some of these features are now available in most software development tools. The *n-dim* system at Carnegie-Mellon University is an innovative research example of a system modeling and design environment which captures many aspects of the design process for later analysis and review [20].

However, in addition to these challenges, any practical CBD method must exhibit another important set of characteristics essential to their success. It would seem that any such method must support at least the following:

- *Multiple entry points.* The method must support the full life cycle from software design, construction, testing, and so on. It must also support organizations starting an application development from scratch in a traditional development, those involved in a series of rapid application developments, and those wishing to update a large existing system.

- *Scaleability to different size tasks.* There is a wide variety of possible usage scenarios for CBD, ranging from small-scale reuse of class libraries, to large-scale mission-critical application building from commercial off-the-shelf (COTS) packages. It must be possible apply the method for either of these extremes, and at points in between.

- *Documentation of engineering decisions and trade-offs.* CBD is based on selection, integration, and evolution of available components. Hence, the method must support the documentation and analysis of the engineering decisions that form the heart of such an approach.

- *Specification and analysis of component interfaces.* Understanding and controlling the interfaces among components is key to CBD. Rather than simply allowing interface signatures to be defined, a CBD method must allow modeling of component interfaces to include modeling of behavior. It seems likely that some formal language may be required to allow reasoning about the behavior and about compatibilities among different component behaviors.

Viewed from a high level, a method satisfying these needs would involve at least the activities illustrated in Figure 4.

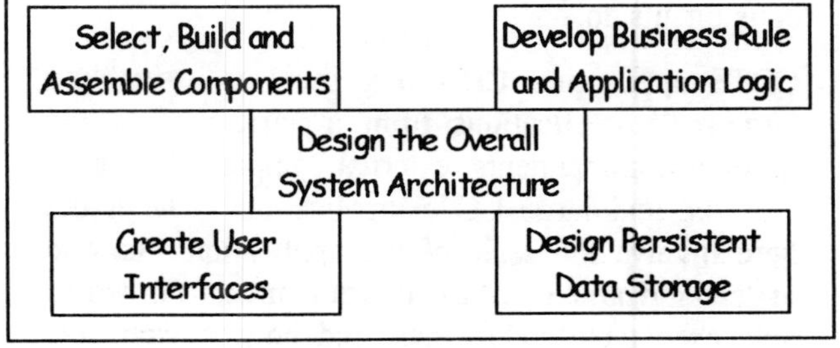

Figure 4. Activities in a CBD Method

It is important to note that the activities in Figure 4 could be carried out in any order. In fact, for a CBD method the user may engage in all of these activities simultaneously throughout the project. The key to a CBD method (and any CASE tool supporting such a method) is the support it provides for managing this concurrent design, the decisions that are made, and the impact of a decision made in one activity on the other activities.

Another key idea from Figure 4 is that business rules and logic are a separate entity that should be managed and maintained in their own right. While the expert systems initiatives of the 1970s and 1980s may have been greatly over-sold, their basic notion of separately managing business logic as a key corporate resource is very valuable.

A final comment on Figure 4 relates to the central role played by the system architecture. It can be claimed that the system architecture forms the backbone of any application. The choices made in defining this architecture dictate to a large extent many of the system's properties (e.g., performance, fault-tolerance, modifiability). If this architecture is poorly chosen, inadequately documented, or unstable, then the resulting application will likely be poorly suited to its task, and difficult to maintain and evolve.

Any CASE tool supporting CBD must provide explicit support for these features. However, the situation is more complex because it is unlikely that a single CBD method will be appropriate for all situations. There may well be at least three different kinds of CBD requiring three different kinds of method:

- Single language CBD that involves building relatively small applications from component libraries that reside locally, or that you purchase off the shelf. Examples are C++ widget libraries and Java applet libraries.
- Multi-language CBD that involves building medium sized applications from components written in multiple languages. The sources to the components are probably available, and there is likely some documentation or local expertise on what the components do.
- COTS application CBD that involves assembling large-scale applications from a variety of locally developed components, external components, legacy systems, and large COTS applications. The issues here involve the scale of the applications, how to understand and interface to components for which only executable code exists, and how to wrap and adapt legacy components to mask unwanted or untrusted behavior.

4.4 Pragmatic Concerns for Established CASE Vendors

In addition to the three primary technical areas of concern for future CASE tool support, there are some particular problems facing established CASE vendors. These are essentially pragmatic issues that inhibit an established CASE vendor from competing in a new market. A few of them are highlighted here.

4.4.1 Competing with the small tool companies

There seem to be an endless stream of small, 2-10 person companies that can quickly produce new CASE tools supporting the latest languages, technologies, and development methods. For an established CASE vendor the life-cycle from concept to product is measured in years and the cost in millions of dollars. At first sight it seems impossible to compete in such a market.

Of course, what the established companies trade on is their reputation, the marketing and support infrastructures they have in place, and the "software engineering" aspects of the tools they develop - support for multiple users, versioning, and so on. Unfortunately, this important separation between the tools is diminishing as the technology changes. In particular, on the surface it seems that the whole premise of CBD is to eliminate that separation completely!

Defining appropriate marketing strategies for tools is a major challenge. This is illustrated by the current approach in many organizations where some pieces of the tools cost many thousands of dollars, smaller versions of those tools (which consist of the main product with some features switched off!) cost only hundreds, and other add-ons are given away free. Simply deciding which part of the tools to sell, which to give away, and in which markets to compete are becoming even more difficult.

There is also an interesting change in development, testing, and release policy that is taking place. Organizations such as Netscape and Microsoft are under such pressure to release new versions of their tools that they reduce their beta testing and field testing to a minimum. Their policy of "release now, fix later" may infuriate some users, but allows them to continually add new functionality to their tools (even at the cost of robustness). Releasing a tool as soon as possible in a narrow window of opportunity is paramount. For established CASE vendors, commitment to quality may be a drawback in obtaining initial market sales!

4.4.2 Dealing with legacy platforms and code

In developing new tools, having an established user base is both an asset and a hindrance. While it provides a ready-market for new products, it also brings obligations with respect to supporting existing methods, platforms, code generators, and so on. The organization may wish to invest heavily in developing new tools that support CBD, new implementation languages, and web-based input and display. However, it has an obligation to make bug fixes to existing products running on MVS, OS/2, and a myriad of Unix operating systems.

The result is that established CASE vendors cannot commit as much resources to developing new products as they would like. Furthermore, any new products must provide a migration path for existing customers. Not doing so severely dents the reputation of the organization in the eyes of existing customers.

4.4.3 Taking on a new mindset

There is always a tendency to stick with what you know. This form of "separation anxiety" is true in every walk of life. For established CASE vendors there is a vast corporate knowledge of how to build, maintain, apply, and consult using the existing tools and techniques. Changing that involves a massive re-education of the workforce.

This problem is amplified if the organization is trying to move into new markets. For example, moving from the enterprise-level CASE tool market to the small application development market requires a completely different approach to how designers work, how the tool is marketed, what is important to long-term revenue, and so on. A significant amount of reeducation is required to overcome these problems.

5. Summary and Conclusions

This paper has examined the future profile of application developers' needs and the changing technology base that will be used to develop and maintain the resultant applications. The paper has described the kinds of applications that will be developed in the future, and the implications for established tools and tool vendors. The response to these challenges will be a major determining factor in the future success of established CASE vendors.

While the rapidly-evolving technology poses many threats, there are also many opportunities for established CASE vendors. Such vendors have an excellent base of tools, knowledge and skills, distribution and marketing channels for future products, and an existing user base that can be an important provider of requirements and new ideas for future products.

There are also significant unanswered challenges to be addressed. In particular, established CASE vendors must address the challenges of:

- understanding the distributed systems design life-cycle, the skills required to build large-scale distributed systems, and the requirements for subsequent tool support;
- investigating how CBD can be realized in practice through appropriate methods and tools;
- analyzing and comparing existing CBD methods and tools, both as a showcase of technology for the software engineering community and as a basis for determining competitive advantage for future CASE offerings.

As the CASE industry continues to consolidate, each of these challenges must be addressed to create a more mature, robust marketplace for the rapid creation of high quality, large-scale, distributed applications.

Acknowledgments

I am grateful to the following people for their comments and feedback on earlier versions of this paper: Fred Long, David Marshall, Doug McCammish, Rajko Milovanovic, Tom Shields, and the anonymous referees.

References

1. G. Booch, "The Future of Software", Presentation slides, http://www.rational.com, 1996.
2. D. Garlan and M. Shaw, "Software Architectures: Perspectives on an Emerging Discipline", Prentice-Hall, Englewood Cliffs, NJ, 1995.
3. D. Garlan et al., "Architectural Mismatch: Why its Hard to Build Systems From Existing Parts", Proceedings of the 17th International Conference on Software Engineering, pp170-185, ACM Press, 1995.
4. P.C. Clements, "A Survey of Architectural Description Languages", Proceedings of the 8th International Workshop on Software Specification and Design, Paderborn, Germany, May 1996.
5. "ASSET: Source for Software Engineering Technology", see http://source.asset.com.
6. J. Solderitsch et al., "The Reusability Library Framework: Leveraging Software Reuse", available at http://source.asset.com/stars/lm-tds/Papers/sses-rlf/symp.html, November 1992.
7. A.W. Brown, D.J. Carney, M. McFalls, Proceedings of the SEI/MCC COTS Symposium, SEI/CMU Technical Report, January 1995.

8. K.C. Wallnau et al, "Correcting, Identifying, and Avoiding Interface Mismatch: Theory and Practice", Software Engineering Institute, Carnegie Mellon University, Submitted to ICSE'97, August 1996.

9. G. Valetto and G. Kaiser, "Enveloping Sophisticated Tools into Computer-Aided Software Engineering Environments", pp40-48, Proceedings of the 7th International Workshop on CASE, IEEE Computer Society Press, July 1995.

10. A.W. Brown (ed.), "Component-Based Software Development", IEEE Computer Society Press, 1996.

11. E. Yourdon, "CASE Update", Application Development Stratiegies, V8, #10, October 1996.

12. P.C. Clements and L.N. Northrop, "Software Architecture: An Executive Overview", pp55-68 in [10].

13. R. Orlafi et al., "The Essential Distributed Object Survival Guide", John Wiley Press, 1996.

14. J. Seigel, "CORBA: Fundamentals and Programming", John Wiley Press, 1996.

15. "WebCenter: Internet for the Enterprise", Texas Instruments White Paper, Version 3, TI Part Number 264117-0001, December 13, 1996.

16. A.W. Brown et al., "Principles of CASE Tool Integration", Oxford University Press, 1995.

17. The Unified Modeling Language (UML), http://www.rational.com/uml.

18. D. D'Souza and A. Wills, "Component-Based Development Using Catalysis", To Appear, Prentice-Hall, 1997. A pre-publication version is available at http://www.iconcomp/catalysis.

19. C. Dellarocas, "Towards a Design Handbook for Integrating Software Components", Proceedings of the 5th Symposium on Assessment of Software Tools (SAST97), IEEE Computer Society Press, June 1997.

20. J. Robertson, E. Subrahmanian, M. Thomas, A.W. Westerberg, "Management of the Design Process: The Impact of Information Modeling", Technical Report, Engineering Design Research Center, Carnegie Mellon University, Pittsburgh, PA, EDRC 06-179-94, 1994.

On the Scope of Relationships

Eur.Ing. Dr. A. Alderson*, Dr. J.W. Cartmell**, A. Elliott**
*School of Computing, Staffordshire University, PO Box 334, Beaconside, Staffordshire, ST18 0DG, UK.
Tel: +44 1785 353468 Fax: +44 1785 353497 Email: cmtaa@soc.staffs.ac.uk
**Lincoln Software Ltd., Marlborough Court, Pickford Street, Macclesfield, Cheshire, SK11 6JD, UK.
Tel: +44 1625 616722 Fax: +44 1625 616780 Email: jc@ipsys.com ae@ipsys.com
Web: http://www.ipsys.com

Abstract

The concept of relationship scope is a valuable modelling concept with a variety of applications. A particular relationships' scope expresses a constraint upon the entities which may validly be linked together by an instance of the relationship. The scoping of relationships has application to validation of reference relationships, imposing semantics upon the data not otherwise expressible directly by the data model. It can be applied to enrich the concept of composite entities. It can define the constraints necessary to direct relational table generation from entity and object oriented data models. It is one of a range of techniques contributing to our meta-CASE programme of managing the complexity of CASE tools by capturing as many aspects as possible through generic functionality parameterised for specific instances by values captured declaratively.

1. Introduction

Those familiar with programming languages will be aware of the notion of the scope of an identifier - the context within which an identifier may be legitimately used. For example, in a block-structured language, an identifier is only accessible from within the block in which it is declared. The scope of relationships has more general applicability in that it is concerned with expressing validity and invalidity of a relationship within some context in which it is used.

We address three applications of the concept of the scope of relationships:

- as a constraint on the creation of relationships. Scope of relationships can be used as a constraint on creating relationships by constraining the connections that are permissible. It may be necessary to limit the entities that can be connected to a given entity by a particular relationship. For example, in a family, the relationship *sister* is constrained to be to an entity of type *female* where that female has the same *mother* as the given entity. It is not valid to link a *male* entity, even with the same *mother*. That the relationship is to a *female* is a **type constraint** and such constraints form the basis of entity-relationship modelling and object modelling. That the *female* in question has to have the same *mother* is a **scope constraint** and such constraints are the subject of this paper.
- as a constraint on reading relationships. Scope of relationships can also be used to define limitations when accessing data. In this sense the limitation relates to which entities can validly be accessed within the context of a given entity through particular relationships, and which cannot. This sense of scope is similar to progamming language scope. It can be used to enrich the notion of composite entities - a group of entities and relationships which for some purpose are to be regarded as a single unit, for example to copy them.
- as a means of defining semantic constraints on logical data models to ensure proper normalisation of a relational design derived from the model, providing the basis for determining primary and foreign keys.

1.1 An example of scope.

Consider the entity model in Figure 1. The diagram shows a fairly typical hierarchical decomposition by use of one-to-many relationships, so called master-detail relationships. To an astute data modeller, this model poses questions about the hybrids:

- can they exist between species of different genera,

- can they exist between species of different families.

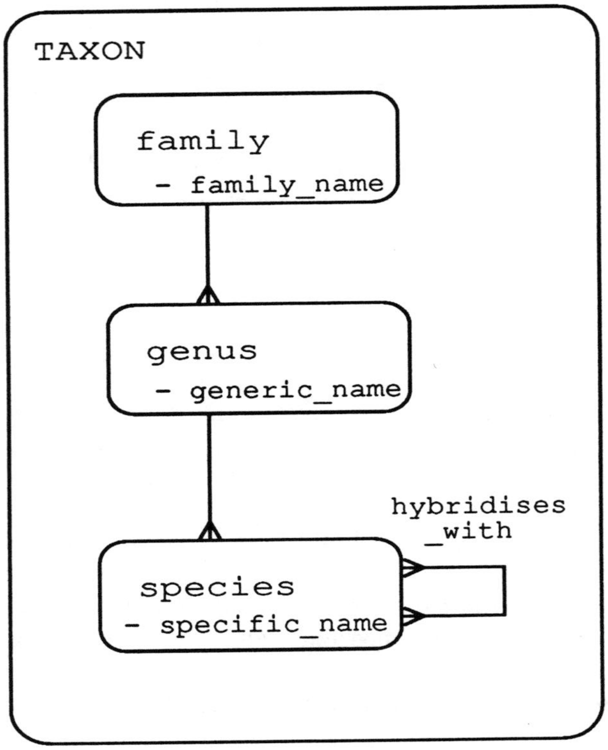

Figure 1 - Taxonomy

In the terminology of this paper, what is at issue is the **scope** of the relationship *hybridises_with.* If inter-generic hybrids do not exist then Figure 2 provides the scope of the *hybridises_with* relationship. This figure, as a **scope triangle**, expresses the constraint that hybridisation is only possible between species of the same genus.

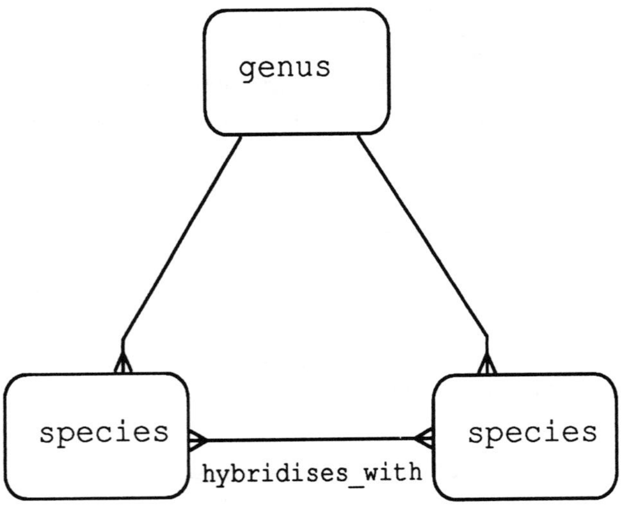

Figure 2 – Scope triangle if strongly constrained

However, if inter-generic hybrids exist, but not inter-family hybrids, then the scope is given by Figure 3. This figure, as a scope triangle, expresses the constraint that hybridisation is possible between different genera, but only of the same family. This is a weaker constraint than that of Figure 2; hybridisation is still possible between species of the same genus (since the common genus has a common family).

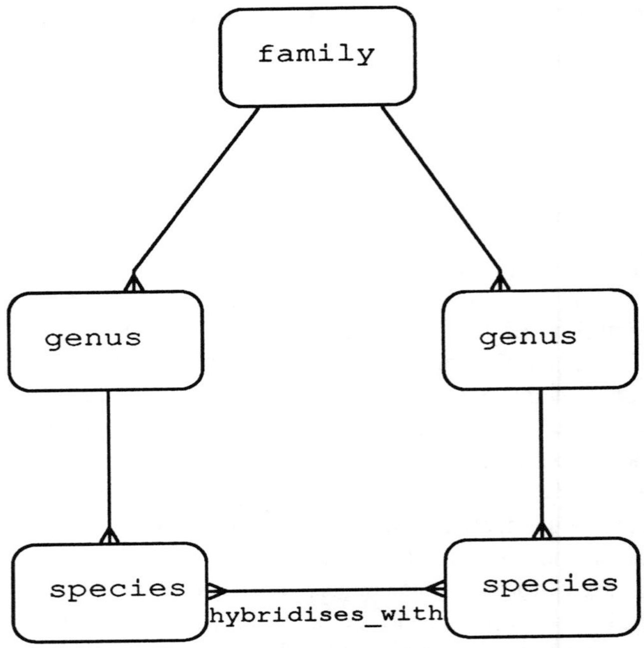

Figure 3 – Scope triangle if weakly constrained

2. Scope of relationships

Our discussion of scope is in the context of Lincoln Software's ToolBuilder metaCASE toolset. ToolBuilder is a metaCASE product -- from a specification of a Computer Aided Software Engineering (CASE) method, it generates a CASE tool supporting that method [1]. The generated CASE tool operates on an underlying database of a form developed by the Eclipse project [2]. This design has been greatly influenced by the Entity-Relationship and Functional models of Data [11, 5].

ToolBuilder views the data of the CASE tool as a collection of entities, each being a uniquely identifiable instance of some entity type. Each entity has attributes and relationships (entity-valued attributes) according to its entity type.

Two categories of stored relationship are distinguished:

- Composition relationships are used to structure data. A composition relationship is one whose destination entity depends on the relationship for its existence. An entity is deleted by removal of a composition relationship of which it is the destination. Its **substructure** is also deleted. The substructure consists of all those entities that can be reached from the entity by traversing composition relationships. All entities of the CASE database are reachable by composition relationships from the root entity of the database.

- Reference relationships are used to cross-reference data. Deleting a reference relationship has no effect on the existence of entities. Reference relationships can be validated against a constraint on their scope, which limits the entities to which they may refer.

Derived relationships are defined in terms of other relationships, and they are derived ultimately from stored relationships. Derived relationships may be defined to be:

- paths in which component relationships are composed together end to end,
- aggregations in which component relationships are put together side by side, the result being determined by union or concatenation of the results of the components,
- user-defined in which a user supplied function provides the derivation.

Paths are like relational joins. Each component relationship is evaluated in the context of the results of evaluating previous component relationships. They may be defined to be followed recursively. A single-valued path is composed from single-valued or many-valued component relationships, and has a single value that is reached by traversing each component relationship in turn. A many-valued path may have single-valued or many-valued component relationships, is evaluated as all entities that are reachable by evaluating each component in turn. Aggregations are like relational unions. A single-valued aggregation may have single-valued or many-valued component relationships. They are evaluated as the union of the results obtained by evaluating the components in turn.

2.1 Scopes of reference relationships

Every reference relationship may have a scope specified for it. The scope of a reference relationship is expressed by a **scope triangle**, in which the constraint on the reference relationship is determined by two further relationships known as the **host base** relationship and the **target base** relationship. The minimal requirements for a host (target) base relationship is that it be single-valued, connecting the host (target) entity type of the reference relationship to a common **base** entity type. Together the reference relationship and the two base relationships form a scope triangle in the entity model, see Figure 4. This way of expressing the constraint is used to generate the possible destinations of a relationship.

The diagram in Figure 4, as a scope triangle, expresses the constraint that for all *b* of type *B*, if relationship *r* exists to entity *c* of type *C* then the value of the host base relationship at *b* is identical to the value of the target base relationship at *c*. Though we have shown *r* to be one-many it may be of any cardinality.

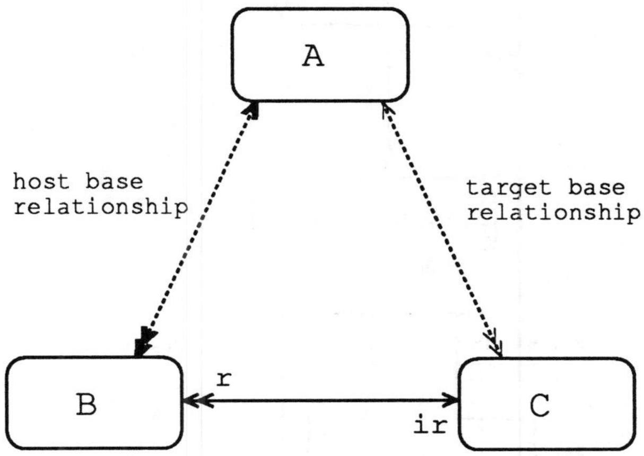

Figure 4 – The general scope triangle

2.2 Scope triangles and scope squares

We will demonstrate the properties of the scope of relationships through an example using the data model for a simple programming language, making the connection with identifier scope in programming languages. Figure 5 shows the data model used by the static analyser for a simple programming language.

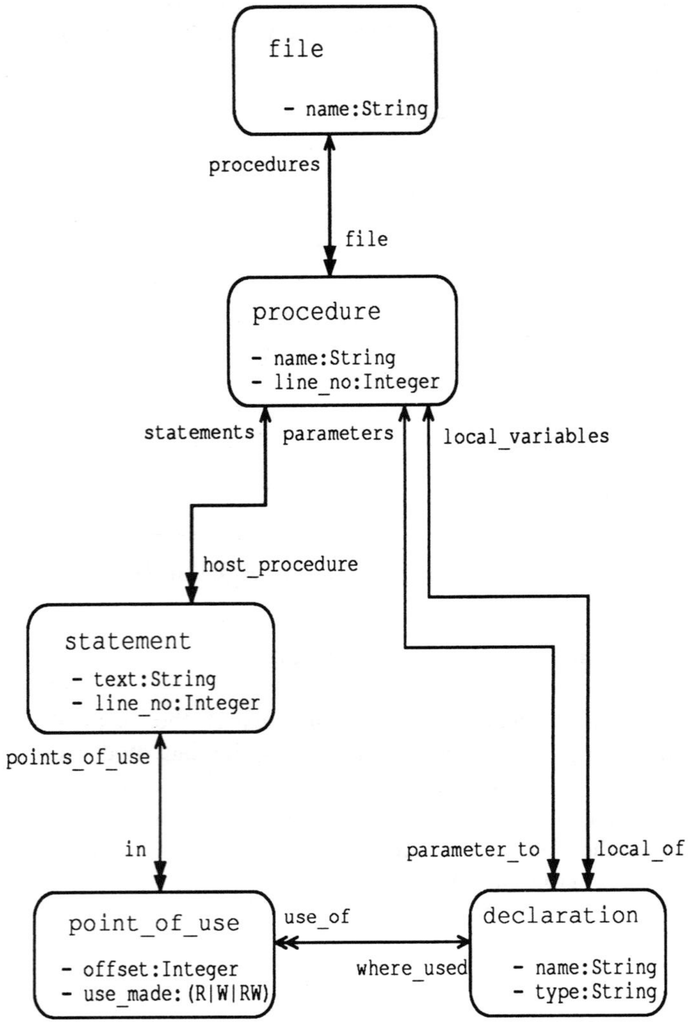

Figure 5 – Data model used by static analyser

Two derived relationships form the sides of a scope triangle for the relationship *use_of - where_used* between a *point_of_use* and the *declaration* used, as shown in Figure 6.

In Figure 6:

I. Shows the scope triangle

II. Shows the derivation diagram for the path, *points_of_use - host_procedure*, between entity types *procedure* and *points_of_use*, derived by composing the relationship *statements - host_procedure*, between entity types *procedure* and *statement*, with the relationship *points_of_use - in*, between entity types *statement* and *points_of_use*, end-to-end

III. Shows the derivation diagram for the aggregation, *declarations - site*, between entity types *procedure* and *declaration* derived from the relationship *local_variables - local_of* and the relationship *parameters - parameters_to* of the same entity types.

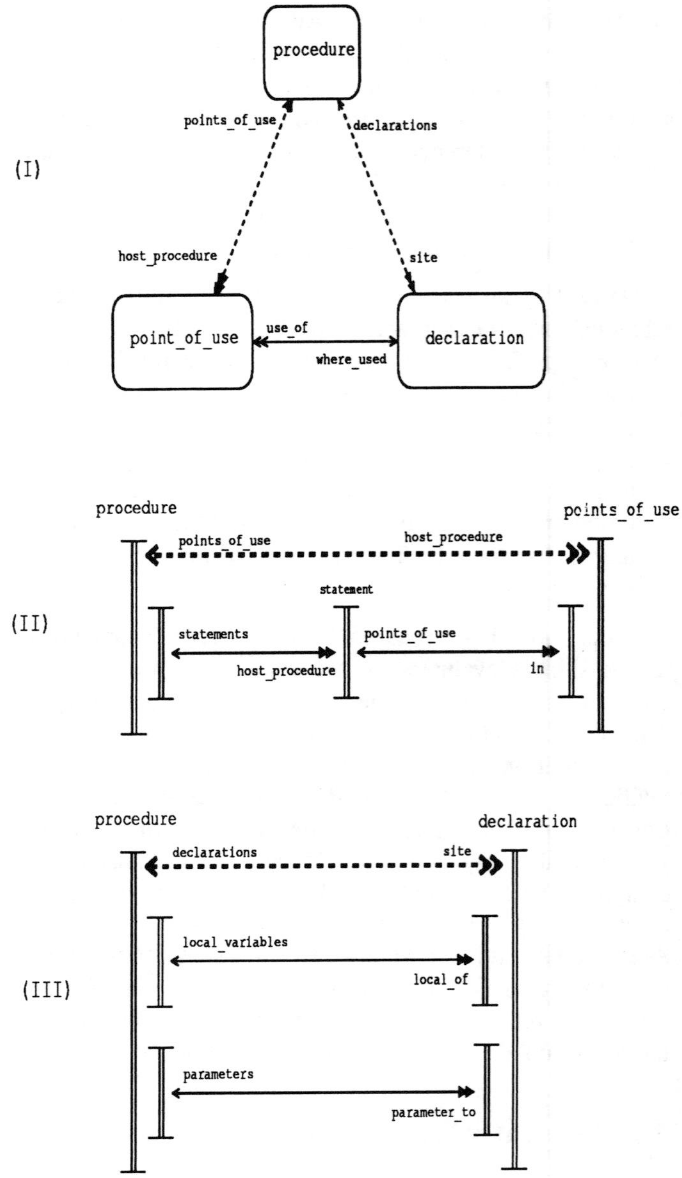

Figure 6 – Scope triangle and base derivations

The meaning of Figure 6(I) as a scope triangle is that a *declaration* may only be used at a *point_of_use* within the scope of the same *procedure*. Conversely, given a *point_of_use* all *declarations* in scope are given by the derived path relationship of *host_procedure* followed by *declarations*. We have constructed a definition of an identifier scope (the scope of *declaration*) using the notion of the scope of a relationship. The relationship *use_of - where_used* is constrained by the host base relationship *points_of_use - host_procedure* and the target base relationship *declarations - site*. We see that scope is a general modelling concept not limited to programming languages.

Suppose now that in our programming language declarations may be made global to files and that such global declarations may be used in statements of any procedure within the same file. In the terminology of the 'C' language these would be known as *statics*. We extend our programming language data model by introducing the abstract entity type *SITE*, which has *file* and *procedure* as subtypes and by adding the composition relationship *statics* between entity types *file* and *declaration*. Figure 7 shows this additional modelling and also shows three derived relationships.

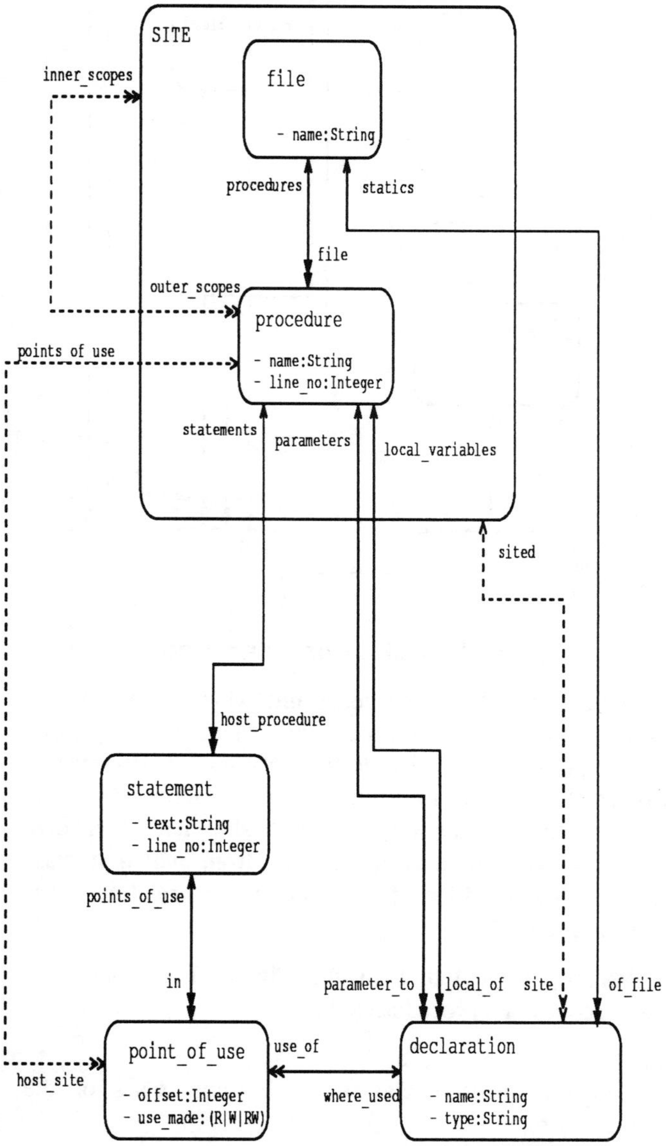

Figure 7 – Extended model

The triangle of relationships of Figure 6(I) is no longer a valid constraint for the *use_of - where_used* relationship. Though a scope triangle with *file* as the base entity type can be defined, it does not express the fact that *locals* within a *procedure* can only be referenced from within that same *procedure*. The scope rules of the language are instead described by a scope square, as shown in Figure 8.

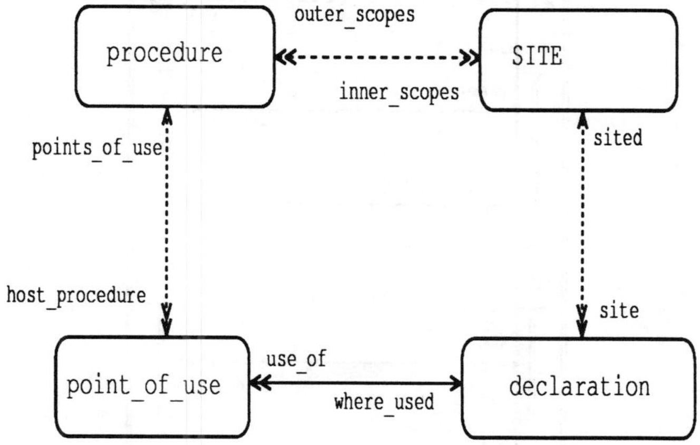

Figure 8 – Scope square

A scope square has a *bridge relationship* between its host base and target base entity types. The bridge relationship will always be a many-many relationship (for if it were single-valued in either direction the scope would revert to a triangle). Figure 8 uses the derived relationships outlined in Figure 7 and whose definitions are given in Figure 9.

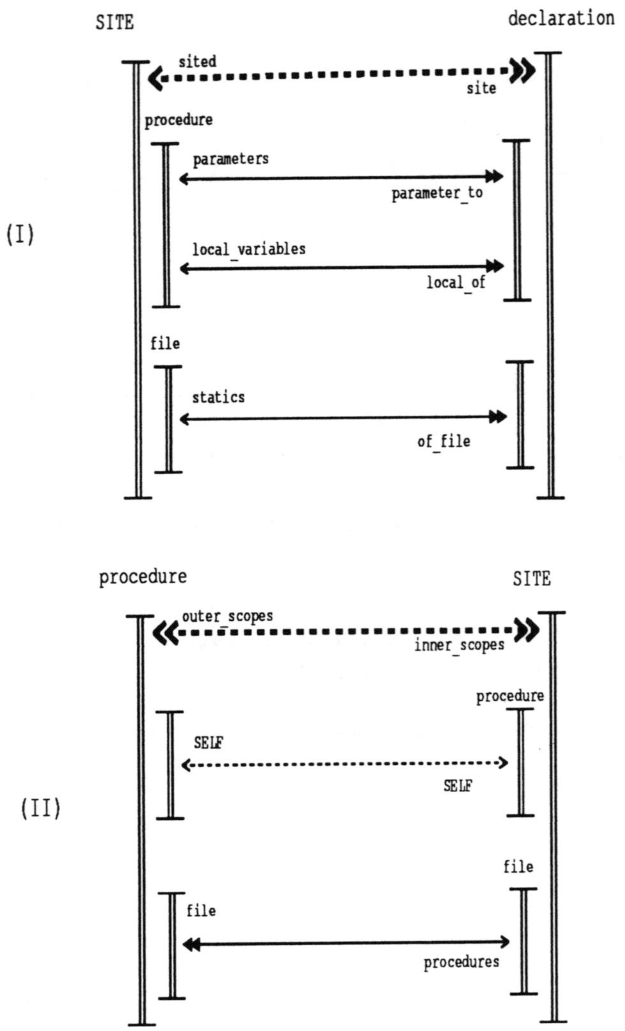

Figure 9 – Derivations in the extended model

Figure 9(II) can be read in two ways:

- left to right - the *outer_scopes* of a *procedure* are the procedure itself (SELF) and the containing *file*.
- right to left - the *inner_scopes* of a *site* are:
    - if the *site* is a *procedure*, then the *procedure* itself (SELF)
    - if the *site* is a *file*, then the *procedures* of the *file*.

As a final example, suppose the language in question is object-oriented and supports classes and class inheritance. The simplest meta-model we can use to scope the *use_of* - *where_used* relationship is as shown in Figure 10.

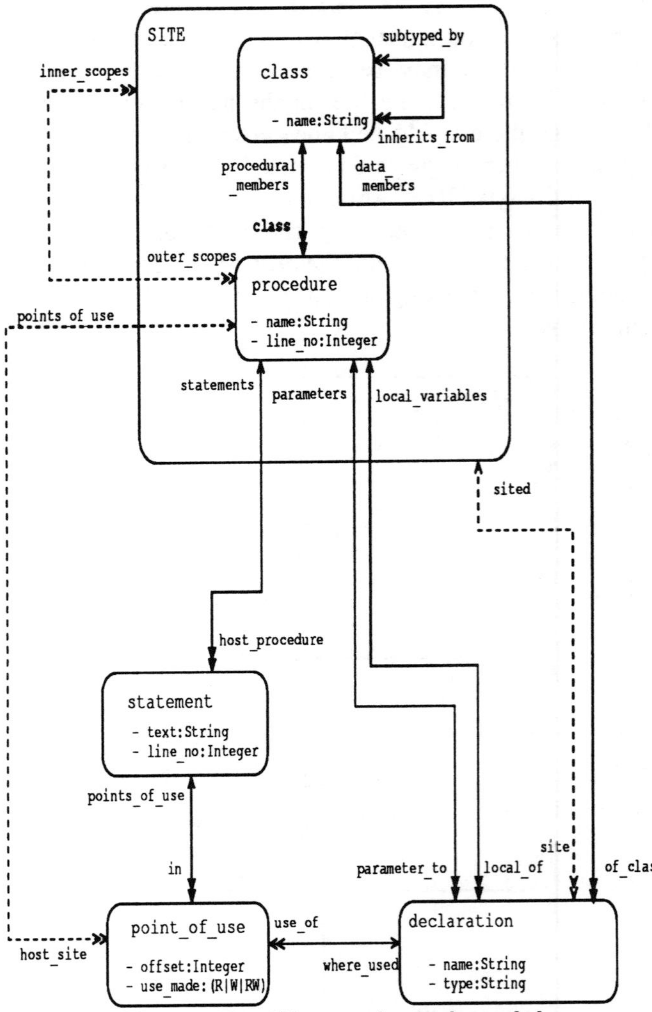

Figure 10 – Class oriented model

In this case the scope constraint which expresses the scope of declarations within the language is still expressed by a scope square identical to that in Figure 8. However in this case to take account of inheritance the definition of the *outer_scopes* - *inner_scopes* relationship has to involve recursion over the ancestor classes from which a class inherits. The definition of a suitable derived relationship is given in Figure 11.

Reading from left to right Figure 11 defines the *outer_scopes* of a procedure to be:

I. the procedure itself and
II. all the ancestor classes of the host class of the procedure,

where the ancestor classes of a class are defined to be classes reachable by zero, one or more traversals of the *inherits_from* relationship.

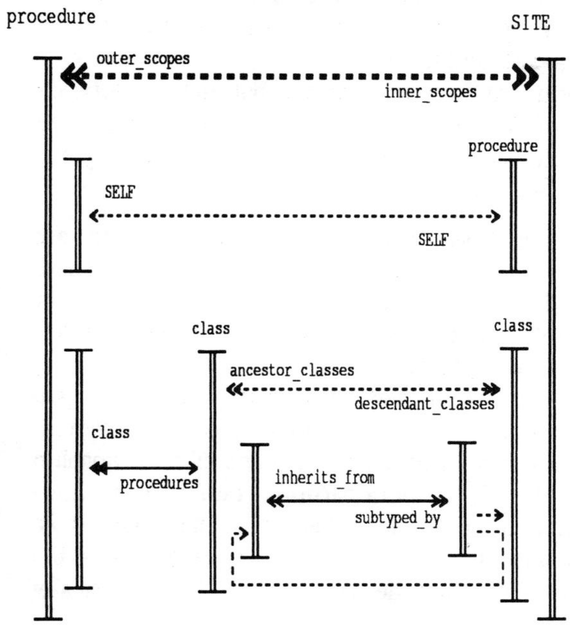

Figure 11 – Recursive derivation from the class oriented model

3. Composite entities

The notion of a composite entity or composite object is common to many database models intended for use by CASE tools, for example Damokles [7], PCTE [9] and ToolBuilder. The idea is that the structure of a complex entity is represented by a group of entities and relationships. Functions, such as copy, are then provided to manipulate the whole structure.

Damokles has the concept of molecular aggregation, allowing the composition of arbitrary entity and relationship instances to form new entities in their own right. These are structured (or complex or composite) objects. The exact semantics of composite objects are defined in the operations of the Damokles database interface. Examples include the retrieval and copying of entire objects. When deleting a composite object, there are several cases depending on whether all its components are to be deleted, or whether the components are to remain in their own right.

In PCTE and ToolBuilder, the structure is determined by distinguished kinds of relationships - the composition relationships.

In ToolBuilder, the entities contributing to a composite entity are all of those entities which can be reached from a given entity which represents (is a placeholder for) the composite entity. The contributing reference relationship instances of the contributing entities are those **dominated** by the placeholder entity. An entity **dominates** a relationship instance if the relationship instance is internal to the substructure of the dominating entity. By internal, we mean that the source and destination entities of the relationship are within the substructure of the dominating entity.

A **strict scope triangle** constraint is one in which the host base and target base relationships are derived entirely from composition relationships; we call them **structural derived relationships.** A strict scope triangle constraint for a relationship ensures that every instance of the relationship is dominated by a base entity of a particular common base entity type at the apex of the triangle. A strict scope triangle constraint for a relationship defines a locality of reference for that relationship. A structural derived relationship of particular interest is the aggregate of all composition relationships recursively. This is predefined by ToolBuilder and is given the name *!children*. This returns every entity in the substructure of a given entity and so determines the structure of a composite entity.

The ToolBuilder operation for copying composite entities copies the attributes of all entities in the substructure. When copying reference relationships there is a different action according to whether the destination entity of the relationship is within the substructure (internal) or not (external).

If an internal reference relationship does not have scope defined then it is copied. If the internal reference relationship has a scope defined and the base entity is internal, then the relationship is copied. If the base entity of the relationship to be copied is external and if the base entity of the copy of the relationship would be the same, then the relationship is copied. If an external reference relationship does not have a scope defined then it is copied. All the remaining external reference relationships whose base entity would be unchanged by the copy are copied.

These rules ensure that scope violations do not occur when composite objects are copied.

The reference relationships to be copied need to be ordered so that there is no attempt to copy relationships before relationships they depend on for their scoping have been copied. If there are circularities in the dependency graph then these are given as errors.

A common use of composite entities in ToolBuilder is to implement of Copy, Cut and Paste operations on diagrams.

4. Converting logical data models to relational data models

The scope concept is applicable in any entity-relationship model and in any object model, such as those of OMT [10]. If the logical model is to be carried forward to relational data design then the expression of scopes at the logical level contributes to a properly normalised table design.

Consider again the logical model in Figure 1 recast in Figure 12 to represent the many-many relationship as a separate entity. In a physical database design targetted at a relational database the *species* table has a composite key consisting of the *family_name,* the *generic name* and the *specific_name.* We have seen that the scope triangle is necessary to describe the constraint upon possible hybridisations. Two possible scopes exist for hybridisation in this example, and these have been represented in Figure 3 and Figure 4. Two related physical designs of the *hybrid* table therefore exist, as shown in Figure 12. The correct one cannot be deduced from the logical model without knowledge of the scope of the *hybridises_with* relationship.

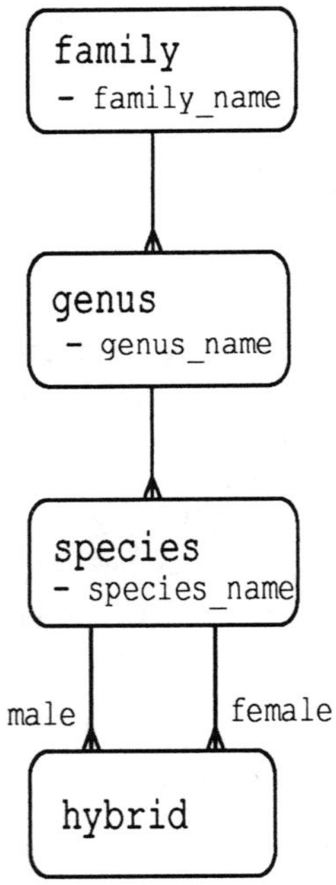


```
   Columns
   -------
a) family_name
   generic_name
   male_specific_name
   female_specific_name

   Columns
   -------
b) family_name
   male_generic_name
   female_generic_name
   male_specific_name
   female_specific_name
```

Figure 12 - Taxonomy - normalised relational model

a) If hybrids cannot be intergeneric then a hybrid is identified by a single generic name and two specific names - male and female.
b) If hybrids can be intergeneric but not be between genera of different families then a hybrid is identified by a male genus and species names and female genus and species names.

The foreign keys of relational database design are replaced by physical pointers in an object-oriented database implementation. The relational model is at the extreme in that each table has its own address space. In ToolBuilder, each physical data partition has its own address space and, therefore, addresses, in their physical implementation, are generally two part addresses containing partition address and address within partition. If the scope of a relationship determines that it is intra-partition rather than inter-partition, then instead a one part address is held. Just as we saw in the discussion of relational implementations the scope of a relationship determines how it is physically implemented.

5. Summary

The scope of relationships is a valuable modelling concept with a variety of applications. It expresses a constraint upon the entities which may validly be linked together by an instance of a particular relationship. It is related to scope of identifiers in programming languages, and we have shown that in a data model of a programming language, scope of relationships can be used to express the semantics of the scope of identifiers. Scope of relationships can be expressed by scope triangles and by scope squares.

As we have presented it, the extended model, Figure 7, is tantalisingly close to the class oriented model, Figure 10, and the general scope square, Figure 8, suggests itself as a common abstract model. However, it is necessary to be wary because more detailed modelling is required to obtain full scope definitions for actual programming languages. Figure 10 falls short of modelling a full OO programming language. For example, the *type* attribute of a declaration should be modelled as a reference relationship to entity type *class.* The models have been kept simple because it has been the intention of the authors to introduce, in a simple way, the abstract concept of scope and supporting notations.

In ToolBuilder, scope of relationships is applied to validation of reference relationships, imposing semantics upon the data not expressible directly by the data model. In this role, it is used in the ToolBuilder data transformation and merging capability to resolve potential addressing ambiguities when loading reference relationships [3]. It is applied to the implementation of operations on composite entities. It is also used in CASE tools generated by

ToolBuilder to implement relational table generation from entity and object oriented data models.

Scope of relationships is one of a range of techniques contributing to our programme with ToolBuilder of managing the complexity of CASE tools by capturing as many aspects as possible through generic functionality parameterised declaratively for specific instances. We have found that the complexity of the algorithms involved can be controlled by factoring it through a data model supported by notions such as scope.

Acknowledgements

We would like to thank Pam Flood of Lincoln Software for cheerfully supporting us in the word processing and graphical production of this paper.

We would also like to thank the referees for their helpful comments.

References

[1] Alderson A., Meta-CASE Technology, *In:* A.Endres and H.Weber (Eds.), *Software Development Environments and CASE Technology*, Lecture Notes In Computer Science, 509, Springer-Verlag,1991.

[2] Alderson A., Cartmell J.W. and Elliott A., The Concepts Underlying a MetaCASE Tool, SOCTR/97/02, School of Computing, Staffordshire University, 1997a.

[3] Alderson A., Cartmell J.W. and Elliott A., Data Transformation Based On Data Model Derivation, SOCTR/97/03, School of Computing, Staffordshire University, 1997b.

[4] Alderson A. and Elliott A., The Eclipse Tool-Builder's Kit and the HOOD Toolset, *In:* K. H. Bennett (Ed.), *Software Engineering Environments: Research and Practice*, Ellis Horwood, Chichester, UK, 1989.

[5] Buneman P., Frankel R.E. and Nikhik R., An implementation technique for database query languages, *ACM Transactions on Database Systems* 7(2), 1982.

[6] Cartmell J.W., Formalising the Network and Hierarchical Data Models - An Application of Categorical Logic, *In: Category Theory and Computer Programming*, Lecture Notes in Computer Science 240, Springer-Verlag, 1989.

[7] Dittrich K.R., The DAMOKLES Database System for Design Applications: Its past, its Present and its Future, *In:* K. H. Bennett (Ed.), *Software Engineering Environments: Research and Practice*, Ellis Horwood, Chichester, UK, 1985.

[8] DoD, Common Ada Programming Support Environment (ASPE) Interface Set (CAIS), MIL-STD-1838A, United States Department of Defense, April 1989.

[9] ECMA, Portable Common Tool Environment (PCTE), Abstract Specification, ECMA-149, 2nd Edition, June 1993.

[10] Rambaugh J.E., Blaha M., Premerlani W., Eddy F. and Lorensen W., *Object Oriented Modelling and Design*, Prentice-Hall, Englewood Cliffs, New Jersey, USA, 1991.

[11] Shipman D.W., The functional data model and the data language DAPLEX, *ACM Transactions on Database Systems* 6(1), 1981.

[12] Earl Waldin and Howard Ricketts, Tailored Case - A Case Study in Metacase, *In: Objects in Europe*, Volume 1, Number 4, Autumn 1994.

Ahead-of-time Debugging, or Programming Not in the Dark

James L. Snell
Snell Software Consultants, Inc.
jsnell@acm.org

Abstract

Code composition is error-prone because it places severe demands on the programmer's cognitive processes. The programmer could benefit from the machine's help at this stage, but conventional programming environments are essentially passive then. The usual assumption is that the programmer does debugging after entering a whole routine, although by this time his/her memory of some details may have decayed. We propose that coding efficiency would be improved if, as soon as a statement is typed, it is executed, and the new program state is displayed. The programmer can see whether the statement has the intended effects, and correct it while the thinking for it is still fresh. We have implemented and informally tested a prototype of this "ahead-of-time debugging" feature. We found that users fix more bugs during code entry and produce code faster and with fewer errors, compared with a conventional environment, and report that using the latter is like "programming in the dark."

1. Introduction and rationale

This project was motivated by two observations:

(1) It is widely recognized that the process of composing program code places heavy demands on human cognition [3, 12, 30]. In coding a single statement, the programmer typically must recall several program states, decide what state changes are needed, choose code to produce them, mentally simulate those changes, typically for several different cases, verify that the changes are the intended ones, and remember the new states. (We use the term "programmer" in a generic sense to mean a person who composes program code or does code-level program design or debugging.) In addition, the programmer must maintain a complex goal structure that relates this statement to others, all ultimately back to the top-level programming goal. As any programmer knows, this finely detailed mental activity can strain the limits of human cognition (e.g., mental workload and memory load [14], stress and fatigue [10]). Given the highly error-prone nature of this process, it is not surprising that programmers write code containing bugs.

(2) Program development environments (PDEs) (and debuggers, which we include in this category for simplicity), provide powerful features for debugging after a program or routine has been entered (breakpoints, single-stepping, watching variables, etc.), but little help during the original entry of program code. This we conclude from an informal survey of some widely used PDEs, including: the Borland C++ and Turbo Pascal Integrated Development Environments; the Microsoft Visual C++ Visual Workbench and Visual Basic programming environment; the DBG debugger supplied with Prime computers; the UNIX debuggers adb, gdb, sdb; and dbx; and the common programming environments for APL, Prolog, and LISP. Some of these provide syntax checking, highlighting, and/or formatting during code entry, which is useful but is no help with logic errors. And some provide an "evaluate mode" that allows a single statement or expression to be typed in, and executes or evaluates it interactively; however, this feature is very limited: It does not display program states automatically, as with a watch window in "debug mode"; and it is completely separate from "entry/edit mode," in which the programmer enters statements to build a new routine. There is apparently an implicit assumption that the programmer will finish composing a routine before starting to test and debug it.

As we juxtaposed these two observations, a new feature occurred to us that could benefit programmers during the initial composition process. This feature would combine "entry/edit mode," "evaluate mode," and "debug mode": As the programmer entered the code for a new routine, as soon as each statement was entered, the environment would execute it and display the new program state. In this way, the programmer would be able to compare the actual consequences of a statement with its intended consequences, and to modify it immediately if necessary. The choice of objects to be displayed as the program state would be specified interactively, as with a debugger watch list. Furthermore, the execution should be able to show the program states for several different test cases. To use the

0-8186-7840-2/97 $10.00

latter feature, the programmer would specify a list of test cases beforehand, and optionally a corresponding list of intended states. The point would be to allow the programmer to offload as much of the memory burden and mental work as possible onto the machine, thereby freeing his/her cognitive resources for more creative tasks. We decided to call this feature "ahead-of-time" (AOT) debugging, since it promotes debugging before a routine is complete, rather than afterwards.

Our main hope and expectation was that use of AOT debugging would reduce time to complete a given programming task, and bug frequency in the code produced. We also expected that discovering and fixing an error in a given statement should help to prevent errors in subsequent statements. Finally, we predicted some affective side-effects of the offloading of cognitive burden: that programmers would experience greater satisfaction and lower levels of stress and fatigue, and might also adopt a freer, more experimental style of programming. The purpose of this project is to test these various hypotheses.

2. AOT debugging and the evolution of programming environments

An analogy with the evolution of other classes of software suggests that the AOT feature is a natural progression from current PDE designs. Consider how text-processing software tools (or "document development environments," by analogy) have evolved in the past four decades. To summarize: In the '60s one typed text on keypunch machines, programmed the formatting using a batch-mode markup language (e.g., Script or SGML), and waited for paper printout. In the '70s video terminals and line editors became common (e.g., Wylbur, QED, ed), allowing the user to edit text interactively, but displaying the changes on only one line at a time. In the early '80s line editors were supplanted by full-screen editors (e.g., XEDIT, emacs), allowing the user to edit anywhere on the screen and immediately see the results, but still only with typewriter text and embedded formatting commands; one had to get printout to see the actual formatting. In the '90s WYSIWYG word processing has become widely available (starting with Apple's MacWrite in 1984, and now with all the major products, e.g., Microsoft Word and WordPerfect); these allow the user to interactively view and edit text of any style, exactly as it will appear when printed—one mode for the entire document development process. Thus there has been a progression of levels of interactiveness, i.e., increasingly immediate visibility of the consequences of user actions, with fewer and fewer modes to switch among, allowing the user to offload more and more memory and cognitive burden onto the computer, and to concentrate on creative tasks.

Programming environments for high-level languages have evolved similarly. In the '60s, the only "programming environment" entailed punch-card input and line-printer output; in the '70s, interactive line-editing of source code became standard, with remote submission and retrieval of batch jobs for compilation and execution; in the '80s full-screen editing and interactive compilation, execution, and symbolic debugging became common, though typically with separate software for each; and in the '90s program development environments have become widely available, providing all four functions in a single software product. As with text processors, there has been a progression of levels of interactiveness. But notice that in current PDEs the functions are not fully integrated (notwithstanding the word "integrated" in some product names): "Edit/entry mode" is still completely separate from "execution/ debugging mode," and from "evaluate mode." The AOT debugging feature removes these boundaries, providing a truly integrated program development environment—as with WYSIWYG text processors, one mode for the entire program development process.

3. A fictitious example of AOT debugging

Consider the following programming problem, as attempted by a fictitious programmer whom we will call Tom. We have chosen an artificially simple problem for the sake of simplicity, but we can partly compensate by supposing that Tom is a relatively inexperienced programmer. The problem is to write a Pascal function, pow, that takes two real arguments, x and y, and returns x^y, computing the result with a loop when the value of y is an integer, otherwise with logarithms. In case the value is undefined, the function should return the predeclared constant undef_real. The function must satisfy the following 14 test cases:

pow(2.5,3)=15.6250	pow(-2.5,3)=-15.6250
pow(2.5,-3)=0.0640	pow(-2.5,-3)=-0.0640
pow(2,1.5)=2.8284	pow(-2,1.5)=undefined
pow(2,-1.5)=0.3536	pow(-2,-1.5)=undefined
pow(0,0)=1	pow(2,0)=1
pow(-2,0)=1	pow(0,1.5)=0
pow(0,-1)=undefined	pow(0,-1.5)=undefined

Suppose Tom begins by writing the following pseudocode, which contains several bugs:

1. If y is an integer: val=1; for n=1 to y, val=val*x
2. If y is not an integer: if x<=0 then val is undefined, else val=$e^{x*\log(y)}$
3. Return val

Working from this pseudocode, in a conventional PDE he might compose the following Pascal code (for simplicity, we will assume there are no syntax problems):

```
function pow(x,y:real):real;      {returns x to the y power}
var  val:  real;                  {value to be returned}
     n:    integer;               {counter for loop}
begin
if y=trunc(y)                     {if y is an integer...}
then begin
     val:=1;                      {init val to 1 before loop}
     for n:=1 to y do             {loop y times}
          val:=val*x              {accum product of val}
     end
else                              {if y isn't an integer...}
     if x<0                       {if x is negative}
     then val:=undef_real         {value is undefined}
     else val:=exp(x*log(y));     {otherwise use log}
pow:=val                               {return val}
end;
```

Notice that in the translation and entry steps, this code inherited all the bugs in the pseudocode, and gained more besides. Using the PDE, Tom adds a driver program around the function to test it, and tests pow(2.5,3), which happily yields 15.625000. He proceeds to test further cases, but soon runs into cases where the function fails. He has trouble understanding which statements are causing which cases to fail, and is not quite sure which statements he intended to handle which cases. After many tests using the debugger's step-through and variable watch features, Tom discovers the bugs: the cases he missed originally (negative integer exponents, negative bases with non-integer exponents), the reversal of x and y and the use of log rather than ln in the original formula, and the miscopied <= symbol. With persistence he fixes them, although while doing so he introduces a new bug (0 with a negative integer exponent), which he also has to fix.

Now let us return to the original pseudocode, this time with Tom starting out using the AOT debugging environment. He first enters the 14 triples of values for x, y, and the required value for pow(x,y) in the test cases window, and specifies "all variables" for the program state variables. He then starts to enter the same code as before:

```
function pow(x,y:real):real;      {returns x to the y power}
var val:       real;              {value to be returned}
    n:         integer;           {counter for loop}
```

In response to each of these three lines, the program state window shows first x and y, then val, and finally n, all as undefined for all 14 cases. Tom continues:

```
begin
if y=trunc(y)                     {if y is an integer...}
then begin
     val:=1;                      {init val to 1 before loop}
```

The environment is passive until Tom types this statement, at which point the program state window updates the value of val to 1 for the eight cases in which y is an integer. Tom continues:

```
     for n:=1 to y do             {loop y times}
          val:=val*x              {accum product of val}
     end
```

Here the program state window shows some new values for those eight cases: n becomes y+1 in each case, and val gets a new value (x^y) in the two cases where y is positive, pow(2.5,3) and pow(-2.5,3). Tom is surprised because he expected val to be updated for the negative y cases too (pow(2.5,-3) and pow(-2.5,-3)). But since he just wrote that statement, his intentions for the loop, the details of its logic, and the relevant variable states are all fresh in his mind, and he easily sees where the bug is, and changes the code to:

```
     for n:=1 to abs(y) do        {loop abs(y) times}
          val:=val*x;             {accum product of val}
     if y<0 then val:=1/val       {if y neg, use reciprocal}
     end
```

Now, to Tom's surprise, the state of val for the case of pow(0,-1), changes to "overflow"! But again, since he has just composed the buggy statement, he quickly understands the cause of the problem and replaces the line with:

```
     if y<0                       {if y negative...}
     then if x=0                  {if x=0, val=0}
          then val=undef_real     {0 to neg pow undefined}
          else val:=1/val         {if x<>0, use reciprocal}
```

Notice how in this situation, fixing one bug introduced another one. In a conventional PDE this second bug might have gone unnoticed for a while, and would likely be approached as completely unrelated to the one from which it propagated. In the AOT environment, that kind of propagation is likely to be caught immediately, while the logic associated with it is fresh in the programmer's mind. Tom verifies that all eight integer-exponent cases are correct, and continues with:

```
else                      {if y isn't an integer...}
    if x<0                {if x is negative}
    then val:=undef_real  {value is undefined}
```

The states of val for pow(-2,1.5) and pow(-2,-1.5) change to undef_real as Tom expects, but he is surprised to see that the same didn't happen for the other two undefined cases. Because these are the x=0 cases, it is immediately obvious that he has copied <= from the pseudocode as <, so he makes the change and the other two cases are now shown correctly. Next he enters:

```
    else val:=exp(x*log(y));   {otherwise use log}
```

The states of val for the two remaining cases change, but to the wrong numbers: 1.422168 for pow(2,1.5) instead of 2.828427, and "overflow" for pow(2,-1.5) instead of 0.353553. Referring to the pseudocode, Tom sees that x and y are backwards and switches them, but still the values are wrong! Using a conventional debugger here, one might assume the bug could be anywhere in the whole routine. But in the AOT environment, Tom knows that all the code down to this point in the routine is already debugged, so he has high confidence that it is worth investing a lot of thought in this one statement. Rethinking the mathematics from first principles, sure enough he realizes his error in the original pseudocode, and replaces the log function with ln. The states of val for the remaining two cases now become correct. He concludes the function with:

```
pow:=val                         {return val}
end;
```

At the instant that Tom is done entering the code, he is also done debugging it.

This example is fictitious, though it is based on observed user interactions with the AOT debugger prototype. It is also unrealistic: Increasingly in modern software development, programmers use object-oriented methodology, working not with language primitives, but with high-level objects, some original but most taken or modified from a standard library; the coding and debugging issues concern the behaviors and interfaces of objects, and the interactions among them. In addition, large software development projects involve programming in teams rather than single authorship. We suspect that the benefits of the AOT environment we have observed will generalize and scale in these ways, but these hypotheses remain to be tested.

4. Experience with a prototype AOT debugging environment

We have built a small prototype programming environment that implements the AOT debugging feature. It incorporates an interpreter/debugger for almost the full Pascal language (written in C) [24], and is driven by a standard graphical user interface running in Windows 95 (written in Delphi). As the user types each line of code into the edit window, the interpreter is invoked automatically and displays in another window the new program state for each of several test cases. The interface includes windows in which the user specifies lists of test data and variables for the program state, which the user can modify interactively at any time. It also includes controls and windows for loading and saving the source file, specifying its name, running the complete program, issuing commands to the debugger, displaying interpreter and debugger messages and program output, etc.

To date we have done only informal testing with a few users (students and colleagues), in the process of refining our hypotheses, factor definitions, methodology, and the software itself. Users are given printed specifications, pseudocode, and test data for short programs, and asked to code and validate the programs as quickly as possible, using either the prototype AOT debugging environment or a conventional PDE (the Borland Turbo Pascal Integrated Development Environment). Before a session each user is asked to rate his/her levels of stress and fatigue, and afterwards the same ratings are requested, as well as level of satisfaction with the programming environment, and any other relevant comments. So far we have made the following general observations:

1. Users detect and fix a substantial number of bugs during initial code entry when using the AOT environment, compared with almost none using a standard PDE.
2. Propagation of logic errors is reduced by using the AOT environment.
3. The AOT users generally produce code faster and with fewer errors in the process, as well as fewer bugs in the end result.
4. AOT users report a higher degree of satisfaction and smaller increases in stress and fatigue than users of the standard PDE.

There are also some anecdotal observations that seem interesting. Some users, when first introduced to the AOT environment, have made remarks like "This makes programming fun" and "This is what I've always needed but didn't know it." Several have stated that they regret having to go back to using other PDEs, since AOT debugging is more productive. And several have said that, in comparison with the AOT environment, using the standard PDE feels like "programming in the dark."

As the project continues, we plan to improve the prototype in several ways, including: (1) Enhancements to the Pascal interpreter, e.g., language extensions and additional debugger commands; (2) Enhancements to the AOT environment itself, in particular, a feature for graphically displaying state changes in linked data structures [31, 28]; and (3) Features for automatically collecting timings, session snapshots, and other data on user interaction with the system, to be used in its evaluation.

We plan to conduct formal trials with a substantial number of subjects to test the validity of our preliminary observations, as well as some other hypotheses. For example, we have not yet had enough experience to suggest whether AOT debugging promotes greater freedom and experimentation in programming style. Nor do we have evidence about whether the apparent benefits for low-level single-author programming generalize to higher-level paradigms (object-oriented programming in particular) and larger-scale multi-author projects. We plan to use as subjects a wide range of programmers, from beginning students to seasoned professionals, to allow analyzing factors such as users' previous experience and training in program design, coding, debugging, mathematics, etc. [18]. We also intend to use state-of-the-art psychometric instruments to measure user satisfaction [6], stress [10, 15], mental workload and fatigue [14, 16, 17, 35], and perhaps other factors [32].

In summary, based on preliminary experience with our prototype, the AOT debugging feature appears to significantly improve programmer productivity and software quality, and would be a beneficial enhancement for any program development environment.

References

1. Barstow, David R., Howard E. Shrobe, and Erik Sandewall, eds. *Interactive Programming Environments.* McGraw-Hill, 1984.
2. Boyle, T. and B. Drazkowski. "Exploiting natural intelligence: Towards the development of effective environments for learning to program." In A. Sutcliffe and L. Macaulay, eds., *People and Computers V* (British Informatics Society), Cambridge Press, 1989.
3. Brooks, R. "Towards a theory of the cognitive processes in computer programming." *Int'l. Jnl. of Man-Machine Studies,* Vol. 9 (1977), pp. 737-751.
4. Brusilovsky, Peter. "Program visualization as a debugging tool for novices." *Adjunct Proc. INTERCHI '93, Human Factors in Computing Systems,* pp. 29-30. ACM, 1993.
5. Card, Stuart K., Thomas P. Moran, and Allen Newell. *The Psychology of Human-Computer Interaction.* Lawrence Erlbaum Associates, 1983.
6. Chin, J.P., V.A. Diehl, and K.L. Norman. "Development of an instrument measuring user satisfaction of the human-computer interface," *Human Factors in Computing Systems, Proceedings of the CHI '88 Conference,* pp. 213-218. ACM Press, 1988.
7. Dix, Alan, Janet Finlay, Gregory Abowd, and Russell Beale. *Human-Computer Interaction.* Prentice Hall, 1993.
8. Eisenstadt, Marc. "Tales of debugging from the front lines." In C. Cook, J. Scholtz, and J. Spohrer, eds., *Empirical Studies of Programmers: Fifth Workshop,* pp. 86-112. Ablex, 1993.
9. Fritzson, Peter, Tibor Gyimothy, Mariam Kamkar, and Hanid Shahmehri. "Generalized algorithmic debugging and testing." *Proceedings of ACM SIGPLAN '91, Conf. on Programming Language Design and Implementation,* pp. 317-326. ACM Press, 1991.
10. Galinsky, Traci L., Roger R. Rosa, Joel S. Warm, and William N. Dember. "Psychophysical determinants of stress in sustained attention." *Human Factors,* Vol. 35, No. 4 (Dec. 1993), pp. 603-614.
11. Gould, J.D. "Some psychological evidence on how people debug computer programs." *Int'l. Jnl. of Man-Machine Studies,* Vol. 7 (1975), pp. 151-182.
12. Green, Thomas R.G. "The nature of programming." In J.-M. Hoc et al., eds., *Psychology of Programming.* Academic Press, 1990.
13. Gugerty, Leo and Gary M. Olson. "Comprehension differences in debugging by skilled and novice programmers." In Elliot Soloway and Sitharama Iyengar, eds., *Empirical Studies of Programmers: First Workshop,* pp. 13-27. Ablex, 1986.
14. Hancock, P.A. and J.K. Caird. "Experimental evaluation of a model of mental workload." *Human Factors,* Vol. 35, No. 3 (Sept. 1993), pp. 413-430.
15. Hancock, P.A. and Joel S. Warm. "A dynamic model of stress and sustained attention." *Human Factors,* Vol. 31, No. 5 (Oct. 1989), pp. 519-538.
16. Hendy, Keith C., Kevin M. Hamilton, and Lois N. Landry. "Measuring subjective workload: When is one scale better than many?" *Human Factors,* Vol. 35, No. 4 (Dec. 1993), pp. 579-602.
17. Hill, Susan G., Helene P. Iavecchia, James C. Byers, Alvah C. Bittner, Allen L. Zaklad, and Richard E. Christ. "Comparison of four subjective workload rating scales." *Human Factors,* Vol. 32, No. 4 (Aug. 1992), pp. 429-439.
18. Holt, Robert W., Deborah A. Boehm-Davis, and Alan C. Schultz. "Mental representations of programs for student and professional programmers." In G. Olson, S. Sheppard, and E. Soloway, eds., *Empirical Studies of Programmers: Second Workshop,* pp. 33-46. Ablex, 1987.
19. Katz, Irvin. R. and John R. Anderson. "Debugging: An analysis of bug-location strategies." *Human-Computer Interaction,* Vol. 3, No. 4 (1987-1988), pp. 351-399.
20. Kline, Paul. *The Handbook of Psychological Testing.* Routledge, 1993.
21. Klint, Paul, Thomas Reps, and Gregor Snelting, eds. "Programming environments / Report on an international workshop at Dagstuhl Castle." *ACM SIGPLAN Notices,* Vol. 27, No. 11 (Nov. 1992), pp. 90-96.
22. Koenemann, Jürgen and Scott P. Robertson. "Expert problem-solving strategies for program comprehension." *Proceedings of INTERCHI '91, Conference on Human*

Factors in Computing Systems, pp. 125-130. ACM Press, 1991.

23. Mackie, R.R., C.D. Wylie, and M.J. Smith. "Comparative effect of 19 stressors on task performance: Critical literature review (what we appear to know, don't know, and should know)." *Proceedings of the Human Factors Society 29th Annual Meeting*, pp. 462-469. Santa Monica, CA: HFES, 1985.
24. Mak, Ronald. *Writing Compilers and Interpreters / An Applied Approach.* Wiley, 1991.
25. Nanja, Murthy and Curtis R. Cook. "An analysis of the on-line debugging process." In Gary M. Olson, Sylvia Sheppard, and Elliot Soloway, eds., *Empirical Studies of Programmers: Second Workshop*, pp. 172-184. Ablex, 1987.
26. Moray, Neville, ed. *Mental Workload: Its Theory and Measurement.* Plenum, 1979.
27. Pennington, Nancy. "Comprehension strategies in programming." In Gary M. Olson, Sylvia Sheppard, and Elliot Soloway, eds., *Empirical Studies of Programmers: Second Workshop*, pp. 100-113. Ablex, 1987.
28. Schreiweis, U., A. Keune, and H. Langedörfer. "An integrated Prolog programming environment." *ACM SIGPLAN Notices*, Vol. 28, No. 2 (Feb. 1993), pp. 53-60.
29. Shneiderman, Ben. *Designing the User Interface / Strategies for Effective Human-Computer Interaction.* Addison-Wesley, 1987.
30. Shneiderman, Ben. *Software Psychology / Human Factors in Computer and Information Systems.* Little, Brown, 1980.
31. Stasko, John and Albert Badre. "Do algorithm animations assist learning? An empirical study and analysis." *Proceedings of INTERCHI '93, Conference on Human Factors in Computing Systems*, pp. 61-66. ACM Press, 1993.
32. Treu, Siegfried. *User Interface Evaluation / A Structured Approach.* Plenum, 1994.
33. Weinberg, Gerald M. *The Psychology of Computer Programming.* Van Nostrand Reinhold, 1971.
34. Wickens, Christopher D. *Engineering Psychology and Human Performance.* Harper Collins, 1992.
35. Wierwille, W.W. and F. Thomas Eggemeier. "Recommendations for mental workload measurement in a test and evaluation environment." *Human Factors*, Vol. 35, No. 2 (June, 1993), pp. 263-282.

Session P4b

Software Reuse, Patterns and Architectures

Reusable project-specific software for industrial control.

J.R.Borer
A.J.Reynolds
Department of Mechanical Engineering, Brunel University, Uxbridge, Middx UB8 3PH

Abstract:

The paper describes a methodology which enables non-software-specialist engineers to specify, design and implement reusable project-specific software for process engineering monitoring and control systems using a suitable real time expert-system. The software, running under a run-time version of the expert-system, is independent of the operating-system software. The inevitable errors and difficulties which normally attend subcontracting can thus be avoided with considerable advantage to integrity, speed of development and project-management.

1. Introduction.

Software for PES-based discrete feedback process control systems, such as those for batch sequence control, equipment monitoring or safety shutdown, falls naturally into two distinct categories; the PES operating-system and project-specific software. Design and implementation of both categories are usually subcontracted to a system-builder or a software house. This, however, is not desirable since it necessitates the transfer of process design information across a contractual interface, which inevitably causes many design or implementation errors. These then persist in the project-specific software as systematic (non-random) faults or 'bugs', which there can be no certainty of discovering before they cause system failure during operation. Neither is it necessary today to subcontract design and implementation of project-specific software, as programming at a high level using a suitable environment can be within the capabilities of process engineers who specify and design the system.

The requirement specification for the project-specific software and its interpretation should be the responsibility of these engineers, who understand the engineering system functions. Software engineers should concentrate on producing, supporting and developing environments which process engineers can then use to generate project-specific software which implements engineering system functions internally. Specification of requirements, design and implementation of project-specific software on the one hand and of the PES operating-system on the other can then be entirely independent of one another. The creativity of both software and process engineers can thus be properly deployed. Transfer of process design information to the system-builder or software house, which is the cause of many systematic errors in the completed software, can be avoided, as can contractual arguments concerning design changes. In this way project management can be made much simpler and development of applications speeded-up.

This paper describes how, using a suitable real-time expert-system, rule-based software can readily be specified and designed by process engineers in the form of a very small number of **generic object-oriented modules** from which independent software components of the project-specific software of a PES-based engineering system can be implemented. It is shown that these modules, subject to minimal modification, can be reused, thus forming the basis of the design of a later system. Integrity of the project-specific software can thus be improved by reuse, which can also reduce design time.

If system configuration is managed in this way, product evaluation can be greatly simplified. There will indeed be two entirely separate products: the PES operating-system and the project-specific software which runs under it, but is entirely independent from it. The generic reusable software modules of the project-specific software can be entirely independent from the non-project-specific software and map only to functions of process engineering mechanisms. They can be validated by functional testing, which can be greatly simplified by defining functionality on two levels; the functions of independent software components being independent of the functions of the system itself, defined in terms of interactions between these components. Thus, each module can be validated (and revalidated if this is made necessary by design changes) at any time during the engineering project design and construction period. Final system acceptance testing need then only address interactions between previously validated components.

Unlike software designed by conventional functional decomposition techniques and implemented in a conventional programming language, project-specific software produced in this way must run under a 'run-time' version of the development system, on a PES which comprises operating software and hardware. Both the operating system and the run-time version of the development system will still have to be validated by conventional means, but can benefit greatly from reuse, unchanged, in other systems.

The original incentive for the work which is the basis of this paper was to overcome problems associated with the safety-critical software of safety shutdown systems in the offshore industry. However, it has become clear that advantages that stem from the techniques developed,

0-8186-7840-2/97 $10.00 © 1997 IEEE

which enable non-software engineers to design and implement project-specific software to run under a standard operating system, and to reuse generic designs of stand-alone project-specific software components, have a much wider appeal. Application of these techniques is indeed appropriate for any PES-based discrete monitoring or feedback control system such as a batch sequence control or plant equipment monitoring system. This paper describes how generic reusable project-specific software modules can be produced for such a system, tested and documented for future use.

2. A formal structure for reusable project-specific software.

Because of the 'top-down' nature of established software design techniques, software engineers traditionally interpret an engineering system specification in terms of the functions of that system: ie. 'functional decomposition'. Other engineers, however, think of an engineering system as a collection of functionally independent component parts which can each perform its own functions in the absence of any of the other components of the system, but which, when assembled together, interact to perform the functions of the system. The dichotomy between this 'bottom-up' approach to engineering system design and the established top-down approach to software system design is responsible for many of the problems which arise when design and implementation of the project-specific software of an engineering system is sub-contracted to software engineers.

These problems can, however, be avoided by designing project-specific software as an 'internal' system which maps to a functionally identical 'external' or real system, **even if the latter only exists as a concept**. The project-specific software of any PES-based discrete feedback control system can thus take the form of a set of transparent software components which each perform, internally, those functions which would otherwise have to be performed externally by equivalent hardware components of an external system. The software specification must therefore define an internal system in terms of these software components and interactions between them. Since each software component of the internal system must correspond **functionally** to a component of the external system which, as already stated, is functionally independent, it follows that the former must also be functionally independent and therefore 'transparent'[2]. We have come to the conclusion that this can only be achieved by specifying the functions of the external system in an object-oriented form, translating this into an object-oriented design of the project-specific software and implementing this design using an object-oriented language. The software implemented from such an object-oriented design would then run on a standard PES to perform the engineering system's functions internally. It must, however, also incorporate the means to communicate values of inputs/outputs from/to an external data-gathering or SCADA system.

Engineers who are not software specialists. think of an engineering system in terms of its component parts which, in this context, can be equated to 'objects'. Any rigorous formal definition of the functions of the external system can, therefore, be translated into an object-oriented form, though it would obviously be better to envisage the system in this way from the outset. 'Cause and effect' diagrams, which are a traditional way to define PES-based emergency shutdown, batch sequence control or equipment monitoring systems, can be readily translated into object-oriented form. Definitions of the functions of each independent system-component in the form of the 'antecedents and consequents' of rules, correspond closely to those provided by 'cause and effect' diagrams. This synergy between the traditional form of specification of the project-specific software of such systems and rule-based software systems is exploited by the techniques described in this paper.

To correspond functionally with each component of the external system a single 'system-object' of the internal system must be defined. This can then perform internally the functions which would otherwise have to be performed externally by an equivalent hardware component of the external system. The means to communicate between this object of the internal system and the plant inputs and outputs can be represented internally as 'interfacing-objects'. The single system-object, together with the requisite number of interfacing objects, constitute a component of the internal system (see figure 1). An interfacing-object will be given a value 'true' or 'false', as a result of the operation of the methods of the system-object, at any time during the course of system operation. Its sole function is thus to enable a change of value to be transferred to or taken from an external SCADA system via a suitable bridge. It serves the same purpose as does an interfacing relay in a hardwired (external) system.

A 'component-relationship' diagram or map (see figure 2), together with an individual functional specification of the single system-object within each component, specifications of each interfacing object and specifications of interactions between components, can together constitute a component-oriented software specification for the internal system.

System-object classes, from which system-objects can

be created at the implementation stage, will normally have some features which can be inherited from a common 'ancestor', and in most cases more than one system-object can be 'created' from a single class definition. Within the system-object class hierarchy, any system-object class definition which does not have more than one subclass, and none of whose inferior classes or subclasses has itself more than one subclass, can thus become the basis of a reusable software module. This principle is illustrated in figure 3 and can be stated formally as follows:-

> **"Any system-object class, which is one of two or more subclasses of its immediate superior class, together with all its superior class/es and subclass/es, can form the basis of an independent software module provided that it does not itself nor any of its subclasses have more than one subclass."**

(It should be noted that the concept of multiple inheritance plays no part in these techniques as currently defined.)

At the software design stage then, a small number of generic modules can be defined, each of which comprises a single 'top' system-object class with its sub-classes, a top interfacing-object class with its sub-classes and definitions of specified 'relationships' which can be created transiently in the course of system operation. Creation of instances of relationships, unlike instances of object-classes, will be a function of system operation rather than of system implementation.

Attributes of a system-object will have to be one of two distinct types. The first type will be given fixed integer values after the system-object has been created, as part of the implementation process. The second type, defined as a logical variable, will also be given a value, 'true' or 'false', initially, as part of the implementation process, but this will subsequently change during system operation. Thus the value of a 'fixed-value attribute' will be a function of the system specification, whilst the value of a 'logical-variable attribute' will be a function of system operation.

The 'features' of system-object classes must also include 'methods' which can reason about the values of interfacing-objects, logical-variable-system-object-attributes or relationships. Input values can be transferred from an external SCADA system into 'input-interfacing-objects' forming parts of an internal-component. The **'internal-methods'** of the system-object which will be part of the same component can then reason about these values and relationships with other system-objects in order to determine values for its 'variable-attributes'. When it takes any given state, the system-object will then carry out all the **'external-methods'** of its class appropriate to that state. These will reason about the values of the system-object's variable-attributes in order to determine values for the 'output-interfacing-objects' of the component and/or relationships with other system-objects. Values transferred from output-interfacing-objects to the external system will thus be the result of operation of the system-object's external-method-rules.

The methods of the system-object class and its subclasses which form the basis of a module can be considered as the project-specific methods of that module. The state of an internal system-component at any time during operation will thus be defined by the values of the variable-attributes of its **single** system-object, which will be determined by the internal-methods of its class. The module, however, must also include definitions of interfacing-object classes whose methods are not project-specific. At the implementation stage each **internal system component** will therefore be generated from one or other of the generic modules by 'creating' a single system-object and all the necessary interface-objects. These objects can be considered as sub-components of the internal system-component.

Identities of input and output interfacing-objects referred to within a method-rule of a system-object **class** will differ between system-objects of the same class, and all references to them within the method-rules of the class must therefore be made 'globally'. It follows that instances of interfacing-object classes can only be 'bound to' the appropriate system-object, **within a system component**, at the implementation stage. This can be achieved, after all the objects or sub-components have been created, by giving the same fixed value to a common fixed-value-attribute, 'component-number', which will have been defined within both the top system-object class and the top interface-object class definitions. During operation, when a method is invoked, these values can then be matched in the antecedent of one of its rules, which will thus act as a filter to ensure that the consequent of the rule is carried out only in respect of those objects which are identified in this way.

Functions of the internal system, as opposed to functions of any of its individual components, can be defined as internal interactions between components. At the design stage a unique relationship will be defined to correspond with an external-method of any class, and a fixed-value attribute which is specific to this relationship can be defined in any system-object class. During system operation, the value of such a relationship-specific fixed-value attribute of system-object 'A' might be matched with the value of the fixed-value attribute 'component-number' of system-object 'B' in the antecedent of one of the external method-rules of the latter's class whose consequent will then set the specified relationship 'true' between the two system-objects. One condition for setting true the logical-variable-attribute of 'A' which corresponds to the specified external-method will thus be satisfied within the antecedent of one of the internal-method-rules of system-object 'A'. This may, however, be only one of several conditions which must be satisfied for this rule to be fired, setting the appropriate logical-variable of 'A' true and thus causing execution of the specified external-method of 'A'. By defining that the external-method-rule/s which constitute/s this method of 'A' shall set the relationship 'false' when fired, the implementation of the relationship can be rendered transient by handshaking.

3. Design of project-specific software.

A written specification of the functions of any one of the components of the external system, which must form part of the latter's object-oriented functional specification, can be used as a basis from which to draw its state logic diagram. 'States' in this diagram will correspond to attributes of the single system-object within the corresponding internal component: 'latched' states will translate into handshaking as defined above. Conditions defined in the diagram for setting or changing states will map to methods of the system-object's class. Each such diagram could thus be translated into a class definition from which one of the system-objects of the internal system could then be 'created'. However, if more than one of these diagrams should have the same topology (see figure 4), it is then possible to define a single class of system-objects, from which, or from a subclass of which, can be created more than one of the system-objects of the internal system at the implementation stage. The number of generic system-object classes defined at the design stage can thus be fewer than the number of system-objects that must be created to correspond, on a one-to-one basis, with the components of the external system. In this way the number of software modules required to comprise the software system design can be minimised. As part of the software design process, therefore, the state diagrams of all the external system components must be compared, in order to identify those which have a common topology.

For instance, if diagram 'A' is found to have states which are not found in 'B' and 'B' to have states that are not found in 'A', then 'A' and 'B' do not have the same topology, and therefore a common class of the internal system-objects, from which both of them can be created, cannot be defined. However, if both 'A' and 'B' do have **any** states in common, they can both be defined as subclasses of a common class which has itself been defined to have only these common states.

Again, the form of a diagram, 'C', is common with that of another diagram, 'D', if it has no state which the latter does not have. If, however, diagram 'D' has states which are not found in diagram 'C' they can be regarded as redundant in the latter. Thus, state diagram 'C' defines a class of system-objects and diagram 'D' its subclass.

A hierarchy of internal system-object classes can thus be constructed on the basis of comparison of the state diagrams for every one of the components which comprise the external system. Within this hierarchy, each system-object class definition which does not have more than one subclass can then form the basis of a reusable software module as described in the previous section (see figure 3). Each module will, however, also include class definitions for all interface-objects, instances of which must form part of any system-component which will be created from it. The module will also include definitions of all relations which are referred to within the methods (internal and external) of the system-object class or any of its superior classes or subclasses which forms the basis of the module.

A hierarchy of interfacing object classes must also be constructed. The top-class 'interface' will have two sub-classes - 'system-input' and 'system-output'. Sub-classes of each of these will have to be defined only if it is necessary to differentiate between different types of plant input or output within the methods of any system-object class. For instance, this will be the case if one method of a class is contingent on satisfactory completion of another. The hierarchy of interface-object classes will thus be determined solely by the functions of system-object classes associated with them within modules.

4. Implementation by development system.

It would, of course, be possible to implement the internal-system design obtained by applying the techniques for software specification and design described in the forgoing sections, in a conventional object-oriented programming language. But implementation in this manner would normally be beyond the capabilities of engineers who are not software-specialists. Without a suitable development system it would, therefore, not be possible to achieve the objective, set out in the introduction to this paper, that such non-specialists should be enabled to design and implement the project-specific software. To achieve this we have found it necessary to use a software development system which is itself designed as a real time expert system, and which, moreover, supports object-orientation in the specificational (though not the dynamic) sense. This section describes implementation under such a system.

Using a real time, expert system, software must be designed and implemented as 'knowledge-bases', which function in conjunction with an 'inference engine'.

Software produced in this way will be entirely different from any that would be produced using a conventional programming language. Unlike the latter it must run under a 'run-time' version of the development system which incorporates the inference engine. However, this, like the PES operating system, will not itself be project-specific and could therefore be reused, unchanged, in later systems.

In order to ensure that it is indeed independent, each module must be constructed as a separate knowledge-base. Before the project-specific software of the system can be implemented, however, these modules will have to be 'merged' to form a single knowledge-base. This merged knowledge base will then constitute the project-specific software system design.

The 'top-class' definitions, 'system' and 'interface', must each inherit features from a basic object-class defined within the development system itself. The functions of these basic object-classes, which will be inherited by the top-class of the internal-system, and all its subclasses, are likely to be coded, within the development system, in a conventional programming language. However, being intrinsic parts of the run-time version of the development system on which the project-specific software to be implemented must run, these basic object-class definitions will not themselves be project-specific, since they will be reused, unchanged, in subsequent systems. The reusable software which **is** project-specific, and is to be created by non-software specialist engineers, will not therefore include this code.

In the first instance, a subclass of one of these basic object-classes must be defined. The development system user, a non-specialist in software, will have to define attributes specific to this subclass of a basic object-class; ie 'system' as a subclass of the basic class definition within the development system, or 'interface' as a subclass of a development system subclass 'logical-data'. Class attributes will have to be bound to a class definition by virtue of the mechanisms of the development system. Subclasses of either of these top-classes of the project-specific software system will then be defined in the same way using the development system. However, methods defined in rule form can be implicitly bound to a class definition solely by virtue of the wording of the rules. For this reason it will not be necessary for the development system to support methods implicitly.

In order to implement a component of the internal engineering system, code must be generated automatically, using the development system, by creating a single instance of the appropriate system-object class definition, which forms part of one of the reusable modules, together with instances of interfacing-object classes which also form parts of the same module. The latter must then be 'bound to' the former **within the component** by allocating the same value to the attribute 'component-number' in the definition tables of each interfacing-object and the single system-object which comprise the system component. By using local names in the antecedents of the generic method-rules of the system-object's class these can be made to refer specifically to input or output interfacing objects: "the value of whose component-number attribute is the same as the value of the component-number attribute of {the system-object}". Thus, during operation, whenever a method-rule of the class of a system-object is fired, its consequent will only be carried out in respect of those interfacing-objects which have the same component-number as the system-object which forms part of the same component.

Relationships between objects must be defined under the development system in a similar way to object classes. As stated in section 3, during operation one system-object will instruct another to carry out one of its external methods by creating, transiently, an instance of a relationship which is specific to that method. So that it is possible to identify, within the external method of the instructing system-object class, both the selected recipient system-object and the external method it is to be instructed to carry out, a fixed-value-attribute which is specific to the relationship and hence to the method to be carried out, must have been defined within the potential recipient system-object's class. After the recipient system-object has been created as an instance of this class, this attribute must be given the same fixed value in its definition table as the 'component-number' attribute of the instructing system-object. Using local names within a rule which constitutes the external method of the latter's class, its consequent can then be made to refer to: "any system-object the value of whose {relationship}-number-attribute is the same as the that of the component-number-attribute of {the instructing system-object}".

Components of the internal system, implemented under the development system as described above, will react to inputs from the plant via a bridge to an external SCADA system, interact with each other by creating transient relationships, and output changes of value to devices in the plant via the bridge and the SCADA system. Changes in the values of interfacing objects can be transferred across the bridge to the external SCADA system, and vice versa, within a single 'iteration period', which will typically be 1 second (but can be less or more).

5. Functional testing and documentation.

As described in section 3, it is possible to condense the state diagrams constructed for each component of the external system into a small number of generic forms. Each of these can then be translated into the design of one of the reusable software modules comprising definitions of system-object and interface-object classes and relationships. Each such generic state logic diagram will constitute a specification of the functions of one of the modules and thus provide a basis for testing all the functions of the internal components created from it that can be exercised within the completed system. In this way functional testing of a small number of software modules will suffice to validate all the components which comprise the internal system. Moreover, the test program for each module will be very much simpler than a normal acceptance test program for an entire system. Software need not be altered in any way by the process of merging, and it is therefore difficult to envisage any systematic fault remaining undiscovered in the project-specific software. Moreover, module testing can be carried out early in the design program and can easily be repeated after any design change, which affects the particular module, has been implemented.

The completed system will, of course, have to be functionally tested for acceptance purposes at project completion, after all design changes have been implemented. However, these tests need address only the system functions, defined as interactions between software components that have already been tested, and will therefore also be very much simpler than normal acceptance tests.

In order that a generic software module can be functionally tested, it will be necessary to add test facilities to it. These, however, must be only temporary and must be deleted before the module is merged with other modules to provide the software design of the entire system. These temporary test facilities include instances of both the system-object and interface-object classes, definitions and instances of other system-object classes to which a component created from the module must be capable of sending messages, and simulated panel push-buttons which, when activated (by 'clicking' on them with a 'mouse' for instance) during test operations, change the values of input interfacing-objects.

Documentation of the design of reusable modules should be generated automatically under the development system and saved, complete with test facilities, for future use as the basis of later, similar, systems. Differences between the functional requirements of a future system and those of the original system for which the modules were designed will be identified, at the design stage, when the state logic diagrams of the new external system have been reduced to the minimum generic forms as described in section 3. Changes to existing reusable modules to produce the design of the new system can then be carried out, functionally tested and saved as design variations in addition to, rather than instead of, the original module designs. New modules can also be designed at this time if necessary. These procedures will be recognised to be in line with normal engineering design practices. Thus, using the techniques described in this paper, the design of components of the project-specific software of PES-based discrete feedback control systems can be seen to be placed on the same basis as physical components of such systems.

6. An example.

To illustrate how this methodology can be applied in conjunction with a suitable development system in order to overcome the problems identified in section 1, a requirement-specification in the form of 'cause-and-effect' diagrams (approximately 50 sheets) for an actual ESD system designed by a major contractor for a platform in the North Sea, will now be considered. Such systems constitute the mechanisms which carry out, not one, but a number of shutdown sequences when dangerous events in the plant operation are detected by one or a number of instruments such as level, flow pressure, temperature, smoke, fire or gas detectors. Some of these sequence control mechanisms serve to shut down certain large items of plant such as compressors or electrical generators, of which there may be several identical examples within a single installation ('unit shutdowns'). Others terminate plant operations safely within sections of the plant, by carrying out operations such as shutting large isolating valves (which may take up to half a minute to close or open) or opening vent valves and stopping or starting pumps. These sequence control operations are then cascaded in certain circumstances so that increasingly larger sections of the plant are shut down according to the 'level' of danger; ultimately culminating in a level sometimes described as 'abandon platform'. It can readily be appreciated that the total system can be very complex; in some respects even more complex than the 'reactor protection system' of a nuclear generator.

Project-specific software to meet this requirement-specification has been designed and implemented using the methodology described in previous sections under version 4.01 of Gensym's G2 development system. It has been comprehensively tested and validated by interfacing it to a simulation of the plant and SCADA operations. This simulation has been constructed as a separate G2 system and runs on a separate platform. Input and output values are exchanged between the ESD system being tested and this system, over a network interface. The simulation uses timers to model the opening and closing of isolating and 'riser' valves on receipt of output signals from the ESD system. Inputs to the ESD system are generated by the simulation system when, after a suitable delay, a valve is deemed to be either 'not fully open/closed', 'fully closed/open' or to have failed to operate. Operation of pressure or level sensors and other shutdown initiating devices is simulated manually, causing plant detector signals to be sent to the ESD system over the network interface. An entirely independent 'operator interface' system has also been constructed which provides 'first-up' alarm features so that a human operator is informed in real time which event/s is/are the 'cause' of an automatic shutdown and which the 'effects'.

Following a HAZOP analysis, it has long been standard practice within the industry to create cause-and-effect diagrams as a formal specification of the ESD system requirements. This is then translated into a specification for monolithic software by a system builder. Using our methodology, it has instead been translated into the object-oriented specification illustrated by Figures 5 and 6 which defines the ESD system as a set of independent objects or components which interact through 'messages' or commands to cause the various mechanisms of the ESD system to operate in a cascade fashion. Under G2, an interface is defined in the form of 'relationships', instances of which can be created transiently representing a message from one object to another. As was envisaged earlier, each project-specific software component of a PES based ESD system can thus be designed, implemented and tested independently.

Figure 5, the 'object/relationship model', shows objects representing the shutdown system mechanisms, messages to be passed between these, inputs from plant sensors and outputs to the plant. Figure 6 illustrates, for one of these internal objects, the definition of its methods in a rule-based form. A complete set of such method definitions, together with lists of inputs and outputs, identified by tag numbers, and messages on an object-by-object basis, completes the formal ESD system requirement-specification. Within this requirement specification, features are necessarily defined for each object, whereas within object-oriented software they must be defined as part of a class or subclass definition.

Methods have been constructed in a 'generic' form and it is not therefore necessary to define a separate subclass for every object. The fewer that are defined the better, since the largest part of the compiled project-specific software represents rules which constitute class methods. Methods have therefore been defined within the most superior class definition possible. An optimum 'hierarchy' of classes and subclasses is thus of the utmost importance in minimising the quantity of code which is ultimately compiled and at the same time maximising its reusability.

Design of a hierarchy of classes starts with definition of one or more 'top-classes' which have no direct superiors. In the system described here, three top-classes were defined:

(i) **'Inhibit-timer'**, which has been defined to provide timers specified in many ESD system requirement specifications in order to give the operator the option to delay a shutdown in certain circumstances, for a strictly limited period.

(ii) **'Interface'**, which is the direct superior of all input and output 'interfacing-object' subclasses, instances of which correspond to interfacing relays in a conventional hardwired ESD system. Their functions are either to copy the states of plant sensors from an external data-gathering or SCADA system to the internal 'system objects' or to copy states of outputs determined by instances of 'system' to the external system.

(iii) **'System'**; which is the direct superior of all subclasses, instances of which together constitute the software which maps to the functions of the ESD system.

Every timer is an instance of the top-class 'inhibit-timer', which therefore has no subclasses. For the sake of simplicity, timers have been left out of the discussion which follows.

From the written descriptions of their methods, a form of state diagram was constructed for each object defined within the ESD system requirement specification (Figures 5 & 6). This is shown in Figure 4. It was found to be common to the equivalent diagrams for the four shutdown objects shown in Figure 5; ESD-system-object, SSD-system-object, electrical-failure-SD-system-object and condensate-SD-system-object. All four were therefore implemented as instances of a generic class, 'plant-SD-system'. The 'permitted' state is actually redundant in instances of this class, but not in instances of its subclass BD-system for reason that are explained later. 'Plant-SD-system' and 'compressor-SD-system' are defined as sub-classes of 'SD-system. The latter is an example of a 'unit-shutdown' which is the term used in the industry for the shutdown procedure for a large self contained (often skid-mounted) unit such as a compressor or a boiler plant. 'Valve-function-system', is the direct superior of all subclasses which represents,within the project-specific software system by feedback from plant sensors, the real time operation of sections of plant throughout the progress of a shutdown sequence. 'SD-system' and 'valve-function-system' were defined as subclasses of the top-class 'system'.

Although they form part of the (internal) project-specific software, subclasses of the top-class 'interface' have no methods and each instance has only one attribute which defines the status of the input from or output to the plant which it represents within the internal ESD system. Means are provided within G2 to force them to adopt the same state as corresponding elements in an external SCADA system.

The class, 'pipeline-valves-system' is identical to the class 'valve-function-system' except that it has additional pressure attributes and the 'permit-blowdown' method. It was therefore defined as the latter's subclass. Both 'import-pipeline-valves-system-object' and 'export-pipeline-valves-system-object' (the 'riser' valves), which have these additional features, were created as instances of this subclass. But 'suction-isolating-valve-system-object' and 'discharge-isolating-valve-system-object', both of which lack these additional features, were created as instances of the parent class 'valve-function-system'. In the same way 'BD-system' was defined as a sub-class of 'plant-SD-system': by defining the 'permitted' attribute in the superior class it was possible to make the form of the 'initiate and permit' method common and define this in the superior class. The value of the permit attribute (see Figure 4), being redundant, is set permanently 'true' in instances of the superior class. However, in instances of 'BD-system' (ESD-blowdown-system-object and TSD), its value is determined by a method which is defined in this sub-class. Defining 'global' classes with their subclass or subclasses in this way has reduced the quantity of compiled code.

The hierarchy of subclasses of the top class 'interface' was determined solely by the need to identify instances which relate to an instance of a subclass of the top class 'system', within a rule which is part of a method of the latter. During system operation therefore, the generic rule/s which constitute this method must refer to specific instances of subclasses of both 'interface' and 'system'. In order to achieve this, an attribute, named 'subclass-number', is defined within the class definitions of both these top classes . This attribute can be given the same value in both instances: a rule need then only refer generically to the values of these attributes in order to 'match' these instances. For example, the instance of the class 'system-output' whose G2 definition is shown in Figure 10 has the same 'subclass number' as has the instance 'SSD-system-object' of the class 'plant-SD-system'. The antecedent of the second rule of the 'plant-SD-system-class-methods' shown in figure 8 defines the condition which fires this rule, ie that these 'subclass numbers' are the same. Instances of sub-classes of the top class 'interface', which map to the inputs from and outputs to the plant, are thus 'bound to' the appropriate instance of a subclass of 'system' by reason of the values given to their identifier-attributes. The reusable software component therefore comprises the definitions of a subclass of 'system' together with definitions of the necessary classes of 'interface', and the definition of 'inhibit-timer' if required.

Similarly, because in the system being described there are four identical compressors, the attribute 'compressor-number', can be allocated a different value (1 to 4) in each instance of the class 'compressor', which is a subclass of 'SD-system', and also in instances of the subclasses of 'interface' which represent its inputs and outputs.

In much the same way, means had to be defined to identify, within the methods of one subclass 'a' of 'system', an instance of another subclass, 'b' , of 'system, to which a message must be sent during the course of system operation. The identity of the recipient object is determined for this purpose by giving a fixed value to an attribute, defined within the class definition of 'b', which is specific to a particular message definition. For the message to be sent, the method rule of the sender object's class, 'a', whose 'consequent' contains the instruction to send the message, must be fired. For this to happen, the value of this attribute of the recipient object must be matched to the value of the 'subclass-number' attribute of the sender object in the antecedent of the same rule. For example, as can be seen from the antecedent of the first rule of the 'plant-SD-system-class-methods whose G2 definition, the class attribute 'valves-sd-number', which is specific to the G2 relation definition 'told-to-close-all-valves-by' enables the identity of a specific instance of the recipient object's class 'valve-function-system' to be matched to a specific instance of the sender object's class 'plant-sd-system' in the external method of the latter class . Thus, an instance of the class 'plant-sd-system' will only send the message 'close-all-valves' to an instance of the class 'valve-function-system' if the value of the 'subclass-number' attribute of the former is the same as the value of the 'valves-sd-number' of the latter.

In addition to the attributes which represent each state, and rules representing, in generic terms, the methods of the class, appropriate fixed value attributes had to be defined as part of the specification of each class or subclass. Attributes of this type, referred to as 'identifier attributes', which are given fixed values within individual instances, have been given names ending in 'number' in order to distinguish them from attributes, referred to as 'logical attributes', which take different values (true or false) during the course of system operation.

Software implementation was accomplished in two stages: first a set of objects was 'created', under G2, from the class and subclasses defined during the design phase; then the interfaces between these internal objects were constructed by allocating matching values to 'identifier-attributes' of the instances created. The system could then be functionally tested. Under the G2 system: the logical-attributes appropriate to each class definition which are shown alongside its icon change value in real time, making this a live display which can be used for testing purposes but is not adequate for operational purposes.

To assist plant operators during normal operation, an 'operator interface' has been built. This provides a 'traffic-light' display of shutdown status, readily interpreted status messages and 'first-up' annunciators. Taken together, this information display informs the operator what is about to take place if inhibit timers are in use, as well as what has taken place, its causes and subsequent results. Rule-based software is particularly well suited to the 'first-up' annunciation which provides information of vital importance to plant operators.

It was noted earlier that construction of the rules representing methods within an object-oriented structure in a generic form leads to great economy of code. The entire system that has been implemented, which is typical of a medium-sized ESD system, comprises less than 5000 lines of compiled code. (excluding the operator interface which is a separate system entirely) Of more importance perhaps is the fact that **the entire system has been implemented from only three generically defined 'software components'**, which can be saved for use, already functionally tested, in the construction of future systems where similar class definitions are apparent, at the software design stage, from

7. Summary.

Software determines the functions of any programmable system. Where these functions must match 'external' ones, as in the case of industrial control systems, software design usually involves the transfer of design information from the engineers who define the external system requirements to software engineers who design and implement an internal system. The latter are unlikely to fully understand them because they are non-specialists in the project-specific software domain. By avoiding this transfer of information, many errors of commission can be avoided. Project-specific software should therefore be separated completely from non-project-specific software in order that it may be designed and implemented, not by software engineers on a contracted-out basis, but by the same team of engineers who define the system requirements from a knowledge of the plant operation. However it is normally beyond the capabilities of the latter to do this using established software design and implementation techniques. It is therefore proposed that they use an expert system as a tool with which to develop rule-based project-specific software to run on a run-time version of the expert-system which is not itself project-specific. The nature of such project-specific software will, of course, be quite different from conventional software since it depends on the inference engine of the expert-system to operate. This proposal, for non-specialists to use 'tools' produced by software specialists to produce project-specific software is in line with current trends in the industry.

In order to reduce still further the incidence of systematic faults, project-specific software should be reusable, which, under established software design techniques, it cannot be. To this end, it is proposed that it should be specified, designed and implemented in an object-oriented form. Techniques for doing this, using a suitable development system which supports specificational object-orientation within a real-time expert system, have been described in this paper.

Acknowledgements:

The authors are grateful to the Amoco (UK) Exploration Company Ltd. and to the Engineering and Physical Sciences Research Council (EPSRC) for funding provided to support this work.

References:

1. BORER J.R.:
'Design and implementation of project-specific software for offshore emergency shutdown systems'.
PhD Thesis, Department of Mechanical Engineering, Brunel University, Uxbridge, Middlesex, 1993

2. I.Pyle, P.Hruschka, M.Lissandre & K.Jackson
'Real time systems and their programming languages'
Wiley series in software based systems - 1993
ISBN 0 201 17529 0

3. 'SO2: A flexible Object-Oriented Data-Base Management system'
Proceedings of the second international conference in Reliability & Robustness of engineering software' - Milan, April 1991
ISBN 1 85312 132 0

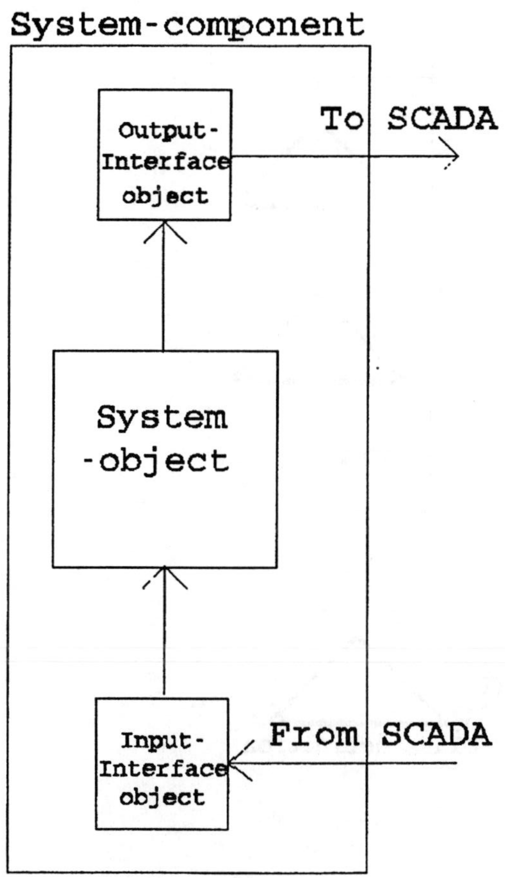

Figure 1

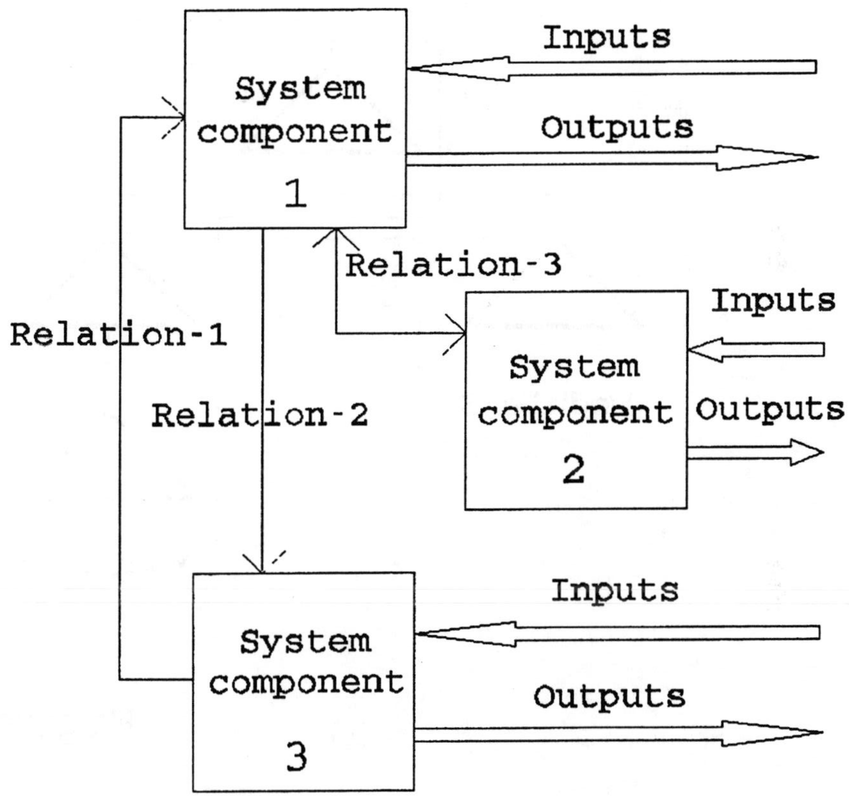

Figure 2

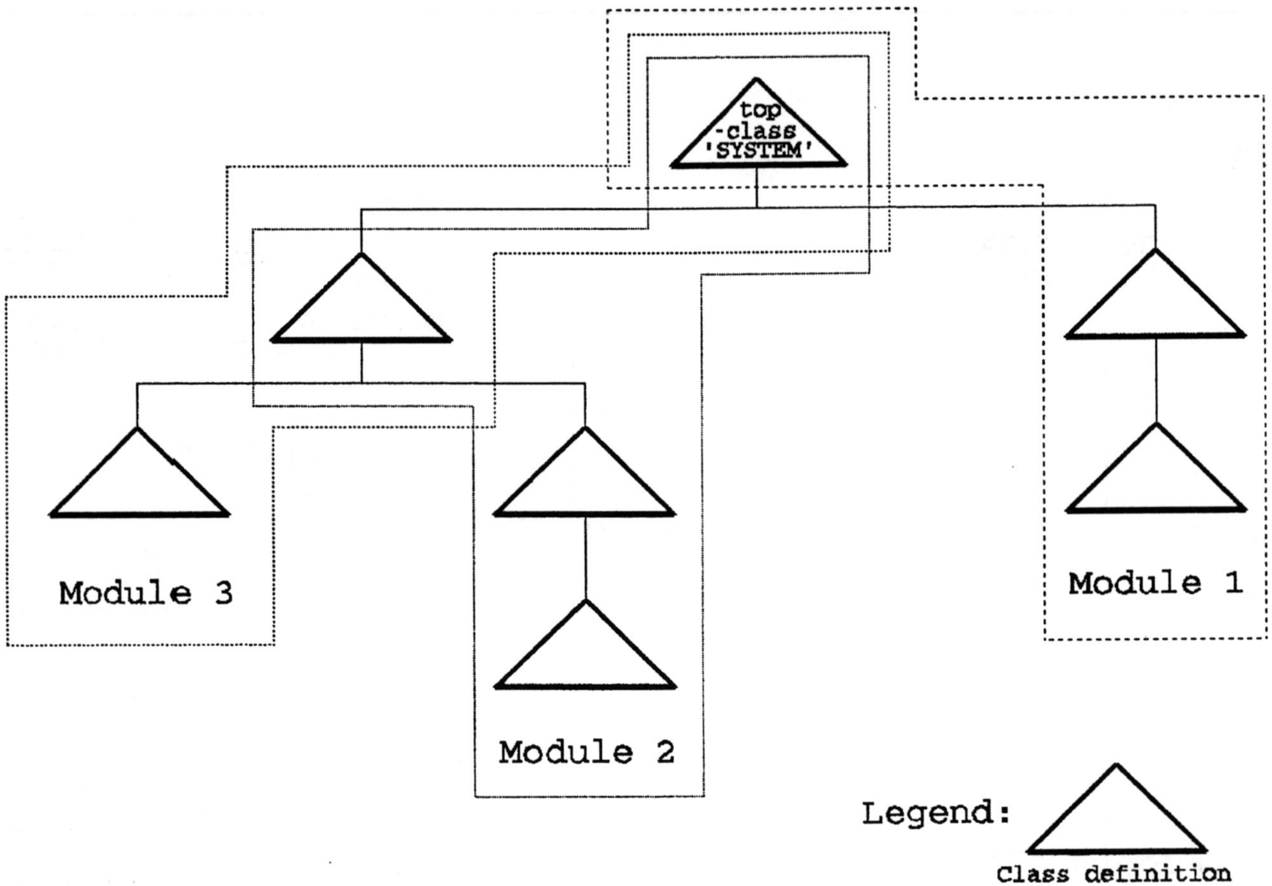
top
-class
'SYSTEM'
Module 3
Module 2
Module 1
Legend:
Class definition

Figure 3

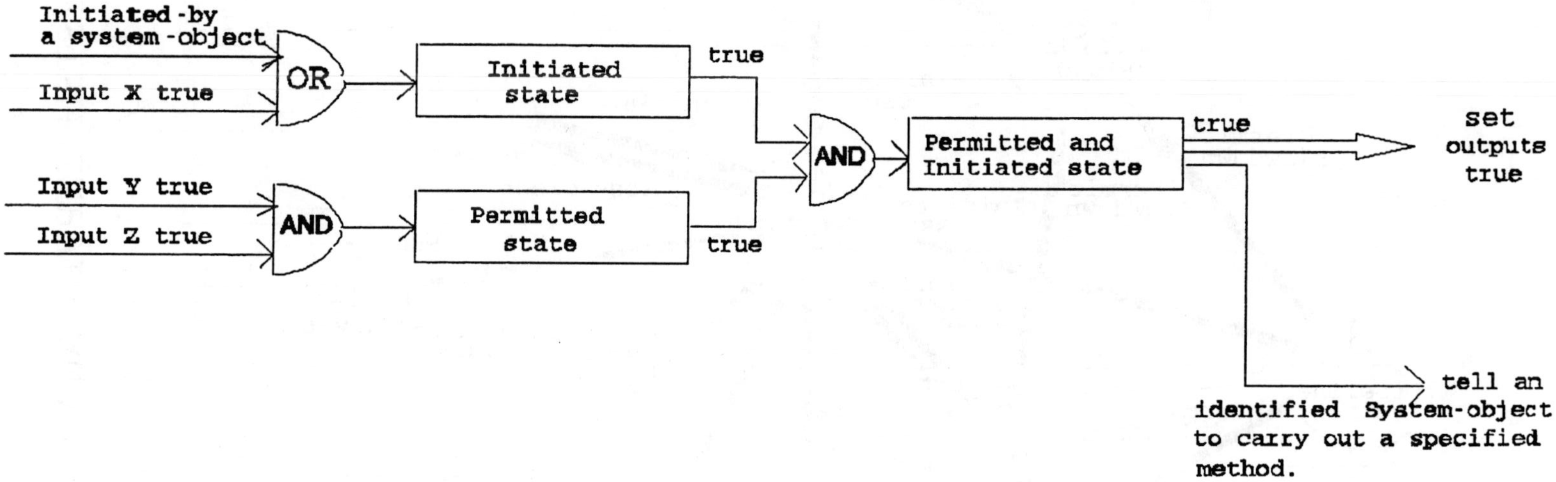

Figure 4 Initiate & Permit method

SYSTEM INPUTS AND OUTPUTS

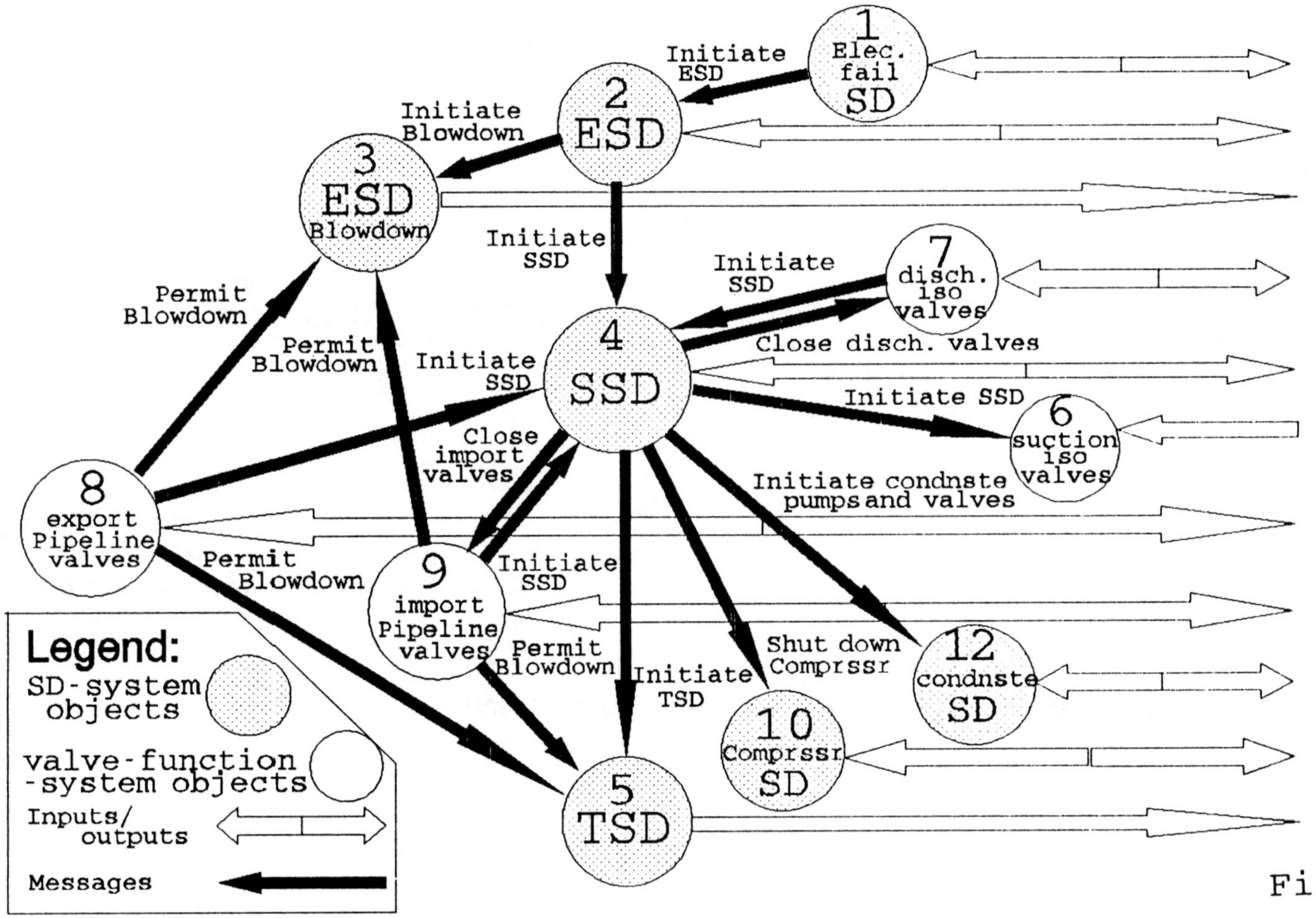

Figure 5

ESD PROJECT-SPECIFIC SOFTWARE SPECIFICATION

INSTALLATION:

PART A - INTERNAL SOFTWARE & I/O INTERFACE

DEFINITION OF OBJECT CLASS No. 4

Name of class: SSD-system.

Superior class: General G2 class definition.

Section No. 2 - Methods of class.

Method 1.

if any system-output is not set:

and SSD-system-object receives a message to initiate it or any system-input is actuated;

and SSD-system-object receives a message to permit initiation from Import-pipeline-valves-system-object

and SSD-system-object receives a message to permit initiation from Export-pipeline-valves-system-object;

then send a message to TSD-system-object to initiate it; and send a message to Condensate-SD-system-object to initiate it; and send a message to every Compressor-system-object to initiate it; and send a message to Import-pipeline-valves-system-object to tell it to close all import valves; and send a message to Discharge-isolating-valves-system-object to tell it to close all discharge isolating valves; and set every system-output.

Figure 6

LV01, a system-output	
Options	do forward chain, breadth first backward chain
Notes	OK
Item configuration	none
Names	LV01
Tracing and breakpoints	default
Data type	truth.value
Initial value	false
Last recorded value	no value
History keeping spec	do not keep history
Validity interval	indefinite
Formula	none
Simulation details	no simulation formula yet
Initial value for simulation	default
Data server	G2 data server
Default update interval	none
G2 to g2 interface name	interface-to-data-gathering-system
Remote g2 expression	lv01
Subclass number	14

Figure 7

PLANT-SD-SYSTEM-CLASS-METHODS-PAGE-2

EXTERNAL-METHODS

for any valve-function-system v if v is not told-to-close-all-valves-by any plant-sd-system and there exists a plant-sd-system s such that (the subclass-number of s = the valves-sd-number of v and the initiation-attribute of s is true and (the inhibit-attribute of s is false or the timed-out-attribute of s is true)) then conclude that v is now told-to-close-all-valves-by s

for any system-output o if o is false and there exists a plant-sd-system s such that (the subclass-number of s = the subclass-number of o and the initiation-attribute of s is true and the permit-attribute of s is true and (the inhibit-attribute of s is false or the timed-out-attribute of s is true)) then conclude that o is true

for any sd-system s if s is not initiated-by any plant-sd-system and there exists a plant-sd-system p such that (the subclass-number of p = the initiation-number of s and the initiation-attribute of p is true) and (the inhibit-attribute of p is false or the timed-out-attribute of p is true) then conclude that s is initiated-by p

for any inhibit-timer t if t is activated-by any plant-sd-system and there exists a plant-sd-system s such that (the subclass-number of s = the timer-number of t and (the initiation-attribute of s is false or the inhibit-attribute of s is false)) then conclude that t is not activated-by s

for any inhibit-timer t if t is not activated-by any plant-sd-system and there exists a plant-sd-system s such that (the subclass-number of s = the timer-number of t and the initiation-attribute of s is true and the inhibit-attribute of s is true) then conclude that t is now activated-by s

Figure 8

A Software Engineering Environment for Configuring Distributed Applications from Reusable Software Architectures

H. Gomaa
Department of Information and Software Systems Engineering
George Mason University
Fairfax, VA 22030-4444
E-mail: hgomaa@isse.gmu.edu
Phone: (703) 993-1652
Fax: (703) 993-1638

G.A. Farrukh
Systems and Technology Division
Technology Research Group
Science Applications International Corporation
Arlington, VA 22203
farrukh@trg1.saic.com

Abstract

In this paper a reuse-oriented perspective is taken to designing and implementing configurable distributed applications. An application domain is defined as a family of systems that have some features in common and others that differentiate them. During domain engineering, reusable specifications, architectures and component types are developed, which capture the similarities and variations of the family of systems that compose the application domain. Target systems are generated by tailoring the reusable specification and architecture given the requirements of the target system, and configuring a target system based on the tailored architecture. The paper describes a software engineering environment for configuring distributed applications from a reusable architecture and library of predefined component types.

1. Introduction

At George Mason University, a project is underway to support software engineering life cycles, methods, and environments to support software reuse at the requirements and design phases of the software life cycle in addition to the coding phase. A reuse-oriented software life cycle, the Evolutionary Domain Life Cycle [3], has been proposed, which is a highly iterative life cycle that takes an application domain perspective allowing the development of families of systems.

Earlier research addressed the analysis and specification phases of the Evolutionary Domain Life Cycle for concurrent and distributed applications [4,6]. This paper describes more recent research investigating the design and implementation phases of the EDLC, with the goal of configuring executable distributed applications from the reusable software architecture and a library of predefined component types. This paper describes the overall approach and then describes the supporting software engineering environment. This research builds on the domain modeling environment described at the last CASE workshop [7], an expanded version of which is given in [8].

0-8186-7840-2/97 $10.00 © 1997 IEEE

2. Evolutionary Domain Life Cycle

The Evolutionary Domain Life Cycle (EDLC) Model is a highly iterative software life cycle model that eliminates the traditional distinction between software development and maintenance. Furthermore, because new software systems are often outgrowths of existing ones, the EDLC model takes an application domain perspective facilitating the development of families of systems [13]. The EDLC consists of the following major activities (Fig. 1):

1) Domain engineering. During domain modeling, the following activities take place resulting in artifacts that are stored in the domain reuse library:

a) Domain analysis and modeling, which involves developing a reusable specification for the family of systems.
b) Domain architectural design, which involves developing a reusable architecture for the family of systems.
c) Implementation of domain specific reusable component types.

2) Target system configuration. During target system generation, the following activities take place resulting in artifacts that are stored in the target system library:

a) Target system specification generation. Given the requirements of an individual target system (one of the members of the family), the target system specification is generated by tailoring the reusable specification.
b) Target system architecture generation. Given the target system specification and the reusable architecture, the target system architecture is generated by tailoring the reusable architecture.
c) Target system component configuration. Based on the target system architecture, the component types to be included in the target system are selected from the domain reuse library. Given the target system configuration parameters, an instance of the target system is then composed by instantiating the target system components, interconnecting them and mapping them onto a hardware configuration.

3. Domain Analysis and Modeling

In a domain model, an application domain is represented by means of multiple views, such that each view presents a different aspect of the domain [4]. The different views are developed iteratively. For a distributed application, the most important views are the object communication view and the feature/object dependency view. The domain modeling approach will be illustrated by means of a factory automation application domain.

As an example of using the domain modeling method for the design of a distributed application, a factory automation domain is considered. This domain encompasses two mutually exclusive kinds of factory systems, high volume low flexibility manufacturing systems and low volume highly flexible manufacturing systems. The domain model is described in [6], so this paper only describes the specific aspects relating to mapping to the target system environment. To fit into this paper, only simplified high volume low flexibility manufacturing systems are described.

3.1. Object Communication Diagrams

In the object communication view, real-world objects are modeled as concurrent tasks, which communicate with each other using messages. Messages between objects may be loosely coupled or tightly coupled. The message communication among objects in the problem domain is shown on object communication diagrams (OCDs), as shown on Figure 2.

In a domain model, object types are classified as:

a) Kernel, i.e., required in every target system.
b) Optional, i.e., only required in some target systems.
c) Variant, i.e., an object type specialized to meet the specific needs of a target system.

Figure 1: Evolutionary Domain Life Cycle Model

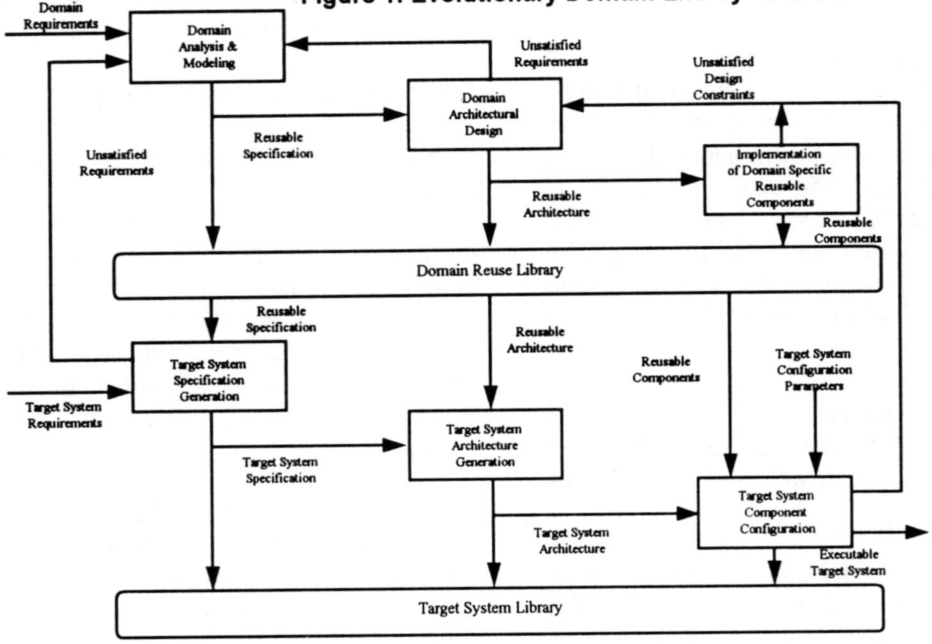

Figure 2: Object Communication Diagram for the High Volume Feature

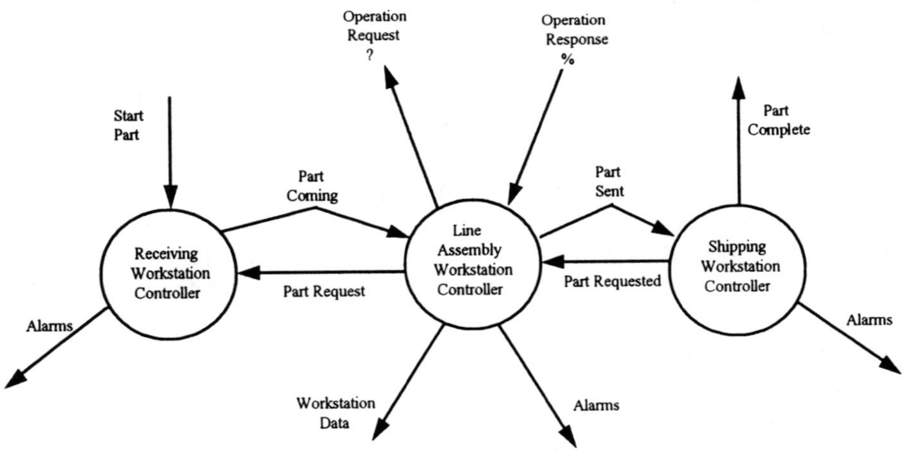

3.2. Feature/Object Dependencies

For each feature (domain requirement), this view shows the object types required to support the feature. In domain analysis, domain requirements are analyzed and categorized as those that support kernel requirements (must be supported in all target systems), optional requirements (only required in some target systems), prerequisite requirements (dependent upon other requirements), and those that are mutually exclusive. This view emphasizes optional features, because it is the selection of the optional features and the object types required to support them that determine the nature of the desired target system. The feature/object dependency view is similar to the use case view [10], extended for families of systems. For each feature, the objects that are needed to support the feature are determined and depicted on an OCD.

3.3. Applying the Domain Modeling Method

3.3.1 Problem Description.

As an example of using the domain modeling method for the design of a distributed application, a factory automation domain is considered. This domain encompasses three mutually exclusive kinds of factory systems, high volume low flexibility manufacturing systems, low volume highly flexible manufacturing systems, and factory monitoring systems. The domain model is described in [6], so this paper only describes the specific aspects relating to mapping to the target system environment. To fit into this paper, only simplified high volume low flexibility manufacturing systems are described.

In high volume systems, manufacturing workstations are laid out physically in an assembly line. Parts are moved between workstations on a conveyor belt. Each manufacturing workstation has an assembly robot and a pick-and-place robot. The manufacturing steps required to manufacture a given part in the factory, from raw material to finished product, are defined in a process plan.

3.3.2 Object Communication Diagrams.

The kernel of the domain consists of three kernel object types, the Alarm Handling Server, Workstation Status Server, and Operator Interface. The Alarm Handling Server and Workstation Status Server objects are both server objects that respond to requests from client objects. Operator Interface is a user interface object that is a client of both the Alarm Handling Server and Workstation Status Server objects. An example of an object communication diagram is given in Figure 2, which shows three objects, the Receiving Workstation Controller, the Line Assembly Workstation Controller, and the Shipping Workstation Controller objects, and their interconnections. In a given target system, there is only one instance of the Receiving Workstation Controller and Shipping Workstation Controller. For this simplified example, there is also only one instance of the Line Assembly Workstation Controller.

3.3.3 Feature/Object and Feature/Feature Dependencies.

The feature/object dependency view shows the optional and mutually exclusive features, as well as the object types and prerequisite features required to support these features. For the factory automation domain the dependencies are as follows:

a) The Factory Production feature requires the optional Process Planning Server and Production Management object types. The Production Management object is a client of the Process Planning Server, which also services other clients.
b) The High Volume Manufacturing feature requires the prerequisite Factory Production feature and the optional Receiving Workstation Controller, Line Assembly Workstation Controller, and Shipping Workstation Controller object types (Fig. 2). In addition to communicating with each other, objects supporting this feature may also communicate with any objects in prerequisite features and with any kernel objects. Thus the Line Assembly Workstation Controller is a client of the Process Planning Server, which is a component of the prerequisite Factory Production feature. All three Workstation Controller objects send alarms to Alarm Handling, which is a kernel object.

There are other features relating to Flexible Manufacturing and Factory Monitoring systems, which are described in [6].

The objects composing the High Volume Manufacturing feature, as well as the objects composing the prerequisite Factory Production feature and the implicitly prerequisite kernel feature, consisting of kernel objects, constitute a High Volume Manufacturing system, one of the target systems that can be generated from the domain model. It should be noted that the Factory Production feature is a feature that represents two objects that are common to both the High Volume Manufacturing and Flexible Manufacturing features, and hence has been factored out as a separate feature.

In the factory automation domain, a feature/feature relationship exists which is captured by the Target Factory Set. Three features are members of this set: the Flexible Manufacturing feature, the High Volume feature, and the Factory monitoring feature. In any target system, only one of these features can be selected, which represents one of the three mutually exclusive kinds of factory systems that can be configured from this domain model.

4. Domain Architectural Design

4.1. Architecture Description

During domain architectural design, a reusable architecture is developed for the family of systems. Each object type in the domain model is mapped to a component type and each feature is mapped to a design fragment showing the composition of interconnected components required to satisfy the feature.

Architectural description languages (ADLs) [14] separate the description of the overall system structure in terms of components and their interconnections (often referred to as "programming-in-the-large") from the description of the internal details of the individual components (often referred to as "programming-in-the-small") [1]. In this paper, components types and design fragments are specified using an ADL, Darwin [11], which is part of the Regis configuration environment [12] for parallel and distributed programming. The Regis environment uses the Darwin ADL for the external specification of each component type, while the internals of component types are programmed in the object-oriented language C++.

4.2. Mapping Object Types to Component Types

A Darwin component specification describes the external specification of the component type. For every simple kernel, optional, and variant object type in the domain model, an equivalent Darwin component type is created. The component interfaces correspond to the object interfaces in the OCDs.

Every Darwin component type is defined in terms of the interfaces it provides and requires from other Darwin component types. The *provide* (or input) interfaces are used to receive messages, while the *require* (or output) interfaces are used to send messages. A Darwin interface consists of an interface name, the type of message interface, and data type of incoming or outgoing message. The Darwin language provides three types of message interfaces: *ports*, *entries*, and *events*, two of which are used in this research. Ports are used for loosely- or tightly-coupled message communication without reply [5]. Entries are used for tightly-coupled message communication with reply.

The Darwin component type equivalent to the Line Assembly Workstation Controller object type is shown in Fig. 3 and described next.

```
component
Line_Assembly_Workstation_Controller (char*
wkst_name)
{
 provide Part_Requested
   <port Part_Request_Type>;
 provide Part_Coming
   <port Part_Type>;

 require Workstation_Data
   <port Part_Type>;
 require Part_Sent
   <port Part_Type>;
 require Part_Request
   <port Part_Request_Type>;
 require Operation_Request
   <entry OpReq_Type, OpRes_Type>;
```

Figure 3: Line Assembly Workstation Controller Component Type

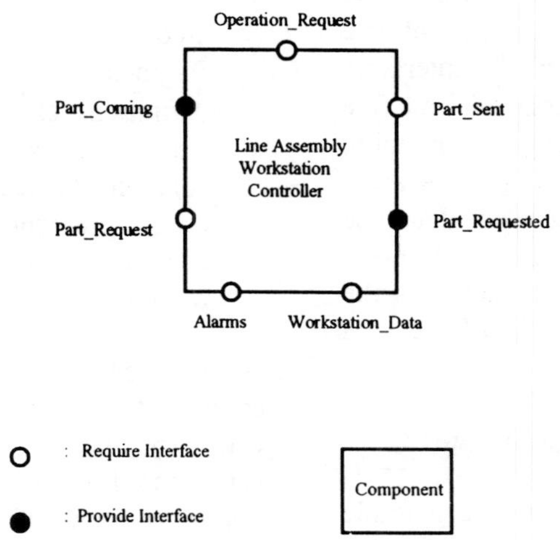

Figure 4: Software Architecture Diagram for the High Volume Fragment

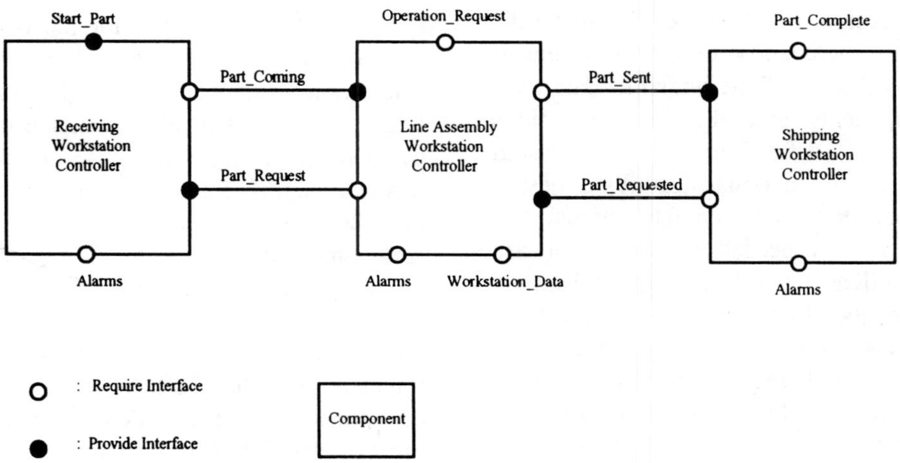

```
  require Alarms
    <port Alarm_Type>;
}
```

The Darwin specification for the Line Assembly Workstation Controller component type shows the definition of two *provide* interfaces (corresponding to incoming messages) and five *require* interfaces (corresponding to outgoing messages) messages. All the interfaces apart from one are *ports* and so they have one data type for their message. The Operation Request interface is an *entry* and therefore contains the data types of both the request, *OpReq Type*, and the response, *OpRes Type*.

4.3. Mapping Features to Design Fragments

To relate the domain features to the reusable architecture, a scenario driven approach [6] (also referred to as the use case approach [10]) is used. Each feature based OCD forms the basis for a design fragment, which is a domain-specific design pattern [2]. A design fragment shows the collaboration among the components required to support a given feature, as well as communication with collaborating components in prerequisite fragments.

For every feature in the domain model, there exists a design fragment in the domain architectural design, which is specified using the Darwin ADL. There is also one design fragment supporting the kernel of the domain. The non-variant components and the interconnections between them are defined in the kernel design fragment. For each optional feature, a design fragment is created, in which the optional and variant components needed to support it are defined as well as the interconnection between these components. In addition, interconnections are defined between the components in the design fragment and any kernel components used by these components. Interconnections are also defined to any optional or variant components defined in prerequisite design fragments.

Specifically, a design fragment contains the following information:

- declaration of component types contained in this fragment
- declaration of fragments required by this fragment, including the kernel fragment
- instantiation of components contained in this fragment
- definition of component interconnections among components contained in this fragment
- definition of component interconnections among components of this fragment and components declared in required fragments (i.e., prerequisite fragments that this component depends on), including the kernel fragment.

In order for a component to be able to communicate with another component, it is necessary that both components be instantiated using the Darwin *inst* statement, and for the *require* interface of the sending component to be connected to the *provide* interface of the receiving component using the Darwin *bind* statement.

4.4. Example of a Design Fragment.

In order for a component to be able to communicate with another component, it is necessary that both the components be instantiated by using the Darwin *inst* statement and their respective interfaces be connected together, using the Darwin *bind* statement.

Fig. 2 shows the OCD for the High Volume feature within the factory automation domain. The feature is mapped to a High Volume design fragment composed of interconnected Darwin components as shown in Fig. 4. and described in this section. Fig. 5 shows the design fragment for the the kernel, called the kernel fragment, consisting of the three kernel components, Alarm Handling Server, Workstation Status Server, and Operator Interface, as well as their interconnections. Fig. 6 shows the design fragment for the Factory Production feature, consisting of the Production Management and Process Planning Server components, as well as their interconnections.

The Darwin instantiation and bind statements for this design fragment are described next. The instantiation statements are used to create one or more instances of a component type. The High Volume fragment has three component types: Receiving Workstation Controller, Line Assembly

Figure 5: Software Architecture Diagram for the Kernel Fragment

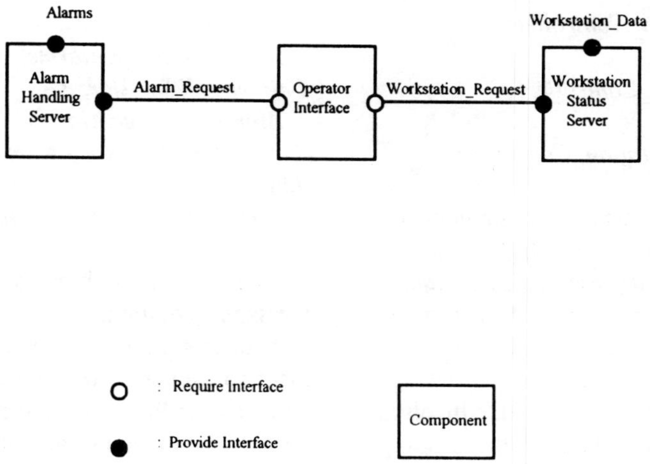

Figure 6: Software Architecture Diagram for the Factory Production Fragment

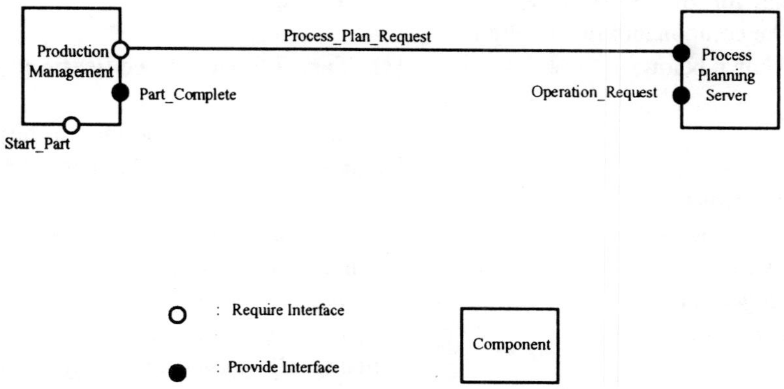

Workstation Controller, and Shipping Workstation Controller, which are instantiated in Darwin as follows:

```
inst
 Receiving_Wkst:
   Receiving_Workstation_Controller;
 Shipping_Wkst:
   Shipping_Workstation_Controller;
 Line_Wkst:
   Line_Assembly_Workstation_Controller;
```

Fig. 4 shows the message communication among components in the High Volume fragment. A message is represented by a *require* interface at the sender side and a *provide* interface at the receiver side, each with the same name as the message name. Message communication between two components involves connecting the *require* interface of the sending component to the *provide* interface of the receiving component using the Darwin bind statement. For example, the Line Assembly Workstation Controller sends the *Part Sent* message to the Shipping Workstation Controller. This is made possible by connecting the Part Sent *require* port of the Line Assembly Workstation Controller to the Part Sent *provide* port of the Shipping Workstation Controller:

```
bind
  Line_Wkst.Part_Sent --
   Shipping_Wkst.Part_Sent;
```

The bind statements for the other messages sent and received by the components in the High Volume fragment are shown below:

```
bind
 Line_Wkst.Part_Request --
   Receiving_Wkst.Part_Request;
 Receiving_Wkst.Part_Coming --
   Line_Wkst.Part_Coming;
 Shipping_Wkst.Part_Requested --
   Line__Wkst.Part_Requested;
```

A design fragment also has to define the interconnections to components in required fragments, which for the High Volume fragment are the kernel fragment and the Factory Production fragment. The following bind statements define the message communication between the three components in the High Volume fragment and two kernel server components, Alarm Handling Server, Workstation Status Server, contained in the kernel fragment (Fig. 5).

```
bind
 Receiving_Wkst.Alarms --
   Alarm_Handler.Alarms;
 Shipping_Wkst.Alarms --
   Alarm_Handler.Alarms;
 Line_Wkst.Alarms -- Alarm_Handler.Alarms;
 Line_Wkst.Workstation_Data --
   Wkst_Status_Srvr.Workstation_Data;
```

The following bind statements define the message communication between the three components in the High Volume fragment and the two components, Production Management and Process Planning Server, in the prerequisite Factory Production fragment (Fig. 6).

```
bind
 Shipping_Wkst.Part_Complete --
   Prod_Mngmnt.Part_Complete;
 Prod_Mngmnt.Start_Part --
   Receiving_Wkst.Start_Part;
 Line_Wkst.Operation_Request --
   Process_Planner.Operation_Request;
```

5. Target System Configuration

A target system is a member of the family of systems that constitute the application domain. It is a tailored instance of the reusable software architecture.

5.1. Target System Specification Generation

A target system is defined in terms of domain features it supports. This consists of the kernel features plus a consistent subset of the optional features - thus there can be no mutually exclusive features in a target system.

The target system specification (Fig. 1) contains all kernel object types (which every member of the family requires), together with the optional and variant object types needed for that specific target system. Selection of the optional and variant object types to include in a given target system is done by selecting those optional features of the domain model desired for particular target system, subject to the feature/object dependency constraints and feature/feature dependency constraints defined in the domain model.

In the Factory Automation domain, a High Volume Manufacturing system (one of the target systems that can be generated from the domain model) consists of three features, the High Volume Manufacturing feature, the prerequisite Factory Production feature and the implicitly prerequisite kernel feature. This system consists of the kernel objects, as well as the objects contained in the two optional features.

5.2. Target System Architecture Generation

To generate a target system, the target system engineer needs to choose features to include in the target system subject to the constraints of the feature/feature dependencies. The corresponding design fragments are then integrated to produce the target system. This integration is necessary because an individual design fragment only specifies a partial target system. However, when merged with all the fragments it depends on, it becomes a specification for an executable target system. The target system architecture generation process uses the reusable architecture and target system specification and generates the target system architecture (Fig. 1).

For a High Volume target system, the High Volume, Factory Production, and kernel fragments are needed (Fig. 7). As a result the component types selected for the High Volume system are:

- The Receiving Workstation Controller, Line Assembly Workstation Controller, and Shipping Workstation Controller, from the High Volume fragment (Fig. 4).
- The Alarm Handling Server, Operator Interface, and Workstation Status Server, from the kernel fragment (Fig. 5).
- The Process Planning Server and Production Management, from the Factory Production fragment (Fig. 6).

Each fragment defines the components contained in the fragment, the interconnections among the components in the fragement, and the interconnections between components in this fragment and components in other required fragments (Section 4.3). Thus Fig. 7 shows:

- Instantiation and interconnection among the three components in the High Volume fragment (derived from the High Volume fragment - Fig. 4).
- Instantiation and interconnection among the three components in the kernel fragment (derived from the kernel fragment - Fig. 5).
- Instantiation and interconnection among the two components in the Factory Production fragment (derived from the Factory Production fragment - Fig. 6).
- Interconnection between components in the High Volume fragment and components in the required Factory production and kernel fragments that the High Volume fragment depends on (derived from the High Volume fragment and shown in Fig. 7).

6. Software Engineering Environment

Fig. 8 shows the software engineering environment that supports the domain engineering activities of domain modeling, domain design, and component implementation, as well as the target system configuration activities of generating target system specifications, architectures, and executable applications. The environment consists of several prototype tools and two libraries: the domain reuse library and the target system library.

6.1 Domain Modeling Environment

Domain analysis and modeling is supported by the proof-of-concept domain modeling environment [7, 8], consisting of an integrated set of software tools. The environment uses commercial-of-the-shelf software as well as custom developed software. The graphical editors supported by the Software Through Pictures CASE tool are used to represent the multiple views of the domain model including the object communication diagrams. The information in the multiple views is extracted, checked for consistency, and mapped to a common underlying representation, which is then stored in a domain reuse library. The feature/object dependencies and feature/feature dependencies are defined using a Feature/Object Editor.

Figure 7: Software Architecture Diagram for the High Volume Target System

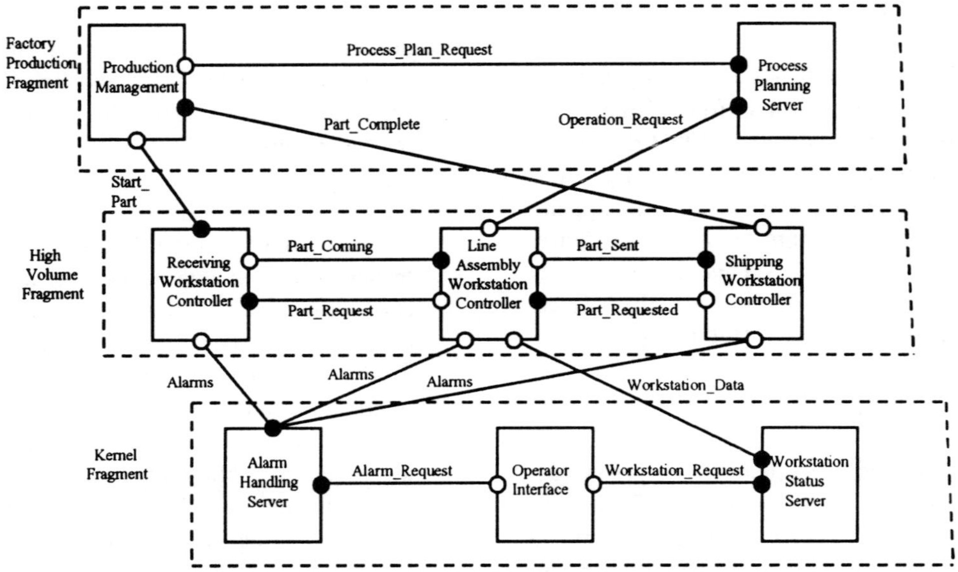

Figure 8: Software Engineering Environment for Reusable Specifications and Architectures

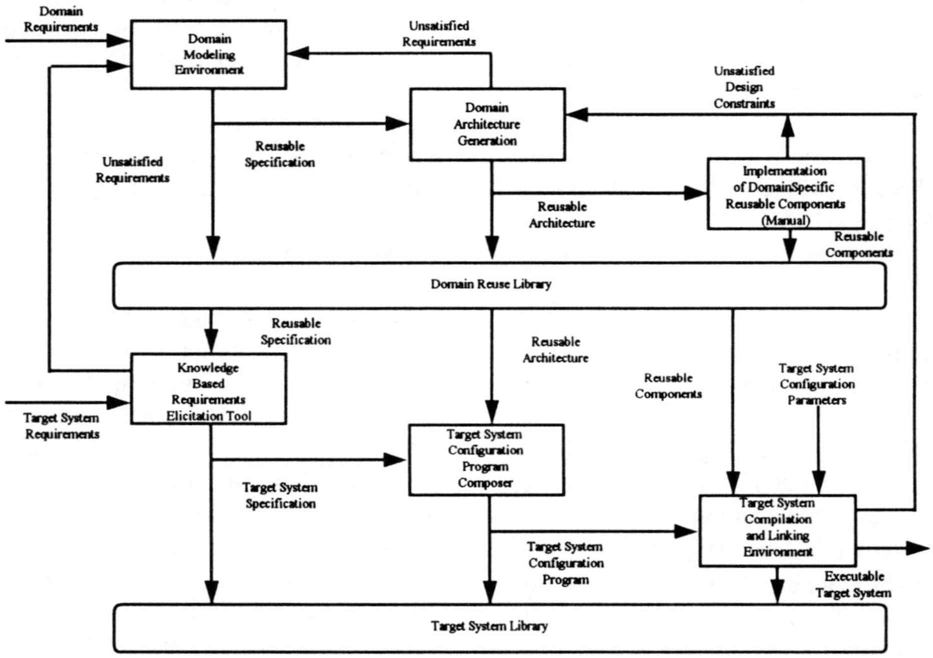

The information needed for generating the domain architectural design is stored in the domain reuse library and consists of domain relations and the domain dependent knowledge base, described in detail in [8].

6.2. Domain Architecture Generation

Generating a reusable architecture for a domain is automated by three tools: the Darwin Components Generator, the Design Fragments Generator, and the Consistency Checker, as described next.

6.2.1 Darwin Components Generator

For every kernel, optional, and variant object type in the domain model, an equivalent Darwin component type is generated and stored in the domain reuse library (Section 4.2). The component interfaces correspond to the object interfaces in the OCDs. The information used to generate the Darwin component types is obtained from the domain relations.

The Darwin Components Generator extracts the necessary information from the domain relations (which capture the underlying representation of the domain model) and generates Darwin component types corresponding to object types in the domain model. The Darwin Components Generator extracts the relevant information from the domain reuse library, namely the object types, messages, and configuration parameters. It generates the *provide* and *require* interfaces for every component type corresponding to the inbound and outbound messages of objects in the OCDs.

6.2.2 Design Fragments Generator

For each feature in the domain model, Design Fragments Generator (DFG) tool creates a design fragment; a design fragment is also created for the kernel components. A fragment contains the Darwin statements for instantiating the components supporting the fragment and defining the binding among these components, as well as the binding between these components and components in prerequisite fragments, including the kernel fragment (Section 4.3). It obtains the necessary information, which consists of the object types, their interconnections, features, feature/object and feature/feature dependencies, from the domain reuse library. Once a design fragment is generated, it is stored in the domain reuse library.

A design fragment generated by this tool contains the names of all required fragments including the kernel fragment, the instantiation statements for supporting Darwin components, and bind statements among different Darwin components. Generating binding statements corresponding to the message communication between components is the most important activity in the process of generating design fragments. The process of generating bindings is divided into three steps: 1) generating bindings statements among components within a given fragments, 2) generating bindings with components in the kernel fragment, and 3) generating bindings with components in prerequisite fragments. The process of generating bind statements is the same for all three steps.

6.2.3 Consistency Checker

When all the design fragments are generated and stored in the domain reuse library, they are checked for internal consistency. A design fragment is considered internally consistent if it contains no Darwin syntax errors and all its required fragments and components are also free from Darwin syntax errors. The process of consistency checking is automated by a tool, the Consistency Checker.

The Consistency Checker tool (Fig. 4) checks every fragment to make sure that it contains correct Darwin syntax for declaration, instantiation, and bind statements for all components in the fragment. It also checks the declaration and instantiation statements for components in all required fragments, including the kernel fragment.

To check the consistency of a design fragment, the Consistency Checker extracts all the include statements and instantiation statements from all prerequisite fragments of a given design fragment and then merges these with the equivalent statements of the design fragment under test. This information is used to create a Darwin component based on the design fragment, which is parsed by the Darwin language parser for syntax errors. The above process is repeated for all design fragments in a domain including the kernel fragment.

6.3. Implementation of Domain Specific Reusable Components

The detailed design and implementation of the domain specific reusable Regis components needs to be performed manually before any target system can be configured and executed. This activity is started after the Darwin component types have been designed and their interfaces defined in the Darwin ADL. The internals of each component type are coded in C++.

Once the reusable components have been developed and tested, they are stored in the domain reuse library. At this stage, the reusable architecture and component types have been developed. Different target system applications can now be configured, as described next.

6.4. Knowledge Based Requirements Elicitation Tool

The Knowledge Based Requirements Elicitation Tool (KBRET) is used to assist with the generation of the target system specification (Fig. 4) [8]. KBRET conducts a dialog with the human target system requirements engineer, presenting the user with the optional features available for selection for the target system. The user selects the desired features, and KBRET reasons about the feature/feature dependencies to ensure that a consistent set of features are selected. Thus KBRET ensures that mutually exclusive feature dependencies and feature prerequisite dependencies are enforced. Based on the selected features, KBRET determines the kernel, optional and variant object types to be included in this target system. This output of KBRET is used to adapt the domain model to generate the target system specification.

6.5. Target System Configuration Program Composer

The Target System Program Composer (Fig. 4) integrates the design fragments, corresponding to the features selected using KBRET, into a Darwin configuration program for the target system. This integration is necessary because individual design fragments only specify partial configurations of target systems. However, when merged with all the fragments it depends on, a design fragment becomes a configuration program for an executable target system. The composed Darwin configuration program has the same structure as a design fragment except for the addition of the target system name and parameter list. The resulting target system configuration program is stored in the target system library.

The Target System Configuration Program Composer extracts all the include statements, instantiation statements, and binding statements from every fragment selected for the target system, including the kernel fragment. These statements are merged to form the configuration program for the target system.

As an example, consider the software architecture diagram for the High Volume Manufacturing target system shown in Fig. 7. This figure shows how components from three fragments, High Volume Manufacturing, Factory Production and Kernel, are interconnected to generate an application.

6.6. Target System Compilation and Linking Environment

The composed target system configuration program is compiled and linked to produce an executable target system application (Fig. 4). It is passed to the Regis compilation and linking environment along with the necessary Darwin and Regis components. The Regis environment creates a "Makefile" for every target system. The GNU "make" utility is then used to compile and link the target system into an executable application. Once the target system is compiled and linked, a target system can be instantiated by passing it the values of the target system parameters.

7. Discussion and Conclusions

This paper has described describes the overall approach and a supporting software engineering environment for configuring distributed applications from reusable architectures. This research builds on the domain modeling environment described at the last CASE workshop. It involves integrating the domain modeling environment with the Regis distributed configuration and programming environment. Thus a target system is composed from predefined design fragments consisting of interconnected components. The environment has been demonstrated with a factory automation domain, a simplified version of which is described in this paper. The environment has also been demonstrated with other application domains, demonstrating that it is application domain independent.

Future research work involves investigating the possibility of replacing the design fragments with higher level Darwin component types corresponding to each feature. We are also exploring other application domains.

7. Acknowledgments

The authors gratefully acknowledge the assistance of L. Kerschberg, C. Bosch, V. Sugumaran, and I. Tavakoli. Thanks are due to J. Kramer and J. Magee for several discussions on Regis. This work was supported in part by NASA Goddard Space Flight Center, the Virginia Center of Innovative Technology and DARPA. The Software Through Pictures CASE tool was donated to GMU by Interactive Development Environments.

8. References

[1] F. DeRemer and H. Kron, "Programming-in-the-Large versus Programming-in-the-Small," *IEEE Transactions on Software Engineering*, June 1976.

[2] E. Gamma, R. Helm, R. Johnson and J. Vlissides, *Design Patterns: Elements of Reusable Object-Oriented Software*, Addison Wesley, 1995.

[3] H. Gomaa, and L. Kerschberg, "An Evolutionary Domain Life Cycle Model for Domain Modeling and Target System Generation," Proc. Workshop on Domain Modeling for Software Engineering, *Intl. Conf. on Software Engineering*, Austin, TX, May 1991.

[4] H. Gomaa, "A Reuse-oriented Approach for Structuring and Configuring Distributed Applications", *Software Engineering Journal*, March 1993.

[5] H. Gomaa, *Software Design Methods for Concurrent and Real-Time Systems*, Addison Wesley, 1993.

[6] H. Gomaa, "Reusable Software Requirements and Architectures for Families of Systems", *Journal of Systems and Software*, April 1995.

[7] H. Gomaa and L. Kerschberg, "Domain Modeling for Software Reuse and Evolution," *Proceedings IEEE Computer Assisted Software Engineering Workshop (CASE 95)*, Toronto, Canada, July 1995.

[8] H. Gomaa, L. Kerschberg, V. Sugumaran, C. Bosch, I. Tavakoli, and L. O'Hara, "A Knowledge-Based Software Engineering Environment for Reusable Software Requirements and Architectures," *Journal of Automated Software Engineering*, Vol. 3, Nos. 3/4, August 1996.

[9] H. Gomaa and G.A. Farrukh, "An Approach for Configuring Distributed Applications from Reusable Architectures, *Proceedings of IEEE International Conference on Engineering of Complex Computer Systems*, Montreal, Canada, October 1996, pp. 442-449.

[10] I. Jacobson, *Object-Oriented Software Engineering*, Addison Wesley, Reading MA, 1991.

[11] J. Magee, N. Dulay, and J. Kramer, "Structuring parallel and distributed programs," *Software Engineering Journal*, March 1993, pp. 73-82.

[12] J. Magee, N. Dulay and J. Kramer, "Regis: A Constructive Development Environment for Parallel and Distributed Programs", *Journal of Distributed Systems Engineering*, 1994, pp. 304-312.

[13] D. Parnas, "Designing Software for Ease of Extension and Contraction", *IEEE Transactions on Software Engineering*, March 1979.

[14] M. Shaw and D. Garlan, *Software Architecture: Perspectives on an Emerging Discipline*, Prentice Hall, 1996.

Reengineering Legacy Applications using Design Patterns

K. Lano
Dept. of Computing, Imperial College, 180 Queens Gate, London SW7 2BZ
Email: kcl@doc.ic.ac.uk

N. Malik
Systems (Private) Limited, Karachi, Pakistan

Abstract

This paper presents a new approach to the use of design patterns for the reengineering of legacy code, using a mapping from procedural design patterns to object-oriented patterns. We show also how object-oriented design patterns can be formalised and correctness conditions for their application derived, in order to justify the preservation of functionality in the reengineering process. We conclude with a case study of reengineering of a legacy COBOL application.

1 Introduction

Design patterns are characteristic structures of classes or objects which can be reused to achieve particular design goals in an elegant manner. For example, the "Strategy" design pattern replaces explicit conditional choices between different algorithm implementations by implicit polymorphic choices given by alternative subtypes of a class. Design patterns are not usually defined in a precise manner, as their very generality makes this difficult. However, if design patterns are to be used to transform legacy applications into functionally equivalent but more maintainable forms, we need to be able to determine when their use results in a correct design step.

The semantics of object-oriented systems has been given in a logical axiomatic framework termed the Object Calculus [6, 7]. Here, we will use an extension of this framework which allows the use of structured actions corresponding to programming language statements, in order to formulate the semantics of the "before" (application of the pattern) and "after" versions of a system, and to show that the "after" version refines (has all the functionality of) the "before" version.

Section 2 describes the Strategy pattern using VDM^{++}, and the informal expression of its correctness. Section 3 describes the case study and the reengineering approach taken. Section 4 introduces the object calculus and describes how patterns such as Strategy can be formalised and shown to be correct design steps. Finally, we conclude with a summary of what has been achieved and what extensions can be considered.

2 Expressing Design Patterns in VDM^{++}

VDM^{++} [5, 14] is an object-oriented formal specification language based on the VDM-SL notation, with extensions to cover concurrent and real-time behaviour in addition to structuring mechanisms such as classes and inheritance. It is suitable for the expression of design transformations such as patterns because it contains both highly abstract specification mechanisms (allowing operations to be defined by pre and post-conditions, akin to the operation schemas of Fusion [3]) and design and implementation-level mechanisms.

Here we will describe in VDM^{++} a "before" and "after" version of a system to which the Strategy pattern can be applied. The papers [13, 9] and thesis [16] together give similar representations of all the patterns described in [8].

Figure 1 describes the general form of the Strategy pattern. The pattern allows multiple algorithms to be used for a particular abstract operation, the choice between these algorithms (embedded in particular **Strategy** subclasses) being made by polymorphism.

Strategy can be used to transform a system of the form of Figure 2 to the form given in Figure 3.

Informally we can reason that the new version of the system achieves the same functionality as the old: the **set_type1** operation of a **Context1** object **obj** results in **obj.strategy** becoming a mem-

0-8186-7840-2/97 $10.00 © 1997 IEEE

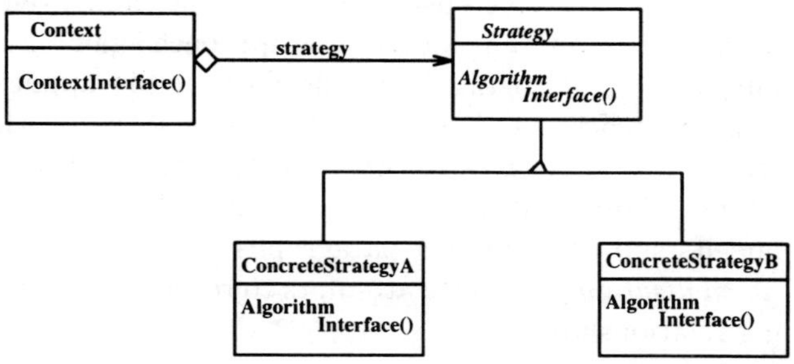

Figure 1. Strategy Pattern Structure

```
class Client
instance variables
  aContext : @Context;
init objectstate ==
  aContext := Context!new
methods
  m() ==
     (aContext!set_type1(); ...
      aContext!ContextInterface())
end Client

class Context
instance variables
  strategy_type : < type1 > | < type2 >
methods
  set_type1() ==
        strategy_type := < type1 >;

  set_type2() == ...;

  ContextInterface() ==
        if strategy_type = < type1 >
        then Code1
        else Code2

end Context
```

Figure 2. Abstract Strategy Structure

```
class Client1
instance variables
  aContext : @Context1;
init objectstate ==
  aContext := Context1!new
methods
  m() ==
     (aContext!set_type1(); ...
      aContext!ContextInterface())
end Client1

class Context1
instance variables
  strategy : @Strategy
methods
 ContextInterface() ==
        strategy!AlgorithmInterface();

 set_type1() ==
        strategy := ConcreteStrategyA!new;

 set_type2() ==
        strategy := ConcreteStrategyB!new
end Context1

class Strategy
methods
   AlgorithmInterface()
          is subclass responsibility
end Strategy

class ConcreteStrategyA
  is subclass of Strategy
methods
   AlgorithmInterface() == Code1
end ConcreteStrategyA
```

Figure 3. Concrete Strategy Structure

ber of $\overline{\textbf{ConcreteStrategyA}}$, the set of existing **ConcreteStrategyA** objects. But this corresponds to the abstract operation of setting **strategy_type** equal to < **type1** >, if we interpret **strategy_type** by the conditional expression

if strategy $\in$ $\overline{\textbf{ConcreteStrategyA}}$
then < **type1** >
else
  if strategy $\in$ $\overline{\textbf{ConcreteStrategyB}}$
  then < **type2** >
  else nil

Likewise, the effect of the **ContextInterface** operation on **obj** results in execution of **Code1** if **strategy** $\in$ $\overline{\textbf{ConcreteStrategyA}}$, and in execution of **Code2** if **strategy** $\in$ $\overline{\textbf{ConcreteStrategyB}}$, which corresponds to the interpretation of the specified behaviour. We can see that there are some informal constraints on the validity of this refinement:

- **strategy** must be an existing object of one of the two subtypes of **Strategy** at the point where **ContextInterface** is called;
- **strategy** cannot change its subclass during an execution of **ContextInterface**.

Other, more precise constraints on the correctness of the step will be derived in Section 4.

3 Reengineering Legacy Applications

Most approaches to the use of patterns in reengineering have focused on the capture of procedural patterns from procedural code [1] or on the capture of OO patterns from OO code [18]. In contrast, we wish to use the existing procedural patterns in the legacy software to create relevant and meaningful OO patterns in the reengineered OO design.

A number of approaches have been developed for reverse-engineering non-object oriented applications into an object-oriented form [21, 17, 11, 15]. The REORG approach of [21] involves a 10-step process to transform a procedural COBOL program into an object-oriented one. Object classes are derived from the existing data structures such as records, database views and working storage sections, and access and update operations allocated to these classes on the basis of data usage analysis in the program. A problem is that analysis of different programs in a system can produce equivalent classes which are not recognised as such because of different data names (ie, attributes that are synonyms are created). The HOOSM approach of [17] addresses these problems. HOOSM is described as a hybrid between conventional OO modelling languages, state-based reactive specification systems and event-driven programming models. The approach again bases initial object recognition on the data of the application, but carries out a detailed alias analysis on the structure and types of records to identify possible synonyms. Additional objects are based on the program and its sub-procedures ("paragraphs" in COBOL). A *normalisation* procedure attempts to recognise subtyping relationships.

Our approach has some elements in common with the REORG and HOOSM approaches, but extends them by using transformations from *procedural patterns* to *object-oriented patterns* as the underlying process. Given the procedural patterns in the source code, we select corresponding OO patterns for the new version of the system, and consequent object classes. In terms of the levels of abstraction for reengineering defined by [2], we are working at the physical design level, although the wide-spectrum nature of VDM^{++} means that higher-level abstractions could also be extracted from applications.

The motivation for this approach is that design patterns are not unique to object-oriented systems: designers have always used some design patterns in the design of procedural systems, however idiosyncratic they may be to their particular environment. In as far as the existence of these patterns assist in program comprehension and maintenance, we do not want to erase or disregard them in the transformation to a new OO architecture, but instead to reuse and adapt them, and use them to select new OO design patterns which achieve the design goals in a more effective way. The loss of maintainer understanding as a result of reengineering is one of the major drawbacks with current reengineering techniques.

In reengineering, it is difficult to identify "design level" objects, i.e., objects other than the ones derived directly from data structures, or files record structures. In our approach the design pattern transformation guides identification of higher level objects in the transformed systems. These objects could be processes, computations or even objects that determine the control flow, as shown in the case study.

A related technique that will also be used is the introduction of object-based interfaces for algorithms [10]. In this case computations that go through distinct phases and use a common set of data are described using a class whose methods initiate the various phases. For example, the process of sorting, which would be usually written as a single function in a language such as C, can be decomposed into operations of **insert**ing an element into an object, changing the object to extract mode or to insert mode, and **extract**ing the **i**-th element in ascending order of size from the object. This interface abstracts away from implementation decisions to carry out the actual sorting process either incrementally during the insertions, in batch mode during the change to extraction, or incrementally during extraction (or a mix of these strategies). This technique is consistent with the attempts at abstraction found in COBOL features such as the report writer and search facilities.

In the following case study we will look at two kinds of control flow structures as examples of procedural patterns.

3.1 The Billing System

3.1.1 Background

The case study used here is extracted from a billing system for water charges used by a utility company. The code is currently being used and hence the case study is illustrative of a "real-world" application. The system, implemented in COBOL, was originally developed in the early 80's for the IBM 4331. In the early 90's the hardware platform was changed to an AIX-based IBM Risc/6000. ISAM files are used for persistent storage, and the system is essentially batch-oriented.

During the platform change the code was reengineered to an extent, with GOTO's being replaced by PERFORM's, and some modularisation added.

Bills are produced bimonthly based on, in the general case, the consumption of water read off from meters. For every billing cycle, first the meter reading data is entered, then the bill processing step is executed. This computes the various charges due and updates the master file with the computed information.

The bill is a sum of water consumption charge, sewerage charges, meter rent and arrears, etc. In the case study we restrict attention to the water consumption charge calculation, as this is the most complex element in the system. For each consumer the water consumption charge is calculated in two main steps. In the first step the consumption is computed and in the second, based on the consumption and other factors detailed below, the charge is calculated.

The consumption calculation involves differentiating several types of consumption: "tariff 5" constant estimated consumption, metered consumption, estimated consumption where either the start or finish meter reading is unknown, etc.

The charge computation involves differentiating commercial and domestic consumption, and different levies for different "slabs" of consumption at various tariffs.

3.1.2 Maintenance Requirements

In many respects for systems that will be frequently maintained, flexibility of the system is a priority at the same level as program efficiency. For the above application the prospective maintenance changes (based on previous experience) include:

- the introduction of new tariff types: this would affect both the consumption calculation as well as the computation of the charges
- the introduction of different control sequences. Under new circumstances the same underlying computations would be invoked under a different set of conditions and possibly after further processing of the variables.

3.2 The Reengineering Process

The information used for reengineering was the source code [16] and the available documentation: a two line description of the purpose of each of the programs.

The first step in reengineering the code was to derive a control flow graph for the programs, and rearrangement of this control flow graph to reveal more systematic structure [12]. Next the code within control flow nodes was divided up on the basis of which files and records (objects) it updated, and utility procedures (often called from several locations) separated out. The data-flow between program variables was examined to determine a formal specification of the functionality of each separated control-flow segment, as described in [12]. Low-level objects corresponding to files, records and screens are recognised, and file accesses, etc are replaced by method calls [11].

For example the record definition

```
05 CONSM-DEL-TAG       PIC X(01)
05 CONSM-KEY
   10 CONSM-TYPE       PIC X(01)
   10 CONSM-TARRIF     PIC 9(01)
   10 CONSM-CONNSZE    PIC 9(02)
05 CONSM-CONSUMPTION   PIC 9(07)
```

for the **Consumption** file results in the class definition:

```
class Consumption_rec
instance variables
  CONSM_DEL_TAG : X1;
  CONSM_KEY : X1N3;
  CONSM_TYPE : X1;
  CONSM_TARRIF : N1;
  CONSM_CONNSZE : N2;
  CONSM_CONSUMPTION : N7
```

```
inv objectstate ==
  CONSM_KEY =
    compose(CONSM_TYPE, CONSM_TARRIF,
             CONSM_CONNSZE)
methods
  delete() ==
      CONSM_DEL_TAG := '1';

  ⋮
end Consumption_rec
```

for the record type, and

```
class Consumption_file
types
  Mode = < input > | < output > |
           < i_o > | < closed >
instance variables
  frec : @Consumption_rec;
  frkey : X1N3;
  ptr : ℕ;
  status : ℕ;
  mode : Mode;
  scontents : seq of @Consumption_rec;
  fcontents : map X1N3 to @Consumption_rec;
  ....
inv objectstate ==
  /* Same records are present in both representations: */
  elems(scontents) = rng(fcontents) ∧

  /* There are no duplicate records in the file: */
  len(scontents) = card(elems(scontents)) ∧

  ⋮
init objectstate ==
  (status := 0; mode := < closed >;
   ptr := 0)
methods
  AT_END() value bool ==
     if (ptr = len(scontents) ∨
         frkey ∉ dom(fcontents))
     then return true
     else return false;

  OPEN(mod : Mode) ==
       if mode = closed
       then
         mode := mod;
         status := 0
       else
         status := 41;

  READ_NEXT() ==
      if mode ∈ { < input >, < i_o >} ∧
         ptr < len(scontents)
      then
        ptr := ptr + 1;
        status := 0;
        rec := scontents(ptr)
      else
        if mode ∈ { < output >, < closed > }
        then status := 47
        else
          status := 23;

  ⋮
end Consumption_file
```

for the class type, which is generated as a renaming of a standard **inddynfile** class [11].

Each program is then converted into a single object, whose methods correspond to significant control-flow nodes such as paragraph start nodes. Subsequent reengineering steps take this as the starting point for the introduction of design patterns and further objects. Examples of such transformation are given below for the two modules.

At the top level the reengineered program will be given an object-based interface with two main methods, **CalculateConsumption** and **CalculateCharge**.

3.3 The Consumption Calculation Module

This module consists of two 'layers'. The top layer consists of the *control* mechanism and the bottom consists of the *computation* procedures. The control layer determines which of the four procedures (metered consumption, average consumption, in-between meter, tariff 5 consumption) in the computation layer will be used. As part of maintenance, both the control mechanism and the computation procedures may change independently. Hence the need for separation of concerns. As the first step in introducing a new object structure for this system, we therefore break the monolithic object that contains the entire program into five finer grain objects, one encapsulating the control mechanism and one for each of the consumption computation procedures. The four procedures are alternatives for the same computation, so it is natural to generalise their interfaces via subtyping.

The control layer is structured as a number of cascading IF-THEN-ELSE statements. The pattern to be observed is that each successive IF statement checks for the non-standard computation case. If such a condition is found the control flow branches off to the relevant procedure in the computation layer. Otherwise it heads forward checking for other non-standard conditions until no such condition remains, in which case the standard computation is performed. Such a procedural pattern could be termed a *sieve* structure.

Our reengineering method tries to identify a suitable corresponding OO pattern to replace this procedural pattern. We select a combination of the *Decorator* and *Chain of Responsibility* patterns [8]. Chain of Responsibility is appropriate because the sieve procedural pattern involves a delegation of a request through a series of entities (conditional tests and processing) until a suitable receiver is found. Decorator is appropriate because each of the conditional handlers may involve specific additional processing which may be changed independently of other handlers.

In this solution, each conditional method in the original class becomes an object of a class **Conditional** (Figure 4).

```
class Conditional
  is subclass of CondHandler
instance variables
  cond: @Condition;
  if_branch: @CondHandler;
  else_branch: @CondHandler
methods
  CalculateConsumption() ==
    (dcl yesno: bool;
       AdditionalProcessing();
       yesno := cond!Condition();
       if yesno
       then
         if_branch!CalculateConsumption()
       else
         else_branch!CalculateConsumption());

  SetConditions(c: @Condition, i: @CondHandler,
                e: @CondHandler) ==
    (cond := c;
     if_branch := i;
     else_branch := e);

  AdditionalProcessing()
    is subclass responsibility
end Conditional
```

Using these conditional objects one can build an arbitrarily complex control structure by class composition. A correctness condition is that each of the chains of responsibility should end with a **ConsumptionCalculation** object (ie, with no further conditional processing) in order to avoid endless loops in the object reference structure. In this program the chaining of conditional objects is shown in Figure 5. Each object **CalcConsumption**, 2000**MetdataConsm** etc is of type **Conditional**, and has an associated **Condition** object (not shown in Figure 5). Terminal nodes in this graph are of type **ConsumptionCalculation**.

The individual conditionals in the program are all based on some variable of either the master file of

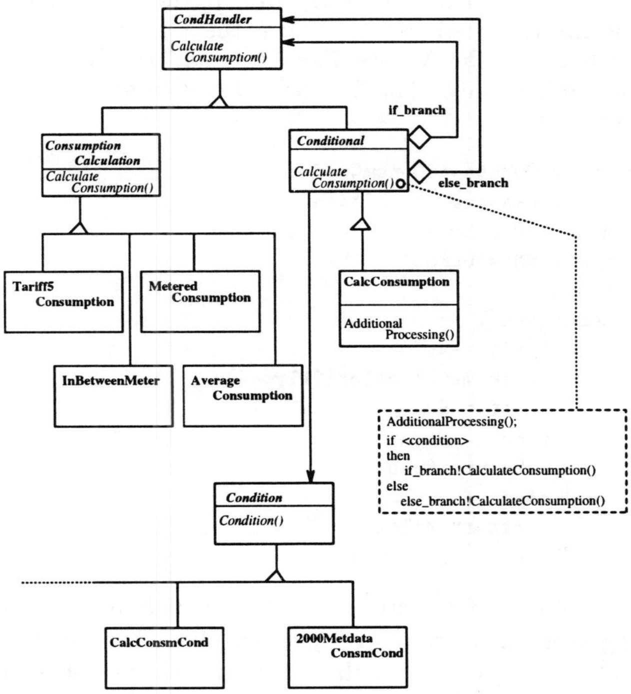

Figure 4. Decorated Chain of Responsibility Structure

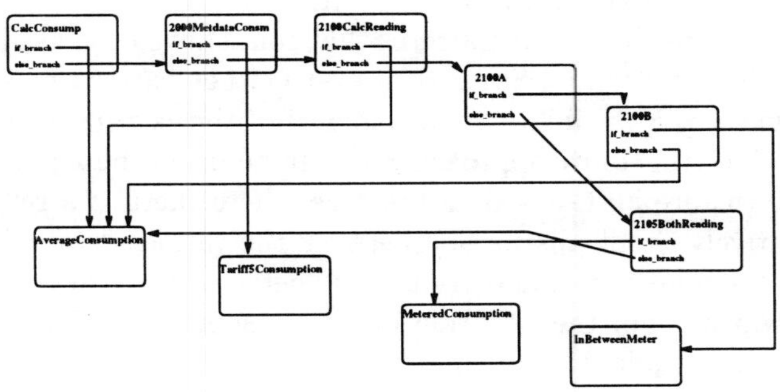

Figure 5. Chain of Conditional Objects in Consumption Calculation

customers or the meter (reading) file. For example, the condition class 2000**MetdataConsmCond** has the condition expression **mast.tariff** = 5 and the class 2100**CalcReadingCond** has the expression **mtr.meter_read** = 0. Hence the former needs a reference to the **MasterRec** class and the latter to **MeterRec** only. The 2000**MetDataConsm** class is as follows:

```
class 2000MetdataConsmCond
  is subclass of Condition
instance variables
  mast: @MasterRec
methods
  Condition() ==
    (dcl tf: nat;
       tf := mast!GetTariffType();
       if tf = 5
       then
         return true
       else
         return false)
end 2000MetdataConsmCond
```

In terms of structure, the conditionals are linked together in a recursive pattern like that of the Decorator pattern, with the **Conditional** objects acting like **Decorator** objects and calling other **CondHandler** (**Component**) objects, and with the consumption calculation objects acting as leaf nodes (**ConcreteComponents**) in the recursion. In terms of behaviour, however, the chain resembles the Chain of Responsibility pattern. Each object in the chain checks for the condition it is equipped to recognise, and forwards requests to either a "if" successor or an "else" successor depending on this condition. The difference between this and the Chain of Responsibility pattern is that the "handling" of a request consists of transferring control to an appropriate object.

Some alternative patterns that could have been used are Strategy and State. However neither pattern provides the flexibility in reconfiguring the conditionals which the above approach gives. In addition these patterns are best suited to the case where there is a relatively simple distinction between the various "states" of a component, and transitions between these states, which is not the situation in the consumption calculation module.

3.4 The Charge Calculation Module

The charge calculation module is quite different in structure from the consumption calculation module. In the latter there was an elaborate control structure which ultimately transfers control to one of four calculation modules, which are mainly independent of each other. That is, the intermediate nodes of the control flow graph (a tree in this case) are primarily for control transfer purposes with relatively little processing, and the "leaves" of the tree contain all the functionality. In contrast the charge calculation module involves significant processing throughout, and the control structure is very much a part of the algorithm (Figure 6).

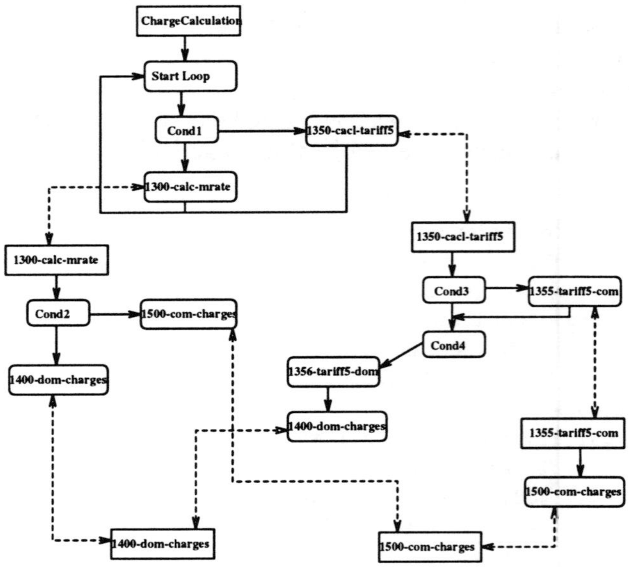

Figure 6. Charge Calculation Module Structure

In the consumption calculation module the reengineering was focussed on achieving greater flexibility in the control mechanism, whilst in the present case it is required in the composition mechanism. Thus the selection of patterns for reengineering reflects this difference.

The initial formal specification, obtained by deriving low-level object classes from the records, files and other data structures of the system, and encapsulating the main program in a single class, with methods for each paragraph [11], has the following form:

```
class MtrRateRec
instance variables
 -- attributes for each field of MtrRateRec
 -- are defined here
methods
 -- update and enquiry methods used on
 -- the record data in the program
end MtrRateRec


class MtrRateFile
instance variables
  scontents: seq of @MtrRateRec;
  ...
```

```
methods
  -- A standard set of operations for
  -- an indexed sequential file
end MtrRateFile

class ChargeCalculation
instance variables
  mtrate: @MtrRateFile;
  ...
methods
  CalculateMeterRate() ==
     (<statements1>;
      for all m in elems(mtrate.scontents) do
        (<statements2>;
         if cond1
         then
           1350_calc_mrate_tariff_5()
         else
           1300_calc_mrate();
         <statements3>);

  1300_calc_mrate() ==
    (<statements4>;
     if cond2
     then
       1400_dom_water_charges()
     else
       1500_com_water_charges() );

  1350_calc_mrate_tariff_5() ==
    (if cond3
     then
       (<statements5>;
        1355_tariff_5_com();
        <statements6>);
    if cond4
    then
      1356_tariff_5_dom());

  1355_tariff_5_com() ==
    (<statements7>;
     1500_com_water_charges() );

  1356_tariff_5_dom() ==
    (<statements8>;
     1400_dom_water_charges() );

  1400_dom_water_charges() ==
    <statements9>;

  1500_com_water_charges() ==
    <statements10>

end ChargeCalculation
```

< **statements**1 > etc represent straight-line segments of code or code containing only utility procedures and straight-line code. The precise details of these segments does not affect the global restructuring of this class.

An important observation here is that at a very early stage the control flow bifurcates into two distinct branches which do not interact until a call is made to 1400_**dom_water_charges** and 1500_**com_water_charges**, at which stage each of the branches terminates. In addition **cond**1 is independent of any of the preceding processing statements and hence is unaffected by them. It can, therefore, be moved out of the loop, and so bifurcate the control at the very start.

3.5 Introducing OO Patterns

We can map the above procedural pattern (alternative algorithms for the same computation, selected on the basis of an initial test) into the Strategy object-oriented design pattern. By introducing this pattern we are able to define an overall structure of the calculation of the consumption charges by using an abstract **ChargeCalculation** class. The two branches of the tree represent the two algorithms (strategies) that can be used to perform the actual calculation. The choice depends on **cond**1 (whether tariff 5 applies or not). The two strategies are encapsulated as **NormalChargeCalculation** and **Tariff5ChargeCalculation** classes, and made subclasses of **ChargeCalculation** (Figure 7).

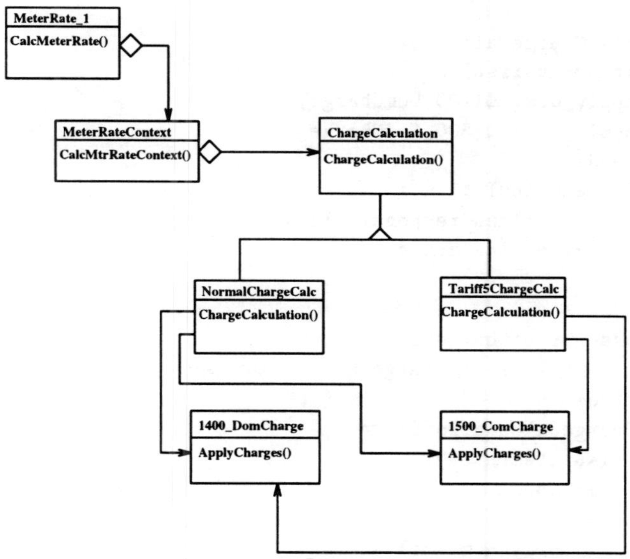

Figure 7. Architecture of Reengineered System

The new set of classes are as follows.

```
class MeterRate_1
```

```
instance variables
  context: @MeterRateContext
methods
  CalculateMeterRate1() ==
    (if cond1
     then
       context!set_tariff5()
     else
       context!set_normal();
     context!CalculateMeterRateContext())
end MeterRate_1


class MeterRateContext
instance variables
  mtrates: set of @MtrRateRec;
  calc: @ChargeCalculation
methods
  set_tariff5() ==
       calc := Tariff5ChargeCalculation!new;

  set_normal() ==
       calc := NormalChargeCalculation!new;

  CalculateMeterRateContext() ==
      (<statements1>;
       for all m in set mtrates do
         (<statements2>;
          calc!ChargeCalculation();
          <statements3>)
end MeterRateContext


class ChargeCalculation
instance variables
  apply_dom: @1400_DomCharge;
  apply_com: @1500_ComCharge
methods
  ChargeCalculation()
    is subclass responsibility
end ChargeCalculation


class NormalChargeCalculation
  is subclass of ChargeCalculation
methods
  ChargeCalculation() ==
    (<statements4>;
     if cond2
     then
       apply_dom!ApplyCharges()
     else
       apply_com!ApplyCharges())

end NormalChargeCalculation

class Tariff5ChargeCalculation
  is subclass of ChargeCalculation
methods
  ChargeCalculation() ==
    (if cond3
     then
       (<statements5>;
        1355_tariff_5_com();
        <statements6>);
     if cond4
     then
       1356_tariff_5_dom() );

  1355_tariff_5_com() ==
    (<statements7>;
     apply_com!ApplyCharges());

  1356_tariff_5_dom() ==
    (<statements8>;
     apply_dom!ApplyCharges())
end Tariff5ChargeCalculation

class ApplyCharge
methods
  ApplyCharges()
    is subclass responsibility
end ApplyCharge

class 1400_DomCharge
  is subclass of ApplyCharge
methods
  ApplyCharges() == <statements9>
end 1400_DomCharge

class 1500_ComCharge
  is subclass of ApplyCharge
methods
  ApplyCharges() == <statements10>
end 1500_ComCharge
```

We assume that the persistent objects such as files which the program manipulates are also declared as instance variables of the appropriate classes in the above pattern structure.

The restructured design of the system is much more complex than a simple definition of new classes for data objects. We have introduced a number of new objects in the system. So the issue is whether this has unnecessarily increased the complexity of the system, or whether there are definite benefits in the new structure. The restructuring has had the following impacts:

An OO Implementation The new system can be more readily implemented in an OO language such as C++ or Object COBOL [22]. However a design only introducing data-based objects would have been sufficient for this.

Improved Maintenance Particularly for the consumption calculation the reengineered system should be more maintainable, as new calculations can be added and the conditions under which calculations are performed can be changed more readily due to the more flexible method (object composition) of combining conditionals in the new system.

Reuse potential The most important benefit of the new designs are their reuse potential. For example, the program structure of the consumption calculation module characterises a large class of batch processing programs, where a complex set of conditions lead to a relatively limited number of processing procedures. By using the "decorated chain of responsibility" design we have decoupled the *logic* of the program from the *functionality*. The programmer simply configures the system with the appropriate conditions and their associated computation procedures. These can be revised for a number of different applications.

Efficiency By introducing a number of objects, the execution path in both modules has become more complicated, compared to a straightforward IF-THEN-ELSE condition checking. Hence, purely in terms of execution efficiency, there might not have been any benefit. At the same time it should be noted that in such batch processing applications, the bulk of the processing time is consumed by database/file access. The computations take up an insignificant proportion of the total time.

The formal justification of such reengineering steps is given in the following section.

4 The Object Calculus

A specification in the object calculus [6, 7] is constructed as a set of linked theories in a temporal logic. Formally, it is a diagram of objects in a category of theories and theorem-preserving morphisms. An object calculus theory consists of collections of *type* and *constant symbols*, *attribute symbols* (denoting time-varying data), *action symbols* (denoting atomic operations) and a set of axioms describing the types of the attributes and the effects, permission constraints and other dynamic properties of the actions. The axioms are specified using linear temporal logic operators such as $\bigcirc$ (in the next state), etc.

The version used here is that defined in [14] in order to give a semantics to VDM^{++}. In this version actions α are potentially durative and overlapping.

In order to give a semantics to a class $\mathbf{C}$, in, for example, OMT [19], Syntropy [4] or VDM^{++}, we define a theory $\Gamma_{\mathbf{C}}$ which has the type symbol $@\mathbf{C}$ representing all possible instances of $\mathbf{C}$, attribute symbol $\overline{\mathbf{C}}$ representing all the existing objects of $\mathbf{C}$, and creation action $\mathbf{new_C}(\mathbf{c} : @\mathbf{C})$ and deletion action $\mathbf{kill_C}(\mathbf{c} : @\mathbf{C})$ which respectively add and remove $\mathbf{c}$ from this set.

Each attribute $\mathbf{att}$ of objects $\mathbf{c}$ of $\mathbf{C}$ is formally represented by an attribute $\mathbf{att}(\mathbf{c} : @\mathbf{C})$ of $\Gamma_{\mathbf{C}}$ (written as $\mathbf{c.att}$ for conformance with standard OO notation) and each method $\mathbf{act}(\mathbf{x} : \mathbf{X})$ is represented by an action symbol $\mathbf{act}(\mathbf{c} : @\mathbf{C}, \mathbf{x} : \mathbf{X})$, written as $\mathbf{c!act(x)}$. Output parameters and local variables of methods are also represented as attribute symbols of $\Gamma_{\mathbf{C}}$.

We can define the effect of methods by means of the "calling" operator $\supset$ between actions:

$$\alpha \supset \beta$$

means that every occurrence of α coincides with an occurrence of β.

Composite actions are defined to represent specification statements and executable code: $\mathbf{pre\,G\ \ post\,P}$ names an action α with the properties that $\mathbf{G}$ is always true at each activation time of α, whilst $\mathbf{P}$, with each "hooked" attribute $\overleftarrow{\mathbf{att}}$ interpreted as the value of $\mathbf{att}$ at initiation of α, holds at the corresponding termination time.

A frame axiom, termed the *locality* assumption, asserts that attributes of an object $\mathbf{a}$ of $\mathbf{C}$ can only be changed over intervals in which at least one of the actions $\mathbf{a!m(e)}$ of $\mathbf{a}$ executes [6]. Likewise, $\overline{\mathbf{C}}$ can only change as a result of $\mathbf{new_C}$ or $\mathbf{kill_C}$ invocations.

Assignment $\mathbf{t_1} := \mathbf{t_2}$ can be defined as the action $\mathbf{pre\,true\ \ post\,t_1} = \overleftarrow{\mathbf{t_2}}$ where $\mathbf{t_1}$ is an attribute symbol. Similarly sequential composition, conditionals and parallel composition "||" of actions can be expressed as derived combinators.

Conditionals have the expected properties:

$$\mathbf{E} \ \Rightarrow\ (\mathbf{if\ E\ then\ S_1\ else\ S_2} \ \supset\ \mathbf{S_1})$$
$$\neg\,\mathbf{E} \ \Rightarrow\ (\mathbf{if\ E\ then\ S_1\ else\ S_2} \ \supset\ \mathbf{S_2})$$

Similarly, **while** loops can be defined recursively.

Some important properties of $\supset$ which will be used in the paper are that it is transitive:

$$(\alpha \supset \beta) \wedge (\beta \supset \gamma) \ \Rightarrow\ (\alpha \supset \gamma)$$

and that constructs such as ; and **if then else** are monotonic with respect to it:

$$(\alpha_1 \supset \alpha_2) \wedge (\beta_1 \supset \beta_2) \ \Rightarrow\ (\alpha_1;\ \beta_1 \ \supset\ \alpha_2;\ \beta_2)$$

and

$$(\alpha_1 \supset \alpha_2) \wedge (\beta_1 \supset \beta_2) \ \Rightarrow\ \mathbf{if\ E\ then}\ \alpha_1\ \mathbf{else}\ \beta_1 \ \supset\ \mathbf{if\ E\ then}\ \alpha_2\ \mathbf{else}\ \beta_2$$

Theories representing subsystems can be composed from the theories of the classes in these subsystems by theory union and renaming. Thus we can compare the functionality of a system (with no distinguished "main" class) with that of another system, via their theories rather than forcing all comparisons to be made between particular classes. This is useful in the case of design patterns, which usually concern sets of classes.

4.1 Interpretations and Refinement

The most important relationship between theories is that of theory interpretation: there is a theory interpretation morphism σ from a theory $\Gamma_{\mathbf{C}}$ to a theory $\Gamma_{\mathbf{D}}$ if every theorem φ of $\Gamma_{\mathbf{C}}$ is provable, under the interpretation σ, in $\Gamma_{\mathbf{D}}$:

$$\Gamma_{\mathbf{C}} \vdash \varphi \;\Rightarrow\; \Gamma_{\mathbf{D}} \vdash \sigma(\varphi)$$

where σ interprets the symbols of $\Gamma_{\mathbf{C}}$ as suitable combinations of symbols of $\Gamma_{\mathbf{D}}$: actions are interpreted by actions (basic or composed), and attributes by terms. For example a single action α of $\Gamma_{\mathbf{C}}$ could be interpreted by a sequential combination $\beta; \gamma$ of actions of $\Gamma_{\mathbf{D}}$. σ is lifted to formulae in the usual way.

This concept will be taken as the basis of *refinement*. We shall say that a system **D** refines a system **C** if there is a theory interpretation from the theory $\Gamma_{\mathbf{C}}$ of **C** to the theory $\Gamma_{\mathbf{D}}$ of **D**.

4.2 Verification of the Strategy Pattern

The theory interpretation in the case of the Strategy pattern is given in Table 1.

Symbol of **Client**	Term of **Client1**
@Client	**@Client1**
@Context	**@Context1**
$\mathbf{new}_{\mathbf{Client}}$	$\mathbf{new}_{\mathbf{Client1}}$
$\mathbf{new}_{\mathbf{Context}}$	$\mathbf{new}_{\mathbf{Context1}}$
obj.aContext	**obj.aContext**
$\overline{\mathbf{Client}}$	$\overline{\mathbf{Client1}}$
$\overline{\mathbf{Context}}$	$\overline{\mathbf{Context1}}$
obj!m	**obj!m**

Table 1. Interpretation of Client into Client1

Additionally, **obj.aContext.strategy_type** will be interpreted by the conditional expression

$$\begin{array}{l}\mathbf{if\ obj.aContext.strategy} \in \overline{\mathbf{ConcreteStrategyA}}\\ \mathbf{then} < \mathbf{type1} >\\ \mathbf{else}\\ \quad \mathbf{if\ obj.aContext.strategy} \in \overline{\mathbf{ConcreteStrategyB}}\\ \quad \mathbf{then} < \mathbf{type2} >\\ \quad \mathbf{else\ nil}\end{array}$$

All actions of the abstract system are interpreted by actions of the same name in the new system. In particular, **(obj.aContext)!ContextInterface** is interpreted as itself. The only significant change in representation is the interpretation of **obj.aContext.strategy_type** by a conditional expression in **obj.aContext.strategy**.

The typing axioms of the abstract system are therefore directly provable, in their interpreted versions, in the concrete system. For example, the constraint that **obj.aContext** $\in$ **@Context** for **obj** $\in \overline{\mathbf{Client}}$ in the theory $\Gamma_{\mathbf{Client}}$ is interpreted by the predicate

$$\mathbf{obj} \in \overline{\mathbf{Client1}} \;\Rightarrow\; \mathbf{obj.aContext} \in \mathbf{@Context1}$$

in $\Gamma_{\mathbf{Client1}}$. But this is a theorem of $\Gamma_{\mathbf{Client1}}$ from its own typing axiom for **aContext**, as required.

The effect of **obj.aContext!set_type1** in **Client** is given by the axiom:

$$\begin{array}{l}\mathbf{obj} \in \overline{\mathbf{Client}} \;\wedge\\ \mathbf{obj.aContext} \in \overline{\mathbf{Context}} \;\Rightarrow\\ \quad (\mathbf{obj.aContext})!\mathbf{set\_type1} \;\supset\\ \qquad \mathbf{obj.aContext.strategy\_type} :=\\ \qquad\qquad < \mathbf{type1} >\end{array}$$

That is, calls of **(obj.aContext)!set_type1** result in **obj.aContext.strategy_type** having the value < **type1** > at their conclusion.

Under the above interpretation this becomes:

$$\begin{array}{l}\mathbf{obj} \in \overline{\mathbf{Client1}} \;\wedge\\ \mathbf{obj.aContext} \in \overline{\mathbf{Context1}} \;\Rightarrow\\ \quad (\mathbf{obj.aContext})!\mathbf{set\_type1} \;\supset\\ \qquad \mathbf{pre\,true\;\;post\,e} = < \mathbf{type1} >\end{array}$$

where **e** is the conditional expression (1):

$$\begin{array}{l}\mathbf{if\ obj.aContext.strategy} \in \overline{\mathbf{ConcreteStrategyA}}\\ \mathbf{then} < \mathbf{type1} >\\ \mathbf{else}\\ \quad \mathbf{if\ obj.aContext.strategy} \in \overline{\mathbf{ConcreteStrategyB}}\\ \quad \mathbf{then} < \mathbf{type2} >\\ \quad \mathbf{else\ nil}\end{array}$$

In other words:

$$\begin{array}{l}\mathbf{obj} \in \overline{\mathbf{Client1}} \;\wedge\\ \mathbf{obj.aContext} \in \overline{\mathbf{Context1}} \;\Rightarrow\\ \quad (\mathbf{obj.aContext})!\mathbf{set\_type1} \;\supset\\ \qquad \mathbf{pre\ true}\\ \qquad \mathbf{post\ obj.aContext.strategy} \in\\ \qquad\qquad \overline{\mathbf{ConcreteStrategyA}}\end{array}$$

But this is provable from the axiom for **obj.aContext!set_type** in **Client1**, which is:

$$\begin{aligned}&\mathbf{obj} \in \overline{\mathbf{Client1}} \ \wedge \\ &\mathbf{obj.aContext} \in \overline{\mathbf{Context1}} \ \Rightarrow \\ &\quad (\mathbf{obj.aContext})!\mathbf{set\_type1} \ \supset \\ &\qquad \mathbf{new}_{\mathbf{ConcreteStrategyA}}(\mathbf{obj.} \\ &\qquad\qquad \mathbf{aContext.strategy})\end{aligned}$$

Similar reasoning shows that the interpretation of the axiom for the effect of **m** in $\Gamma_{\mathbf{Client}}$ is provable from the corresponding axiom for **m** in $\Gamma_{\mathbf{Client1}}$.

We can now make more precise the assumptions required for the transformation to be correct:

- **obj.aContext.strategy** $\in \overline{\mathbf{Strategy}}$ at the point where **ContextInterface** is called;
- **obj.aContext.strategy** must remain in the same subclass of **Strategy** during the execution of **ContextInterface**.

In addition, because the frame axiom of **Context** must also be true in interpreted form in **Context1**, **strategy** can only change its existence or subclass during the execution of **set_type1** or **set_type2**. In particular, although a **Strategy** object could, in principle, be shared between two or more **Context** objects, these objects must simultaneously set its type. Otherwise, there could be time periods [**t1**, **t2**] over which an object **obj** $\in \overline{\mathbf{Context1}}$ will be idle (not executing any action) but during which the type of **obj.strategy** changes, which contradicts the interpretation of the frame axiom for **Context** (which asserts that the **strategy_type** attribute can *only* be changed during executions of the **set_type1** or **set_type2** actions of **obj**).

In the case of the charge calculation restructuring, we have the interpretation of actions given in Table 2, in addition to the standard interpretation for the Strategy pattern. The notation **obj!Class'Method** denotes the action which behaves as the version of **Method** defined in class **Class**, provided **obj** $\in \overline{\mathbf{Class}}$, and which is otherwise undefined in its behaviour.

This interpretation provides a formal trace of the origin of the elements of the reengineered system back to the initial system. It can be directly checked that the properties of the abstract actions are also true of the concrete actions that interpret them.

Symbol of **ChargeCalculation**	Symbol of **MeterRate_1**
CalculateMeterRate	**CalculateMeterRate**
1300_calc_mrate	**calc!NormalChargeCalculation'ChargeCalculation**
1350_calc_mrate_tariff_5	**calc!Tariff5ChargeCalculation'ChargeCalculation**
1355_tariff_5_com	**calc!Tariff5ChargeCalculation'1355_tariff_5_com**
1356_tariff_5_dom	**calc!Tariff5ChargeCalculation'1356_tariff_5_dom**
1400_dom_water_charges	**(calc.apply_dom)!ApplyCharges**
1500_com_water_charges	**(calc.apply_com)!ApplyCharges**

Table 2. Interpretation of ChargeCalculation into MeterRate_1

5 Conclusions

We have shown that a formal justification for the transformations of class and object structures produced by design patterns can be given, in terms of an established formalism for temporal reasoning. We have also shown that reengineering based on design patterns can extend the capabilities of existing methods of reengineering into object-oriented descriptions.

We believe that tool support for the reengineering method illustrated in this paper is possible, along the lines of the REFORM tool [23]. Such a tool would be equipped with a number of procedural and OO design patterns. The tool would provide assistance in the discovery of procedural patterns by using pattern-matching. Given a procedural pattern, it could also suggest the valid transformations to OO patterns that could be applied, and would carry out the selected transformation. Existing OO reengineering techniques (for example, control-flow restructuring, creation of object-based interfaces, or the postulation of inheritance structures on the basis of multiple record types in a file) could be incorporated.

Trials of formalised approaches to design patterns using the object calculus have been carried out within Alcatel in Brazil.

References

[1] E. Burd. Extracting Reusable Modules from Legacy Code: Considering the Issues of Module Granularity, *Proceedings of 3rd Working Conference on Reverse Engineering*, IEEE Press, 1996.

[2] E. Chikofsky, J. Cross. Reverse Engineering and Design Recovery: A Taxonomy, *IEEE Software*, January 1990.

[3] D. Coleman, P. Arnold, S. Bodoff, C. Dollin, H. Gilchrist, F. Hayes, and P. Jeremaes. *Object-oriented Development: The FUSION Method.* Prentice Hall Object-oriented Series, 1994.

[4] S. Cook and J. Daniels. *Designing Object Systems: Object-Oriented Modelling with Syntropy.* Prentice Hall, Sept 1994.

[5] E. Durr and E. Dusink. The role of VDM^{++} in the development of a real-time tracking and tracing system. In J Woodcock and P Larsen, editors, *FME '93*, Lecture Notes in Computer Science. Springer-Verlag, 1993.

[6] J. Fiadeiro and T. Maibaum. Describing, Structuring and Implementing Objects, in de Bakker *et al.*, *Foundations of Object Oriented languages*, LNCS 489, Springer-Verlag, 1991.

[7] J. Fiadeiro and T. Maibaum. Sometimes "Tomorrow" is "Sometime". In *Temporal Logic*, volume 827 of Lecture Notes in Artificial Intelligence, pages 48–66. Springer-Verlag, 1994.

[8] E. Gamma, R. Helm, R. Johnson and J. Vlissides. *Design Patterns: Elements of Reusable Object-oriented Software.* Addison-Wesley, 1994.

[9] S. Goldsack, K. Lano. Annealing, Object Decomposition and Design Patterns, *TOOLS Pacific 1996*, Melbourne, Australia, 1996.

[10] K. Lano. *The B Language and Method: A Guide to Practical Formal Development*, Springer-Verlag, 1996.

[11] K. Lano, H. Haughton. *Reverse Engineering and Software Maintenance*, McGraw-Hill, 1993.

[12] K. Lano. Transformational Program Analysis, *Journal of Software Testing, Verification and Reliability*, December 1994.

[13] K. Lano, J. Bicarregui, S. Goldsack. Formalising Design Patterns, *BCS Northern Formal Methods Workshop*, EWIC Series, Springer Verlag, 1997.

[14] K. Lano, S. Goldsack, J. Bicarregui, S. Kent. Integrating VDM^{++} and Real-time System Design, *Z User Meeting*, LNCS, Springer-Verlag, 1997.

[15] H. Lividas, T. Johnson. A New Approach to Finding Objects in Programs, *Software Maintenance, Research and Practice*, Vol. 6, 249–260, 1994.

[16] N. Malik. *Design Patterns and Reengineering*, Dept. of Computing, Imperial College, 1996.

[17] P. Newcomb, G. Kotik. Reengineering Procedural into Object-oriented Systems. *Working Conference on Reverse Engineering*, Toronto, Canada, July 1993. IEEE Press, 1993.

[18] L. Prechelt. Design Recovery by Automated Search for Structural Design Patterns in Object-oriented Designs, *Proceedings of 3rd Working Conference on Reverse Engineering*, IEEE Press, 1996.

[19] J. Rumbaugh, M. Blaha, W. Premerlani, F. Eddy, and W. Lorensen. *Object-Oriented Modelling and Design.* Prentice Hall, 1991.

[20] M. Ryan, J. Fiadeiro, T. S. E. Maibaum. Sharing Actions and Attributes in Modal Action Logic. In T. Ito and A. Mayer, editors, *Proceedings of International Conference on Theoretical Aspects of Computer Science (TACS '91).* Springer-Verlag 1991.

[21] H. Sneed. Migration of Procedurally Oriented COBOL programs in an Object-oriented Architecture, *IEEE Conference on Software Maintenance*, 1991.

[22] E. Yourdon. Object-Oriented COBOL, *American Programmer*, Vol. 3, No. 2, February 1990.

[23] K. Bennet and M. Ward. Using Formal Transformations for the Reverse Engineering of Real-Time Safety Critical Systems, *Proceedings of Safety Critical Systems Club Meeting*, Springer-Verlag Workshops in Computer Science, 204–223.

Understanding Resistance to Software Reuse

A. Lynex & P.J. Layzell
Software Management Group
Department of Computation
UMIST, PO Box 88
Manchester, UK, M60 1QD
andy.lynex@umist.ac.uk

Abstract

Reuse technology is no longer solely restricted to the research domain. Companies that have adopted its techniques to enhance their development process have reported useful improvements in development productivity and quality. We looked at why these improvements are not being exploited more widely within industry as a whole.

By means of questionnaires and interviews with selected senior IT personnel at organisations with large IT requirements we have been able to identify factors preventing or inhibiting reuse adoption. Proposing solutions to eliminate the causes of these, enables us to suggest how companies looking at reuse techniques may adapt in order to better their chances of success.

1. Background

Although an established topic amongst the research community, reuse technology still has to make its predicted impact on industry. Yet almost every business with a sizeable IT requirement reports software quality and productivity problems, exactly the two issues systematic reuse processes claim to solve.

While some areas have had a great deal of success with reuse schemes, as documented in the literature, these tend to be within small development teams working in niche areas of IT focused organisations. We wanted to look at what effort, if any, was being made within large non-IT companies to follow these successes in their in-house IT functions.

Where organisations have adopted reuse as part of their development process, attempts have been made to model this (i.e.[1]) in order to provide a prototype for other organisations. These however, tend to look at individual sections of IT departments working in specific areas. Of more interest is the effect overall structure of an organisations IT function has on opportunities for reuse, the role reuse has as a component of IT strategy as a whole and the attitudes towards adopting reuse techniques.

Our aim being to establish the current state of reuse within the organisations involved in this survey and to look at what inhibitors reduce this from the ideal suggested in the literature. From this information we hope to extrapolate what relationships exist between an organisation and the reuse opportunities available to it and to suggest actions to cure the inhibitors described.

2. Aims of Investigation

Technical solutions to the problems of reuse are often reported in computing literature[2, 3]. In particular knowledge of the classifications, approaches, benefits and supporting technology of reuse seems to have been around for some time:

- Classification of reuse is often based on the level of abstraction at which the reuse occurs. For instance code segments, designs or requirements specifications.
- Approaches to reuse include policies for organising development teams to encourage reuse [4, 5] well as methods for actually delivering reuse. Most of the common methods falling into one of five categories:
    - Source code components[6] - for instance REBOOT[7].
    - Reusable software patterns [8] - for instance The Programmer's Apprentice[9].
    - Transformation Systems[10, 11].

0-8186-7840-2/97 $10.00 © 1997 IEEE

    - Application Generators[6, 12] - for instance UNIX's YACC.
    - Very high level languages[6] - for instance SETL[13].
- Technologies incorporating some aspects of the reuse concept such as Object Orientation, standard programming component libraries and platform independent operating systems seem to becoming common place[3].

Surveys of benefits actually achieved from the introduction of reuse are also well documented [14, 15].

Our survey aims to investigate why with all this effort being made to extol the virtues of reuse and to make it part of everyday software development process, many companies with large software requirements are so far behind in their implementation of these techniques.

Within the time available, the sample size used has been very restricted and this paper does not claim any statistical significance for the results presented. However even within this small sample population, there are clear signals as to why software reuse has been resisted or hard to promote within given organisations. The nature of the companies selected as representative of large IT users as a whole make it likely that these signals will be held in common by many other companies.

3. Investigation Procedure

This review is based primarily around interviews with key managerial personnel within the IT functions of large British companies(see section 4). It was also stipulated that these should not be companies for whom IT is a core business (as data already exists for these). Before the interviews, preparatory questionnaires were sent to companies of interest to identify appropriate participants and gain an initial overview of their current position. Data collated from all responses to these was also used in drawing the reports conclusions.

Interviews were conducted around a list of topics drawn from issues raised by the questionnaire answers to give structure and to ensure the areas addressed covered all relevant issues.

Five companies were selected for interview; additionally a further fourteen were involved in the questionnaire stage. The following general topics were used as a basis for our discussions:

- Background and structure of the organisation - To determine the companies function, how it is organised and how this reflects on the structuring of the IT function. What responsibilities and roles does the IT function play and how is it organised.

- Organisation of software development - To discuss the process of software development employed, specifically concerned with how business requirements are derived and dealt with.

- Future of software development - How might development processes change in the future with reference to organisation structure changes and improving the process itself.

- Reuse Processes - Have any attempts been made to investigate or establish formalised reuse processes. What successes and failures have been recorded. Are there any instances of informal reuse in operation. What inhibitors prevent establishment/advancement of systematic reuse.

4. Background of Participant Organisations

The following sub-sections provide a brief overview of the organisations visited and their general attitude and approach to reuse.

4.1. Organisation 1

The interview was conducted with the central applications architect at a large regional transport operator. Originally the companies IT function was centrally based and divided between three areas; Passenger Services, Engineering Services and Engineering Operations. Within each of these a further breakdown of function occurred; for instance Passenger Services was divided by routes operated and Engineering Operations by engineering disciplines.

A number of years ago it was decided to look at out-sourcing IT functions to concentrate on the core business. Initially this only extended as far as support and desktop systems for all three areas of IT provision. As this proved successful so a move was made to out-source further; this resulted in the internal central IT function being reduced to three managers overseeing the operation of the three IT areas. Each manager had the role of specifying requirements to the contracted IT suppliers. Additionally some services needing intimate understanding of the business remained in-house; for instance maintenance of the business process model, data model, data standards and security issues.

These changes had the outcome that the business units became very autonomous with their own IT budgets. The only restriction to them spending this how they pleased was that projects that may affect corporate data had to be submitted to the business systems managers for consistency checking to prevent resource collision between units. Additionally projects thought to fulfil some central business requirement may receive funding from centralised budgets as an enticement to submit projects that may have a remit wider than an individual unit for further central checks.

4.2. Organisation 2

This interview was conducted with the deputy to the IT director at a major regional utility company. Three managers head up the separate sections of the companies IT strategy reporting to an IT director sitting on the board. The first section was Software Delivery responsible for providing the infrastructure to operate the software. Second was a support function providing helpdesk type facilities and attempting to keep the systems up and functioning. Finally Special Projects handled in-house software development. Special Projects was itself sub-divided into two development functions; Engineering Systems which produces complete software solutions to support business functions and Customer Systems which implements small projects to add functionality to the main software systems. Due to this developments within the section may span anything from one week to twenty man years.

Special projects has tried a resource pool arrangement for staffing of developments as this would seem to fit well with their need to bring in large numbers of contract staff for major development projects. However a return was made to fixed teams, this being more in the interests of permanent staff. In this way experts tend to stay with the systems they know and if they are moved this is done in such a way that they may be recalled if required. A vast knowledge base is recognised to be held by staff who have been with projects right through their development cycle.

IT is responsible to the business as this is where all its work comes from. It is also specified that all IT should be procured through the IT section in order that support may be provided. To these ends development projects are owned by a manager from outside IT, who commits to them by allocating funds from his/her budget. Control of projects is however the responsibility of a board made up from a senior IT person, a senior representative of the user community and someone nominated by the project owner.

4.3. Organisation 3

In this organisation, the IT strategy manager for the defence division of a major engineering company was interviewed. The main IT functions were outsourced to a single IT supplier over ten years ago; including data centre management, network infrastructure and applications development. A retained IT presence maintains the link between supplier and user community, develops strategy, handles development of systems for inclusion in products and deals with systems used in product design and development. In essence while business support systems are outsourced the technology requirements of the actual business are met in-house.

Within business support systems most of the legacy past over to the supplier was in the form of off-the-shelf products with heavy customisation. Cumulative changes to these had lead to vast annual maintenance costs which had become by far the largest part of the IT budget. Installation of upgrades had become almost impossible due to the sheer quantity of customisations.

The division is spread over a number of largely autonomous sites. Within each of these working practices tend to vary and this maps to differences in the way the systems have been customised. A willingness between the sites to co-operate on future development of these systems is identified.

4.4. Organisation 4

In this organisation, the Deputy to the IT director at major nation-wide retailing business was interviewed. Here IT is seen as a support function rather than part of the actual business and so while it is headed by a director he does not sit on the main board.

Four sections deliver all the businesses IT requirements; Operations looks after the central corporate IT infrastructure including networking, database & hardware maintenance and helpdesk support for business support software systems. Central Development develops the businesses support systems and those for the companies depots. Store Development develops systems for the companies retail outlets and provides support for these. Finally, Project Support manages the projects of the development sections; including planning, quality assurance and resourcing. As part of project management it is the responsibility of this section to maintain central business architectures, business data and application portfolios.

All business IT requirements are handled by Project Support, fulfilled by one of the development sections and maintained by the support facilities making IT delivery possible from a central site.

4.5. Organisation 5

Finally, the head of IT function for a major financial services company was interviewed. The business is divided into two autonomous units handling differing financial products. IT is a group at the sub-directorate level responsible to the finance director. Although division of the group mirrors that of the company the head of the smaller units IT function is responsible to the head of IT at the larger division. Both units' IT is split between operations and development.

Software systems are estimated to be split evenly between in-house developments and off-the-shelf procurements within the main unit while within the smaller unit in-house systems represent about two fifths of the total number. Off-the-shelf products generally fulfil business support roles whereas in-house developments are more orientated towards business critical functions.

Developments tend to be initiated within the IT function as a result of close user interaction or specific support requirements from the business. This follows the view held that IT should be closely bound to the business process as a facilitator.

Some consideration had been given to adoption of reuse, but this occurred in a limited piecemeal fashion.

5. Overview of Current Practice

We looked into what efforts were being made by the organisations involved to investigate and implement reuse processes. Our findings break down into two areas the experiences of reuse within the organisations and the managerial concerns over their development process and how this process may change in the future.

5.1. Reuse Experiences

Unsurprisingly current reuse processes were restricted almost entirely to reusing executable code components with little thought for higher lifecycle artefacts. In particular, while companies considered reusing complete applications a priority, there was little attention to formal reuse within the development process for new software.

This became apparent when actual occurrences of reuse were considered as these seemed to revolve around adaptation of complete applications to similar requirements in other areas of the business.

The structure of the organisations seemed to play the largest role in determining the level at which reuse occurred. For two of the participants (Organisations 1 & 3) the companies consisted of a number of largely autonomous business units with strongly similar functionality (see section 4). In both cases this division caused the IT function to be split along these lines also. Recognition of the difficulties this imposed on catering for the IT needs of the individual units tended to lead to identification of cases where reuse could occur.

For instance the requirement that central data could be accessed by multiple business units lead to the creation of a corporate data model and data standards for these organisations. As all projects to use central information then had to be checked for compliance with the data standards it became possible to locate projects performing similar functions on common data. For Organisation 1 this manifested itself as a central IT function performing the checks and then being able to liase between business units with similar requirements in order to introduce reuse of existing applications or co-operation on new developments. In the case of Organisation 3 the business units (sites) themselves were sufficiently committed to the maintenance of data standards that they themselves identified projects fulfilling common requirements and rolled out the resultant applications across all appropriate areas.

The problem experienced by these companies is that where opportunities for shared development are located it is still difficult to convince the separate business units to co-operate on development. Indeed where one unit has developed an application that the others could equally well apply getting them to use it is complicated due to a reluctance to take on systems developed elsewhere. An example cited (by Organisation 1) where two business units were found to be producing applications that overlapped extensively was in the development of systems for keeping inventories of resources and for managing maintenance of those resources. An inventory application was underway within one business unit when the central IT function of the organisation found that a second unit was planning the system to manage maintenance; obviously these would operate on very similar information and would have to communicate. The first business unit was not willing to delay its development progress until the second had determined their requirements and the second was not willing to adopt the first's system upon which to build their own and so no compromise could be reached.

The remaining three organisations had more integrated IT sections divided firstly between development and support/maintenance and then within development on a business function basis rather than by the physical divisions within the company. In these cases reuse seemed to be considered less, possibly due to the reduced prominence of shared information.

These three companies had no specific reuse policy in place and they cite common reasons for this being the case. They state that their systems are very large long term ventures which are replaced in their entirety. This only happens very rarely and thus means that technology will have moved on between developments and that any investment in building reusable components will be wasted as new techniques will make them obsolete. Systems are targeted for specific business areas and rolled-out throughout the organisation and thus their is little of the overlap of functionality found in the other companies to exploit as reuse opportunities.

There is however, opportunity here for reuse of requirements as the systems developed often replace existing versions in order to update technological aspects of their implementation or to add new functionality. Although this was recognised by the companies it was argued that requirements for their systems were well known within the domain and that to record these for future use rather than recapture them each time the systems were redeveloped was of little consequence in the running of the development projects.

Informal reuse was identified as being present within development teams by all participants and interestingly one suggested that formalising this would actually reduce its effectiveness. This reuse was seen as being at the level of developer knowledge and experience and as such very hard to mandate as part of the development process.

Overall data seemed to be the main driving force behind what reuse did occur. Organisation wide data models gave insight into what data was available and where this was processed leading to identification of shared areas of responsibility.

It was often the case that only when a shared interface to some data was involved that shared functionality requirements were detected between separate projects.

As these methods of identification mean that reuse opportunities are detected when a project is in early stages of development reuse tended to focus upon either adapting a complete solution previously developed or co-operating on development of a new solution with another business unit with similar requirements.

5.2. Reuse Management

Our priority here was to determine the level at which reuse had been considered within the organisations interviewed and what effect, if any, this had had on their development process. We also aimed to discover how the participants considered there development processes may change in the future.

We were pleased to find all of the organisations interviewed had considered reuse at a senior management/directorate level. At two of these, this had lead to some form of policy being established. This tended however to be of an informal nature and thus not necessarily promoted throughout the company. For example the use of a central IT function within Organisation 1 to locate reuse opportunities across separate business units was a well planned strategy, however the actual working of this was not sufficiently specified and while there was some knowledge of its existence within the business units co-operation was not mandated upon them. Its operation took the form of questionnaires sent to managers at the inception of projects to gauge their scope. From these a register of projects allowed identification of overlap. However, details on questionnaires were often found to be vague or misleading due to the managers indifference to and suspicion of the task.

One issue uncovered within the participants view of their development process was that the developments occurring had little commonality to be exploited for reuse. As already mentioned the organisations rejecting reuse cited replacement of existing systems as their main development task. Additionally Organisation 4 brought up an interesting factor. It was stated that much of their effort was expended in evolutionary development of existing systems. Legacy systems had become reliable and bug free as a result of cumulative maintenance and so when additional functionality was required it became more cost effective to tack this on as additional layers rather than to redevelop as this protected the investment made in maintaining these systems. This type of development may well be seen as very large scale reuse and more effective then any alternative process for redeveloping the systems. This also underlines the fact that reuse of components from existing systems can vastly reduce the maintenance costs associated with new software developments.

All participants noted the difficulties in monitoring what reuse went on whether this was formal or not. It was generally stated that an unmeasurable saving was not worth pursuing.

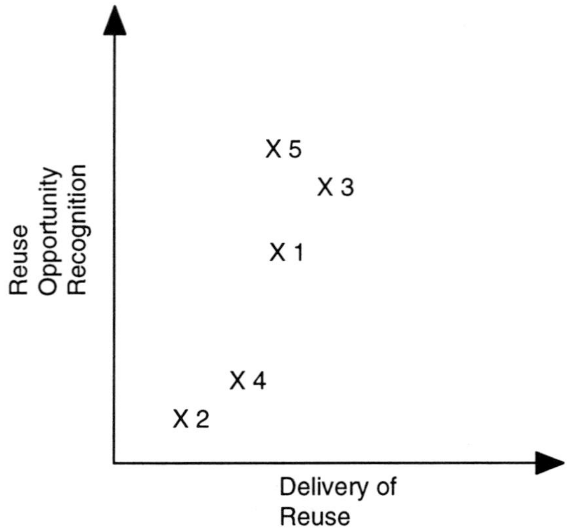

Figure 1. Comparison of recognition and delivery of reuse opportunities.

Figure 1 illustrates how the organisations compared in terms of recognising and delivering reuse opportunities (number references relate to aliases assigned in section 4). As mentioned reuse measurement was considered difficult by all involved, however, estimates could be achieved from examples given.

Although most of the companies were able to recognise the opportunities for reuse available to them, few were able to capitalise on these to deliver the expected benefits. Details of this are given below:

Organisation 1 - Some reuse between business units as identified by the central control function's standards section. This tends to be of entire applications but it is often hard to follow opportunities through to results due to the divided nature of the business.

Organisation 2 - No formalised reuse, claimed to be due to development mainly of one off systems, do reuse requirements for systems that are being directly replaced.

Organisation 3 - Reuse of common processes from systems for products within business units and reuse of common applications for support systems between business units. Heavy customisation tends to occur to reused systems rather than co-operation on the development.

Organisation 4 - little formalised reuse, again due to development of one off systems. Some development effort is targeted towards enhancing existing systems which when considered as an alternative to redevelopment introduces considerable reuse.

Organisation 5 - Reuse of existing systems knowledge for development areas is good. Little formality introduced as most effort is focused upon producing novel systems which do not tend to have much commonality.

A number of the participants mentioned that they intended to look at introducing alternative development methods in the future. These methods seemed aimed at moving the companies development strategies from formal lifecycle models towards faster and more customer orientated development. In particular Rapid Application Development (RAD) [16] and Joint Application Design (JAD) [17] techniques, with shorter requirements capture and design stages but longer prototyping phases and more user involvement, were seen as the way forward for development of most small support systems. The main business support systems on the other hand would continue to be built in much the current way for most of the companies. RAD techniques were expected to lead to better fulfilment of customer requirements.

Consideration of further outsourcing seems prominent amongst plans for most of the companies as they feel they should concentrate on their core businesses. It was recognised however that IT strategy could only be dictated internally and that that this would involve holding a minimum amount of data for management of the business and keeping a careful check on the work of suppliers. It was felt by all companies that careful IT strategy management would become increasingly important to maintain market position in the face of stronger competition. Organisations 3 & 5 mentioned that IT was looked to by senior management to provide a competitive edge over rivals.

Organisation 2 provided an interesting insight into management strategy when describing development of their customer billing system (which was currently under way). Realising the opportunities provided by the opening up to competition of the regional domestic utility provision market in the UK, senior management had identified that the possibility existed for them to expand their supply business into other domestic utility services. This lead to the inclusion within the billing system of the ability to handle supply of multiple products with differing natures. However, rather than creating a general system which could have billed for the supply of any product the decision had been made to determine those markets into which the company was most likely to expand and to include facilities only for supplying in those areas. While this shows elements of long term strategy in IT planning it also demonstrates the reluctance to perform development of software able to provide generic functionality and therefore be reused. This is largely due to the increased initial development costs and demonstrates a major barrier to adoption of reuse technology, namely that of reluctance to make an up front investment in return for possible benefits long term.

The long term nature of IT strategy planning was again raised by Organisation 4 whose ten year systems development plan was not seen as unrealistic in length. This aimed to specify all major systems development to be undertaken in the period and underlined the notion that requirements of individual developments were easily captured from the existing systems providing the functionality and from the staff working in those areas. Organisations 2 & 4 particularly saw their software production almost entirely as redevelopment of existing systems to update the technology employed with little new functionality.

Organisation 5 made the interesting point that they find the requirements generated by their business too complex for developers to understand well and that in the future it may well pay them to have the expert users actually perform the implementation themselves. This extends the JAD approach, involving user participation in preparation of initial prototypes, advocated by the other businesses to its limit where users are trained in development techniques rather than training software engineers in the concepts of the business processes.

6. Identification of Inhibitors

From the information gathered about the participant organisations it is possible to identify a number of inhibiting factors that prevent reuse meeting its full potential within these companies. These are detailed below:

- Organisations structure - Problems relating to organisational structure are most noticeable for companies with autonomous or physically split business units(Organisations 1 & 3). There is often some notion of competition between units with control over their own budgets and this tends to obscure the advantages that may be gained by sharing information or resources between units. This problem is particularly acute in business units with similar areas of operation. Even without physical divisions companies can suffer from a lack of openness and co-operation between units over IT strategy. Any of these reasons may cause division of the IT provision. Without some central control co-ordinating efforts this can mean the business wide picture is lost, together with opportunities for large scale reuse.

- IT structure - Even in companies with only one IT source and no problems of divided user communities there is the question of the IT departments own organisation. Studies of successful reuse programs tend to highlight the division of IT supply into producers and consumers[1] of reusable components. None of the participant IT departments were organised in this way and thus complete restructuring would be required. The advantage cited for the success of producer/consumer relationships is that role definition is enhanced reducing the developers disincentives to be involved with reuse.

For the organisations surveyed attainment of a producer/consumer structure for software development was considered impractical mainly due to the reluctance of upper management to commit funds up-front to the production of software to meet a future need.

Organisation 2 previously had experience of trying to restructure development staff in attempting to move from fixed teams to a resource pool arrangement. This failed due to eventually being seen as against the interests of permanent staff when considering that their developments often involved the hiring of large numbers of contract staff. It is likely that similar situations would occur for other companies when trying to alter team relationships. These issues must be addressed in order to attain a suitable structure for effective reuse or they may increase the disincentives for staff to be involved with reuse.

For companies unable or unwilling to restructure not having a dedicated team developing reusable components implies the components must be sourced from existing projects, even with this approach however, there needs to be some work done in co-ordinating and managing these. This suggests that some form of restructuring will still be necessary to put in place some form of reuse manager.

With a producer/consumer structure surveys still show problems in organisation as managerial structures still need to be well thought out. For instance a producer and consumer reporting to different managers may well have contrary priorities causing failure to work effectively on the same project.

- Inertia - The main anti-reuse complaint from the project managers perspective seemed to be that the pressure to complete developments was sufficient to prevent them having time to implement any scheme put forward. In particular each project had to meet such exacting deadlines that the introduction of any slack time to allow developer training or introduction of new techniques was impossible.

  Only at Organisation 5 had an attempt been made to introduce an overhead to project resources to be used in assessing reuse opportunities. Although at an early stage of introduction this did make it possible for projects to produce small libraries of components which they felt may be of future use, these tended to be small utilities that then remained within development teams. Thus reuse levels were low and even when it did occur the small component size meant that little effect was made.

- Knowledge - In a significant number of cases the level of knowledge of the issues and technologies for reuse was prohibitively low. Most information had come from general computing publications and thus contained insufficient detail to present a true picture of current techniques or how to apply them.

  It was felt by all participants that other technologies held more promise for development process improvement in the short term and that investigating and implementing these would provide more visible benefits. In particular RAD and JAD techniques were considered to be better directions for altering the development process as these would have a more direct effect on the face IT presented to its customers. For instance by giving them more influence in development and providing them with prototype products earlier in the development cycle. While reuse was seen as a technology which would only benefit IT internally and not very visibly.

- Commitment - Underlying all the issues inhibiting introduction of systematic reuse is a requirement for all involved to be committed to the cause. Little reliable data is available to justify cost/benefit statements for reuse and so faith is required to introduce programs when in all probability jobs may be at stake if they fail. From the questionnaire responses interest in the whole reuse issue seemed limited, again possibly due to the lack of data relating to the effect of reuse on the development process of non-IT companies.

- Measurement - As with any engineering activity measurement of reuse is vital to its success in a business environment. Unless measures of progress and success can be made funding will quickly dry up. A common complaint from the participants was that any reuse that did occur could not be measured and so did not promote further investigation of those techniques.

  Organisation 5 found this hampered the expansion of their current attempts at introduction of reuse techniques as it was hard to show a rate of return on the investment made in resourcing the overheads allowed on projects.

- Management - While uncoordinated reuse may work for experienced solitary developers in a constant domain this is not good enough for business wide use. In order to implement any systematic method there will need to be management buy-in. Previous studies[15] have concluded that the only way to introduce large scale changes in working practices is top down. This again derives from the lack of reliable information on reuse as without external justification for its introduction only high level support can authorise the changes and expenditure necessary to make reuse programs successful.

  Organisations 1, 3 & 5 which had this support in principal can be seen to have achieved higher reuse delivery ratings in Figure 1. There is still a need even here however for better visibility of this support throughout the companies in order to make further improvements.

- Economic - It is well recognised through out the literature[15] that establishment of a reuse program requires up-front investment before any dividend will be seen. For many companies and indeed all those involved here this is hard to justify with IT budgets already being squeezed in an increasingly competitive marketplace. Hewlett Packard report costs of producing reusable components to be between 111% and 480% relative to standard software products[18] this together with costs of actually reusing the components demonstrates the requirement to invest before any benefits will be seen. Similarly another study found components often had to be reused over 13 times before extra development costs were recovered[19].

  While Organisation 5 do make a budget assignment to achieving reuse, Organisations 1 & 3 rely on identifying reuse opportunities amongst existing development work. This again shows up in the achieved reuse delivery rating of Figure 1.

Changes to the economics of development are also necessary once reuse is introduced in order to keep the program rolling. Costs incurred in creating and managing reusable assets must be recovered from the projects which exploit those assets in order that reuse may be assessed for its worth and does not become a constant overhead to all development.

- Disincentives - Among the staff who would be potentially involved in any introduced reuse scheme there are a number of reasons why they may consider this not in their interests[20]. Most often cited is the 'not-invented-here' rejection of reusable resources made available, this recognises that developers often do not trust components that they have not built themselves to be reliable and to fulfil the functions specified. Less common is the fact that many developers actually consider engineering components more 'fun' than integrating them into a system.

  The first of these factors into the problems experienced by Organisations 1 & 3 in achieving results from the detected opportunities for reuse. This shows up as business units not wishing to adopt applications developed in other units.

Table 1 lists the identified inhibitors together with the symptoms of these recognised within the businesses and actions that may resolve them.

Inhibitor	Symptoms	Actions
Organisations Structure	Competition amongst business units. Unwillingness to co-operate or share strategy information. Overlap of responsibility on corporate data and process models.	Restructuring. Introduce central co-ordination of IT developments. Mandate Co-operation.
IT Structure	Lack of role definition for staff within the reuse process. No co-ordination of development efforts between overlapping projects to look for common areas. Priority conflicts between producer and consumer teams.	Again central co-ordination of development may help. Reorganise to introduce more common development between projects. Look to introduce methods for collaborative development of components to meet multiple sets of requirements. Ensure overall project goals and deadlines are communicated to all involved.
Inertia	Current developments are always top priority over process engineering. Previous process changes still have to be implemented.	Introduce regular review of development process. Encourage participation from development teams in process reengineering. Make identification of reuse opportunities a stage within the development cycle and assign project time to it.
Knowledge	Discussion of reuse process is restricted to parties with personal interest. No research into new techniques has been sanctioned.	Educate key personnel and arrange for dissemination of the information. Publish articles in company news letters.
Commitment	Lack of co-operation. Continued support voiced for old processes.	Make reuse a company goal to attach status to those involved. Implement incentive scheme for staff involved in reuse - perhaps providing a small bonus to providers of components each time they are reused.
Measurement	Costs of reuse not assigned to projects that receive benefit of it. Overhead from reuse processes becomes part	Look at methods of assigning value to reuse opportunities. Have developers estimate savings made.

	of costs for development section as a whole, raising their expenditure.	Implement metrics on code to compare that written from scratch to that imported from reuse libraries.
Management	Tried and tested processes cannot be made into standard practice. Project managers have differing views on the best way forward.	Educate senior managers. Where non IT managers control development projects ensure they understand that there budgets are made more effective by co-operation with other development projects.
Economic	Project managers have tight budgets which do not allow for extra investment in developing reusable components.	Fund reuse studies and then back these up by investing in the results. Take on expert personnel to manage reuse program where non suitable exist.
Disincentives	Quality issues are continually raised with previously developed components. Even standard third party libraries are ignored in favour of development from scratch of basic functionality.	Recognition system for creators of reusable components and their reusers. Implement some form of certification scheme for reusable components. Again, make reuse a company goal. Educate developers in methods of reuse.

Table 1. Inhibitors to better systematic reuse.

7. Key Messages

Agreement of opinion amongst the participants over the issues raised by our survey tends to suggest that many other organisations will be in similar positions to those involved. For these organisations the promises of reuse are largely unfilled due to the difficulties of integrating such a technology into traditionally structured organisations.

Identified symptoms of failing reuse will not be unfamiliar to managers at these organisations as they may well have been experiencing these already when trying to implement other large changes to well established business processes. Perhaps however, the inhibitors causing these symptoms are more of a surprise and are not as easily identified. Hopefully organisations will be able to learn from the experience of those surveyed by making the suggested actions in order to give a better chance of systematic reuse succeeding.

The key lesson from the survey is that integrating systematic reuse into the development process is a difficult problem to which the answer will vary from organisation to organisation. In particular each company will have different expectations from the technology and will need to remove different impediments. There is no single path to reuse success which can be followed by all, instead each company must tailor the experiences of others to find a solution that will work for them. Only by looking for symptoms of possible problems in their development process can organisations hope to eliminate these problems to ease the way for introduction of their own reuse processes.

It became increasingly clear that most identified problems were not with the technology itself but with integrating this into the business. With a process whose results are not likely to be seen for some time it is important that everyone concerned with its implementation is committed to making it work, the best way to achieve this is by lending full management support and making it clear that this is the case.

Future development trends such as those suggested by the participants (RAD, JAD) are driven by increasing time-to-market pressures and are likely to lead to effective reuse only being achievable at the component level. Involving users in development will cause applications to be excessively specialised. Reuse of such specialised applications would require massive alteration equivalent to redevelopment and so make it not worth while. In these cases reuse must be achieved either by building the applications from standard components that may be reused elsewhere or co-ordinating development by reengineering requirements from all those who may wish to use the application and then building a common process. Many companies have realised in the past it can be much more effective to buy off-the-shelf packages to provide functionality rather than developing in-house solutions to meet all requirements. This mind set must be transferred to the development of all applications by buying in components to meet standard requirements. However, the software industry must first realise the potential for standard component supply as a new form of business.

8. Acknowledgements

The authors wish to thank the organisations and their employees upon whom this study is based.

References

[1] D. Fafchamps, "Organizational Factors and Reuse," in *IEEE Software*, vol. 11, 1994, pp. 31-41.

[2] C. W. Krueger, "Software Reuse," School of Computer Science Carnegie Mellon University Pittsburgh Pennsylvania 15213 June 1992 1992.

[3] T. Biggerstaff and A. Perlis, "Software Reusability," *Volume 1, Concepts and Models*: ACM press, 1989.

[4] J. W. Hooper and R. O. Chester, "Software Reuse - Guidelines and Methods," New York: Plenum Publishing, 1991, pp. 17-47.

[5] M. Griss, J. Favaro, and P. Walton, "Managerial and Organisational Issues in Starting and Running a Software Reuse Program," , W. Shafer, R. Prieto-Diaz, and M. Matsumoto, Eds.: Ellis Horwood, 1994, pp. 51-78.

[6] C. W. Krueger, "Software Reuse," *ACM Computing Surveys*, vol. 24, pp. 131-183, 1992.

[7] J. M. Morel and J. Faget, "The REBOOT Enviroment," presented at Selected Papers from the 2nd International Workshop on Software Reusability Advances in Software, Lucca, Italy, 1993.

[8] C. T. Jones, "Reusability in Programming: A Survey of the State of the Art," *IEEE Transactions on Software Engineering*, vol. 10, pp. 488-494, 1984.

[9] C. Rich and R. Waters, "The Programmers Apprentice: A Research Overview," *Computer*, pp. 1-25, 1988.

[10] P. Freeman, "Reusable Software Engineering: Concepts and Research Directions," in *Tutorial: Software Reusability*, P. Freeman, Ed., 1987, pp. 10-23.

[11] T. E. Cheatham, "Reusability Through Program Transformations," *IEEE Transactions on Software Engineering*, vol. 10, 1984.

[12] J. M. Neighbors, "DRACO: A Method for Engineering Reusable Software Systems," in *Software Reusability - concepts and methods*, vol. one, T. J. Biggerstaff and A. J. Perlis, Eds. New York: ACM Press, 1989, pp. 295.

[13] P. Kruchten, E. Schonberg, and J. Schwartz, "Software Prototyping Using the SETL Programming Language," *IEEE Software*, vol. 1, pp. 66-75, 1984.

[14] V. Basili, G. Caldiera, F. McGarry, R. Pajerski, G. Page, and S. Waligora, "The Software Engineering Laboratory - An Operational Software Experience Factory," presented at 14th International Conference on Software Engineering, Melbourne, Australia, 11-15th May, 1992, 1992.

[15] R. Joos, "Software Reuse at Motorola," in *IEEE Software*, vol. 11, 1994, pp. 42-47.

[16] D. Hough, "Rapid Delivery: An Evolutionary Approach for Application Development," *IBM Systems Journal*, vol. 33, pp. 397-419, 1993.

[17] J. Wood and D. Silver, *Joint Application Design - How to design quality systems in 40% less time*. New York: John Wiley & Sons, 1989.

[18] W. C. Lim, "Effects of Reuse on Quality, Productivity, and Economics," in *IEEE Software*, vol. 11, 1994, pp. 23-30.

[19] J. Favaro, "What Price Reusability?," *Ada Letters*, vol. 1991, pp. 115-124, 1991.

[20] M. Lenz, H. A. Schmid, and P. F. Wolf, "Software Reuse through Building Blocks," in *Software Reuse: Emerging Technology*, W. Tracz, Ed.: Computer Society Press, 1987, pp. 100-108.

Session P4c

Process Modeling

End User Computing: How an Organisation can Maximise Potential

D. R. Lawrence *, H U Shah ** and P Golder ***

** School of Computing and Information Technology, University of Wolverhampton, Wolverhampton, WV1 1SB, UK.*
email: cm1994@wlv.ac.uk

*** School of Computing, Staffordshire University, Stafford, ST18 0DG. email:H.Shah@soc.staffs.ac.uk*

**** Dept. Computer Science and Applied Mathematics, Aston University, Birmingham, B4 7ET, UK.*
email: p.a.golder@uk.ac.aston

keywords: *end user computing, modelling, effectiveness prediction, activity profiles*

0-8186-7840-2/97 $10.00 © 1997 IEEE

Abstract

End user computing (EUC) is an activity that is attracting increasing interest from information systems (IS) researchers and business organisations. The vast increase over recent years of the use of IT as part of everyday business activities, and the growing direct involvement of business users in application development, clearly has implications for modern organisations. We discuss how an organisation might best approach the task of optimising the effectiveness of end user developed applications, and also of maximising the contribution that can be made by IT specialists. As part of this discussion we outline a modelling approach which is designed to enable the prediction of the impact of changes to identified success factors on the effectiveness of end user developed applications. We discuss the results of a questionnaire survey of 69 business users.

We show how business users can be categorised by their levels of IT/Business/IS knowledge and expertise, and how this can be used to identify which users are best suited to taking part in end user centred development projects.

1. Introduction

Our research concerns improving the understanding and performance of end user computing (EUC) - which has been defined as being *user* reliance on IT to personally develop software [3].

It is claimed that EUC has the following important advantages over the more traditional approaches to systems development [2;3;13] :-

* eliminating the problems associated with ineffective communications between analysts and end users.
* ownership transfer to end users
* enhanced productivity and effectiveness
* improved user-friendliness in systems

A survey in 1991/2, of UK's top 2000 IT consumers found that 12% of systems were developed by end-users, and that this was expected to rise to 18% by 1994 [8]. The introduction of networked workstations in recent years, together with the proliferation of PC based software and general exposure of society at large to computers and their uses, has precipitated the trend of transferring powers of choice and operation of software away from centralised IT departments to business users [14;3]. The benefits and potential of EUC have been recognised by many researchers and practitioners [15;6], but also attention has been drawn to associated *risks* [18].

Some warn that applications produced by end users are prone to problems of poor design, documentation, and integration and that guidance and control is needed to effectively address these problems [2;22;9].

EUC is a term which does not strongly imply direct involvement of users in the *development* of software systems, and so we prefer to use the term Business User Development (BUD). The BUD term also emphasises that the individuals concerned primarily have a *business* role in an organisation.

There is also what is perhaps a largely 'hidden' concern - how will the further empowerment of end users affect the role and status of IT specialists ? It is important that further investigation and exploration is carried out in this area so that we can move towards the optimisation of the potential of increased user empowerment, but at the same time make the most effective use of the skills and experience of IT specialists.

2. Optimising BUD Effectiveness

There has been a great deal of published work on the improvement of the quality of end user developed applications [7;20]. Much of this work involves the consideration of providing training for users, and of providing an appropriate support framework for end user development activities. The following recommendations have been made [1] aimed at improving the quality of end user developed applications:-

i) Documented quality policies which are actively implemented and also supported by all levels of management.

ii) Quality assurance reviews should be made of BUD products, especially where systems are multi-user and/or business critical systems. A quality assurance group (perhaps comprising members of an BUD support unit) could provide a service to the end users.

iii) End users could prototype the design of a required system, which could then be 'refined' and fully implemented by an end-user support group.

iv) High quality reusable software modules should be made available to end user developers.

v) End users should receive training in areas such as systems development techniques, use of IT tools, and general problem solving.

We feel that these recommendations have warranted a much greater prominence in recent reviews of research in this area (and indeed a greater degree of use as a basis for further research). It is a sobering thought to note that these recommendations are now over 10 years old, and just as necessary to be implemented in many of today's organisations. We support the spirit of the recommendations, but would like to add the suggestion that business users should be provided with more usable and powerful BUD tools; to move towards obviating the need for users to gain excessive degrees of IT specialist expertise and/or support. Our research into BUD modelling (which is outlined later) will lead to the prototyping of advanced tool support for BUD participants.

Many have raised the issue of end user applications having deficiencies due to poor use of data validation, documentation, structured design techniques, and security [3]. It has been proposed that users should adopt comprehensive guidelines [22] - we are concerned that the level of systems development skills targeted would require an excessive amount of training, and also possibly reduce the focus that the user would normally have on business issues. This concern is supported elswhere, [4], who recommend the use of a suitably 'non-rigorous' methodology to encompass detailed design, implementation and testing of applications.

The aforementioned list [1] includes mention of a quality assurance group - this concept is taken up by others [4] who propose a quality framework for end users developing software. The framework focuses on the use of a 'quality agent' who has the role of helping with:-

* identifying which projects need to be developed within a quality management system (QMS)
* approving requirements specification documents and detailed project plans
* assisting with managing departmental and organisational support systems

We feel that this approach could pay very high dividends, with the proviso that business users are involved in debating and agreeing with the standards and procedures to be adopted, and the criteria to be used when making the various decisions.

In general there appears to have been insufficient involvement of business users in the recent open debates about BUD, and how to best manage and control the processes involved. To an extent this also applies to IT specialists. We feel that it is time now for IT specialists and business users in particular organisations to get together and discuss the issues. IT specialists have played an important role in information systems development (ISD) for many years now and it would be foolish to even consider casting this vast experience aside; to be 'recklessly' replaced by BUD. It is important to move from an era of centralised IT specialist domination, to one in which business users are empowered, but the potential of IT specialists is also maximised.

3. Maximising the Potential of IT Specialists

It is understandable for IT specialists to have been somewhat 'protective' about their position over recent years as BUD has grown in importance. The immediate assumption is that the role of the traditional specialist analyst/designer/programmer is threatened by business users taking on BUD activities. We feel that this is an over simplification, and that far from being threatened, IT specialists have the opportunity of an enhanced existence. Traditionally there has been a divide between IT specialists and business users - essentially attributed to the culture gap [23]. As the ISD understanding and awareness of those business users that participate in BUD increases, this culture gap will begin to close - which will help to alleviate some of the problems of communication (between the analyst/designers and users). This is important, because we feel that even with full empowerment of business users it is not likely (and not in the interests of organisations involved) to result in the disappearance of the IT specialist role in ISD. Even if we reached a scenario in the future whereby business users were able to enjoy 'ideally' powerful and usable BUD tools, a consistent and thorough corporate policy on BUD support and quality control, and appropriate training and management support, the role(s) that we would envisage for IT specialists are as follows:-

i) consulting with BUD tool designers (in conjunction with business users) with regard to recommendations of design and other systems development standards built into the tools.
ii) helping to manage and provide technical and skills support for BUD participants.
iii) developing application systems within projects (internal and external to the organisation) deemed to not be suitable for BUD (or simply those projects which are part of a BUD 'backlog' and which are high priority projects).
iv) providing training and consultancy to business users in ISD skills.

Individual IT specialists also have the opportunity to gain business skills in particular areas of need and interest, and so possibly become very effective in BUD - by operating as part of a business department rather than a centralised IT department.

4. Modelling BUD effectiveness

Although the presence of BUD continues to increase in organisations [10;17;11;12], and even though research into EUC has been extensive [21;14;18;7;19] there is as yet no clear model of how contributing factors lead to outcomes. Our research addresses this issue by studying the measurement of BUD contributing factors and linking them to measured BUD outcome effectiveness. We are also interested in categorising business users in terms of business/IS/IT expertise - an indication of BUD potential.

We have developed a simple research model which illustrates our view that the following factors contribute to BUD effectiveness:-

* User IT Sophistication - measure of a users IT skills and experience
* Business/IS knowledge - extent to which a user understands the complexities and business issues involved in an IS
* Role/Authority - power and freedom of a user to take part in BUD
* BUD tool support - extent to which tools available meet needs of a business user developer, and are suitable for their use

These factors were initially selected mainly on the strength of practical personal experience in the ISD area. The aim was to utilise factors that were perceived as significant contributors to BUD effectiveness, and also were *measurable* within a research study. We have also ensured that our model is in harmony with conclusions made by previous investigations and studies - which have been comprehensively collated and summarised in other work [7;5].

BUD effectiveness outcomes is viewed as the culmination of how User IT Sophistication, Business/IS knowledge, Role/Authority, and BUD Tool Support interact together.

We regard the primary importance of the model as being a vehicle to enable the effects (on outcomes) of changes to one or more contributing factors to be predicted. To facilitate this predictive feature we have developed a means of measuring the various aspects and identifying links between contributors and outcomes. The model is likely to be useful in assisting businesses in the task of creating effective strategies relating to BUD resourcing, training and tool/infrastructure support provision. This would form part of a wider IT/IS strategy for an organisation (which includes identifying the most appropriate role(s) for IT specialists).

We have used a questionnaire (previously validated in a pilot study - [16] survey to gain measures of the various factors for particular individuals. The questionnaire incorporates the concept of measuring contributing factors and BUD effectiveness via participant's ordinal responses to questions which target each of the various aspects involved.

5. Results and conclusions of the Survey

The results are based on a total of 69 completed questionnaires received from the 80 organisations contacted. Most of the questionnaires were sent out to (UK) student placement sites - this was expected to improve chances of questionnaire completion and also had the advantage that these organisations were more likely to utilise computerised information systems. Others were sent to large UK organisations working within a mixture of market sectors. In all cases, the contacts were asked to arrange for questionnaires to be completed by personnel who *primarily* had a *business* role within the organisation, and also had some interaction with IT.

5.1 Relationship between factors and outcome effectiveness

The statistical analysis of the results confirm that the consideration of these aspects as contributing factors to BUD effectiveness is valid, and that the factors of *Role* and *Tools* seem to be particularly significant (see Table 1).

Table 1: Significance of contributing factors

	p value (correlation with BUD effectiveness)	
IT Knowledge/expertise	0.55	*** (very highly significant)
Business/IS knowledge	0.38	* (significant)
Role (freedom+power)	0.62	*** (very highly significant)
Tools (suitability)	0.64	*** (very highly significant)

where '*' denotes significance at 5% level:-$p < 0.05$
'***' denotes significance at 0.1% level:-$p < 0.001$

A linear regression analysis further confirms that role (power and freedom) and Tools (suitability) appear to be the dominant factors (see Table 2).

Table 2:- Regression analysis of contributing factors

	p value (< 0.05 is significant)
IT Knowledge/expertise	0.096
Business/IS knowledge	0.858
Role (freedom + power)	0.007 ** (highly significant)
Tools (suitability)	0.021

The use of *path analysis* indicates that all of the factors (i.e. including Business/IS knowledge) have both direct and indirect influences on the BUD outcome effectiveness.

The regressional analysis of the survey results provides an equation, which can be used to calculate (predict) the expected level of BUD effectiveness, based on measures of the contributing factors (-10.3 + (0.22*IT factor) - (0.0157*Business/IS factor) + (1.26*role factor) + (0.397*tools factor)). The shape of the equation is expected to be refined as we gather and utilise more data, but already it is showing a promising (in statistical terms) level of explanation (51%).

The availability of a reliable instrument to measure the effect of contributing factors on BUD outcome effectiveness means that organisations are now able to carry out impact analysis relating to BUD effectiveness due to planned changes to the factors. This provides a useful facility to organisations who are interested in building up a profile of the BUD potential within the organisation, and/or wish to direct investments in end user training, tool support, etc. such that the resulting impact is optimised.

5.2 Categorisation of business users

The sub-totals of ordinal values for questions relating to 'IT knowledge/expertise' and to 'Business/IS knowledge' have been used to categorise the survey participants. Carefully chosen values were used to act as boundaries to define *naive, fair*, and *expert* delimiters (averages of 'less than 2.5', '>= 2.5 and <3.5', and '3.5 and above' per question - each question having a maximum response of 5 - were chosen to represent the three ranges respectively). Table 3a shows that most of the participants (44/69) in the survey have levels of IT experience of either 'fair' or 'expert' - which is to be expected as computerisation is no longer a new phenomenon in business. However, a number are rated as 'IT-naive' which is a little surprising. Table 3b shows the relatively high number (20 out of 69) of participants who seem to have low levels of Business/IS knowledge (rated as 'naive') - this could be of concern to business managers, in that it would seem that expertise in this area is a fundamental BUD success factor, and may need early attention by organisations.

Table 3a: IT expertise levels

Total IT expert	=	17
fair	=	27
naive	=	25

Table 3b: Business/IS expertise levels

Total Business/IS expert	=	36
fair	=	13
naïve	=	20

The analysis enables the survey participants to be placed into categories of varying business/IS/IT 'expertise'. The categories can be listed in order of increasing potential for high BUD effectiveness. The view taken is that the higher the level of business/IS knowledge, the higher the potential, and within any level of this knowledge (i.e. naive, fair, or expert) the potential is increased with increasing IT experience. Table 4 shows that the nine categories can be translated into three major sections of 'strong', 'good', and 'weak' characteristics of personal BUD effectiveness potential. People within each section can be placed at one of three sub-levels according to the amount of IT specialist support/training required for them to capitalise on their business/IS knowledge.

Table 4: Business User Categorisation Results

Business+IS/IT expert:	13 :	STRONG BUD Potential(level a)
Bus+IS expert/IT fair:	14 :	" (level b)
Bus+IS expert/Naive IT:	9 :	" (level c)
Bus+IS fair/IT expert:	1 :	GOOD BUD Potential (level a)
Bus+IS fair/IT fair:	7 :	" (level b)
Bus+IS fair/ IT naive:	5 :	" (level c)
Bus+IS naive/IT expert:	3 :	WEAK BUD Potential (level a)
Bus+IS naive/ IT fair:	6 :	" (level b)
Business+IS/IT Naive:	11 :	" (level c)

(where: level a => minimal IT specialist support/training needed
level b => moderate IT specialist support/training needed
level c => significant amount of IT specialist support/training needed)

The majority of the survey participants (27 out of 69) are placed in the top two categories - suggesting that organisations generally are likely to employ many people who have high levels of potential for successful involvement in BUD. The top two categories represent business users who are likely to be very well suited to being involved in user centred development projects. As BUD tools are developed to be more advanced then the level of IT skills required will reduce.

Table 5: Role/Tools ordinal scores

	Role	Tools
No. of High Scores (3.5+ out of 5)	14	9
No. of Medium Scores (2.5-3.5 out of 5)	15	13
No. of Low Scores (<2.5 out of 5)	40	47

Table 5 shows a summary of the ratings of scores for role (power and freedom) and tools (suitability). It shows that the large majority of users have BUD tools which have limited scope and suitability, and indicates that a significant proportion of users seem to be constrained in BUD activities by the nature of their role/authority. These conclusions are generally supported by the free text responses received.

6. Survey conclusions

i). The analysis of the survey results suggest that there are clear links between BUD outcome effectiveness and the measured contributing factors; 'IT expertise'; 'Business/IS knowledge'; 'Role power/freedom'; and 'BUD tool support'. Results so far indicate that it is the latter two factors which are dominant in terms of determining the effectiveness of BUD outcomes, but that all the factors both direct and indirectly influence outcome effectiveness.

ii) We have shown that regressional analysis provides an equation which can be used to calculate an expected BUD effectiveness level (based on measured contributing factors). The equation has a promising level of explanation (51%). This is encouraging - especially at this stage of the research.

iii) We expect organisations to be able to use the model to predict the impact (on BUD outcome effectiveness) of making planned changes to the contributing factors. The modelling of factors contributing to BUD effectiveness will assist with strategic decisions regarding business user empowerment; in matching business users to appropriate development work, in identifying desired improvements in the various factors, and in monitoring effects of such improvements.

iv). It has been demonstrated that the survey results can be used to categorise the participants into one of nine levels of IT and business/IS expertise - placing business users in order of potential for high BUD effectiveness.

v). There are indications that many business users could be constrained in terms of BUD due to role restrictions, and unsuitable tool support.

7. References

1. Alavi M. (1985), "Some Thoughts on Quality Issues of End User Developed Systems", *Proceedings of the Computer Personnel and Business Data Processing Research conference*, Minneapolis USA, May 1985, ACM, pp. 200-207.

2. Alavi, M. & Weiss, I.R. (1985), "Managing the risks associated with end-user computing", *Journal of Management Information Systems* **2**(3), Winter 85-86, 5-20.

3. Amoroso D.L. & Cheney P.H. (1992), "Quality End-user Developed Applications: Some Essential Ingredients", *Data Base*, **23**, Winter 1992, p.1-11.

4. Barr S., Foley R.W. & McMullan M. (1994). 'Towards a Quality Management System for end-user application development', *Proceedings of Software Quality Management II*, Edinburgh. July 1994, Volume 1.

5. Blili S., Raymond L. & Rivard S. (1996), "Definition and Measurement of End User Computing Sophistication", *Journal of End User Computing*, **8**(2), pp. 3-12, 1996.

6. Boone G. H. & Merlyn V.P. (1988), "The CASE Experience: Annual CASE Survey 1988", *CASE Research Corporation*, Bellevue W.A., 1988.

7. Brancheau J.C. & Brown C.V. (1993), "The Management of End User Computing:

Status and Directions", *ACM Computing Surveys*, **25**(4), December 1993.
8. Bray P. (1992), "The Software Time Bomb", *WHICH Computer,* September 1992.
9. Cale E.G. Jr (1994): "Quality issues for end-user developed software", *Journal of Systems Management*, **45**(1), Jan 1994, USA, p.36-9.
10. Davies D. & Davies D. (1990): "The Effect of Training Techniques and Personal Characteristics on Training End Users of Information System", *JMIS(7:2)*, Fall 1990, pp. 93-110.
11. Guimaraes T. & Igbaria M., " Exploring the relationship betwen IC success and company performance", *Information and Management*, **26**(3), pp.133-141, March 1994.
12. Guimaraes T. (1996). "Assessing the impact of information centres on end-user computing and company performance", *INFORMATION RESOURCES MANAGEMENT JOURNAL*, 9(1), pp6-15, Winter 1996.
13. (van) Heusden, G.H.P.J. & Wijnen G.C.W. (1994): "End user computing from I and A departments, *Informatie*, **36**(2), Feb 1994, pp.118-124, Netherlands (in Dutch).
14. Huff S.L., Munro M.C. & Marcolin B. (1992): "Modelling and Measuring End User Sophistication", *Proceedings of ACM SIGCPR conference*, April 1992, Cincinnati, Ohio, ACM Press, 1992.
15. Khan E.H. (1992), "The Effects of Information Centres on the Growth of End User Computing", *Information and Management*, **23** (5), pp.279-289.
16. Lawrence D.R., Shah H.U. & Golder P.A. (1995), "A Study to Validate an End User Computing Model - Towards Predictive Quality", *Proceedings of Software Quality Management III*, Vol 1,pp.457-468, April 3-5th, 1995, Seville.
17. McLean E. R. & Kappelman L.A. (1992), "The Convergence of Organisational and End-User Computing", *Journal of Management Information Systems*, Winter 1992-3, **(9)** No. 3, pp.145-155, 1993.
18. Panko, R.R.; Halverson, R.P., Jr. (1994),"Individual and group spreadsheet design: patterns of errors", *Proceedings of the Twenty-Seventh Hawaii International Conference on System Sciences. Vol.IV: Information Systems: Collaboration Technology Organizational Systems and Technology*, 4-7 Jan 1994, Wailea USA, IEEE, p. 4-10.
19. Pentland B. T. 1989, "Use and productivity in personal computing: An empirical test", *Proceedings of the 10th International Conference on Information Systems*, ACM, New York, pp. 211-222.
20.Rivard, S., Poirier, G., Raymond, L. & Bergeron, F. (1994): "Development of a measure to assess the quality of user-developed applications", *Proceedings of the Twenty-Seventh Hawaii International Conference on System Sciences. Vol.IV: Information Systems: Collaboration Technology Organizational Systems and Technology*, Wailea (HI) USA, 4-7 Jan 1994, IEEE, USA, p. 522-31
21. Rockhart J.F. & Flannery L.S. (1983), "The Management of End User Computing", *Communications of the ACM*, **26** (10), Oct 1983, pp.776- 784.
22. Salchenberger, L. (1993) "Structured development techniques for user-developed systems", *Information and Management***24**(1), 41-50.
23. Shah, H.U.; Dingley, S.; Golder, P.A. (1994), "Bridging the culture gap between users and developers", *Journal of Systems Management*, **45**(7), July 1994, p. 18-21.

Balancing Acts: Reconciling Competing Visions of the Way Software Technologists Work

Stuart Shapiro and Steve Woolgar
Centre for Research into Innovation, Culture and Technology (CRICT)
Brunel University
Uxbridge, Middlesex UB8 3PH
United Kingdom
S_Shapiro@acm.org

Abstract

The practice of software development has been viewed by some as marked by anarchy and fragmentation and by others as characterized by order and universalism. How is it that two essentially opposite stereotypes of the way software technologists work have gained such prominence? This paper argues that both characterizations are valid and explores them in the context of an ethnographic and historical investigation of software process standards in a computer company. These tendencies toward order and disorder manifest themselves in several different ways which suggest that both forces are an inescapable concomitant of working with software. As a result, these tendencies must be managed in tandem to achieve an equilibrium rather than dealt with in isolation. This is likely to require sophisticated forms of professional judgment on the part of practitioners.

1. Introduction

Computer software development has always exhibited a split personality. On the one hand, practice often seems naturally disordered. This is epitomized by the "not invented here syndrome," a marked reluctance on the part of developers to use relevant designs and program code which someone else has previously produced. This tendency toward disorder pushes software technology toward fragmentation and a multiplicity of everything, be it programming languages, development techniques, or solution strategies. On the other hand, practice often seems naturally ordered. In this case, imperatives such as the "silver bullet syndrome" hold sway, involving the search for a single magical solution such as formal methods or object-oriented techniques which will dramatically ameliorate or solve the problems associated with software development. This tendency represents comprehensiveness and universality with respect to the very same things for which the tendency toward disorder represents fragmentation, thus pulling practitioners toward single languages, techniques, and strategies.

Life would be a good deal easier if we could simply brand one of these tendencies as manifestly undesirable in opposition to the other. Unfortunately, both these tendencies are usually thought of as troublesome. Each syndrome is seen as a problem to be overcome rather than as a property to be embraced. Equally important, they represent fundamentally opposed views of the way practitioners in software technology work. How can these views co-exist side by side? How can they be reconciled?

2. Methodology

The research reported here combined ethnographic and historical study of software process standards within a large commercial organization. Originally a means of studying and understanding primitive tribal peoples, ethnography as been used as a basis for gaining new insights into the practice of science and technology (e.g., [7]). This approach encompasses a variety of techniques including participant observation, interviews, the examination of documentary evidence, and the audio and video recording of interaction. Furthermore, the approach taken here was marked by dialogue with those in the setting. We thus provided feedback to those who were interested and treated the resulting interactions as further material for analysis. The upshot of this is a kind of practical relevance different from the explicit recommendations which are the traditional hallmark of policy-oriented research. Instead, we sought to sensitize individuals and the organization to key cultural processes which undergird their technological practice.

The setting in which this research took place is a large (more than 100 employees) software development facility in Britain which is part of a multinational computer company producing both hardware and software.

0-8186-7840-2/97 $10.00 © 1997 IEEE

Development activities at this facility encompass multiple product lines on multiple platforms and utilize a variety of methods and languages. The principal author was attached to a project involving development of a relatively small (~ 10,000 lines of code) communications option which would augment the main product (~1,000,000 lines of code). As a result, the project team was atypically small (six people). High-level languages were used and the principal development method was a modified form of Literate Programming [5]. The entire facility has BS 5750 certification.

The principal author was with the project team for approximately eighteen months over which time he spent one or two days a week on site attending team meetings, examining project documents, and interacting informally with team members. Formal interviews were also conducted with the team members and several lines of management. In addition, developers in two other product lines were informally interviewed, providing useful points of comparison. Moreover, we sought not only to understand how the existing process standards are used in practice but to uncover their origins well. In other words, an explicit attempt was made to understand the history behind the process standards. This included obtaining and examining past versions of the standards as well as related company directives and memoranda.

3. Findings

We have divided our findings and arguments into three threads. The first, contingent practice, refers to how the process that practitioners followed reflected the surrounding circumstances. These circumstances included not just the attributes of the specific project at hand but also organizational strategy and history as well as conceptions of professionalism. The second thread, community versus individual standards, reflects a key distinction we observed but which was not sufficiently appreciated by those involved. We contend that these two aspects of standardization are equally important, but that process standards only address one of them. The third thread, reification, describes what happens when process standards become disengaged from the process which actually takes place. The result is not unlike the case of a legal or moral stricture that is widely endorsed yet frequently violated. We conclude with some thoughts on the implications of our findings for the janus-faced nature of software development practice.

3.1 Contingent practice

The software process standards within the firm we studied resulted primarily from internal concerns and efforts over the last decade. Although broad standards existed before this in the form of a corporate development guide, work over the last ten years produced a multi-tiered standards structure covering the corporate, site, product division, and product line levels with significant scope for process "tailoring" at the project level. While the initial impetus behind the development of these standards was firmly situated inside the company, the growing prominence of general QA process standards around the middle of this period provided additional momentum.

Around 1990, the firm committed itself to a standards strategy of devolution. As a company document notes, "the implications of this was that the programming community would end up with many customized development processes rather than a single process that would be uniformly followed throughout the community." (Because anonymity was promised as a condition of access to the firm, sources that would identify the company are not given.) A clear and conscious effort has been made to keep the firm's multi-tiered standards structure hierarchical, yet it is explicitly stated in the relevant documentation that when a conflict arises, local standards take precedence. In acknowledging the importance of flexibility and local contingencies (i.e. the immediate circumstances surrounding the development of a particular product), the company has reflected a general sentiment evident in public domain reports of the software process standards in other companies (e.g., [3] and [4]). This sentiment resonates (though not perfectly) with the notion of "situated action" in the social sciences. According to this theory, actions—however much planned—are inescapably taken within particular, concrete circumstances which will require unforeseen adaptations [10]. The firm we studied appears to stand out in the strength of its commitment to a broad strategy of process devolution under which process decisions are made at the lowest practicable level.

The most visible contingencies governing process tailoring, both formal and informal, within the product lines were projected size of the resulting code (an indication of complexity and required effort), time pressure, and prior experience with the types of function being developed. Small sized elements, those with commercially critical deadlines, and those embodying familiar types of functionality might well undergo abbreviated design processes. Inspections beyond those of high level designs suffered even more than design processes, which was hardly surprising given that the time required to properly inspect a component exploded as design detail increased. When some of these contingencies demanded conflicting responses, resolving the conflict within the development process became a matter of professional judgment . This was a key problem for the project we observed, which had to cope with both time pressure and inexperience implementing certain kinds of functionality. Distinct differences of opinion surfaced regarding an appropriate response vis-a-vis the development process.

The notion of "commercial pressure" featured prominently in participants' representations of their work practices which in turn reflected contingent definitions of professionalism. Individuals repeatedly drew comparisons between the activities in our project's product line, the activities in the other product lines in the division, and the activities in other product divisions. Tales of the less structured, more casual processes followed by other teams in these areas were almost invariably accompanied by observations that these products were relatively young, struggling to establish and maintain their commercial viability, and therefore couldn't afford to engage in elaborate development processes with long lead times. Such characterizations contrasted with the product line to which we were attached—a well-established market leading middleware product whose users depend on and expect extremely high quality.

These contrasts connoted differing definitions of professionalism. Thus, for the well-established product, professionalism was understood in terms of one's ability to follow a highly structured process; in the case of the younger product, professionalism was first and foremost about getting the job done to a reasonable standard on time. The point here, and it's one which the practitioners themselves appreciate, is that both conceptions of professionalism appear appropriate within their respective contexts. In the "mature" and highly reputable product which has traditionally enjoyed plenty of development resource (although this is now changing) and has a well-elaborated development process, the overriding imperative is maintaining the quality which has been painstakingly built into the product over many years. In the context of a product fighting for market position with short development cycles and a more informal development process, the central thrust must be to meet deadlines without slipping beneath a quality threshold. Clearly, development in the former context can be viewed as more orderly than development in the latter. Nevertheless, each makes sense under the particular circumstances surrounding it. Conversely, each would prove problematic in the other's context.

3.2 Community versus individual standards

A central and long standing cultural stereotype of the software community has been the "cowboy" programmer. This stereotype arose in the early years of commercial programming (late 50s - early 60s) and represents the idiosyncratic, seat-of-the-pants programming style which became the sworn enemy of those seeking to transform software development into a disciplined, professionalized process more like formal engineering as they perceived it. Both the academic and trade literature from that time on has routinely and plaintively observed the need to control the seemingly natural anarchic tendencies of software developers. A programmer, a 1964 editorial in *Datamation* contended, "wants his specs in black and white . . . complains if they are. He doesn't believe in flowcharting or overlays, creating specific parameters for test data . . . complains about the furnished live data. He can't tolerate any systems work other than his own. Anyone else's program is incapable of modification" [2]. Here was a typical vision of the problem of programmers out of control. The answer, it logically followed, was to exert control, to constrain the procedures and activities of practitioners. Similarly, albeit in less incendiary terms, prominent computing experts declared in 1978 that "even though we talk about the 'engineering' of software, the implementer (programmer) still has too much freedom to be regarded as practicing engineering, in the sense that an aeronautical or civil engineer does" [11]. This has remained to a large extent the conventional wisdom regarding managing software development and software process standards have reflected it.

This attitude is embedded in the process standards of the firm we studied at all levels: corporate, site, product division, and product line. A decade ago, when the company began the effort which has led to the current state of its process standards, the introduction to a topical issue of the firm's in-house research journal noted that "programming has evolved from a highly individualistic profession into an orderly engineering process." Individualism and anarchy were clearly perceived as the problem, discipline and control the solution. A few years later, suspicion arose that perhaps things had gone too far in this direction. For example, a corporate document describing a set of good programming "imperatives" observed in its introduction that management had developed "a strong feeling that people were hiding behind the [corporate programming guide] and only doing what it said." It suggested that the firm "had to 'remove the shackles and chains' of the current process and give our people a chance to be innovative and creative." Still, implicit in this rhetoric was the conventional view that there existed a natural tendency toward innovation and creativity which would respond to a loosening of the overly constraining process standards with the development of local, customized processes.

The ethos the company wanted to foster was nicely summed up by Dan Bricklin, one of the developers of the groundbreaking spreadsheet program VisiCalc. In an interview published in 1986, Bricklin responded to a question regarding his own personal style of software development by observing that "you simply do whatever is appropriate for the particular situation" [6]. In other words, the developer alters his or her procedures depending on the circumstances surrounding a specific project. If one can take this as a working assumption, which is essentially what process standards do, then one can be confident that within the controlling boundaries of the standards developers will alter the process to match the circumstances. Too much disorder, too much fragmentation, too much *entropy* produces problems. But as long as limits are imposed, natural fragmentation will help ensure that the process varies as appropriate.

There is, however, another side to this. As one of the people in our firm told us, people get in a rut. Just as individuals tend to follow the same route between home and work each day, so too do individuals sometimes follow the same development route on each project. This mindset is clearly displayed by Gary Kildall, the late developer of the CP/M operating system, in an interview from the same source as Bricklin's. In response to the question about his personal approach to programming, Kildall declared that "I follow very definite procedures which work for me, though they may not work for other people" [6].

We found numerous manifestations of this desire for continuity. For example, one manager complained that "we as a management community keep thinking that our people are always going to try to shirk the process, they are always going to try [to] avoid as much work as they can, and yet I have to beat these guys into doing less work. My arguments with them are always along the lines 'Do you really have to go into this level of rigor . . .?'" Similarly, a programmer noted that "if people have particular methods which they used in the past and get to know, they will tend to favor those and try and use those throughout and I am sure that they think that about me and I am sure it's true for me as well." Indeed, we witnessed clues to this kind of behavior on our project. The process standards specified a three phase design process. However, the option existed to combine the second and third design phases into a single phase. One of the key debates that took place on the project was whether or not to use a combined design phase. Those in favor of separate and distinct design phases argued on the basis of good experiences with this approach on previous projects they had worked on. Those against it, whose experiences were largely or wholly with combined phases, argued that a combined phase worked perfectly well. In the end, separate phases were used. While in this case an important process issue was placed in high relief due to the clash of different experiences, it is easy to imagine a situation in which a preponderance of similar experiences leads to the automatic adoption of a particular approach. Several people alluded to just this sort of occurrence.

Software development organizations, as one would expect given the assumptions embedded in the larger software development culture, concern themselves principally with achieving standardization across the community. They can't afford to have people doing things too many different ways, so they concentrate on achieving a certain degree of commonality across the organization. This is what software process standards aim to accomplish. However, standardization also takes place at the level of the individual over time. ***Within the boundaries of the process standards,*** individuals may very well end up employing the same approach repeatedly without due consideration of the specific circumstances of each project. Software process standards are designed to contend with entropic tendencies, not these *self-ordering* ones.

An illuminating metaphor is the cabin doors on an airliner. As an airplane climbs, of course, the differential between the internal and external atmospheric pressure increases. The external pressure drops dramatically while the internal pressure must be maintained at something much closer to sea level. As a result, the stress on the doors is from the inside out. Therefore, the door seats such that those forces seal the door tighter rather than weakening the seal. The door is designed to more effectively resist stresses pushing outward than stresses pushing inward. Similarly, software process standards are designed to resist the stress of entropic rather than self-ordering tendencies.

It turns out therefore that personal experience, both good and bad, ends up being a key contingency governing process tailoring. Individuals who have suffered a particularly bad experience with a certain technique are loath to use that approach again. Likewise, individuals who have used a particular technique with great success will be eager to return to it. Thus, one of the principal contingencies is effectively disconnected from the context of the project at hand. Rather, it is connected to previous projects which may or may not have had comparable contexts.

As previously noted, software development is increasingly acknowledged as a contingent process with appropriate actions dependent on the circumstances of a specific project. Process standards assume that practitioners will operate within the entire "space" of the standards, employing particular methods and techniques as circumstances dictate. Yet this is a problematic assumption. Therefore, developing optimal process standards is not simply a matter of determining the appropriate level of constraint. Rather, it is a matter of equilibrium management, of finding a means of counteracting and balancing entropic and self-ordering forces.

3.3 Reification

While process standards may focus on controlling entropic rather than self-ordering tendencies, their success in doing even this much cannot be taken for granted. A constant and key issue concerning process standards is the extent to which practitioners actually adhere to them. In our firm, both internal company audits and external audits (relating to QA certification) are regularly conducted to ascertain this. The limitations of such exercises are such, though, that they cannot guarantee detailed workaday adherence. One programmer, for instance, pointed out the existence of "proof pieces" toward which auditors could be steered.

Although we heard the inevitable stories of rogue programmers and projects conducting their affairs with scant regard for the process standards, the consensual view was that almost everyone followed the standards to some degree, be it in broad terms or as precisely as possible. Indeed, in many cases the constraints imposed by the support tools help ensure this. Nevertheless, it was not especially unusual for shortcuts and informal modifications of varying degree to be used in response to contingencies such as those discussed above. This tendency was reinforced by substantial cutbacks in staffing levels owing to corporate "downsizing" and by increasingly intense competitive pressures.

Observing and discussing the ways the practitioners circumvent and alter the process, we were struck by how relatively sensible (at least with our modest expertise) many of these actions seemed. Most of them appeared to be pragmatic responses to the contingencies at hand. To the extent that some of these responses were becoming de facto standards, they could have been justifiably inserted into the standards. Yet they weren't and as a result the standards failed to accurately mirror what was actually taking place. For example, one programmer noted that on his project "we haven't fed back anything to anybody to say this is how it ought to work, and I don't expect we will unless someone asked us." Likewise, a manager mentioned that "one of the things I think we are poor at is because of the pressures that we're put under . . . we don't go back and say we've just stripped that out because we don't need it and we don't put a note there to say 'You only need to do this if. . . .'"

This seems to represent a major shift in the cultural interpretation of the process standards. The standards themselves clearly spell out the notion that these are meant to be "living" standards in the sense that it is assumed that they will be continuously reviewed and modified to reflect actual best practice in the firm. General QA standards such as BS 5750 make somewhat the same point, although their rhetoric seems to emphasize adherence and control more than organic change. The process standards both guide and reflect the activities of practitioners. This latter aspect, though, seems to have suffered diminished significance relative to the former.

In other words, the process standards have become *reified* and have thus taken on a relative immutability which lends them a cultural aura more akin to legal or moral strictures than to an organic means to an end. This was brought home to us by the number of times individuals would preface comments regarding adherence to the standards with the caution "don't tell anyone I said this." Similarly, when making introductions, one manager invariably emphasized to his programmers that the researcher was not an auditor of any type, that their remarks would not prompt any sort of management "comeback," and that they should therefore be sure to tell the researcher what they actually did rather than what the standards said they did. The divergence between What We're Supposed to be Doing and What We're Actually Doing, as one programmer characterized it, was a very touchy business and very difficult to speak about with any sort of public voice. Everybody (or virtually everybody) knew what was going on, but saying it out loud was simply not done.

Of course, a modicum of deviation from official social norms is often accepted if not outright expected in a given culture. Who among us has never exceeded a speed limit or crossed against a traffic light or committed any of a large collection of common violations of various cultural strictures? As long as the divergence between actual behavior and established norms remains relatively modest in character or frequency, the community can go about its business with minimal disruption or difficulty. However, when that divergence widens in scale and/or scope it may significantly impede the operation of that community.

Deviation from the standards, even for reasons which seem defensible in their local contexts, has become in some sense equivalent to actual moral or legal deviance of a common sort. Virtually everybody does it, but no one feels very comfortable admitting it. This deviance has taken on the air of a dirty little secret: something which isn't all that secret, but simply isn't talked about in polite company. The ad hoc character of these deviations reflects the nature of situated actions, but ad hoc development is also strongly connected with the cowboy programmer stereotype and all its negative connotations. Thus the character and frequency of deviation combine to produce an atmosphere which retards frank and open discussion of the process and the process standards.

This point is related to, but different from one raised in the literature, namely the failure to improve process standards continuously once they have been established [1]. In this case, the process arguably *is* being improved (or at least rendered contextually more effective) through the informal adaptations of practitioners as they respond to certain kinds of contingencies. The problem is not that everyone is content with the standards as they exist and unaware of a need for any kind of modification, for clearly they do modify them in practice. Those modifications, though, and the contingencies which prompt them, are not fed back into the process standards, thus fostering a dysfunctional deviance rather than simple stagnation.

Reification of the process standards, moreover, has permitted them to serve as a mask which conceals the true impacts of company cutbacks. As previously noted, these cutbacks have forced staff to make hard choices regarding their adherence to the process. A number of people suggested, though, that upper management has been able to turn a blind eye to the quality impacts of these actions at least partly because they can point to the standards as proof that effective quality assurance practices are still being carried out. Effective quality assurance practices may possibly still be taking place, but reified process standards which do not mirror actual practice provide a shaky foundation for such an assumption. If management does not appreciate that this reification has taken place, they can come to the potentially erroneous conclusion that cutbacks are not having any significant deleterious effects on product quality. As one manager put it, "I think again it is a lack of willingness to face up to the fact that if you used to have 300 people doing something and now you only have 90, things have to change . . . but nobody wants to admit to that. . . . [T]here is a selective deafness . . . so the sort of things that suffer are adherence to policy, adherence to processes, and updating of processes . . ." Reified process standards can be instruments of self-deception.

4. Conclusions

The silver bullet syndrome and the not invented here syndrome represent two opposing views of the way software technologists work. Each may be true, but each is incomplete. In actuality, they are manifestations of two opposing trends or forces. Reconciling these competing visions of the way practitioners work requires explicitly acknowledging the existence, the inescapability, and the legitimacy of both perspectives. Software technologists are cowboys *and* team players, anarchists *and* disciplinarians, yin and yang. As with yin and yang, the choice is not between one or the other but in how we attempt to balance the two. It's all too easy to fall into the trap of focusing exclusively on controlling either entropic or self-ordering tendencies in software development or of wildly alternating between the two. It is always easier to obsess about one thing at a time.

Managing the equilibrium between entropic and self-ordering tendencies in software development is a dynamic process which amounts to an ongoing balancing act. As one manager observed, "it's a bit like a tight rope I guess. You are forever trying to balance and keep on that tight rope and probably if somebody comes and audits you or reviews you at any point in time they would criticize you . . . because you're either [on] one side or the other . . . but there may be good reasons for that." That balancing act revolves around a number of factors, but the crux of the matter is professional judgment. As much of the preceding has suggested, the practitioners we observed actively resorted to various forms of professional judgment in determining tradeoffs, interpreting the process standards, and responding to contingencies generally. Yet, we also saw aspects of practitioner behavior which revealed that some facets of practitioner judgment remain problematic. This was not a matter of practitioners making decisions they should have recognized as unwise or inappropriate; we are not in a position to pass judgment on the quality of specific decisions. Rather, this was a matter of what might be termed systemic problems—the failure to fully explore or consider alternative approaches within the space of the standards and the failure to sufficiently feed contingent behaviors back into the standards. Again, we must stress that what concerns us here is not the behavior of specific individuals but cultural behavior. These systemic problems indicate that the conception and operation of professional judgment in this particular culture and probably in the larger culture of software technologists is in some respects inadequate and relatively unrefined.

Achieving a practical and beneficial balance between entropic and self-ordering tendencies demands a sophisticated form of professional judgment. As Henry Petroski has argued, this "does not necessarily come from a deeper understanding of theory or a more powerful command of computational tools. The traditional engineering sciences are servants and students but not masters and teachers of engineering judgment . . ." [8]. The nature and development of professional judgment is something with which established engineering fields have explicitly concerned themselves [9]. Yet there has been very little explicit discussion of this in the software community.

This is not merely a philosophical issue. It is very much a practical one as well. It cuts to the heart of professional development and effective practice. Here are three things software professionals and their employers can do to nurture professional judgment:

- Plan for experience. Attempt to systematically vary work assignments so as to foster not only an inventory of technical skills but an inventory of experience with different contexts and contingencies.
- Develop and support formal mentoring programs.
- Develop a case study approach to education and professional development by compiling and studying project case histories.

Unfortunately, though, all of these tasks demand professional and organizational time and resources in an era characterized by unrelenting pressure to make do with less. But even simple sensitization can help. Holding up a mirror through ethnographic study and feedback can enhance self-awareness and potentially change behavior. But achieving even this much requires a willingness on the part of software development organizations to expose themselves and their practices to an outsider, an always delicate business.

Working effectively with software requires an especially sophisticated view of professional judgment and how it interacts with experience and contingency. Clearly there is a role for software process standards in this, just as no one would deny the importance of the codes of practice which figure prominently in the work of other types of technologists. But process standards can only work properly if they are recognized as based on an incomplete view of the way practitioners operate. The silver bullet syndrome and the not invented here syndrome represent opposite yet equally valid perceptions of practitioner behavior. Reconciling these competing visions is straightforward once one recognizes the inescapable and probably necessary existence of both entropic and self-ordering tendencies. Reconciling is one thing, however, and coping another. Effectively coping with these contrary forces will demand greater and more sophisticated understanding and appreciation of the processes that really count: the processes of practitioner judgment.

Acknowledgments

The research on which this paper is based was supported by ESRC grant no. R000234269.

References

1. Coallier, François, 1994. How ISO 9001 Fits Into the Software World. *IEEE Software* 12 (January): 98-100.
2. *Datamation*, 1964. Checklist for Oblivion. 10 (September): 23.
3. Dion, Raymond, 1992. Elements of a Process-Improvement Program. *IEEE Software* 10 (July): 83-85.
4. Henry, Joel and Bob Blasewitz, 1992. Process Definition: Theory and Reality. *IEEE Software* 10 (November): 103-105.
5. Knuth, Donald E. 1992. *Literate Programming*. Stanford, CA: Center for the Study of Language and Information. CSLI Lecture Notes, No. 27.
6. Lammers, Susan. 1986. *Programmers at Work: Interviews*. Redmond, Washington: Microsoft Press.
7. Latour, Bruno and Steve Woolgar. 1986. *Laboratory Life: The Construction of Scientific Facts*. Princeton: Princeton University Press.
8. Petroski, Henry. 1994. *Design Paradigms: Case Histories of Error and Judgment in Engineering*. Cambridge: Cambridge University Press.
9. Shapiro, Stuart. Forthcoming. Degrees of Freedom: The Interaction of Standards of Practice and Engineering Judgment. *Science, Technology, & Human Values*.
10. Suchman, Lucy A. 1987. *Plans and Situated Actions: The Problem of Human-Machine Communication*. Cambridge: Cambridge University Press.
11. Wasserman, Anthony I., Laszlo A. Belady, S. L. Gerhart, Edward F. Miller Jr., William M. Waite, and William A. Wulf, 1978. Software Engineering: The Turning Point. *IEEE Computer* 11 (9): 30-41.

BOOTSTRAP: Five Years of Assessment Experience

Hans Stienen *, Franz Engelmann *, Ernst Lebsanft
* SYNSPACE AG, Rottmannsbodenstrasse 30, CH - 4102 Binningen
Phone: (41) 61 4220240, Fax: (41) 61 4220933
Email: stienen@synspace.ch

Abstract

The main characteristics of the BOOTSTRAP method are briefly described, i.e. the reference framework, the assessment procedure, the structure of the questionnaires and the rating and scoring mechanisms used.

The major part deals with the results of the BOOTSTRAP assessments performed worldwide over the last 5 years. In this part, major experiences from over 40 sites and 180 projects are analysed in detail and summarised. The empirical data support the basic concepts of the Capability Maturity Model (CMM), but demonstrate that the more detailed profiles the BOOTSTRAP method provides are an excellent instrument to identify strengths and weaknesses of an organisation. BOOTSTRAP proved to be a very efficient and effective means not only to assess the current status of software process quality but also to initiate appropriate improvement actions.

The last part deals with future trends in software process assessment approaches, i.e. the development of a common framework for performing assessments.

1 Introduction

A software product is always the result of a process. A careful design and control of the software development process is therefore essential in order to prevent errors in the resulting work products and to produce quality instead of attempting to achieve it only by (late) testing and verification activities [13]. There is an urgent need for sound software process improvement techniques.

A Software Process Assessment is a comprehensive examination and evaluation of all engineering and management processes that appertain to Application Development, Product Installation and Operational Support including Software Maintenance. It results in a set of metrics (profiles), that encourage an organisation to recognise its major strengths and weaknesses. The resulting profiles enable the determination of feasible targets for software process improvements. An assessment provides a solid baseline for measuring progress.

The software process assessment and improvement method BOOTSTRAP has been developed in an ESPRIT project, which was partially funded by the European Commission [8], [9]. The approach evolved on the basis of CMM [10], [11], the ISO 9000 Series and the European Space Agency's Software Engineering Standards. Since 1991, over 100 assessments have been performed, the majority of them in Europe mostly by members of the Bootstrap Institute but also by licensees of the method. Based on these experiences, the assessment instruments have been revised and refined repeatedly. Additional criteria that originated from the Total Quality Model issued by the European Foundation for Quality Management [3] have been incorporated recently.

The resulting assessment and improvement method is characterised by the following points:

- It provides detailed maturity levels and capability profiles of both organisations and projects,
- It allows optionally to determine the degree of fulfilment of the 20 elements of ISO 9001,
- It allows benchmarking, i.e. the comparison with specific industrial sectors, countries and other assessment data stored in the BOOTSTRAP database, and
- It includes through its standardised procedure immediate feedback to the organisation and support for initiating improvement actions.

From past experiences with software process assessment methods it appears that a major problem encountered is that deviations from a reference framework like the one advocated by SEI may be so large that few of the specified characteristics may be observed, although the organisation performs evidently well on the market. This is especially true for small software development organisations with short communication and reporting lines and an informal organisational structure. The basic assumption that only one way to perform the development process exists is not accepted. A major challenge for an assessment method is therefore the incorporation of appropriate mechanisms for tailoring individual assessments to the actual needs of an organisation. BOOTSTRAP is flexible enough to account for the various application areas, the typical size and cultural differences across organisations and countries [7].

2 Main Features of BOOTSTRAP

BOOTSTRAP has been initiated primarily as a project to encourage technology transfer. Assessments were identified as an excellent vehicle for that purpose. Rather than

0-8186-7840-2/97 $10.00 © 1997 IEEE

to perform a plain survey of the status, the main objective of a BOOTSTRAP assessment is to reach consensus about a feasible improvement action plan. Improving software process quality requires measuring it. BOOTSTRAP recognises that there may exist several obstacles to overcome. Mean features of BOOTSTRAP are:

- Uniform procedure, mandatory assessor qualification and training scheme,
- Carefully designed questionnaires for both site and project evaluations,
- Constructive, not normative approach,
- Open questions, granular scoring and rating mechanism, and
- Immediate feedback and action planning.

Organisations often report severe difficulties in managing organisational and technological change. Investments may be quite high and many risks are encountered. Transitions should take place step by step. The fact that the BOOTSTRAP method does not assume strict adherence to a distinct key practice model like CMM, but allows for alternative approaches, is a key factor to its success.

3 The Reference Model

In order to identify good software engineering and management practices, it is necessary to have the appropriate instruments available for the classification, measurement and analysis of these practices.

For the examination and evaluation of the actual practices within an organisation, it is useful to be guided by a reference model that describes the typical software development practices. In many organisations, such a reference is at least partially available in the form of a standards and procedures manual. However, completeness and depth may vary. There also exist a number of generic standards, which are relevant for software development.

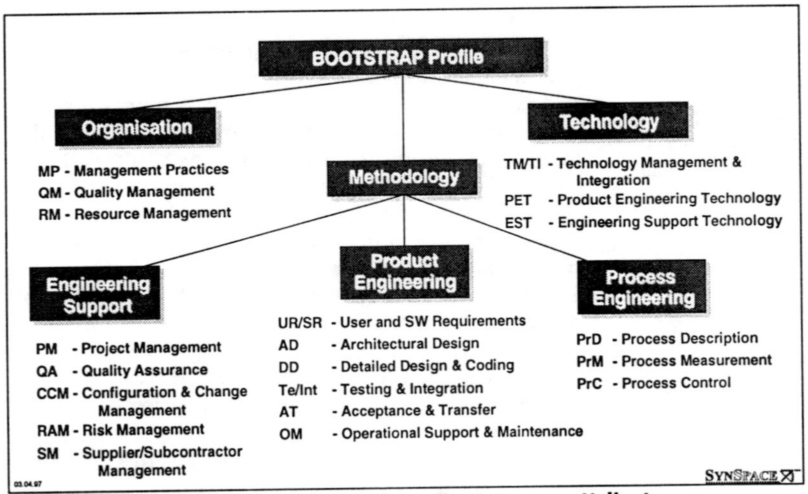

Figure 1: Overview of the BOOTSTRAP attributes.

One example is the international standard ISO 12207 Information Technology - Software Life Cycle Processes [5]. In this document, three distinct primary process areas consisting of 18 main processes, each subdivided in a number of activities are identified. The disadvantage of such very explicit models is their tremendous level of detail. The BOOTSTRAP approach is therefore a very pragmatic one. The scope of applicability is neither limited to any specific software development approach nor to any specific application domain. Reference for a description of all software engineering and management activities covered by the method are basically the two questionnaires used. An organisation and its process quality are evaluated with respect to organisation, methodology and technology, as shown in Figure 1.

The first group refers to the processes that describe the organisational aspects of a software producing unit or a project team. This group is characterised by 3 key attributes: The attribute Management Practices describes how well the communication, command and control structures as well as reporting lines and procedures fit into the organisational framework, the attribute Quality Management covers all activities concerning the establishment and use of an effective quality management system, whereas Resource Management supports the optimal allocation of personal skills and organisational assets. Under heading Methodology 3 areas are combined, i.e. Engineering Support, Process Engineering and Product Engineering. The first area evaluates procedures and techniques applied in more than just one life cycle phase. Explicitly addressed in the form of distinct quality attributes are Project Management, Quality Assurance, Risk Analysis and Management, Configuration and Change Management as well as Supply Management. The second area concentrates on process definition, modelling, measurement and deployment. The last group addresses the primary software production processes for each of the life-cycle phases. In addition to these aspects also tool support is taken into account. Provisions for selecting and introducing new technologies into the organisation are covered as well as the typical tools for supporting the software development process.

The technology attributes are excluded from the computation of the capability level of an organisation or project. BOOTSTRAP assumes that an organisation has to satisfy basic organisational requirements first, and then to take care of engineering methods before making investments in technology as third priority [6]. The underlying model guides organisations to a mature, disciplined and stable way of producing software of a level of quality that satisfies the users' needs.

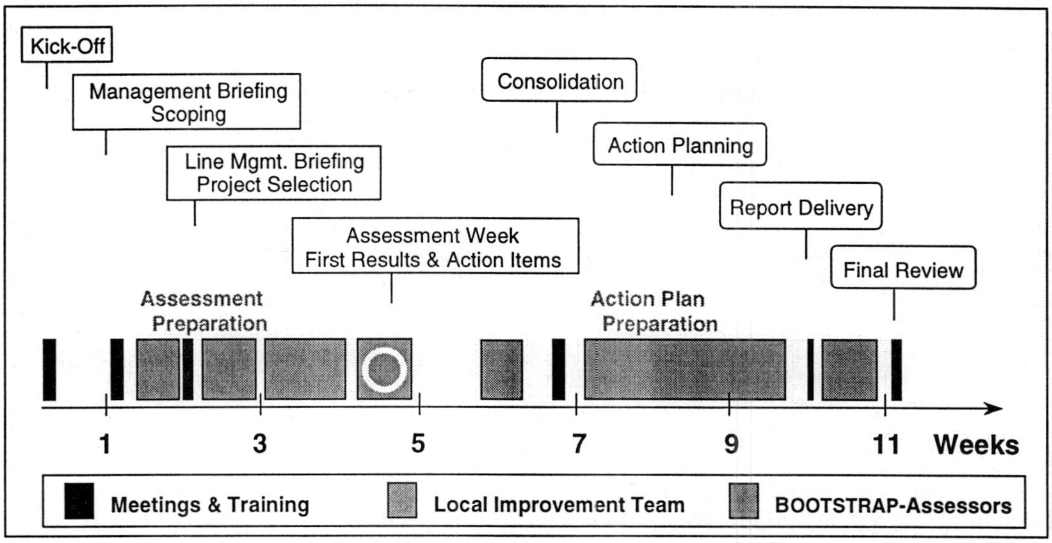

Figure 2: A typical BOOTSTRAP assessment schedule.

4 The BOOTSTRAP Procedure

Even with sophisticated assessment instruments, rating and scoring answers given during the interviews always contain an element of judgement. For this reason strict adherence to the established procedures is expected in order to keep variance as small as possible. The Bootstrap Institute maintains a strict qualification scheme for BOOTSTRAP assessors. The curriculum encompasses at least one week of training, followed by 10 days of apprenticeship in real assessments. Applicants are expected to be experienced software engineers with at least 5 years of industrial practice. The Bootstrap Institute founded by the original partners of the ESPRIT project also reviews all assessment data. Results are stored in the BOOTSTRAP Database, which may be accessed by members of the institute and licensees of the method for providing benchmarks and comparative analyses to their clients.

As initiation and continuous support for improvement actions is the prime goal of BOOTSTRAP, a cooperative approach is used in order to characterise and analyse a software organisation or project. In order to get true commitment and support on all levels, the perspectives of management and engineering staff are equally important. Therefore, a typical schedule of a full assessment includes several briefing and debriefing activities as well as a full-day action-planning workshop, as shown in Figure 2.

Main objective of the first steps of an assessment, the briefings, is to agree on the objectives and scope of the assessment and to obtain commitment from both senior and line management as well as engineering staff. During the initial phase, a pre-assessment questionnaire is distributed in order to prepare the interviews and to collect that kind of information that is otherwise not readily available.

Core activity of a BOOTSTRAP assessment is the on-site week. To emphasise the importance of team-oriented processes, group interviews are the central part of this period. For the interviews, two nearly symmetrical questionnaires are used, which take between 3 and 6 hours of time. Between 110 and 150 questions are discussed, which cover all key aspects of the software development process at that level of detail that is needed to determine candidate areas for further improvement and to provide a baseline to be able to demonstrate progress.

Using computer-based tools, a preliminary evaluation is already made on-site, immediately after the interviews. First results are presented and discussed at the end of the on-site week. Results of individual projects are presented only to the project representatives during the debriefings. Beyond this, to a wider audience only aggregated figures are presented and discussed to preserve confidentiality.

Improvement action planning starts immediately after the on-site period with a one-day consolidation and action-planning workshop with the local improvement team in order to ensure full acceptance of the findings and recommendations proposed. The assessment part of the improvement process is formally finished with the delivery of the assessment report and a joint review of the achieved results.

Most organisations appreciate that BOOTSTRAP reduces initial costs and lead-time to a minimum required for establishing a solid baseline for necessary improvement actions and corresponding investments. Participants experience BOOTSTRAP as a motivating exercise and as a real support in order to make improvements really happen and to become a more mature organisation without increasing the amount of paperwork.

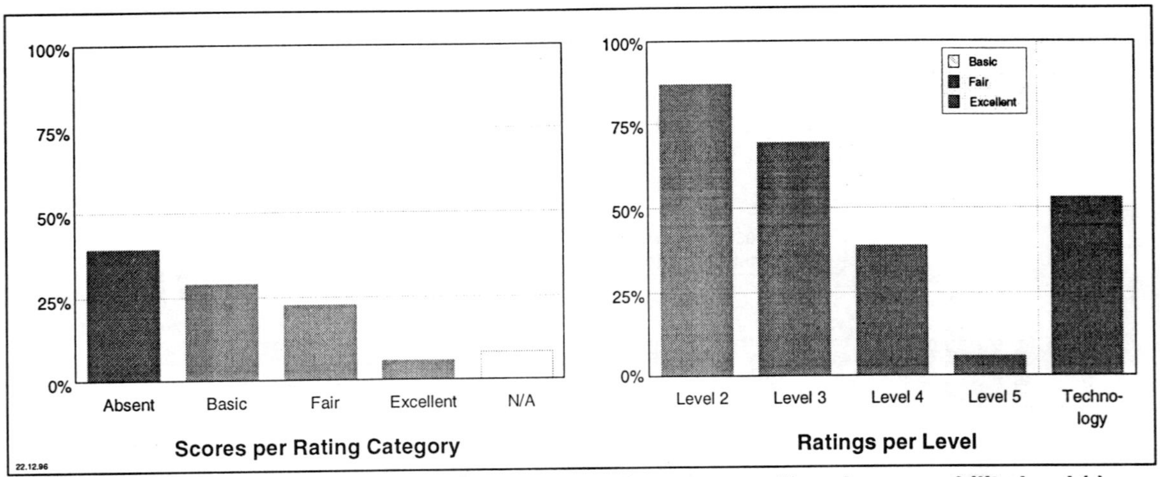

Figure 3: Typical distribution of the scores per rating category (l) and per capability level (r). On the average about 30% of all processes are absent, whereas less than 10% fulfil all criteria. In this case 85% of all level 2 and already 70% of level 3 processes are existent.

5 Rating and Scoring

An important feature is that BOOTSTRAP uses open questions to examine the actual situation and to solicit opinions of the key players that will influence the success of the software improvement activities. By using well designed questionnaires it is guaranteed that no critical points are missed and particular strengths and weaknesses are revealed. A scheme with a fine granularity is applied to judge the relative importance of each aspect.

To achieve a common agreement upon improvement actions by all member of the organisation is rather difficult, as different opinions will occur inevitably. Hence, to generate confidence in the obtained results consistent scoring is vital. The purpose of a scoring mechanism is to reach consensus, so the algorithms for aggregating the large amount of data collected during the interviews must be robust enough to support intuition.

In order to obtain a clear and true picture of current practices responses must be evaluated in several dimensions. BOOTSTRAP uses mainly the following measures:

- Overall process capability,
- Quality profile of the applied processes.

Mere existence of a process doesn't say too much about an organisation's capability to develop quality software within given time and budget constraints. Therefore, BOOTSTRAP requires that existing processes are analysed in detail during the interviews and responses are scored in one of the categories basic, significant or excellent. Whenever the process or activity addressed by a given question is not relevant, that question is said to be not-applicable and, as a consequence, excluded from further evaluation. As shown in Figure 3 (l), in a typical case about 10% of the generic processes that are identified by BOOTSTRAP may be not relevant, but also that nearly 40% of the relevant ones are not practised at all.

With each question BOOTSTRAP assigns a number indicating a distinct capability level. Questions belonging to a particular process area may span several levels. Evaluation of the responses leads to a quantitative assessment of the fulfilment of specific requirements for each level. Figure 3 (r) shows the average existence and quality of the processes for the various levels. The charts provide a first indication, whether effort is spent in a balanced way. It is frequently observed that organisations pay attention to all processes, irrespective of their maturity. The reference model is designed in such a way that mastering the lower level processes is assumed to be a prerequisite for establishing the higher ones. Therefore, it is obvious that

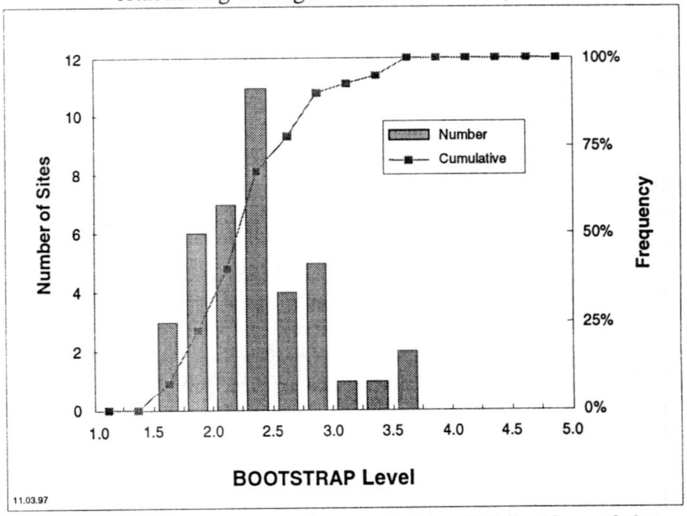

Figure 4: Histogram and cumulative distribution of the observed BOOTSTRAP levels (n=40).

higher values are found on the lower levels, but it is too rigid to expect that all effort is concentrated on practices belong to a particular level, until all criteria for that level are satisfied.

Experience has shown that there may exist good reasons for an organisation to emphasise some processes that belong to the higher levels or to skip some lower level processes. Typical examples are on one hand processes that address quality, i.e. quality management and quality assurance and on the other hand, some of the product design processes. The first is often the case in organisations that concentrate on ISO 9000 certification. The latter is often observed in software development units that produce different kinds of systems. In this case, the responsibility for defining certain engineering activities is delegated to each of the software engineering teams within such a unit. If during the assessment, it was found that this approach works well, responses in the site questionnaire that address particular management concerns belonging to these aspects were set to 'not applicable'. For the matching project questions, the same procedure has been applied. By doing so, criteria associated with these questions were excluded from the computation of the overall BOOTSTRAP rating. This unique feature of BOOTSTRAP permits a fair comparison between individual projects in different application domains or organisational units operating in different business sectors.

6 State of Practice in Software Development

As there is now ample data available from past assessments, it is possible to evaluate typical strengths and weaknesses of the approach. During the last 5 years, SYNSPACE has visited more than 50 sites in Europe, the USA and India. A survey of 40 software development units is presented here. Staff number ranged from 6 to 850. Development units in the industrial sector tend to be smaller than in other areas, i.e. about 60 viz. 120 staff members. The total number of development projects examined amounts to 160.

The population of the participating organisations may not be representative for the software industry in general. Most organisations that performed a BOOTSTRAP Assessment are already aware of the importance of process quality: About half of them were ISO 9001 certified, which is clearly far above the average for the industrial sectors they belong to. In our sample, the public sector is completely absent, although it is estimated that 40% of the total software development effort in Europe is spent here. Even more surprising is that independent software houses are not well represented. Nearly all participants are Product Development or IT Departments, equally distributed over the industrial and the (financial) service sector.

The reduction of all assessment data into one single number is however rather controversial. The scores for each level and each attribute result in real indicators for the performance of an organisation or a particular project. To reduce the large amount of data resulting from an assessment to a single number, it is necessary to associate numeric values with each of the rating categories. BOOTSTRAP uses values ranging from 0 (absent) to 4 (excellent) for this purpose. The ratings for the individual questions are summed up and divided by the maximum rating possible. The overall outcome is then mapped on an equidistant scale ranging from 1 to 5. This scale has been made extremely popular by SEI. At least until the typical strengths and weaknesses are well understood, BOOTSTRAP does not put much emphasis on this number. To track progress a single figure like the overall rating of an organisation or project may be useful.

To get a first impression of the actual situation in software industry, the overall BOOTSTRAP rating of an organisation provides a useful measure. As a continuous scale is used for evaluating the assessment responses, results may be expected of being (approximately) randomly distributed around a mean value. Confirmation can be derived from Figure 4. The overall BOOTSTRAP ratings observed so far range from 1.5 to 3.7, but most organisations end up in the range between 2 and 2.5. Less than 10% of all organisations are found able to achieve level 3.

Several other interesting aspects of how software organisations work can be examined using the BOOTSTRAP database that contains the key data of a large variety of organisations. A frequently asked question for example is whether performance is dependent from the software development unit size. Indeed, from the data presented in Figure 5 a trend towards higher ratings for larger organisations can be observed.

It may be true that in larger organisations project teams are larger, and therefore the supporting processes are more visible. However, this does not imply that productivity is lower under these circumstances. A detailed analysis of our data reveals that in the larger organisations software engineers are working in the same area over a longer time, have more years of practical experience and tend to be higher educated [2]. In our sample also excel-

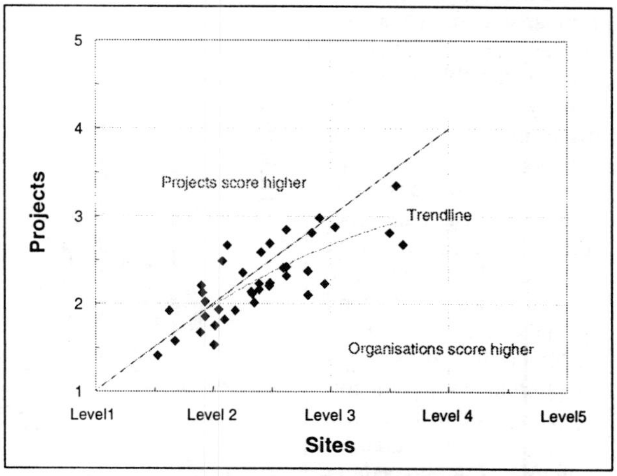

Figure 5: Average project performance vs. management view.

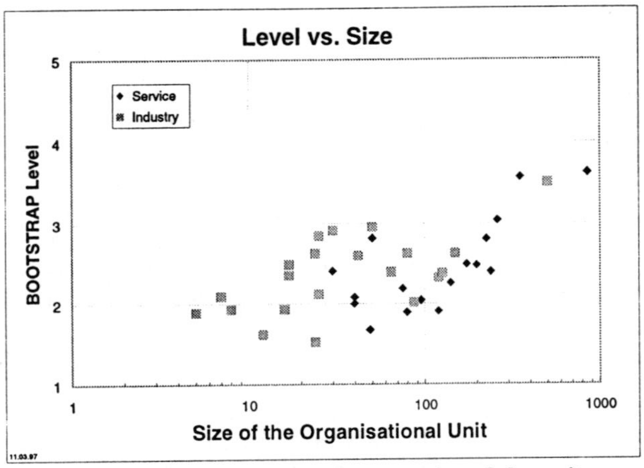

Figure 6: BOOTSTRAP level versus size of the unit.

lent performing small engineering teams are present. Organisational stability, clear customer focus and permanent staff training seem to be the dominant factors for attaining excellent results.

Within most organisations, it can be observed that some individual projects perform far better than one would really expect from the organisational framework. However, above level 2 project averages tend to be lower than may deduced from the global interview, which reflects the opinion of the line management. This trend becomes visible in Figure 6. A general tendency to over-estimate the effectiveness of the software development processes by senior management can be noticed.

Not only the overall BOOTSTRAP rating varies from case to case, it may be expected that the existence and quality of the particular software processes will vary accordingly. The perception of executives and software engineers is often quite different. A comparison of capability profiles as shown in Figure 7 provides a valuable input for objectively raising awareness of that issue. An analysis of the average profiles reveals that most organisations have difficulties in areas, like process description, measurement and control (PrD, PrM and PrC) as well as architectural design and testing, i.e. AD and Te. Also the lack of a proper quality system visibly supported by executive management (QM) is a major source of complaints. QA procedures are accordingly low in most cases. Weaknesses in these areas are frequently compensated (at high costs) by both extensive integration and acceptance testing (AT) as well as by rigorous maintenance and repair procedures for errors reported from the field (OM).

Differences between the overall ratings (sites) and the project averages are more subtile. In most cases they can only be explained by an examination of the responses collected for each particular question.

7 Outlook

Ten years ago, the Software Engineering Institute (SEI) started the development of a software process framework [4]. This framework, later referred to as the Capability Maturity Model (CMM), has become the basis for software process assessment and improvement [11]. According to CMM a software development organisation evolves from an "initial" level to an "optimising" level. For each level a set of key process areas is defined that every organisation must be able to perform, before the next level can be approached. CMM assumes that 80% and in some cases 90% of all processes belonging to the areas associated with that particular level must exist, before capabilities on the higher levels are awarded. This approach has often been criticised.

From Figure 8 (l) it can be observed that indeed most organisations concentrate on level 2 and 3 processes before starting to implement level 4 or even level 5 practices. The interpolated lines indicate that a typical organisation with an overall rating of 2 will perform not only nearly 80% of all level 2 practices, but also already 60% of all level 3 practices and even 20% of the level 4 practi-

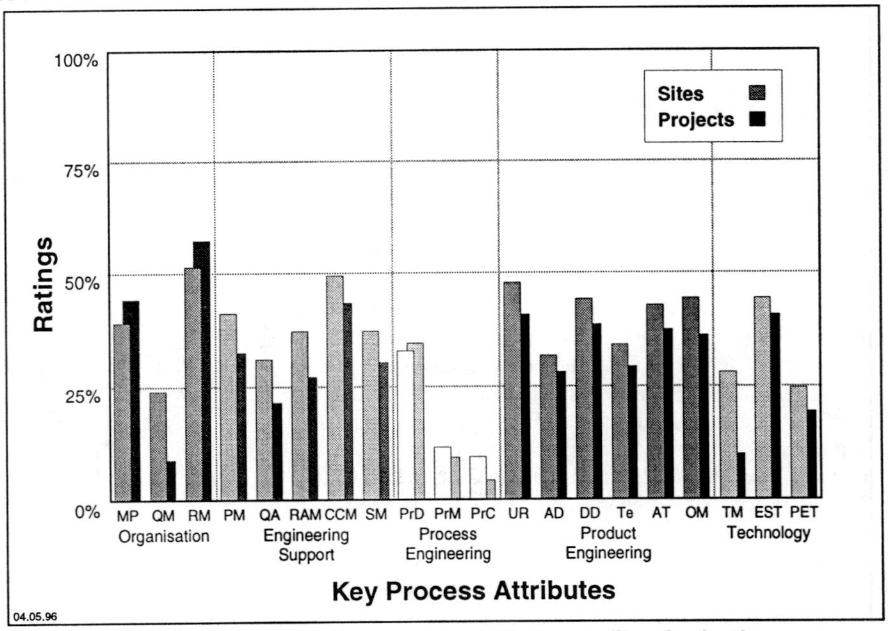

Figure 7: Average BOOTSTRAP attribute profiles for both organisations and individual projects (n=40/166).

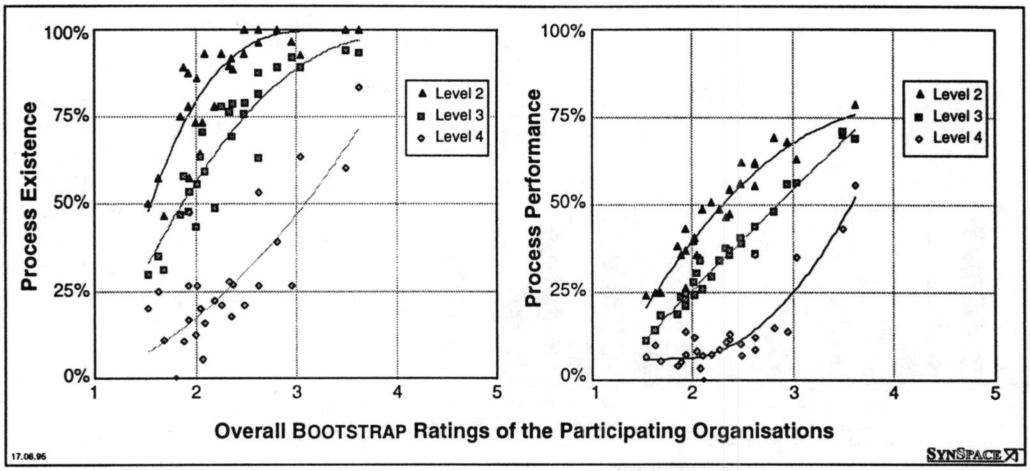

Figure 8: Process existence (l) and quality (r) on the various maturity levels vs. overall BOOTSTRAP rating.

ces. The same trend can be observed for an organisation with an overall rating of 3. On average, such an organisation will perform in some way all basic processes that belong to level 2 and about 80% of the level 3 practices. On that capability level, the importance of level 4 practices is growing fast. Level 5 practices are virtually nonexistent in all but a few organisations. The observations made here are exactly in line with CMM, which assumes for the completion of each level the existence of 80% of the key processes associated with that level. The difference is that BOOTSTRAP doesn't assume that practices belonging to a particular level are concentrated in a few key process areas.

The mere existence of a process is doesn't say too much about the capability of an organisational unit or project team to produce quality software within the given constraints. This is illustrated in the right hand part of Figure 8. It can be observed here that in an organisation with an overall BOOTSTRAP rating of exactly 2 about 80% of the level 2 practices are existent, but merely in a rudimentary form, as only 40% of all level 2 criteria are fulfilled. For level 3 or level 4 practices the differences between process existence and process quality are even more apparent. Both aspects discussed earlier in this section are essential elements of the BOOTSTRAP method. This has been recognised by SPICE.

In 1993, a joint ISO/IEC working group established a project called SPICE, Software Process Improvement and Capability Evaluation [1] aimed at the harmonisation of the various software process assessment methods. SPICE's Baseline Practices Guide currently contains a very detailed framework called Model for Process Management (MPM) which is based on the recent ISO Standard 12207. MPM organises software development activities in 5 process categories, encompassing 35 base practices, each subdivided in 3 to 10 separate activities[1]. For each of the base practices, 6 levels of management practices are defined. With such a comprehensive framework, it is not a straightforward task to develop an assessment method [12].

During the last five years, the BOOTSTRAP assessment instruments are refined several times. From our regular analysis of assessment profiles as shown in Figure 7, it becomes clear that the establishment of a stable software development process within an organisation is equally important as it was 5 years ago when the first version of BOOTSTRAP was developed. However, in some areas questions could be dropped. Nowadays, questions addressing the working environment and the technical infrastructure are no longer relevant, as at least in Europe the conditions improved significantly. Also due to the proliferation of PC-based development the configuration management of both code and design documents is now state-of-practice in most organisations where we have performed an assessment (Figure 7). Attention is shifting to other areas. Mainframe development is the exception now. It is therefore not surprising that organisations frequently signalise that they have serious problems in adopting client-server technology. Applications are no longer developed from scratch but assembled from standard components. Development cycles become shorter and shorter. Establishing good relations with customers and users on one hand and product design on the other hand are a major concern today. Assessment methods have to recognise that.

An assessment is not a goal in itself. The purpose of an assessment is to reveal the software producing capabilities of an organisation and to identify areas for further

1 In SPICE V2.0 which has been submitted recently to the International Standardization Organization as Preliminary Draft Technical Report (PDTR ISO 15 504) the number of base practices has been reduced to 29. The subdivision of the base practices in individual activities are now excluded form the normative part of the standard.

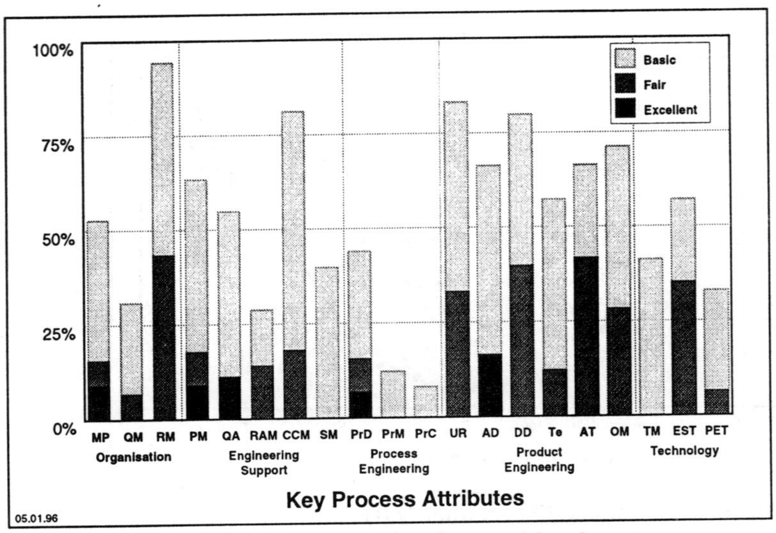

Figure 9: A typical example of a combined process existence and quality profile.

improvement of the processes practised. A major concern must be that an assessment should disturb a software organisation no longer than the bare minimum and only consume a reasonable amount of effort.

Although the SPICE framework is extremely detailed, BOOTSTRAP can be made compliant without loosing its simplicity. A first impression of how a BOOTSTRAP Profile in the near future may look like is given in Figure 9. What is needed in order to meet the requirements of the new ISO Standard, is mainly the addition of some more attributes and a few more specific questions as well as an extension of the rating categories. Also the scoring mechanism should be modified using the slightly different categorisation and evaluation scheme of ISO 15504.

BOOTSTRAP, and originally also CMM to some extent, claim to be suitable for any type of software development. As assessment methods become increasingly sophisticated, this objective is hardly to achieve. BOOTSTRAP allows for that reason to decide that some processes are not applicable. This approach may make sense in organisations that have already established a comprehensive baseline for software process improvement. ISO/SPICE envisages also providing a tailoring procedure in order to reflect the kind of application and the needs of a particular customer. The real challenge for SPICE will be to make assessments results to be comparable and therefore suited for benchmark exercises as BOOTSTRAP is already now.

8 Conclusion

Nearly in all cases, the driving force behind the assessment came either from engineering staff members or from executives responsible for software development. Major reason was the feeling of leading persons that software development processes could be improved, but that it was unclear what kind of activities would be the most promising ones. For a decision, it was felt, an objective picture of the current state was needed.

Another important reason for performing an assessment is ISO 9000. BOOTSTRAP is able to large extent to decide whether a software development unit satisfies the criteria for an ISO 9001 certificate. For many organisations, the BOOTSTRAP assessment was the starting point of an ISO 9000 certification process. But also organisations already certified since several years were visited. As the regular audits required by ISO 9000 frequently failed to address those issues that staff members conceived to be relevant in software engineering practice, users, software engineers and management as well were more or less frustrated. It was expected that a software process assessment would demonstrate that the current situation was not as good or bad as senior management or user departments may think, and that as a result of the BOOTSTRAP assessment resources and funding would be made available by management to improve the situation. Their primary motivation was to better define appropriate actions for further improvement efforts.

9 References

[1] A. Dorling. Software Process Improvement and Capability Determination, *Software Quality Journal*, Vol. 2, Nr. 4, pp. 209-224, 1993.

[2] F. Engelmann, W. Schynoll, H. Stienen. BOOTSTRAP Software Process Assessment - Experiences and Further Developments, *Proc. SafeComp '95*, Belgirate, Italy, 1995.

[3] C. Hakes. The Corporate Self-Assessment Handbook. *Chapman & Hall*, 2nd ed., London, 1995.

[4] W. D. Humphrey. Managing the Software Process, *Addison Wesley*, New York, 1989.

[5] International Organization for Standardization. *ISO/IEC 12 207 Information Technology - Software Life Cycle*, Processes. Genève, 1995.

[6] G.R. Koch. Process Assessment: the BOOTSTRAP Approach, *Information and Software Technology,* Vol. 35, Nr. 6/7, pp. 387-403, 1993.

[7] G.R. Koch. Quality Improvement as a Multicultural Challenge - The European View, *First World Congress of Software Quality*, San Francisco, June, 1995.

[8] P. Kuvaja et. al. BOOTSTRAP: Europe's assessment method, *IEEE Software*, Vol. 10, Nr. 3, pp. 93-95, 1993.

[9] P. Kuvaja et. al. Software Process Assessment & Improvement - The BOOTSTRAP Approach, *Blackwell*, 1994.

[10] M. Paulk, B. Curtis, M. Crissis, C. Weber. Capability Maturity Model for Software, Version 1.1, Technical Report CMU/SEI-93-TR-24, Software Engineering Institute, Pittsburgh, Febr. 1993.

[11] M. Paulk et. al. The Capability Maturity Model - Guidelines for Improving the Software Process, *Addison Wesley*, New York 1995.

[12] M. Paulk, M. Conrad, S. Garcia. CMM versus Spice architectures, *IEEE Software Process Newsletter*, Nr. 3, pp. 7 – 11, 1995.

[13] R. Stevens. Creating Software the Right Way. *Byte*, pp. 31 – 38, Aug. 1991.

Session P4d

Software Engineering Education

Systems Development with Java: Experiences from a Practical Project Course in Software Engineering*

Klaus Bergner
Technische Universität München,
Institut für Informatik,
D-80290 München, Germany
bergner@informatik.tu-muenchen.de

Franz Huber
Technische Universität München,
Institut für Informatik,
D-80290 München, Germany
huberf@informatik.tu-muenchen.de

Abstract

This paper describes our experiences in using the Java programming language in a student software engineering project. We focus on the suitability of Java for developing large-scale software systems in teams, and on the tools and techniques used for design and implementation. Furthermore, we comment on the significance of our experiences for future educational software engineering projects as well as for industrial projects.

1. Introduction

Developing large software systems in teams is a skill best learnt by practical experience. In order to make this experience available to our students at the informatics department of Technische Universität München, we have been giving practical project courses in software engineering for three years. Each of these courses comprised a complete software development project and was intended to deliver a usable software product to a customer at the end of the project. The time available for the students to realize the project was one semester (three months).

This paper summarizes the experiences gained in the 1996 summer term, during which we developed a CASE tool for distributed systems engineering with a team of 14 students. Aside from organizational issues we will put special emphasis on how the concepts of our implementation platform, the Java [7] programming language and its libraries, work together with standard object-oriented software engineering techniques.

We think that most of our experiences from this course are of interest not only for other university projects, but for industrial software development as well.

*This work was partly carried out within the Subproject A6 of the "Sonderforschungsbereich 342" and the Project SysLab, sponsored by the German Research Community (DFG) under the Leibniz program and by Siemens-Nixdorf.

2. The Project – Goals, Results, Future Work

2.1. The Goal: A Tool for the FOCUS Method

The goal of the project was to develop AUTOFOCUS, a working prototype of a CASE tool for distributed systems engineering, comprising graphical editors for the different views of a system. The description formalisms for these views are embedded in the semantical framework of FOCUS [5], a formal development method for distributed systems. FOCUS is based on a mathematical foundation using semantical concepts like stream processing functions [4] to describe the components of a system. It provides precise mechanisms for refining system specifications, enabling a developer to prove the correctness of development steps. The concept of AUTOFOCUS is described in detail in [11] and [10]. Its description formalisms, for which appropriate editors had to be implemented, are

- system structure diagrams (SSDs), which describe the static structure of a system by a network of interconnected components exchanging messages over channels,
- state transition diagrams (STDs, or automata) to describe the behaviour of system components, and
- extended event traces (EETs, basically a subset of Message Sequence Charts as standardized in ITU Z.120 [12]) used to specify exemplary system runs.

It should be obvious that a tool that complex can hardly be implemented entirely in an educational course during a period of three months. Therefore, it was the goal of the course to act as a starting point for the whole project and to implement the basic components of the tool.

0-8186-7840-2/97 $10.00 © 1997 IEEE

2.2. Project Results

2.2.1. Tool Prototype

The main result of the project course is a working prototype of AUTOFOCUS. As can be seen from the architectural

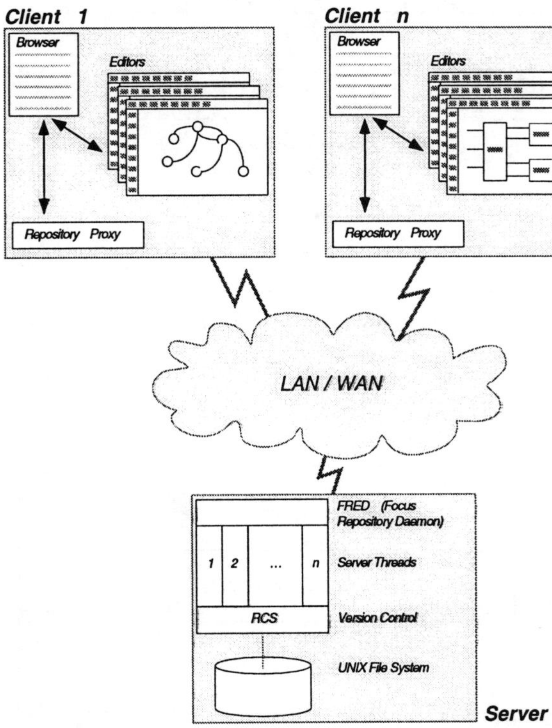

Figure 1. Architectural View of the Current AUTOFOCUS Implementation

view in figure 1, AUTOFOCUS is a typical client/server application with a central repository where all development documents are stored. An arbitrary number of clients can connect to the repository over a network using TCP/IP-based sockets. Within the server process, a dedicated thread is running for each client. The repository is currently document-based, mapping development documents to files on a UNIX file system. Access and version control is provided by the UNIX revision control system RCS [3].

The AUTOFOCUS client contains a project browser used to navigate through the development projects and documents in the repository, and three graphical editors necessary to edit the different diagram types. Both the clients and the server, which encapsulates the RCS system, are completely implemented in Java.

To provide an impression of the current status of AUTOFOCUS, a screen hard-copy of some parts of the client application is shown in figure 2.

2.2.2. Documentation

Besides the tool prototype, a set of documents has been produced in the project: the system specification document [20], the system design document [19], and class design documents (the latter suffered from the time pressure in the final stages of the project and must still be completed), as well as a user's guide for the AUTOFOCUS tool, from which an HTML online help was generated.

2.2.3. Statistics

The results just outlined were achieved by a group of 14 students within three months, with one and a half months used for implementation. The whole project thus spans 42 person months with implementation consuming 21 person months. The documents produced in the project comprise roughly 100 pages, not including the partially incomplete class design documents. The current size of the AUTOFOCUS prototype is around 32 kLoC (900 kByte) written entirely in Java.

2.3. Further Development

Based on the current status, we are planning a series of further development activities that will mostly be carried out in student projects.

Currently, AUTOFOCUS is re-designed, mainly because of two reasons: First, all user interface parts will be reworked to fit into the new version 1.1 API [24] of Java, and second, there is some amount of "runaway code" which has been implemented in the final stages of the project under heavy time pressure and is thus not very well structured and documented.

Although AUTOFOCUS can be used for real work in its current state, most of its potential as a tool based on formal foundations has not been realized yet. Extensions of AUTOFOCUS to be implemented are

- consistency checks for all documents in a development project,
- interfaces to external verification tools, like model checkers and theorem provers,
- simulation, and
- code generation.

While the consistency checks are based on the well-defined abstract syntax and context conditions of the AUTOFOCUS description techniques, the latter three extensions build upon the formal semantics defined for them.

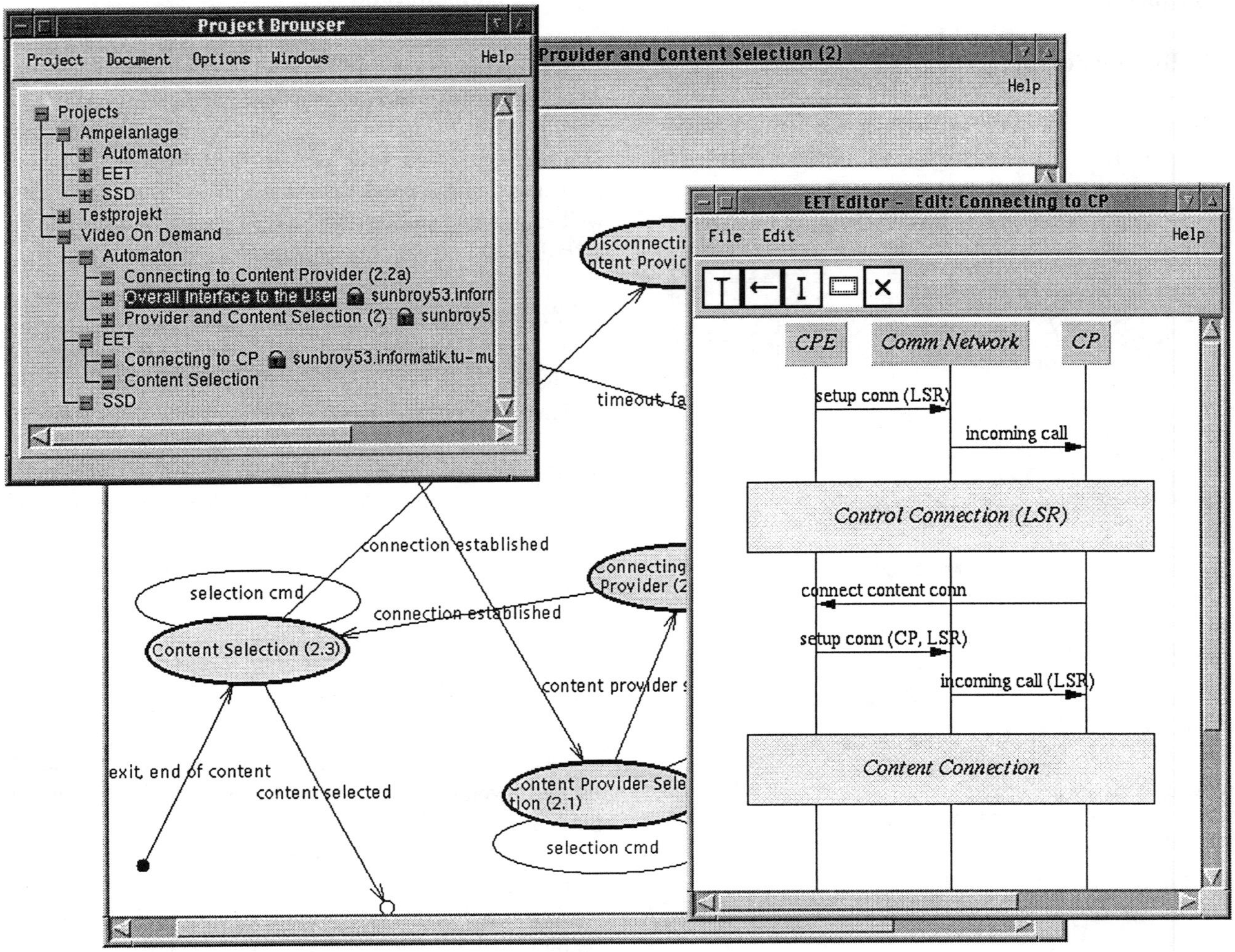

Figure 2. Project Browser, STD Editor, and EET Editor of the AutoFocus Client

3. Project Organization

As in the former runs, we tried to keep the course as close as possible to a real industry project [1, 2]. The announcement of the course, published in our local university news groups and web pages, was for instance formulated like typical job offerings found in newspapers. After the registration we ran application interviews with the students in order to assign them to developer teams according to their interests and their knowledge in specific areas.

However, a number of circumstances usually found in industry projects could not completely be reproduced in our course. In contrast to "reality", where requirements of a new system are often unclear and keep changing even during the actual development process, the requirements for our tool were clearly stated at the beginning of the course, following a few months of conceptual work by the tutors. Furthermore, our student developer team was mostly unexperienced in software engineering issues, and many of them as well in object-orientation. We tried to alleviate this problem by extensive training during the first weeks of the course (two sessions per week, which were later used for project meetings). Probably the biggest difference to industry projects was our decision to base the development of a new software product on a technology, namely the Java platform, that was completely new for us and not yet evaluated.

The latter two issues were not felt as drawbacks compared to real-world development because they made the project situation even more challenging for our participants.

3.1. Developer Teams

The architectural view of the AutoFocus tool depicted in figure 1 already implies a coarse modularization into the following subsystems:

- a central repository,
- a set of graphical editors for
  - extended event traces and
  - system structure diagrams and state transition diagrams, both of which are basically editors for binary graphs and thus similar to implement,
- a central component on the client side coordinating the editors and providing a graphical interface to organize the documents in the repository.

In order to achieve a consistent internal data representation for all development documents, the actual data in the documents were kept separate from the editors and grouped together in an own module, following the Model-View-Controller paradigm [13]. The resulting five subsystems were each implemented by a team of two to three students.

3.2. Development Process

The development process we followed in the course was influenced by Denert [6] and had furthermore grown out of the experiences of the former two runs of the course. Our recommendations in that respect are summarized in [2].

We spent two weeks on system specification, three weeks on system design, six weeks on implementation, and two weeks on test and integration. Each phase was concluded by a milestone with a set of deliverables. Following each milestone, reviews were held for quality assurance.

We intended to make extensive use of prototyping, especially for the user interface parts of AUTOFOCUS, where we planned to use an evolutionary GUI prototype as a foundation for the final user interface of the system. Due to the poor quality of the user interface builders available for Java at that time (see also section 5), this was not possible; instead we started coding the user interface classes directly in Java very early.

4. Experiences

The reasons we chose Java as development language for AUTOFOCUS arose from former experiences with C++ and `itcl` [14], which were used in the first two runs of the course. Each of these languages had its deficiencies: C++ suffered from long turnaround times, the complexity of the language, and the necessity to manage storage by hand. Furthermore, the C++ implementations available to us suffered from the absence of easily usable, stable, and portable libraries and did not support important features of the language, like exception handling. `itcl`, an object-oriented variant of the `tcl` scripting language, did not have most of these drawbacks, but the language is, especially for teaching purposes, not very elegant, has no strong typing, and the programs run very slowly.

Java seemed to incorporate the virtues of both of these languages, avoiding their disadvantages. Another reason to choose Java was that the novelty, and the attention it was gaining in the media made it an interesting and appealing language for attracting interested students for the practical course.

In the following, we will examine whether Java could fulfill our expectations and also how well it supported the design process and the transition from analysis to design.

4.1. The Java Platform

In the whole, Java could be easily learnt by the students of our course, most of which had experience with C, but were not familiar with object-oriented languages. This experience differs from the one with C++ in the first course, where it took a long time before the students could master more than a basic set of features. Surprisingly, with Java the transition seemed easier because here it is hard to write "non-object-oriented" programs and developers are forced to change their habits quite radically.

4.1.1. Safe Execution Environment

We think that Java's safe execution environment and automatic garbage collection saved a lot of time because it considerably reduced the number of errors compared to our first project. In addition, most of the bugs were relatively harmless, and finding and fixing them did not need much time: Many bugs in our bug list were fixed by the responsible developers the day they were reported. The only "hard" bug during the course, taking nearly one week to find and fix, was caused by a bug in the standard `InputStream` class, whose objects were sometimes corrupted when the server's load was high. In contrast, the C++ project in the first course suffered from sporadic memory corruption errors which in rare cases needed weeks to hunt down.

4.1.2. Platform Independence

The platform independence of Java could only partly fulfill its expectations: In principle, the code (which we developed under Solaris) could be run on other platforms. However, there were some serious deficiencies and numerous small inconsistencies, mainly concerning the user interface area. Currently, we have verified the versions for Solaris, Linux and HP-UX 10, whereas it is not possible to run the AUTOFOCUS client on HP-UX 9, Microsoft Windows, or MacOS due to bugs of the AWT implementation. In the case of Windows, there exist some "standard" workarounds [26, 21] to fix the problem (modal dialogs do not suspend the execution of the calling method), but since they all deteriorate the structure of the code, we chose not to implement them, but to wait for SUN fixing the problem instead.

4.1.3. Performance

In spite of these negative experiences, we were satisfied with the speed of the resulting code. Although the tool in its present form has serious drawbacks with respect to its performance, they are mostly due to the use of RCS as repository: For most actions involving the repository, a new process has to be scheduled on the server and a file has to be read, parsed and transmitted over the network. Actions concerning only the client side are surprisingly fast, even when they impose interactive repositioning of some graphical elements and redrawing the screen of an editor. The precaution measure to provide two modes of moving graphical objects with the mouse, one with instant diagram update during the move, one with update only at the end of the move, is hardly necessary even for larger documents.

4.1.4. Single Inheritance

Compared to C++, Java supports only single inheritance, but additionally offers so-called interfaces. This was not felt as a deficiency: The syntactical elements of FOCUS' description techniques could be (meta-)modeled as Java classes in a natural way. Single inheritance was used only for factoring out graphical information common to some elements. For example, the `Edge` class is used as a base class both for channels in SSDs and for transitions in STDs. Interfaces were rarely used: Only three were introduced overall, and two of these are only repositories for system constants and have no methods. The remaining "real" interface `TreeNode` captures the common functionality of the different entries (like projects or documents) in the project browser.

In some cases, the standard interfaces provided by the Java framework were implemented: `Runnable` was used to create runnable menu commands, and `Observer` was used for realizing the update mechanism between the clients and the server. We suspect that during the redesign of AUTOFOCUS, interfaces will be used more often because we expect that more features common to some classes can be factored out.

4.1.5. Lack of Parametric Types

Java's lack of parametric types was first felt as a serious drawback by us because it requires the use of dynamic casts at runtime, especially when using the powerful container classes of the `util` package, and therefore adversely affects the type safety of the system. At some time during the course we thought about solving this problem via a simple, macro-based template mechanism based on the substitution of a type parameter with an actual type, similar to the heterogeneous translation scheme proposed in the Pizza approach [15]. In the end, we did not choose this solution because it would have required the reworking of the already implemented uses of container classes. Furthermore, the students did not have any difficulties with it and there were hardly any `ClassCastException` runtime exceptions. One explanation for this is that most such casts follow a certain pattern and concern closely related methods in the same class: For example, the "standard" implementation of a 1-to-many association between classes `Foo` and `Bar` uses the `Vector` class and involves a `private Vector barElems` attribute in class `Foo` and `Foo` methods `void addBarElem(Bar)`, `void removeBarElem(Bar)`, and `Enumeration barElems()`. This way, care has to be taken only when iterating over the `Bar` elements because the enumeration provides no explicit type information about its elements.

4.1.6. Exception Handling

The exception handling concept of Java proved to be valuable, especially with respect to evolutionary prototyping. We were able to implement a first prototype that lacked most of the exception handling and could handle only the "easy" standard cases. Later on, when the design was stabilized, the code for exception handling could be added with relatively few problems.

4.1.7. Package Mechanism

The package mechanism was very useful because it made it possible to clearly structure the code following the responsibilities of the developer teams. We provided one package per team (and therefore also per subsystem, see section 2.2) and an additional utility package for code usable for all teams. The package mechanism and the visibility modifiers were quickly understood by the students and they used them as intended to hide their internal classes from the other teams to provide shallow and comprehensible interfaces. This approach may, however, lead to multiple implementations of similar functionality, worsened by the lack of some basic functionality in the standard libraries: At one time in the project, two teams each built their own simple dialog class, thus performing unnecessary work and compromising the uniformity of user interaction. Later on, this functionality was integrated into our `util` package. We recommend the installation of a person or team responsible for identifying, factoring out, and implementing possible `util` classes.

Another difficulty with packages is the lack of a tool for re-working their structure: If it is necessary to move classes between packages (or even to move whole packages), much manual editing is needed because all classes importing the class (or package) have to be changed.

4.1.8. Libraries

As mentioned above, one of the main reasons to use Java was the presence of a library of standardized and easy to use classes. To build a distributed CASE tool like AUTOFOCUS, libraries for concurrency, network, GUI, and graphics programming are indispensable. Apart from minor flaws, the functionality provided by the Java libraries was sufficient for our project in most areas. However, we were missing some basic functionalities in the area of GUI programming. Programming simple dialogs, toolbars, scrollable panels, and print support did consume much time during the course, and the migration to standard classes in new releases of the Java libraries will also consume much time in the future.

Two very useful facilities were not available in the standard libraries at the time of the course: For the communication and the transmission of commands between the clients and the server one team had to invent special, simple versions of features that will be contained in the "Remote Method Invocation" and "Object Serialization" standards of the next release of the JDK [25]. Although that was not particularly difficult given the standard libraries, it did cost quite some effort.

Another feature we were missing was the lack of powerful mechanisms for managing persistent storages. Our decision to use RCS with a flat file representation of the respective documents was very adequate for the repository of the prototype, since we got the sophisticated locking and revision control facilities of RCS "for free". The granularity level of a repository document, however, is too coarse for some of the planned extensions of AUTOFOCUS. Given our present design, complex queries like, e.g., "return all channels on which a message with a certain datatype can be transferred" involve the transfer of all documents from the repository server to the client. This is not acceptable, especially given the poor performance of the Java-RCS-connection, which requires the creation of a new server process for each repository action. We think that upcoming approaches like Java APIs for object-oriented databases [16] or orthogonal persistency [27] will fulfill our needs in the future.

4.2. Analysis and Design Techniques and Java

4.2.1. Analysis and Design Techniques

Due to the strict schedule of the course, the most important requirement for analysis and design techniques was ease of use. Some techniques turned out to be very useful and were well accepted by the participants: Among the notations provided by the Object Modeling Technique (OMT, [18]), we mainly used class diagrams to develop a first meta-model of the AUTOFOCUS description formalisms. This supported the participants in gaining insight into how the concepts of these formalisms work together and thus served to establish a level of common understanding among the participants. The meta-model was subsequently refined and could be translated almost without structural changes into Java (see also sections 4.1.4 and 4.1.5).

The lack of useful GUI prototyping tools for Java (see section 5) forced us to apply "handmade" rapid prototyping: To describe user interface behaviour at an abstract level, we used automata similar to the interaction diagrams from [6] together with mock-up "screen shots" that were produced using standard drawing software. Data and control flow between the different subsystems of AUTOFOCUS were specified at a high level using a notation similar to OMT's data flow diagrams.

4.2.2. Design Patterns

Design patterns played an important role during the development of AUTOFOCUS. Apart from their advantages for educational purpose [2], their knowledge (especially of those from [9]) is very helpful in understanding the architecture of the Java libraries because they were designed using a pattern approach (an overview over some of the patterns built into the AWT framework is given in [8]). In some cases, the Java libraries go one step further and provide explicit support for special patterns, thus turning an "immaterial" pattern into a standard framework mechanism. This is, e.g., the case for the `Observer` pattern from [9].

For our system, the `State` pattern from [9] turned out to be the most important one. We used it to create a `Behavior` class representing the actual mode of a graphical editor, and containing methods to handle user events like `singleClick` and `mouseDrag`. Special subclasses — like `ViewOnlyBehavior` and `SetChannelBehavior` — override them to provide a behavior according to the current mode of the editor, which can be selected via the toolbar. During the run of the AUTOFOCUS client, all reactions on events arising inside the canvas of an editor are performed by its actual `Behavior` object.

The `State` pattern was particularly useful because it allowed to clearly separate GUI-related code from the code responsible for handling user events, a concept not directly supported by the standard event handling mechanisms of the first version of AWT [22]. The new version 1.1 [24] provides an improved mechanism based on the delegation of events to special `EventListener` objects. This fits very well to our approach (a possibility is to make `Behavior` an implementation of the `EventListener` interface) and will make the transition to the new API smooth. Furthermore, the separation of the code for the different modes of the editors made it easy to develop the editors step by step, using evolutionary prototyping.

5. Tools

Although the tools provided by Sun's Java Developer's Kit [23] make up just a very basic set of development tools, they proved to be sufficient for the development of AUTOFOCUS. Among the tools we found missing, the most important ones were a graphical, windowed debugger, a tool for managing and visualizing the inheritance and association structures of the classes and packages, and a decent GUI development tool. We hope that the upcoming integrated development environments will fulfill our needs in this respect.

Our experience with the JFactory GUI Builder V1.0 for Solaris [17], which we wanted to use for building an evolutionary prototype of the user interface, was less satisfactory: We could not use the generated code because it did not fit very well into the code structure of our project, the screen layout during the design sometimes did not match the screen layout of the generated programs, there were some serious flaws with respect to multi-user capability, and the tool crashed frequently. Therefore, we stopped using it for evolutionary as well as for explorative prototyping (see also section 4.2.1) very early in the development process. In the current JFactory version V1.1, however, some of these flaws were fixed.

Fortunately, the lack of a decent GUI builder was not a critical point because only a relatively small fraction of the program would have benefited from such a tool: Most of the code concerning the user interface went into the implementation of the editor behaviors and the custom components (like the toolbar and the tree browser). A GUI builder is not useful at all here. However, some of the AUTOFOCUS dialogs are not very appealing because optimizing the look of a "hand-crafted" GUI is very tedious and consumes too much time, especially given the poor infrastructure of the current AWT version.

6. Conclusion

To summarize our experiences gained in the project course, we can clearly state that Java is indeed more than an applet-only programming language. Despite its current deficiencies, which are, in our view, mostly problems of the current implementations, Java turned out to be a viable platform for implementing large and complex real-world applications. Compared to C++, it offers essentially greater ease of use, making it especially suitable for educational programming projects.

References

[1] W. Bartsch, K. Bergner, R. Hettler, and B. Paech. Studenten Entwickeln Universelles Hochschulinformationssystem: Erfahrungen aus einem Softwaretechnik-Praktikum. In *SEUH '95, Report 44 of the German Chapter of the ACM*. Teubner-Verlag, 1995.

[2] K. Bergner. Under pressure – recommendations for managing a practical course in software engineering. In *Proceedings of Software Engineering: Education & Practice (SE:E&P'96)*. ACM Press, 1996.

[3] D. Bolinger and T. Bronson. *Applying RCS and SCCS: From Source Control to Project Control*. O'Reilly & Associates, Inc., 1995.

[4] M. Broy. Functional specification of time sensitive communicating systems. In M. Broy, editor, *Programming and Mathematical Models*. Springer, 1992. NATO ASI Series F: Computer and Systems Science, Vol.88.

[5] M. Broy, F. Dederichs, C. Dendorfer, M. Fuchs, T. Gritzner, and R. Weber. The design of distributed systems - an introduction to FOCUS. TUM-I 9202-2, Technische Universität München, 1993.

[6] E. Denert. *Software-Engeneering*. Springer, 1991.

[7] D. Flanagan. *Java in a Nutshell: A Desktop Quick Reference for Java Programmers*. O'Reilly & Associates, Inc., 1996.

[8] E. Gamma. Java und Design Patterns – Eine vielversprechende Kombination. *Java Spektrum*, pages 18–24, September/October 1996.

[9] E. Gamma, R. Helm, R. Johnson, and J. Vlissides. *Design Patterns: Micro-Architectures for Reusable Object-Oriented Design*. Addison-Wesley, 1994.

[10] F. Huber, B. Schätz, A. Schmidt, and K. Spies. AutoFocus – A Tool for Distributed Systems Specification . In J. P. Bengt Jonsson, editor, *Proceedings FTRTFT'96 – Formal Techniques in Real-Time and Fault-Tolerant Systems*, pages 467–470. LNCS 1135, Springer Verlag, 1996.

[11] F. Huber, B. Schätz, and K. Spies. AutoFocus – Ein Werkzeugkonzept zur Beschreibung verteilter Systeme . In U. H. H. Hermanns, editor, *Formale Beschreibungstechniken für verteilte Systeme*, pages 165–174. Universität Erlangen-Nürnberg, 1996. Erschienen in: Arbeitsberichte des Insituts für mathematische Maschinen und Datenverarbeitung, Bd.29, Nr. 9.

[12] International Telecommunication Union, Geneva. *Message Sequence Charts*, 1996. ITU-T Recommendation Z.120.

[13] G. E. Krasner and S. T. Pope. A cookbook for using the Model-View-Controller user interface paradigm in Smalltalk-80. *Journal of Object-Oriented Programming*, 1(3):26–49, August/September 1988.

[14] M. J. McLennan. [incr Tcl] — *Object-Oriented Programming in Tcl*. AT&T Bell Laboratories, 1247 Cedar Crest Boulevard, Allentown, PA 18103 (USA), 1993.

[15] M. Odersky and P. Wadler. Pizza into Java: Translating theory into practice. In *Proceedings of the 24th ACM Symposium on Principles of Programming Languages*, January 1997.

[16] Poet Software. Poet Homepage, 1996. `http://www.poet.com`.

[17] Rogue Wave Software, Inc., 850 SW 35th St., Corvallis, OR 97333 USA. *JFactory – The Visual Interface Builder for Java*, 1996. http://www.roguewave.com/products/jfactory/jfactory.html.

[18] J. Rumbaugh, M. Blaha, W. Premerlani, F. Eddy, and W. Lorensen. *Object-Oriented Modeling and Design*. Prentice-Hall International Inc., 1991.

[19] STP-96 Team. AutoFocus Systementwurf Version 2.1, 1996. http://autofocus.informatik.tu-muenchen.de/Results/systementwurf21.ps.gz.

[20] STP-96 Team. AutoFocus Systemspezifikation Version 2.0, 1996. http://autofocus.informatik.tu-muenchen.de/Results/systemspez20.ps.gz.

[21] SUN Microsystems, 2550 Garcia Ave., Mountain View, CA 94043-1100 USA. *AWT Modal Dialog Blocking Bug & Workaround*, 1996. http://java.sun.com/products/JDK/1.0.2/AWTModalBug.html.

[22] SUN Microsystems, 2550 Garcia Ave., Mountain View, CA 94043-1100 USA. *Java AWT: Delegation Event Model*, 1996. http://java.sun.com/products/JDK/1.1/designspecs/awt/events.html.

[23] SUN Microsystems, 2550 Garcia Ave., Mountain View, CA 94043-1100 USA. *The Java Developer's Kit, Version 1.0.2*, 1996. http://java.sun.com/products/JDK/1.0.2/.

[24] SUN Microsystems, 2550 Garcia Ave., Mountain View, CA 94043-1100 USA. *JDK 1.1 Preview*, 1996. http://java.sun.com/products/JDK/1.1/designspecs/index.html.

[25] SUN Microsystems, Inc., 2550 Garcia Ave., Mountain View, CA 94043-1100 USA. *Java Distributed Systems*, 1996. http://chatsubo.javasoft.com/current/.

[26] T. Tempelmann. Modaldialogs.java, 1996. http://www.muc.de/~tt/java/ModalDialogs.java.

[27] University of Glasgow, Department of Computer Science. *PJava – The Persistent Java Project*, 1996. http://www.dcs.gla.ac.uk/pjava/.

A Course in Software Engineering and Project Management at University Level for Industrial Needs

Some Reliable Results after Ten Years of Experiences

Stefan Biffl, G. Thomas
Vienna University of Technology, Department of Software Engineering, Vienna, Austria
Stefan.Biffl@tuwien.ac.at

Abstract

This paper reports on the structure of a two-semester workshop accompanied by lectures on software engineering (SE) methods and on major issues in project management (PM). The course is taught to 300 students per year as part of a master degree curriculum in Computer Science (CS). During the last ten years the technical content of the course as well as structure, style and schedule have been reviewed regularly in order to achieve a high degree of practical effectiveness.

Form and contents of the software engineering labs are described. Teaching project management in parallel with experiencing PM in team-work is presented as a major factor in tayloring SE education towards practical needs. The authors' experiences in SE consulting and project management in industrial practice have gradually tuned the course design towards the following priorities.

C1: Caution with 'latest' methods. C2: Caution with (brand-)new tools. F1: Focus on (experiencing) roles in SE teams. F2: Focus on work organization on team-level. F3: Focus on work organization of the team members on the individual level. F4: Focus on rigid selection of team supervisors.

Keywords: *Software Engineering Education, Experience Report, Workshop Design, Project Management, Teamwork, Roles, Reviews.*

1. Introduction

University teachers regard the statement 'At least 80% of knowledge in software engineering is in practice, the rest in academia' as rather uncomfortable. The reason behind this is a low priority on real industrial project experience during the process of faculty member selection. The risk of this strategy concerning the theme at hand is an educational establishment, which, while meeting the standards of scientific correctness, does not meet the actual problems of software engineering (SE) in practice in a consistent way (see [6], [14]).

During several industrial consulting SE projects and a few 'in charge' SE development experiences the authors of this article have gradually tuned the priorities of their educational responsibility from a rather classical focus on state-of-the-art SE methodology as well as a mapping of actual scientific standards towards the needs of industrial projects groups (see [3], [9], [12]). These needs have been experienced personally and they have been reported by professionals in numerous talks and discussions. According to our empirical investigations actual requirements in practice for software engineers coming freshly from university are:

1. Fair knowledge of *state-of-the-art technology* in hardware and in operating systems.
2. Fair knowledge in *theoretical background* of computer science (CS).
3. Ability to understand new *methods and tools* supporting these methods within a fair time (e.g. four to six weeks).
4. Above average familiarity with the *current major paradigms* of SE and information technology (today e.g. object-orientation, Java, NT, SQL; ten years ago e.g. SADT, Pascal, UNIX, DOS, index-sequential files).
5. Understanding of the whole *process* of software engineering from analysis to maintenance, including quality assurance and project management.
6. The ability and modesty to *do any job within that process*, even though its outside image is not high (e.g. maintenance).
7. The ability and modesty to *do any job within the team* by understanding the own role as well as the role of other team members, while respecting their responsibilities.
8. Understanding and respecting the *value of actual project experience* of senior software engineers and project managers, while seeing their own knowledge of state-of-the-art tools and methods in a realistic context.

The skills described in the first four items of the above list are covered by other courses within a mainstream CS curriculum (see [7], [13]). Or, these skills are typical for the special social group 'CS students', as they usually love experimenting with new tools. Therefore the achievement of these skills need not be considered as a primary guideline for the design of a SE course.

The last three of the above requirements may seem to be pure personality factors, which can not be influenced in the educational framework at universities. This is not necessarily so. According to our experiences the underlying metaphor on the theme 'What software engineering is about' contributes largely to the personal attitudes team members actually bring out. Whether the mental metaphor for a SE project is that of rather routine engineering team work or that of a rather adventurous enterprise for heroes is a central message to the students and should be chosen carefully rather than occur by accident. The project metaphor 'in this course we will be the first landing on Mars' may sound much more attractive and motivating than 'let's build a house where four families can live comfortably', but SE projects in practice tend to follow much more the second line.

2. Priorities for a SE course

The following list of priorities for a SE course is the outcome of a regular review process of matching practicioners' needs to the results of the course.

C1) Caution with 'latest' methods. It is important for participants to learn at least one representative method for each of the main activities in SE, so they can understand its use and value within a project and within the whole SE process. There is no need to introduce recent scientific suggestions too quickly. This actually will cause a lot of logistic risks for the stability of the course. E.g. introducing object-oriented methods before 1991 would not have been of use with respect to practical SE needs.

C2) Caution with (brand-)new tools. Participants are not to waste too much time on understanding development tools, as this is not the main focus of serious SE education. However it is important to understand the use and value of tools within a SE project and the SE process. While tools should be simple and effective, they should not be too outdated, as the personal satisfaction of participants correlates strongly with the look and feel of their final product. Just like in industrial environments participants must be protected from being misused as second level test people for new development environments. Moreover the use of tools widespread in industry contributes to the market value of the participants.

F1) Focus on roles in SE teams. Understanding the different tasks during a full SE process is a necessary condition for a serious SE workshop. Apart from the functionally natural grouping along the phases of the SE process (analysis, design, coding, test and integration, maintenance) grouping tasks and activities around specific roles for team members has turned out to be one of the most effective means of teaching and learning SE. Understanding the model of a certain role – like programmer, designer, tester, administrator, QA-specialist, project coordinator – within a SE team creates personal identification, well-defined responsibilities in the team, and matches the requirements 5 to 8 listed in the introduction.

F2) Focus on work organization on team-level. Young software engineers by nature are keen on engineering products and thrive on the satisfaction derived from being able to create new products. Nevertheless CS students are used to working alone in technical problem solving, while group work is often rather alien to them. In addition to telling participants that group work is important, we have included a variety of simple group shaping tasks right from the beginning of the workshop. The solution of these tasks includes the sharing of documents and providing services for each other which over time creates mutual respect and a feeling for the team as a new entity.

F3) Focus on work organization of the team members on individual level. While discussing behavior in a group as well as its to-do's and don'ts can be a novel personal experience for students, problems in actual work arise from the fact that CS students often lack essential basics in personal work organization. To strengthen the view that everybody should contribute to the final results at his best, simple skills in personal working and communication techniques (e.g. time planning, mindmapping[1], product presentation, negotiation styles) are taught. We have found time for these issues in the course schedule by e.g. teaching only one OO-design technique instead of presenting three approaches plus a discussion of their advantages and disadvantages.

F4) Focus on rigid selection of team supervisors. The following sections will show that regular discussion and supervision is essential to that type of SE course. Because of the large number of students involved, this cannot be handled by the regular faculty staff alone. Senior students (about 20 for 50 teams) do the main job. Obviously the task of selecting and motivating them as well as auditing their performance is a key issue, for they are in frequent (often daily) contact with their teams and serve as major communication partners in the process of *experiencing* SE project work. Moreover student supervisors do a lot of detailed method teaching to team members, as lectures can only provide overview and basic examples. After years of mixed results, the selection process has matured and is efficient now.

---

1 Mindmapping is a notation to help capture ideas and concepts in a non-linear pictorial form (see [2]).

3. General workshop design

3.1. Pedagogical goals and methods

Setting. The department of SE at the Vienna university of technology has been in charge of the software engineering workshop for more than ten years. Each year 300 students complete the course in their second year of computer science. Fifty teams of 5 to 7 persons are guided by 5 professors together with 20 (senior student) supervisors.

Specific goals of the course for students are to 1. Understand and exercise a range of software engineering methods. 2. Develop a working commercial product for a real customer. 3. Work in and cooperate with a team. 4. Manage the time for meeting the review schedules. In summary 'Live through a real-life project with coaching but without the financial risk.' (see [4]).

Timeline structure. The overall workshop takes eight months and consists of three main phases. *Phase A* in October is a four-week entry 'technical fitness' test, where the individual students have to show or aquire a minimum level of programming skills. *Phase B* is a three-month team workshop from November to January, where the teams complete a pre-designed product to get aquainted with group-work, methods and tools. *Phase C* consists of a four-month team project from March to June, where each team has to find a suitable commercial task with a real customer outside the university and develop a complete system from specification to acceptance test.

Methods and Roles. The course curriculum aims to teach a broad range of basic software engineering methods to groups of students, who are used to individually solving small programming assignments. Group work needs to be an integral part of disseminating software engineering practices in order to prepare students for team work in industry.

Quality Assurance (QA)			
Analysis	Design	Implement.	Test
Project Management (PM)			

Fig. 1: Development Phases with QA and PM.

Figure 1 shows the four software development phases that structure the timeline of phases B and C and put the range of methods into perspective as well as accompanying quality assurance and project management supporting activities. During the course the professor takes the role of middle management, the supervisor acts as quality assurance person, and the team members are to work as project management and software engineers.

Lecture. According to [8] there is a loose coupling of the workshop to an accompanying lecture, where the theory of methods and their use in industry are discussed. To help students start working on SE methods, a string of *tutorials* has been introduced into phases A and B, where senior students show and discuss small examples.

Grading. Each student can earn 1000 grading points in a term, where 10 points roughly equivalent one working hour. In winter term the points are distributed on the entry-test (20%), product quality (60%), and answers to questions on products and software engineering methods (20%).

3.2. Phase B – getting used to team-work, new methods and tools

Phase B is the most delicate part of the course, where individual students and groups acquire work patterns that are applied for the rest of the course. The quality of these work patterns shapes recurring success or problem situations. Phase B starts with assembling the teams from individual students who have passed phase A. As soon as possible the teams get acquainted with their objectives and negotiate the distribution of work among themselves and make a *work contract* with their supervisor.

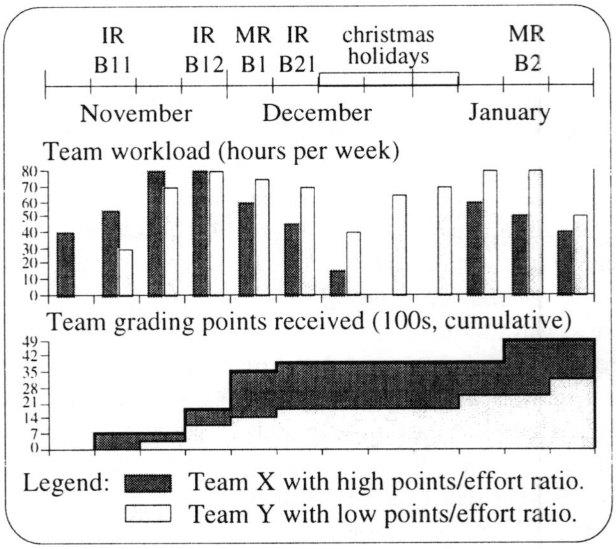

Fig. 2: Review timeline, workload and grading example.

To show and enforce good object-oriented architecture teams of students get a *framework with frozen interface specification* for a pre-designed product 'to fill out'. The pre-defined project for the workshop this year is called named 'Mail-Order'[2] (MO). Preparation of course mate-

2 The main tasks of project MO are to support a fictive Mail-Order company in processing orders from clients, shipping items, billing cus-

rial, tools and software for this project took six senior students 1500 hours over six months. This approach enables the teaching staff to exchange components between teams and to give components to teams that severely lag behind schedule. On the average phase B takes a group of seven some 500 work-hours, which roughly are distributed on team organization and meetings (10%), learning new methods (20%), implementation (40%), documentation (10%), testing (20%).

Figure 2 shows phase B of the workshop in fall 1996. The timeline shows five planned review points in the weeks from November to January. There are two *management reviews* (MR) where the team presents work products to a professor. In preparation for each MR there are one or more *internal reviews* (IR) where a supervisor gives feedback to the team in form of a discussion over the products submitted. Moreover the supervisor asks questions to determine the team members' understanding of the product and SE methods. On this basis he assigns grading points to products and individuals. Students get feedback on contracts and points received at reviews via a spreadsheet model.

Timing and workload. Figure 2 shows examples for the workload of two student teams and the sum of grading points received at reviews. Team X (dark shading, thick line) has ideal timing and reaches the maximum points available while keeping workload around the planned level. Team Y (light shading, thin line) with bad timing reaches only 60% of the maximum grading points and exceeds the planned workload by over 20%. Team Y has a late start leading to postponed reviews, re-reviews and work sessions during christmas holidays to make up for lost time.

3.3. Information exchange at the lab

Most students work at their computers at home and use the university lab as communication center. The lab provides one meeting room and twelve networked computers with modem and internet access for all students of the course. The computers are used mainly to show and explain work products, to exchange large pieces of software that would take too long to send over a telephone line, and to integrate parts of a work product together with coworkers.

Figure 3 shows the work spaces of groups and exchange spaces with communication paths between them. The senior student developers for the internal 'mail-order'-

---

tomers, maintaining stock and suppliers, and organizing users in branch offices.

product-templates (MO) integrate updated versions of their executables, basic and advanced components and release them to the lab. Supervisors can download and test all components, while students use only the basic components to develop their own versions of the advanced components as a course task. These new components are handed in to the supervisors, who can recommend original good work to the component marketplace for distribution to other supervisors. Teams with performance problems can 'buy' advanced components from their supervisor by trading course points for program functionality.

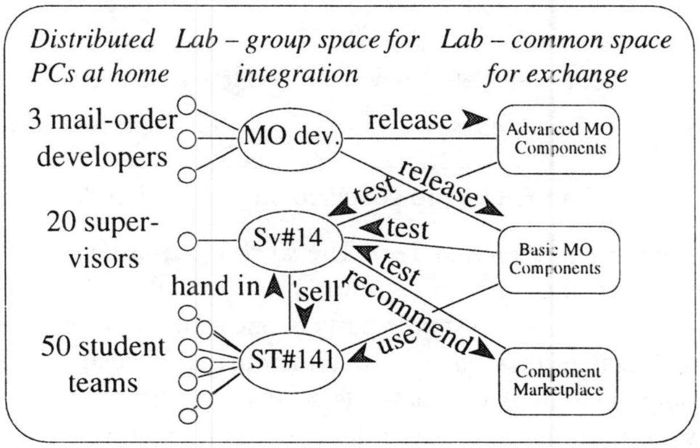

Fig. 3: Product integration and exchange at the lab.

4. Software engineering products and methods

The final products of course phases B and C are administrative commercial applications that help a group of users in a small office domain like ambulance scheduling, accounting for a construction bureau, or lending cars.

The three central parts of these applications are a database fitting the problem, an object model, and a user interface (UI) design capable of carrying out all necessary business transactions in a convenient way.

Analysis. In phase B all teams are given a worked-out specification and design to show how good documents in early phases help implementation and testing. The specification includes a description of the domain, a list of prioritized business transactions, object-oriented analysis (OOA) model, and entity-relationship (ER) diagrams with integrity rules for the database (see fig. 4).

In phase C in the spring semester each team has to find a customer and elicit the information needed to draw up the specification.

Design. An architecture (OOD) and user interface design (UID) have to be created that bridge the requirements from analysis to the chosen tool set for implementation. This includes proper error handling, a workable plan for integration, and a tracability matrix to verify the design against the analysis documents.

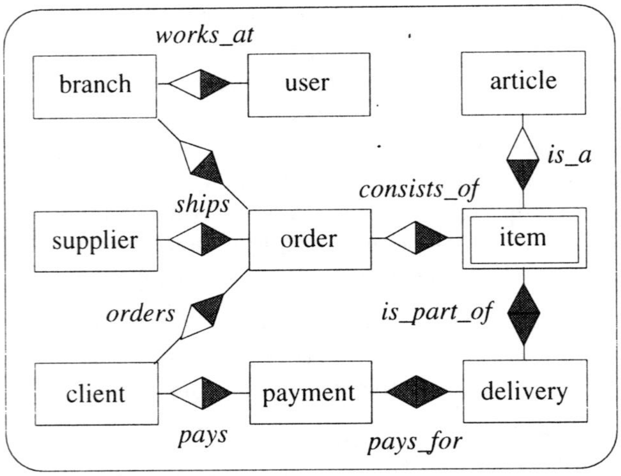

Fig. 4: Part-ER for pre-specified project 'Mail-Order'.

Implementation and Test. The work group usually implements the objects at home on distributed PCs. Integration of the system's parts is one of the most exciting events of the course, where the quality of design and discipline in implementation determines the difference between building a successful system and spending long hours on diagnosis and rework.

In parallel with design and implementation a test plan and black-box (BB) test cases and test data sets are prepared. As soon as possible parts of the system get tested and the results are reported within the team and to the supervisor. The testers build a utility program to check the database for compliance with the integrity rules defined during analysis.

User Support. For the user an online-help, a basic user-manual, and an installation package are prepared.

5. Project management and quality assurance

While exercising and understanding the engineering methods is the main aim of the course, PM and QA shape the group and keep the focus on progress.

Project Management consists of all activities that communicate to the members of the group what has happened as well as what is to be done by whom and by when. Quality assurance attends to that all products can be verified and validated, checks products for their characteristics and gives feedback to the creators. During the course project management includes assigning responsibilities to individuals and reporting on project progress, while quality assurance relates the products to grading points necessary for students to pass the course.

5.1. Planning and negotiation

Team Building. The assembling of the team is an event with a great influence on the further workshop. Students can sign up for teams. Usually a quarter of the people have known each other before. Each team names a *team coordinator* to channel the communication and an *administrator* to keep all documents in order. The supervisor tries to rearrange groups with a bad mix of skills and may exchange students with other supervisors.

	Students		St1	St2	St3 ...	St7
	max.	*points*	710	680	670	700
Product items	*points*	*recvd.*	450	360	490	610
Design UI	*300*	*240*	R60	C20	C20	
Design reports	*60*	*60*				R100
...	...	...				
Impl. Sales	*320*	*210*	C30		R40...	
Impl. Clients	*360*	*180*	C40	R60		
...	...	...				
Test Data	*160*	*20*		C40	...	
Test Cases	*420*	*0*	C30	C20	C20	R30
...	...	...				

Legend: R60 ... responsible for product, 60% of work
C20 ... co-worker for product, 20% of work

Fig. 5: Cut from a feedback spreadsheet.

Work contracts for responsibility. For the final grading of students' work there is a list of products and their maximum worth in grading points. At the start of each phase of the course the team is asked to assign each work product to one person, who is responsible for the completion of this product (see fig. 5). While this person can have co-workers, this measure makes sure that for each product there is somebody 'whose level of adrenaline will rise with the approaching deadline' and who will take steps to start work on this item. Moreover the supervisor and team members know who can tell them about progress on each work product, which makes communication faster and loss of information less likely.

5.2. Work packages

The master plan of the course schedules the reviews and their engineering content, while the teams are to distribute and schedule the work packages necessary to produce the program parts and documents on time with the required quality.

Steps for solving a Work Package. 1. Get and read the assignment and time table. 2. Discuss problems and unclear parts. 3. Negotiate contract with supervisor. 4. Plan and distribute work packages. 5. Execute work packages. 6. Collect and integrate work products. 7. Check work products against assignment.

Most items in this list get triggered by meetings, need intermediate communication, and end with team or subgroup meetings.

Work distribution. The worth of each work product in grading points reflects the time necessary to build it and the importance of the product for the project. Distributing the work evenly among the team members insures against excessive individual workload and team problems should a team member quit the course. In practice the supervisor adapts his level of coaching and management to his perception of the team's internal management abilities.

Functional role models. Over time these approaches in most groups lead to a relatively stable distribution of work-tasks on members with special skills and/or knowledge. Typical roles are coordinator, administrator, report writer, document designer, user interface designer, system designer, analyzer and tester, database specialist, and toolsmith.

Scheduling. While work distribution usually is not a problem, the proper timing of activities and the integration of several parts into one product (like a program or text document) can be tricky. The drawing of a PERT-diagram to find the critical path through a set of activities helps to set the priorities right when under deadline pressure.

5.3. Assessment

Feedback. A spreadsheet containing the relations of products to people working on products or responsible for a product (see fig. 5) answers four crucial questions. 1. What am I responsible for? 2. Who works with me? 3. How many grading points have I earned so far? 4. Could I do better? This information is the basis for re-negotiation of work contracts within the team in case of severe problems.

Reporting. All members of the team, the supervisor and professor need to know what has been done, which products have been completed successfully and where unexpected difficulties need special attention. Journals on project meetings and current versions of documents as well as reports on reviews capture this information.

Reviews. The succession of internal and management reviews serves as a project pace-maker for formal and informal feedback on project accomplishments, grading and trouble-shooting. At each review the supervisor asks one or two students to explain an aspect of a product and how methods are used to construct or analyze products. This helps to keep the team members reflecting on the idea of these methods and disseminates knowledge within the team.

Recognizing and handling conflicts. Most of the few teams that quit the course do not fail because of technical problems but due to unsolved conflicts that have smoldered long enough to prevent meaningful coordinated work. One of the most important tasks of the supervisor is to watch for signs of disharmony in the group, diagnose the cause and suggest a constructive way to solve the latent crisis while the team has a chance to keep up the schedule.

6. Practical course organization

In a course with many teams there is little room for adhoc organization in the large, since the time lag to inform everyone involved takes at least a week. An important focus for course organization is to provide a role model to disseminate central responsibilities, communication channels, and backup plans.

6.1 Formal roles

All persons participating in the course have a time budget that limits their regular contribution to the course to a maximum of a day per week. Figure 6 from [1] shows the roles and numbers of people involved and the main paths of communication between these roles during the course.

Professors. Assistance professors who see students every month for feedback and trouble-shooting. Each professor covers four supervisors.

Supervisors. Senior students who are in touch with individual students and teams on a weekly basis to provide guidance and feedback.

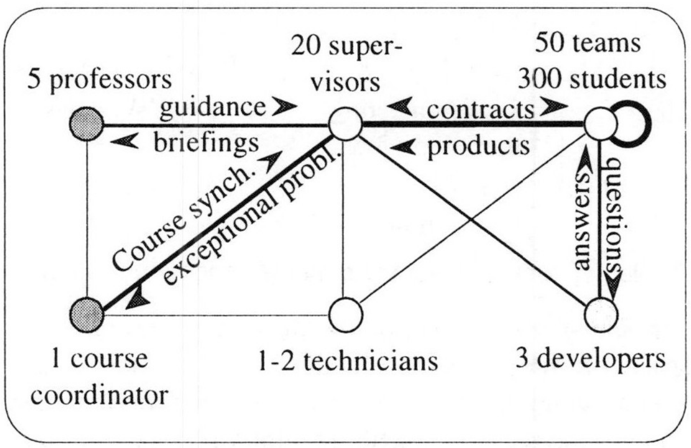

Fig. 6: Main communication paths between roles.

Teams and Students. Each team consists of up to seven students and has a dedicated supervisor. Teams organize their work on their own. The bulk of information exchange stays within the group's boundaries.

Course coordinator. The course coordinator is one of the professors. He looks after the preparation of the course material, briefs supervisors and professors, and keeps an ear on the ground to anticipate and defuse potential sources of big trouble.

Technicians. Senior students who keep the lab hardware and network in service.

Developers. Senior students who have specified, designed, and implemented the software, part of which is to be completed by the student teams. They service a mail hotline and a file with frequently asked questions in the lab.

6.2 Communication channels

The large number of students leads to a steady flow of information like programs and software components, documentation, work plans, work packages and work products, status messages, technical and organizational questions and answers, discussions and polls via e-mail.

This information in many cases needs timely recognition and an answer within two days to keep the work going smoothly. Any person in the course can handle 20 interactions (equivalent to an e-mail needing an action of five minutes or more) per week without problem, 50 of such interactions take up almost a day. The supervisors act as filters for professors and course coordinator to prevent information overload.

Similarly the pre-designed product must show a sufficiently high level of documentation and technical maturity to prevent a flood of questions pouring in to the developers, frustration for students and setting a bad example.

	Communication (C)	
Mode of	synchronous C	asynchronous C
pull C	invited meeting, tutorial, review	ftp, WWW, news
push C	phone, ad-hoc meeting	mail, e-mail, voice mail

Table 1: Possible modes and media of communication.

Modes of communication. Table 1 shows examples of the use of communication media in a workshop. *Synchronous* communication is suited for negotiation, fast decision-making, or conflict-resolution. *Asynchronous* communication gives the receiver the possibility to 'think it over' and react at his own pace. *Pull* communication needs active search of receivers and is suitable for channels with high volume of messages with low priority. *Push* communication delivers messages into the receiver's information space, which is convenient for important information. In the workshop asynchronous communication as structured use of e-mail and ftp is strongly encouraged for normal information exchange and typically follows the channels in figures 3 and 6. Meetings are prepared by e-mail briefings.

6.3 Maintaining supervisors

Selection and training. At the end of the academic year candidates for supervisors in the following year are asked to pass an acceptance test. Usually at least half of the supervisors do another term as a supervisor the following year. New supervisors from the group of successful workshop participants are recommended by their supervisor or professor. Central criteria for choosing a supervisor are good knowledge on methods and tools as these are the means to build up initial credibility with the workshop participants. Further criteria are personal integrity, communication skills, and the ability to complete projects.

The candidates share interest to increase their knowledge on SE, to have the opportunity to guide a group, and to earn some $2000 per year while studying. An internal workshop prepares them to use the supervisor's material given to them in meetings, tutorials, and reviews.

Internal coaching. Supervisors are in the most direct contact with the student teams, teaching details in project context, giving practical advice, and moderating discussions and grading issues. These activities need sensitivity for situations, whether to help or to demand. In addition to the direct feedback from the team member each supervisor can seek guidance from his dedicated professor or the course coordinator. The four supervisors of a professor build a group that arranges common matters like dates for management reviews among themselves. For issues that concern the overall workshop all supervisors come together about once a month or as the occasion demands.

Typical Career Path. Each year some of the established supervisors work together to build the workshop example for phase B in the following term. Successful supervisors typically stay with the workshop for about three years. Others who like variety take up supervising assignments in other graduate courses. To give a chance for reflection on the events during the SE workshop in the following year we provide a lecture and workshop on quality assurance. Students can focus their electives on SE in the second part of the CS curriculum when taking relevant practical work assignments in industry. Every year around four former supervisors work on their graduating thesis in a joint project of the department and an industrial partner. Graduate students return from their positions in industry to seek advice on an innovative project or to take up Ph.D. studies.

7. Results and feedback

In a regular review process we ask for feedback from course participants, supervisors and graduate students who work in industry to keep the focus of the course on a balance between academic basis and practitioners' needs. In the following section 7.1 deals with results and feedback from the last term. Section 7.2 summarizes industrial feedback during the last 6 years. Section 7.3 aims at outlining the major lessons learned during the last 10 years being in charge of the course.

7.1. Feedback from course participants

Data to evaluate the impact of the course is gathered from spreadsheets with grading information, feedback from students at key reviews on their role in the team, skills learned, workload, opinion on course materials and tools. The supervisors keep journals on their workload, reports on reviews and remarkable events.

Grading and effort. Around 90% of the teams pass the workshop. Typically the team grades reflect the grading of the team members, only in rare cases differs the grade of an individual student more than one grade from the team average. A team of seven puts in winter term 500 to 800[3] work hours and 300 to 500 hours in spring term, while their supervisor spends 100 to 130 hours in fall term and 80 to 100 hours in spring term.

Common problems. Some teams had initial problems with the tools and dated computers at the university lab, most commented on shortcomings with the documentation of the frozen interfaces in phase B. A number of teams doubted the effect of questions on understanding at the reviews.

Mixed reactions. Most teams complained that the workshop was significantly more work than they were credited for in their curriculum, while conceding that they would be able to use the experience in coming projects. Some people questioned the value of all the measures taken in the workshop that went beyond programming, especially documentation and reviewing it. The relation of grading points to work products was generally regarded as a very good guide to distribute the work parts, while some mismatches of points were found and the observed effort for specific products gave rise to discussion and local redistribution of grading points.

Positive feedback. For the majority of students the workshop was their first opportunity to practice their skills on a medium-size product and within a project. In this context they commended the positive feeling of working in a productive group, the novelty of real project management with negotiated contracts and reviews. The overall impression was to have worked hard for a new understanding of mostly usable and practical issues.

Success factors for students and teams. Students and supervisors ranked the following list of abilities weighed to their impact on passing the course. 1. Core programming abilities. 2. Information exchange in a timely fashion. 3. Ability for communication. 4. Teamwork, especially conflict resolution at reviews or integration of product parts. 5. Access to technical facilities. 6. Ability to find somebody who has a working part of the solution and can explain it. A local survey showed that teams who have severe deficiencies with more than two of these factors have a significantly lower ratio – up to 1:6 – of grading points per work-hour than well equipped teams.

7.2. Feedback from industry

The small market for software engineering in Austria provides us with ample opportunity to stay in contact with former students who are active in innovative projects which benefit from university cooperation. Moreover the department traditionally seeks a strong connection to industrial practice to mix and transfer relevant know-how in both directions.

More than 40% of all software development in Austria is going on in and around Vienna. Moreover the Vienna University of Technology is the only graduating institution on university level for computer scientists in Vienna. Apart from the authors' personal and institutionalized feedback with industry, two broad studies on the experience of earlier graduates [10, 11] have strengthened and structured our views on requirements for SE education in practice.

As far as educational effectiveness in SE is observable, at least two valuable effects have shown evidence. 1. Participants who have worked as *team supervisors* turn out to be highly effective in actual industrial SE-practice, as we can see from routine inquiries of firms for former supervisors. 2. The requirements of industry for software engineers from university – as stated in the introducing section – are shared across market divisions, like administrative information processing, industrial engineering, or telecommunications. Students with qualifications in these areas are sought after, even when these needs are not men-

[3] One team reported 1300 work hours during winter term, but admitted to have built an elaborate tool-box besides solving the workshop problems.

tioned expressly in advertisements.[4]

7.3. Lessons learned

Over the years the workshop has seen lots of major and minor adjustments.[5] The course has grown from 'Structured programming under DOS with a character-oriented display' in the 1980s to the current course in the mid-1990s which uses dated 486 in a Windows-NT network to run a Client/Server environment with an SQL-database. The technical complexity is rising sharply while stability and manageability of the lab computers improves after a chaotic period when using Windows around 1990.

When introducing the object-oriented paradigm in the form of 'just another programming language' in 1991, we found out the hard way to *'be cautious with latest methods'*. It took over two years to pervade the supervisors at that time thoroughly with the idea. When the course aims to teach a variety of methods then every single one must be stable and practical.

The technical knowledge of the average student entering the workshop has improved with the growing complexity of PC-systems in the home sector, while a person without fundamental technical knowledge who has to learn all the basics during the course faces technical hurdles of increasing number and size. More than once colleagues have persuaded us to introduce enhanced tool-technology (e.g., EasyCase in 1991 or Nextstep in 1993) at least for part of the course participants. Very often the groups concerned had to be excluded from the general schedule as more than half of their time went into learning and handling the new tool. This experience has lead to the general guideline *'Caution with (brand-)new or overly complex tools'*.

Active team member selection. In an early phase of the workshop the criteria 'people who are able and interested only' is enforced. This measure reduces the spread in the quality of final results and minimizes the number of teams and individuals failing to pass the course.

Appropriate material/experience schedules. Reasonable timing of the distribution and examination of technological and managemental know-how keeps the students focused on key issues. Learning, applying, and experiencing have to be coupled tightly.

Appropriate communication distribution. Reasonable communication path planning and its disciplined enforcement on actual communication ensures a satisfying distribution of information, communication events, and communication load for students, supervisors and professors.

Work organization on team-level and on individual level is a basic ingredient to keep the work going smoothly. On the average, CS students have a rather low level of theory and practice in that particular field. Therefore we have to establish a basic level. Without investing time into professional team-work and individual work, a larger number of teams tends to 'socio-dramatize'[6] at tough milestones.

Rigorous supervisor selection. The supervisor often acts somewhere between first-line-management and adviser, which needs a careful pick from the available candidates. The supply of supervisors to choose from can diminish suddenly, if the technical platform of the course gets changed radically for an unfamiliar operating system and development tool. In such a situation you have to choose people with the necessary technical qualifications. This has resulted in a much higher workload for professors, as the average social-service performance of these supervisors tended to be seriously reduced.

In summary *common sense* in software engineering and project management has improved for the majority of participants, the *major roles* within a SE-team are understood or at least respected, *'uncreative' requirements* like enhanced documentation, project management infrastructure or means of quality assurance are truly less alien to most students after experiencing their benefits.

8. Conclusions

In this paper we have reported on structure, style, schedule and contents of a software engineering course aiming at meeting industrial needs, while maintaining good academic standards. Special focus has been given to an appropriate balance between learning a method/technology and learning by doing.

Teaching software engineering and project management to a rather large number of participants without drain of quality or intensity is achieved by a couple of measures, which have been described above. Among these you can find purely organizational criteria, which turned out to be the very essential.

Teaching SE and PM is about teaching methods and

4 Advertisements generally just look for 'software engineers fluent in language X on operating system Y with database Z', which reflects the rather tool-oriented view of project staffers.

5 ... and has passed through many an experiment – like Cobol under VMS, multi-user application development on two DEC VAXes, or Modula-2 on early Apple Macs.

6 This effect, well-known to professors and managers alike, makes a team or individual, who did not complete a negotiated assignment for any reason, display a behavior like trying to find a scapegoat, finding some kind of excuse, or plain wailing, rather than trying to constructively find a solution through re-negotiation within the team and with the professor or manager.

techniques, too. Teaching SE and PM well is about enforcing some experience with the need, use, and scope of these methods and techniques within a project. You can not simulate real practice in a SE course at university, but you can practice real engineering action in teams. The underlying metaphor we suggest is rather unheroic – 'a team meets and organizes itself in order to engineer a useful service for a customer'.

References

1. Biffl St., Grechenig Th. Teaching Software Engineering and Project Management to 300 Participants without Drain of Quality or Intensity, Short Paper, ACM SIGCSE, *Proc. of Integrating Technology into Computer Science Education, Uppsala, Sweden*, June 1997.

2. Buzan T., Buzan B. *The mindmap book.* BBC Worldwide Publishing, 1993.

3. Crow G.B., Rariden R.L. Strengthening the computer information systems curriculum through cooperative education, *J. of Computer Information Systems 32(3):52-55*, Spring 1992.

4. Finkelstein A. (ed.) Software Engineering Education Resources, *Proc. of ACM/IEEE Int. Workshop on SE Education*, May 1994, Sorrento, Italy.

5. Habermann A.N. Software engineering practice, research and education, *Applied Computer Science and Software. Turning Theory into Practice* p. 83-90 Schwartzel H. Springer-Verlag Berlin, Germany, 1991.

6. Joyce D.T. Education and experience: Partners in producing Software Engineers, *International Symposium on Engineering Software Systems.* 1993, D.W. Russell (ed.), World Scientific, p. 4-7, May 1993.

7. Knight J.C., Prey J.C., Wulf W.A. Undergraduate Computer Science Education: A New Curriculum Philosophy and Overview, *Proc. of ACM SIGCSE Conf.*, Phoenix, AZ, March 1994.

8. Knox D. et al. Use of Laboratories in Computer Science Education: Guidelines for good Practice, Working Group Report, *Proc. of Integrating Technology into CS Education'96*, Barcelona, Spain, pp. 167-181, June 1996.

9. Olson G.M., Olson J.S., Carter M.R., Storrosten M. Small group design meetings: An analysis of collaboration. *Human Computer Interaction 7(4)*, 1992.

10. Rapf K. et al. *Informatikabsolventenbefragung 1989 – Study on the professional needs of practicing software engineers,* Hochschülerschaft an der Technischen Universität Wien, 1990.

11. Sax G. *Wirtschaftsinformatiker zwischen universitärer Ausbildung und beruflicher Praxis.* Diplomarbeit Universität Wien, 1990.

12. Sharon S. (ed.). *Handbook of Cooperative Learning Methods*, The Greenwood Educator's Reference Collection, Greenwood Press, 1994.

13. Tucker A.B. (ed.) et al. Summary of the ACM/ IEEE-CS Joint Curriculum Task Force Report Computing Curricula 1991, *Comm. of the ACM*, 34(6):68-84.

14. Walz D.B., Elam J.J., Curtis B. Inside a Software Design Team: Knowledge Acquisition, Sharing, and Integration, *Comm. of the ACM* 36(10):63-77, 1993.

Session P5a

System Development Methods II

Software Technology for Embedded Systems

Peter Green, Derrick Morris and Gareth Evans
Computer System Design Group,
Department of Computation,
UMIST.

Abstract

The MOOSE approach to the engineering of embedded systems is discussed in this paper. MOOSE is a full-lifecycle, model-based approach which is based on extensions to Object Oriented technology to apply to both software and hardware. The paper describes how early lifecycle models that represent the logical behaviour and architecture of a system can be transformed into representations that allow implementation source for both software and hardware to be synthesised.

1. Introduction

Embedded systems provide control in an enormous variety of products from consumer electronic goods (for example mobile phones) through to high integrity applications such as flight control systems. The economic importance of such systems is considerable, with the market for third party embedded system software alone being worth US$0.5 billion in 1995, and this is projected to increase to US$1.1 billion in 1999 [1].

However, the development of embedded systems is a particularly difficult task, a core problem being the provision of highly complex functionality involving concurrency, in the context of strict non-functional requirements (NFRs) relating to issues such as timing, memory requirements, cost etc. Additional complications arise since embedded systems often require the development of software, the hardware base on which the software executes, and application-specific hardware. Indeed, the issues of meeting requirements (both functional and non-functional) and the need to implement embedded systems in both hardware and software are becoming increasingly interrelated. Whereas traditionally the software in a system provided the functionality and the hardware determined performance, this is now no longer wholly true. The advent of hardware description languages and ASIC (Application-Specific Integrated Circuit) technology on the one hand, and high performance RISC processors on the other, means that there are now important trade-offs to be made between hardware and software implementations which need to be investigated. This can only be realistically done in the context of the whole system.

Although many successful embedded systems products exist, the discipline for developing them is not mature or stable, and their development can lead to serious difficulties [2]. Whilst the design and implementation of software and hardware components is reasonably well understood, there has only been limited progress in development methods which address the system as a whole. Many current approaches partition the system between hardware and software at an early stage, which means that it is usually not possible to examine the overall functional behaviour of the complete system until it is finally implemented, and that trade-offs between hardware and software solutions in the context of the NFRs are not possible.

This paper presents an approach to embedded system development which delays the separate treatment of hardware and software until a stage when high level implementation source can be automatically synthesised from a complete system design. The method begins with the construction of a model that specifies the behavioural requirements of a complete product. This Behavioural Model is then made executable in order to support functional validation of the complete system and hence provides an environment for investigating system-wide issues before making technology commitments on which an implementation will be based. The method draws upon many ideas embodied in a variety of graphical approaches to software development and is based on Object Oriented models that deal with mixed software/hardware systems. Since models play a central role in the method, the approach is called Model-based Object Oriented System Engineering (MOOSE). The paper focuses on the overall development paradigm and the use of an Object Oriented approach to represent complete embedded systems. Details of hardware-specific issues can be found in [3] and [4].

Although MOOSE was developed specifically for embedded systems, it has been used with some success to develop software-only systems and to model hardware-only systems. In particular, all the tools that support the method (see Section 4) have been developed

0-8186-7840-2/97 $10.00 © 1997 IEEE

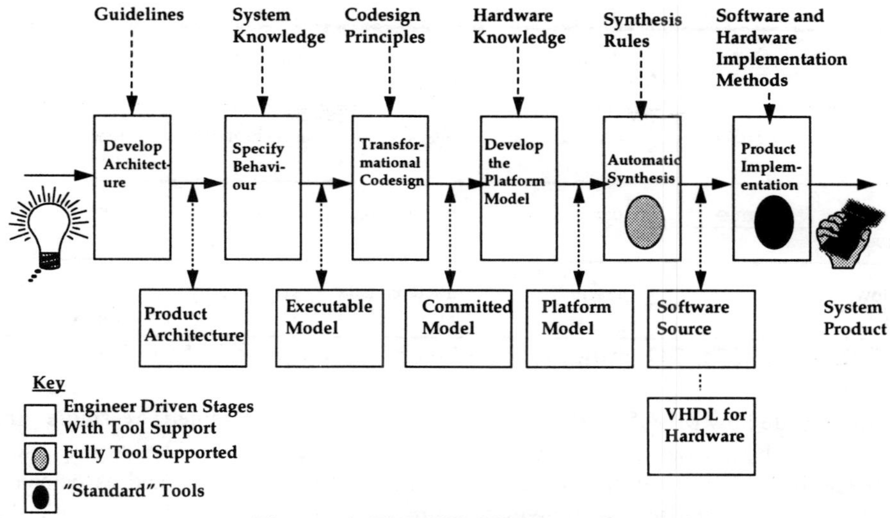

Figure 1: The MOOSE paradigm

using the method, and it appears that it does have a more general applicability, especially to the development of CASE, and other similar, tools.

A number of other 'whole system' approaches have been proposed, including those which seek to integrate existing analysis and design methods and tools to provide a seamless approach to complete system development [5, 6]. These have the advantage of using well tried methods at the expense of introducing tool and method integration problems. Alternative paradigms attempt to devise homogenous methods and tools that provide an integrated route to system development [3, 7, 8]. These have the advantage of being focused directly on the problem area, but have the corresponding disadvantage of needing either to invent new methods or to provide extensions to existing methods, often requiring the development of supporting tools. For the reasons outlined in [3], the research introduced in this paper falls into the latter category, and so is concerned with the construction of a uniform system model which is validated by simulation prior to being partitioned into hardware and software elements that are separately implemented.

2. Overview of the MOOSE paradigm

Figure 1 shows the MOOSE paradigm, which begins with a product idea, and ends with the synthesis of implementation source code for both software and hardware. The source forms the input to the final stage shown in Figure 1, which uses standard software and hardware implementation tools for building the product.

The current implementation language for software is C++ and the 'standard tools' are compilers and debuggers for that language. However, this choice of language is not fundamental to the approach and it can be adapted to alternative languages. If necessary, multiprocessor implementations can be developed, and the automatic synthesis mechanism produces separate source code for each processor. The objects placed in different processors, hence different programs, interact through communication mechanisms that are either developed or selected in the final stages of model development.

For hardware, representations in the hardware description language VHDL are generated and the 'standard tools' are those that provide simulation and automatic manufacture of ASICS from VHDL specifications. Again, this choice is not central, and MOOSE can handle other styles of hardware implementation.

Four phases of incremental development precede the synthesis of the implementation source. The first phase develops an architecture having three parts, a Behavioural Model (which is the primary component), a Domain Model (which is an Object Oriented Analysis model of the problem domain intended to support the construction of the Behavioural Model), and a textual analysis and classification of requirements, both functional and non-functional. The Behavioural Model captures the system's functional requirements, and in the second phase it is extended into an Executable Model, so that the behaviour can be dynamically validated. In the third phase experiments are performed with the Executable Model and transformations are applied that capture the decisions committing objects to a software or hardware implementation. This phase is concluded by associating both kinds of objects with specific processors. At this stage there is enough detail in the Committed Model to synthesise the complete C++ source for each processor in the implementation, with the exception of system software components. In the fourth phase system software and hardware components are added or, if necessary developed, in a Platform Model to support the complete synthesis of the implementation source, for both the software and hardware. Further details of the Platform Model can be found in [4].

Connection Type	Symbol	Time Behaviour	Information Carried	Communication Behaviour	Usage Restrictions
Interaction	name ↔	discrete	parameters and result	synchronous	none
Event	name - - →	discrete	none	asynchronous	none
Information Flow - Time Continuous	name →→	continuous	structured data	asynchronous	none
Information Flow - Time Discrete	name →	discrete	structured data	asynchronous	To/From External Objects

Table 1: MOOSE Communication Mechanisms used in this Paper

It is perhaps helpful to indicate how MOOSE relates to Object Oriented methods for software development (for example [10]). MOOSE has been developed specifically for the engineering of complete embedded systems requiring the concurrent development of both software and hardware. Hence the method provides abstractions and communications mechanisms appropriate to objects of both kinds. This is in contrast to methods such as [10] which are aimed solely at software development. In addition, the needs of an overall *systems* development process, rather than a *software* development process, necessitate the inclusion of stages (such as Transformational Codesign) not present in software lifecycles. These matters are explored in more detail in [3].

3. Overview of the MOOSE notation

A MOOSE model consists of a hierarchy of diagrams called Object Interaction Diagrams (OIDs), which collectively represent the operation of a system as an interacting set of objects in which each object has responsibility for a specialised and cohesive share of the system's total functionality. At the higher levels of the hierarchy, the objects represent subsystems whose decomposition is given on subordinate diagrams. Decomposition ends when an object is considered simple enough to be treated as *primitive*. Class definitions for the primitive objects are then provided, and it is these that are used to produce an Executable Model.

Although there is a superficial similarity between the appearance of OIDs and Data Flow Diagrams (DFDs) in Structured Analysis [9], the semantics of OIDs, based on a network of communicating objects, are completely different and are much closer to those of Booch's object diagrams [10] used for defining message flows in Object Oriented software. However, it is important to understand that in the Behavioural and Executable models, the OIDs depict uncommitted rather than software (or hardware) objects, and the semantics of the inter-object connections reflect this.

The kinds of connections used in this paper are summarised in Table 1. Each connection has a name, and the use of an upper case indicates that the connection is a *bundle*, i.e. a set of primitive lines that are gathered together and represented as single line on an OID to enhance readability. The names should be chosen to indicate logical purpose, and associated dictionary entries provide further detail. For example, the dictionary entry for a bundle names its constituents. Entries for interactions and parameterised events define their parameters, and entries for information flows show the information structure.

4. An example MOOSE model

An embedded Video Controller is used to demonstrate the MOOSE approach. The Video Controller digitises, compresses and stores video input from a local cluster of video cameras. Compressed images from each camera form a time ordered sequence of a user specified length, captured at a rate fast enough for a replay to approximate to moving video. In the steady state each new frame added to a sequence replaces the oldest previously captured frame. Several Video Controllers will be connected, via a LAN, to a Control Station to provide a distributed surveillance system. The Control Station will configure, control and access the information in the Video Controllers by sending commands over the LAN. The available commands will allow for the setting of various parameters such as the frame rate and the length of the captured sequence for each camera.

The Video Controller must also handle digital inputs from presence sensors, and cameras are associated with individual sensors. Inputs from a sensor are interpreted as incidents and the image sequence from the associated camera prior to, and immediately following, the incident are retained as an Incident Record, after which the cameras involved continue capturing new images. The Control Station is to be notified when sensor inputs occur, and any associated Incident Record can be relayed to the Control Station on demand.

In addition to linking cameras to sensors, they may be designated 'on-line' in which case their images are transmitted to the Control Station as soon as they are captured. All images transmitted to the Control Station must be labelled with time, date, incident identifier and the identity of the originating camera.

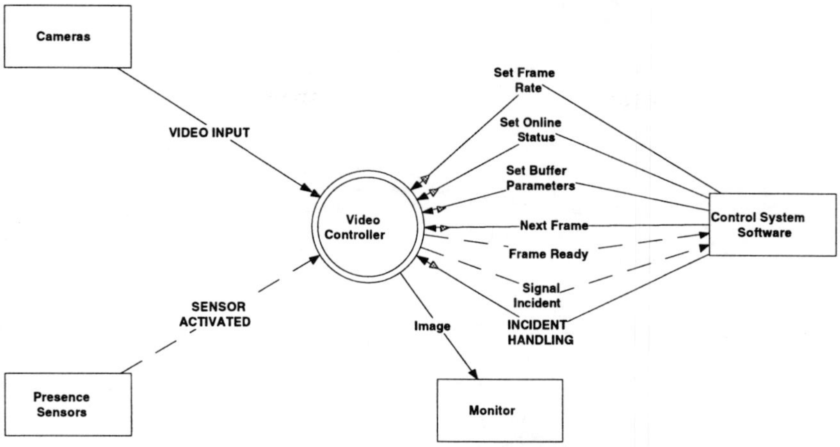

Figure 2 External View of Video Controller

Space constraints dictate that only the key elements of the MOOSE method can be illustrated in the following sections, and so a number of the stages in the method will only receive passing comment. Further details of these aspects can be found in [3].

4.1 Product architecture : the Behavioural Model

The OID hierarchy for a model begins with an External View, which shows the system as a single object (the double-edged circle) interfaced to objects of the external environment (the rectangles) that have contact with it. The system object encapsulates every item of hardware and software that will result from the development, including appropriate interfaces to the external objects. For the Video Controller, Figure 1, the environment includes cameras, sensors and the surveillance application software in the Control System. A video monitor is added to the model so that it may generate visible results although this would, in practice, be associated with the application software.

Connections to externals usually depict logical behaviour, leaving open the decision on how the physical connection will be implemented. Figure 2 therefore represents commands from the Control System as logical interactions rather than as messages placed on the LAN, the design of which will be developed within the model. Figure 2 also shows that Images sent to the Monitor are time discrete (packeted) information flows. In contrast the Camera connections are shown as a bundle of time continuous information flows, defined in the model dictionary as PAL encoded video inputs on the assumption that cameras of this specification have already been selected.

Figure 3 shows the decomposition of the Video Control System into six objects, which encapsulate the system's functionality into cohesive units communicating via interactions or events. Interactions usually request actions, pass parameters and return results, and are synchronous, in that a sending object pauses until the receiving object accepts the message and returns a response. Depending on the design of the receiving object a response may be

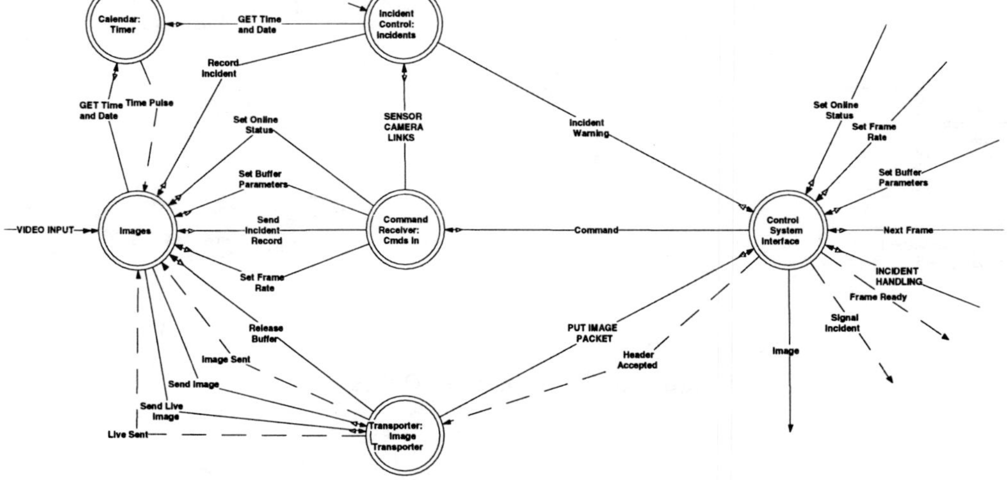

Figure 3 First Level Expansion of the Video Control System

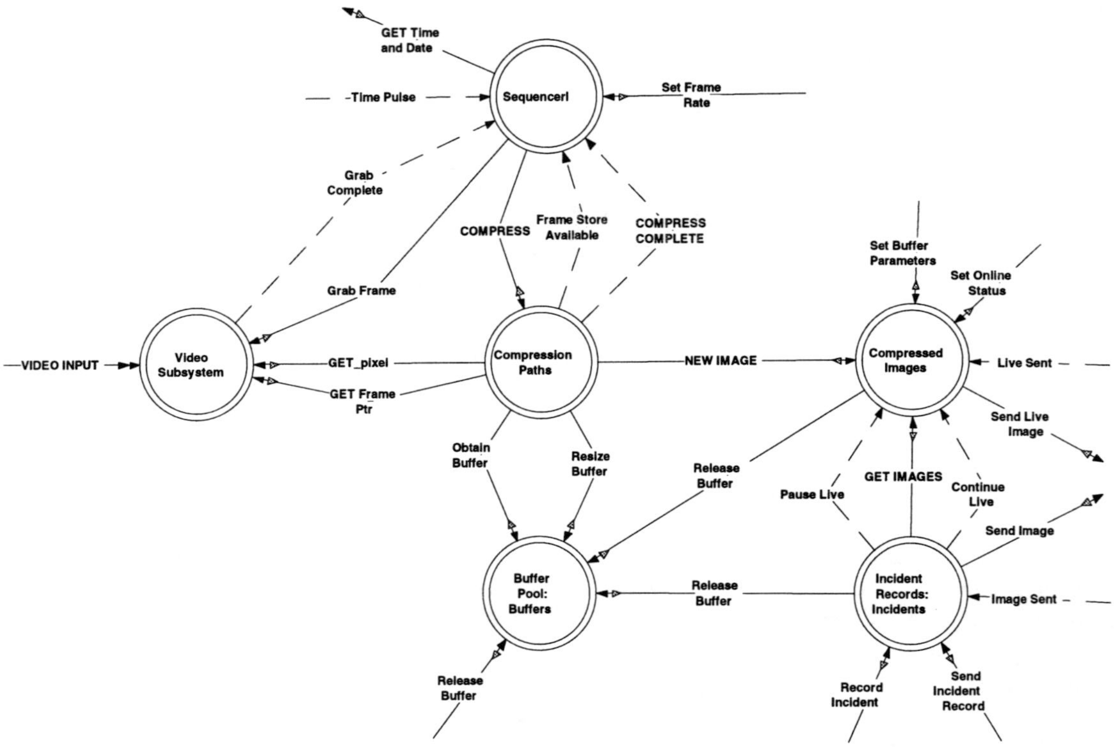

Figure 4 The decomposition of the Images object

provided after the requested action is complete or as soon as parameter transfer is complete. The latter approach is typically used where actions take a significant time, and the returned results are not of direct use in determining the immediately following activity of the sender. For example, the Images object, which captures and compresses video input, and sends compressed images to Transporter by the Send Image interaction, can continue capturing other images when a response is returned, which may be before the transmission is complete.

Events are used to signal significant state boundaries, thus in order that Images knows when a further image transfer can be requested an Image Sent event is raised on completion of each transmission. In any model of a system where performance requirements impose a need for concurrency, designers should use techniques

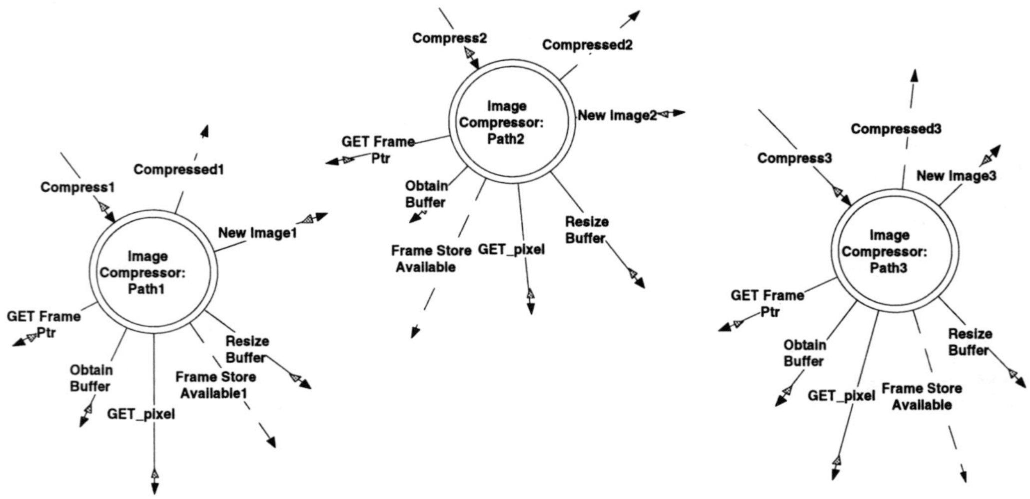

Figure 5: Compression Paths

such as the above to avoid critical threads of activity waiting for other services to complete. However, the integrity of the system's behaviour must be assured by providing appropriate interlocking via event signals.

Four objects in Figure 3 are primitive, indicated by their object names being preceded by class names (:). The others, Images and Control System Interface, require further expansion and Figure 4 gives the expansion of the former. Figure 5 gives the expansion of the Compression Paths object, which appears on Figure 4. It is not necessary for the purpose of this paper to complete the model by giving expansions of the remaining non-primitive objects, but it should be noted that the Compression Paths object has a separate (concurrent) compressor object for each camera as shown in Figure 5.

4.2 Specify behaviour : Creating an executable model

After the completion and approval of the Behavioural Model, the next step is to create an Executable Model which provides an emulation of the system's behaviour. The Executable Model is created by providing class definitions for each primitive object on the OIDs. The first component of a class definition is a Class Interface Specification (CIS), which defines the detail of all the connections to objects in the class. A CIS has a simple tabular layout in which the essential information is given for a C++ class interface to be generated.

The implementation of a class is based on a Class Implementation Diagram (CID), which has a similar appearance to an OID except the 'bubbles' have only a single outline and represent the functions of the class. There are also 'store' symbols (parallel lines) that represent private data structures in objects of the class. Connections in the CIS appear as entries or exits on the CID and are connected to the functions that handle them. Other connections between functions on a CID denote function calls whereas those between functions and stores represent data accesses. See for example Figure 6, and note that three instances of this class appear on Figure 5.

Figure 6 depicts the (*interaction*) function servicing the compress interaction, and this function simply sets the Compression Status variable which is periodically monitored by the *active* function compressor. Active functions are permanently executing centres of concurrent activity, and are distinguished by the fact that they do not receive interactions or events. Thus, if a frame is to be compressed and the compressor is not already occupied and notes through the Compression Status variable that a compress is required, then it will obtain the image, compress it in stages, and write the compressed image to a buffer in the Buffers object shown in Figure 4. If the compressed image exceeds a predefined size then the compressor function can call for additional buffer space to be made available via the interaction resize_buffer. After a complete frame has been compressed, the compressed event is produced. The function Image Compressor is the *constructor* function for the class.

Further class definitions are not needed for the purposes of illustrating the method. However, it should be noted that with the aim of providing a meaningful execution of the model, the Video Digitiser on Figure 5 is given a definition that simulates the cameras by taking previously captured images from files, and the implementation of the Control System Interface on Figure 2 copies every frame it receives into a window created in the model execution environment to represent the Monitor.

The actions of CID functions are defined by sequences of C++ code that must be supplied by developers. However, for *state machine functions* (not shown in Figure 6) the source code can be synthesised directly from a state transition diagram. Once code is supplied for all the functions in the classes of primitive objects in the model, the extended model can be processed by a synthesis tool which generates a Windows-based C++ program which implements the Executable Model. This can then be used to evaluate the functional behaviour of the system.

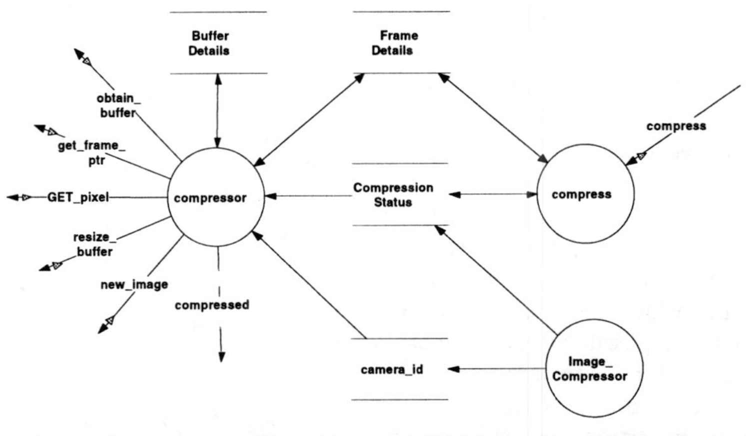

Figure 6: The Class Implementation Diagram (CID) for the Image Compressor

It is important to understand the nature of the Executable Model. In essence, it is a software emulation of an abstract model of an embedded system, where the components (objects) are uncommitted to implementation in software or hardware. However, for those objects which are eventually committed to software, the code developed for the executable model can be carried forward into the final implementation. Objects which eventually become hardware can be developed in a straightforward fashion from their software emulation.

When timing estimates or actual timing data are available, they may be added to class definitions in the form of timing models which specify the stimulus-response timing characteristics. If this is done, the tools which synthesise the executable model will produce a time-aware model from which the overall timing characteristics, performance and responsiveness of the system can be assessed.

From the material presented in this section it might appear that MOOSE models are object based rather than object oriented. For example, the Video Controller System contains no class hierarchy based on inheritance. However, the Video Controller System is simple enough not to require a class hierarchy. In the fully documented MOOSE method [3] inheritance is available. In addition the notation allows the specification of dynamically created objects and repetitive patterns of objects.

4.3 Transformational Codesign

This is the phase of the MOOSE paradigm where implementation decisions are incorporated into the Executable Model. The goals are to make decisions that provide a 'best fit' with the NFRs, and incorporate them by changes that are of a transformational nature, thereby safeguarding the 'proven' behaviour of the model. Since the model remains executable its logical behaviour and performance characteristics can still be investigated.

Typically the steps to be taken in transforming an Executable Model into a Committed Model are:

- Design of the Interface Mechanisms (requiring addition of objects and transformation of connections)
- Commitment of Objects to Hard or Soft Implementations (requiring modification of object inter-connections)
- Decisions on the Number of Processors (and the association of objects with them)
- Analysis of Threads of Execution

The design of the interface mechanisms is the first step because it often requires the addition of new objects, and these are best added to the model before other decisions are taken. This stems from the MOOSE policy of keeping external interfaces as flexible as possible (unless the exact form of the interface is specified in the requirements). This provides developers with the freedom to decide upon the most appropriate interfaces as part of the system design. However, it is important to note that the changes introduced by adding further objects only produce small, localised disturbance to the model and the changes that are not purely additive involve only localised transformations.

Next the commitment of objects to either software or hardware is decided. The essential problem here is to satisfy the NFRs. The MOOSE tools do not make the decisions but they assist in identifying the need for change and they provide, through the Executable Model (particularly the time-aware version), a means to investigate the consequences of various commitments. Finally they allow implementation decisions to be captured in a manner that carries them through to synthesised implementations. Commitment is marked on an OID by shading the objects; shaded objects with a black border are hardware, with a white border are software and non-primitive objects that contain both hardware and software objects are left uncoloured. Examples of committed models can be found in [3] and [4].

Following the hardware/software commitment, a review of inter-object connections is required and transformations are made to produce the preferred hardware to hardware connections (usually based on information flows and events) and software to software connection style (using interactions and events). Hardware/software connections may involve interactions driven by software and events produced by hardware.

The next step is to decide on the processors that will be required, and several factors influence this choice. Obviously the decision determines the actual concurrency in the software, and this has to be matched with the need for intrinsic concurrency. Requirements for physical distribution of are also of importance in this regard. Clearly the choice of processor types combined with their number determines the performance available, which must be sufficient to meet peak demands and response times. Other NFRs, such as power consumption, may be the deciding issue on processor type, and this may impact the number of processors required to meet the performance requirements. The assignment of objects to processors is indicated by writing a logical processor name on the object.

After the processors have been chosen and objects have been assigned to them, the consequences for the threads of execution running through the soft objects have to be analysed. This analysis has to recognise that each processor provides a sequential (but interruptable) execution mechanism for the functions of the software objects assigned to it, whereas in the model prior to processor commitment each object was considered to be concurrent. Checks to be made concern, for example, deadlines and times to service events, reachability, integrity, and freedom from deadlock and livelock. Various transformations of the model may be needed if problems are highlighted by the above analysis. Again the Executable Model is a vehicle that supports the analysis.

The next stage in a MOOSE development is the creation of a Platform Model which provides the system's execution environment, including the hardware base

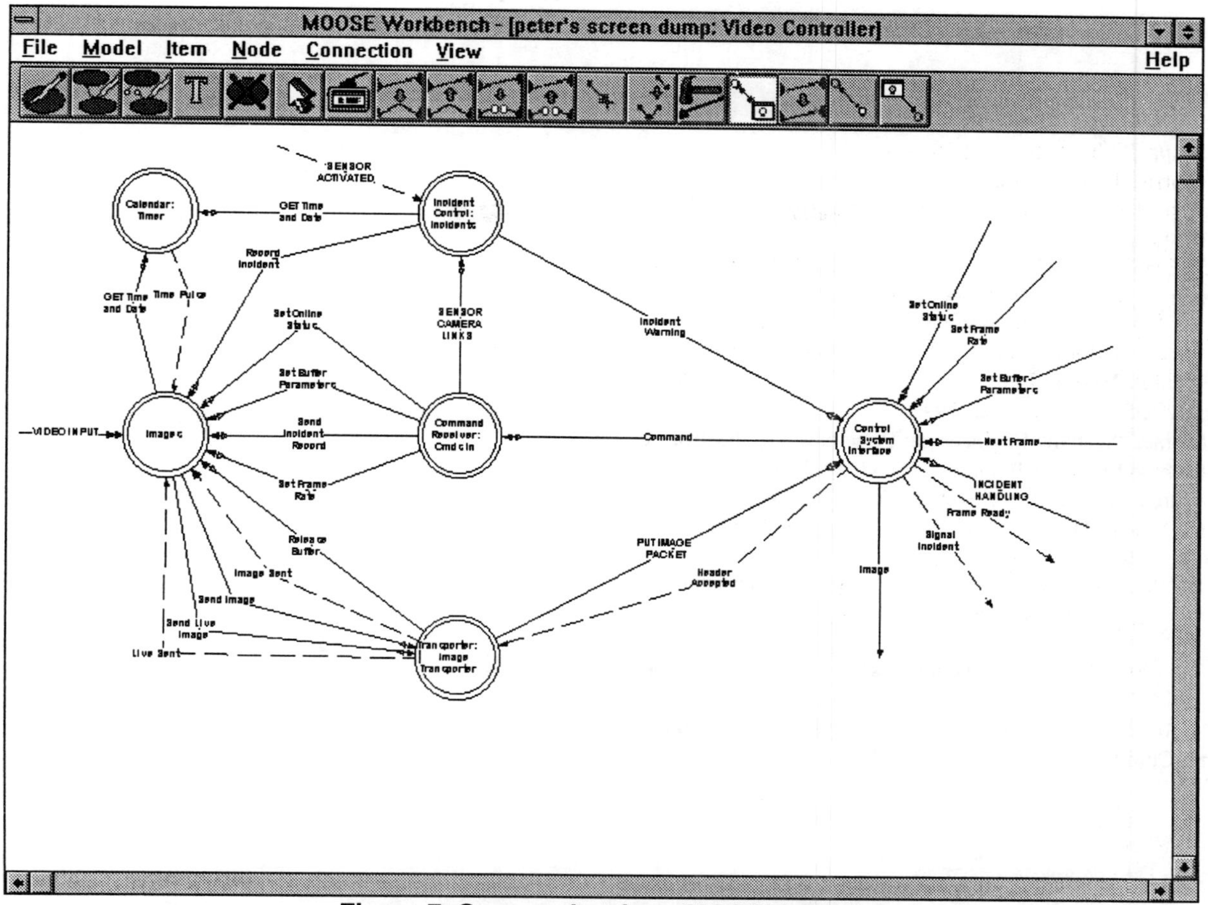

Figure 7: Screen-shot from MOOSEbench

(processors, memories, busses etc) and operating system components (schedulers, device drivers etc). For further details see [3] and [4].

4. Current status

This paper discusses ongoing work and so a status report is more appropriate than conclusions. The notation and basic approach to the development of embedded computer systems is stable and is documented in a book [3], and a supporting toolset (known as MOOSEbench) is available. MOOSEbench runs under Microsoft Windows, and the original version provides facilities for the capture and editing of models, and the synthesis of Executable Models. A Windows-based model execution environment is also provided. Further information and a trial version of the workbench is available on the World Wide Web at http://www.cl.co.umist.ac.uk/moose, and a screen-shot from the tool is shown below in Figure 7.

An updated version of the toolset is now available that provides a number of new features including libraries, implementation source synthesis, and time-aware model execution. The major objective of providing support for libraries is the re-use of designs and implementations, and so the MOOSE libraries contain both re-usable objects (i.e. their class definitions) and subsystems (i.e. object networks specified by OIDs). The MOOSE project is developing libraries catering for the use of implementation technologies developed within the ESPRIT Open Microprocessor Initiative (OMI) and selected application areas such as vision and multi-media.

The synthesis of implementation source code produces code for the final system implementation in C++ (for software) and VHDL for hardware. A slightly longer-term objective is to synthesis C rather than C++ for the software in the system, as there are sometimes no C++ compilers for microcontrollers used in embedded systems, whereas C compilers are usually available.

A number of case studies, based on real embedded systems products and in collaboration with industry, are currently in progress to assess the method.

5. Dedication and Acknowledgements

This paper is dedicated to the memory of Professor Derrick Morris who died suddenly in January 1997.

Partial funding for the work has come from the EC (projects OMI/DE 6909 and OMI/MODES 20.592) and the EPSRC (project GR/J07631).

6. References

[1] ESPRIT Project 20.592 (OMI/MODES), "MODES Exploitation Plan", Deliverable TR 2.1.2, GPS Ltd., Roborough, Plymouth, UK, November 1996.

[2] W. W. Gibbs, "Software's Chronic Crisis", Scientific American, pp. 72-81, September 1994

[3] D. Morris, D. G. Evans, P. N. Green and C. J. Theaker, Object Oriented Computer System Engineering, Springer Verlag, 1996.

[4] D. G. Evans, P. N. Green, D. Morris and P. B. James-Roxby, "A Systems Approach to Embedded System Development", Embedded Microprocessor Systems, eds. C. Muller-Schloer, F. Geerincks, B. Stanford-Smith, R. van Riet, IOS Press, 1996.

[5] K. Kronlof, Method Integration: Concepts and Case Studies. John Wiley & Sons, Chichester, 1993.

[6] B. Thome, "Systems Engineering: Principles and Practice of Computer-based Systems Engineering", Wiley, 1993.

[7] D. Harel, "Biting the Silver Bullet: Towards a Brighter Future for System Development" *IEEE Computer*, Vol. 25, No. 1, pp. 8-20, 1992

[8] N. S. Woo, A. E. Dunlop,. and W. Wolf, "Codesign from Cospecification", *IEEE Computer*, Vol. 21, No. 1, pp 42-47, 1994

[9] E. Yourdon, "Modern Structured Analysis" Prentice Hall, Englewood Cliffs, 1989.

[10] G.Booch, "Object-Oriented Analysis and Design", Benjamin-Cummings, Redwood City, 1994.

Software Engineering Support for Reliably Interconnecting Legacy Virtual Environments*

Don Welch
Department of Computer Science
University of Maryland
College Park, MD 20742
dwelch@cs.umd.edu

James Purtilo
Institute for Advanced Computer Studies and
Department of Computer Science
University of Maryland
College Park, MD 20742
purtilo@cs.umd.edu

Abstract

As the power and utility of virtual reality environments increases, so do the potential benefits found from combining several such environments. The U.S. Department of Defense currently uses over 2000 simulators, and has mandated that they all be inter-operable through its High Level Architecture. Modifying these legacy systems to interact through an abstract software layer presents the developer with a host of difficult software engineering issues. Not the least of which is how to build a system that will remain configured to provide realistic behavior in spite of system anomalies.

This paper explores some of these issues such as coordinate translation and event mapping and gives our suggestion for automating the construction of an abstraction layer. It also examines how we keep an interconnected virtual environment properly configured regardless of system anomalies. We relate our successes to date in overcoming these problems by means of various automated tools.

1. Introduction

Interconnecting legacy programs is laborious and prone to errors. There is a significant amount of new development associated with the interconnection software as well as the modifications required to the legacy software. Interconnected systems by their nature are more complicated than their component parts. Building robust interconnected computer systems from existing applications requires developers to overcome many types of problems not normally encountered when developing new software from scratch. We are intensely interested in finding methods and support tools that will lower the cost of building reliable systems out of legacy components. Our approach in this research has been to focus on a specific domain, wherein we can examine issues for dealing with legacy systems in depth, with the intent of abstracting these lessons later.

The specific domain that we are focusing on is Virtual Environments (VEs). The U.S. Department of Defense (DoD) has mandated that all its distributed simulations must be adapted to use its emerging High Level Architecture (HLA) for interconnection. This means over 2000 legacy simulations must be modified in the near future to interact with each other through this software abstraction architecture. Interconnected Virtual Environments (IVE) are a particularly interesting problem since they have all the usual problems associated with program interconnection plus domain-specific issues such as coordinate system translations, performance constraints, data filtering and object grouping.

IVE builders are not only responsible for gluing existing VEs together, but IVEs also require support utilities to perform functions that were not needed in standalone VEs. If the IVE is large then VEs must be able to join and leave the IVE while it is running. Controllers must be able to unobtrusively monitor the virtual world and they must be able to intervene to insure that the goals of the exercise are being met. The IVE must be robust, and network anomalies must have minimal effect on the IVE participants. We think that the most interesting of these support functions is reconfiguring the IVE in the presence of anomalies to maintain realism.

To illustrate some of the added complexity involved in maintaining a configuration to support realism, consider the failure of a component VE. It is unrealistic to remove the effected virtual entity or to let it continue under the control of only a *dead-reckoning* algorithm. Some type of computer controlled simulation must take control. Deciding which simulation depends not only on types (e.g., tank for tank) but on the state of the spares (spare already in use or not). Once

*This research was funded by Office of Naval Research contract number N000149410320

0-8186-7840-2/97 $10.00 © 1997 IEEE

the IVE reconfigures to compensate, what if the original VE comes back up? Ideally the IVE should give control back to the human-in-the-loop VE, unless the entity has already been destroyed in the virtual world. The decision is not straight forward and requires advanced logic to be made properly. We call the process of automatically reconfiguring the IVE in response to external conditions *Compensating Reconfiguration*.

1.1. Related Work

Research in distributed virtual environments has been mostly confined to multi-user virtual environments built from scratch to work together or distributing the processing of VE tasks to improve performance. The *EM toolkit* and *DIVE* environment are two of the best known systems that provide an environment for building the entire distributed VE. [17] [8] *Virtual Design* is another complete VE software engineering environment that also focuses on using a wide array of input data and hardware. [1] *DGPSE+* is an experimental environment supporting distributed graphics support. [13] None of these systems supports the reuse of legacy VEs.

This work draws on the experience with code generators, interconnection tools, and packagers. Hofmiester and Purtilo [9] have built the SURGEON system for dynamic reconfiguration and Chen and Purtilo [2] have built tools for mapping events in event based interconnected systems.

The gluing together of disparate heterogeneous distributed systems forms the foundation on which we built this work. Using standard interconnection abstractions makes the development of a software engineering environment practical. Our solution supports interconnection abstractions like POLYLITH,[14] HLA,[5] and CORBA.[15] These abstractions make it easy for our framework to tap into existing systems without changing any of the component VEs.

The end-result of Compensating Reconfiguration is the dynamic reconfiguration of the IVE. There are two primary approaches to dynamic reconfiguration. The CONIC approach moves the application to a quiescent state prior to reconfiguration.[10] This approach requires logic located in each component that will migrate a component to a quiescent state in finite time. A quiescent state is not realistically achievable for CVEs. Hofmeister's approach is better for CVEs.[9] She requires the components involved to divulge their internal state, then loads this into the new component. Since VEs in a CVE continuously divulge their internal state (the part that the rest of the simulation cares about anyway), the software is ready for dynamic reconfiguration without change.

Since our work in compensating reconfiguration results from our investigation of fault-tolerance, we have examined these techniques and found them too specialized for Compensating Reconfiguration problems. [3] Because of the time constraints imposed by virtual reality, we designed our Compensating Reconfiguration framework to trade-off between consistent state and reaction time. Fault-tolerance acts on the loss of some required service, where Compensating Reconfiguration handles losses as well as gains. The choice of compensating action is straight forward in fault-tolerant systems; while in a Compensating Reconfiguration system, a combination of system state and application state may dictate divergent compensating actions.

2. Requirements

To clearly identify what we are trying to accomplish, we discuss the requirements for a software engineering environment that supports IVE construction. We first look at generating the interconnection software. This includes the IVE runtime and the interface modules for each of the component VEs. Then we take a close look at one of the support utilities IVEs need: Compensating Reconfiguration.

2.1. Interconnection Generator Requirements

For the interconnection generator to be useful, it must be easier and faster for the IVE builders to create a functioning IVE with it than without. Since numerous iterations will be necessary to tighten up the requirements, it must also be easier to modify. The generator must be capable of incorporating design decisions and departing from defaults as more is understood about the system. It must create robust modifiable code that can serve as the basis for a production system, because exploiting the work done in prototype development can reap large benefits if the pitfalls can be avoided. The interconnection code produced must expose hinge points [1] to the software engineers that are isolated from the rest of the code. Changes to the legacy VEs must be minimized and isolated so as to reduce the complexity of IVE construction. Finally, the engineers assembling an IVE must deal with a wide array of topics across many technical areas. The generator must allow the engineers to reason about the interconnection as abstractly as possible.

The interconnection software must provide a full range of services that you would expect in any large heterogeneous distributed system. First and foremost the interconnection must be independent of any architecture or programming language. The interconnection software must handle all communication between VEs. Bindings between VEs and the runtime must be dynamic. During execution the IVE must be able to change its configuration to adapt to changing needs and requirements.

[1] Places where change is likely throughout the life-cycle.

The resulting IVE must also be able to provide IVE specific services. The most computationally intensive is coordinate translation. The VEs will most likely use different coordinate systems. Placing the translation code in the interconnection avoids the difficult task of changing the coordinate system used in the legacy VE. Another important service the interconnection software must provide is event mapping. All events in the component VEs will not map nicely to single events among the other VEs. The interconnection software must seamlessly map these events so the legacy VEs can continue to use their original events. Finally, IVEs have unique dynamic data grouping that may vary between legacy VE designs. When the interconnection software manages this grouping, each VE can continue to work with its own view of data grouping. The more work done in the interconnection software, the fewer changes to the legacy VEs, but also more latency in the interconnection.

The perception of human users is the performance driver. Human perception can be quite forgiving in that it perceives a 100 ms response as instantaneous. It can also be demanding in that techniques such as suspending the IVE or rolling back the events will manifest unrealistic behavior. Humans can tolerate small deviations from realistic behavior and still continue to successfully interact in the virtual world, although IVE builders must minimize these lapses. IVEs will need some technique such as *Dead-Reckoning* to over come network latency.

2.2. Compensating Reconfiguration Requirements

A Compensating Reconfiguration component participates in the IVE architecture as shown in Figure 1. It provides the ability to restructure the running IVE in accordance with a set of rules and the current states. As it executes, it monitors the IVE unobtrusively, until it notices a system anomaly. Then using the rules provided by the designers it determines what compensating reconfiguration is necessary and implements it through the interconnection software. The driving principle for Compensating Reconfiguration is maintaining *coherence*, which means every virtual object is controlled by one and only one VE.

To provide this service the Compensating Reconfiguration utility must perform a set of interrelated functions. The Compensating Reconfiguration utility must detect system anomalies in order to react to them. It also must keep its own copy of the system and application state. This eliminates network latency during the decision process, but more importantly eliminates the requirement for VEs to save their state prior to reconfiguration. Additionally, it must be able to use a simple form of the application state when it makes reconfiguration decisions. The decision itself must be driven by domain-based rules as well as the current IVE state. The decision process must be fast enough to avoid unrealistic behavior, while sophisticated enough to handle complex situations. The Compensating Reconfiguration utility must be able to use loops, conditionals, and waits when invoking the reconfiguration primitives. It must be able to modify the structure, geometry, or implementations of the IVE. Whatever order or frequency of reconfigurations the Compensating Reconfiguration implements, the IVE must always end up in a coherent state.

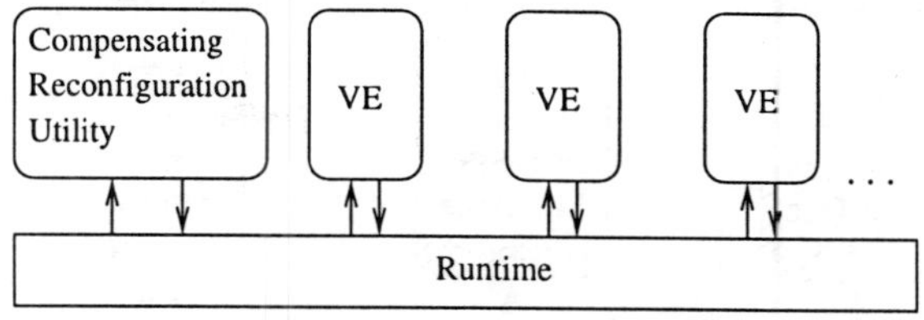

Figure 1. IVE with Compensating Reconfiguration Utility

3 Toolkit

We have built a prototype environment based on meeting these requirements. It has three facets: an interconnection generator *Zubin* that creates the interconnection runtime and the interface software, a Compensating Reconfiguration framework *Bullpen* and a tailored methodology that exploits these tools.

3.1. ZUBIN: the Interconnection Generator

The runtime interconnection abstraction is highly customized to fit the design of the legacy VEs and the requirements of the IVE. The runtime and interface modules can be built by hand, but we feel that this design and coding process can be effectively captured and reused by an interconnection generator.

All communication in the system is between the interface modules and the runtime. When an event occurs in a legacy VE, it uses the interface module API to notify the runtime. Messages from the runtime are received by the interface which calls the appropriate routines in the legacy code.

The Zubin Language description gives a mostly non-procedural description of the software glue that holds the IVE together. However, there are some places to record design decisions in the IVE description. Additionally, there are also sections where developers can insert code escapes. The reasons we departed from a purely non-procedural specification was to support iteration in development and the complexity of some of the algorithms used in VEs.

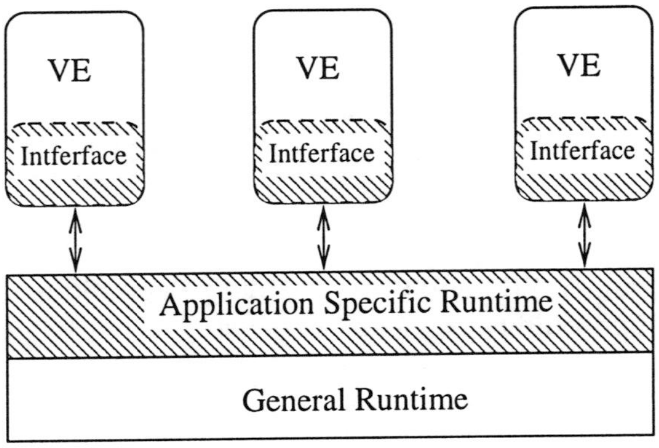

Figure 2. IVE Interconnection Infrastructure Created by Zubin (shaded)

```
OBJECT obTank ACTIVE:
# Comments that go in the source code
# for the Tank Virtual Object
ATTRIBUTES :
  FLOAT atTurretDir, # in radians
  FLOAT atDir,
  BOOLEAN atDrawPlow = FALSE;
RULES rnMove(atX, atY)
  FOR ALL ACTIVE
  {* if ((atX + atMaxSizeX) >=
              ($atX - $atMinSizeX) &&
      (atX - atMinSizeX) >=
              ($atX + $atMaxSizeX) &&
      (atY + atMaxSizeY) >=
              ($atY - $atMinSizeY) &&
      (atY - atMinSizeY) >=
              ($atY + $atMaxSizeY))
   *} VIOLATION evCrash(atObId, $atObId);
HOLDS
  obTurret;
CAN HOLD
  obMinePlow[atDrawPlow = TRUE:FALSE];
```

Figure 3. Example Virtual Object Description

Since many different coordinate systems can be in use in the IVE, the translation algorithms to convert between each coordinate system in use are described in the *Translation Section.* The algorithms are defined as code escapes because the coordinate system translation is not always a single mathematical formula. The spherical earth does not transfer well to a flat map, therefore converting geographic coordinates requires conditionals and lookup tables.

Interconnection and configuration information for the runtime are described in the *Component Section* of the description. In addition, the initialization information required for component VEs to join the IVE is also related here. It also contains information about the different types of component VEs that may participate in an IVE session. Zubin uses much of this information to generate the interface modules.

The environmental states, such as weather or lighting conditions are defined in the *Environment Section.* Zubin automatically generates events to change the IVEs environmental states.

Data Filtering and message routing is described in the *Areas of Interest Section.* Areas of Interest may be declared based on spatial constraints (the most popular), or functional alignments. This partitioning—to reduce message traffic—can be handled by the runtime using multicasting which is useful in large IVEs, or by it selectively sending messages to the appropriate VEs.

The *Objects Section* describes the objects shared by the VEs. Objects are described using inheritance which provides less repetitive descriptions, but more importantly allows more intuitive descriptions of things such as collisions. A set of default attributes automatically is included with each object. These attributes vary with the object type but primarily include the location (in three dimensions), the orientation (3 degrees of freedom), and the size (minimum and maximum along each dimension) of the object.

Figure 3 shows an example of a virtual object description in the Zubin description language. This simple example shows the description of a tank virtual object. The tank is declared to be an active object, therefore the runtime is aware that the tank can move about the virtual world influencing other virtual objects. Those attributes that are not part of the default attribute set are declared here. One rule is shown, and this states that no two active objects can occupy the same space at the same time. All default attributes are used in this calculation. If this rule is violated, the runtime generates the *Crash* event. Finally object grouping is declared through the *HOLDS* and *CAN HOLD* declarations.

The *Events Section* contains descriptions of the functionality of the IVE. Each event in the IVE has a list of messages that are sent or received when the event occurs. The messages can be synchronous, which require confirmation from the runtime or asynchronous. The developer also designates whether or not a message is to be filtered based on *Areas Of Interest.* Finally, the content of the message is also defined.

Figure 4 shows an example of an event description in the Zubin description language. There are two messages associated with this event, there may be many more because messages are tailored for the VEs with which they communicate. The first message is from the VEs to the runtime. It is a synchronous message, which means that the runtime must

```
evMove (INT obId, INT X, INT Y, FLOAT dir):
  MESSAGE SYNCH rnMove;
    FROM cmTankSim, cmBradleySim;
    CONTENT (INT obId, INT X, INT Y,
             FLOAT dir);

  MESSAGE ASYNCH;
    TO cmTankSim SPATIAL;
    PRIORITY REGULAR;
    RELIABILITY UNRELIABLE;
    CONTENT (INT obId, INT X, INT Y,
             FLOAT dir);
```

Figure 4. Example Event Description

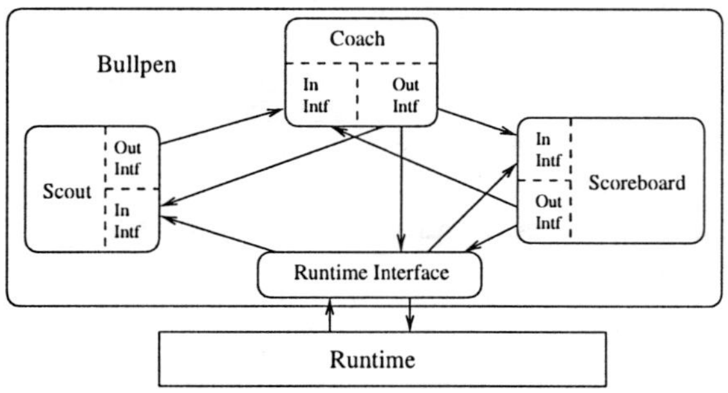

Figure 5. Bullpen Structure and Data Flow

check the *Move* rule before it can acknowledge the message. If the rule is not violated, the appropriate *to* messages will be sent to the other VEs. This message is an update of the object location and receipt is not critical to the IVE therefore it is an asynchronous method that is sent by unreliable (less bandwidth) means.

3.2. Bullpen: Compensating Reconfiguration Framework

Our approach to solving this problem is a software engineering environment called Bullpen. A key part is the Bullpen framework, which includes three components. Figure 5 shows the data flow between the Bullpen Framework components and the simulation. Bullpen gets its policies at runtime through the use of various files.

We have developed the Bullpen prototype on a simulation architecture based on DoD's High Level Architecture (HLA). Bullpen runs as a support utility; it only inserts itself into the simulation when required. Most of the time it will monitor all the message traffic of the simulation and do nothing. If the simulation is using multicast or broadcast then there is no overhead. With unicast there is the slight penalty of an additional network message per simulation message. When it detects an event of interest, Bullpen then makes two decisions. The first decision determines a compensating reconfiguration, while the second decides how to implement the reconfiguration.

Bullpen has three independently executing components. It is Scout's mission to detect events of interest and report them along with any preliminary information to Coach. Coach contains the decision-making logic for both the end-state and how-to reconfiguration decisions. Coach directly executes the reconfigurations by using the simulation architecture API and remote system calls. Scoreboard is responsible for keeping a valid copy of the application and system state. In our prototype this includes implementation of the dead-reckoning algorithm.

Bullpen has at least five major threads running whenever it is executing. Scout continues to handle incoming messages and to test for absent VEs regardless of what else Bullpen is doing. This way Bullpen can identify an event when it happens. Coach manages simultaneous events by spawning a new thread for each event it handles. Scoreboard deals with queries and updates in one thread while updating the database through dead-reckoning in another. This way we insure that the database always represents an accurate picture of the state.

We designed Bullpen to work in a wide array of heterogeneous environments. We wrote Bullpen in Java^{TM} to make it portable across platforms. We designed it to function in a HLA type environment without change. The only coding required is the implementation of the reconfiguration strategies. Bullpen itself may run on one, two, or three separate hosts to support scalablity. To support this we encapsulated inter-component communication to allow easy migration to and from a distributed architecture.

Scout. Scout reifies the event detection function. It keeps its own small lists, but otherwise relies on Scoreboard for application state information. Anytime Scout observes a message from a VE it updates that VE's heartbeat. Scout is also party to reconfigurations made by Coach so that it understands the current structure of the simulation. It detects events two ways: by discovering messages from VEs that Bullpen has reconfigured out of the simulation, and by detecting an expired heartbeat.

Coach. Coach uses a separate type of Decision-Maker for each type of event that it handles. Each Decision-Maker uses the rules defined by the simulation developers and the current state to choose a compensating action. Compensating actions are implemented as a Strategy, which can be a Java^{TM} method or a *Planner*. When the Strategy is a method, it can use conditionals, loops, and waits while it executes the reconfiguration. It also has the ability to query

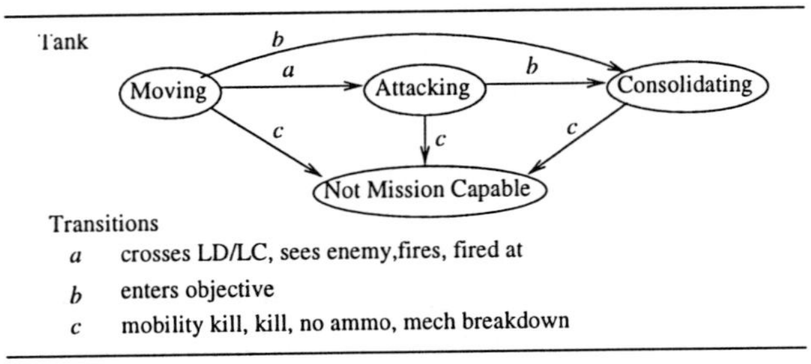

Figure 6. State Transition Diagram for an Individual Tank

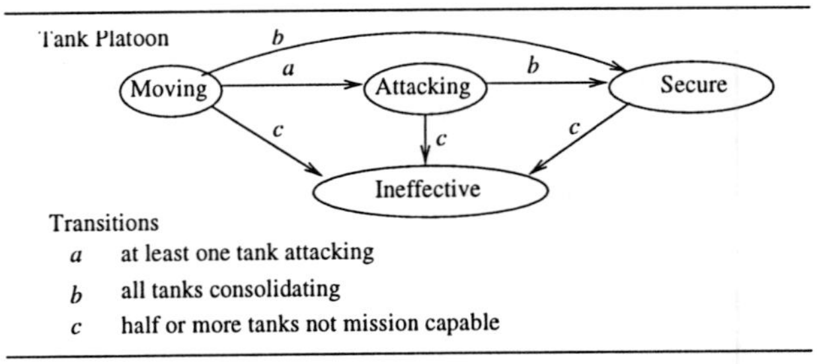

Figure 7. State Transition Diagram for a Grouping of Tanks

for system and/or application state. This is very powerful, but forces the developer to deal with the reconfiguration protocol. A planner works off a set of rules and is easier to reason about, but may be slower. Coach also uses a locking protocol to ensure that reconfiguration actions are atomic and leave the federation structure consistent.

Scoreboard. Scoreboard's purpose is to keep an accurate version of the system and application state and provide an interface for queries. Scoreboard monitors message traffic updating itself, to include using triggers to keep accurate meta-states. The federation's dead-reckoning algorithms are part of Scoreboard.

Bullpen needs access to the application meta-state while making a decision. In large simulations making decisions using the state of entities can be very complex. When stating requirements, simulation users will tend to think in terms of aggregate states of virtual object groups. These we call meta-states.

To better explain meta-states look at figures 6 and 7. Figure 6 shows the transitions and rules for a single virtual entity—a tank. Figure 7 shows the state transitions for a unit—a tank platoon—containing four tanks. The individual tanks change state based on their location, status, or the actions of other virtual entities. The tank platoon changes state when all or some of the member tanks change state. If we were to follow this hierarchy to division level (~5000 vehicles) you can see that the complexity of the conditionals required to use the state would be enormous. This makes using the application state unrealistic. However, by encoding state changes and relationships in the database through the use of a trigger, the use of meta-states of the levels in the hierarchy becomes very convenient.

Performance. Assessing the performance of a Compensating Reconfiguration component is difficult. Its primary goal is to avoid unrealistic behavior. Unrealistic behavior springs from a player not being controlled by one and only one simulation. However, with dead reckoning unrealistic behavior will not manifest itself until some time after the actual event. Because the user's judgment determines unrealistic behavior, it is difficult to define. Additionally, unrealistic behavior is application and situation dependent. Without control, virtual aircraft in close combat will misbehave sooner than trucks traveling at constant speed on a straight highway.

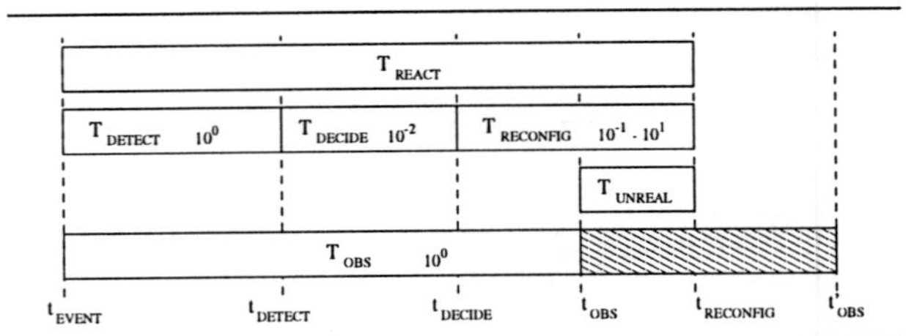

Figure 8. Reconfiguration Timeline (not to scale)

We are satisfied that Bullpen meets performance requirements. It will never force unrealistic behavior on the IVE, even if it cannot guarantee that unrealistic behavior will not occur. A coherent configuration has every entity controlled by one and only one VE. Under Bullpen, the IVE will always reach a coherent configuration—if one is possible. Although brief interludes of unrealistic behavior are undesirable, users can tolerate them and still have a successful IVE experience.

Figure 8 shows the timeline for a reconfiguration. These times are all very hardware dependent so we limit ourselves to an order of magnitude analysis. t_{event} is the time the event occurs. t_{detect} is when Bullpen detects that event. With heartbeats, this will average half the heartbeat expiration, measured in seconds.[7] t_{decide} marks the completion of Bullpen's decision process. The elapsed time T_{decide} is the only part that is attributable to Bullpen. Usual values are in hundredths of a second. $t_{reconfig}$ indicates the completion of the reconfiguration. In the best case where the simulation builders dedicated a *hot spare* to this event $T_{reconfig}$ would have a duration measured in tenths of a second. At the other end of the spectrum, loading and initializing a VE would give $T_{reconfig}$ a value measured in tens of seconds.

t_{obs} will occur at some non-deterministic interval (usually seconds) after t_{event}. If it is also after $t_{reconfig}$, say at t'_{obs} then no unrealistic behavior occurs. If it is before $t_{reconfig}$ then the simulation will display unrealistic behavior during the interval T_{unreal}. The duration of T_{unreal} is dependent on T_{react}. $T_{detect}(10^0)$ dominates T_{react} in the best case, and $T_{reconfig}(10^1)$ dominates in the worst case. T_{decide} is never the dominant term.

Example Scenario To help illustrate how a Compensating Reconfiguration component generated by Bullpen works we will go through a simple scenario. Our example is a military simulation that integrates manned simulators and computer generated forces (CGF) to create a rich training environment. An aviation section (one observation helicopter, two attack helicopters) supports a platoon (four tanks) during an attack. The tanks and helicopters are crewed simulators, while the rest of the friendly and enemy forces are CGFs.

The goal of this exercise is to train the users. Therefore a goal of the simulation builders is to insure that a system failure will not result in the rest of the participants noticing unrealistic behavior. Additionally, the simulation must bring a manned system that becomes available again back into the exercise as quickly and seamlessly as possible. The simulation builders write the rules to achieve these goals. Figure 9 shows a portion of the rules for replacing a VE that fails.

The exercise starts and all participants are taking part in the war game. A tank simulator drops its network connection. The uncontrolled virtual tank continues to behave according to its dead-reckoning algorithm. This is only acceptable for a situation-dependent period of time.

Scout detects that the virtual tank's heartbeat has expired. Scout sends the information to Coach, which spawns a process to decide how to compensate. The decision-maker collects information as it refines its decision. Scout has told it that the missing player is a tank. Scoreboard tells it that a manned tank simulator controlled the virtual M1. In this scenario, the exercise developers allocated the resources to support a hot spare for the tanks, so Scoreboard also tells Coach that the hot spare is still available. Coach picks a Strategy that changes ownership of the virtual tank to the hot spare software/host.

Should a second M1 also fail, the hot spare would not be available, and Bullpen would restructure the simulation differently. Bullpen is adaptive in this way because it has a dynamic picture of the system and application state.

The exercise continues with the virtual tank controlled as a CGF rather than by a crew. The network problem clears and the tank simulator reenters the IVE, trying to control its original virtual tank. Scout detects this and notifies Coach, which then spawns another decision-maker. Scoreboard tells Coach that a CGF currently controls the disputed virtual tank, and the returning component has human users. Therefore it executes a Strategy that replaces the CGF with the crewed tank simulator. This includes not only changing ownership of the virtual tank, but stopping the CGF, and updating the tank simulator with the latest state information from Scoreboard.

```
SWITCH (FEDERATE TYPE ==) {
CASE  "M1"
  SWITCH ("federate" ID APP ==) {
  CASE "tank_sim"
    SWITCH ("Host" "host_11" "M1_CGF" ==) {
    CASE "hot" "CS_StartM1HotSpare"
    ELSE "CS_StartSimpM1CGF"
    }
  CASE "m1_cgf"
    SWITCH ("Unit" "tank_plt" ==) {
    CASE "aslt"
      SWITCH ("Host" "host_11" "M1_CGF" ==) {
      CASE "hot" "CS_StartM1HotSpare"
      ELSE "CS_StartSimpM1CGF"
      }
    ELSE "CS_StartSimpM1CGF"
    }
  CASE "simple_m1_cgf" "CS_StartSimpM1CGF"
  ELSE "CS_StartSimpM1CGF"
}
:
```

Figure 9. Replacement Rules

This scenario did not use meta-states, nor did it show how Bullpen handles canceling events. It only used two basic events, an absentee, and a reentry. Bullpen is capable reacting to more complicated situations, but this example presents a flavor for what it can do and how it does it.

3.3. Methodology

To properly tie our toolkit together we have developed a tailored methodology to exploit the strengths of these tools. This methodology focuses on extracting the salient features of the existing systems and juxtaposing those with the new requirements of the IVE to create a description of the interconnection. This description is used to quickly create a prototype system. The user and developer then assess the IVE and measure it against user needs. After a number of iterations, the requirements stabilize and both user and software engineer should be confident that the system represents an executable specification for the IVE. At this point the executable specification can be used to build a production system. The IVE code already carries a high degree of assurance that it accurately translates the description into interconnection code. Techniques can now be applied to optimize the simple interconnection code so that performance requirements can be met. These techniques can be automatic or manual.

Phase 1: Requirements Analysis The first phase has two major super-tasks: *Legacy System Analysis* and *IVE Requirements Gathering*, each with their own task list. The former concentrates on understanding the legacy systems within the context of the IVE, while the latter focuses on understanding how the interconnected system is to act. These two activities cannot be performed in isolation since they are heavily influenced by the results of the other.

Super-task a: Legacy System Analysis The tasks of Legacy System Analysis start with understanding the basics such as architecture, system and programming language. The developers must examine each legacy VE to determine which aspects of its architecture are interesting to the rest of the IVE. Each VE may use numerous coordinate systems, so the developers must identify a single coordinate system for communication with the IVE. They must also identify and understand the environmental states used locally well enough to allowing mapping across the IVE at a later stage. They must examine the events of the legacy VE events and decide which are related to the IVE and which only have local consequence. Finally, they must canvass virtual objects in each VE. From this study they must understand enough about each virtual object to be able to map it to virtual objects in each of the other VEs. Some objects will not be shared with the IVE; normally environmental objects such as terrain, buildings, etc.

Super-task b: IVE Requirements Gathering One of the tasks the IVE builders must accomplish as part of this super-task is determining what, if any functionality must be added to each legacy VE. Once they identify the functionality, the design, implementation and test of this added functionality is handled using a traditional maintenance process, which is beyond the scope of this paper.

The other tasks the software engineers do as part of this super-task are assimilate the products of Legacy System Analysis into a coherent set of requirements for the interconnection software. Most of this assimilation involves mapping items between the legacy VEs through the interconnection software. However, a significant portion is devoted to strictly IVE wide functions. There are seven major tasks they must accomplish.

The developers must choose a single coordinate system for communicating with the runtime. This way each VE will have to translate to at most one other coordinate system. Additionally, this limits the total number of translations algorithms to $\mathcal{O}(n)$. For each translation identified, they must

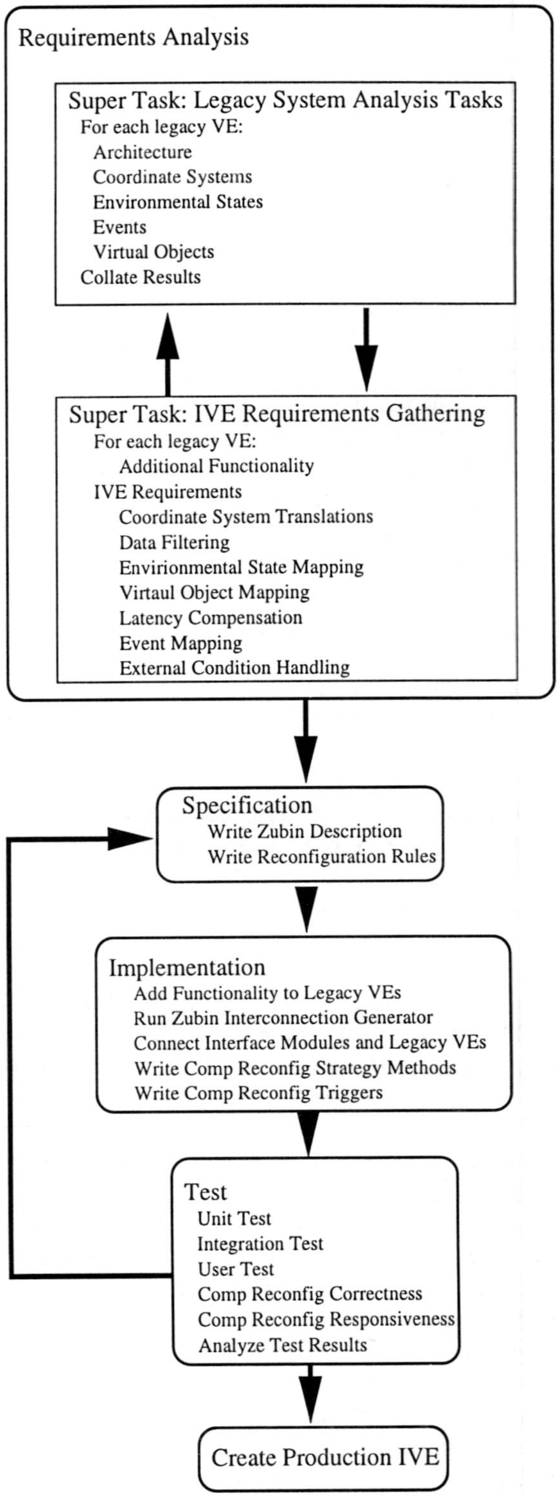

Figure 10. Methodology

identify or develop the translation algorithm.

If the IVE is to reach any size, message traffic can create a bottleneck in network bandwidth and at the component VE's cpu. To scale, the IVE must filter the messages to insure that a VE receives all the messages it needs, but few of the messages it does not need. The data filtering scheme involving spatial proximity and functional areas of interest is developed during this phase.

Another task they must do is map all the environmental states identified in the legacy VEs to each other. Environmental states can be exceeding complex in some VEs and mindlessly simple, or even not represented in others. Weather has great impact on aircraft, and might not even be represented in a VE with infrared sensors. The states must be distilled to their most basic components while still meeting the user's requirements for realism.

Object mapping involves identifying how each of the objects in the IVE will be represented in each other VE. Objects will not always map directly to each other. A virtual battle may involve all friendly forces in reality, but they may see each other as "bad guys" for training purposes. Additionally, the way each VE handles grouping will differ and the software engineers must identify the "lowest common *grouping* denominator." In addition to mapping the objects, they identify the coherency rules along with an algorithm that determines when they have been violated.

In standalone VEs network latency is not an issue, but in interconnected VEs handling it is critical to the success of the IVE. The most common techniques are *dead-reckoning* and *forward-reckoning*. Both continuously update the state of non-local objects based on the last reported state. The developers must choose a technique for handling network latency and develop the necessary algorithms for inclusion in the individual VEs.

Event mapping is critical and the software engineers must look at events from three different perspectives. First they must look at all events in the component VEs and determine which ones are salient to the IVE. Next they must identify events that do not exist in any of the component VEs but nevertheless, are needed for the IVE. These form the set of IVE events. Finally, they must take the newly identified IVE events and determine how each VE will import each event and map it to one of its own. Not all IVE events need be brought into each VE; a radar simulator will not care if it is day or night.

The IVE builders must identify system anomalies that can have catastrophic effect on the IVE and determine how to counteract them. They must examine each failure that can effect the IVE and determine its probability of occurrence and impact on the IVE. They must also look at the substitute resources available and the kind of performance they can expect with each possible configuration. Armed with this knowledge they perform a cost/benefit analysis and allocate resources for spares appropriately. Additionally, they must analyze the impact of reentering VEs that have been reconfigured out of the IVE. The conditions under which the VE regains control of its original objects, what happens when it does not.

Phase 2: Specification The major task of this phase is to take the products from phase 1 and put them into a formal preliminary description of the interconnection software. The IVE builders write the description of the interconnection in the Zubin description language. They also write the rules governing a coherent IVE for Bullpen to build its decision logic.

Phase 3: Implementation This phase is significantly shortened by using our toolkit. However, there is some coding that must be finished during this phase. Any functionality that must be added to the legacy VEs must be completed by this point. The Zubin description is turned into an instantiation of the runtime and the interface modules are built by running the interconnection generator. The interconnection generator builds the interface modules in the legacy VE's programming language consequently providing a tailored application programming interface (API) to each individual VE. Using the API each legacy VE is linked into the rest of the IVE.

The developers use the Bullpen framework to build a Compensating Reconfiguration utility. Besides the rules that have been developed in phase two, some programming has to be done. The actual methods that implement the reconfigurations must written. In addition, the triggers of the database must incorporate the state transition rules into to meta-states.

Phase 4: Test Once the legacy code has been modified and the executables built the system can be tested by the software engineers. They must test the functionality added to the legacy VEs—if any. Because we are reusing the process with a code generator, there is a high degree of assurance that the system meets the specifications as stated in the Zubin description. Therefore they can focus testing on determining whether or not the specifications capture the true IVE requirements (Validation and Verificaiton). In addition, any changes to the requirements can be documented at this time.

Testers must insure the Compensating Reconfiguration utility reacts correctly and quickly enough. Testing the correctness of a reconfiguration includes making sure it executes the proper reconfiguration in response to an event. It also means insuring that the reconfiguration will actually compensate for the event. In the IVE Requirements Gathering phase the analysts did a cost/benefits analysis of compensating actions. Assumptions and conclusions from that analysis must be confirmed through testing during this phase.

With the additional knowledge gained at this point, the developers go back to the specification phase and modify the description. Design decisions can be put into the system such as where coordinate translation will occur. Reconfiguration rules and implementations are changed if needed. When the system has been rebuilt it can again be presented to the user. Eventually the system becomes an executable specification for the IVE.

Phase 5: Creating a Production System Armed with this executable specification for the IVE the software engineers can then set about building a production quality system. There are two tracks that they can follow: starting from scratch, or reusing the prototype. Normally, trying to build quality and performance into a prototype system is a recipe for disaster. In this instance we feel that it is possible. The interconnection code generated by Zubin is robust code that has been used and tested numerous times. The interconnection code is modular and as long as the interfaces are kept intact it should be possible to keep changes isolated.

4. Conclusions

In our experiments so far we have found that the performance of software built with our framework is comparable to hand-built interconnection code. Additionally, the Domain-Directed Reconfiguration component imposed very little overhead on the IVE under normal circumstances and was able to provide anomaly compensation fast enough for human-in-the-loop systems.

Our preliminary work verifies that Zubin requires less effort than creating equivalent interconnection code by hand. The process for using Zubin mirrors manual coding up through specification. Savings of effort begin to show during implementation and test. We used Zubin to turn a simple walkthrough IVE a description of about 400 lines into approximately 5000 lines of C++ source code. If nothing else we have saved the clerical work of creating 5000 lines of source code. We saved effort testing, because we focused on overall IVE behavior, and did not spend the time verifying that the interconnection code met specifications. However, the real savings came when as a result of test, major changes were made to the IVE. In one instance we decided to change the coordinate system used by the runtime which effected almost every module in the interconnection. Using Zubin took less than a hour as compared to the many hours spent doing it manually.

We have also been successful in using Bullpen to reduce the effort needed to add Compensating Reconfiguration to IVEs. We do this through our framework and the abstract encapsulation of the decisions required to build the function. We feel that the real advantage to our approach will come with reuse and hope to confirm this soon.

The time that an IVE takes to reconfigure itself to compensate for a system event is composed of three parts, only one of which is attributable to the decision. If resources are allocated for *hot spares* the dominating term is the time it takes to detect the event (a function of IVE design). If significant resources are not available then the time to start a replacement process dominates, but never the time that the Compensating Reconfiguration utility takes to decide.

We have developed a set of tools for building an interconnected virtual environment from legacy standalone virtual environments. We used a runtime implementation of a software bus abstraction that has been automatically specialized for a specific application to interconnect the IVE. We built the interconnection software with an interconnection generator that creates the interconnection runtime as well as the applications programming interface. We also developed a software framework for developing a Compensating Reconfiguration utility. We have wrapped this all together with a tailored methodology that exploits the strengths of these tools to create a rapid prototyping environment for the virtual environment domain.

The executable specification that results is useful to developers of production systems in two ways. By having an executable specification much more can be understood about the target system by the developers than just working from paper documents alone. The users have had an opportunity to see what the final system will look like, and both users and requirements engineers can have higher assurance that the correct system is being built.

The interconnection code is robust since it is the result of process reuse, therefore it may be possible to modify the prototype to create a production quality system. Our system does not replace the difficult reasoning about IVEs. Instead it automates the more mundane aspects of IVE creation, allowing the software engineers to focus on the core problems facing the IVE builder.

References

[1] P. Astheimer, W. Felger, and S. Müller. Virtual Design: A generic VR System for Industrial Applications. *Computers and Graphics*, 17(6):671–677, November/December 1993.

[2] C. Chen and J. Purtilo. Event Adaptation for Integrating Distributed Applications. In *Proceedings of the Conference on Software Engineering and Knowledge Engineering*, June 1995.

[3] F. Cristian. Understanding Fault-Tolerant Distributed Systems. *Communications of the ACM*, 34(2):57–78, Feb. 1991.

[4] Defense Modeling and Simulation Office. High Level Architecture Rules, Aug. 1996. Version 1.0.

[5] Defense Modeling and Simulation Office. High Level Architecture Interface Specification , Feb. 1997. Version 1.1.

[6] Defense Modeling and Simulation Office. High Level Architecture Object Model Template , Feb. 1997. Version 1.1.

[7] DIS Steering Committee. The DIS Vision, A Map to the Future of Distributed Simulation, May 1994. Version 1.

[8] M. Green. Environment Manager. Technical report, Department of Computing Science, University of Alberta, Feb. 1994.

[9] C. R. Hofmeister and J. M. Purtilo. Dynamic Reconfigureation of Distributed Programs. In *Proceedings of the 11th International Conference on Distrubuted Computing Systems*, pages 560–571, 1991.

[10] J. Kramer and J. Magee. The Evolving Philosophers Problem: Dynamic Change Management. *IEEE Transactions on Software Engineering*, 16(11):1293–1306, Nov. 1990.

[11] J. Magee, J. Kramer, and M. Sloman. Constructing Distributed Systesm in Conic. *IEEE Transactions on Software Engineering*, 15(6):663–675, June 1989.

[12] H. Mili, F. Mili, and A. Mili. Reusing Software: Issues and Research Directions. *IEEE Transactions on Software Engineering*, 21(6):528–561, June 1995.

[13] Z. Pan, J. Shi, and M. Zhang. Distributed Graphics Support for Virtual Environments. *Computers and Graphics*, 20(2):191–197, March/April 1996.

[14] J. M. Purtilo. The POLYLITH Software Bus. *ACM Transactions on Programming Languages*, 16:151–174, Jan. 1994.

[15] J. Siegel. *CORBA Fudamentals and Programming*. Wiley Computer Publishing Group, New York, 1996.

[16] Under Secretary of Defense (Acquisition and Technology). Modeling and Simulation Master Plan, Jan. 1995. Draft.

[17] Q. Wang, M. Green, and C. Shaw. EM - An Environment Manager For Building Networked Virtual Environments. In *Proceedings of the IEEE Virtual Reality Annual International Symposium*, pages 11–18, Research Triangle Park, NC, March 11-15 1995.

[18] R. M. Weatherly, A. L. Wilson, B. S. Canova, E. H. Page, A. A. Zabek, and M. C. Fischer. Advanced Distributed Simulation through the Aggregate Level Simulation Protocol . In *29th International Conference on System Sciences*, pages 407–415, Wailea, Hawaii, 3-6 January 1996.

Managing the Human-Software Environment

Valentina Plekhanova and Ray Offen

CSIRO - Macquarie University
Joint Research Centre for
Advanced Systems Engineering (JRCASE)
Sydney, NSW 2109, Australia
+61 (0)2 9850 91 07 and +61 (0)2 9850 91 09

valentin@mpce.mq.edu.au; roffen@mpce.mq.edu.au

ABSTRACT

In this paper a software development team is characterised by a Human-Software Environment (HSE) model, which captures the individual characteristics of the participants in a project such as their professional and specialisation skills and knowledge. This paper presents some practical applications of the HSE model for the Human Resource Management (HRM) activities in support of the Software Development Process (SDP). We show how managing the Human-Software Environment facilitates the determination of available and required human resources with respect to the project task(s) and finds an optimal allocation of human resources in the context of economic constraints and customer requirements, etc. The proposed approach is based on mathematical modelling. Illustrative examples are presented.

KEYWORDS

software development process, human resource management, skills, knowledge, cost reduction strategy, mathematical modelling

0-8186-7840-2/97 $10.00 © 1997 IEEE

INTRODUCTION

The software development process, like many other human activities, depends very much on the intellectual capabilities and practical skills of participants. Managing the skills and knowledge of project participants facilitates all aspects of the software development processes, and allows one to regulate and define these. The people involved in a project form a team with a specific structure, which reflects the professional capabilities of the people involved and corresponds to the project's particular parts. The interrelationships between team members, the structures of a team and its project, with the quantitative and qualitative changes and developments in the process, all constitute a complex environment. A description of this environment was introduced by the Human-Software Environment (HSE) model [11]. The environment of each software project can be determined and uniquely characterised with reference to its requirements, context and constraints which vary from one project to another. Final product quality and project productivity (among other factors) depend on the strategy which is preferred, such as an innovation strategy, a quality enhancement strategy, or a cost-reduction strategy [6].

It is a well known fact that it is not only the skills and knowledge of the people involved that affect the project's artifacts but also the human resource management process(es) which make a profound impact [2]. Human resource management should be judged against four measurable goals: the development of employee commitment, the pursuit of flexibility, the achievement of quality performance through quality personnel, and the strategic integration of people policies [14]. Thus, human resource management is considered as a support process to the Software Development Process (SDP).

This paper is concerned with an approach to the solution of some of the most critical human resource management problems [7], such as

- definition of available and required human resource with respect to project task(s);
- allocation of human resources to project task(s);
- comparison of human resources with each other or with previous resource allocations;
- optimal allocation of human resources on the basis of task characteristics, in the context of economic constraints and customer requirements;
- decision making, etc.

The rest of the paper is organised as follows. Firstly, we introduce development team factors *via* a Human-Software Environment model in which knowledge and skills are the focus. The next step is HSE modelling in order to define the feasible combinations of participants on the basis of human capabilities to perform the project task. Then, on the basis of HSE model optimisation task models are introduced by illustrative examples. The concluding section presents a summary and indicates some directions for future work.

BASIC NOTIONS OF HUMAN-SOFTWARE ENVIRONMENT

We define **knowledge** as the range of information, experience and understanding that someone must possess to perform a given task efficiently and effectively, and **skill** as the ability to perform a given task reliably and with facility (achieving expected outcome(s)). Human factors, such as the combined skills and knowledge of the development team's members exert major and controlling influences on the software development process. We define the knowledge and skill-related factors as factors that represent the professional and specialisation knowledge and skills of the software development team members. These knowledge and skill-related factors form and generate a capability-based environment in which software development processes are performed, mediating the manner in which various project roles accomplish the tasks which create or modify development artefacts.

We define the Human-Software Environment (HSE) *as a set of knowledge and skill-related factors that influence the evolution and behaviour of software development activities.*

HSE characteristics

There are three distinct types of data that can be used for the descriptions of the development team's capabilities: **attribute data, ideational data** and **relational data** [1], that are rooted in professional knowledge and skill values. We represent these data in the following ways:

Attribute data capture the knowledge and skill factors, for example, the length of required skill experience, the knowledge of computer languages, the skills associated with technical systems, etc. Attribute data can be introduced in two ways: qualitative and quantitative depending on data availability.

Ideational data can present the properties of team specialisations or a kind of application domain and any required supplementary or special capabilities for task performance. We define team specialisation as the application domain(s) or the subjects(s) which the team activities concentrate on, for example, finance, medicine, ecology, etc.
Relational data are concerned with the static or dynamic interrelationships that exist between the task participants. These interrelationships introduce a structural context to the HSE, in that the relational data inherit the project tasks' interrelationships or can be represented by the team structure in the case of undefined project tasks.

The three types of data, described above, can be collected alongside one another as integral aspects of the same investigation. Typically, questionnaires, interviews, participant observation or documentary sources can be used to collect the data. The attribute data items can be collected through interviews, surveys, tests and questionnaires. The relational data can be obtained from the project task's work-breakdown-structure and availabilities of human resources. The ideational data can be derived from task performance and/or team specialisations within a particular application domain.

Capabilities profiles

Let us define the capabilities profile (c_p) semantically as a set of knowledge and skill-related factors possessed by a particular individual and/or through a given task, i.e. $c_p = \{ e_1, e_2, \ldots, e_n \}$, where e_i $(i = \overline{1,n})$ is an element of c_p which characterises either skill or knowledge, n is the number of factors. The overall HSE is formed by data defining the human resources involved in the project, that is the *available* capabilities, on the one hand, and by the software development process and project tasks on the other hand, that is the *required* capabilities. We define a **required** capabilities profile (b_0) as a requisite set of knowledge and skill-related factors that are required for performance of given task with expected outcome(s). An **available** capabilities profile (b) is a set of the knowledge and skill-related factors that are available to perform a given task. Depending on data availability, the presentations of required and available capabilities profiles can be introduced on qualitative or quantitative level.

Such a semantic presentation of capabilities profiles readily allows for not only the comparison and analysis of the available capabilities profiles with respect to each other and/or to required capabilities for a task performance but also for the modelling of a development team by various approaches. This modelling is made possible by using set theory [8], and the theory of topological and metric spaces [9].

Required factors that are provided by the available capabilities profile for the performance of a given task are represented by the intersection I_p of available capabilities profile b and required capabilities profile b_0: $I_p = b \cap b_0$, thus $I_p = \{ e \mid e \in b \text{ and } e \in b_0 \}$.

If $b \cap b_0 = \varnothing$ the sets b, b_0 are said to be disjoint with respect to the required capabilities profile and an available capabilities profile *does not satisfy, even partially, the required capabilities profile*, for the performance of a given task.

Combining of available capabilities profiles b_1 and b_2 for the performance of a given task is defined by the union U_p of two available capabilities profiles b_1 and b_2: $U_p = b_1 \cup b_2$, thus

$$U_p = \{ e \mid e \in b_1 \text{ or } e \in b_2 \}.$$

Capabilities in reserve are represented by the complement of b_0 relative to b, denoted by R_c :
$R_c = b \setminus b_0$, such $R_c = \{ e \mid e \in b,\ e \notin b_0 \}$ or $R_c = b \setminus (b \cap b_0)$.

Missing capabilities with respect to a given available capabilities profile are defined by the complement of b relative to b_0 denoted by m_c: $m_c = b_0 \setminus b$, such

$$m_c = \{ e \mid e \in b_0,\ e \notin b \} \text{ or } m_c = b_0 \setminus (b \cap b_0).$$

A missing capability is a capability which is *essential* for the task performance, but is absent from the required set of capabilities for the given task performance.

Illustrative example 1 - Capabilities profiles

As an example let us consider the typical newspaper advertisement for a job:

```
ANALYST/PROGRAMMER

Exciting new development project within leading investment bank.  Work with Sybase,
V/B and C++.   3-4 yrs IT exp with V/B or C++ (Windows) and a keen interest in
financial markets will provide this career opp.
```

Advertised skills and knowledge factors can be introduced as the required capabilities profile $b_0 = \{ e_1, e_2, e_3, e_4, e_5, e_6, e_7, e_8 \}$, which consists of the following observable key factors represented by *attribute data* (qualitative and quantitative levels):

e_1 - knowledge of Windows: 3-4 years;

e_2 - knowledge of Visual Basic (V/B): 3-4 years;

e_3 - knowledge of C++: 3-4 years;

e_4 - knowledge of Sybase: 3-4 years;

e_5 - knowledge of unit testing: 3-4 years;

e_6 - coding skills: 3-4 years;

e_7 - unit testing skills: 3-4 years.

and an *ideational data*

e_8 - financial market (supplementary knowledge).

Consider an illustrative comparison and analysis of the capabilities profiles. Suppose that

- available capabilities profiles b_1, b_2, b_3, b_4 are introduced by the available knowledge and skill-related factors;
- these factors have the required ranges of time experience;
- and are associated with persons:

Bob with $b_1 = \{ e_1, e_2, -, e_4, e_5, e_6, e_7, -, -, - \}$;

Liz with $b_2 = \{ e_1, e_2, -, e_4, e_5, e_6, e_7, -, -, e_{10} \}$;

Rod with $b_3 = \{ -, -, e_3, e_4, e_5, e_6, e_7, e_8, e_9, - \}$;

Con with $b_4 = \{ -, -, -, -, -, -, -, -, e_9, e_{10} \}$,

where

e_9, e_{10} are not required knowledge and skills factors;

"- " - no knowledge and skill of particular required factor,
then the missing capabilities, the capabilities in reserve, the combining of available capabilities and other practical applications of this presentation of capabilities profile are illustrated by Table 1.

$b_1 \cap b_0$	I_p	$\{e_1, e_2, e_4, e_5, e_6, e_7\}$	skill and knowledge intersection
$b_2 \cap b_0$	I_p	$\{e_1, e_2, e_4, e_5, e_6, e_7\}$	skill and knowledge intersection
$b_3 \cap b_0$	I_p	$\{e_3, e_4, e_5, e_6, e_7, e_8\}$	skill and knowledge intersection
$b_4 \cap b_0$	I_p	$\varnothing$	b_4 does not satisfy to b_0
$b_1 \setminus b_0$	R_c	$\varnothing$	does not have capabilities in reserve
$b_2 \setminus b_0$	R_c	$\{e_{10}\}$	e_{10} - capabilities in reserve
$b_3 \setminus b_0$	R_c	$\{e_9\}$	e_9 - capabilities in reserve
$b_0 \setminus b_1$	m_c	$\{e_3, e_8\}$	missing capabilities
$b_0 \setminus b_2$	m_c	$\{e_3, e_8\}$	missing capabilities
$b_0 \setminus b_3$	m_c	$\{e_1, e_2\}$	missing capabilities
$b_1 \cup b_2$	U_p	$\{e_1, e_2, e_4, e_5, e_6, e_7, e_{10}\}$	a union of skill and knowledge
$b_2 \cup b_3$	U_p	$\{e_1, e_2, e_3, e_4, e_5, e_6, e_7, e_8, e_9, e_{10}\}$	a union of skill and knowledge
$b_1 \cup b_3$	U_p	$\{e_1, e_2, e_3, e_4, e_5, e_6, e_7, e_8, e_9\}$	a union of skill and knowledge
$b_1 \cup b_2 \cup b_3$	U_p	$\{e_1, e_2, e_3, e_4, e_5, e_6, e_7, e_8, e_9, e_{10}\}$	a union of skill and knowledge

Table 1. *Comparing the qualitative data of capabilities profiles allows us to analyse the capabilities of the candidates. For example, Bob, Liz and Rod have very similar qualitative data contained in the capabilities profiles and can be considered as a candidates for the advertised position (Fig. 1). Bob and Liz have the same capabilities attributes intersections with required capabilities profile and the same missing capabilities (e_3, e_8). Rod does not have knowledge of Windows (e_1) and Visual Basic (e_2), but he has knowledge of financial market (e_8) and knowledge of C++ (e_3) while Bob and Liz do not have them. Liz and Rod have some capabilities in reserve that can be considered as useful for a particular project (Fig. 2). Con is not the right person for this position because he does not have the required capabilities. The final decision requires more detailed consideration of these profiles by using quantitative data like duration (or range) of experience, skill levels, priority of capabilities factors for the project, etc.*

a) b)

Fig. 1. *Bob, Liz and Rod have the same "length" of a) available skills and knowledge intersections and b) missing factors.*

Remarks

For practitioners, there are different ways of obtaining and identifying key skills and knowledge factors of a capabilities profile for a given task performance. We briefly mention some possible approaches.

Available capabilities profile: Companies utilise a variety of different types of staff evaluation, based on interviews, questionnaires and tests. There are several well-known software packages, that support skills and knowledge evaluation. Examples are the basic typing tests or Microsoft's Certification Assessment Exams, which includes Access Application Development, Visual Basic, Windows for Workgroups, SQL Exams and many others. As a rule, the results of such tests are included in a staff-skills database and can be considered as available data for the description of an available capabilities profile.

Required capabilities profile: In most organisations there is an implicit sense of the key skills on which success depends. This is important in refining skills because it can help to identify common, transferable skills. Understanding the commonalities, involving transferable attributes and aptitudes among individuals can effectively enlarge the definition of key skill factors for new projects.

Moreover, there are a number of techniques that can be utilised to define and identify the key factors for a required capabilities profile. For example, the quasi-classical (QC) logic [12], [13] or/and *Delphi method* [3], [4], [5] approach(es) can be applied to define the *key knowledge and skill - related factors* for a required capabilities profile, and to determine the *required task characteristics.* Analysing and identifying the inconsistencies that arise between experts is made possible by the quasi-classical (QC) logic that allows for reasoning with inconsistent factors. In this context the role of the Delphi study is to augment any contribution from 'learning' based on past experience.

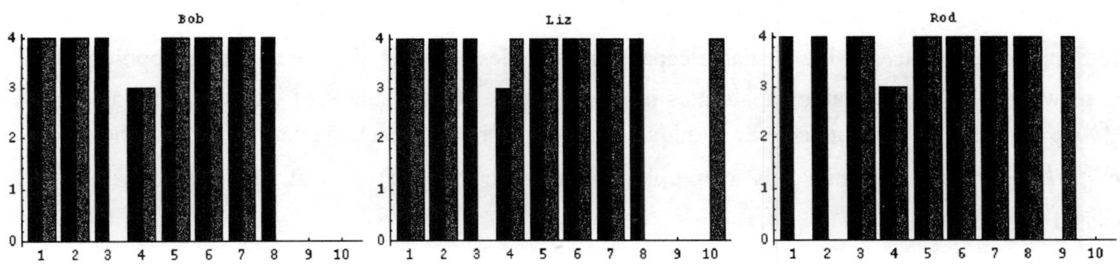

Fig. 2. *Bob and Liz have the same capabilities attributes intersections with required capabilities profile and the same missing capabilities (* e_3, e_8 *). Rod does not have knowledge of Windows (* e_1 *) and Visual Basic (* e_2 *), but he has knowledge of financial market (* e_8 *) and knowledge of C++ (* e_3 *) while Bob and Liz do not have them. Liz and Rod have some capabilities in reserve that can be considered as useful.*

Performance profile - Horizontal representation of performance factors

We define **performance factors** as the characteristics that represent task performance attributes like, for example: cost, time, reliability, productivity and so on; an **available performance profile** (a) as a set of a-priori estimated performance factors $a_j, j = \overline{1, j_a}$; **required performance profile** (a_0) as a set of required performance factors $a_j^0, j = \overline{1, j_0}$. Most of the characteristics of a required performance profile can be obtained from customer requirements, such as cost and time of performance. Characteristics like reliability, quality and the productivity should be assigned in a-priori as the 'best' ones. The available performance characteristics can be obtained from different performance. We associate each of the available and required capabilities profiles with the corresponding available and required performance profiles.

Representation

The HSE is represented semantically as the union of N available capabilities profiles where N is a number of people in the development team) of the project team: $E = \bigcup_{i=1}^{N} b_i$. We define the HSE as a space E of available capabilities profiles and F as a subset of available capabilities profiles of E for a particular task performance. Since the subset F can be represented by different numbers of available capabilities profiles and may consist of different available capabilities profiles, the given space E has a finite number of different combinations, in terms of topological space theory [9], different topology (F_i , $i = \overline{1,k}$, k is a number of topology). Then there are a number of feasible combinations of the capabilities profiles that form the topology. We can evaluate the suitability of each combination by computing its characteristics like cost, reliability and/or time of task performance, etc., by means of optimisation with respect to economic constraints and/or customer requirements.

Therefore we can use the theory of topological and metric spaces in order to solve a number of practical problems.

Mapping - Vertical representation of performance factors

In order to generalise the presentation of economic constraints or required performance characteristics we consider the notion of *mapping*. We denote by $\omega = \{\omega_i, i = \overline{1,N}\}$ the **set of weights** that may represent either cost, time or the task performance reliability of the available capabilities profiles. Each available capabilities profile $b_i \in E$ is associated with the weight $\omega_i = a^i_j$, $j \in \{1,\ldots,j_a\}$, $i = \overline{1,N}$, where a^i_j is the $j\,th$ element of the available performance profile. Let (E,F) be a discrete topological space of the available capabilities profiles and (Ψ,W) be a discrete topological space of weights of the available capabilities profiles, where W is a subset of weights (a topology). By f we denote a rule that associates a unique element of Ψ with each element of E . Then we write $f\colon E \to \Psi$ and say that f is a **mapping** of E into Ψ. If $b \in E$, the weight in Ψ associated with b, is denoted by $f(b)$.

Hence, performance factors can be presented in two ways:
horizontal representation introduces the performance profile of a capabilities profile: i.e. an available or required capabilities profile is associated with an available or required performance profile;
vertical representation identifies one of the available performance characteristics: i.e. an available or required capabilities profile is associated with one of the available or required performance characteristics.

Horizontal representation allows the description of all available performance factors. Vertical representation permits the consideration of an available capabilities profile with respect to one of the required performance factors, which we call "**weight**". We choose the available capabilities profile "**based on weight**". This vertical representation of performance factors allows for the evaluation of a combination of available capabilities profiles with respect to one of the required characteristics for performance assessment. Therefore, it permits the definition of a combination of available capabilities profiles with respect to the corresponding weights (or from practical viewpoints to combine a group of people on the basis of required performance factors).

OPTIMISATION TASKS: DESIGN AND SOLUTION

All organisations have to make decisions about how to allocate their limited resources. Management should continually allocate scarce resources in order to best achieve the required goals, whatever they might be. Let us consider an example of a possible optimisation task for finding the best allocation of human resources that can be solved by making use of linear programming [10]. In this section we illustrate the application of the proposed approach to modelling the software development team. The optimisation tasks are introduced, based on the HSE models presented in [11]. Modelling the HSE by means of topological and metric spaces allows the consideration of human resource management problems: *the definition of all feasible combinations of individuals to perform a project task; the definition of a metric on the HSE which represents a measure of available staff capabilities profile suitability with respect to project task performance.* These approaches to the HSE allow the *determination of an optimal allocation of people for achieving a given task performance.* In this paper we shall restrict attention to a cost-reduction strategy, among others, for the human resource management process.

Illustrative example 2 - Optimisation task on the topological space

Since the topology for E may consist of different available capabilities profiles, we should base the evaluation on parameters such as cost, reliability and so on, rather than the number of available capabilities profiles. To obtain the optimum solution to the problem, it is necessary first to determine all possible "capabilities settings" for a given task performance and then generate all the feasible combinations of available capabilities profiles. Although generating all feasible combinations may not be too difficult, the determination of all the capabilities settings may be a formidable task and can be solved, for example, by means of a *Delphi method*, though in general this is not a simple task.

Suppose, that a mapping $f: E \rightarrow \Psi$ associates an available capabilities profile with a corresponding cost, the standard cost of b_i available capabilities profile has a *range* c_i *per unit of time* and then the weight can be represented by cost $\omega_i = c_i$ of the *i'th* available capabilities profile. We define the **cost profile** C ={ c_i, $i = \overline{1,k}$ }, as the set of cost performance a particular task by the combination of the k available capabilities profiles. Assume that the cost of any task performance is affected by the amount of time available to complete the task or we can say that decision variable is a time. We will use the following definitions [10]:

Crash Time: This is the minimum time required to complete a task.

Optimistic Time ($\mathbf{t}^0$): This is the time that would be required to perform a task under unusually favourable (ideal) circumstances.

Most-Likely Time ($\mathbf{t}^m$): This is the best estimate (or most realistic estimate) of the time required to complete a task.

Pessimistic Time ($\mathbf{t}^p$): This is the time that would be required to perform a task under unusually adverse conditions.

Expected Time ($\mathbf{t}^e$): This is the average time required to complete a task under normal circumstances.

It is important to note that circumstances like favourable (ideal), adverse, normal should be, as much as is possible, identified and adequately defined in specific contexts.

Mathematical representation of the optimisation task:

Suppose, that all the feasible combinations of available capabilities profiles are known: $F = \{ F_j : F_j = \{ b_i, i = \overline{1, k_j} \}, j = \overline{1, K} \}$, where k_j - a number of available capabilities profiles that form the *j'th* combination; *K* - a number of feasible combinations of capabilities profiles for a given task performance; the optimistic time and the pessimistic time can represent the characteristics, that capture factors like economic constraints and/or customer requirements and are estimated by T_i^o and T_i^p correspondingly: $t_i^o \leq T_i^o$ and $T_i^o < t_i^p \leq T_i^p$ for the *i'th* available capabilities profile. The expected time t_i^e is a weighted average computed as follows [10]:

$$t_i^e = (t_i^o + 4t_i^m + t_i^p) / 6 .$$

Each combination F_j is associated by the cost profile $\mathbf{C}_j = \{ c_i, \ i=\overline{1,k_j} \}, \ j=\overline{1,K}$. The cost of applying the combination of available capabilities profiles can be computed as follows:

$$C_j = \sum_{i=1}^{k_j} c_i t_i^e \ , \ j=\overline{1,K}.$$

Therefore, an objective is to find the combination of available capabilities profiles $F^* \in F$ which gives the minimum of cost, subject to the constraints. This combination we will call an **optimal combination** of available capabilities profiles.

Thus, the general model on a topological space can be written as

$$\min_{F=\{F_j\}} imize \ C_j = \sum_{i=1}^{k_j} c_i t_i^e \ , \ j=\overline{1,K} \ ,$$

subject to linear inequalities for each combination:

$$t_i^e = (t_i^o + 4t_i^m + t_i^p)/6 \le T_i^e \ ;$$
$$0 < t_i^o \le T_i^o \ ; \ T_i^o < t_i^p \le T_i^p \ ; \ t_i^m > 0 \ ;$$
$$T_i^e > 0 \ ; \ c_i > 0 \ ; \ T_i^o > 0 \ ; \ T_i^p > 0 \ .$$

The optimisation problem, which has been described with a mathematical language above, means that we seek to minimise the objective function over choices of *F*, the combinations of available capabilities profiles, subject to linear inequalities (constraints) or some given conditions. The objective function is a numerical representation of the quality, efficiency, productivity or cost of the variable(s) selection. In the manner described in this illustrative example it is the cost of a combination of the available capabilities profiles. The optimisation task becomes the selection of a topology $F^* \in F$ "based on weight", which represents an optimal combination of available capabilities profiles for a given task performance. Practically, this allows for more than the allocation of human resources to the project task(s). It also provides for the optimal allocation of human resources on the basis of the task characteristics, capturing factors such as economic constraints and/or customer requirements. This allocation we will call an **allocation "based on weight"**.

Illustrative example 3 - Optimisation tasks on the metric space

In order to select all combinations of available capabilities profiles which satisfy the required one, we represent the HSE as a metric space [9]. The concept of a metric is used to define a notion of distance on a space and carries with it a certain structure. In [11] we define

- the power of cover $\rho(b)$ as a "deviation" of available capabilities profile $b \in E$ from a required capabilities profile b_0 which is measured by

$$\rho(b) = \rho(b, b_0) = \frac{m}{n}, \ \ 0 \le \rho(b) \le 1 \ ,$$

  where m is a number of available factors that belong to an intersection of available capabilities profile b and required capabilities profile b_0: $b \cap b_0 \ne \varnothing$; n is the number of required factors for the performance of a given task;
- a metric on a set E of available capabilities profiles of the HSE as the "distance" between two profile's powers $d(b_i, b_j) = |\rho(b_i) - \rho(b_j)|$; the distance between an available capabilities profile and a required capabilities profile is defined by $d(b, b_0) = |\rho(b) - 1|$;
- a metric space (E, d) with the metric $d(b_i, b_j)$; the topology for E is generated by the metric;
- the radius r as the power of "uncover" of a required capabilities profile by an available capabilities profile.

Thus, in order to define the metric on the HSE and define all feasible combinations of participants to perform the project task, that satisfy the "metric", the HSE is represented by a metric space (E,d). In this section let us consider an example of the possible optimisation task on the metric space.

Mathematical representation of optimisation task: There are a number of feasible combinations of the capabilities profiles that form the topology generated by a metric d for metric space. Suppose, that all the feasible combinations of available capabilities profiles that are generated by a metric d are known and represented by a set:

$$B=\{B_j\},\ B_j(b_0)=\{b_i \mid b_i \in E:\ d(b_i,b_0)<r\ ,\ r>0\,,\ i=\overline{1,k_j}\ \}_j\ ,\ j=\overline{1,K}\,.$$

As in illustrative example 2, let us assume that weight is represented by cost $\omega_i = c_i$ of the *i'th* available capabilities profile. An objective is to find the combination of available capabilities profiles $B_j^* \in B$ generated by d and gives the minimum cost of cost profile C.

Continuing as before, the problem can now be summarised in a mathematical form:

$$\min_{B=\{B_j\}} imize\ C_j = \sum_{i=1}^{k_j} c_i t_i^e\ ,\ j=\overline{1,K}\ ,$$

subject to the constraints for each combination:

$$t_i^e = (t_i^o + 4t_i^m + t_i^p)/6 \le T_i^e\ ;$$
$$0 < t_i^o \le T_i^o\ ;\ T_i^o < t_i^p \le T_i^p\ ;\ \ t_i^m > 0\ ;$$
$$T_i^e > 0\ ;\ c_i > 0\ ;\ T_i^o > 0\ ;\ T_i^p > 0\,.$$

Since the objective is to minimise cost, the optimal combination is found by selecting that combination which has the most appropriate match to the required cost value. The optimisation task allows the reduction of choices among the different topologies that give the optimal (best) combinations of available capabilities profiles for a given task performance. In practice, this means that we can make decisions about who is permitted to perform a given task. These decisions can be made on the basis of the use of certain mathematical techniques (linear programming, comparison and analysis of available and required human resources) to get the best possible solution to a problem (minimize cost) involving limited human resources.

CONCLUSION

In this paper we have described theoretical work being undertaken for modelling the management of skills and knowledge factors of software project participants. The skills and knowledge factors define (mediate) an environment within which the software development process proceeds and are the core characteristics of the development team represented by the Human-Software Environment model. Theoretical notions along with illustrative examples have been presented in order to introduce the critical task of human resource management. That is, we have represented the definition of the most appropriate candidates for the job by means of analysis and comparisons of their available skills and knowledge. The optimisation tasks have been obtained in order to provide the optimal allocation of human resources to task performance on the basis of task characteristics, in the context of economic constraints and customer requirements. These tasks of human resource management that arise in the software development process are captured by means of the proposed mathematical modelling of the development team and yields the tools to support improved development activities.

REFERENCES

1. Scott, J.: Social Network Analysis: a Handbook, SAGE Publications, 1992.
2. Curtis, B., Hefley, W. and Miller, S.: People Capability Maturity Model (CMU/SEI-95-MM-02), Pittsburgh, PA: Software Engineering Institute, Carnegie Mellon University, 1995.
3. Dalkey, N. and Helmer, O.: An experimental Application of the Delphi Method to the Use of Experts, Management Science, v. 9, 1963, p.458.

4. Shannon, R.E.: Systems Simulation: the art and science, Prentice-Hall, Inc., Englewood Cliffs, New Jersey, 1975.
5. Quade, E. S.: An Extended Concept of Model, Proceeding of the 5th International O.R. Conference, J.R. Lawrence (ed.), Tavistock Publ., Ltd., London, 1970.
6. Schuler, R.S. and Jackson, S. E.: Linking competitive strategies with human resource management practices, Academy of Management Executive, 1(3) August, 1987, pp. 207-219
7. Kochan, T.A. and Barocci, T.A.: Human Resource Management and Industrial Relations: Text, Readings and Cases, Boston, Little Brown, 1985.
8. Levy, A., Basic set theory, Berlin, 1978.
9. Burrill, C.W.: Measure, Integration, and Probability, McGraw-Hill Book Company, 1972.
10. Siemens, N., Marting, C.H. and Greenwood, F.: Operations Research: Planning, Operating, and Information Systems, The Free Press, 1973.
11. Plekhanova, V. and Offen, R.: Fine-Grain Modelling of the Software Development Process: a People-Centred Approach, JRCASE Research Report Number 96/10, July 1996.
12. Hunter, A. and Nuseibeh, B.: Analysing Inconsistent Specifications, (to appear in) Proceedings of 3rd International Symposium on Requirements Engineering (RE97), Annapolis, MD, USA, 5-8th January 1997.
13. Hunter, A. and Nuseibeh, B.: Managing Inconsistent Specifications: Reasoning, Analysis and Action, Department of Computing Technical Report Number 95/15, Imperial College, London, UK, October 1995.
14. Guest, D.E.: Human resource management and industrial relations, Journal of Management Studies, 24, 5, 1987, pp.503-521.

Session P5b

Employing COTS Technology

The SYNTHESIS Environment for Component-Based Software Development

Chrysanthos Dellarocas
Sloan School of Management
Massachusetts Institute of Technology
Room E53-315, Cambridge, MA 02139, U.S.A.
Tel. +1 (617) 258-8115
dell@mit.edu

Abstract:

Component-based software development places an emphasis on identifying and managing interdependencies among preexisting pieces of software in order to integrate them into new systems. Traditional software development methodologies, on the other hand, place an emphasis on representing components, leaving the description and management of component interdependencies implicit, or distributed among the components. To support component-based software development, we need new methodologies and tools which elevate the representation and management of software component interdependencies to a distinct design problem, orthogonal to the specification and implementation of the core functional pieces of an application. A core element of such methodologies will be a "design handbook" of software component interconnection, which catalogues common software interconnection dependencies and sets of alternative protocols for managing them. SYNTHESIS, a component-based software development environment based on this perspective, has been developed and successfully used to minimize the manual effort required to integrate independently developed components into new applications.

1. Introduction

During the past few years a range of technical, economic, and social factors have come together to encourage a new way of software engineering that is often referred to as component-based software engineering. This approach bases system development on the definition of software architectures that capture the needs of a given organization and on the selection and integration of components that implement the pieces of these architectures. The big promise of component-based software engineering lies in the possibility to reuse independently developed, off-the-shelf components in order to build new applications more rapidly, economically, and reliably than with traditional approaches.

Despite the significant economic potential and substantial research effort that has been put into component-based software engineering, so far this new paradigm of software development has failed to gain a significant presence in large-scale, commercial development projects [2, 6]. Part of the reason is related to the difficulty of locating appropriate components and the legal issues surrounding their reuse. But even when such issues have been resolved, the lack of software development methodologies specifically designed to support component-based development is discouraging many software engineers from adopting it.

This paper argues that traditional software development methodologies are not well suited to the requirements of component-based software development. It identifies the treatment of interdependencies among software components as one fundamental area where component-based development poses new requirements, not met by traditional methodologies and tools. It proposes a new perspective for developing software systems which treats the interconnection of components in a software system as a separate design problem, entitled to its own representations and design frameworks. It introduces SYNTHESIS, a software development environment based on our perspective and reports on experience gained by using the system to develop new applications from sets of existing components. Finally, it discusses related work and presents some directions for future research.

2. Requirements for Component-Based Software Development

In this section we identify a fundamental difference between traditional and component-based software development. We argue that this difference merits the

0-8186-7840-2/97 $10.00 © 1997 IEEE

development of new methodologies specifically tailored to the needs of the new paradigm. Finally, we introduce a perspective on which such methodologies can be based.

Both traditional and component-based software development methodologies need to specify the requirements and overall architecture of the target software system. However, from then on the two paradigms of software development focus on a different set of design activities.

The objective of traditional software development methodologies is to facilitate the *creation* of one or more implementation-level modules which, together, implement the functionality and data of a software system. Despite the diversity of the various methodologies in use today, they are all essentially providing models and techniques that help answer the following questions:

- How can we best divide the required functionality and data of a system into a set of components.
- How can we best encode the required interactions among components of a system into component interfaces.

Traditional methodologies focus on defining components, leaving the definition of interdependencies among components implicit, and the implementation of protocols for managing them fragmented and distributed among the interacting components. At the implementation level, software systems are sets of modules in one or more programming languages. Although modules come under a variety of names (procedures, packages, objects, clusters etc.), they are all essentially abstractions for components.

Most programming languages directly support a small set of primitive interconnection mechanisms, such as procedure calls, method invocation, shared variables, etc. Such mechanisms are not sufficient for managing more complex dependencies that are commonplace in today's software systems. Complex dependencies require the introduction of more complex managing protocols, typically comprising several lines of code. By failing to support separate abstractions for representing such complex protocols, current programming languages force programmers to distribute and embed them inside the interacting components [14]. Furthermore, the lack of means for representing dependencies and protocols for managing them has resulted in a corresponding lack of theories and systematic taxonomies of interconnection dependencies and ways of managing them.

In component-based development, the components are usually pre-existing and fixed, or customizable in a limited way. The design focus then lies on *integrating* existing components to form new systems. The essential design questions that methodologies must help answer become the following:

- How can we best select existing components to implement a system's functional pieces.
- How can we best manage the interdependencies and mismatches among the selected components and integrate them into a seamless system.

In this paper we will focus on the second question. Traditional methodologies do not provide much help with answering this question because they do not recognize interdependencies as a distinct design entity, nor do they provide any systematic guidance for designing coordination protocols for managing such interdependencies. As a result, most component integration projects today are carried out in an ad-hoc manner, resulting in frequent time and budget overruns and the general perception that component integration is more difficult than it should be [5].

As a response to the previous observations, this paper proposes a new perspective for specifying and implementing software systems. This perspective can form the basis for practical component-based software development methodologies. It is based on coordination theory [12] and applies concepts developed in the Process Handbook project [4, 11]. Unlike current practice, our perspective emphasizes the explicit representation and management of dependencies among software activities as distinct entities. The two main principles of our perspective can be stated as follows:

- *Explicitly represent software dependencies.* Software systems should be described using representations that clearly separate the core functional pieces of an application from their interdependencies, providing distinct abstractions for each.
- *Build design handbooks of component integration.* The field knowledge on component integration should be organized in systematic taxonomies that provide guidance to designers and facilitate the generation of new knowledge. Such taxonomies will catalogue the most common kinds of interconnection relationships encountered in practice. For each relationship, they will contain sets of alternative coordination protocols for managing it. In that way, they can form the basis for *design handbooks of component integration,* similar to the well-established handbooks that assist design in more mature engineering disciplines.

3. The SYNTHESIS Application Development Environment

The coordination perspective on software design introduced in the previous section has been reduced to practice by building SYNTHESIS, an application development environment based on its principles. SYNTHESIS is particularly well suited for component-based software development. This section presents a brief introduction to the SYNTHESIS system. A detailed description can be found in [3].

The current implementation of SYNTHESIS runs under the Microsoft Windows 3.1 and Windows 95 operating systems. SYNTHESIS itself has been implemented by composing a set of components developed using different environments (Intellicorp's Kappa-PC, Microsoft's Visual Basic, and Shapeware's Visio).

SYNTHESIS consists of three elements:

- SYNOPSIS, a software architecture description language
- an on-line design handbook of dependencies and associated coordination protocols
- a design assistant which generates executable applications by successive specializations of their SYNOPSIS description

3.1 SYNOPSIS: An Architecture Description Language

SYNOPSIS supports graphical descriptions of software application architectures at both the specification and the implementation level. The language provides separate language entities for representing software *activities* and *dependencies*. It also supports the mechanism of *entity specialization*. Specialization allows new entities (activities and dependencies) to be defined as variations of other existing entities. Specialized entities inherit the decomposition and attributes of their parents and can differentiate themselves by modifying any of those elements. Specialization enables the incremental generation of new designs from existing ones, as well as the organization of related designs in concise hierarchies. Finally, it enables the representation of reusable software architectures at various levels of abstraction (from very generic to very specific).

Activities

Activities represent the main functional pieces of an application. They *own* a set of ports, through which they interconnect with the rest of the system. Ports represent interfaces through which resources are produced and consumed by various activities.

An activity can optionally decompose into patterns of simpler activities and dependencies which implement the functionality intended by the composite activity. An activity can have an optional association with a code-level component which implements its intended functionality. Examples of code-level components include source code modules, executable programs, network services, etc. SYNOPSIS provides a special notation for describing the properties of software components associated with activities.

Activities are distinguished into generic and executable. *Executable* activities are activities which have either a direct association to a code-level component, or a decomposition whose members are all executable. *Generic* activities are activities that do not have a direct association to a code-level component and/or have a decomposition where at least one member is not executable.

Dependencies

Dependencies describe interconnection relationships and constraints among activities. Like activities they can optionally decompose into patterns of simpler dependencies. They can have optional associations with *coordination protocols*. Coordination protocols are activities that introduce the additional code required in order to manage their associated dependency.

Like activities, dependencies are also distinguished into generic and executable. *Executable (or managed)* dependencies are dependencies which have either a direct association to an executable coordination protocol, or a decomposition whose members are all executable. *Generic (or unmanaged)* dependencies are dependencies that do not have a direct association to an executable coordination protocol and/or have a decomposition where at least one member is not executable.

Using the above definitions, SYNOPSIS can be used both to describe system specifications (sets of generic activities and dependencies) as well as system implementations (sets of executable activities and dependencies). Furthermore, implementations can be derived from specifications by successive specializations of generic elements into executable. Figure 1 shows an example of a software application specification and implementation in SYNOPSIS.

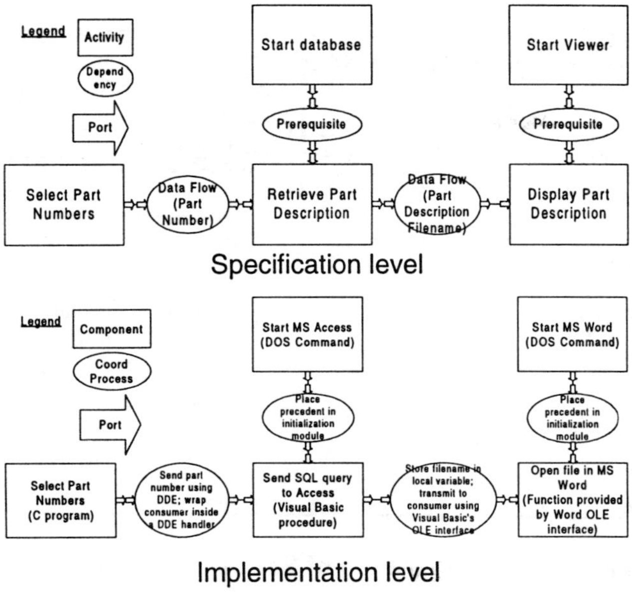

Figure 1: Representation of a simple file viewer application using SYNOPSIS.

3.2 A Design Handbook of Software Component Integration

The ability to represent dependencies and coordination protocols as distinct entities from the components they interconnect allows the construction of taxonomies that systematize the field knowledge in integrating software components, and provide guidance for solving such problems in a routine manner. Such taxonomies should contain:

- a catalog of the most common kinds of interconnection dependencies encountered in software systems
- for each kind of dependency, a catalog of sets of alternative coordination protocols for managing it

An important decision in making a taxonomy of software interconnection is the choice of the generic dependency types. If we are to treat software interconnection as an orthogonal problem to that of designing the core functional components of an application, dependencies among components should represent relationships which are also orthogonal to the functional domain of an application. Fortunately, this requirement is consistent with the nature of most interconnection problems: Whether our application is controlling inventory or driving a nuclear submarine, most problems related to connecting its components together are related to a relatively narrow set of concepts, such as resource flows, resource sharing, and timing dependencies. The design of associated coordination protocols involves a similarly narrow set of mechanisms such as shared events, invocation mechanisms, and communication protocols.

After making a survey of existing systems, and building on earlier results of coordination theory [12], we have based the taxonomy of dependencies presented in this paper on the assumption that component interdependencies are explicitly or implicitly related to patterns of resource production and usage. In other words, activities need to interconnect with other activities, either because they use resources produced by other activities, or because they share resources with other activities.

Based on this assumption, the most generic dependency families in our taxonomy include:

- *Flow dependencies.* Flow dependencies represent relationships between producers and consumers of resources. They are specialized according to the kind of resource, the number of producers, the number of consumers, etc. Coordination protocols for managing flows decompose into protocols which ensure accessibility of the resource by the consumers (usually by physically transporting it across a communication medium), usability of the resource (usually by performing appropriate data format conversions), as well as synchronization between producers and consumers.
- *Sharing dependencies.* They encode relationships among consumers who use the same resource or producers who produce for the same consumers. Sharing dependencies are specialized according to the sharing properties of the resource in use (divisibility, consumability, concurrency). Coordination protocols for sharing dependencies ensure proper enforcement of the sharing properties, usually by dividing a resource among competing users, or by enforcing mutual exclusion protocols.
- *Timing dependencies.* Timing dependencies express constraints on the relative flow of control among a set of activities. Examples include *prerequisite dependencies* and *mutual exclusion dependencies.* Timing dependencies are used to specify application-specific cooperation patterns among activities which share the same resources. They are also used in the decomposition of coordination protocols for flow and sharing dependencies.

A detailed description of our taxonomy of dependencies and coordination processes can be found in [3].

Our SYNTHESIS prototype contains an on-line version of our taxonomy of dependencies and coordination processes. The design spaces of our taxonomy have been

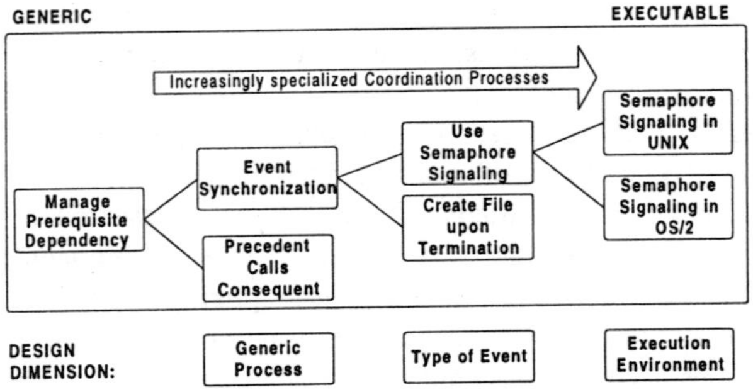

Figure 2: A hierarchy of increasingly specialized coordination protocols for managing prerequisite dependencies.

implemented by hierarchies of increasingly specialized SYNOPSIS entities. For example, Figure 2 shows a partial hierarchy of increasingly specialized processes for managing prerequisite dependencies. Each process contained in the handbook contains attributes that enable the system to automatically determine whether it is a compatible candidate for managing a dependency between a given set of components.

3.3 A Design Process for Generating Executable Applications

SYNTHESIS supports a process for generating executable systems by successive specialization of their SYNOPSIS descriptions. The process can be summarized as follows:

1. Users describe their application using SYNOPSIS, as a pattern of activities connected through dependencies.
2. The design assistant of SYNTHESIS scans the application description and iteratively does the following for each generic (i.e. not executable) application element:
   a) It searches the on-line design handbook for compatible specializations.
   b) It selects one of the compatible specializations found, either automatically, or by asking the user. If no compatible specialization can be found, it asks the user to provide one.
   c) It replaces the generic application element with the selected specialization and recursively applies the same process to all elements in the decomposition of this element.
3. After all application elements have been replaced by executable specializations, the design assistant integrates them into a set of modules in one or more languages and generates an executable application out of the collection.

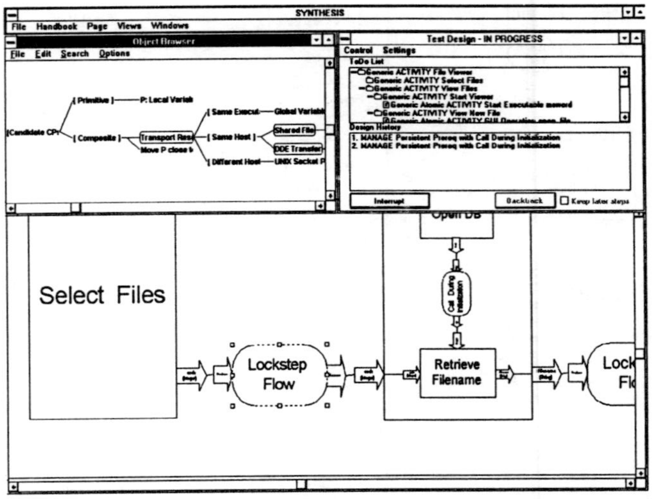

Figure 3: Configuration of SYNTHESIS windows during the design process

Figure 3 shows the configuration of SYNTHESIS windows during the design process.

The above design process minimizes the manual effort required to integrate software components into new systems. Users only need to participate in the specialization process by making the final selection when more than one compatible specializations have been found. In the rare cases when no compatible specialization can be found, users need to provide the code for such a specialization. Specializations thus provided become a permanent part of the repository.

4. Using SYNTHESIS to Facilitate Component-Based Software Development

4.1 Overview

We have tested the capabilities of SYNTHESIS by using it to build a set of applications by integrating independently written pieces of software. Each experiment consisted in:

- describing a test application as a SYNOPSIS diagram of activities and dependencies
- selecting a set of pre-existing components exhibiting various mismatches to implement activities

Experiment	*Description*	*Components*	*Results*
File Viewer	A simple system which retrieves and displays the contents of user-selected files.	User interface component written in C; filename retrieval component written in Visual Basic; file display component implemented using commercial text editor.	SYNTHESIS integrated components suggesting two alternative organizations (client/server, implicit invocation); all necessary coordination code was automatically generated in both cases.
Key Word in Context	A system that produces a listing of all circular shifts of all input lines in alphabetical order [18].	Two alternative implementations for each component (both written in C): as a server and as a UNIX filter.	3 different combinations of filter and server implementations were each integrated in 3 different organizations (see Table 2). SYNTHESIS generated most coordination code; users had to manually write 16 lines of code in 2 cases
Interactive TEX	A system that integrates the standard components of the TEX document typesetting system in a WYSIWYG ensemble.	Standard executable components of TEX system.	Target application was completely described in SYNOPSIS. SYNTHESIS was able to generate coordination code automatically.
Collaborative Editor	A system which extends the functionality of existing single user editors with group editing capabilities [7].	Micro-Emacs [10] source code was used to implement single-user editor.	Same system description was specialized in two different ways to generate micro-Emacs-based group editors for Windows and UNIX.

Table 1: Summary of experiments of using SYNTHESIS to facilitate the integration of existing software components in new applications.

- using the design process outlined above to semi-automatically manage dependencies and integrate the selected components into an executable system
- exploring alternative executable implementations based on the same set of components

The results of our experiments are summarized in Table 1. Overall, we used SYNTHESIS to build 4 test applications. Each application was integrated in at least two different ways. For example, for one application we built one implementation where components were organized around client/server interactions, and a second where the same components were organized around peer-to-peer interactions. This resulted in a total of 14 different implementations. SYNTHESIS was able to build all 14 implementations, typically generating between 30-200 lines of additional glue code in each case in order to manage interdependencies and integrate the components. In only 2 cases, users had to manually write 16 lines of code (each time), to implement two data conversion routines that were missing from the design handbook. Reference [3] contains a detailed description of our experiments.

4.2 Example: Building a Collaborative Editor by Integrating Existing Components

This section presents one of our experiments in more detail. It also serves as an example of how SYNTHESIS can form the basis for a methodology for component-based software development.

In our experiment, we used SYNOPSIS to create a collaborative editor architecture, loosely based on the ideas of Knister and Prakash [7]. Collaborative editors allow the joint concurrent editing of the same document by a group of people. We selected an existing single-user editor and mapped the activities of our architecture to source code modules of that system. Then, we used SYNOPSIS and its on-line design handbook of coordination protocols in order to manage the dependencies of our architecture and integrate the resulting set of components and coordination protocols into an executable collaborative editor application for Microsoft Windows. Finally, we reused the same collaborative editor architecture and used SYNTHESIS in order to generate an equivalent application for UNIX.

Our collaborative editor architecture implements a collaboration protocol loosely based on the one presented in [7]. The following is a brief description of the protocol:

The protocol is based on the designation of one of the participants in an editing session as *master*. Master participants have complete editing capabilities. The remaining participants are *observers*, with no editing capabilities. Observers see every change and cursor movement made by the master; the observer's cursor is in "lock-step" with the master's cursor. Observers cannot perform any operations which change the text. If attempted, such operations simply have no effect.

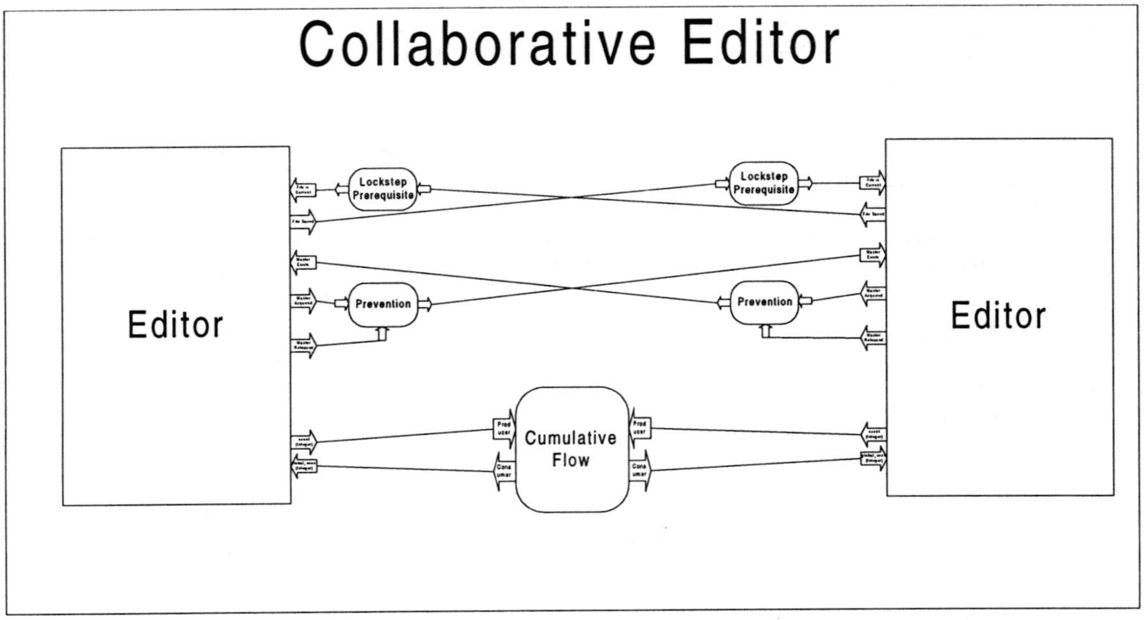

Figure 4 : Top level decomposition of collaborative editor architecture with two participants.

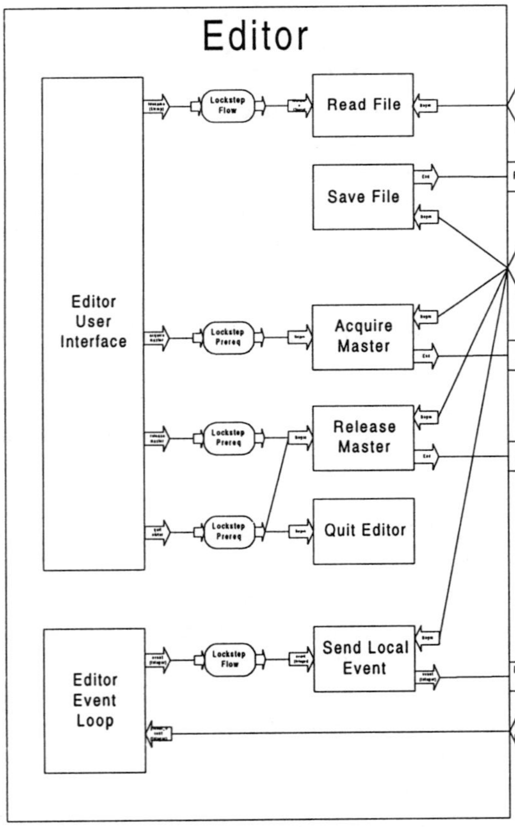

Figure 5: Decomposition of Editor activity.

At all times, at most one participant can be the master. All others are observers. When an editing session starts, there is no master. During that time, any participant can take control and become the master by pressing a designated key-sequence (which might be editor-dependent). During the session, a master may relinquish control by pressing another key-sequence. Once there is no master, all participants are once again allowed to take control.

During time periods when there is no master, all participants are allowed to individually edit their buffers. Each local editing activity is then propagated to all participants. The result is a truly egalitarian mode of collaborative editing.

Any number of users can participate in a collaborative editing session. Participants can enter and leave the session at will, simply by starting or quitting their instance of the editor program. When a new participant enters the session, if there is a master, the current contents of the master's buffer are written back to disk, before they are loaded into the new participant's buffer. In this way, it is ensured that the buffer contents of all participants are identical at all times.

A SYNOPSIS architecture for describing a collaborative editor system which supports the collaboration protocol described above is given in Figure 4. The architecture interconnects a set of simpler Editor activities, corresponding to individual session participants. The decomposition of Editor activities is given in Figure 5.

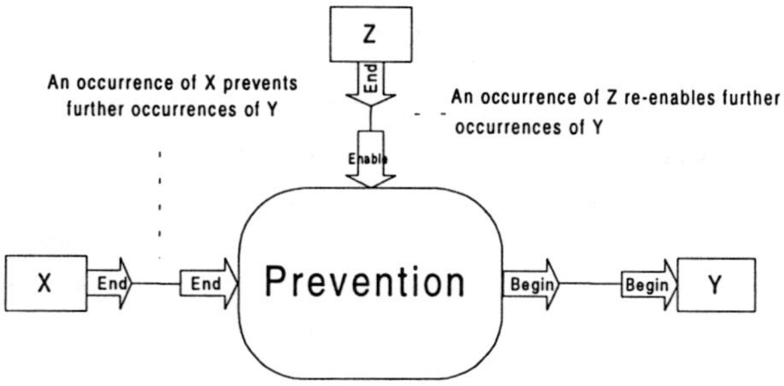

Figure 6: Prevention dependencies.

The operation of the overall system is based on a Flow dependency for broadcasting a participant's keystrokes to all participants, and a set of Prevention dependencies, each connecting a participant to all other participants (except itself). Prevention dependencies belong to the general family of timing dependencies of our taxonomy. They specify that the occurrence of an activity X (enabler) prevents further occurrences of an activity Y until a third activity Z (disabler) occurs, in which case occurrences of Y are re-enabled (Figure 6).

In our system, each Prevention dependency is "enabled" whenever a participant acquires master status. It is "disabled" whenever that same participant releases master status. It connects to the Master Exists port of all other participants. While "enabled", a Prevention dependency prevents the execution of all Editor subactivities connected to the Master Exists port of all participants except the one who acquired master status. These subactivities include the ability to broadcast a participant's local keystrokes, as well as the ability to acquire and release master status. The resulting effect is that only the current master can make its keystrokes visible to everyone's local editor copy and only the master can release master status.

Each Editor activity can be based on an existing single-user editor component. The source code of the editor must be available in order to use it in this system. The activities depicted in Figure 5 must be mapped to source code modules of the single-user editor using the component description language of SYNOPSIS (see [3] for details).

In our experiment we used MicroEmacs [10] as our single-user editor component. MicroEmacs is written is C and its source code is available for free. There exist versions of the system for both UNIX and Windows environments.

Each version of MicroEmacs was "fitted" into our generic architecture with a minimal need for manual modifications, very similar to those described in [7]. Then SYNOPSIS was able to manage the same set of dependencies with coordination protocols specific for each execution environment in order to generate two alternative executable implementations of the same system (one for UNIX, one for Windows).

The experiment provided an excellent example of how component-based software development can facilitate the reuse of software architectures in order to facilitate the generation of applications for multiple platforms.

5. Related Work

5.1 The Process Handbook Project

The work reported in this paper grew out of the Process Handbook project at MIT's Center for Coordination Science [4, 11]. The Process Handbook project applies the ideas of coordination theory [12] to the representation and design of business processes. The goal of the Process Handbook project is to provide a firmer theoretical and empirical foundation for such tasks as enterprise modeling, enterprise integration, and process re-engineering. The project revolves around a software tool, called the "process handbook", which contains rich descriptions of how different organizations perform similar processes, including the relative advantages of the alternatives. SYNOPSIS has borrowed the ideas of separating activities from dependencies and the notion of entity specialization from the Process Handbook. SYNOPSIS has moved beyond the Process Handbook in refining the process representation so that it can describe software applications at a level precise enough for code generation to take place, and in defining a repository of dependencies and coordination protocols for the specialized domain of software systems.

5.2 Architecture Description Languages

Architecture Description Languages (ADLs) provide support for representing software systems in terms of their components and their interconnections [8, 15]. They often provide separate abstractions for representing components and their interconnections. SYNOPSIS shares many of the goals and principles of many recent ADLs, most notably UniCon [16]. However, whereas previously proposed architectural languages only provide support for implementation-level connector abstractions (such as a pipe, or a client/server protocol), SYNOPSIS is the first language which also supports specification-level abstractions for encoding interconnection relationships (dependencies). Furthermore, apart from introducing a new architectural language, this work proposes a more general perspective on designing systems which also includes the development of design handbooks for activities and dependencies as well as a design process for generating executable systems by successive specializations of their architectural descriptions.

5.3 Component Frameworks

Component frameworks such as OLE, CORBA, OpenDoc, etc. [1] facilitate the interoperation of independently developed components by limiting the kinds of allowed interactions and by providing a standardized infrastructure for managing them.

Component frameworks and our coordination perspective represent two very different philosophies in component-based software development. Component frameworks, once again, place the emphasis on components. They provide a fixed infrastructure for managing component interdependencies (middleware) and require components to adhere to a specific set of standards in order to interoperate.

Our coordination perspective, in contrast, is based on the belief that the identification and management of software dependencies should be elevated to a design problem in its own right. Therefore, dependencies should not only be explicitly represented as distinct entities, but furthermore, when deciding on a managing protocol, the full range of possibilities should be considered with the help of design handbooks. Components in SYNOPSIS architectures need not adhere to any standard and can have arbitrary interfaces. Provided that the right coordination protocol exists in its repository, SYNTHESIS will be able to interconnect them. Furthermore, SYNTHESIS is able to suggest several alternative ways of managing an interconnection relationship and thus possibly generate more efficient implementations. Finally, open interconnection protocols defined in specific component frameworks can be incorporated into SYNTHESIS repositories as one, out of many, alternative ways of managing the underlying dependency relationships.

6. Discussion and Future Work

Component-based software engineering builds new software systems by integrating existing components. Identifying and properly managing the interdependencies among components becomes a central concern in this new paradigm. Software engineering methodologies specifically geared towards component-based development need to elevate the representation and management of interdependencies among software components to a distinct design problem, entitled to its own abstractions and design taxonomies.

SYNTHESIS is one such methodology and toolset. It is based on an architecture description language that clearly separates software activities and dependencies, and on a design handbook that contains the most common types of dependencies encountered in software systems, as well as sets of alternative coordination processes for managing them.

The practical advantages of SYNTHESIS include:

- *Easier integration of code-level components.* SYNTHESIS can take advantage of its on-line design handbook (a systematic codification of field knowledge in component integration) in order to minimize the need for additional manually written code to bridge mismatches and manage dependencies among software components.
- *Support for rapid multi-platform development.* When applications are ported to a new execution environment, their abstract architecture (activities and dependencies) remains unaffected. The parts most likely to require modification are the coordination protocols that manage their dependencies. By expressing new applications as SYNOPSIS diagrams, dependencies can be managed using alternative coordination protocols in order to generate code for multiple platforms beginning from a single system description. The experiment discussed in Section 4.2 provided an example of how SYNTHESIS can be used to generate code for multiple platforms from a single SYNOPSIS description.
- *Superior insight into the range of alternative implementations.* The explicit representation of dependencies as distinct entities which are subsequently managed by consulting a design handbook, encourages designers to consider a wide range of alternative ways of implementing their systems. We are confident that this will result in a more systematic and rational way of organizing large-scale systems.
- *Easier application maintenance.* Designers often need to change the implementation of activities, in order to reflect changes in functional requirements or evolutions in component implementation. Applications will be easily reconstructed after such changes, by reusing the same architectural diagram and simply managing again the dependencies of the affected activities with the rest of the system.

Our initial experience with SYNTHESIS has provided positive evidence to support our claims on small-scale systems. With our future research we plan to demonstrate the advantages of our approach as a basis for building and maintaining large-scale software systems out of existing parts.

References

1. Richard M. Adler. Emerging Standards for Component Software. *IEEE Computer*, March 1995, pp. 68-77.
2. T. J. Biggerstaff and A. J. Perlis. *Software Reusability.* Volumes 1 and 2, ACM Press/Addison Wesley, 1989.
3. Chrysanthos Dellarocas. *A Coordination Perspective on Software Architecture: Towards a Design Handbook for Integrating Software Components* (Ph.D. Thesis). MIT Center for Coordination Science Working Paper #193, February 1996. Also available from http://ccs.mit.edu/ccswp193/main.html
4. C. Dellarocas, J. Lee, T. W. Malone, K. Crowston and B. Pentland. Using a Process Handbook to Design Organizational Processes. In *Proceedings, AAAI Spring Symposium on Computational Organization Design*, March 21-23, 1994, Stanford, CA, pp. 50-56.
5. D. Garlan, R. Allen and J. Ockerbloom. Architectural Mismatch or Why it's hard to build systems out of existing parts. In *Proceedings, 17th International Conference on Software Engineering*, Seattle WA, April 1995.
6. T. Capers Jones. Reusability in Programming: A Survey of the State of the Art. *IEEE Transactions on Software Engineering*, Vol. 10, No. 5, September 1984, pp. 488-494.
7. M. J. Knister and A. Prakash. DistEdit: A Distributed Toolkit for Supporting Multiple Group Editors. In *Proceedings, CSCW 90*, Los Angeles, CA, October 1990, pp. 343-355.
8. Paul Kogut and Paul Clements. Features of Architecture Representation Languages. Carnegie Mellon University Technical Report CMU/SEI. Number to be assigned. Draft of December 1994.
9. Charles W. Krueger. Software Reuse. *ACM Computing Surveys*, Vol. 24, No. 2, June 1992, pp. 131-183.
10. D. M. Lawrence and B. Straight. *MicroEmacs Full Screen Text Editor Reference Manual, version 3.10*, March 1989.
11. T.W. Malone, K. Crowston, J. Lee and B. Pentland. Tools for Inventing Organizations: Toward a Handbook of Organizational Processes, In *Proceedings, 2nd IEEE Workshop on Enabling Tech. Infrastructure for Collaborative Enterprises*, April 20-22, 1993.
12. Thomas W. Malone and Kevin Crowston. The Interdisciplinary Study of Coordination. *ACM Computing Surveys*, Vol. 26, No. 1, March 1994, pp. 87-119.
13. D. L. Parnas. On the Criteria to Be Used in Decomposing Systems Into Modules. *Communications of the ACM*, Vol. 15, No. 12, December 1972, pp. 1053-1058.
14. Mary Shaw. Procedure Calls Are the Assembly Language of Software Interconnection: Connectors Deserve First-Class Status. Carnegie Mellon University, Technical Report CMU-CS-94-107. January 1994.
15. Mary Shaw and David Garlan. Characteristics of Higher-level Languages for Software Architecture. Technical Report CMU-CS-94-210. Also appears as CMU/SEI-94-TR-23, ESC-TR-94-023.
16. Mary Shaw, Robert DeLine, and Daniel Klein. Abstractions for Software Architecture and Tools to Support Them. IEEE Transactions of Software Engineering 21, 4, April 1995, pp. 314-335.

Feature Modelling of Component-Based Embedded Software

Jarmo Kalaoja, Eila Niemelä and Harri Perunka
VTT Electronics
P.O. BOX 1100, FIN-90571 Oulu, Finland
Tel. +358 8 551 2111, Telefax +358 8 551 2320
email: { jarmo.kalaoja, eila.niemela, harri.perunka }@vtt.fi
www: http://www.ele.vtt.fi/

Abstract

The electronic and automation industries develop and maintain software embedded in computer-controlled products. Higher software productivity can be achieved by a systematic software engineering process and an environment that supports automatic software mass-customisation. Existing methods are too narrow and commercial tools are often too closed to be suited for component-based software tailoring.

Integrating feature and object-based models and providing a distributed environment - based on commercial tools - feature models of embedded software are utilized in reuse-oriented product development, maintenance and sales. Reuse of product knowledge is based on layered feature models. Configuration data for product variations is automatically derived and mapped to software design and implementation components and assemblies.

1. Introduction

Embedded computer systems, incorporated in different types of products, are common in everyday goods, industrial equipment and machine automation systems. The increasing number of product features and diversity of customer requirements have resulted in the need to change development and production processes. Instead of designing a single product, mangement of product families and software tailoring are required.

The main characteristics of embedded software, e.g. hard real-time requirements, limited memory size, hardware interfaces and low-level languages - like assembly or C - are obstacles in designing generic solutions for embedded application software. Different kinds of object-oriented modelling methods - like OMT and ROOM - and graphical programming tools have been used for early prototyping and software component design [1]. Visualisation and early verification of designs - with modern CASE-tools - have speeded-up the software development process, but CASE-tools have not resolved the problems of how to create components for mass-customised software.

Software tailoring is done by selecting a desired group of product features which can easily be implemented with add-on software components. Software tailoring is possible when customised product features are designed in a systematic way using graphical product feature models and support tools for the creation, maintenance and selection of feature models. If a support environment automatically links feature models to component designs and application assemblies, feature models can be utilised in different organisational levels, e.g. software design, production, maintenance and sales.

A feature model specifies all features of product families and relationships between them. The structure of mechanical systems is often described as feature models [2]. The results of domain analysis are sometimes represented as features, modelled e.g. by frames [3]. However, most environments only support the viewpoints of an analyst and a designer, the needs of production, customers and sales are omitted. Feature models are applied in [4] [5] for application software by combining domain analysis and feature modelling. Also this technique supports analysts and designers. However, utilisation of a feature model can be much more comprehensive, if it integrates design, implementation, and configuration knowledge in the same model which is also used by sales managers and customers.

Commercial database-tools for configuration management do not satisfy the requirements of the component-based software development process. First,

0-8186-7840-2/97 $10.00

these tools are closed and expensive. Openness is required, because the data derived from product feature models are used for component configuration and for producing feature selection lists to help customisation. Secondly, the notations of the modelling methods of commercial tools support only the selection of high-level components. Software features, however, cannot be encapsulated in components but are normally propagated to a group of components in a different way, e.g. by parameters or inter-component connections.

This paper emphasises the feature modelling and customisation of embedded software. We present a reuse-oriented development process, a feature modelling method, and a prototype environment supporting feature and component-based software development.

2. Features in Embedded Software Development

Varying customer needs result in the features of embedded software products. Different markets, users, usage types and product types, for example, contribute to the features of a product, and finally to software adaptability requirements. Software adaptability - like features - has to be considered regarding the application domain, product families, and customisation [6]. The purpose of software feature modelling is to:

- identify customer needs in family-based products,
- create a basis for the design of software components for product families, and
- support customised software production and delivery.

In order to achieve the goals of feature-based software development, some preliminary analysis work is necessary. The analysis tasks are illustrated in Figure 1.

Application Domain Analysis. Application domain analysis is a pre-study to collect varying customer needs as well as software adaptability requirements. Application domain knowledge is obtained, for example by studying existing systems. Diversity of customer needs, information about feasible implementation technologies and development processes are collected and analysed.

The needs of end-users are identified and different solutions are considered in order to analyse the benefits and the constraints of various technologies. QFD (Quality Function Deployment) can be used as a feasibility analysis method [7]. In this phase, domain and technology-dependent product knowledge with the estimated feasibility is mapped to the requirements of the main user groups. A study of least three to five existing applications is necessary for successful domain analysis. Reverse-engineering is often required because of the low maturity of the development process and poor software documentation [8].

Software Architecture Analysis and Design. The objective is to identify the partitions of basic and customisable software, to determine the scope of adaptability, and to define mechanisms and principles, how the generic product family software architecture supports the creation of adaptive systems.

Software Component Design. Guidelines and preliminary candidates for software components are specified before generalisation according to product variations.

Feature Modelling. The primary issue of feature modelling is to provide a grouped, hierarchical structure of features for a product family and to describe the relationships between the features. The software architecture and documentation of candidate components are updated with the results of feature models. Usually some iterations have to be carried out before the model is complete. A stable feature model and a software architecture are required to automate the mapping of feature and component models. Later, development and production processes use the feature models as the basis for product families. The scope and the basic manners of software adaptability are determined in the feature modelling phase.

Software Production. Component selections and configuration data are derived from the feature models of a product family. Configuration of design components can be resolved by the following way:

- Features define the components that are necessary to implement defined customer needs.
- Feature values define component configuration parameters which are used to select the final functionality or connections of a generic or application domain component.
- Finally, features are transformed or mapped to source code implementations and the final feature-based software is built by compiling. The executable code thus includes only the selected features.

Feature-based software development is a strongly iterative process. This is mainly due to the fact that several models interact. Firstly, feature models serve as a link between non-technical customer needs and the technical software architecture and component designs, and secondly, the software architecture and component designs are affected by the features. It is also essential to keep separate models consistent during the product development.

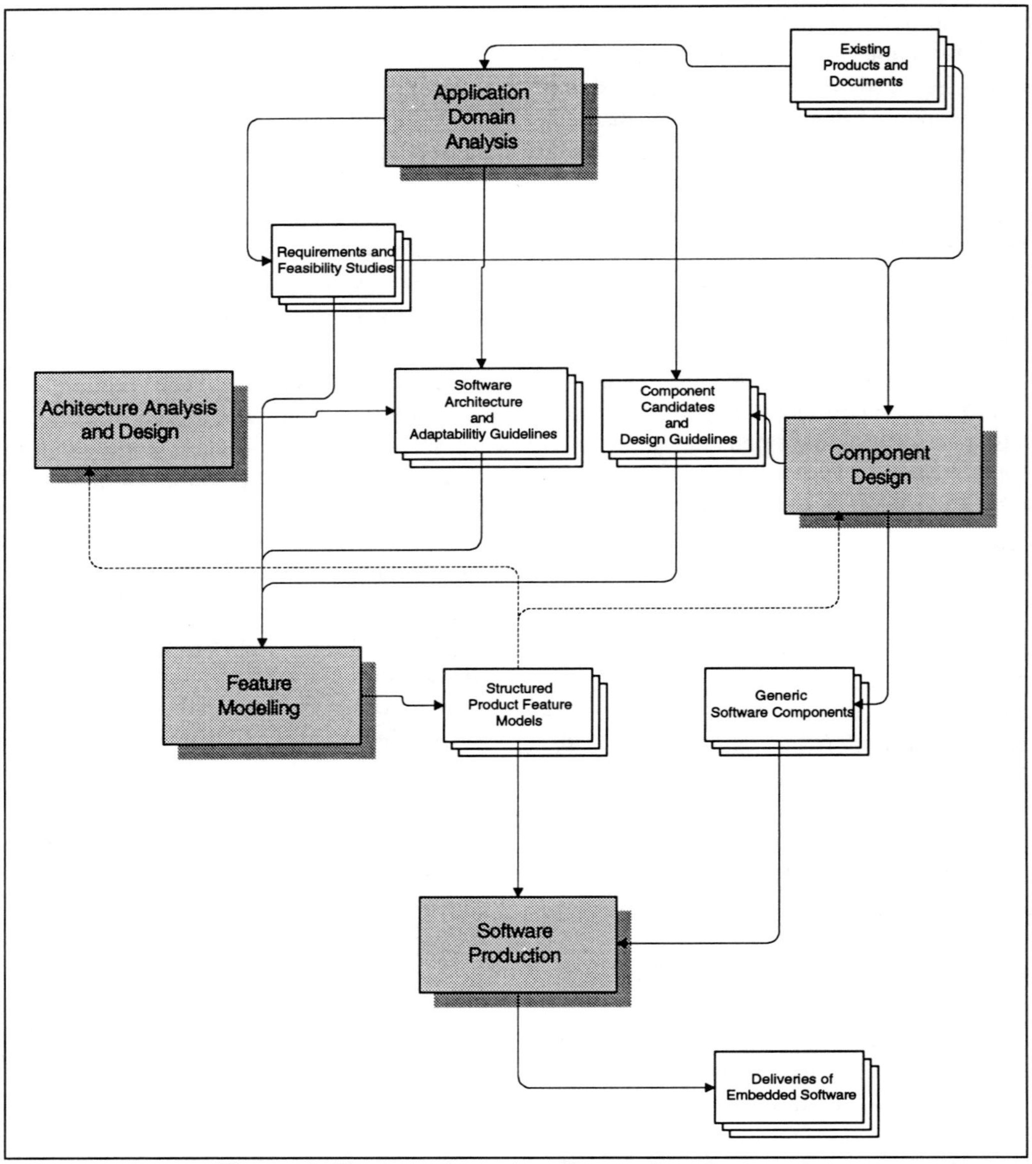

Figure 1. Feature-based software development.

Evolution of delivered applications requires support for computer-aided application assembly, version control and traceability checking for software components and identified features [9] [10]. Therefore, the models should be stored in a database under version control.

3. Practical Feature Modelling

Product family feature models illustrate the characteristics of products derived from customer needs as well as from technical constraints covered during the application domain analysis.

To visualise features and feature interrelationships, graphical notations have been developed. For example, the MICOM method [4] presents such a notation. As an example, consider a feature model illustrating some features of a taxi-meter (Figure 2).

In this case, the MICOM notation has been enhanced with sub-diagram reference (UserInterface) and graphical inter-feature relationships (*requires* and *excludes*). The MICOM notation describes inter-feature relationships as comments.

A feature model is presented graphically as a tree with nodes and links. A node of the tree represents either a feature, mutual exclusion between features or a value of a feature. The source node of a link is called a parent feature. If a link is connected to another feature (sub-feature), the parent feature controls when that feature can be selected.

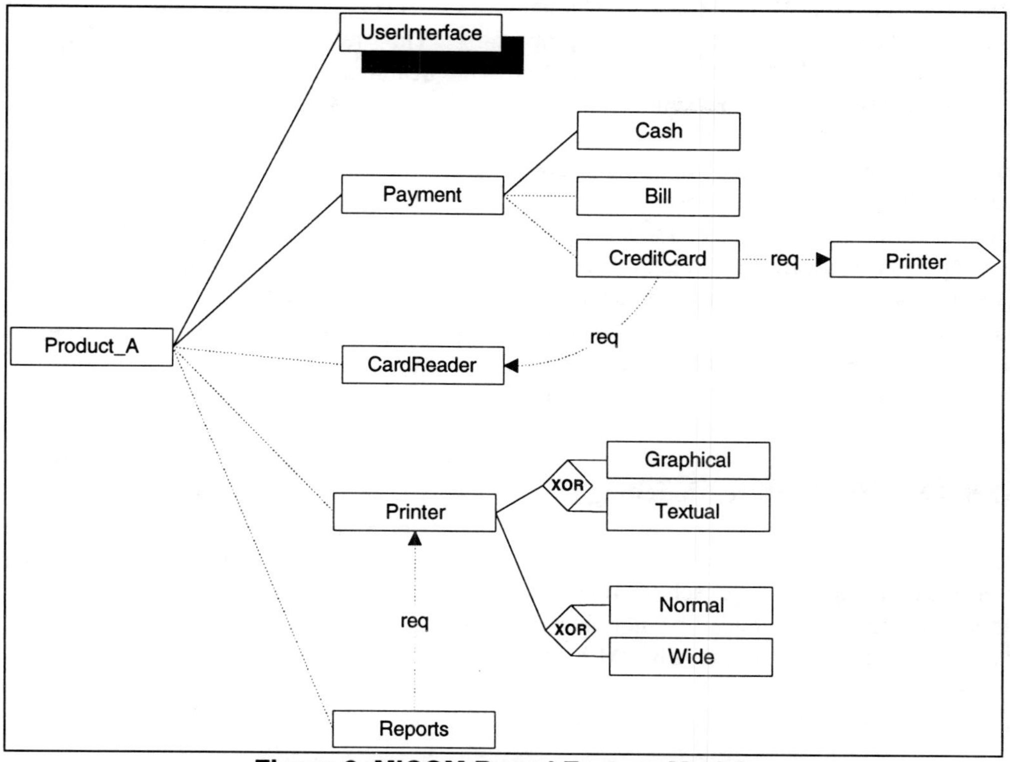

Figure 2. MICOM Based Feature Model.

If a feature prevents selection of another feature with the same parent feature, the relationship is modelled as an XOR-node. An OR-node defines a list of optional features at the same hierarchical level. An AND-node describes the transitive relation where one selection requires also another feature or features to be selected. An optional feature is presented as a dashed link.

To avoid contradictions feature modelling consists of many iterations and regrouping before the model has an understandable form for designers, sales managers and customers.

In addition to links, feature model symbols can be connected by relations between features. A relation specifies a restriction between two features or feature values. Relations cannot be expressed as a tree structure.

The feature model is also linked to software components and component parametrisations. Mapping from non-technical customer needs to product features in a feature model and further into selections of software components and parameters of components may not be straightforward. Four types of relationships between product features and software components and component parameters exist:

- one feature to one component/parameter
- one feature to many components/parameters
- many features to one component/parameter
- many features to many components.

Naturally, one-to-one relationships are easy to manage, and should be encouraged whenever possible. Unfortunately, this very seldom works in practical software implementations. Many-to-many relationships are very complex and lead to error-prone designs and implementations with unpredictable side-effects in reuse and customisations. These relationships should be avoided, but in many cases they are unavoidable. In such cases clearly designed algorithms are required to solve the mapping. Our on-going research addresses this problem.

In practical designs, one to many relationships are common. Such relationships require some attention in design. When one feature affects several components or several parameters in a component, it should be verified that all the required components with the defined parameters may co-exist and will be well-behaving in the implemented system.

Many features affecting a single component or a parameter are easy to handle, due to localization of the influences of customization. However, the size of the component design and the implementation is prone to grow. Large components are therefore hard to keep free of non-conflicting parameters in the long term. This is especially true, when the originating features are not related to each other.

As a general rule component designs and feature models should be kept identical with one-to-one mapping relationships. As feature models reflect the application domain view, a similar view should also be encouraged in component designs. Also in object-oriented modeling the application domain view is highlighted. Identical views in both of the modelling phases minimises imbalance between the models. Therefore, object modelling is preferred for component identification. Flexibility and reusability of design increases. A drawback is, however, that optimised functionality may be lost with objects. Thus, instead of pure one to one relationships, good compromises of one to one and one to many relationships are preferred.

3.1 Extended Notation for Feature Modelling

For expressing complex feature and component mapping relationships an extended approach is proposed. Formal description of the feature modelling notation is shown in Figure 3. As an extension to the MICOM-based notation it includes:

- A feature model diagram defines a feature block type.
- The default selection status of a feature is presented.
- The relation (mutual exclusion) between child features is presented in the parent feature.

These enhancements provide the following benefits:

- Possible selections can be clearly presented for customers in standard selection form.
- Information about selected features can be stored as well-structured data.
- Feature blocks are used for reuse and recurring structures.

In the proposed notation a feature name must be unique inside a feature diagram. A data value feature has a new symbol. A link from a feature symbol to a value symbol represents a choice for the value of the parent feature. The value name must be unique in the context of the range of choices that represent the possible values of the same feature.

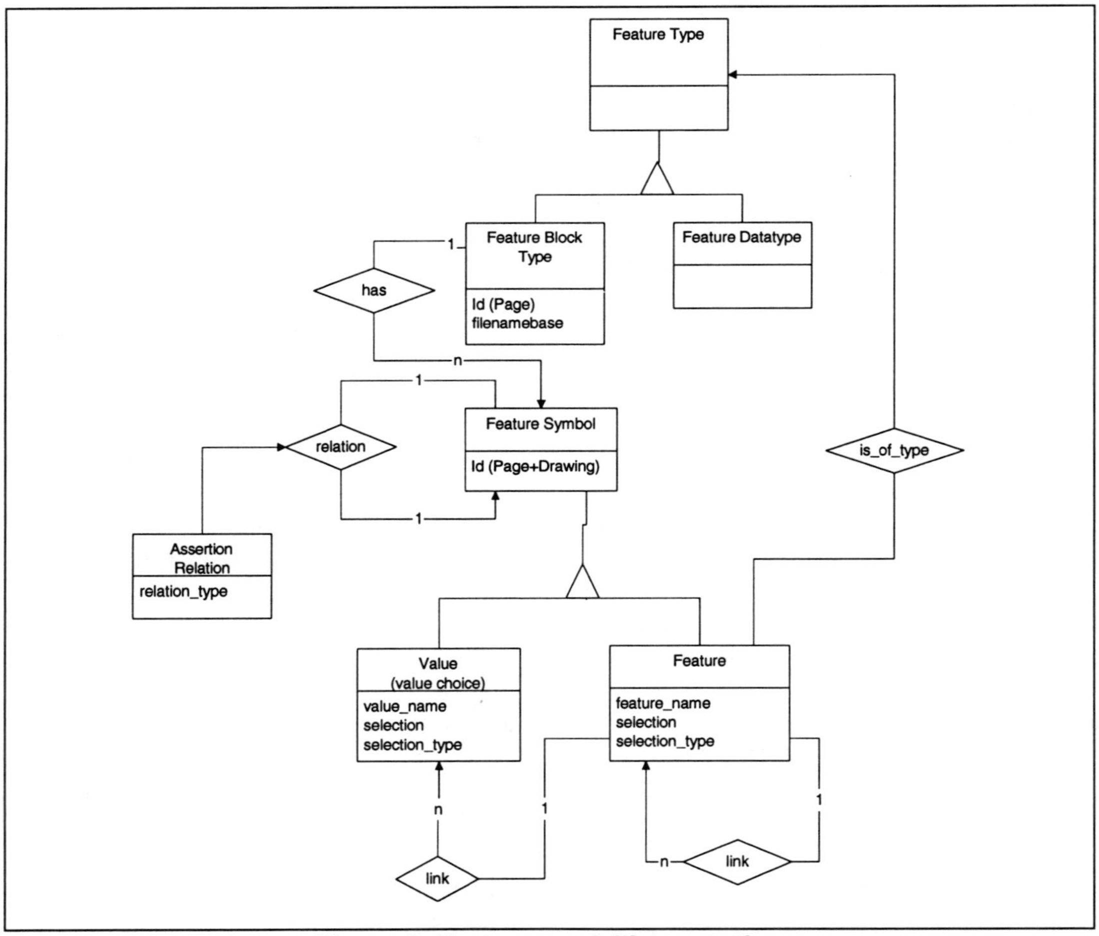

Figure 3. Feature modelling notation.

A feature with no parent feature in the diagram is called the root feature. A feature diagram can have several root features and thus more than one separate tree structure.

A node representing a feature has the attributes *selectable* and *selects*. The *selectable*-attribute defines if the feature can be selected, not selected or if it is always selected. The *selects*-attribute defines the relation between child nodes, i.e. how they can be selected together. The possible choices are 'only one', 'zero or more', or 'at least one'. The value of the attributes are represented graphically in the symbol.

If a node (feature) in the tree is selected, its child nodes (subfeatures) may also be selected. The default value of selection for each feature can be defined in the model. This means that even if a parent feature is not selected by default, a default value for the selection of its child feature can be given, if the parent is selected later.

In addition to feature tree links, a relation can be defined between any two nodes at adjacent tree branches. The possible relations are 'requirements', 'require each other', 'excludes' and 'include each other'. These are needed because the feature space cannot always be described as a simple tree.

The maintainability of a feature model is improved by structuring the model into blocks. A feature model block is a part of the feature model tree describing a group of related features and restrictions for their selection. For example, the user interface (UI:UserInterfaces) is presented as a feature block in the extended feature model of the taxi-meter (Figure 4). A restriction between features can only be expressed inside the same feature model block. A feature block type can be used as a type of the feature in some other higher level feature blocks.

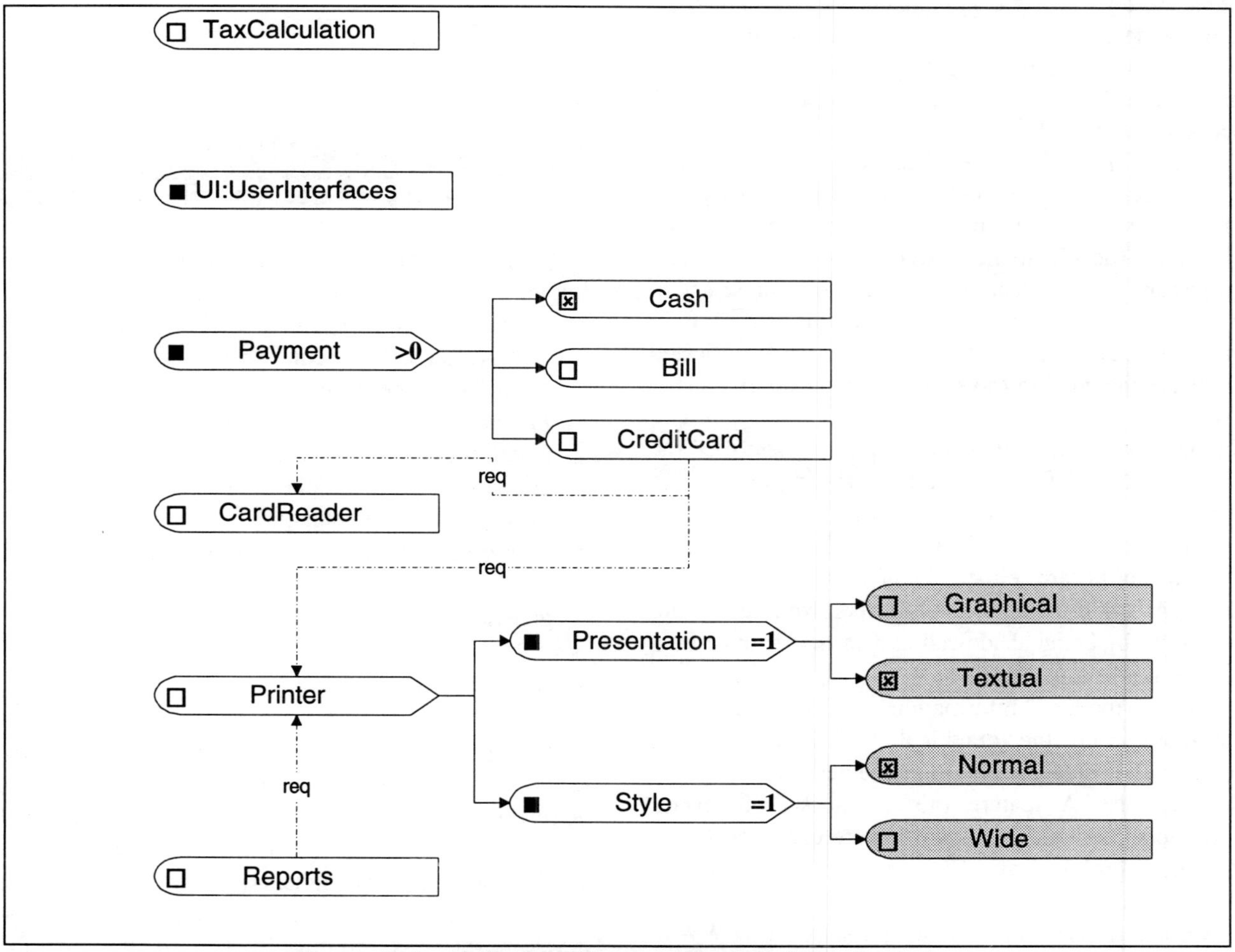

Figure 4. An Extended Feature Model of Product_A.

4. Use of Feature Models in Software Development

The objective of component-based design is to define a set of parametrized software components that implement all the features identified in the feature model. In product deliveries, only the necessary components with proper parameter values implementing the required features of a single customised product are included.

Object-based notations are preferred in modelling software components. Objects provide attributes for parametrisation and methods for the interfaces and services of the components. Structured methods based on functional modelling lack such notations. Object-oriented methods like ROOM [11] and OOA/OOD [12] are appropriate for modelling component designs.

However, to link feature models and component designs closely, software components in our prototype system are designed using experimental EON (Embedded Object Notation). EON is a light-weight notation, suitable both for drafting and for final component design. It supports both object-based and structured design.

The experimental tool environment integrated with EON connects feature models, component design phase models and software building activity into an integrated application development environment. The tool environment enables feature-based component selection and sets up configurable parameter information in components. A code generator takes care that the selected features are included in the source code of the executable software.

In our prototype system the graphical syntax of the feature models is defined so that the resulting feature tree can be easily converted into an HTML form for feature selection. A feature model is a graphical tree-like model in which nodes are either features or feature value choices. A value node symbol differs from a feature symbol only by being shadowed and in that it must be a leaf node of a feature tree.

Feature model information is automatically transformed from the graphical tool into a feature database. The database is implemented as a textual prolog-database. A feature model consists of several feature model components. Each feature component in a graphical or prolog form can be handled as a separate unit in version control. This helps to track the changes in the feature database. The features are selected by WWW HTML forms which are generated from the feature component database by a prolog program. In the feature selection tool, a feature component is represented as an HTML form for the user. In addition to these forms, a number of other forms are created with commercial HTML editors to handle customer identification and product feature documentation (Figure 5).

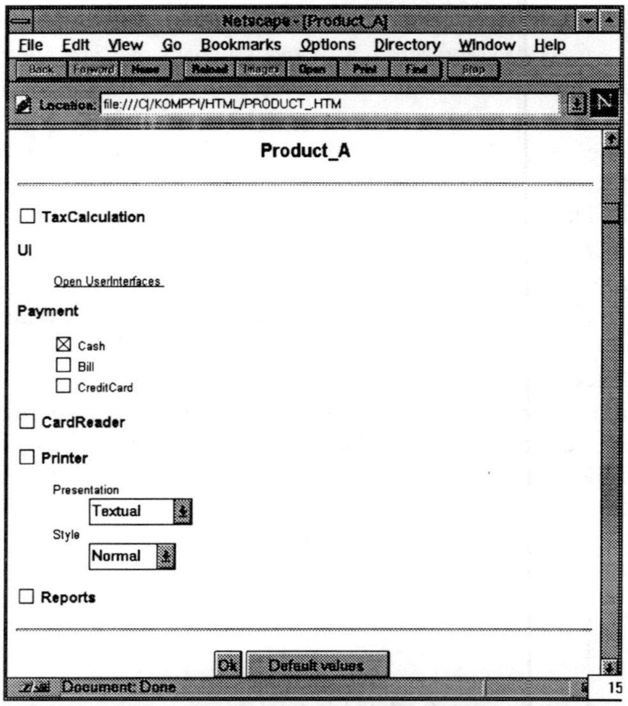

Figure 5. Feature selection form of Product_A.

Product features can be mapped to a software implementation for example in the following way:

- *Feature-based component selection.* The system is constructed by the components which are selected according to the features.
- *Feature-based component configuration.* Configuration of generic components is fixed by a generator or a compiler by setting the values of instantiation parameters.
- *Feature-based automatic programming.* The final application software is generated automatically using generic customizable component models.

5. Discussion

The approach improves product quality and customer satisfaction. Quality is improved by avoiding faulty deliveries due to insufficient and vague product specifications. A feature model is a product family specification that is understood by salesmen, R&D engineers, and customers. Efficiency of software development is improved, due to the reusability encouraged by parametrisable software components.

To achieve these improvements, however, some requirements have to be fulfilled. Firstly, application domain experience is necessary to identify product family features. Secondly, software architecture supporting adaptability with components and parameters is required, and finally, a mechanism to link features and software components in a consistent manner is expected. Unfortunately, there is no generic solution which fulfills all these requirements. Instead, company-specific, even product family-specific solutions are followed.

Our future work focus on the interconnections of software components, trying to apply different interface description languages, such as CORBA IDL and MIL (Module Interconnection Language). The characteristics of embedded real-time software sets some special requirements and restrictions for the required interface description language. Design for testability is a major issue and requires more attention to be paid when reusable software components are to be used for various product families and mass-tailored software deliveries.

In summary, the productivity of the development of embedded software can be increased by a reuse-oriented process, a feature modelling method, and an analysis and design environment supporting feature and component-based software development. Diversity of customer needs, information about feasible implementation technologies, and development processes are collected and analysed in the domain analysis phase.

Feature models describe customized product features derived from customer requirements analysis, technical feasibility studies and constraints as a hierarchical feature-tree structure. A feature-tree is a link between non-technical customer needs, technical requirements, and the software architecture and component designs. A feature modelling method and its graphical notation supports the creation of a common understanding between software developers, salesmen and customers. The maintainability of feature models is supported by grouping related features in blocks, and describing them as a part of a feature-tree.

Component-based design results in a set of parametrisable software components that implement all the identified features. The EON-notation supports the linking of a feature model and component designs. The required features of a single customised product are selected via the feature model form of an integrated tool environment. The prototyping environment supports automated software application deliveries by integrating feature models, component design phase models and software build mechanisms. However, model integration is always a company-specific or a product family-specific solution.

References

[1] Seppänen, V., Niemelä, E. & Taramaa, J. 1995. CACE + CASE = Better Reuse of Mechatronic Software. 1995. Proceedings of CASE'95 workshop. Toronto: IEEE Computer Society. pp. 289-295.

[2] Liu, T-H. & Fisher, G. W. 1993. An Approach for PDES/STEP Compatible Concurrent Engineering Applications. Concurrent Engineering: Tools and Technologies for Mechanical System Design. Haug, E. J. (eds.) NATO ASI Series. Berlin: Spring-Verlag. pp. 433-464. ISBN 0-397-56532-9.

[3] Ihme, T. 1991. Reuse-oriented structured analysis for embedded systems. VTT Publications 85. VTT Offset: Espoo. 141 p. ISBN 951-38-4063-8.

[4] Kang, K-C & Jang, S-C. 1994. A Model-Based MICOM Application Software Development Model. In the Proceedings of 1st Asia-Pacific Software Engineering Conference, 7-9 Dec. 1994, Tokyo, Japan. IEEE Comput. Soc. Press, Los Alamitos, CA. pp. 124-132.

[5] Zeller, Andreas 1994. Configuration Management with Feature Logics. Braunsckweig: Technische Universität Braunsckweig, Arbeitsgrouppe Softwaretechnologie, Informatik-Bericht No. 94-01. 48 p.

[6] Ihme, T. & Niemelä E. 1997. Adaptability in Object-Oriented Embedded and Distributed Software. In Muhlhäuser M. (ed.). Special Issues in Object-Oriented Programming. Heidelberg: Dpunkt Verlag. Workshop reader of the 10th European Conference on Object Oriented Programming ECOOP'96. pp. 29-36. ISBN 3-920993-67-5.

[7] Day, R. 1993. Quality Function Deployment. Linking a Company with Its Customers. ASQC Quality Press: Milwaukee, Wisconsin. 245 p. ISBN 0-8739-202.

[8] Ihme, T., Niemelä E. & Salmela M., 1995. Object-Oriented Re-engineering of Embedded Software. Mechatronics. Vol. 5, No. 1, pp 73-86.

[9] Taramaa, J., Lintulampi, R. & Seppänen, V. 1994. Automated Assembly of Machine Control Software. Mechatronics, Vol. 4, No. 7, pp. 753-769.

[10] Taramaa, J., Seppänen, V. & Mäkäräinen, M. 1996. From Software Configuration to Application Management - Improving the Maturity of the Maintenance of Embedded Software. Software Maintenance: Research and practice. Vol. 8. pp. 49-75.

[11] Selic, B., Gullekson, G. & Ward, P. 1994. Real-time object-oriented modeling. New York: John Wiley & Sons. 525 p.

[12] Shlaer, S. & Mellor, S. 1992. Object Lifecycles, Modelling the World in States. Englewood Cliffs, New Jersey, Prentice Hall Inc. 250 p.

Component-based Systems Development: Challenges and Lessons Learned

Vu Tran[1]
ArcQuest Corporation

Dar-Biau Liu
California State University, Long Beach

Brad Hummel[1]
ArcQuest Corporation

Abstract

The continuing increase of interest in Component-based Software Engineering (CBSE) signifies the emergence of a new development trend within the software industry. Unlike preceding software engineering models, CBSE heavily relies on the utilization of commercial off-the-shelf (COTS) products as the underlying foundation for new product development. Its emphasis is on the identification, selection, evaluation, procurement, integration, and evolution of reusable software components to provide complex integrated solutions at shorter development time and minimum cost. Compared to traditional development-centric software engineering approaches, CBSE promises a more efficient and effective approach to the delivery of software solutions to the market. However, underestimating the technical risks associated with the selection, evaluation, and integration of these software components has often resulted in longer schedule delay, and higher development/ maintenance cost, often experienced in integrated system development projects. This paper describes an experience at the Mitsubishi Consumer Electronics Engineering Center (CEEC) in implementing embedded Internet/Television systems using CBSE. It also describes the procurement-centric model that we have utilized to support project planning and to guide the development process. The COTS-based Integrated System Development (CISD) model identifies key engineering phases and their sub-phases that are often ignored, or merely implicit, in existing development-centric models. From the initial results of this project, the paper presents the various lessons learned at the CEEC in CBSE.

1. Introduction

The prospect of increased product reliability and stability, at shorter development time and reduced cost, has led to a recent surge of interest in component-based software engineering. This engineering approach emphasizes the acquisition and integration of reusable COTS products over in-house development for constructing complex and large-scale software solutions. The key driving factors that support this increasing interest in CBSE include:

1. The increasing industrial competition for delivery and provision of higher quality and more reliable software solutions in shorter time frames.
2. The increasing demand for larger and more complex software solutions, which often can not be effectively implemented in a timely manner by a single software development organization.
3. The increasing availability of both generic and domain-specific reusable COTS software components.
4. The increasing degree of interoperability and standard compliance among COTS software products that enables significant reduction in product integration time and effort.
5. The increasing research in, and support for development of, better software component "packaging" techniques and approaches, which form the basis for production of complex reusable components. Some emerging techniques and approaches include Design Patterns [GAMM94], Domain-based Modeling [SHLA92] [AWAD96], and Software Architecture [GARL94].
6. The increasing recognition that software reuse is one of the most important means to achieve better software solutions with minimum development cost. For instance, a recent empirical study by Basili, Briand, and Melo identifies software reuse as a key contributor to the reduction of development errors and rework in object-oriented development projects [BASI96].

At the CEEC, component-based software engineering has received very close attention early on. It has been

[1] Vu Tran and Brad Hummel were Project Lead and Chief Software Architect at Mitsubishi CEEC, responsible for the early development of the DiamondWeb Internet/Television product family for North America.
[2] DiamondWeb™ is a registered trademark of Mitsubishi Corporation.

0-8186-7840-2/97 $10.00 © 1997 IEEE

chosen as the approach for developing the DiamondWeb™[2] Internet/Television product family. The DiamondWeb project is an ambitious attempt by Mitsubishi to provide fully integrated Internet/Television solutions for the consumer electronics market in North America. Some technologies chosen for the end-product include Java, World-Wide-Web, TV HTML, Netscape-like plug-ins, Netscape Secured Socket Layer (SSL), TV image and Web HTML printing, Web page zooming and panning , and many others. Future technologies that are being investigated include digital television, and plasma display television. The first shipment for North America consists of all the Internet technologies mentioned above, embedded in existing large-screen Mitsubishi television product families.

The key reasons behind the selection of CBSE as the approach to engineering the DiamondWeb system include:

1) **To meet a demanding development schedule.** The existing fierce competition between television and computer vendors in the Internet/Television market requires the company to release a product within one year after its inception. For the DiamondWeb system, envisioned as a full integrated system rather than a standard set-top box solution, this is an especially demanding schedule. As a result, developing the system with available COTS products seems to be a more viable approach than developing it from scratch.

2) **To reduce the need for engineering specialists to support the development of the various technologies.** With the continuing shortage of engineers, especially specialists, in key areas of computer technology such as embedded system development, object-oriented software with Java and C++, multimedia, distributed systems, and Internet software, adopting available COTS products enables leverage of the expertise provided by the product vendors.

3) **To leverage the reliability of existing COTS products.** COTS product integration would enable us to take advantage of the reliability of existing products in building the DiamondWeb system. It is perceived that the same level of product reliability would be difficult to achieve otherwise with a small available staff and a short development schedule.

Recognizing the limitations of currently existing development models, a procurement-centric engineering model was adopted as a framework to support both project planning and product development. The COTS-based Integrated Systems Development (CISD) model describes a systematic approach to development of integrated software solutions using commercial off-the-shelf components [TRAN97a] [TRAN97b]. Unlike development-centric models, the CISD model is designed specifically to reflect the development steps associated with the development of COTS-based integrated systems.

In the next section, this paper summarizes the limitations of using development-centric models to support component-based software development. The paper then describes various key efforts associated with CBSE. Subsequently, the paper summarizes the CISD model, and its integration with a development-centric model, used in the DiamondWeb project. Finally, the paper presents the lessons learned regarding CBSE from this project.

2. Review of existing software engineering models

In order to ensure the success of the DiamondWeb project, we started the project with the selection of a unified and appropriate approach to system development with CBSE. Two prominent development-centric models selected for evaluation were the Waterfall [ROYC70] and Spiral models [BOEH88]. The Waterfall model, and its derivatives, describe the software development process as an ordered sequence of engineering phases, ranging from requirement definition to operation (Figure 1). In this model, each engineering phase has to be completed prior to the start of the subsequent phase. In Figure 1, this orderly process is illustrated with the forward pointing arrows. The backward pointing arrows capture the necessary reworks that are often experienced in software development projects. In the Waterfall model, these reworks are considered exceptions to the overall development process.

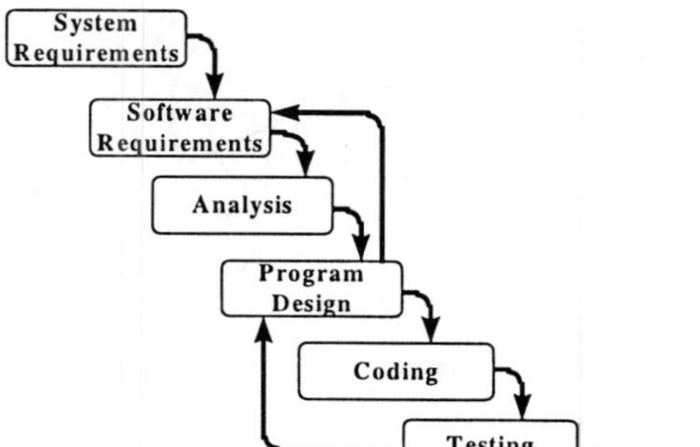

Figure 1 The Waterfall Model

A limitation of this model is its inadequate reflection of the iterative and incremental nature of modern software development processes. These iterative and incremental development characteristics are often needed to accommodate the uncertainty that exists at the beginning of most software projects [PRES92]. This problem is especially troublesome in implementing component-based systems where the system requirements and architectures are often driven by the capabilities and structures of the final set of COTS product components selected for integration. However, these components can not be identified prior to the product selection and evaluation. Furthermore, as a development-centric model, the process described in the Waterfall model completely ignores the extensive effort of selecting, evaluating, and integrating COTS products often experienced in component-based software development. Other limitations of the Waterfall model are summarized in [HUMP90].

The Spiral model, and its derivatives, attempt to address some inherent limitations of the Waterfall model. This model captures the need to "analyze a little, design a little, implement a little" as a normal part of the software development process [BOEH88]. The iterative and incremental development dynamics described in the Spiral model provide a framework for modern object-oriented development methodologies including [RUMB91] [SHLA92] [AWAD96] and [BOOC94]. However, like the Waterfall model, this model is also development-centric. Its main focus is to capture the spiral process of developing a software solution from scratch. As a result, the model fails to reflect the procurement-centric nature of the component-based software engineering process. Other development-centric variations of the Waterfall and the Spiral software development models are further described in [McCO96].

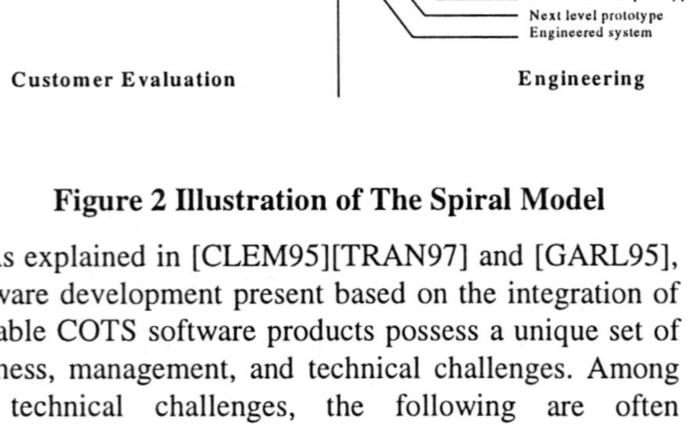

Figure 2 Illustration of The Spiral Model

As explained in [CLEM95][TRAN97] and [GARL95], software development present based on the integration of reusable COTS software products possess a unique set of business, management, and technical challenges. Among the technical challenges, the following are often experienced:

1. Adoption of a new COTS product into an integrated software system means incorporating additional constraints inherent in that product into the system's overall architecture, functionality and performance.

2. Integration of COTS software products means incorporating multiple inconsistent architecture frameworks within a single system. This architectural mismatch has been recently identified as a fundamental obstacle to component-based software development in [GARL95]. Underestimating these problems often resulted in higher cost of development, performance, and maintenance [GARL95][FAIR94].

3. Insertion of a COTS software product into a system also means inheriting its architectural, functional, and performance defects in the final system. In the worst case, the number of defective execution paths in the overall system can increase exponentially as more defective products are integrated [TRAN97].

4. Usage of COTS software products means taking risks that future system extensions might be limited due to dependence on the support of other COTS product vendors for the required capabilities. In addition, there is no guarantee of long-term technical support from vendors, or of compatibility between versions of the selected COTS products newer than those originally integrated in the system [CLEM95].

5. Maintenance of a system of integrated COTS products often requires additional cost for continuing staff training on the different behaviors, architectures, protocols, and messaging formats among these products. In addition, replacement of a particular unusable COTS product in the future can result in expensive redesign and reimplementation of the system to enable interoperability between the new product and the rest of the system.

In order to effectively address the potential technical problems identified above, a more procurement-centric model was needed for the DiamondWeb project. In addition, we felt that key engineering efforts experienced from working with CBSE needed to be identified explicitly to support effective project management and scheduling. Based on the collective experience of our engineering staffs and results of literature research in CBSE, a common recurring set of engineering efforts were identified. In the next section, these efforts will be described in more detail.

3. Analysis of the COTS product evaluation, selection, and integration process

The key engineering efforts often encountered in a software integration process include:

1. Classifying and deriving domain requirements in order to drive the early COTS product selection effort.

2. Partitioning the system into domain-specific subsystems to enable concurrent COTS product evaluation.

3. Defining an overall system architecture that is based on the architectures of the selected COTS products.

4. Defining an overall COTS product evaluation strategy and criteria that reflect the available time and resources.

5. Identifying and prioritizing candidate COTS product sets for evaluation.

6. Evaluating the prioritized candidate COTS product sets.

7. Integrating the selected candidate COTS product combination into the final system.

3.1 Classifying and deriving domain requirements

The evaluation and selection of COTS products can not be effectively implemented without understanding the requirements associated with the system to be developed. However, system requirements often do not directly address the characteristics of a particular application or service domain that are needed in COTS product evaluation. Rather, these requirements often describe the functional, performance, and interoperability needs of the entire system from a "black box" perspective. In CBSE, understanding of the overall system requirements is often not enough. These system-level requirements need to be broken down, extracted, derived, and organized into collections of domain-specific requirements. This effort is necessary to separate the system's overall requirements into loosely coupled sets to support subsequent concurrent product evaluation and selection efforts. For instance, requirements regarding the system's information persistence should be derived, extracted, and collected to define the criteria for selecting COTS database storage products. Similarly, communication-related functional and performance requirements need to be extracted, derived, and collected for the selection of COTS communications products. This domain-specific requirement derivation and classification process is mostly overlooked in existing software engineering models, yet often implemented in component-based software development projects.

3.2 Partitioning of the system into domain-specific subsystems

Modern methodologies emphasize the importance of partitioning a large-scale software system into multiple manageable subsystems for concurrent analysis, design and implementation. To ensure maximum internal cohesion and minimum external coupling between these subsystems, the partition should reflect the various application and service domains associated with the system [AWAD96]. According to [SHLA92], a domain is "a separate real, hypothetical or abstract world inhabited by a distinct set of objects that behave according to the rules and policies characteristic of the domain." From our experience, this effort is imperative to support early identification of candidate COTS products for evaluation. More importantly, it also enables early identification of subsystems that cannot be supported by the procurement of COTS products. These subsystems will be implemented using a development-centric approach. Figure 4 illustrates an example of the domain-based partitioning of those portions of the DiamondWeb™ system[1] that resides in the Mitsubishi television. The shaded boxes identify subsystems that can be implemented totally or partially by the procurement of COTS products. The white boxes identify subsystems that will be developed entirely in-house. The stand-alone boxes are generic utilities or services that will be used by other subsystems as needed.

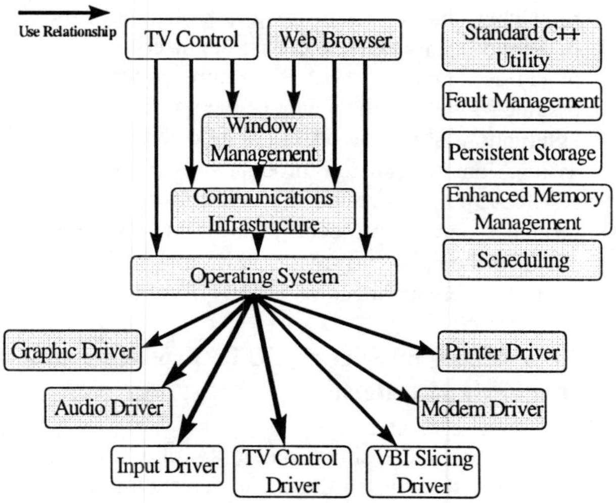

Figure 3 The DiamondWeb Internet/TV subsystems

3.3 Defining an overall system architecture

A high quality, reliable, and maintainable large-scale software system can not be built without a consistent overall system-level architecture framework. This recognition has contributed to an emerging discipline of software engineering research and application known as Software Architecture. The goal of this discipline is to

[1] Many details have been omitted to protect company proprietary and confidential information.

recognize and capture elegant system and subsystem-level software architectural solutions to recurring system construction problems [GARL94] [SHAW95]. In general, defining consistent, extensible, and robust software architectural solutions has always been a challenging task in software engineering. In CBSE, this task is much more difficult. First, as discussed in [CLEM95] and [TRAN97a], the architecture of a component-based integrated system is often influenced significantly by those of the selected components. Thus, the selection of different software components, as a result of the product evaluation and selection effort, often has a significant impact on the overall architecture of the system. For instance, defining a communication infrastructure to support distributed system development might require selection among COTS products supporting different standards and protocols, such as (1) the HP OpenView®[2] (SNMP/CMIP/CMOT protocols), (2) the Talarian RTWorks®[3] (a proprietary protocol), or (3) the IONA Orbix®[4] (CORBA protocol). As a result the final architecture of the system to be developed often continues to evolve throughout the COTS product evaluation effort. Second, as described in [GARL95], overcoming architecture mismatch among selected COTS software products is another challenging task often not experienced in development-centric software engineering. This is due to (1) assumptions about the nature of the product, (2) assumptions about the nature of the product interfaces, (3) assumptions about the overall system architecture, and (4) assumptions about the product's construction process [GARL95]. As a result, the architecture of the selected products, and the protocol, control, and data mismatches between them, often provide additional challenges to the overall system architecture design effort in CBSE.

3.4 Defining an overall COTS product evaluation strategy and criteria

With the increasing availability of COTS products, evaluating them is an endeavor demanding considerable time and energy. Furthermore, there are often no obvious winners among the candidate products that are being evaluated. Selecting an appropriate product typically requires tradeoff analysis among the available products in which only a "better than others" solution is available. As a result, establishing the criteria for the selection of these products is a very important task in CSBE. These product evaluation and selection criteria always extend beyond those defined by the system functional requirements. Some criteria are concerned with the product vendors, such as (1) the level of product support expected for the life of the system, and (2) the stability of the company. Others reflect the limitation of time and resources to support the evaluation effort, such as (1) the deadline associated with the final product selection decision, (2) the resources that can be allocated for the evaluation effort, and (3) the number of products to be evaluated. COTS evaluation strategies, such as first-fit or best-fit evaluation, and product comparison criteria are also defined during this effort. From our experience, large-scale integrated system development often requires concurrent evaluations of multiple software domains, with multiple engineers across multiple development organizations. As a result, early establishment of these criteria provides a uniform guideline for timely and consistent evaluation of COTS software products.

3.5 Identifying and prioritizing candidate COTS product sets

The COTS product identification phase typically requires extensive effort and time spent in attending conferences, reviewing literature, training, traveling and communicating with product vendors. Unfortunately, current development-centric models do not explicitly recognize these as normal parts of the development effort. In procurement-centric development, the efforts to support COTS product identification often require a large amount of dedicated human resources and time. In addition, the selection of an inappropriate candidate product for integration can result in an enormous amount of extra time and effort to re-evaluate and re-implement the system with another product. To support realistic cost analysis and project planning, the process of identifying candidate COTS products should be captured as part of the component-based software development.

During a product identification effort, an important criterion for early elimination of candidate products is their inherent dependency. Products that depend on others which violate the system requirements can be eliminated from the evaluation effort early. For instance, products that do not work with the required operating system should be rejected.

While identification of appropriate candidate products for evaluation is an important task, *prioritizing* them enables subsequent "on-schedule", and often time-optimized, product evaluation. As described in subsection 3.4, the criteria used for prioritizing the candidate products are often extensive and subjective. They are dependent on many non-technical issues such as product costs, available time, product preference, product vendor's history, etc. From a technical perspective, two important guidelines for prioritizing candidate products

[2] OpenView® is a registered trademark of Hewlett-Packard Corporation

[3] RTWorks® is a registered trademark of Talarian Corporation.

[4] Orbix® is a registered trademark of IONA Technologies Ltd.

for evaluation include: (1) the product's ability to inter-operate with other products, and (2) its ability to support multiple identified application and service domains. Selecting products that are readily inter-operable enables reduction in the overall integration time and effort. In contrast, selecting a group of products that are not readily inter-operable means additional time and effort will be needed for product integration. Products that can support multiple domains should receive higher priority since they enable a reduction in the number of inter-product interfaces that need to be interconnected. Products that provide maximum support for both criteria above are often those that provide the widest coverage of the system requirements at minimum additional development cost.

In a system integration project, there are often multiple software products selected for a concurrent and integrated product evaluation effort. This approach is needed in order to support selection of an optimal COTS product combination for the system to be implemented. From our experience, in the short-term, the limitations of a particular product might not be as important as its ability to collaborate with others to perform the required system-level functionality. In the long-term, however, the limitations of individual products can negatively impact the extensibility of the entire integrated system. As a result, the evaluation effort needs to address all candidate software products' capabilities as individuals and in collaboration.

3.6 Evaluating the prioritized candidate COTS product sets

The typical process for evaluating a COTS product includes (1) the acquisition of the product and its dependent products, (2) the design of the appropriate prototype and test plan, (3) the configuration of the development environment to support the product evaluation, (4) the installation of the product and other dependent products, (5) the actual coding of prototype, (6) the evaluation of the product, and (7) the generation of the appropriate product evaluation report. In [BROW96], Brown and Wallnau provided additional discussions of these activities to support a COTS software product evaluation. For CBSE, the level of complexity regarding COTS product evaluation increases significantly since multiple products will have to be evaluated in combination.

In general, there are three important areas in COTS product evaluation. These include (1) functionality, (2) interoperability and architecture, and (3) performance. Functionality evaluation encompasses both evaluation of functionality of the individual products and of their integration. Interoperability and architecture evaluation ensures that all candidate COTS products can be integrated according to their product specifications. Performance evaluation addresses the performance of the integrated COTS products in supporting system-level functional threads. During this evaluation process, adequate prototype software is implemented to support all necessary integration and testing. Although the role of software prototyping has always been recognized as an important part of modern software development processes, software prototyping in CBSE takes on a much more important role: it is the only mechanism available for discovering the capabilities and the limitations of candidate COTS products within the context of the system to be developed.

3.7 Integrating the final selected candidate COTS product combination

Once a set of candidate COTS software products has been selected, the development effort enters the product integration phase. This phase consists of the following efforts: (1) developing the software adapters needed to interconnect all the selected COTS products, (2) developing the necessary enhancements to these products, (3) developing other parts of the system that can not be supported by available COTS products, and (4) integrating and testing the final system. Since these efforts often require in-house development and testing, a development-centric approach such as those that are derived from the Waterfall or Spiral model should be utilized. A collection of development-centric software engineering approaches are described in [McCO96].

4. Introducing the COTS-based Integrated System Development (CISD) Model

The CISD model developed at the CEEC is our attempt to generalize the technical process of selecting, evaluating, and integrating COTS products to support procurement-centric software development. The model encompasses all technical efforts associated with CBSE. The CISD model consists of three distinct phases: Product Identification, Product Evaluation, and Product Integration. The ***Product Identification*** phase includes the process of collecting and understanding the overall system requirements, identifying and classifying COTS product into product sets, and prioritizing them for the subsequent evaluation. The ***Product Evaluation*** phase includes the process of integrating, evaluating, and comparing these product sets to select the most optimal combination for integration. The ***Product Integration*** phase includes the building of all necessary software adapters and enhancements to the selected COTS product set to implement the required integrated system. The overall product selection, evaluation, and integration process is often iterative in nature, depending on the size of the system to be developed and the engineering resources available. Subsequent sections describe each phase in more detail.

4.1 The Product Identification phase

The Product Identification phase includes all technical activities that are required to generate a prioritized collection of product combinations for subsequent evaluation. The major activities during this phase

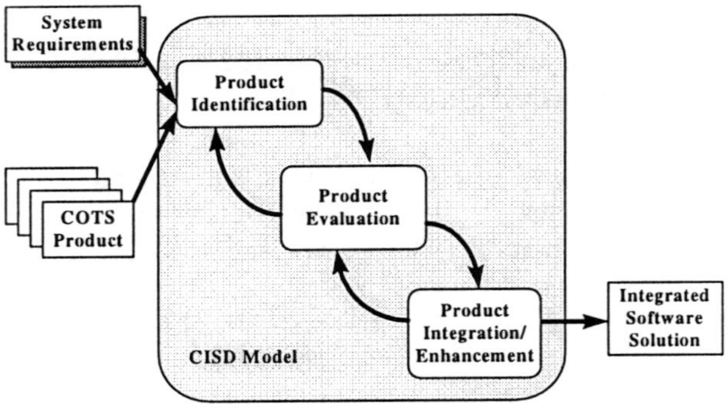

Figure 4 The CISD Model

include: (1) Requirement Analysis and Classification, (2) Product Identification and Classification, and (3) Product Prioritization. The ***Requirement Analysis and Classification*** stage encompasses the process of understanding the system requirements and partitioning these requirements into various application and service domains. The ***Product Identification*** stage encompasses the process of collecting information on candidate COTS products and grouping these products into different product combinations, or sets, for further evaluation. Subsection 3.5 describes various activities implemented during this stage, including the identification of subsystems that have to be built from scratch. These subsystems will subsequently be implemented using a development-centric software engineering method. The ***Product Prioritization*** stage includes the review of all candidate product sets to generate a prioritized list for further evaluation.

The outputs of the initial COTS product identification effort also include updates to the system's overall architecture.

4.2 The Product Evaluation phase

The Product Evaluation phase encompasses the process of creating prototype software for temporary integration and testing of the candidate COTS products (Figure 6). The goal of the Product Evaluation phase is to compare and identify an optimum set of collaborative COTS products for the final integrated system. As a result, this effort needs to include, at a minimum, the following evaluations: (1) functionality of each individual product and product sets, (2) architecture/interoperability of product sets, and (3) performance of each individual product and product sets. The ***Evaluation Preparation*** stage includes all the activities from the initial acquisition of selected products for evaluation to the design of the overall experiment and the configuration of the evaluation environment.

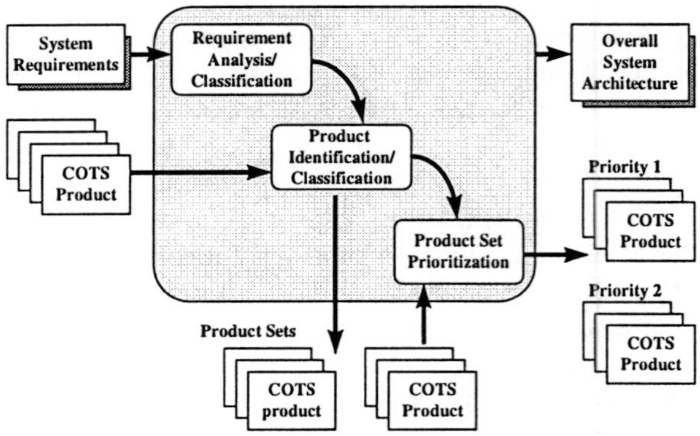

Figure 5 The Product Identification Phase

The ***Functionality Evaluation*** stage enables actual verification and validation of the overall capabilities of each individual product and product sets. Prior to this effort, our understanding of these products is based primarily on past experience, marketing literature, conference information, technical discussions with vendors, and product training. The Functionality Evaluation stage can often be performed initially on an individual product basis, thus requiring a minimum level of configuration support. The complete functionality evaluation often can not be implemented prior to the completion of the next stage. The ***Architecture/ Interoperability Evaluation*** stage evaluates the connectivity and architecture of the candidate COTS products. Specifically, some issues to be addressed during this stage include: (1) the interactions of software components along the identified system critical paths, (2) the extensibility of the overall integrated architecture, and (3) the compliance with required standards by the integrated components. During this stage, the entire candidate product set, and its dependencies, are installed for evaluation. Furthermore, additional software adapters are often required to support their integration. Once they are integrated, the Functionality Evaluation effort can be completed. The ***Performance Evaluation*** stage is often performed last since the performance criteria are often system-level requirements and can not be easily divided into subsystem-level requirements. If time permits, performance evaluation for each interacting component should also be done to provide detailed understanding of the impact of each individual component to the overall system's performance.

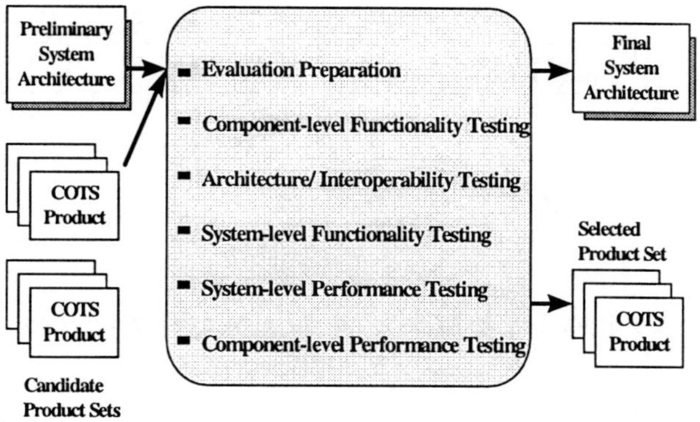

Figure 6. The Product Evaluation phase

From our experience, there are multiple approaches to organizing the COTS product evaluation phase. At the two extremes are the Comprehensive Evaluation (CE) and First-Fit Evaluation (FE) approaches. For the CE approach, illustrated in Figure 7, all candidate product sets are evaluated through all identified stages. The result is a prioritized list of these product sets, ranked by their overall performance. The goal of the CE approach is to ensure that an optimal product set will be selected for the final integration at the cost of additional evaluation time and resources. The FE approach, on the other hand, ensures minimal cost to the evaluation effort by eliminating product sets that failed a particular evaluation stage and selecting the first one that passes all evaluation stages. However, the product set selected might not be the optimal solution (Figure 8). Other product evaluation approaches fall between these two extremes.

The result of the Product Evaluation phase is the optimum product set to be used in the final integrated system. In addition, a final System Architecture specification capturing the overall integrated architecture supported by the chosen product set is delivered.

4.3 The Product Integration/Enhancement phase

The Product Integration/Enhancement Phase encompasses all development efforts required to interconnect different selected COTS products into a single integrated system. As described in subsection 3.7, an appropriate development-centric software engineering approach should be utilized to ensure the high quality and reliability of all software to be developed.

Figure 9 summarizes the complete CISD model. The additional backward pointing arrows between stages and phases reflect the iterative and incremental development often experienced in large-scale component-based software projects.

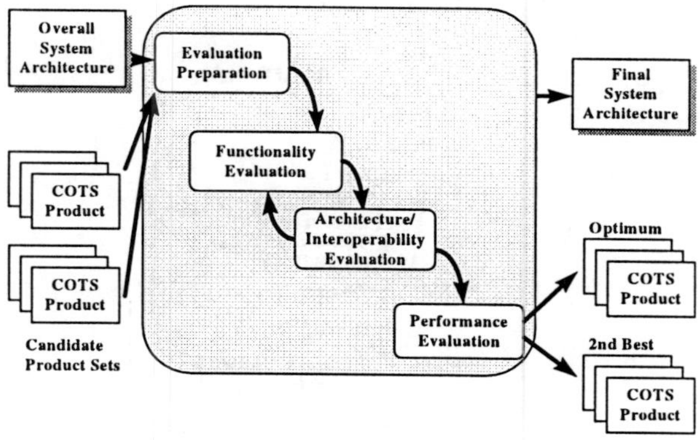

Figure 7. The Comprehensive Evaluation (CE) approach

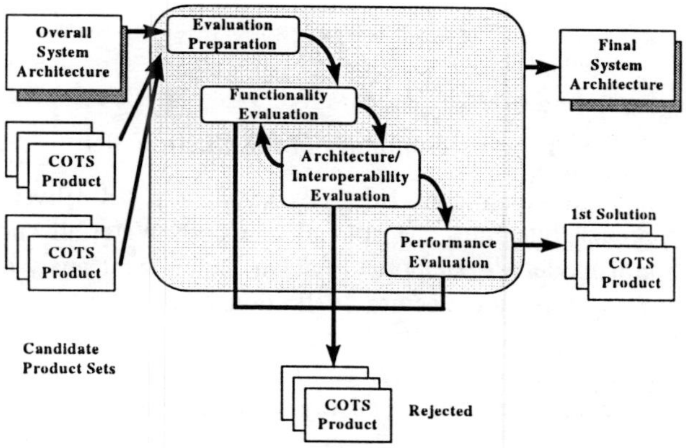

Figure 8. The First-Fit Evaluation (FE) Approach

5. Integration of development-centric and procurement-centric models

Implementation of large-scale integrated systems often requires the combination of both development-centric and procurement-centric engineering models. Defining a single development approach that incorporates both development-centric and procurement-centric models enables effective handling of projects that require both extensive integration of COTS products and in-house software development. For the DiamondWeb project, the modified staged-delivery (MSD) approach is utilized (Figure 10).

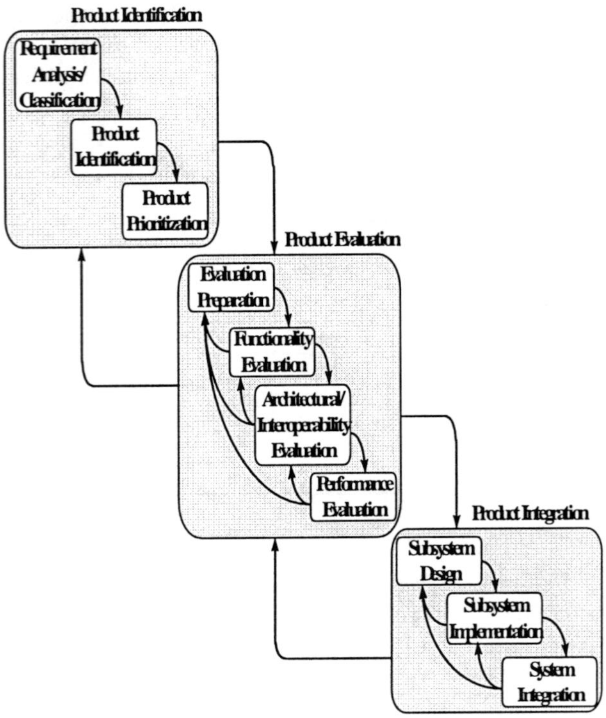

Figure 9 Summary of the CISD model

As described in [McCO96], the staged-delivery approach integrates the strengths of both Waterfall and Spiral models to support top-down requirement analysis and system architecture definitions, and bottom-up iterative/incremental development at the subsystem level. For the DiamondWeb project, the methodology adopted to support the staged-delivery approach was Octopus [AWAD96], an extension, for real-time system development, of the OMT [RUMB91] and Fusion [COLE93] methods. The MSD includes both staged evaluation/selection of COTS products and staged software development at the subsystem level. The arrow from the product evaluation stages to the subsystem development stages reflects the adoption of a development-centric approach to implement the additional software needed to support COTS product integration and enhancement. The feed-back arrows from COTS product evaluation stages to System Architecture and Requirement Analysis reflect the dependency of these phases on the COTS product evaluation results. The System Integration and Delivery stages emphasize the incremental and iterative integration of all subsystems, both COTS-based and development-based, into a final system for delivery.

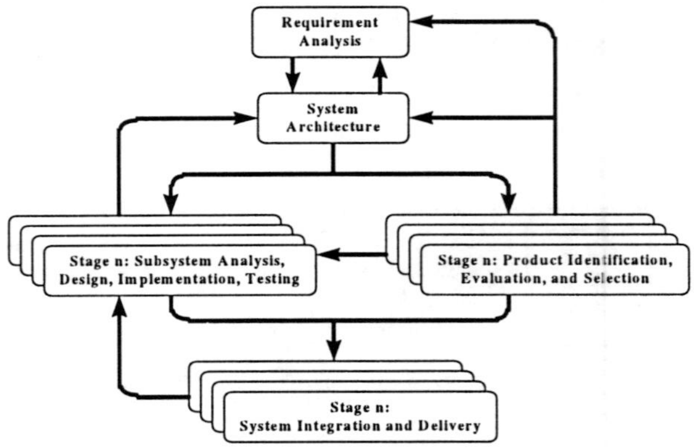

Figure 10 Modified Staged Delivery Development Framework

6. Lessons Learned on the DiamondWeb project

The initial result of the DiamondWeb system implementation was encouraging. Despite the multiple CBSE-related technical and management problems that emerged throughout the development effort, appropriate risk anticipation and mitigation have resulted in an on-time delivery of the first version of the product. The following are key lessons learned from this CBSE effort:

1. **A risk-based approach to management of requirement changes is needed.** The continuing requirement changes during the DiamondWeb development lengthened the product identification and evaluation efforts far beyond what was initially estimated. Overall, these efforts consumed more than half the total development time (starting from requirement analysis). The impact of requirement changes to component-based software development until now has been largely ignored within the research and development community. From our experience with the DiamondWeb project, and many others previously, requirement changes often have a much more serious impact on the overall schedule in CBSE than in other development approaches. This is due to the difficulty with customizing components that are purchased off-the-shelf for integration. As a result, new product identification, evaluation, selection, and integration efforts would be needed to support the new requirements. In the DiamondWeb project, the risk-mitigation strategies that were utilized included: (1) early domain analysis to

identify and capture common domain-specific requirements to ensure early establishment of those that are keys to the system, (2) establishment of a requirement change control board to assess the impact of a particular requirement change and determine when the change should take place with minimum impact to the overall development effort, (3) development of alternative product integration strategies to ensure rapid replacement and deployment of new solutions in response to major changes in requirements, (4) agreements with product vendors to provide custom support for key products such as the real-time operating system, device drivers, Java, and the Web browser, to ensure that these components will evolve to meet the changed system requirements. Although the CISD model used identified a gap between system-level requirements generated during analysis and the subsystem-level requirements needed for early COTS product evaluation, it does not adequately reflect the important relationship between requirement changes and development efforts in CBSE. Efforts are underway to incorporate these information into the model.

2. **Management of architecture mismatch among different products is needed.** The architecture mismatch among these products was another source of difficulty during our development. Each COTS product selected varied significantly in its functionality and interface making it very difficult to determine the appropriate level of abstraction. Correct abstraction was necessary to ensure that future replacement would not impact the rest of the system. Furthermore, many products selected were unique and could not be replaced when changes occurred later. For instance, during the DiamondWeb development, our replacement of the underlying operating system caused the replacement of several COTS products and in some cases there were no alternative ones available altogether. Additional in-house development had to be undertaken for these irreplaceable products in a much shorter time frame in order to maintain the existing schedule. As a result, the entire engineering staff had to increase its work hours, sometimes to 80 hours/week, to compensate for the shortened allowable development time. As mentioned in previous sections, the issues of architecture mismatch between COTS products are currently being aggressively addressed within both research and development communities.

3. **Management of engineering skill mixes for CBSE is important.** As COTS products were being replaced during the development, the required technical expertise of the in-house development staff also changed. This change in engineering expertise has caused tremendous management difficulty in the DiamondWeb project. During the beginning of the project, our intention was to allocate all in-house engineering resources at the application development level while relying on COTS products for core services such as the operating system, device drivers and Web browser. The decision to change the underlying operating system during the middle of the development had a tremendous impact on the task assignment of the staff. Since the new operating system came with an sophisticated television control application, there was almost no need for in-house development at the application-level. Instead, because the vendor of this operating system did not provide support for porting it onto some of our specialized hardware devices, in-house development at the device driver level was needed. Since the engineering staff was previously hired and trained for application-level development, retraining was necessary to support device driver development and operating system porting. With the project already under a tremendous schedule constraint, it was very difficult to allocate additional time for the retraining.

7. Summary

The prospect of shorter development schedule, lower resource cost, and higher product quality has led to the increasing adoption of component-based software engineering as a more viable alternative to the traditional development-centric software development approaches. However, underestimating the technical risks associated with integrated system development and management has produced disappointing results. A factor contributing to the current limited success of integrated system development is the absence of a model that explicitly captures the nature and characteristics of this new software engineering approach.

The early adoption of the COTS-based Integrated Systems Development (CISD) model in the DiamondWeb project provides a much better understanding of the efforts needed to support its implementation. This is because it explicitly identifies the key efforts required in integrating COTS software components that are often ignored in other development-centric models. In addition, the model integrates well with the iterative and incremental nature of current development-centric approaches. Work on extending this model to capture the impact of requirement changes is presently our key area of concentration.

8. Acknowledgement

The authors would like to thank Robert Green from Motorola Inc. for his valuable comments and suggestions to the earlier versions of this paper.

Vu Tran can be reached at tran_v@sat.mot.com

Dar-Biau Liu can be reached at liu@engr.csulb.edu
Brad Hummel can be reached at hummel_b@sat.mot.com

9. Reference

[AWAD96] M. Awad, J. Kuusela, and J. Ziegler, "Object-Oriented Technology for Real-Time Systems: A Practical Approach Using OMT and Fusion," Prentice-Hall, 1996.

[BASI96] V. R. Basili, L. C. Briand, and W. L. Melo, "How Reuse Influences Productivity in Object-Oriented Systems," Communications of the ACM, Oct. 1996.

[BOEH88] B. Boehm, "A Spiral Model for Software Development and Enhancement," Computer, May 1988.

[BOOC94] G. Booch, "Object-Oriented Analysis and Design with Applications," Benjamin-Cummings, 1994.

[BROW96] A. W. Brown and K. C. Wallnau, "A Framework for Evaluating Software Technology," IEEE Software, Sept. 1996.

[CLEM95] P. C. Clements, "From Subroutines to Subsystems: Component-Based Software Development," The American Programmer, Nov. 1995.

[COLE93] D. Coleman, P. Arnold, S. Bodoff, C. Dollin, H. Gilchrist, F. Haynes, and P. Jeremaes, "Object-Oriented Development - The Fusion Method," Prentice-Hall, 1993.

[COPL95] J. O. Coplien, and D. C. Schmidt, "Pattern Languages of Program Design," Addison-Wesley, 1995.

[FAIR85] R. Fairley, "Software Engineering Concepts," McGraw-Hill, 1985.

[FAIR94] R. Fairley, "Risk Management for Software Projects," IEEE Software, May 1994.

[GAMM94] E. Gamma, R. Helm, R. Johnson, and J. Vlissides, "Design Patterns: Elements of Reusable Object-Oriented Design," Addison-Wesley, 1994.

[GARL94] D. Garlan, and M. Shaw, "An Introduction to Software Architecture," CMU Software Engineering Institute Technology Report CMU/SEI-94-TR-21, ESC-TR-94-21, Jan. 1994.

[GARL95] D. Garlan, R. Allen, and J. Ockerbloom, "Architectural Mismatch (Why it is hard to build systems out of existing parts)," Proceedings of the 17th International Conference on Software Engineering, April 1995.

[HUMP90] Humphrey, W. S., "Managing The Software Process," Addison-Wesley, 1990.

[McCO96] McConnell, S., "Rapid Development: Taming Wild Software Schedules," Microsoft Press, 1996.

[PRES92] R. S. Pressman, "Software Engineering: A Practitioner's Approach," McGraw-Hill, 1992.

[ROYC70] W. W. Royce, "Managing The Development of Large Software Systems," Proceedings on IEEE WESCON, Aug. 1970.

[RUMB91] J. Rumbaugh, M. Blaha, W. Premerlani, F. Eddy, and W. Lorensen, "Object-Oriented Modeling and Design," Prentice-Hall, 1991.

[SHAW95] M. Shaw, D. Garlan, R. Allen, D. Klein, J. Ockerbloom, C. Scott, and M. Schumacher, "Candidate Model Problems in Software Architecture," CMU Software Engineering Institute White Paper, Jan. 1995.

[SHAW96] M. Shaw, "Some Patterns For Software Architectures," in J. M. Vlissides, J. O. Coplien, and N. L. Kerth (eds.), "Pattern Languages of Program Design II," Addison-Wesley, 1996.

[SHLA92] S. Shlaer, and S. J. Mellor, "Object Lifecycles: Modeling the World in States," Yourdon Press Computing Series, Prentice-Hall, 1992.

[TRAN97a] V. Tran and D. B. Liu, "A Risk-Mitigating Model for The Development of Reliable and Maintainable Large-Scale Commercial-Off-The-Shelf Integrated Software Systems," Proceedings of the 1997 Annual Reliability and Maintainability Symposium - The International Symposium on Product Quality and Integrity, Jan. 1997.

[TRAN97b] V. Tran and D. B. Liu, "A Procurement-centric Model for Engineering Component-based Software Systems," Proceedings of the 1997 Fifth International Symposium on Assessment of Software Tools and Technologies, Jun. 1997.

[VLIS96] J. M. Vlissides, J. O. Coplien, and N. L. Kerth (eds.), "Pattern Languages of Program Design II," Addison-Wesley, 1996.

[WHIT94] I. White, "Using The Booch Method: A Rational Approach," Benjamin-Cummings, 1994.

[YOUR89] E. Yourdon, "Modern Structured Analysis," Yourdon Press Computing Series, 1989.

Session P5c

Requirements Specification

Getting the Requirements Right - A Professional Approach

Dr. L.B. Hunt
Computer System Architects Limited
CSA House
Worplesdon - Surrey GU3 3PP - United Kingdom
Tel: 44(0)1483 236061 - Fax: 44(0)1483 236028

Abstract

Software engineers and system analysts are continually inundated with demands to adopt this design methodology or that implementation support tool. There is no shortage of options. However, unless it is very clear what it is that is supposed to be designed and/or implemented, such techniques and tools are likely to be wastefully employed producing the wrong thing. It is incumbent upon all professional engineers, before committing other people's money and resources, to be able to confirm that they are setting to work with a good requirement specification.

What is a 'good' requirements specification and how may we ensure that we have one?

This paper describes a radically new approach to producing re-usable requirements specifications which achieves levels of clarity and precision hitherto unattainable. Above all the approach provides the ability to demonstrate clearly to a client the **actual** *content of a specification as opposed to its* **supposed** *content - in an information sense. Such ability is vital if the professional engineer is to be able to carry his client with him or if the client is to be convinced when changes are required - before any serious commitment to consequential or candidate design is made.*

1 Introduction

All software engineering activity should proceed from a clear, quality assessed, statement of requirements. When embarking upon the production of a system whose requirements need to be formally stated, either as a basis for inviting tenders, responding to tenders or as the starting point for design or implementation, one cannot overestimate the importance of producing a good requirements specification document or the importance of ensuring its completeness, consistency and correctness or of the impact of all three attributes on long term costs and productivity.

Errors in requirements are pervasive, dangerous and costly **[Faulk, 1995]**. It is beginning to be appreciated that the majority of software errors are introduced during the requirements definition phase of any project **[GAO, 1992]**. There is also growing evidence that errors in requirements can be the cause of serious accidents. A 1992 study concluded that the major source of software related errors in NASA's Voyager and Galileo spacecraft were errors in functional and interface requirements **[Lutz, 1993]**. If requirements errors are not corrected until the system has been implemented the cost can be extremely high. It has been estimated **[Boehm, 1981 and Fairley, 1985]** that correcting requirements errors during implementation can cost up to 200 times as much as if they were corrected during requirements definition.

Given the high incidence of requirements errors the seriousness of accidents that may be caused and the high cost of late corrections, techniques for improving the quality of requirements documents, and for early detection of requirements errors, are crucial.

This paper describes some of the fundamental concepts which underlie the Generic Model Approach to Requirements Capture (GMARC). These concepts were developed and integrated into a requirements engineering methodology **[Hunt,1992]** by a team of professional software and system engineers for use by the same kind of people. This methodology is now commercially available and is supported by a PC based software package whose use ensures adherence to the methodology and without which the associated manual workload would be impossibly complex.

The importance of the investment involved in the production of a Requirements Specification is almost invariably underestimated - to the ultimate detriment (in both financial and performance terms) of the system concerned. With modern, highly complex systems the need for properly structured, carefully controlled, system specifications, which are internally correct, consistent and complete and which adequately satisfy the requirement, is vital. Further there is a need to ensure that such specifications can be readily modified and re-used without

0-8186-7840-2/97 $10.00 © 1997 IEEE

incurring either too much consequential effort and delay or without introducing spiralling increases in cost and complexity. In order to approach this virtual Nirvana, computer aided support is essential. This is the case primarily because of the enormous decrease in routine manual calculation and information sorting that is thereby achieved. The human participants in the process are correspondingly relieved of the error-prone, tedious and, more often than not, fruitless series of trial solutions which are nearly always necessary in order to generate an adequate context for balanced judgements to be made during the development of a system specification.

2 Problem Areas

Aside from the usual project management issues there are a number of other areas of consideration which need to be taken into account by the professional software engineer when setting up the conceptual framework which defines a particular task. Three of the most important of these areas are:

- Psychological
- Philological
- Acceptance

Firstly, Psychological considerations involve a proper understanding of the limitations to which everyone's thinking is subject. These limitations become manifest when attempting to describe a new idea during the process of passing it on to someone else - as in a requirements specification. We are all constrained in this context by our previous experience. As a consequence we tend to describe things in terms of our previous experience and, in so doing, we inadvertently close the door to other possibilities. The professional engineer needs to be aware of such issues in order to be able to take appropriate precautionary measures during the process of interpreting incoming information.

Another area of psychological difficulty is the problem that everyone has to confine any given set of comments to the same level of detail. Again and again in almost any technical description that may be selected it will be found that there are passing comments and observations which properly belong to some other level of detail. The presence of such passing comments, far from improving clarity, only serves to divert attention from those issues that should be being addressed at the current level of detail.

Secondly, Philological considerations include all those difficulties that arise when setting down natural language descriptions of anything. Formal, mathematically provable, languages are not sufficiently useful. This is because it has been finally demonstrated that it is not possible to use mathematically provable languages for open systems [Hogan, 1995]. Open systems are those which incorporate non-deterministic processes - ie all natural systems!

We are all encouraged to make our documents 'readable'. Thus, it is hoped, others will find it easy to read such documents and will thereby be encouraged to learn more about the subject matter. The problem with readable documents is that they encourage a narrative style which leads to compound and complex sentences. An example of a compound sentence in this context is:

The system will exchange invoices, receipts and special billing instructions with regional offices.

This sentence is compound because it can readily be rephrased in the form of three simple sentences; one referring only to 'invoices', one to 'receipts' and one to 'special billing instructions'. Such simple sentences are referred to as 'atomic' sentences. Complex sentences on the other hand are not capable of being so easily decomposed. Complex sentences typically need to be completely rephrased in order to make their meaning unambiguous and in order to be able to decompose them into atomic components.

Non-atomic sentences can be, and indeed are, difficult to assign contractual liability to in a precise manner. This is because their meaning is obscured by grammatical complexity. Professional engineers should employ their utmost endeavours to eliminate spurious complexity of this kind if they are to minimise and manage the real complexity of any consequential design. By so doing the opportunity for error is minimised and long term costs are reduced. All of this surely must be in the interests of the client and therefore of the professional software engineer.

Another philological problem is the cavalier over-use of certain words to which we are all prone. We all use the same word to mean many different things (eg the word 'system') and we often use different words to refer to the same thing. Such looseness inevitably introduces confusion into descriptions which need to be, by virtue of the financial consequences of misinterpretation, as precise and unambiguous as we can possibly make them.

Thirdly and finally - acceptance considerations. Every specification document that the author of this paper has examined to date has been found to contain a large number of subjective requirements. These are requirements whose intention is inevitably subject to interpretation by the reader. Examples of such requirements are:

- The system must be user friendly.
- The hardware must be easy to maintain.
- Rapid response is essential.

The ultimate realisation of requirements of this kind, in the system that is being specified, is incapable of being verified in any objective manner without recourse to other more definitive information. If such information is not provided, or referred to, at the outset then uncertainty will exist and there is potential for error. The above examples are necessarily rather obvious - in order to make the point. In practice much more subtle forms exist to plague the activities of the professional engineer intent on identifying a particular need.

Another important aspect of acceptance is that associated with the dynamic viability of the system being specified. This issue is associated with the problem of demonstrating that the given specification will lead to the realisation of a system that will perform in the correct manner. That is: does the requirement call for something which is dynamically viable - and if not why not?

All the above issues - and more - are capable of being addressed and resolved prior to any commitment to design **[Collins, 1994]**. Therefore, if the ability exists, it must surely be in the interests of the client (and therefore the professional engineer) to carry out such resolution - at least to some extent.

3 The Methodology

3.1 General

The previous section has outlined just a few of the problems that beset the professional engineer's attempts to obtain a clear and objective statement of requirements. In this section the GMARC approach to resolving such problems is introduced.

All good engineers know that, when first presented with any new body of information, a valuable first step is to attempt to identify patterns and/or structure in the raw information. The presence of structure invariably improves the ability to process and relate information content - one component with another - and, consequently, to identify omissions, inconsistencies and errors as well as carry out many other processes of a similar nature.

How should we go about identifying structure and content in a statement of requirements? In order to answer this question we need firstly to have identified some form of generalised framework - upon which each application can be hung - and secondly we need to identify the components of the given application in order that we can categorise them using the framework. Once they have been categorised the components can thereby be readily compared and related both to each other and to generic forms. Such generic forms develop with time and constitute the application area expertise repository or knowledge base. The professional engineer often has an informal knowledge base of this kind in his head where it is invisible to others. GMARC provides the ability to capture generic knowledge explicitly and thereby makes it available to other practitioners **[Peltu, 1995]**. As a result the opportunity for mutual benefit and consensus is dramatically improved.

3.2 The Basic Framework

The research that formed part of the GMARC development work led to the conclusion that there is a fundamental and generally applicable framework into which all requirements information can be sorted prior to identifying and analysing the structure of the system being specified. In order to get a feel for the nature of this framework let us imagine that we can define a three dimensional array where the three dimensions are:

- Application Aspect
- Support Layer
- Detail Level

Figure 3.2:1 overleaf illustrates a simple example where the three dimensions have each been assigned three category names. As can be seen the category names can be interpreted as defining an array of small rectangular regions, each such region corresponding to a particular combination of category names.

Having identified a framework let us now turn to the components which we wish to arrange within this frame. Firstly let us imagine that all the sentences in a given specification document have been reduced to a set of atomic requirements - as indicated in Section 2 above. Every member of this set of atomic requirements may be categorised by assigning to it a three digit code (where each digit is either a 0,1 or 2) and where each digit indicates a category name (attribute) in the corresponding dimension. Thus the code 112 for example would be assigned to any atomic requirement which has the three attributes:

Function, Facilities, Component.

When each requirement has been assigned an appropriate categorisation code, it will have been effectively assigned to one of the small rectangular regions illustrated in Figure 3.2:1. Some of the regions will be empty, some will have a few entries and some will have a lot. The 'density distribution' of requirements in the array will then be found to reveal some very interesting facts about the document - but see Section 4.

It has been established in fact that there are four dimensions rather than three, the fourth one being 'Viewpoint'. The corresponding four dimensional array is illustrated in Figure 3.2:2 overleaf. Therefore, to fully categorise each atomic requirement, we actually need to attach to it a four digit code of the form 0112. This particular code means any requirement which has the following attributes:

Operations, Function, Facilities, Component.

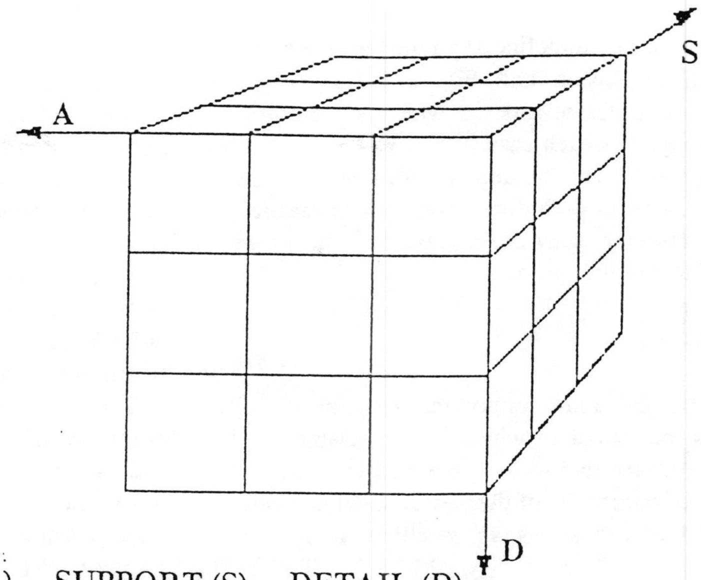

	ASPECT (A)	SUPPORT (S)	DETAIL (D)
0	Purpose	User	Context
1	Function	Facilities	Subsystem
2	Principle	Utilities	Component

Figure 3.2:1 **THREE DIMENSIONAL ARRAY**

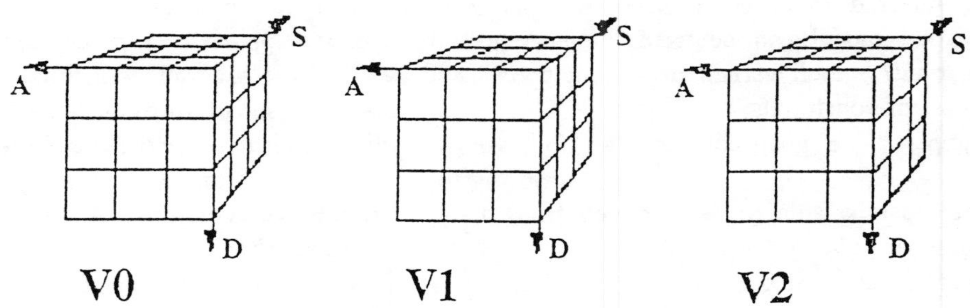

	VIEWPOINT (V)	ASPECT (A)	SUPPORT (S)	DETAIL (D)
0	Operations	Purpose	User	Context
1	Maintenance	Function	Facilities	Subsystem
2	Administration	Principle	Utilities	Component

Figure 3.2:2 **FOUR DIMENSIONAL ARRAY**

We are able, of course, to define any number of category names in each dimension and Figure 3.2:3 overleaf indicates a possible framework in which six category names are employed in each case.

There is no reason why the number of category names needs to be the same in each dimension and, in practice, it is often the case that they are indeed different as we will illustrate later in this paper.

3.3 Evolution

Perhaps one of the most important aspects of any specification is the extent to which it is re-usable. All professional engineers should be concerned to maximise the re-usability of the results of their efforts. This applies equally well to specifications as much as it does to designs and to production.

Any set of requirements can be divided into two subsets: those which identify goals and those which identify constraints. The Goals are the aspirations of the system specifier. They refer to things that need to be achieved - even though some of them may come into conflict with each other. The Constraints are the limitations imposed upon the Goals by virtue of real world, environmental or implementation considerations. It is the constraints which realise a particular instance (ie an application) of a given set of Goals. Different sets of constraints realise different instances of the set of concepts identified by the Goals. The set of Goals for any system is referred to in GMARC as a 'pivotal model! A pivotal model can be used to generate a multitude of variants - each variant dependent upon its own particular set of constraints.

As an example of a goal consider the following requirement:

'Any record must be able to be retrieved from the database within 5 seconds'.

An example of an associated constraint could be:

'All database records must be held on magnetic tape units - type xyz'.

These two requirements would doubtless come into conflict with each other for databases of any useful size. All such clashes need to be detected and reconciled - preferably before embarking on any consequential design.

The set of goals for any system (the pivotal model) constitutes the only truly portable (re-usable) part of the system by virtue of its constraint-free nature. Figure 3.3:1 illustrates the separation of Goals and Constraints for the purpose of being able to identify and possibly reconcile any adverse effects of one upon the other. The extent to which a set of constraints causes a pivotal model to change is the extent to which the resulting system is not re-usable under different circumstances.

The Pivotal Model should initially be produced in isolation in order to obtain a constraint-free view of the structure of the system being specified. If we consider only one layer at a time, starting at the highest, then the constraints should be applied to each layer, one detail level at a time (top down) to produce a constrained specification for the layer. At each level of detail, in each layer, it will be possible to make informed decisions as to which course to pursue as the reconciliation process unfolds - modifying as necessary or, at least, drawing attention to consequences in each case.

The major advantage that results from the production of the pivotal model first, and then the application of the constraints to it, is the fact that the impact of the constraints becomes highly visible and, in particular, those constraints that cause unacceptable changes to the pivotal model can be rapidly identified and, if necessary, removed or modified. It is precisely these constraints which impair re-usability. Of course it is not possible to eliminate the effects of all constraints - otherwise the system would not be realisable. But we frequently have the power to change their form or to ameliorate their influence when it impacts on the re-usability of any part of the system.

The above argument applies equally well to each one of the support layers and thus, as we progress down the development path, and each support layer moves into the foreground of consideration, we are able to review re-usability in the above way and in the light of knowledge gained from preceding layers. When every layer of the specification has been processed we should not only have a complete and well structured specification, we should also have one in which the non-re-usable components have all been clearly identified and the reasons why.

As an illustration of what happens during conventional progressive evolution, let us consider the all-too-typical situation where the goals have not been separated from the constraints at specification time. Therefore the impact of either set on the behaviour and fabric of the resulting system is not able to be separately identified. Imagine also that the first implementation has been a success. So much so that the manufacturer (or the client) is encouraged to develop a variant for another situation. Imagine finally that the goals for the second variant remain more or less the same, thus it is only the constraints which change.

What actually happens in practice is that the system, as designed and built for the first variant, is modified - to save time and resources. The outcome is that the fabric and the behaviour of the new variant has influences built into it which not only result from the set of system goals and the new set of constraints, but also from the old and now out of date constraints from the first variant (V1). These out-of-date constraints come into conflict with the

	VIEWPOINT	ASPECT	SUPPORT	DETAIL
0	Operations	Purpose	User	Level 0
1	Maintenance	Performance	Facilities	Level 1
2	Administration	Function	Utilities	Level 2
3	Development	Principle	Infrastructure	Level 3
4	Training	Location	Equipment	Level 4
5	Security	Existence	Environment	Level 5

Figure 3.2:3 GENERIC FRAMEWORK

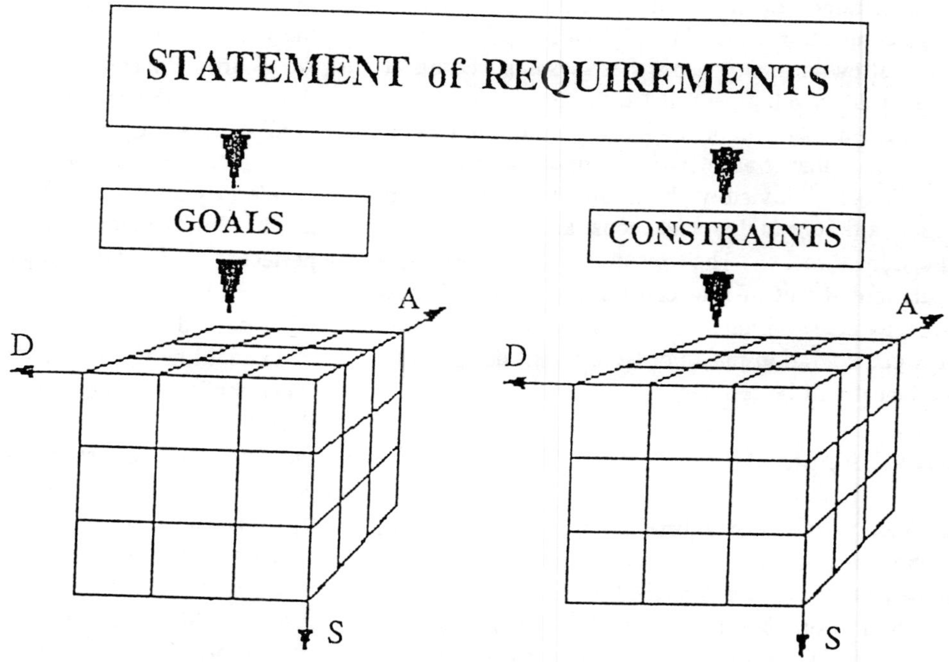

Figure 3.3:1 SEPARATING GOALS FROM CONSTRAINTS

new (V2) constraints in quite invisible ways and, consequently, debugging of development changes takes longer than expected because the system reacts to such changes in a slightly unpredictable manner. Nevertheless the resulting V2 variant performs reasonably well and the client (or manufacturer) is subsequently encouraged to consider investing in a further (V3) variant.

V3 suffers from similar debugging difficulties to those experienced when producing V2. However in this case the problem is much more pronounced and debugging takes much longer. We now have three sets of constraints built invisibly into the fabric and behaviour of V3 - two of them inappropriate!

If the above process is continued, with each new variant utilising the previous one (to take advantage of the most recent thinking and technology), it will not be long before the debugging process becomes so lengthy that everyone involved will become afraid to make any change at all. This is because each change causes so many unpredictable consequences that the time required to arrive at a stable state each time becomes unacceptably high and the associated resource costs too great.

The history of Software and System engineering is littered with examples of situations of the above kind ranging from mainframe operating systems, through stock exchange applications, to fighter aircraft autopilots. After a number of evolutionary steps, these systems became so fragile that all development had to be terminated. It is believed that a major contribution to this result was, in each case, that accelerating obsolescence was unavoidably, and invisibly, built into the development process by a failure to dissociate constraints from goals at specification time. The resulting and inexorable accumulation of out-of-date constraints, with each new variant, guaranteed limited evolutionary potential. Re-usability consideration must not be left until design time. If it is then it will be too late.

4 A Real Application

In this section we take a brief look at the results of subjecting a real requirements specification document to the classification process described in Section 3.2 above.

The application chosen to exemplify the process is a military air traffic control system. The document used was part of an Invitation To Tender that was put out to a worldwide bidding contest by the air force of a European country. Figure 4.1:1 overleaf contains part of the result of subjecting the document to GMARC classification. Only the Operations viewpoint is presented in Figure 4.1:1 and, as can be seen, only four support layers, five application aspects and six levels of detail were employed. The numbers in the boxes represent the numbers of goals and the number of constraints that were assigned the corresponding set of attributes. Thus, for example, in the User layer, in the Function column and in the fourth level of Detail, there are 91 goals and 48 constraints ie 139 requirements in total.

The most obvious benefit arising from Figure 4.1:1 is that it provides a succinct view of the coverage of the subject provided by the document. In addition attention is drawn to a multitude of features of the information in the document which would otherwise not be visible. For example:

It is clear that the thinking of the person (or persons) who wrote the document is dominated by previous experience. We can see this because the largest proportion of the requirements are positioned in the Function Aspects column with very few in the Purpose Aspects column. This implies that the specifier knows, from previous experience, 'how' the system should work but not 'why'. Inevitably, therefore, we are impelled to ask how can it be verified that the system is appropriate to the task?

Similarly it is clear that the specifier is a low level details type person. In the User layer (as mentioned above) there are 139 function requirements at the 4th level of detail but not a single one in either the zero level or the first level of detail. This implies the conclusion that the writer does not know what the overall function of an Air Traffic Control System is - nor indeed what are the functions of the major subsystems. This conclusion is hardly credible in a document of this stature. Nevertheless this is the actual content of the document.

We may also ask why there are no requirements at all in the Infrastructure layer. This situation may be perfectly valid and the subject may have been intentionally left for one of the other viewpoints to handle. On the other hand there may be a genuine oversight here.

In addition, it is rather alarming to note - with so much functionality having been specified - that so few Performance Aspects have been specified. Referring to the 139 Function Aspects, we are able to see that there are only 3 associated Performance Aspects. How can we be expected to know the intended performance therefore?

There are many more questions of a similar nature that it is possible to raise as a result of the information that is made visible in Figure 4.1:1 - and this is just one viewpoint. The essential point that attention is drawn to here is the huge increase in visibility that results from the production of a GMARC requirements density matrix.

Having separated the requirements, in each location of the requirements density matrix, into goals and constraints - for say the function aspects - it is then possible to group similar requirements together to identify re-usable objects. Figure 4.1:2 illustrates an object hierarchy that could typically be developed from say the four levels of

Support Layers	Detail Levels	Purpose	Performance	Function	Principle	Existence
USER	0	31/2	2/8		2/-	
	1					
	2			1/0		
	3	2/0	15/8	11/9		14/2
	4	5/3	3/0	91/48	7/1	27/0
	5			21/0	20/0	
FACILITIES	0					
	1			1/0		
	2		4/0	1/8	3/0	
	3			5/8		
	4		3/0	8/6		
	5			10/0		
INFRASTRUCTURE	0					
	1					
	2					
	3					
	4					
	5					
EQUIPMENT	0		1/0			0/1
	1					
	2					
	3				1/0	1/0
	4			4/0		4/0
	5					0/1

Application Aspects

OPERATIONS VIEWPOINT

Figure 4.1:1 **REQUIREMENTS DENSITY MATRIX**

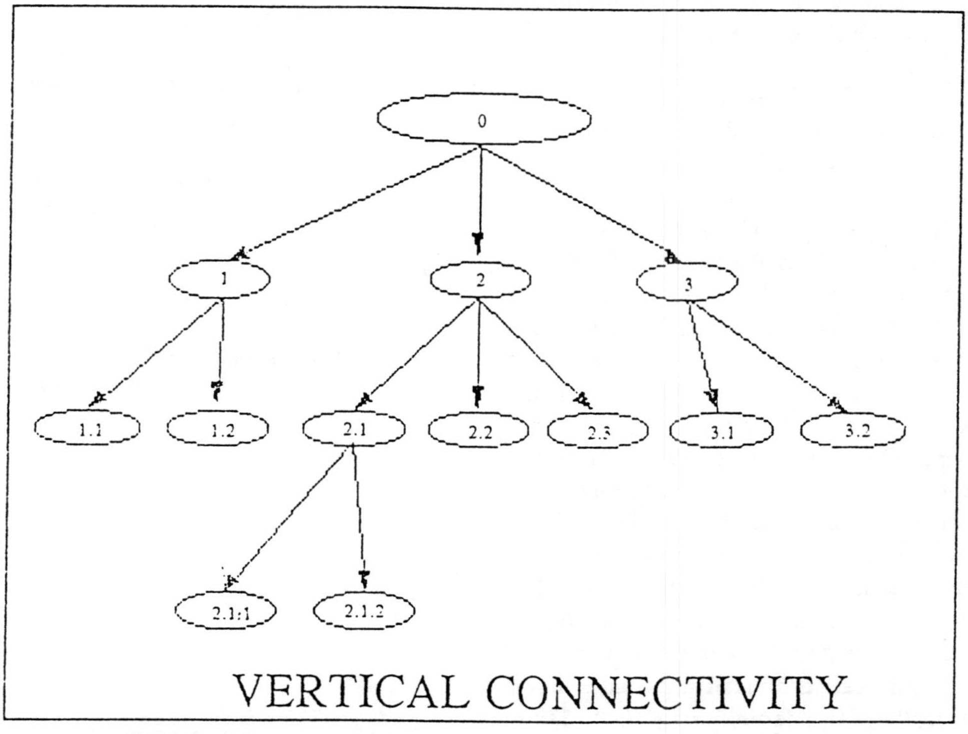

Figure 4.1:2 **OBJECT HIERARCHY**

functional goals that are present in the User layer of Figure 4.1:1. A similar hierarchy could then be developed for the constraints. Overlaying the two hierarchies will draw attention to any obvious differences and/or conflicts. Furthermore, each level of detail in the hierarchy can be regarded as a model of that aspect of the system being specified. The GMARC tool enables its Users to automatically create and animate such models in order to explore the dynamic viability of the specification at each level of detail. In fact the GMARC tool contains many more facilities of this kind - including knowledge accumulation and direct elicitation of requirements from the minds of its users. However these are subjects of other GMARC papers.

5 Concluding Comments

This paper is aimed at drawing attention to the fact that it is possible to considerably improve the quality of a requirement specification prior to its adoption by system designers or software engineers. In particular it is suggested that the Professional engineer has a duty to his client to ensure the production of such high quality specifications prior to the commitment of resources to design and implementation. There is a great deal that it is possible to achieve in this context. However there is - perhaps understandably - detectable reluctance to expend resources on specification improvement. There is reluctance by procurement organisations - who wish to pass on to their suppliers as much responsibility as possible - and there is reluctance by supplier organisations - who wish to leave the door open for possible price increases (as a result of changes) at a later date. In addition, few will want to spend time improving a specification until they have been awarded the contract. After contract award all the pressure is then devoted to producing the system as quickly as possible. Such pressures have always held back the development of high quality specifications. Nevertheless, with the increasing move towards fixed price contracts, it is becoming more important to initiate projects with specifications which are consistent, complete, coherent and correct if overall risk is to be minimised.

It is also important to recognise that, if indefinite evolutionary potential is ever to be achievable, the professional engineer must encourage his clients, when specifying a variant of a system, to recognise the need to return each time to the underlying set of the goals before applying a new set of constraints. This process will not only encourage the re-use of requirements information it will lead to the identification of really re-usable design components and really re-usable products **[Hugo, 1995]**.

Finally this paper draws attention to the fact that, due to the rising perception of the need to produce improved specifications, appropriate tools are now being developed. The professional engineer should be aware of these tools and their capabilities. At this point in time there are very few requirements analysis tools that directly address the issue of reusability of requirements. GMARC is one of the first.

6 References

[1] Boehm, B.W. (1981), Software Engineering Economics, Prentice Hall, Englewood Cliffs, N.J.

[2] Collins, A (1994), Systems Disasters can be avoided; Computer Weekly, 08-12-1994.

[3] Faulk, S.R. (1995), Software Requirements: A Tutorial. Tech. Rep. NRL-7775, Naval Research Laboratory, Washington, D.C.

[4] Fairley, R. (1985), Software Engineering Concepts, McGraw-Hill, New York.

[5] GAO (1992), Mission Critical Systems: Defence attempting to address major software challenges, Tech. Rep. GAO/IMTEC-93-13, U.S. General Accounting Office, Washington, D.C. Dec.

[6] Hunt, L.B. (1992), GMARC - Final Report of Project IED4/1/1151. Produced under the auspices of the Department of Trade & Industry's Information Engineering Advanced Technology Programme (IEATP) of the Joint Framework for Information Technology (JFIT).

[7] Hugo, I (1995), Back in circulation; Computing, 17-08-1995, page 16.

[8] Hogan, J (1995), From Complexity to Perplexity; Scientific American, June 1995, pages 74-79.

[9] Lutz, R.R. (1993), Targeting safety-related errors during software requirements analysis. In Proceedings of the first ACM SIGSOFT Symposium on the Foundations of Software Engineering (Los Angeles, Cal., Dec.), ACM, New York.

[10] Peltu, M (1995), Make yourself re-useful; Computing, 09-02-1995, page 40.

Developing Component-Based Tools for Requirements Reuse: A Process Guide

W. Lam
Department of Computer Science, University of Hertfordshire
College Lane, Hatfield, AL10 9AB, UK
Tel: +44 1707 284337, Fax: +44 1707 28303
W.Lam@herts.ac.uk

Abstract
The reuse of requirements has received little attention in the literature, especially in relation to genuine industrial problems. This paper describes the efforts that have been made to promote the reuse of requirements for aero-engine control systems at Rolls-Smiths Engine Controls Limited (RoSEC). In the approach here, the notion of the requirements "component" is first introduced as a structure for reuse, and the process of component engineering used to create such components is examined. The role of requirements components in the development of reuse tools is investigated, particularly from the viewpoint of tool evolution. The COMPASS (COMPonent ASSistant) framework is presented as a development strategy for component-based requirements reuse tools. The paper closes with an initial evaluation of the approach and a summary of lessons learnt.

Keywords: Requirements, components, reuse, reuse tools, generalisation, families.

1. Introduction

Software procurement often begins with a statement of requirements. Requirements have a pivotal role in the software development process — Davis [22] notes that detecting and repairing an error during the implementation stage can cost ten times as much as in the requirements stage. However, the elicitation of requirements, their capture and analysis, and the production of a requirements document, can be an extremely time-consuming process.

Increasingly, developers are looking towards reuse and Component-Based Software Engineering (CBSE) methods to increase development productivity; a strategy recognised as early on as 1969 by McIlroy [11]. This paper discusses how a CBSE approach can assist the requirements engineering process. In particular, the notion of the requirements component is presented, which differs form the traditional view of a component as an implementation artefact. The format for the paper is as follows. Section 2 describes the industrial background for this work. Section 3 introduces the CBSE approach and presents a process model. Section 4 describes the component engineering phase of the approach and the process by which requirements components are created. Section 5 describes the toll construction phase of the approach and the process by which reuse tools are developed. Section 6 provides an initial evaluation of the CBSE approach and summarises the main lessons learnt. Finally, Section 7 concludes with a summary of the work and draws attention to related work.

2. Industrial Background

The initial groundwork for the paper was done when the author was based at the Rolls-Royce University Technology Centre (at the University of York, UK), and involved in the development of reuse methods for RoSEC (Rolls Smiths Engine Controls Limted).

2.1 Aero-Engine Controls Systems

RoSEC develop aero-engine management systems known as FADECs (Full Authority Digital Engine Controllers). Figure 1 shows a schematic view of a FADEC, at the heart of which is an electronic engine controller (EEC).

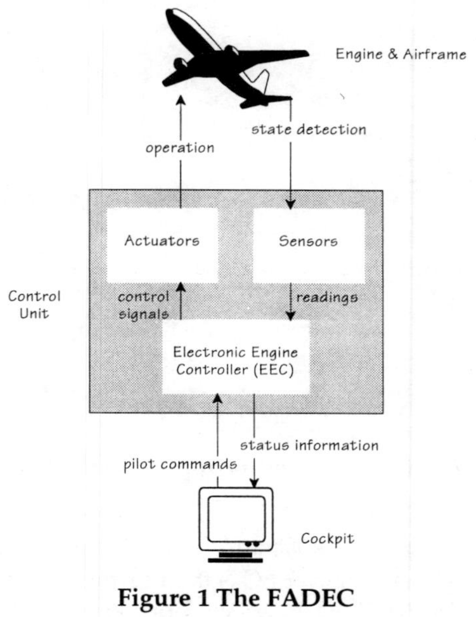

Figure 1 The FADEC

In short, the EEC uses sensors to monitor the engine and other components on the airframe (the aircaft body). The EEC controls the engine via the operation of actuators, such as valves, igniters and pumps. The FADEC also accepts commands from the pilot, and provides status information about the engine back to the cockpit. The FADEC is embedded and safety-critical, and is physically located as a 'black-box' on the engine casing.

2.2 The Families Concept

It was Parnas [12] who first introduced the concept of program 'families'. Recent work by those in the reuse community (see for example, WISR [21] and WSRET [20]) have extended the original concept of program family to that of the system family. Here, a domain is characterised by a family of systems, and reuse is achieved by the definition of generic family members which can be specialised into specific family members, i.e. applications in the domain [4].

The families concept closely mirrors how aero-engines are actually manufactured. Aero-engines are typically developed in an engine series. An engine in a specific series is termed a mark, where each mark differs in engine functionality and performance. A mark then has one or more variants, tailored for a specific airframe and set of customer requirements. It would seem plausible then, to extend the family concept to the development of software systems; in particular, the EEC at the heart of the FADEC (Figure 2).

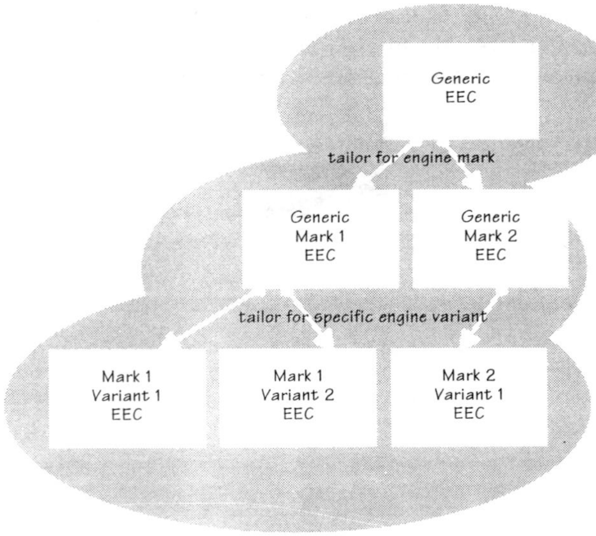

Figure 2 The families concept applied to the EEC

Here, there is a generic EEC software system for each engine series, which is specialised to give generic mark EECs. A generic mark EEC is then further specialised into a variant of a mark, which represents the final EEC software delivered to the customer. As commercial motivation, it was envisaged that such a families approach would support two key market factors — cheaper development costs and more rapid development timescales — mainly via high levels of reuse and a reduced testing load.

3. CBSE Approach

In theory, applying a family concept to EEC software development is an appealing idea. However, the practicality of doing so raises a number of technology transfer issues:

- How does a families approach affect the way in which the organisation captures requirements from the customer?
- How does a families approach affect existing, tried-and-trusted development methods used by the organisation?
- The EEC is part of a safety-critical system, so what assurances can be made that software developed using a families approach is at least as safe as the existing approach?
- How does a families approach affect the testing and certification process?

It is clear that making radical and wholesale changes to a 'live' development process carries with it a high level of risk, particularly for those working on safety-critical software such as FADECs. As such, it was necessary to carefully consider the technology transfer strategy.

3.1 Technology Transfer Strategy

It has been argued that reuse at the requirements level can significantly increase reuse at later stages of development [15], [1]. Given this, we decided to investigate how a families approach could be applied at the level of requirements for the FADEC, before trying to scale the approach up to cover the entire lifecycle. A complete FADEC requirements document, however, can easily exceed 100 pages of A4. For this reason, we decided to focus efforts on one particular domain of aero-engine control: aero-engine starting. Aero-engine starting involves the rotation of the engine shafts from a still position to a self-sustaining idle speed. This includes control over the fuel flow into the engine and subsequent ignition of fuel. The aero-engine starting domain was chosen as the requirements in the domain are relatively complex, for which increased reuse was highly desired.

It was also envisaged that tools would play an important part of the technology transfer process, acting as 'trojan horses' for carrying the families concept into projects in a way that has more direct impact than say a research or method document.

3.2 The Requirements "Component" Concept

Because there was likely to be a large number of individual reusable requirements, the idea of the requirements "component" was adopted as a means of grouping related generic requirements and treating them as a single managed unit. This raises the level of software engineering abstraction somewhat from existing work in the area of CBSE, which tends to view components as things which reside at the level of implementation.

3.3 CBSE Approach Overview

To set the overall scene, Figure 3 shows a general overview of our approach. Three roles are identified:

- *Component engineer*: who studies the domain to identify and create reusable requirements components.
- *Domain expert*: who provides domain knowledge and advises the component engineer.
- *Tool end-user*: who is typically someone who develops applications in the domain.

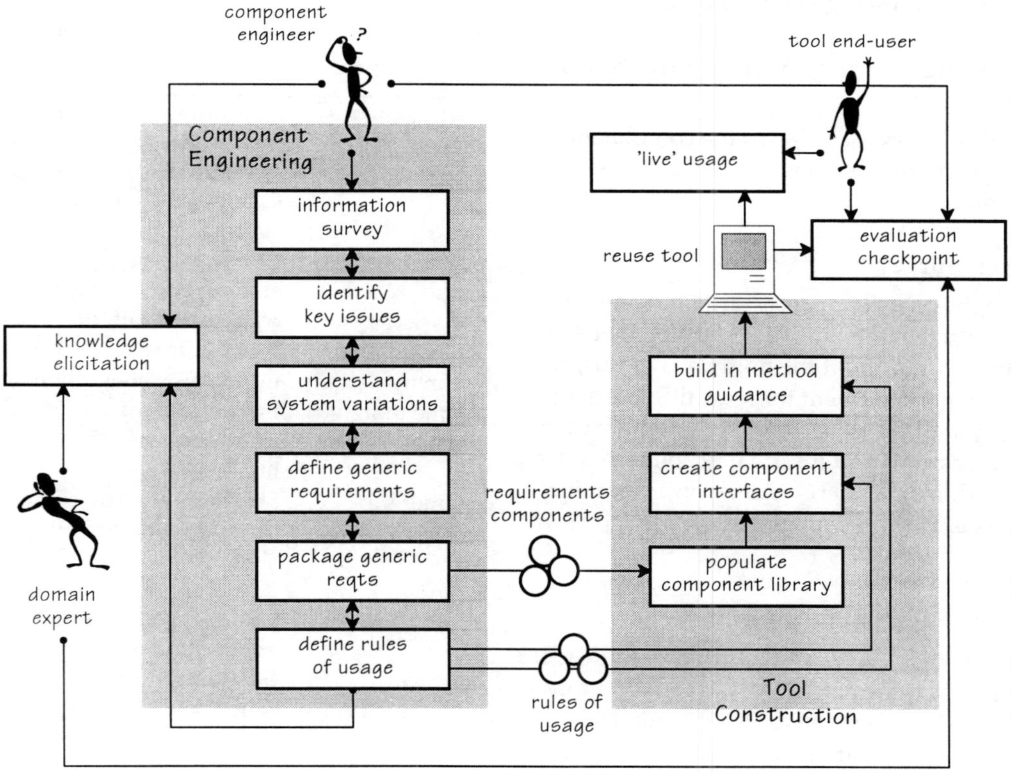

Figure 3 CBSE approach overview

There are two main phases in the approach: component engineering and tool construction. In component engineering, the job of the component engineer is to identify and define requirements components. In tool construction, the aim is to develop a tool which supports the use of those requirements components on application projects. Briefly, the specific tasks in the component engineering phase are:

- *Information survey:* Learn about the domain by studying the requirements documents of different systems in the domain and speaking to domain experts.
- *Identify key issues:* Pinpoint critical areas of functionality in the domain.
- *Understand system variations:* Understand how systems in the domain can vary from one to other. Begin to distinguish the non-variable (or core) elements from the variable elements. The nature of the non-variable elements makes them good candidates for reusable components.
- *Define generic requirements*: Now identify common or typical requirements in the domain, i.e. requirements which pertain to the majority of systems. Abstract from concrete requirements the generic and reusable elements.
- *Package generic requirements:* Group together closely-related generic requirements into a requirements component. This affords a larger-grain level of reuse.

- *Define rules of usage:* Make explicit the constraints and restrictions on how a requirements component may be used.

During the component engineering phase, the component engineer is likely to consult frequently with domain experts. The specific tasks in the tool construction phase are:

- *Populate component library*: Store the requirements components in a component repository.
- *Create component interfaces*: Develop a structured means of accessing and using the requirements components.
- *Build in method guidance*: Develop procedures to ensure that a requirements component is used properly, and is not abused.

The tool construction phase is geared towards our own particular development methodology that enables us to rapidly build prototype reuse tools. This in part, has been influenced by the use of Windows on a PC platform and the Microsoft Visual Basis development environment which encourages rapid prototyping. More details about the tool construction phase is given later on in this paper.

4. Component Engineering: Aero-Engine Starting

In this section, we discuss each step in the component engineering phase in greater detail with respect to the aero-engine starting domain.

4.1 Information Survey

A component engineer will not necessarily be someone who is familiar with the domain. The first step therefore is to acquire information about the domain. For this, we read the requirements document for four different aero-engine starting systems. Discussions, both in the form of formal interview sessions and informal telephone contact, were held with 3 domain experts. An avionics reference book, "Aircraft Gas Turbine Engine Technology" [18] was also consulted.

4.2 Identify Key Functional Areas

It is sensible to establish early on some kind of framework which helps organise information. We have found that identifying the key functional areas in a domain facilitates the information acquisition, organisation and reasoning process, especially for the domain novice. It was evident from the way in which requirements documents were organised, and from discussions with domain experts, that the aero-engine starting domain could be structured in terms of a number of key functional areas (Figure 4).

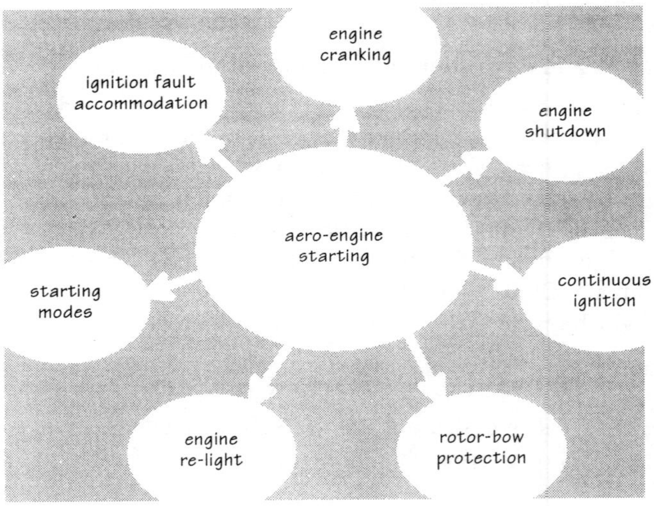

Figure 4 Key functional areas in the aero-starting domain

This identification of the key functional areas was also helpful in defining the scope of the aero-engine starting domain. A short description of each of these key functional areas in give in Table 1.

Table 1 Short description of key functional areas

Issue	*Description*
starting modes	Depending upon where the aircraft is, its altitude, speed, and the receipt of the appropriate cockpit signals, an engine can be started in one of many different starting 'modes'.
continuous ignition	Continuous ignition, if a feature of the starting system, enables an engine to be continuously lit for a period of time.
ignition fault accommodation	Specific procedures are carried out in the event of an ignition failure.
engine re-light	Engine re-light prevents a 'flame-out' condition when the engine becomes unlit.
engine shut-down	Shutting-down an engine requires that certain engine components become disabled.
Cranking	'Cranking' is an engine maintenance feature, and refers to the starting of an engine but without the engine actually becoming ignited.
rotor-bow protection	Rotor-bow protection prevents excessive damage being done to the motor in the event of the rotor-blades becoming locked.

Each key functional area acted as focal areas for the remainder of the component engineering phase.

4.3 Understand System Variations

For each key functional area, we investigated how requirements differed between individual systems in the domain. For example, one major area of system variation that we found was that the pilot-to-system interface (essentially the cockpit) for each system was different. As a consequence, requirements were often tied to a particular cockpit arrangement, such as "to start a crank, press button X followed by button Y" (to use an example from the key functional area of cranking). There were also differences in functional capabilities. For example, in the key functional area of continuous ignition, some systems incorporate features to preserve the life of the igniters. Understanding the variations between systems in the domain placed me in a better position for working out what was and was not reusable — an essential part of the next step.

4.4 Define Generic Requirements

By understanding system variability, one has a platform for identifying requirements which are common to systems in a domain, and separating these from requirements which are of a more optional or novel nature. However, even with common requirements, it was necessary to factor out the system-specific details to formulate truly generic requirements; Table 2 shows an example of this.

Table 2 Use of abstraction to formulate generic requirements

Element in Abstraction Process	*Example*
concrete requirement from system A	When the engine is not in the process of being started, cranked or run, if the fuel switch is in the OFF position and the master crank switch is in the ON position, and the engine start switch is then turned to the ON position then a dry crank will be initiated.
Equivalent concrete requirement from system B	When the engine is not in the process of being started, cranked or run, if the fuel switch is in the OFF position and then the engine start switch is turned to the CRANK position, then a dry crank will be initiated.
Constant requirement part	When the engine is not in the process of being started, cranked or run, if (X) and then (Y), a dry crank will be initiated.
Variable requirement part	X and Y are cockpit-specific signals.
Abstraction reasoning	Cockpits are specific to a particular system, and not all systems will have the same cockpit layout. Hence, this aspect is a variable requirement part and must be factored out of the generic requirement.
generic requirement	When the engine is not in the process of being started, cranked or run, if (cockpit signal 1) and then (cockpit signal 2), a dry crank will be initiated.

Here, the generic requirement takes a number of parameters, represented by the brackets, which captures the system-specific elements which make the generic requirement into a concrete requirement.

4.5 Package Generic Requirements

Closely-related requirements are often treated as a group rather than individually. For example, it does not make much sense to have a requirement for starting a crank, without also having a requirement for terminating a crank. As such, a decision has been made to group closely-related requirements together to form 'self-standing' requirements components. For example, the requirement component for engine re-light is a collection of four generic requirements:

When the aero-engine re-light is armed, a flameout is deemed to have occurred when (flameout criteria) is true.
When the aero-engine is running, engine re-light shall be armed when (set of cockpit signals) are received.
When the engine re-light is armed, it shall be disarmed when (set of cockpit signals) are received.
When a flameout is detected, the EEC shall command (which igniter) to ON for a period of time equal to (delay period).

This approach has two significant effects. First, it has raised the level of reuse granularity from that of the single requirement to a set of requirements. Second, and perhaps more significantly, it has introduced a strong component-oriented view to the construction of a requirements specification.

4.6 Define Rules of Usage

There is more to requirements reuse than simply the specialisation of generic requirements. With the concept of a requirements component, there are often rules and constraints about how the requirements component could be legitimately used. To illustrate, in a requirements component for 'continuous ignition', there was a constraint of a mandatory choice of mutually exclusive options:

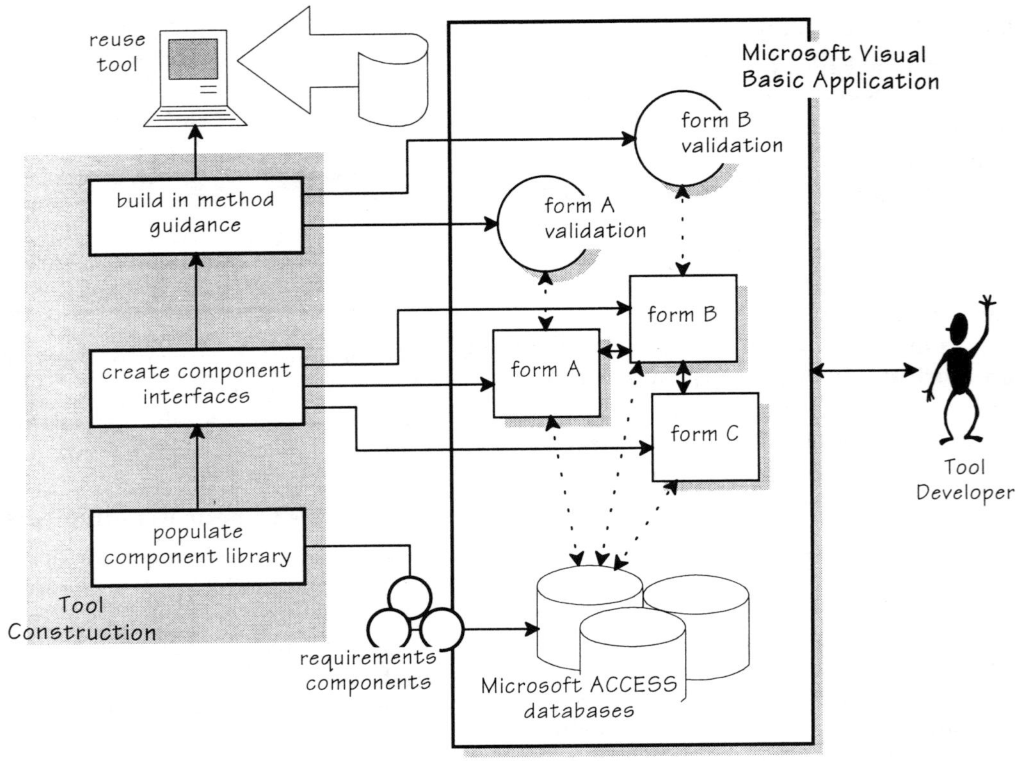

Figure 5 The COMPASS framework

1. The igniters are energised for a minimum specific period of time.
2. The igniters are energised for a maxium specific period of time.
3. The igniters are energised for a minimum and maximum specified period of time.
4. The igniters are energised until manually switched off by the pilot.

Here, the mandatory choice of an option represents an explicit rule of usage associated with the requirements component.

4.7 Scale of Component Engineering

For the aero-engine starting domain, one man-month was spent on the initial component engineering phase, where 13 requirements components were produced. Consultations were held with three different domain experts; these took the form of weekly 1-hour interview sessions and short discussions by phone. Of the 13 requirements components, the 'largest' component included 6 generic requirements, and the smallest component included 2 generic requirements.

5. Tool Construction: Aero-engine starting

The motivations for reuse and CBSE at RoSEC include reductions in cost and time-scales for FADEC development. As a research project, one of the central objectives here was to demonstrate to managers and software development personnel at RoSEC how the families concept and technology of reusable requirements components could streamline the existing requirements engineering process. In addition, it was felt that a tool which individuals could themselves experiment with, as opposed to a 'proposed new methods' document, would provide a tangible and more effective vehicle for demonstrating the potential benefits of the new technology.

5.1 The COMPASS Framework

The COMPASS (COMPonent ASSistant) development framework is a strategy for rapidly building reuse tools, and centres around the concept of the requirements component. Figure 5 shows the COMPASS framework and how it relates to the tool construction phase of the approach.

The COMPASS framework is tied in with the rapid prototyping capabilities afforded by the Microsoft Visual Basic development environment running on the PC under Microsoft Windows. In implementation terms, a reuse tool is a Visual Basic executable. Requirement components are placed, in a textual format, in a Microsoft ACCESS database. An interface to the component is then created (by the tool developer) as a 'form' (Visual Basic terminology for a window) which can be likened to a data-entry screen. These forms are linked, and collectively provide the interface for using and specialising the requirements components 'underneath'. Method guidance is built into the reuse tool as form validation procedures. The end-result is a reuse tool which is easy to evolve (in Visual Basic, forms are easily modified, added or deleted) in the face of on-going component engineering and tool evaluation feedback.

To continue with the example, the COMPASS framework has been used to develop a reuse tool, called COMPASS-S (COMPASS for Starting), to enable the reuse of requirements components in the aero-engine starting domain. In the following sections, we describe the COMPASS-S tool in more detail.

5.2 The Component List

One special kind of form in COMPASS-S is the Component-List, which is a selection list of available requirements components. Figure 6 is a screen-capture of the Component-List form from COMPASS-S, showing the list of requirements components currently available.

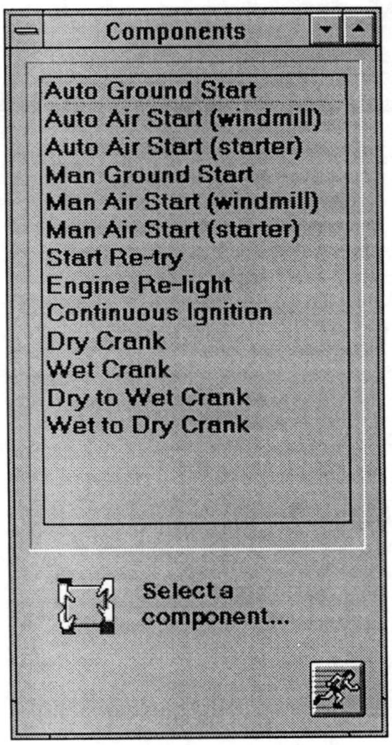

Figure 6 The Component-List

When the user clicks on a list-item in the Component-List, the form for the selected requirements component is displayed.

5.3 The Engine Re-light Requirements Component

Assume the user clicks on the 'engine re-light' list-item in the Component-List; this causes the form for the engine re-light component (discussed previously in Section 4) to be displayed, which is shown in the screen-capture of Figure 7.

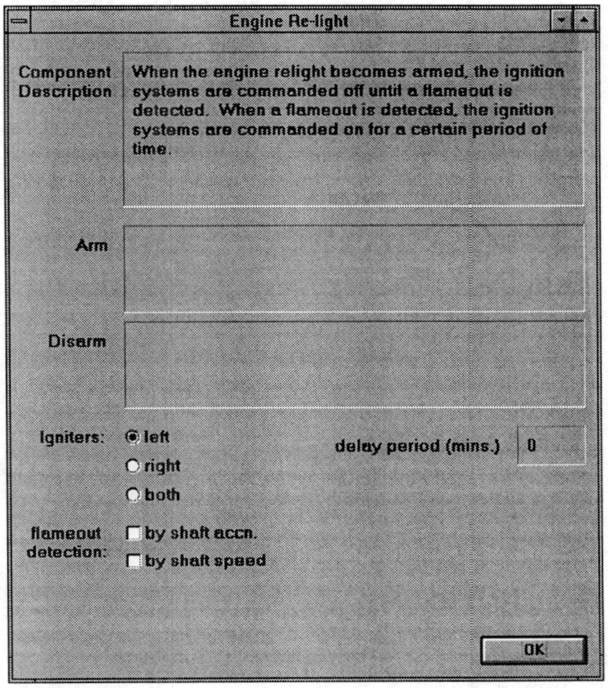

Figure 7 The form for the engine re-light component

The form provides a number of 'fields' for the user to fill-in, options and check-boxes. Note here that there is a component description field, which provides a brief description of the component to tool-users. Table 3 describes how the fields, options and check-boxes relate directly to the generic requirements encapsulated by the engine re-light component.

As one can see, the form provides a structured approach for tailoring and reusing requirements components. This helps ensure that a component can only be used in its intended manner, an essential point when the application is a safety-critical system.

5.4 Method Guidance

The design of each form, and the sensible use of option buttons and tick-boxes, minimises to a large extent erroneous use of a requirements component. The rules of usage for a requirements component, defined in the component engineering phase, strongly influences a form's design. In addition, forms will often have a number of associated validation procedures. For example, typing anything other than a number in a numeric field causes a simple error message to be displayed, alerting the user to the misuse of the requirements components. Clearly, the capability to enforce such rules and constraints is a distinct advantage of a tool over an entirely manually-driven process.

Table 3 Link between form and generic requirements

Form Field	*Field Type*	*Generic Requirement*
Flameout detection: there are two ways to detect a flameout: by a drop in engine shaft acceleration or by a drop in engine shaft speed. Both methods may be used.	Checkbox	When the engine re-light is armed, a flameout is deemed to have occurred when (flameout criteria) is true.
Arm: what the pilot does to turn on engine relight.	Text	When the engine is running, engine relight shall be armed when (cockpit signals) is received.
Disarm: what the pilot does to turn off the engine relight	Text	When the engine is armed, it shall be disarmed when (cockpit signals) is received.
Igniters: the igniter which is operated under engine relight; this is either the left or right igniter, or both.	Option	When a flameout is detected, the EEC shall command (which igniter) to ON for a period of time equal to (delay period).
Delay period: the length of time the igniter(s) remain on for after being turned on.	Numeric	

5.5 The Wet Crank Requirements Component

Figure 8 shows a less complex form, for the 'wet crank' requirements component. Engine cranking is often performed during the maintenance of an aero-engine. A wet crank refers to the situation when an aero-engine is rotated, but where the fuel is not ignited (as opposed to a dry crank where the fuel is completed shut off).

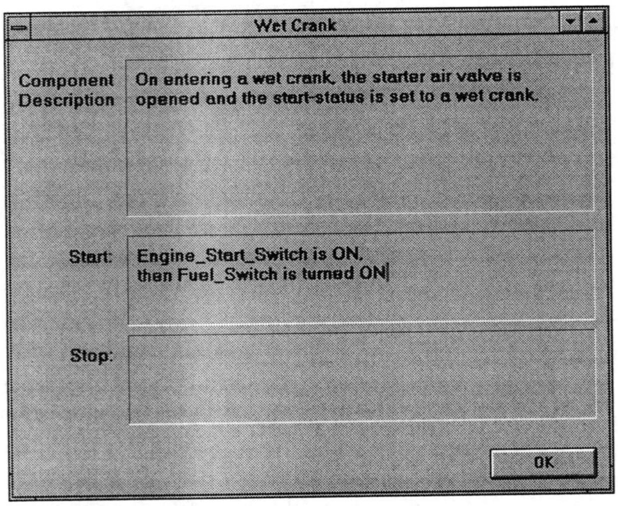

Figure 8 The form for the wet crank requirements component

5.6 Generation of a Requirements Document

A key deliverable from the requirements engineering process is a requirements document, which often has a contractual role. As part of the technology transfer strategy, it was important to demonstrate to managers and software developers at RoSEC how component technology could accelerate the production of requirements documents. In the current version of COMPASS-S, when the user fills in a form for a requirements component, the generic requirements are instantiated or associated with a selected option, and placed in a separate database. Querying over this database can then used to generate a simple requirements document in the form of query-search output. Although not complete, this is the core of a document production facility.

6. Initial Evaluation

It should be evident that efforts have been concentrated not only on advancing the technology of requirements engineering, but also on its industrial institutionalisation. The work described here is at a formative stage. As such, the evaluation and refinement of the ideas is an on-going process. However, a number of observations that have been made about the utility of the ideas.

6.1 COMPASS-S Release

A prototype of the COMPASS-S tool was released for evaluation to a number of engineers at RoSEC and demonstrated to management on a number of occasions. Some of the most significant comments which motivate future work are as follows:

- *"The requirements components are too simple, and need to be made more flexible":* This points to the quality of the component engineering. Were all the generic requirements within the intended scope of a requirements component identified? Can the generic requirements which make up a particular requirements component be made more flexible in terms of additional parametisation?
- *"Novel requirements are not really catered for":* It would seem that any reuse-oriented approach is based on the reuse of *typical*, rather than novel requirements which are by their very nature reuse resistant. Simply 'tagging' on novel requirements appears one easy way to deal with this problem, but may introduce inconsistencies with requirements derived from generic requirements.
- *"The automatic generation of the requirements document is inadequate":* At present, the requirements document from COMPASS-S is based on the dump of a query-search. However, one area under investigation is the integration of the report generation feature with Microsoft Word; this would make documents more visually appealing. More powerful query-search mechanisms are also under investigation.

6.2 The COMPASS Framework

The COMPASS framework provides a loose method for creating component-based reuse tools. The development and refinement of COMPASS-S took the author, an experienced Visual Basic programmer, less than 15 days. In many cases, changes to the requirements components require only simple changes to a component's form. Much of this owes to the simplicity of the reuse tools which are a product of the COMPASS framework, which can be likened to data-entry and validation screens. However, it would seem that this simplicity is a strength, as the underlying concept is not a difficult one for tool users to grasp. It is also questionable whether in such situations, having more complex tools would significantly improve the overall reuse process.

6.3 The Family Concept Applied to Requirements Engineering

It would seem that organisations which specialise in developing many kinds of similar applications in a particular domain can benefit from applying a families approach to requirements engineering. This statement seems justified on the basis of the experience here. The identification and creation of requirements components, a process which we call component engineering, is one way of encouraging the reuse of a generic family components. However, some lessons here are:

- There are limits to reuse: All systems will have differences; sensible reuse is about finding the right balance between typical and non-typical functionality.
- Be aware of over and under-abstraction: Over-abstraction often leads to requirement components which include too many parameters and options, making them more difficult to understand. Under-abstraction, however, will make requirement components seem rather inflexible.
- For the component ideology to work at the requirements level, requirements components should be viewed as independent units. This means a low level of cohesion with other requirements components and the separation of distinct functional areas.
- Component engineering is an iterative process. It does, however, rely on the component engineer having a certain level of domain knowledge. Here, domain experts must play an active part in facilitating the component engineering process.
- Worthwhile reuse tools can only be developed when there has been competent component engineering. Avoid jumping straight into tool development before this has been achieved.

7. Conclusions

This paper has reported on the use of Component-Based Software Engineering (CBSE) methods to assist the requirements engineering process in the domain of aero-engine control systems. Here, the use of CBSE methods at the requirements level is a radical departure from the traditional view of the component as an implementation artefact.

In the literature, a number of approaches have been suggested for achieving reuse at the requirements level. These approaches include analogy [3], [8], case-based reasoning [7], difference-based reasoning [10] and domain modelling [2], [9]. A closer examination of these approaches reveals all are based on the specialisation or adaptation of generic constructs. Here, a similar approach is followed, but the concept of the requirements component has been employed both as the primary unit of reuse and as a mechanism for packaging together related requirements. Within RoSEC, the requirements component has been instrumental in raising the thought process from one where systems are developed 'from scratch' to one where systems are built from pre-defined components. This is very much a cultural as well as technical transition.

The main contribution of this paper, however, has been in the description of how requirements components can be used as a basis for creating reuse tools at the requirements level. An approach has been described which views the overall process as the combination of two-phases: a component engineering phase and a tool construction phase. The component engineering phase can be seen as a form of 'domain analysis', a term used by those in the reuse community to refer to *"the process by which information used in developing software systems is identified, captured and organised with the purpose of making it reusable when creating new systems"* [13]. A number of domain analysis methods currently exist, such as Feature-Oriented Domain Analysis (FODA) developed at the SEI [6] and Organisational Domain Modelling (ODM) developed on the STARS project [16]. However, the form of component engineering suggested in this paper is specific to requirements, not to software engineering artefacts in the general way that the above domain analysis methods are. This we feel is one particularly novel aspect of the work — there is currently little in the literature which suggests a process for how one might go about 'getting hold of' requirements which are reusable. The component engineering phase is a step in this direction.

we have elaborated in some detail how the COMPASS framework facilitates reuse tool development in the tool construction phase. These reuse tools do bear some resemblence to the idea of domain-specific kits suggested by Griss and Wentzel [5]. While there are many different development methods for developing systems, there is far less by way of development methods for developing tools (for developing systems). This has been a strong motivation for the COMPASS framework, which is targeted specifically at component-based requirement reuse tools. Perhaps one drawback of the COMPASS framework is that it is too closely-tied in with the development tool Microsoft Visual Basic. However, it is in fact this close tie that has made the rapid development and evolution of reuse tools possible in the first place.

The work here is still at a formative stage. However, it is felt that the ideas discussed so far will be of value to other organisations embarking on reuse projects, particularly where the focus is on improvements in the requirements engineering process. Future work will be directed on the validation and refinement of the approach in other domains outside of aero-engine control systems.

8. References

[1] Biggerstaff, T. and Ritcher, C. (1987), Reusability framework, assessment and directions, IEEE Software, 41(3), March, 1987.

[2] Bolton, D., Jones, S., Till, D., Furber, D. and Green, S. (1994), Using domain knowledge in requirements capture and formal specification construction, In Jirotka, M. and Goguen, J. (Eds.), "Requirements Engineering: Social and Technical Issues", Academic Press, London, 1994.

[3] Finkelstein, A. (1988), Reuse of formatted requirements specifications, Software Engineering Journal, 3(5):186-197, 1988.

[4] Gomaa, H. (1995), Reusable software requirements and architectures for families of systems, Journal of Systems and Software, 28:189-202, 1995.

[5] Griss, M.L. and Wentzel, K.D. (1995), Hybrid Domain-Specific Kits, Journal Systems and Software, 30:213-230, 1995.

[6] Kang, K., Cohen, S., Hess, J., Novak, W. and Peterson, S. (1990), Feature-Oriented Domain Analysis Feasibility Study, CMU/SEI-90-TR-21, Software Engineering Institute, Carnegie-Mellon University

[7] Lam, W. (1994), Reasoning about requirements from past cases, PhD thesis, Kings College, University of London, 1994.

[8] Maiden, N. and Sutcliffe, A. (1993), Exploiting reusable specification through analogy, Communications of the ACM, 35(4):55-64, 1993.

[9] Maiden, N. (1996), Acquiring Requirements: a domain-specific approach, In Proceedings of IFIP Working Groups 8.1/13.2 Conference, Domain Knowledge for Interactive System Design, (Eds. Sutcliffe, A.G., Benyon, D. and Assche, F.V.), Geneva, May 8-10, 1996.

[10] Miriyala, K. and Harandi, T.H. (1991), Automatic derivation of formal software specifications from informal descriptions, IEEE Transactions on Software Engineering, 17(10):1126-1142, 1991.

[11] McIlroy, M.D. (1969), Mass-produced Software Components, Proceedings of the 1969 NATO Conference on Software Engineering, 1969.

[12] Parnas, D.L. (1976), On the design and development of program families, IEEE Transactions on Software Engineering, Vol SE-2, March, 1976.

[13] Prieto-Diaz, R. (1990), Domain analysis: an introduction, ACM SIGSOFT Software Engineering Notes, 15(2):47-54, 1990

[14] Ryan, K. and Mathews, B. (1993), Matching conceptual graphs as an aid to requirements reuse, In Proceedings of the IEEE International Symposium on Require-

ments Engineering, ISBN 0-8186-3120-1, page 112-120, 1993.

[15] SPC (1992), Software Productivity Consortium Reuse Adoption Guidebook, Version 01.00.03, SPC-92051-CMC, November, 1992.

[16] STARS (1995), Organisation Domain Modeling Guidebook, STARS-VC-A023/011/00, March, 1995.

[17] Svoboda, F., Maymir-Ducharme, F. and Poulin, J. (1996), Domain Analysis in the DoD, Software Engineering Notes, 21(1):55-67, January 1996.

[18] Treager, I.E. (1994), Aircraft Gas Turbine Engine Technology (2nd Edition), ISBN 0-07-065158-2, Glencoe, Ohio.

[19] Wartik S. and Prieto-Diaz P. (1992), Criteria for comparing reuse-oriented domain analysis approaches International Journal of Software Engineering and Knowledge Engineering, 2(3):403-431, 1992.

[20] WSRET (1995), Proceedings of the 4th International Workshop on Software Reuse Education and Training, Morgantown, West Virginia, 14-18th August, 1995.

[21] WISR (1995), Proceedings of the 7th Annual Workshop on Software Reuse, August 28-30, St. Charles, Illinois, 1995.

[22] Davis, A.M. (1993)
Software Requirements: Objects, Functions and States
Englewood Cliffs NJ, Prentice-Hall.

Terminologies and Terminology Servers for Information Environments

S. K. Bechhofer, C.A. Goble, A.L. Rector, W.D. Solomon, W.A. Nowlan
and the GALEN Consortium
Medical Informatics Group
University of Manchester
Oxford Road
Manchester M13 9PL
seanb@cs.man.ac.uk
Tel: +44 161 275 6239

Abstract

Terminologies, or constrained vocabularies, are a potentially rich means of representing the metadata required for applications that have partially structured and incomplete dynamic data to describe, and exploratory and inexact queries to express. Such applications include digital libraries and multimedia repositories and software management; specific application communities include medicine and art. We propose that terminologies are ideal for meeting today's information requirements and that a dynamic terminology service is the appropriate architectural approach. We present the requirements of a terminology server, and describe the implementation and practical use of one developed by the authors that uses a Description Logic, GRAIL, *to represent the terms. The Terminology Server has been extensively used in applications relating to medicine and is being used in the integration of diverse information sources for Molecular Biology.*

1. Introduction

Terminologies, or constrained vocabularies, are important as they provide a framework within which communities can communicate and express ideas in a consistent manner, and are essential where standardisation and unambigous information sharing is important. A terminology is a collection of terms or concepts with relationships between them, particularly the *is-a* or *subsumption* relationship, which is used to build a *classified hierarchy* of concepts. Classification supports notions such as generalization and specialization – descriptions can be refined, incrementally adding more detail when necessary, and queries can use the subsumption hierarchy to ask general questions. The use of terminologies is widespread within communities which have a need or desire to share standardised information, including systems for such diverse purposes as:

- classification of medical conditions (e.g. SNOMED) [7],
- descriptions of works of art (e.g. Iconclass) [33],
- library cataloguing (e.g. Dewey Decimal).

The application of terminologies is now receiving attention from the more general information management community because they appear particularly powerful for describing semi-structured information flexibly but with coherence and rigour. Furthermore, they are extensible in that data instances described by a collection of terms can incrementally collect those terms and be continually reclassified or indexed – extremely useful if we cannot always predict how we wish to describe a data instance at the outset. Thus terminologies are a promising representation for metadata for three main areas:

- *content-description of semi-structured information*: the description of content of information instances as documents or images cannot necessarily be strictly typed at the outset to fit with a pre-typed but static database schema where instances populate a predefined and complete schema. Application examples include: digital libraries and document/image archives [31], broadcast video archives [11] and open hypermedia systems;
- *the description of highly complex domains*: domains such as medicine and art are so complex, and the variability of description of instances is so great, that a static type system is impracticable without massive loss of descriptive richness [22];

0-8186-7840-2/97 $10.00 © 1997 IEEE

- *ontologically-supported mediation between diverse information sources*: a terminology can be used to represent a common ontology that different information sources can map to. The common description must be rich enough to be all encompassing, and the mappings will be incomplete, imprecise and changeable as sources have missing data or are altered. As sources are described they should be classified with respect to one another to support imprecise cross-mappings [2].

All the above applications have similar requirements of their metadata:

- the data to be described is *complex* and frequently unstructured or semi-structured requiring a rich and expressive metadata model;
- the data is gathered and processed *incrementally* over time, collecting metadata (e.g. images collect annotations) so that the fundamental assumption that all metadata is known at data capture time is flawed;
- information is *incomplete* and *imprecise* as we cannot always predict how we wish to describe a data instance such as a document, unlike conventional databases where the data instances are strictly typed at the outset;
- data descriptions are *dynamic* and *evolutionary*. Flexible extensible descriptions are required as the same data may be reused from many different perspectives, and dynamically classified by many different, unpredictable, and possibly contradictory interpretations of the same contents, requiring data to be multiply classified as descriptions are elaborated and data is reused;
- incomplete descriptions lead to *imprecise queries* and *incomplete results* where the answer to a question might well just be an initial reduction of the search space. For example, (1) we may wish to present an example description and answer the question "retrieve objects that are similar to this" where the similarity is a metric of how closely the descriptions are classified w.r.t. to one another; (2) upon presentation of a request for an image containing a male politician, if the answer is empty we would like to be offered images of politicians as a more general alternative by relaxing the query constraints.

Terminologies can be seen to sit somewhere between the world of unstructured free text documents where there is no domain model or content metadata other than keywords, and more rigorous database schema for specific solutions, where highly coherent models exist but are inflexible and not painlessly extensible. Strictly-typed data schema, as in OODBMS give us sharing, consistency checking, indexing and query retrieval, but are inflexible. Attaching keywords to documents is a more flexible descriptive mechanism but the keywords used by different users are usually arbitrary and do not tend to converge – hence the terms do not form a standard interchangeable domain description. Recent work in Semantic Hypermedia systems proposes the reintroduction of database conceptual models to hypermedia systems [20] otherwise links are rarely typed or represent any rigorously expressed semantic model.

We suggest that terminologies are well suited to applications where the challenge is how to describe information intelligently and flexibly, how to evolve descriptions, how to reuse information by viewing it from multiple perspectives and how to search and browse for incomplete, inconsistent information using imprecise and exploratory/interactive questioning.

In this paper we propose the use of terminologies implemented through Terminology Logics (or Description Logics as they are also known) for describing metadata, and a service-oriented architecture that encapsulates the description logic in a **Terminology Server** – a resource that delivers a range of terminological services. We have built a terminology server for a clinical environment and report on our practical experiences from that effort.

Section 2 describes Terminology Logics and the requirements for a Terminology Server and Section 3 describes the architecture of a Terminology Server and the implementation for the GALEN [27] project and other programmes. Section 4 describes applications making use of the GALEN server. Section 5 discusses related work and Section 6 presents our conclusions. The paper deals primarily with the architecture and motivation for a terminology server, and where possible avoids detailed discussion of the description logic used within the implementation. Sections 3 and 4, however, make reference to the GRAIL description logic [26] developed during GALEN, as the techniques described there make use of special features of GRAIL.

2. Terminology Logics

Conventional approaches to managing terms pre-date computation (medical terminologies have been in use since the 18th Century) and do not in general have a great deal of underlying structure. A common method is to use a *coding scheme* – a tree-like structure of terms, with each term having an attached alphanumeric code, uniquely identifying the term. The subsumption relationship is then based on code substrings. An example of a coding scheme is shown in Figure 1. This is a simple hierarchy which is intended to represent types of cars and the features they can have. The example will be used to illustrate points throughout the paper.

A1 Car
A11 Estate Car
A11X Estate Car, 1000 cc
A11Y Estate Car, 1500 cc
A12 Sports Car
A12X Sports Car, 1000 cc
A12XA Sports Car, 1000 cc, alloywheels
A12Y Sports Car, 1500 cc
...

Figure 1. A simple coding scheme

Such schemes do provide a certain amount of support and have proved useful over the years, but they suffer from problems. With many modifiers, the number of terms required quickly grows, producing a combinatorial explosion and schemes that are too large. All the information in the representation is asserted, and must be given by a modeller or coder producing the representation. Because of this, the semantics can be unclear, leading to problems of interpretation. A lack of structure in the representation hampers navigation through the scheme, and associated activities such as data entry or the recording of information using the terms from the terminology are troublesome. At the same time, schemes can be too small, leading to insufficient coverage – as all the terms must be defined pre hoc there may not be a term appropriate to a certain situation.

An approach to providing a computational solution to term building and term management is to use a *compositional* representation which has a richer structure than the simple tree-like structures supported by traditional schemes. Such representations are provided by Description Logics (DLs), also known as Terminological Logics. These have enjoyed considerable attention from the Knowledge Representation section of the AI community in the last few years and there are a number of well known prototype DLs, descendants of the KL-ONE language, including CANDIDE, BACK, CLASSIC, and LOOM; for an overview see [5].

All DLs define complex entities in terms of composite descriptions made up of a limited set of elementary concepts assembled according to explicit rules. DLs can be viewed as languages obtained by term composition using recursive *term constructors*, where some terms are *concepts* (denoting a collection of instances or individuals) or *roles* (relationships between, or attributes of, concepts or instances). DLs distinguish between *primitive* concepts and *defined* concepts.

The concepts define a subsumption lattice. Primitive concepts have no characterising attributes and memberships and are placed in the lattice by the system designer. Defined concepts are placed *automatically* by a *classifier* based on their compositional structure. Subsumption relationships are determined primarily using structural rules, but classification also employs some inference based on cardinalities of relationships. Classified concept descriptions are a form of implied, more specific subtype of their base supertype, inheriting the properties of their supertype. This automatic classification allows us to incrementally elaborate and specialise descriptions (or terms) without having to worry about maintaining a consistent hierarchy explicitly. Recent work has provided a sound formal basis for several description logics along with results concerning their complexity [4].

The power of DLs is derived from the automatic determination of subsumption between compositional descriptions. If a descriptive model is constructed using highly compositional defined concepts wherever possible, we can navigate the resulting lattice to reveal, for example, the direct parents and children of any specific description and the least common parent and greatest common child of a pair of descriptions.

To return to our example, we would need to supply definitions for elementary concepts such as Car, Engine and so on, along with relationships to represent having an engine, an engine being of a certain size and so on. The composites such as Estate Car with 1000cc engine would then be constructed using these elementary concepts and relationships. The fact that this is a kind of Car would then be inferred by the classifier (along with other subsumption relationships – for instance this concept is also a kind of Vehicle with an Engine). Figure 2 gives an example of a Description Logic model for the Cars hierarchy given in Figure 1. This segment is given in pseudo-GRAIL syntax. The basic operations used here are those for introducing new concept and attribute definitions and adding new constraints. Car is a primitive concept. A defined concept is characterised by a set of attributes or role-fillers whose presence makes an object belong to this concept. A composite expression is generally of the form (topic which rel value), where topic and value are concepts and rel is a relationship. Expressions can be nested, with value or topic being a composite. A defined concept (in the style of GRAIL) could be GermanCar which is a Car with Germany as a role-filler for the role hasCountryOfOrigin. SportsCar which ⟨hasCountryOfOrigin Germany, hasWheelType Alloy⟩ is said to have a Concept topic SportsCar and two role-filler pairs called criteria. This composite defined concept is classified as a subtype of SportsCar which hasCountryOfOrigin Germany, SportsCar which hasWheelType Alloy, SportsCar, Car which hasCountryOfOrigin Germany, Car which hasWheelType Alloy, and Car.

"primitive concepts"
TopCategory newSub Car.
TopCategory newSub WheelType.
TopCategory newSub Country.
Country newSub [Germany, France].
WheelType newSub [Alloy Steel].
Car newSub [EstateCar SportsCar].
"role definition (inverse not shown)"
Attribute newAttribute hasEngineSize.
Attribute newAttribute hasWheelType.
Attribute newattribute hasCountryOfOrigin
"role between concepts (sanctioning not shown)"
Car hasEngineSize Number.
Car hasWheelType WheelType.
Car hasCountryOfOrigin Country.
"defined concepts"
(Car which hasCountryOfOrigin Germany)
  name GermanCar.
SportsCar which
  ⟨ hasCountryOfOrigin Germany, hasWheelType Alloy ⟩.

Figure 2. A Description Logic Model in GRAIL

2.1. Benefits of a Description Logic

Description logics have two functions that make them particularly attractive as models for describing semi-structured and complex information [5].

A type system. *Expressivity*: Description Logics make it possible to express the semantics of information systems and are often more expressive than traditional Semantic Data Models or Object Oriented data models;

Type checking: type refinement is provided automatically through the subsumption ordering on descriptions and hence provably correct subsumption algorithms can be used for type checking;

Schema verification: by checking whether a compositional concept's description will classify we are able to verify the schema's consistency;

Type equivalence: each compositional description contains only the necessary and sufficient descriptions for the concept. Hence terms that are expressed in different ways but come down to the same description are equivalent and redundancy is reduced.

The type system forms an ontology that can be browsed, queried and can drive interfaces.

An indexing/query system. *Automatic multiple classification*: Description Logics form a dynamic multiaxial classification scheme to support incremental elaboration and partial information. Concepts can be incrementally specialised, with the automatic classification capabilities of a Description Logic taking care of relationships between concepts. As more information is attributed to the description, the concept migrates through the classification hierarchy;

Query formulation: imprecise querying and query generalisation/specialisation is supported by a) generalising or specialising concept terms; b) relaxing or restricting cardinality constraints or c) adding or removing terms to navigate through the concept hierarchy and explore potential relationships between terms and their associated instances;

Data exploration: Description Logics are naturally suited for expressing queries and defining views, as the subsumption relationship can be used to organise queries automatically and views, hence supporting data exploration and query optimisation.

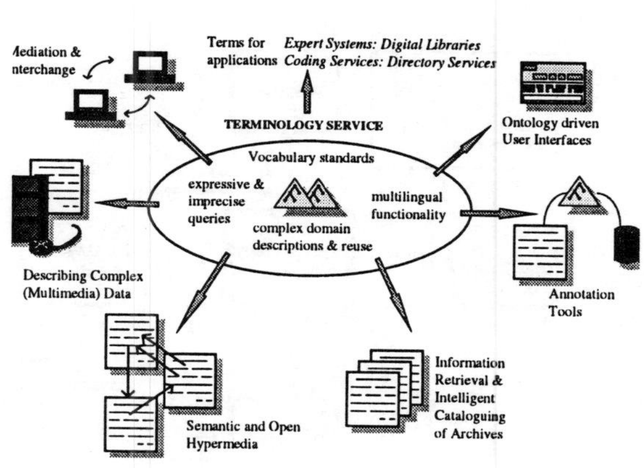

Figure 3. The utility of a terminology service

Description Logics have been used in a wide variety of applications including the representation of complex schemas for cars [30], software management [8] and medicine [27], data archaeology [6], mediation between heterogeneous data stores [2] and database querying [16]. However, interacting with Description Logic implementations can often prove difficult. In the past, solutions involved embedding the logic in large monolithic systems with all the attached problems of maintenance and implementation, lack of consistency, and the hampering the exchange of terms between applications. As Figure 3 suggests, a "terminology server" can be used to drive, or interact with, a number of different systems and therefore should be perceived as a separate component.

3. A Terminology Service

We propose a move towards a service-oriented architecture and the encapsulation of a Description Logic in a **Terminology Server** or TeS – a resource that delivers a range of terminological services. These services are used by a variety of applications such as modelling tools, query engines, data entry interfaces and so on. Figure 4 illustrates some of the services one would expect distributed servers to de-

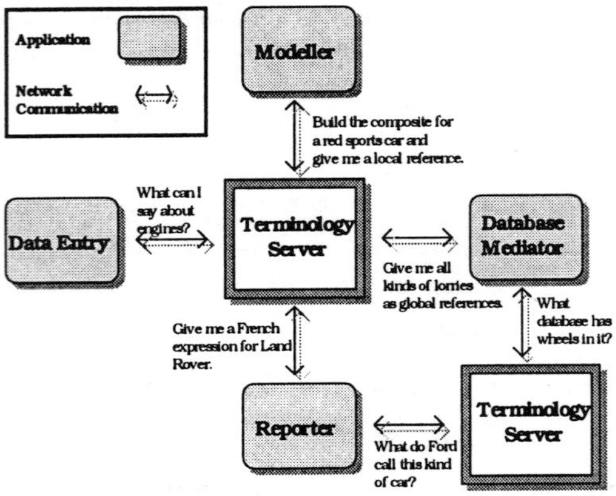

Figure 4. Resources Delivering Terminological Services

liver. A terminology server approach is essential if we are to build generic "plug and play" mixed systems, for example if a semantic hypermedia system is to use the TeS as a link resolution service along with conventional link following or information retrieval services [23].

3.1. Services

The services can be broken down into three main types: pure terminological or *concept* services, language or *linguistic* services, and *extrinsic information* services.

Concept Services. Along with maintaining the representation of the concepts, the services include operations which both extend and query the content of the model; these operations are commonly known as TELL and ASK [5]. Operations for extension include the introduction of new primitive concepts, the introduction of new relations, and the addition of new constraints on roles. Queries include those to determine the primitive concepts and relations; requests for the parents (generalizations) or children (specializations) of a concept definition (w.r.t. the subsumption hierarchy); usage of concepts and information about how concepts and relations can be combined to create new potential composite concepts. A description logic provides us with a *generative* framework where new conceptual definitions can be constructed by applying modifiers to base concepts. Classification operations take a conceptual definition and determine its place in the hierarchy (according to the rules defined in the logic). Such an operation may also perform validity checking that the concept is consistent and fits with any constraints the model imposes – in this way the server is providing a form of type-system (see section 2.1). Table 1 includes some examples of a concept service's operations.

ASK *Type Based*	*Type checking*: Is this a legal expression? Are these two definitions the same? *Type exploration*: what further can be said about the expression - i.e. how can I specialize it?
Index-based	*Classification*: Where does the expression sit in the hierarchy? *Query relaxation*: How can I generalize the expression? *Query tightening*: How can I specialize the expression?
Other	*Language rendering*: What are the natural language expressions for this concept? *Mediation & Translation*: How does this expression correspond to some external representation I have?
TELL	Introducing new elementary concepts; Introducing new rules about term composition; Naming concept definitions; Providing maps to external representations

Table 1. Concept Services

Linguistic Services. The server deals with terms. In order to aid interaction with the terminology, and for user interfaces, these terms should be available in representations other than the underlying one used by the description logic. Thus the server should offer linguistic services which provide the conversion to and from natural and other language expressions.

Extrinsic Information Services. Concept and linguistic services deal with the terminology in isolation. In addition to these, we may expect to be able to relate terms from the terminology to objects from the rest of the world. As this information associated with the terminology has no effect on the underlying classification, we refer to these as extrinsic information services. These operations are of course not completely divorced from the terminological operations – services may well use the classification in order to sparsely decorate the hierarchy and allow general querying.

We require the ability to relate terms from the terminology with terms from existing hierarchies or classifications. Such functionality is essential if a new system is to prove compatible with existing work. Domains in which a terminology server would prove useful are often those domains which already have existing terminologies – thus legacy systems must be supported [24].

In addition, terminologies can be used as mediators between information sources – the server can provide information about the concrete representation of a conceptual definition in a particular information source. These mappings to other representations can be seen as examples of extrinsic information services [2].

As examples, the concept (EstateCar which hasEngineSize 1000cc) could be mapped to code **A11X** from the scheme presented earlier. Alternatively we may know that details of sports cars are kept in a particular database – information about the location of this database and the format of entries can be associated with the concept SportsCar. When searching for instances of sports cars, we can use this information to determine where to look.

3.2. Client Applications and Concept Referencing

We can envisage multiple Terminology Servers in a distributed environment with applications coupled to a local server occasionally using other servers. A server might also support multiple concept models. This leads to two possible forms of referencing concepts:

- Persistent global references, interchangeable between servers: a collection of servers may exist, all sharing the same ontology. Concepts are exchanged between servers and must be server and session independent.
- Persistent local references for a particular server: a server may be coupled with a collection of applications using that server; such applications require fast references with reasonably tight coupling and so those references persist beyond any particular client-server session.

These assume that references are persistent and independent of any client-server session; we can also see the requirement for transient but fast session-dependent references for a particular server – for optimum efficiency a server and client application might be tightly coupled with transient references to concepts.

References provide a naming service, with local references forming a local name space (valid for a particular server) and global references a global name space (valid for all servers). These references refer to concepts in an internal representation; applications will also need to refer to them as (natural) language expressions and in terms of existing hierarchies or schemes.

By encapsulating the logic and operations as a collection of services, the terminology can be used as a resource in a distributed system; for example as a common facility in a CORBA distributed environment.

3.3. The Galen Terminology Server

The GALEN and GALEN-IN-USE [25] EU-funded projects have developed a Terminology Server for the support of medical applications. The Terminology Server

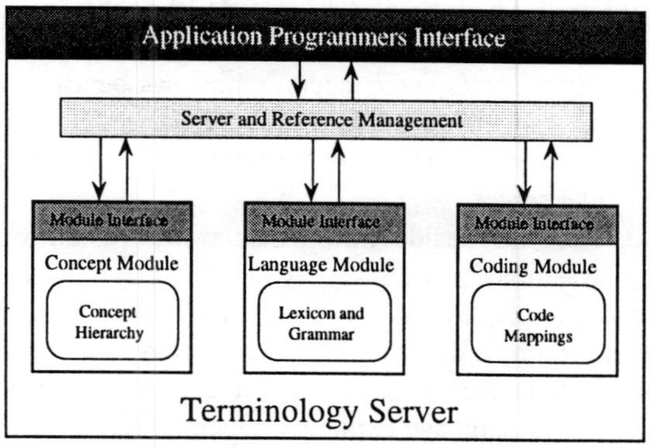

Figure 5. The architecture of a server

presents clinical concepts to applications which may then use the concepts to drive content-sensitive user interfaces, to mediate between medical classification systems or to act as types for medical records. The server is now being used to support applications from Biological Sciences, Art and Hypermedia.

Here we present and discuss the particular architecture of our terminology server and present a scenario to illustrate its usage. The server is implemented as a collection of modules, each with a distinct responsibility, along with a server manager. The server management layer brokers requests from the outside world, and delegates them to the appropriate modules (some requests may require services from more than one). It also deals with reference management and output scheme production as discussed in Section 3.4.

There are several modules in our current implementation, each with a rough responsibility for a class of services as described above. Figure 5 shows the three principle ones – the Concept Module, Language Module and a specific example of an Extrinsics Module for managing Clinical Coding Services.

As an example, we consider the functioning of a client tool, the purpose of which is to present a user with an interface allowing the construction of a composite concept description, and the subsequent storage of this concept in a variety of formats. An example of such a tool is the SCUI [1], which provides clinicians with the facility to append detailed clinical information to a clinical record.

We describe the dialogue which takes place between the client application and the server.

1. The client requires an initial entry point into the conceptual model. This may be either a collection of *global references* held by the client, or may be represented by marking or annotating concepts held by the server – thus allowing multiple clients access to the same entry points.

2. For each entry point X, the client is interested in how the concept can be specialised. A request "what can I say about X?" is made to the server. This request is recognised by the server manager and delegated to the concept module. A collection of references will be returned to the client, representing the roles and concepts which can be used to construct specializations of X. These references will usually be *local references* – valid only for a particular connection to a particular server.

3. The client decides how to display the available options - e.g. as buttons, picking lists, or in some graphical notation. In order to display the concepts, it may need language expressions which describe them – the references are simply pointers to concepts held within the conceptual model, and do not have language explicitly attached. Thus further requests to the server may be made of the form "provide me with a language expression for concept Y". These will be delegated to the language module.

4. The client builds an interface based on the relationships and language provided by the server. The user selects appropriate concepts to build a particular composite. A request may then be made to the server to classify this description. Again this is passed on to the concept module, where the concept is classified – the module determines the concept's place in the hierarchy – and a reference is passed back to the client.

5. At this point, there are several things the client can do. We may wish to specialize further, in which case the process is repeated. It may be that the client application needs to store a persistent reference or *global ID* for the new composite. In this case, further requests to the server will be made, requiring format conversion of references. Such format conversions may require calls to modules or may be dealt with entirely by the server manager. Alternatively, the user may want to know how the built concept is represented in some other scheme. In the example of the SCUI, requests could be returned as codes from the ICD or SNOMED classifications. This requires a call to the server which is passed to the coding services module (See Section 3.6).

Code conversion is an example of inter-module communication. In order to determine a "closest matching code", the code conversion module needs to know about the parents of a concept, information provided by the concept module. All such communication is through the server manager and module interfaces.

3.4. Client Coupling, Reference Management and Name spaces.

The discussion above introduces the notion of concept references. The server is a *dynamic* resource. Rather than having applications hold on to conceptual definitions which contain all the required information, the server hands out references to concepts held in the Concept Module. When further information about a concept is required, the application will query the server. This does mean that the references are in some ways useless without the server, so care must be taken that information is not lost, particularly when dealing with volatile references.

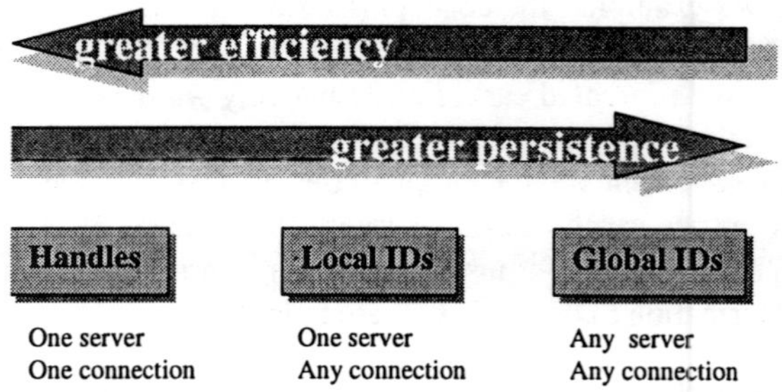

Figure 6. Reference Types

Caching policies. References and query results can be cached by both the server and clients, allowing more efficient answering of queries. This is particularly useful for operations such as language generation – in most circumstances, once the server has been queried for a string representing a concept, it is unnecessary to regenerate the string.

Caching can cause problems during the process of modelling. If new information is being added, the answers to questions, particularly those concerning the concept hierarchy, can change. Thus both clients and server must be careful to initialize and clear caches when information is updated.

As described earlier, references can be roughly split into two categories: persistent global references and local references. In the example above, the client made use of local references when building a data entry form but would require global references for persistent storage.

Our current implementation actually provides three levels as shown in Figure 6.

Handles are the most transient of references, and are valid for a single connection to a particular server. Handles cannot be stored persistently.

Local IDs are valid for a particular server and will exist over multiple connections. A local ID table is maintained by the server relating references to concepts. Local IDs can be stored, as long as the application will be connecting to the same server at a later date. Local IDs could be implemented using a table in the server relating references to concepts in the hierarchy or as references to a database if the concept module chooses to store the representation externally.

In the current implementation, there is very little difference between the efficiency of handles and local IDs. The performance of local IDs was considered good enough for most purposes, so little attempt has been made to improve handles. As the conceptual models grow, however, or if the conceptual hierarchy is stored externally, the performance of local IDs may deteriorate. We may then make use of the knowledge that handles are transient in order to employ caching or other techniques to improve the performance of handles.

Global IDs are interchangeable between many servers containing the same model. As each server may represent the hierarchy in different ways, Global IDs are implemented as a "decompiled" representation of the concept, which is then reclassified when presented to the server. Because of this, Global IDs are the least efficient of the references and should only be used when references are to be interchanged between servers.

Other Output Schemes. In addition to references, answers to questions can be requested using other representations, such as natural language or coding schemes, as illustrated in Figure 4. These formats are currently "one-way" – in our present implementations, we cannot present a natural language expression or code to the server and expect it to be treated as a concept reference. However there are operations to allow us to convert from coding scheme codes to concepts and (to a certain extent) from natural language expressions to concepts.

References, Natural Language expressions and Codes together form what are known as *Output Schemes*. A request to the server will specify the desired output scheme (or schemes) for the result. Calls will often request multiple output schemes for results. For example, a browser application will ask for children of a concept as both handles (so that further manipulations can be performed on the child concepts) and as natural language, so that a representation of the children can be presented to the user. Specifying multiple schemes in cases like this can increase performance by cutting down the overheads present in both the conceptual operations of the server and the underlying transport mechanisms of the network.

3.5. GRAIL sanctions.

GRAIL has been specifically devised for medical terminologies, which has influenced its range of term constructors. In contrast to some representations, certain constructs are excluded (for example, negation). GRAIL chiefly differs from its KL-ONE relatives in that it has: conceptual assertions (concept inclusions) that take part in classification; the management of part-whole relationships and limited expressions of cardinality [26]. For the purposes of this paper only one of GRAIL's differences needs explanation, as it is used by the linguistic and interface building services, namely *role sanctioning*. A sanction is an assertion that two concepts may be related via some role. Compositions of terms cannot be formed unless an appropriate sanction is present. Sanctioning serves two purposes, although they are both really different views on the same operation:

- It constrains the formation of compositional terms, ensuring that only *semantically valid* compositions are formed, preventing misnomers such as Country which hasEngineSize 1000cc.
- It provides answers to questions such as "what can I say about X?" To answer this question we examine the sanctions applying to the term X, and return an answer based on these.

Note that sanctioning has no effect on the classification process – the sanctions present or absent on a concept will not change its place in the concept hierarchy. Sanctioning is thus an operation which could be quite easily added to description logics other than GRAIL; other DLs rely on role restriction. The position of a concept in the hierarchy does effect the sanctioning process however, as sanctions are inherited. This inheritance of sanctioning allows us to place sanctions around the hierarchy in a sparse manner, allowing the construction of many compositions with a single assertion. For example, we could assert that Mammals can have a gender which is Male or Female, allowing the formation of Men, Bulls, Tom Cats etc. without having to explicitly assert that the relationship holds for Humans, Cattle, Cats and so on.

GRAIL supports two levels of sanctioning – the first represents general relationships while the second represents those things that can really be formed. To use a medical example, we may say that in general, Conditions occur in Body Parts. This is not to say that every condition can occur in every body part, but it is useful to be able to express the idea. Then at a more specific level, we can assert that Fractures occur in Bones, allowing the formation of a fracture of a bone. Sanctioning is hierarchical – a high level sanction must be present before a low-level sanction can be asserted. The levels of sanctioning provide flexible control over the formation of compositional concepts.

3.6. Server Modules

Here we discuss the core modules of the server in more detail.

Concept Module. The Concept Module, as it is responsible for the core terminological functionality of the server, includes the maintenance of the representation of the concept hierarchy and support of classification operations as

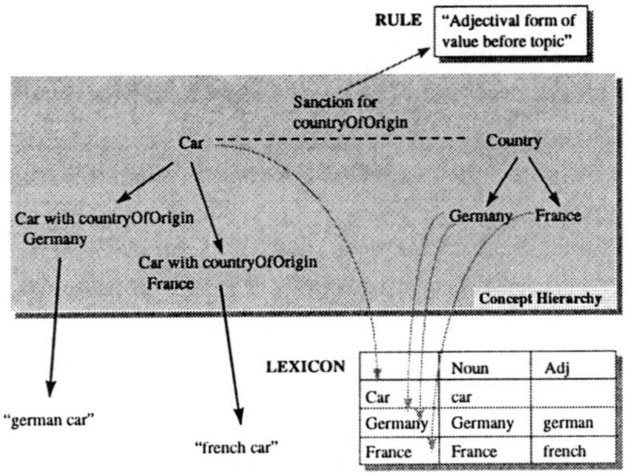

Figure 7. Language Generation

discussed in Section 3.1. The hierarchy is kept as a graph or semantic network, with nodes representing concept definitions and arcs represent relationships such as subsumption (the specialisation or "is-a" relationship), usage and so on. The network may actually be held in an external database, as in K-Rep [17].

Subsumption test algorithms. Classification depends primarily on a subsumption test – a test which determines when one concept definition is a generalization of another. The current implementation of the concept module uses a *normalize and compare* or *structural* style of subsumption algorithm [35]. Such algorithms have been shown to have problems with incompleteness – the classifier may not spot all subsumption relationships that hold. The algorithms are sound however, in that any subsumption relationships determined by the classifier will hold – and research is ongoing in the development of *tableaux-calculus* based algorithms for classification which exhibit better behaviour with respect to completeness [4].

Our architecture will enable us to replace the subsumption algorithms without any visible difference to client applications.

Language Module. The Language Module is responsible primarily for the generation of natural language expressions for concept definitions. Language generation uses a lexicon containing words or phrases for elementary concept definitions, along with grammar rules which describe how phrases should be combined together. The concept hierarchy is used extensively, allowing the addition of general rules which describe phrase construction for a large number of situations [34].

Figure 7 shows the workings of the Language Module. The central grey area represents the conceptual hierarchy (as stored and represented in the Concept Module). There are some elementary concepts such as Country, Car, Germany, along with some composite definitions (which will have been placed in the hierarchy by the classifier). Concepts can have attached to them specific lexical information, such as noun and adjectival forms. We have also shown a *sanction* – a constraint allowing the formation of a composite sanction by asserting that it is valid to form a composite using the concepts and relationship. The rule associated with the relationship hasCountryOfOrigin describes how to form a natural language expression from an expression using the relationship. The attachment is actually made to the sanction. Using the rule and the basic words in the lexicon, we can construct a phrase corresponding to the concept Car with countryOfOrigin Germany, i.e. "German Car". If an additional country France is introduced into the model, in order to ensure that phrases are produced for composites using the term, we need only provide the appropriate forms of phrase for the concept itself.

Generic Extrinsic Information Module. The Extrinsic Information Module allows us to attach information which is in some way "external" to the conceptual model. This includes information which has no terminological significance, but which should be associated with particular conceptual definitions. The model is used as a framework upon which we can hang useful facts, exploiting the inheritance hierarchy to decorate the model sparsely.

An example of the use of extrinsics is a drug interaction model produced as part of PEN & PAD [22]. A taxonomy of drugs was defined, and using extrinsic information, known interactions between different classes of drugs were recorded. This information was not considered to be important in terminological terms, but it is useful to be able to rely on the hierarchy for retrieval.

Various policies for retrieval of extrinsic information can be used including:

Exact Only information attached to the concept in question is returned;

Lowest The hierarchy is traversed in a breadth first manner from the concept, returning the first pieces of information encountered;

All All information attached to the concept or any of its ancestors is returned.

Coding Services Module.

The Coding Services Module was built for the specific purpose of relating the GALEN conceptual model to existing coding schemes for medicine [24]. It is in fact a specialised example of the more general Extrinsic Information Module. Coding Schemes are a limited form of terminology which generally consist of a collection of terms arranged in a (single-axial) hierarchy, with all relationships between terms explicitly asserted.

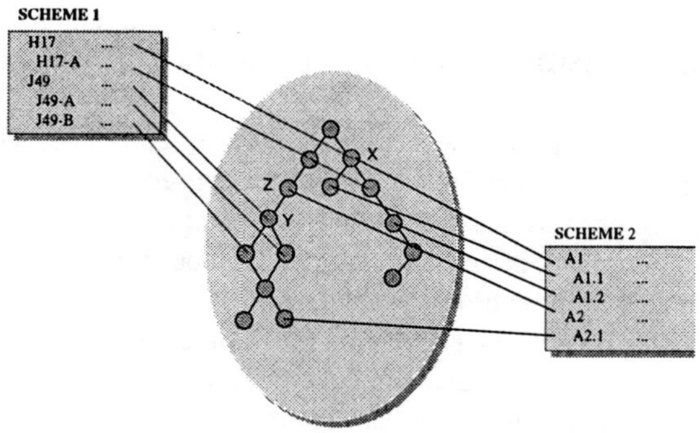

Figure 8. Code Conversion

If a coding scheme and the conceptual model held in the server have similar coverage, we can provide *mappings* from one to another, indicating concepts which are represented in both models. This maintenance of the mappings (along with associated functionality) is the responsibility of the Coding Services Module.

Once a collection of mappings have been defined, we can perform various retrieval operations. For example, given a code, we can ask for the concept(s) to which it has been mapped. More interesting, however, is the conversion in the opposite direction, providing codes for concepts. Given a concept X, we can ask whether the concept has an associated code mapped to it or a related concept, using one of the policies described above.

This is particularly useful when the conceptual model has more coverage or more depth than the static coding scheme. As an example, the coding scheme may not have an entry for green estate car but may have one for estate car, which is a parent of the term we need coded.

When more than one coding scheme has been mapped, an extension of this technique can provide *mediation services* between the two representations, as shown in Figure 8. The oval area represents the conceptual model held in the server with the coding schemes on either side. Starting with a code in **Scheme 1**, we can map into the representation, then out again to **Scheme 2** – even when there is no direct match. For example, starting with code H17, we can map to concept X. This has an explicit mapping to code A1 in Scheme 2, providing us with an easy conversion. Starting with code J49, and mapping to concept Y, we find no direct correspondence with **Scheme 2**. We then look up the hierarchy, and find that concept Z (a parent of Y) does have a mapping to code A2 from **Scheme 2**, and this provides us with our conversion, or "nearest corresponding code".

Traditional methods of code conversion involve crafting conversions between each pair of schemes. For each new scheme, conversions must be provided into every other scheme. With the technique described above and the use of the conceptual model as an *interlingua*, we need only provide a single mapping to and from the central representation for each coding scheme.

Scheme Validation. The use of mappings as described above can assist in the process of *validating* a coding scheme. If a scheme has been provided with a mapping to a representation held in the server, we can check that the subsumption relationships in the scheme are coherent, i.e. that if terms occur as parent and child in the scheme, then the corresponding terms in the model are also ancestor and descendant.

3.7. Application Programmer's Interface

Access to the server is via a well-defined Application Programmer's Interface, available as a library of C functions. The `xdr` notation – a data representation language suitable for remote procedure calls which forms the basis of Sun RPC – is used to describe the underlying concrete representations and to define operations for serialising and deserialising data as it is transmitted over a network. We have simply used `xdr` for data encoding, and have implemented a simple remote procedure call on top of this. The use of `xdr` ensures the availability of a C interface, and solves some of the problems caused by differences between data representations on different platforms. However, `xdr` is quite dated, and we are considering a move to a system such as CORBA.

The notion of a terminology server fits well into the CORBA framework – by encapsulating the logic and operations as a collection of services, the terminology can be used as a resource in a distributed system. CORBAMed, a subgroup of OMG, will be putting out an RFP on terminology services later this year – the aim being to specify the services that a CORBA compliant Terminology Server must support.

Client applications have been built in C and Smalltalk on both PC and Unix based platforms, and have communicated successfully with the server over both local- and wide-area networks. Work is also being undertaken on a Java binding to the C API.

4. Case Studies

To illustrate the use of a server and to highlight interesting areas of open questions and further work, we present two example *case studies* which provide real examples of the server technology in use. The first deals with the use of the server and its terminological logic to drive the data entry and query process. The second is concerned with the use of

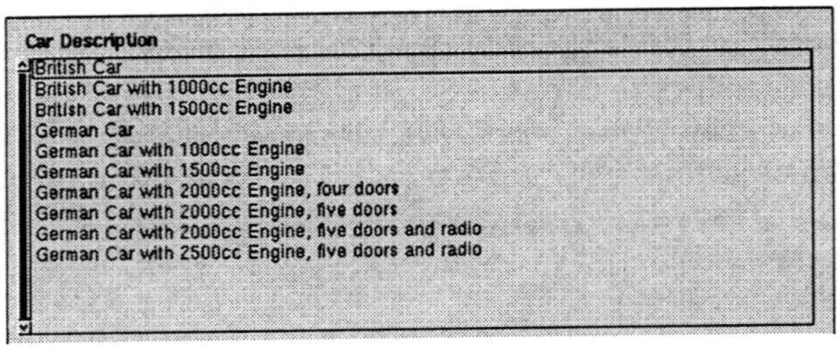

Figure 9. A Picking List Interface

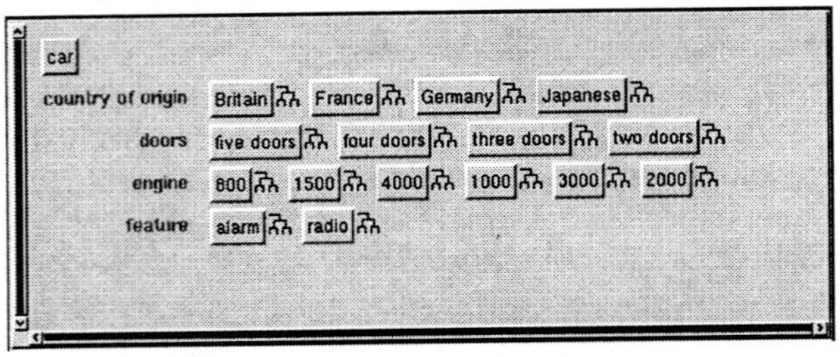

Figure 10. A Compositional Data Entry Interface

the server to aid in the co-ordination of the building of large scale traditional static terminologies.

4.1. PEN & PAD

Several applications have been built which rely on server functionality to support data entry. An example is PEN & PAD, a product which has evolved from experiments with user interface requirements for clinical data entry [22] and now forms part of the latest version of a major computer package for General Practitioners [15].

The application relies on the notion of controlled data entry, where interfaces are built according to the information present in the conceptual model. In particular this constrains the construction of complex expressions, ensuring that incoherent expressions cannot be generated.

As discussed in Section 2, GP systems had previously used static coding schemes such as SNOMED to represent clinical information. Interfaces are generally based on the notion of a *picking list*, as shown in Figure 9 where a selection of alternatives are offered to the user – note the duplication of modifiers (a by-product of the underlying structure of the representation). When several modifiers are present, many similar terms will have to be coded and presented to the user, often causing confusion.

The solution to this is a user interface that allows the *compositional* construction of terms, as shown in Figure 10.

Figure 10 shows an interface which uses controlled data entry, and allows construction of the same terms in a *compositional* manner. This second interface presents a great deal more information to the user – the picking list has only allowed a small subset of the possible combinations. If it were to contain all combinations, the list would be so long as to be unusable.

Once expressions have been built up and classified (as described in Section 3.3, the server is used to provide language expressions and codes from existing systems. These references, codes or language can then be stored in external databases for later retrieval.

The emphasis here is very much on data *entry* and capture. The added value gained from the use of the server is that language and codes can be produced quickly and found without having to resort to the usual methods of navigation through such systems which can be troublesome, as described earlier.

4.2. GALEN-IN-USE

GALEN-IN-USE [25] is a follow on project to GALEN [27]. The intention in GALEN-IN-USE is to use a terminological model to aid in the building of the next generation of coding schemes for medicine. Although the ultimate goal is to provide clinical terminology via a dynamic server, GALEN-IN-USE goes some way towards achieving consistent hierarchies which are to be delivered via traditional means.

GALEN-IN-USE faces several interesting challenges, many concerned with the *modelling* process. The project requires a conceptual model on a large scale – current estimates put the size of the model in the region of 10,000 concepts. This is simply the number of named and elementary concept definitions – as the representation is *generative*, the actual number of concepts which can be described using the model is huge. Contrast this with the size of most knowledge bases which seldom rise above the hundreds.

Tools are thus required which help in the various activities associated with building and maintaining the model. These currently take the form of a variety of *knowledge browsers* providing both textual and graphical representations of the structure of the model.

The project is collaborative, involving several international partners on the modelling side. Support is thus required for the process of *harmonising* sections of model. This occurs at both the *technological* level, where tools are needed to allow verification and consistent integration of new knowledge and at the *management* level, where modellers at different sites must be co-ordinated. This is supported through a variety of means including e-mail and WWW forums.

Population of the model is helped by the use of existing corpora (which will ultimately be mapped to concepts in the central model) as sources for terms and constraints. Some of this process has been automated, with natural language processing techniques being used on the rubrics associated with codes. In addition, much use is made of metadata and *templates*. Intermediate representations are used to insulate modellers from the complexities of the underlying representations. Rubrics are "dissected" into an intermediate format which can then be translated into GRAIL expressions using tools such as the SPET and TIGGER [29].

The modelling process is often *interactive*, requiring a certain level of performance from the classification engines which form the heart of the terminology server. Early implementations were built in Smalltalk – a language supporting rapid prototyping and the easy construction of user interface tools. However, as the models grow larger, the performance of the Smalltalk implementations becomes unacceptable. Alternative implementations of the core conceptual functionality have been built in C++ [28]. The modular nature of the server internals allowed the replacement of the classification engine with a minimum of disruption.

5. Related Work

A considerable amount of work has been undertaken in the area of Description Logics that has largely fallen into two divisions: theoretical work with little or no implementation and practical systems with little view to extensible services or the application to large scale concept models. None have adopted the approach of a terminological server; instead they concentrate on the details of the classifier rather than taking an overall systems architecture view.

Workers in the area of information integration have taken a more architectural viewpoint, for example those working within the I3 (Intelligent Information Integration) initiative. The I3 reference architecture [3] proposes four families of services; co-ordination and management, semantic integration and transformation, functional extensions and wrapping. A terminology service would appear to be orthogonal to these families and contribute to all of them: ontologies for service brokering; terms for describing the semantic content of different services; terminological inferencing etc.

SIMS [2], and Observer [19], part of the InfoQuilt programme [14], use the Description Logics LOOM and Classic respectively to mediate between heterogeneous information sources. SIMS still seems to perceive the terminology as an embedded component rather than an information service. However, Observer describes an *ontology server* – an application providing access to ontologies represented using a description logic, and mappings from terms in the ontologies to data repositories. This can be seen as a kind of terminology server as described here.

The InfoQuilt project [14] advocates the use of an ontology to describe multimedia and although does not suggest Description Logics or an ontology server as an approach one presumes from their work in integration that this is an approach that they are considering. Some forays have been made into the application of DLs to document description, e.g. CANDIDE [21], but this work is not described in detail and there is little evidence of its practical application. Likewise [18] theoretically applies a terminology logic to information retrieval but without any view on a terminological service architecture.

Farquhar et al [10] present the case for an *ontology server* that supports the ability of users to publish, browse, create and edit ontologies through the World Wide Web. The main purpose behind this is the support of collaborative development of ontologies and the process of achieving consensus on common ontologies by distributed groups. In our GALEN-IN-USE project similar support is achieved through web-based discourse tools. Farquhar et al's emphasis is on a shared ontolingua that supports assembly and reuse of existing ontologies from a repository by way of batch loading and translations from the ontology server to stand-alone applications – this is in direct contrast to our approach of a dynamic integrated terminology server serving individual concepts to client applications. From an application viewpoint, that of digital libraries, [9] discusses the need for an *authority tool* which is an application providing a knowledge service and the functionality of a thesaurus; this can be interpreted as a terminology server.

6. Conclusions and Further Work

In this paper we have presented the case for terminologies to be used as a means of richly representing the metadata for applications that have partially structured and incomplete dynamic data to describe, and exploratory and inexact queries to express. Applications with these characteristics are the applications of interest in this decade. Such terminologies represent ontologies that should not be embedded in client applications but should be shared and reused as a distributed resource. To make this possible the terminologies should be implemented as a service through a terminology server offering a number of sub-services: conceptual, linguistic and extrinsic. We have described a particular implementation of a service using a particular technique known as Description Logics; however, there is no reason to presume that this is the only representation for terms. Indeed, ConceptBase [13] could be considered as a terminological service where the concepts are represented in a deductive frame-based model, although it happens that DLs are particularly suited to interface building. We have shown how a terminology service can support a wide range of applications, and how one might form a useful component in a distributed information system. However, several open questions still remain.

Tools. Further support and tools are required for the modelling process, addressing both the managerial and technical problems associated with distributed and collaborative model building. The use of a terminological model provides added value, but there is a price to pay in that a conceptual model of the domain must be produced.

Interacting Servers and Models. The provision of Global IDs suggests that architectures with multiple terminology servers are possible. So far, however, our experiences have been with an architecture containing a *single* server. Global IDs are still useful though, as that single server may change. In addition, all the reference types described above are presumed to be references to concepts in a single conceptual model. How would servers interact if they had differing conceptual models with a degree of overlap? Preliminary investigations into image catalogues suggest that multiple, disjoint terminologies are required. How are these to be provided?

Query. So far no real attempt has been made to consider the process of retrieval. The use of the conceptual model can provide powerful query facilities, with queries being formed at abstract levels and the conceptual model providing a space around which we can navigate. For instance, if a query proves too general, we can consider specializing the concept (or possibly sub-concepts or sub-queries). Alternatively, if the query is too specific, sections of a query could be replaced with parent concepts, broadening the search space.

The use of the model for querying rather than data entry poses new problems in terms of user interfaces which are being addressed as part of the TAMBIS project [32]. In general, the level at which queries can be asked will differ to the level at which information must be specified for data entry. For example, it is generally the case that a medical Condition will occur in a Body Part, and so asking for all the instances or occurrences of Condition located in Body Part is reasonable. However, we are unlikely to allow the recording of such a concept in a record. Thus data entry and data retrieval place *different* requirements on the controlling user interfaces.

Performance. Expressive DLs are known to have problems with tractability. If a terminology server is to be used in an *interactive* fashion as we suggest, the performance of the classifier must be adequate. We have investigated the benefits of parallelism [28], and research is ongoing into optimisation techniques for classification [12].

Instances. Using a terminology as a query language requires the full integration of an instance space with the classification operations offered by the concept model. Although acknowledged widely throughout the Description Logic community, this has been an area of some neglect, with few implementations of Description Logics providing complete reasoning due to the practical problems of tractability. We are currently pursuing research in this area, and there are questions as to how much completeness is really required in the reasoning over instances in order to support practical and useful applications.

7. Acknowledgements

The authors would like to acknowledge the other members of the Medical Informatics Group and GALEN consortium. We would like to thank Graham Riley for his invaluable comments on this paper. This research is supported by the European Union under the Advanced Informatics in Medicine (AIM) project 2012 (GALEN) and HealthCare Telematics project HC 1018 (GALEN-IN- USE), and by the UK through EPSRC grant GR/J98820 (PAEPR), BBSRC grant BIF/05344 (TAMBIS), and EPSRC/DTI grant TCS VAMP GRH 48811.

References

[1] L. L. Alpay, W. A. Nowlan, W. D. Solomon, C. Lovis, R. H. Baud, T. Rush, and J.-R. Scherrer. Model-Based Application: The GALEN Structured Clinical User Interface. In *AIME 95*, 1995.

[2] Y. Arens, C. Y. CHee, C.-N. Hsu, and C. A. Knoblock. Retrieving and Integrating Data From Multiple Information Sources. *International Journal on Intelligent And Cooperative Information Systems*, 2(2):127–158, 1993.

[3] Y. Arens, R. Hull, and R. King. REFERENCE ARCHITECTURE for the Intelligent Integration of Information, Version 2.0, 1995.

[4] F. Baader and B. Hollunder. A Terminological Knowledge Representation System with Complete Inference Algorithms. In *Processing declarative knowledge: International workshop PDK'91*, number 567 in Lecture Notes in Computer Science, pages 67–86. Springer-Verlag, 1991.

[5] A. Borgida. Description Logics in Data Management. *IEEE Transactions on Knowledge and Data Engineering*, 7(5):671–782, 1995.

[6] R. Brachman, P. Selfridge, L. Terveen, B. Altman, A. Borgida, F. Halper, T. Kirk, A. Lazar, D. McGuinness, and L. Renick. Integrated Support for Data Archaeology. *International Journal of Applied and Cooperative Information Systems*, 2(2):159–185, 1993.

[7] R. Cote, D. Rothwell, J.L.Palotay, R. Becket, and L.Brochu. *The Systemised Nomenclature of Medicine: SNOMED International.* College of American Pathologists, Northfield, IL, 1993.

[8] P. Devanbu, R. Brachman, P. Selfridge, and B. Ballard. LaSSIE: A Knowledge-based software information system. *Communications of the ACM*, 34(5), 1991.

[9] M. Doerr. Authority Services in Global Information Spaces. Technical report, Institute of Computer Science, Foundation for Research and Technology - Hellas, Heraklion, Crete, Greece., 1996.

[10] A. Farquhar, R. Fikes, W. Pratt, and J. Rice. Collaborative Ontology Construction for Information Integration. Technical report, Knowledge Systems Laboratory, Dept of Computer Science, Stanford University, 1995.

[11] C. Goble, C. Haul, and S. Bechhofer. Describing and Classifying Multimedia using the Description Logic GRAIL. In *Conference on Storage and Retrieval of Still Images and Video IV*, San Jose, 1996. SPIE Vol 2670.

[12] I. Horrocks. Optimisation Techniques for Expressive Description Logics. Technical Report UMCS-97-2-1, University of Manchester, Department of Computer Science, 1997.

[13] Jorke, Matthias and Gallersdörfer, Rainer and Jeusfeld, Manfred A. and Staudt, Martin and Eherer, Stefan. ConceptBase - A Deductive Object Base for Meta Data Management. *Journal of Intelligent Information Systems*, 3:167–192, 1994.

[14] V. Kashyap and A. Sheth. Semantic Heterogeneity in Global Information Systems: The Role of Metadata, Context and Ontologies. In G. Papazoglou, M. & Schlageter, editor, *Co-operative Information Systems: Current Trends and Directions*. (to appear).

[15] J. Kirby. PEN & PAD: The Next Generation. In *Primary Health Care Specialist Group*, Cambridge, UK, 1995.

[16] T. Kirk, A. Y. Levy, Y. Sagiv, and D. Srivastava. The Information Manifold. In *AAI Spring Symposium on Information Gathering in Distributed Heterogeneous Environments.*, Stanford, California, 1995. AAAI.

[17] E. Mays, R. Dionne, and R. Weida. K-Rep System Overview. *SIGART Bulletin*, 2(3):93–97, 1991.

[18] C. Meghini, F. Sebastiani, U. Straccia, and C. Thanos. A model of information retrieval based on a terminology logic. In *Proc ACM SIGIR93. Pittsburg, USA*, pages 298–307, 1993.

[19] E. Mena, V. Kashyap, A. Illaramendi, and A. Sheth. Managing Multiple Information Sources through Ontologies: Relationship between Vocabulary Heterogeneity and Loss of Information. In *Knowledge Representation meets Databases KRDB '96, ECAI '96*, Budapest, Hungary, 1996.

[20] J. Nanard and M. Nanard. Should Anchors Be Typed Too? An Experiment with MacWeb. In *Hypertext '93*, pages 51–62, 1993.

[21] S. Navathe, A. Savasere, T. Anwar, H. Beck, and S. Gala. Object Modelling Using Classification in CANDIDE and its Applications. In A. Dogac, T. Ozsu, A. Briliris, and T. Sellis, editors, *Advances in Object-Oriented Database Systems*, volume 130 of *ASI Series*, pages 435–476. NATO, 1994.

[22] W. A. Nowlan, A. L. Rector, S. Kay, B. Horan, and A. Wilson. A Patient Care Workstation Based on User Centred Design and a Formal Theory of Medical Terminology: PEN & PAD and the SMK Formalism. In *Fifteenth Annual Symposium on Computer Applications in Medical Care. Proceedings of SCAMC91*, pages 855–857. McGraw-Hill Inc., 1991.

[23] J. O'Neill. *An Investigation into the use of GRAIL as a Hypermedia Authoring Tool.* University of Manchester, Department of Computer Science, 1996.

[24] P. Pole and A. Rector. Mapping the GALEN CORE Model to SNOMED III:Initial Experiments. In *1996 AMIA Annual Fall Symposium (Formerly SCAMC)*, 1996.

[25] A. Rector, P. Zanstra, and The GALEN Consortium. The GALEN-IN-USE Project. *To appear in: European Health Telematics Observatory Journal 1996*, 1996.

[26] A. L. Rector, S. K. Bechhofer, C. A. Goble, I. Horrocks, W. A. Nowlan, and W. D. Solomon. The GRAIL Concept Modelling Language for Medical Terminology. *Artificial Intelligence in Medicine*, (9):139–171, 1997.

[27] A. L. Rector, P. Zanstra, W. D. Solomon, and The GALEN Consortium. GALEN: Terminology Services for Clinical Information Systems. In M. Laires, M. Ladeira, and J. Christensen, editors, *Health in the new Communications Age*, volume 24 of *Health Technology and Informatics*. IOS Press, 1995.

[28] G. D. Riley, J. M. Bull, and A. P. Nisbet. Parallelisation of a Semantic Network Classifier. In *2nd European School of Computer Science, Parallel Programming Environments for High Performance Computing,*, l'Alpe d'Huez, 1996.

[29] J. E. Rogers, S. W. D., A. L. Rector, P. Pole, P. Zanstra, and E. van der Haring. Rubrics to Dissections to GRAIL to Classifications. In *To appear in: MIE 97*, 1997.

[30] N. Rychtyckyj. DLMS: An Evaluation of KL-ONE in the Automobile Industry. In *KR' 96*, pages 588–596, 1996.

[31] J. Schmidt, G. Schroder, C. Niederee, and F. Matthes. Linguistic and Architectural Requirements for Personalized Digital Libraries. *International Journal of Digital Libraries (JODL)*, 1(1), 1996.

[32] TAMBIS. Tambis www home page. http://www.cs.man.ac.uk/mig/tambis/index.html, 1996.

[33] H. v. d. Waal. *ICONCLASS: An Iconographic Classification System.* Koninklijke Nederlandse Akademie van Wetenschappen, 1973-1985.

[34] J. C. Wagner, R. H. Baud, and J.-R. Scherrer. Generating Noun Phrases from a Medical Knowledge Representation. In *MIE 94*, pages 218–223, Lisbon, Portugal, 1994.

[35] W. Woods. Understanding Subsumption and Taxonomy: A Framework for Progress. In J. Sowa, editor, *Principles of Semantic Networks: Explorations in the representation of knowledge*, pages 45–94. Morgan Kaufmann, San Mateo, CA, 1991.

Author Index

NOTES

IEEE Computer Society Publications

The world-renowned Computer Society publishes, promotes, and distributes a wide variety of authoritative computer science and engineering texts. These books are available in two formats: 100 percent original material by authors preeminent in their field who focus on relevant topics and cutting-edge research, and reprint collections consisting of carefully selected groups of previously published papers with accompanying original introductory and explanatory text.

Submission of proposals: For guidelines and information on Computer Society books, send e-mail to cs.books@computer.org or write to the Acquisitions Editor, IEEE Computer Society, P.O. Box 3014, 10662 Los Vaqueros Circle, Los Alamitos, CA 90720-1314. Telephone +1 714-821-8380. FAX +1 714-761-1784.

IEEE Computer Society Proceedings

The Computer Society also produces and actively promotes the proceedings of more than 130 acclaimed international conferences each year in multimedia formats that include hard and softcover books, CD-ROMs, videos, and on-line publications.

For information on Computer Society proceedings, send e-mail to cs.books@computer.org or write to Proceedings, IEEE Computer Society, P.O. Box 3014, 10662 Los Vaqueros Circle, Los Alamitos, CA 90720-1314. Telephone +1 714-821-8380. FAX +1 714-761-1784.

Additional information regarding the Computer Society, conferences and proceedings, CD-ROMs, videos, and books can also be accessed from our web site at http://computer.org/cspress

4/15/97